BROWNING

POETICAL WORKS
1833–1864

D1639705

Oxford University Press, Ely House, London W. 1

GLASGOW   NEW YORK   TORONTO   MELBOURNE   WELLINGTON
CAPE TOWN   IBADAN   NAIROBI   DAR ES SALAAM   LUSAKA   ADDIS ABABA
DELHI   BOMBAY   CALCUTTA   MADRAS   KARACHI   LAHORE   DACCA
KUALA LUMPUR   SINGAPORE   HONG KONG   TOKYO

BROWNING

POETICAL WORKS
1833–1864

EDITED BY
IAN JACK

LONDON
OXFORD UNIVERSITY PRESS
NEW YORK TORONTO

ROBERT BROWNING

Born London, 7 May 1812
Died Venice, 12 December 1889

*Robert Browning's Poems were first published in the
Oxford Standard Authors in 1905, reset with additions
in 1940, and many times reprinted.*

This edition of the Poetical Works, 1833–1864, *was
first published in 1970 and reprinted in 1975.*

ISBN 0 19 254165 X

*Printed in Great Britain
at the University Press, Oxford
by Vivian Ridler
Printer to the University*

O.S A.

CONTENTS

INTRODUCTION

BROWNING's career falls into three periods. From the publication of *Pauline* in 1833 to that of *Sordello* in 1840 his greatest ambition was to write a long poem describing 'the incidents in the development of a soul', because—as he immediately added—'little else is worth study'. In these two poems, and in *Paracelsus* (1835), Browning is concerned with the meaning of human life, and in particular with the problems that confront a poet or intellectual as he strives to find his true role in society. Browning himself once said that not a single copy of *Pauline* had been sold. His statement that *Paracelsus* had proved a 'dead failure' was an exaggeration, however, since the poem was well received by two or three discriminating reviewers, and its publication gained him the entrée to the literary society of the day. The publication of *Sordello* was an unequivocal failure. Hardly anyone had a kind word for the poem, and the best-known comment remains that of Jane Welsh Carlyle, who read the entire work without being able to make out whether Sordello was a man, a city, or a book. Ten years were to pass before Browning ventured to publish another long poem.

The other great interest of Browning's early period was the poetic drama. In 1836–7, flattered by Macready's request that he should 'write a play . . . , and keep [him] from going to America', Browning had written *Strafford*, which was performed on the 1st of May 1837 and published the same day. During the next ten years he wrote five plays intended for the theatre, as well as two closet dramas. Macready rejected the first two of these, *King Victor and King Charles* and *The Return of the Druses*, commenting on the latter in the privacy of his diary:

Read Browning's play, and with the deepest concern, I yield to the belief that he will *never write again*—to any purpose. I fear his intellect is not quite clear.

When Browning made a third attempt, however, with *A Blot in the 'Scutcheon*, Macready allowed himself to be persuaded by the enthusiastic praise of Dickens, who told him that he knew 'nothing . . . so affecting' in any book he had ever read 'as Mildred's recurrence to that "I was so young—I had no mother" '. Unfortunately the poet and the actor quarrelled during the rehearsals, and the play proved a complete failure. 'If to pain and perplex were the end and aim of tragedy,' wrote a reviewer in *The Athenæum*, 'Mr. Browning's poetic melodrama called *A Blot in the 'Scutcheon* would be worthy of admiration, for it is a very puzzling and unpleasant piece of business.'

These and other plays were published between 1841 and 1846 in a series of pamphlets called *Bells and Pomegranates*.[1] Printed by Moxon in double columns, in a format that recalled his editions of the Elizabethan dramatists, these low-priced publications (from 6*d*. to 2*s*. 6*d*.) may be regarded as a sign of the enforced modesty consequent upon the failure of *Sordello*. Browning's original intention was to confine the series to dramas, but fortunately he allowed himself to be persuaded by his publisher to include a number of shorter poems, a handful of which had already appeared in periodicals. This explains the 'Advertisement' printed opposite the first page of the text of *Bells and Pomegranates, No. III* (*Dramatic Lyrics*):

> Such Poems as the following come properly enough, I suppose, under the head of 'Dramatic Pieces;' being, though for the most part Lyric in expression, always Dramatic in principle, and so many utterances of so many imaginary persons, not mine.

No. VII contains a similar collection, with the title *Dramatic Romances and Lyrics*.

Two of the shorter poems included in the *Dramatic Lyrics*, 'Johannes Agricola' and 'Porphyria's Lover', had been written as early as 1834 or 1835, so anticipating by seven or eight years the second and most important period of Browning's poetic career, that in which he concentrated on writing brief dramatic poems of various types, notably those which are now usually referred to as his 'dramatic monologues'. The years from 1846 to 1861, during which he lived in Italy with his wife Elizabeth Barrett, were the happiest of Browning's life, and the harvest of that time is to be found in the collection of short and middle-length poems published in 1855 under

---

[1] Browning was persuaded to give the following explanation of the meaning of the title: 'I only meant by that title to indicate an endeavour towards something like an alternation, or mixture, of music with discoursing, sound with sense, poetry with thought; which looks too ambitious, thus expressed, so the symbol was preferred. It is little to the purpose, that such is actually one of the most familiar of the many Rabbinical (and Patristic) acceptations of the phrase; because I confess that, letting authority alone, I supposed the bare words, in such juxtaposition, would sufficiently convey the desired meaning.' *Bells and Pomegranates, No. VIII*, before *A Soul's Tragedy*.

the title of *Men and Women*. In these two volumes 'Fra Lippo Lippi', 'Bishop Blougram's Apology', and 'Andrea del Sarto' made their first appearance. *Dramatis Personæ*, which contains 'Abt Vogler' and 'Caliban upon Setebos', marks the end of this phase of Browning's life. About the time of the publication of this volume, in 1864, he began work on *The Ring and the Book*, the longest and most ambitious of all his poems, and the bridge between his dramatic poetry and the more didactic work of his later years.

Browning's reputation was slow to develop, but once it began to grow it grew steadily. In 1867 he was made an Honorary M.A. by the University of Oxford, and elected to an Honorary Fellowship at Balliol. The foundation of the Browning Society in 1881 is another significant date. What most of its members seem to have wanted was a moral teacher, and as it happened this desire coincided with the waning of Browning's dramatic powers and his increasing wish to promote his own reading of human life. In the period of reaction after his death there is no doubt that his reputation suffered most unfairly because his name was associated with an optimistic philosophy which many men of the new age, not least the influential T. S. Eliot, found temperamentally unsympathetic. So it came about that a poet who had much more in common with the poets of the first half of the present century than had his rival Tennyson suffered at least as severely from depreciation and neglect. While poets as various as Hardy, Kipling, Ezra Pound, and Eliot himself all learned from Browning's exploration of the possibilities of dramatic poetry and of colloquial idiom, his reputation among professional critics remained distinctly lower than it deserved. He was remembered as the author of such masterpieces as 'My Last Duchess' and 'The Bishop Orders his Tomb at Saint Praxed's Church', but critics did not trouble to ask themselves what position the authorship of such poems entitled him to in the hierarchy of the English poets. It is hoped that the present edition will encourage a new generation of readers to explore and appreciate the work of this enigmatic and greatly gifted poet.

The aim of this edition is to present all the volumes and pamphlets of poetry which Browning published up to the year 1864, in the order in which they first made their appearance. The text, however, is that of the collected edition which he published at the end of his life.

Like a number of other poets of the nineteenth century, Browning rearranged and reclassified his poems in later life, as well as revising them. An editor is therefore obliged to choose between preserving the poet's final arrangement of his poems and reverting to a more chronological presentation. In the present edition the editor has ventured to retain the arrangement of the poems in three important collections, *Dramatic Lyrics* (1842), *Dramatic Romances and Lyrics* (1845), and *Men and Women* (1855). As the poet's final revision of the text of these poems is reprinted, the editor may be accused of eclecticism; but it seems to him that the advantages of this procedure outweigh the disadvantages. The student is now enabled to read Browning's poems in the order in which they first appeared in volume form, though with such improvements to the text as the poet made when he collected his poems later in his life.

The alternative would have been to reprint the first seven volumes of the 1888–9 edition as they stand. If the arrangement of the poems had been strictly retained, that would have meant printing *Sordello* (1840) before *Paracelsus* (1835)—an arrangement clearly due only to the convenience of the printer[1]—and giving the poems originally published in *Dramatic Lyrics*, *Dramatic Romances and Lyrics*, and *Men and Women* under three separate categories which most confusingly retain the same titles: although the sections entitled 'Dramatic Romances', 'Dramatic Lyrics', and 'Men and Women' in the final collected edition contain between them all the poems in the three collections referred to above, the arrangement and classification are quite different. Of the 51 poems first published in the two volumes of *Men and Women* in 1855, for example, only 7 are to be found in the small class of 13 poems entitled 'Men and Women' in the final edition: the rest are distributed among the 'Dramatic Romances' and 'Dramatic Lyrics'.[2]

Although Browning's attempt to classify these poems in the collected editions of 1863, 1868, and 1888–9 throws a certain amount of light on his own thinking about his poetry, as I have tried to show elsewhere,[3] it is clear that he was less than whole-hearted about the rearrangement. 'In a late edition [i.e. that of 1863]', he

---

[1] 'The poems that follow are . . . printed in chronological order; but only so far as proves compatible with the prescribed size of each volume, which necessitates an occasional change in the distribution of its contents' (additional preface to *The Poetical Works*, 1888–9, vol. i).

[2] One poem, the long dramatic scene called 'In A Balcony', is printed separately, as a category of its own.

[3] 'Robert Browning' (Warton Lecture on English Poetry), in *Proceedings of the British Academy* (*1967*), 1968.

wrote in the *Poetical Works* of 1868, 'were collected and redistributed the pieces first published in 1842, 1845 and 1855, respectively, under the titles of "Dramatic Lyrics", "Dramatic Romances", and "Men and Women". It is not worth while to disturb this arrangement.'[1] He made no attempt to classify and redistribute the contents of the *Dramatis Personæ* volume, as consistency would have demanded.

In the present edition a table (pp. 941–3) lists the poems in the three categories of 'Dramatic Lyrics', 'Dramatic Romances', and 'Men and Women' in the collected editions, so that the reader can easily follow Browning's own attempt at classification. It would have been much more difficult to have attempted to rearrange the poems chronologically, from a similar table, if the alternative method of arrangement had been adopted. No textual apparatus is included, but changes in the titles of the poems are carefully recorded. For background information the reader is referred to *A Browning Handbook*, by William Clyde DeVane (second edition, New York, 1955).

Sordello is so difficult a poem that I have printed in the margin the helpful running-summary given at the top of the pages in the editions of 1863 and 1868, but omitted in 1889. In many places reference to the early editions has enabled me to correct minor errors, mainly of punctuation, which occur in some or all copies of the edition of 1889 (in later printings the type became very worn). My principal verbal emendations are as follows: 'the next life' for 'next life' in 'Cristina', l. 63 (p. 397 below); 'its' for 'his' in 'The Flight of the Duchess', l. 730 (p. 463); 'allowed of it' for 'allowed it' in *Christmas-Eve and Easter-Day*, l. 729 (p. 508); 'soil' for 'soul' in 'Bishop Blougram's Apology', l. 608 (p. 661); 'other' for 'others' at l. 759 of the same poem (p. 665); and 'off' for 'oft' in 'Saul', l. 328 (p. 730).

For help with the translations in Appendix E, I am indebted to the Master of Pembroke College, Cambridge, and to Mr. William K. Glavin, of St. Mark's School, Southboro, Massachusetts.

IAN JACK

Pembroke College
Cambridge
1970

---

[1] Vol. iii, p. [74].

CHRONOLOGY

1812 (7 May) Born at Southampton Street, Camberwell, the son of Robert Browning and Sarah Anna Wiedemann Browning.

c. 1820–6 At school near his home, taught by the Misses Ready and the Revd. Thomas Ready.

c. 1824 Early poems, *Incondita*, submitted to publishers by his parents, but without success.

1826 Reads Voltaire and Shelley.

1828–9 Attends some lectures at the new London University, but soon abandons them.

1832 (22 October) Inspired by Kean's performance of *Richard III* with the ambition of writing a poem, a novel, an opera, etc., under various assumed names: hence *Pauline*, 'the first work of the *Poet* of the batch'.

1833 (March) *Pauline* published. (30 October) Browning reads Mill's criticisms of the poem.
Begins *Sordello*.

1834 (March–April) Accompanies the Chevalier George de Benkhausen, the Russian consul-general, on a brief visit to St. Petersburg.
Begins *Paracelsus*.

1834 or 1835 Writes 'Johannes Agricola' and 'Porphyria's Lover'.

1835 *Paracelsus* published.

1836 (26 May) Meets Landor and Wordsworth at a dinner given by T. N. Talfourd; invited by Macready to write a play.

1837 *Strafford* published, and performed five times.

1838 First visit to Italy, in search of material for *Sordello*.

1840 Publication and failure of *Sordello*.

1841 (April) Publication of *Pippa Passes*, the first of eight pamphlets of verse under the general title *Bells and Pomegranates*.

1842 (March, November) Publication of *Bells and Pomegranates, Nos. II–III* (*King Victor and King Charles*, and *Dramatic Lyrics*).

1843 (January, February) *Bells and Pomegranates, Nos. IV–V* (*The Return of the Druses* and *A Blot in the 'Scutcheon*): *A Blot in the 'Scutcheon* fails on the stage.

1844 Second (more leisurely) journey to Italy.
      (April) *Bells and Pomegranates, No. VI (Colombe's Birthday).*

1845 (10 January) First letter to Elizabeth Barrett Barrett.
      (20 May) First visit to Wimpole Street.
      (November) *Bells and Pomegranates, No. VII (Dramatic Romances and Lyrics).*

1846 (13 April) *Bells and Pomegranates, No. VIII (Luria and A Soul's Tragedy).*
      (12 September) Secret marriage in Marylebone Church.
      (19 September) Leaves England with his wife, and settles in Pisa.

1847 The Brownings move to Florence, and soon settle in Casa Guidi.

1849 Birth of 'Pen' Browning.
      Death of the poet's mother.
      Publication of *Poems* (in two volumes).

1850 *Christmas-Eve and Easter-Day.*

1855 *Men and Women* (two volumes).

1860 (June) Buys 'the old Yellow Book' on a stall in Florence.

1861 (29 June) Death of Elizabeth Barrett Browning: Browning leaves Florence in August and returns to England in October.

1863 *The Poetical Works* (in three volumes).

1864 *Dramatis Personæ.*

1866 Death of the poet's father.

1867 Honorary M.A. of the University of Oxford, and Honorary Fellow of Balliol College.

1868 *The Poetical Works* (in six volumes).
      (21 November) Publication of *The Ring and the Book*, vol. i.
      (26 December) Publication of *The Ring and the Book*, vol. ii.

1869 (30 January) Publication of *The Ring and the Book*, vol. iii.
      (27 February) Publication of *The Ring and the Book*, vol. iv.
      Unsuccessful proposal of marriage to Louisa, Lady Ashburton?

1871 *Balaustion's Adventure, Including a Transcript from Euripides.*
      Prince Hohenstiel-Schwangau, Saviour of Society.

1872 *Fifine at the Fair.*

1873 *Red Cotton Night-Cap Country or Turf and Towers.*

1875 *Aristophanes' Apology.*
      The Inn Album.

I DEDICATE these volumes to my old friend John Forster, glad and grateful that he who, from the first publication of the various poems they include, has been their promptest and staunchest helper, should seem even nearer to me now than almost thirty years ago.

R. B.

London: *April* 21, 1863.

THE poems that follow are printed in the order of their publication. The first piece in the series I acknowledge and retain with extreme repugnance, indeed purely of necessity; for not long ago I inspected one, and am certified of the existence of other transcripts, intended sooner or later to be published abroad: by forestalling these, I can at least correct some misprints (no syllable is changed) and introduce a boyish work by an exculpatory word. The thing was my earliest attempt at 'poetry always dramatic in principle, and so many utterances of so many imaginary persons, not mine,' which I have since written according to a scheme less extravagant and scale less impracticable than were ventured upon in this crude preliminary sketch—a sketch that, on reviewal, appears not altogether wide of some hint of the characteristic features of that particular *dramatis persona* it would fain have reproduced: good draughtsmanship, however, and right handling were far beyond the artist at that time.

R. B.

London: *December* 25, 1867.

I PRESERVE, in order to supplement it, the foregoing preface. I had thought, when compelled to include in my collected works the poem to which it refers, that the honest course would be to reprint, and leave mere literary errors unaltered. Twenty years' endurance of an eyesore seems more than sufficient: my faults remain duly recorded against me, and I claim permission to somewhat diminish these, so far as style is concerned, in the present and final edition where 'Pauline' must needs, first of my performances, confront the reader. I have simply removed solecisms, mended the metre a little, and endeavoured to strengthen the phraseology—experience helping, in some degree, the helplessness of juvenile haste and heat in their untried adventure long ago.

The poems that follow are again, as before, printed in chronological order; but only so far as proves compatible with the prescribed size of each volume, which necessitates an occasional change in the distribution of its contents. Every date is subjoined as before.

R. B.

London: *February* 27, 1888.

PAULINE

A FRAGMENT OF A CONFESSION

Plus ne suis ce que j'ai été,
Et ne le sçaurois jamais être.

MAROT.

NON dubito, quin titulus libri nostri raritate sua quamplurimos alliciat ad legendum: inter quos nonnulli obliquæ opinionis, mente languidi, multi etiam maligni, et in ingenium nostrum ingrati accedent, qui temeraria sua ignorantia, vix conspecto titulo clamabunt Nos vetita docere, hæresium semina jacere: piis auribus offendiculo, præclaris ingeniis scandalo esse: . . . adeo conscientiæ suæ consulentes, ut nec Apollo, nec Musæ omnes, neque Angelus de cœlo me ab illorum execratione vindicare queant: quibus et ego nunc consulo, ne scripta nostra legant, nec intelligant, nec meminerint: nam noxia sunt, venenosa sunt: Acherontis ostium est in hoc libro, lapides loquitur, caveant, ne cerebrum illis excutiat. Vos autem, qui æqua mente ad legendum venitis, si tantam prudentiæ discretionem adhibueritis, quantam in melle legendo apes, jam securi legite. Puto namque vos et utilitatis haud parum et voluptatis plurimum accepturos. Quod si qua repereritis, quæ vobis non placeant, mittite illa, nec utimini. NAM ET EGO VOBIS ILLA NON PROBO, SED NARRO. Cætera tamen propterea non respuite . . . Ideo, si quid liberius dictum sit, ignoscite adolescentiæ nostræ, qui minor quam adolescens hoc opus composui.—*Hen. Corn. Agrippa, De Occult. Philosoph. in Præfat.*

London: *January* 1833.
V. A. XX.

[This introduction would appear less absurdly pretentious did it apply, as was intended, to a completed structure of which the poem was meant for only a beginning and remains a fragment.]

PAULINE

1833

[*Omitted from the editions of 1849 and 1863. Slightly revised in 1868, and further
revised in 1888-9. For the 1833 text see Appendix A below.*]

PAULINE, mine own, bend o'er me—thy soft breast
Shall pant to mine—bend o'er me—thy sweet eyes,
And loosened hair and breathing lips, and arms
Drawing me to thee—these build up a screen
To shut me in with thee, and from all fear;   5
So that I might unlock the sleepless brood
Of fancies from my soul, their lurking-place,
Nor doubt that each would pass, ne'er to return
To one so watched, so loved and so secured.
But what can guard thee but thy naked love?   10
Ah dearest, whoso sucks a poisoned wound
Envenoms his own veins! Thou art so good,
So calm—if thou shouldst wear a brow less light
For some wild thought which, but for me, were kept
From out thy soul as from a sacred star!   15
Yet till I have unlocked them it were vain
To hope to sing; some woe would light on me;
Nature would point at one whose quivering lip
Was bathed in her enchantments, whose brow burned
Beneath the crown to which her secrets knelt,   20
Who learned the spell which can call up the dead,
And then departed smiling like a fiend
Who has deceived God,—if such one should seek
Again her altars and stand robed and crowned
Amid the faithful! Sad confession first,   25
Remorse and pardon and old claims renewed,
Ere I can be—as I shall be no more.

I had been spared this shame if I had sat
By thee for ever from the first, in place
Of my wild dreams of beauty and of good,   30

Or with them, as an earnest of their truth:
No thought nor hope having been shut from thee,
No vague wish unexplained, no wandering aim
Sent back to bind on fancy's wings and seek
Some strange fair world where it might be a law;   35
But, doubting nothing, had been led by thee,
Thro' youth, and saved, as one at length awaked
Who has slept through a peril. Ah vain, vain!

Thou lovest me; the past is in its grave
Tho' its ghost haunts us; still this much is ours,   40
To cast away restraint, lest a worse thing
Wait for us in the dark. Thou lovest me;
And thou art to receive not love but faith,
For which thou wilt be mine, and smile and take
All shapes and shames, and veil without a fear   45
That form which music follows like a slave:
And I look to thee and I trust in thee,
As in a Northern night one looks alway
Unto the East for morn and spring and joy.
Thou seest then my aimless, hopeless state,   50
And, resting on some few old feelings won
Back by thy beauty, wouldst that I essay
The task which was to me what now thou art:
And why should I conceal one weakness more?

Thou wilt remember one warm morn when winter   55
Crept aged from the earth, and spring's first breath
Blew soft from the moist hills; the black-thorn boughs,
So dark in the bare wood, when glistening
In the sunshine were white with coming buds,
Like the bright side of a sorrow, and the banks   60
Had violets opening from sleep like eyes.
I walked with thee who knew'st not a deep shame
Lurked beneath smiles and careless words which sought
To hide it till they wandered and were mute,
As we stood listening on a sunny mound   65
To the wind murmuring in the damp copse,
Like heavy breathings of some hidden thing

Betrayed by sleep; until the feeling rushed
That I was low indeed, yet not so low
As to endure the calmness of thine eyes.   70
And so I told thee all, while the cool breast
I leaned on altered not its quiet beating:
And long ere words like a hurt bird's complaint
Bade me look up and be what I had been,
I felt despair could never live by thee: 75
Thou wilt remember. Thou art not more dear
Than song was once to me; and I ne'er sung
But as one entering bright halls where all
Will rise and shout for him: sure I must own
That I am fallen, having chosen gifts   80
Distinct from theirs—that I am sad and fain
Would give up all to be but where I was,
Not high as I had been if faithful found,
But low and weak yet full of hope, and sure
Of goodness as of life—that I would lose   85
All this gay mastery of mind, to sit
Once more with them, trusting in truth and love
And with an aim—not being what I am.

Oh Pauline, I am ruined who believed
That though my soul had floated from its sphere   90
Of wild dominion into the dim orb
Of self—that it was strong and free as ever!
It has conformed itself to that dim orb,
Reflecting all its shades and shapes, and now
Must stay where it alone can be adored.   95
I have felt this in dreams—in dreams in which
I seemed the fate from which I fled; I felt
A strange delight in causing my decay.
I was a fiend in darkness chained for ever
Within some ocean-cave; and ages rolled,   100
Till through the cleft rock, like a moonbeam, came
A white swan to remain with me; and ages
Rolled, yet I tired not of my first free joy
In gazing on the peace of its pure wings:
And then I said 'It is most fair to me,   105
'Yet its soft wings must sure have suffered change

'From the thick darkness, sure its eyes are dim,
'Its silver pinions must be cramped and numbed
'With sleeping ages here; it cannot leave me,
'For it would seem, in light beside its kind,   110
'Withered, tho' here to me most beautiful.'
And then I was a young witch whose blue eyes,
As she stood naked by the river springs,
Drew down a god: I watched his radiant form
Growing less radiant, and it gladdened me;   115
Till one morn, as he sat in the sunshine
Upon my knees, singing to me of heaven,
He turned to look at me, ere I could lose
The grin with which I viewed his perishing:
And he shrieked and departed and sat long   120
By his deserted throne, but sunk at last
Murmuring, as I kissed his lips and curled
Around him, 'I am still a god—to thee.'

Still I can lay my soul bare in its fall,
Since all the wandering and all the weakness   125
Will be a saddest comment on the song:
And if, that done, I can be young again,
I will give up all gained, as willingly
As one gives up a charm which shuts him out
From hope or part or care in human kind.   130
As life wanes, all its care and strife and toil
Seem strangely valueless, while the old trees
Which grew by our youth's home, the waving mass
Of climbing plants heavy with bloom and dew,
The morning swallows with their songs like words,   135
All these seem clear and only worth our thoughts:
So, aught connected with my early life,
My rude songs or my wild imaginings,
How I look on them—most distinct amid
The fever and the stir of after years!   140

I ne'er had ventured e'en to hope for this,
Had not the glow I felt at His award,
Assured me all was not extinct within:
His whom all honour, whose renown springs up

Like sunlight which will visit all the world,   145
So that e'en they who sneered at him at first,
Come out to it, as some dark spider crawls
From his foul nets which some lit torch invades,
Yet spinning still new films for his retreat.
Thou didst smile, poet, but can we forgive?   150

Sun-treader, life and light be thine for ever!
Thou art gone from us; years go by and spring
Gladdens and the young earth is beautiful,
Yet thy songs come not, other bards arise,
But none like thee: they stand, thy majesties,   155
Like mighty works which tell some spirit there
Hath sat regardless of neglect and scorn,
Till, its long task completed, it hath risen
And left us, never to return, and all
Rush in to peer and praise when all in vain.   160
The air seems bright with thy past presence yet,
But thou art still for me as thou hast been
When I have stood with thee as on a throne
With all thy dim creations gathered round
Like mountains, and I felt of mould like them,   165
And with them creatures of my own were mixed,
Like things half-lived, catching and giving life.
But thou art still for me who have adored
Tho' single, panting but to hear thy name
Which I believed a spell to me alone,   170
Scarce deeming thou wast as a star to men!
As one should worship long a sacred spring
Scarce worth a moth's flitting, which long grasses cross,
And one small tree embowers droopingly—
Joying to see some wandering insect won   175
To live in its few rushes, or some locust
To pasture on its boughs, or some wild bird
Stoop for its freshness from the trackless air:
And then should find it but the fountain-head,
Long lost, of some great river washing towns   180
And towers, and seeing old woods which will live
But by its banks untrod of human foot,
Which, when the great sun sinks, lie quivering

In light as some thing lieth half of life
Before God's foot, waiting a wondrous change;   185
Then girt with rocks which seek to turn or stay
Its course in vain, for it does ever spread
Like a sea's arm as it goes rolling on,
Being the pulse of some great country—so
Wast thou to me, and art thou to the world!   190
And I, perchance, half feel a strange regret
That I am not what I have been to thee:
Like a girl one has silently loved long
In her first loneliness in some retreat,
When, late emerged, all gaze and glow to view   195
Her fresh eyes and soft hair and lips which bloom
Like a mountain berry: doubtless it is sweet
To see her thus adored, but there have been
Moments when all the world was in our praise,
Sweeter than any pride of after hours.   200
Yet, sun-treader, all hail! From my heart's heart
I bid thee hail! E'en in my wildest dreams,
I proudly feel I would have thrown to dust
The wreaths of fame which seemed o'erhanging me,
To see thee for a moment as thou art.   205

And if thou livest, if thou lovest, spirit!
Remember me who set this final seal
To wandering thought—that one so pure as thou
Could never die. Remember me who flung
All honour from my soul, yet paused and said   210
'There is one spark of love remaining yet,
'For I have nought in common with him, shapes
'Which followed him avoid me, and foul forms
'Seek me, which ne'er could fasten on his mind;
'And though I feel how low I am to him,   215
'Yet I aim not even to catch a tone
'Of harmonies he called profusely up;
'So, one gleam still remains, although the last.'
Remember me who praise thee e'en with tears,
For never more shall I walk calm with thee;   220
Thy sweet imaginings are as an air,
A melody some wondrous singer sings,

Which, though it haunt men oft in the still eve,
They dream not to essay; yet it no less
But more is honoured. I was thine in shame,   225
And now when all thy proud renown is out,
I am a watcher whose eyes have grown dim
With looking for some star which breaks on him
Altered and worn and weak and full of tears.

Autumn has come like spring returned to us,   230
Won from her girlishness; like one returned
A friend that was a lover, nor forgets
The first warm love, but full of sober thoughts
Of fading years; whose soft mouth quivers yet
With the old smile, but yet so changed and still!   235
And here am I the scoffer, who have probed
Life's vanity, won by a word again
Into my own life—by one little word
Of this sweet friend who lives in loving me,
Lives strangely on my thoughts and looks and words,   240
As fathoms down some nameless ocean thing
Its silent course of quietness and joy.
O dearest, if indeed I tell the past,
May'st thou forget it as a sad sick dream!
Or if it linger—my lost soul too soon   245
Sinks to itself and whispers we shall be
But closer linked, two creatures whom the earth
Bears singly, with strange feelings unrevealed
Save to each other; or two lonely things
Created by some power whose reign is done,   250
Having no part in God or his bright world.
I am to sing whilst ebbing day dies soft,
As a lean scholar dies worn o'er his book,
And in the heaven stars steal out one by one
As hunted men steal to their mountain watch.   255
I must not think, lest this new impulse die
In which I trust; I have no confidence:
So, I will sing on fast as fancies come;
Rudely, the verse being as the mood it paints.

I strip my mind bare, whose first elements   260

I shall unveil—not as they struggled forth
In infancy, nor as they now exist,
When I am grown above them and can rule—
But in that middle stage when they were full
Yet ere I had disposed them to my will;   265
And then I shall show how these elements
Produced my present state, and what it is.
I am made up of an intensest life,
Of a most clear idea of consciousness
Of self, distinct from all its qualities,   270
From all affections, passions, feelings, powers;
And thus far it exists, if tracked, in all:
But linked, in me, to self-supremacy,
Existing as a centre to all things,
Most potent to create and rule and call   275
Upon all things to minister to it;
And to a principle of restlessness
Which would be all, have, see, know, taste, feel, all—
This is myself; and I should thus have been
Though gifted lower than the meanest soul.   280

And of my powers, one springs up to save
From utter death a soul with such desire
Confined to clay—of powers the only one
Which marks me—an imagination which
Has been a very angel, coming not   285
In fitful visions but beside me ever
And never failing me; so, though my mind
Forgets not, not a shred of life forgets,
Yet I can take a secret pride in calling
The dark past up to quell it regally.   290

A mind like this must dissipate itself,
But I have always had one lode-star; now,
As I look back, I see that I have halted
Or hastened as I looked towards that star—
A need, a trust, a yearning after God: 295
A feeling I have analysed but late,
But it existed, and was reconciled
With a neglect of all I deemed his laws,

Which yet, when seen in others, I abhorred.
I felt as one beloved, and so shut in   300
From fear: and thence I date my trust in signs
And omens, for I saw God everywhere;
And I can only lay it to the fruit
Of a sad after-time that I could doubt
Even his being—e'en the while I felt   305
His presence, never acted from myself,
Still trusted in a hand to lead me through
All danger; and this feeling ever fought
Against my weakest reason and resolve.

And I can love nothing—and this dull truth   310
Has come the last: but sense supplies a love
Encircling me and mingling with my life.

These make myself: I have long sought in vain
To trace how they were formed by circumstance,
Yet ever found them mould my wildest youth   315
Where they alone displayed themselves, converted
All objects to their use: now see their course!

They came to me in my first dawn of life
Which passed alone with wisest ancient books
All halo-girt with fancies of my own;   320
And I myself went with the tale—a god
Wandering after beauty, or a giant
Standing vast in the sunset—an old hunter
Talking with gods, or a high-crested chief
Sailing with troops of friends to Tenedos.   325
I tell you, nought has ever been so clear
As the place, the time, the fashion of those lives:
I had not seen a work of lofty art,
Nor woman's beauty nor sweet nature's face,
Yet, I say, never morn broke clear as those   330
On the dim clustered isles in the blue sea,
The deep groves and white temples and wet caves:
And nothing ever will surprise me now—
Who stood beside the naked Swift-footed,
Who bound my forehead with Proserpine's hair.   335

And strange it is that I who could so dream
Should e'er have stooped to aim at aught beneath—
Aught low or painful; but I never doubted:
So, as I grew, I rudely shaped my life
To my immediate wants; yet strong beneath   340
Was a vague sense of power though folded up—
A sense that, though those shades and times were past,
Their spirit dwelt in me, with them should rule.

Then came a pause, and long restraint chained down
My soul till it was changed. I lost myself,   345
And were it not that I so loathe that loss,
I could recall how first I learned to turn
My mind against itself; and the effects
In deeds for which remorse were vain as for
The wanderings of delirious dream; yet thence   350
Came cunning, envy, falsehood, all world's wrong
That spotted me: at length I cleansed my soul.
Yet long world's influence remained; and nought
But the still life I led, apart once more,
Which left me free to seek soul's old delights,   355
Could e'er have brought me thus far back to peace.

As peace returned, I sought out some pursuit;
And song rose, no new impulse but the one
With which all others best could be combined.
My life has not been that of those whose heaven   360
Was lampless save where poesy shone out;
But as a clime where glittering mountain-tops
And glancing sea and forests steeped in light
Give back reflected the far-flashing sun;
For music (which is earnest of a heaven,   365
Seeing we know emotions strange by it,
Not else to be revealed,) is like a voice,
A low voice calling fancy, as a friend,
To the green woods in the gay summer time:
And she fills all the way with dancing shapes   370
Which have made painters pale, and they go on
Till stars look at them and winds call to them
As they leave life's path for the twilight world

Where the dead gather. This was not at first,
For I scarce knew what I would do. I had   375
An impulse but no yearning—only sang.

And first I sang as I in dream have seen
Music wait on a lyrist for some thought,
Yet singing to herself until it came.
I turned to those old times and scenes where all   380
That's beautiful had birth for me, and made
Rude verses on them all; and then I paused—
I had done nothing, so I sought to know
What other minds achieved. No fear outbroke
As on the works of mighty bards I gazed,   385
In the first joy at finding my own thoughts
Recorded, my own fancies justified,
And their aspirings but my very own.
With them I first explored passion and mind,—
All to begin afresh! I rather sought   390
To rival what I wondered at than form
Creations of my own; if much was light
Lent by the others, much was yet my own.

I paused again: a change was coming—came:
I was no more a boy, the past was breaking   395
Before the future and like fever worked.
I thought on my new self, and all my powers
Burst out. I dreamed not of restraint, but gazed
On all things: schemes and systems went and came,
And I was proud (being vainest of the weak)   400
In wandering o'er thought's world to seek some one
To be my prize, as if you wandered o'er
The White Way for a star.

                        And my choice fell
Not so much on a system as a man—
On one, whom praise of mine shall not offend,   405
Who was as calm as beauty, being such
Unto mankind as thou to me, Pauline,—
Believing in them and devoting all
His soul's strength to their winning back to peace;
Who sent forth hopes and longings for their sake,   410

Clothed in all passion's melodies: such first
Caught me and set me, slave of a sweet task,
To disentangle, gather sense from song:
Since, song-inwoven, lurked there words which seemed
A key to a new world, the muttering   415
Of angels, something yet unguessed by man.
How my heart leapt as still I sought and found
Much there, I felt my own soul had conceived,
But there living and burning! Soon the orb
Of his conceptions dawned on me; its praise   420
Lives in the tongues of men, men's brows are high
When his name means a triumph and a pride,
So, my weak voice may well forbear to shame
What seemed decreed my fate: I threw myself
To meet it, I was vowed to liberty,   425
Men were to be as gods and earth as heaven,
And I—ah, what a life was mine to prove!
My whole soul rose to meet it. Now, Pauline,
I shall go mad, if I recall that time!

   Oh let me look back ere I leave for ever   430
The time which was an hour one fondly waits
For a fair girl that comes a withered hag!
And I was lonely, far from woods and fields,
And amid dullest sights, who should be loose
As a stag; yet I was full of bliss, who lived   435
With Plato and who had the key to life;
And I had dimly shaped my first attempt,
And many a thought did I build up on thought,
As the wild bee hangs cell to cell; in vain,
For I must still advance, no rest for mind.   440

'Twas in my plan to look on real life,
The life all new to me; my theories
Were firm, so them I left, to look and learn
Mankind, its cares, hopes, fears, its woes and joys;
And, as I pondered on their ways, I sought   445
How best life's end might be attained—an end
Comprising every joy. I deeply mused.

And suddenly without heart-wreck I awoke

As from a dream: I said ' 'Twas beautiful,
'Yet but a dream, and so adieu to it!'   450
As some world-wanderer sees in a far meadow
Strange towers and high-walled gardens thick with trees,
Where song takes shelter and delicious mirth
From laughing fairy creatures peeping over,
And on the morrow when he comes to lie   455
For ever 'neath those garden-trees fruit-flushed
Sung round by fairies, all his search is vain.
First went my hopes of perfecting mankind,
Next—faith in them, and then in freedom's self
And virtue's self, then my own motives, ends   460
And aims and loves, and human love went last.
I felt this no decay, because new powers
Rose as old feelings left—wit, mockery,
Light-heartedness; for I had oft been sad,
Mistrusting my resolves, but now I cast   465
Hope joyously away: I laughed and said
'No more of this!' I must not think: at length
I looked again to see if all went well.

My powers were greater: as some temple seemed
My soul, where nought is changed and incense rolls   470
Around the altar, only God is gone
And some dark spirit sitteth in his seat.
So, I passed through the temple and to me
Knelt troops of shadows, and they cried 'Hail, king!
'We serve thee now and thou shalt serve no more!   475
'Call on us, prove us, let us worship thee!'
And I said 'Are ye strong? Let fancy bear me
'Far from the past!' And I was borne away,
As Arab birds float sleeping in the wind,
O'er deserts, towers and forests, I being calm.   480
And I said 'I have nursed up energies,
'They will prey on me.' And a band knelt low
And cried 'Lord, we are here and we will make
'Safe way for thee in thine appointed life!
'But look on us!' And I said 'Ye will worship   485
'Me; should my heart not worship too?' They shouted
'Thyself, thou art our king!' So, I stood there

Smiling—oh, vanity of vanities!
For buoyant and rejoicing was the spirit
With which I looked out how to end my course;   490
I felt once more myself, my powers—all mine;
I knew while youth and health so lifted me
That, spite of all life's nothingness, no grief
Came nigh me, I must ever be light-hearted;
And that this knowledge was the only veil   495
Betwixt joy and despair: so, if age came,
I should be left—a wreck linked to a soul
Yet fluttering, or mind-broken and aware
Of my decay. So a long summer morn
Found me; and ere noon came, I had resolved   500
No age should come on me ere youth was spent,
For I would wear myself out, like that morn
Which wasted not a sunbeam; every hour
I would make mine, and die.

                      And thus I sought
To chain my spirit down which erst I freed   505
For flights to fame: I said 'The troubled life
'Of genius, seen so gay when working forth
'Some trusted end, grows sad when all proves vain—
'How sad when men have parted with truth's peace
'For falsest fancy's sake, which waited first   510
'As an obedient spirit when delight
'Came without fancy's call: but alters soon,
'Comes darkened, seldom, hastens to depart,
'Leaving a heavy darkness and warm tears.
'But I shall never lose her; she will live   515
'Dearer for such seclusion. I but catch
'A hue, a glance of what I sing: so, pain
'Is linked with pleasure, for I ne'er may tell
'Half the bright sights which dazzle me; but now
'Mine shall be all the radiance: let them fade   520
'Untold—others shall rise as fair, as fast!
'And when all's done, the few dim gleams transferred,'—
(For a new thought sprang up how well it were,
Discarding shadowy hope, to weave such lays
As straight encircle men with praise and love,   525

So, I should not die utterly,—should bring
One branch from the gold forest, like the knight
Of old tales, witnessing I had been there)—
'And when all's done, how vain seems e'en success—
'The vaunted influence poets have o'er men!   530
''T is a fine thing that one weak as myself
'Should sit in his lone room, knowing the words
'He utters in his solitude shall move
'Men like a swift wind—that tho' dead and gone,
'New eyes shall glisten when his beauteous dreams   535
'Of love come true in happier frames than his.
'Ay, the still night brings thoughts like these, but morn
'Comes and the mockery again laughs out
'At hollow praises, smiles allied to sneers;
'And my soul's idol ever whispers me   540
'To dwell with him and his unhonoured song:
'And I foreknow my spirit, that would press
'First in the struggle, fail again to make
'All bow enslaved, and I again should sink.

'And then know that this curse will come on us,   545
'To see our idols perish; we may wither,
'No marvel, we are clay, but our low fate
'Should not extend to those whom trustingly
'We sent before into time's yawning gulf
'To face what dread may lurk in darkness there.   550
'To find the painter's glory pass, and feel
'Music can move us not as once, or, worst,
'To weep decaying wits ere the frail body
'Decays! Nought makes me trust some love is true,
'But the delight of the contented lowness   555
'With which I gaze on him I keep for ever
'Above me; I to rise and rival him?
'Feed his fame rather from my heart's best blood,
'Wither unseen that he may flourish still.'

Pauline, my soul's friend, thou dost pity yet   560
How this mood swayed me when that soul found thine,
When I had set myself to live this life,
Defying all past glory. Ere thou camest

I seemed defiant, sweet, for old delights
Had flocked like birds again; music, my life,   565
Nourished me more than ever; then the lore
Loved for itself and all it shows—that king
Treading the purple calmly to his death,
While round him, like the clouds of eve, all dusk,
The giant shades of fate, silently flitting,   570
Pile the dim outline of the coming doom;
And him sitting alone in blood while friends
Are hunting far in the sunshine; and the boy
With his white breast and brow and clustering curls
Streaked with his mother's blood, but striving hard   575
To tell his story ere his reason goes.
And when I loved thee as love seemed so oft,
Thou lovedst me indeed: I wondering searched
My heart to find some feeling like such love,
Believing I was still much I had been.   580
Too soon I found all faith had gone from me,
And the late glow of life, like change on clouds,
Proved not the morn-blush widening into day,
But eve faint-coloured by the dying sun
While darkness hastens quickly. I will tell   585
My state as though 'twere none of mine—despair
Cannot come near us—this it is, my state.

Souls alter not, and mine must still advance;
Strange that I knew not, when I flung away
My youth's chief aims, their loss might lead to loss   590
Of what few I retained, and no resource
Be left me: for behold how changed is all!
I cannot chain my soul: it will not rest
In its clay prison, this most narrow sphere:
It has strange impulse, tendency, desire,   595
Which nowise I account for nor explain,
But cannot stifle, being bound to trust
All feelings equally, to hear all sides:
How can my life indulge them? yet they live,
Referring to some state of life unknown.   600

My selfishness is satiated not,
It wears me like a flame; my hunger for

All pleasure, howsoe'er minute, grows pain;
I envy—how I envy him whose soul
Turns its whole energies to some one end,   605
To elevate an aim, pursue success
However mean! So, my still baffled hope
Seeks out abstractions; I would have one joy,
But one in life, so it were wholly mine,
One rapture all my soul could fill: and this   610
Wild feeling places me in dream afar
In some vast country where the eye can see
No end to the far hills and dales bestrewn
With shining towers and towns, till I grow mad
Well-nigh, to know not one abode but holds   615
Some pleasure, while my soul could grasp the world,
But must remain this vile form's slave. I look
With hope to age at last, which quenching much,
May let me concentrate what sparks it spares.

This restlessness of passion meets in me   620
A craving after knowledge: the sole proof
Of yet commanding will is in that power
Repressed; for I beheld it in its dawn,
The sleepless harpy with just-budding wings,
And I considered whether to forego   625
All happy ignorant hopes and fears, to live,
Finding a recompense in its wild eyes.
And when I found that I should perish so,
I bade its wild eyes close from me for ever,
And I am left alone with old delights;   630
See! it lies in me a chained thing, still prompt
To serve me if I loose its slightest bond:
I cannot but be proud of my bright slave.
How should this earth's life prove my only sphere?
Can I so narrow sense but that in life   635
Soul still exceeds it? In their elements
My love outsoars my reason; but since love
Perforce receives its object from this earth
While reason wanders chainless, the few truths
Caught from its wanderings have sufficed to quell   640
Love chained below; then what were love, set free,

Which, with the object it demands, would pass
Reason companioning the seraphim?
No, what I feel may pass all human love
Yet fall far short of what my love should be.   645
And yet I seem more warped in this than aught,
Myself stands out more hideously: of old
I could forget myself in friendship, fame,
Liberty, nay, in love of mightier souls;
But I begin to know what thing hate is—   650
To sicken and to quiver and grow white—
And I myself have furnished its first prey.
Hate of the weak and ever-wavering will,
The selfishness, the still-decaying frame . . .
But I must never grieve whom wing can waft   655
Far from such thoughts—as now. Andromeda!
And she is with me: years roll, I shall change,
But change can touch her not—so beautiful
With her fixed eyes, earnest and still, and hair
Lifted and spread by the salt-sweeping breeze,   660
And one red beam, all the storm leaves in heaven,
Resting upon her eyes and hair, such hair,
As she awaits the snake on the wet beach
By the dark rock and the white wave just breaking
At her feet; quite naked and alone; a thing   665
I doubt not, nor fear for, secure some god
To save will come in thunder from the stars.
Let it pass! Soul requires another change.
I will be gifted with a wondrous mind,
Yet sunk by error to men's sympathy,   670
And in the wane of life, yet only so
As to call up their fears; and there shall come
A time requiring youth's best energies;
And lo, I fling age, sorrow, sickness off,
And rise triumphant, triumph through decay.   675

And thus it is that I supply the chasm
'Twixt what I am and all I fain would be:
But then to know nothing, to hope for nothing,
To seize on life's dull joys from a strange fear
Lest, losing them, all's lost and nought remains!   680

There's some vile juggle with my reason here;
I feel I but explain to my own loss
These impulses: they live no less the same.
Liberty! what though I despair? my blood
Rose never at a slave's name proud as now. 685
Oh sympathies, obscured by sophistries!—
Why else have I sought refuge in myself,
But from the woes I saw and could not stay?
Love! is not this to love thee, my Pauline?
I cherish prejudice, lest I be left 690
Utterly loveless? witness my belief
In poets, though sad change has come there too;
No more I leave myself to follow them—
Unconsciously I measure me by them—
Let me forget it: and I cherish most 695
My love of England—how her name, a word
Of hers in a strange tongue makes my heart beat!

Pauline, could I but break the spell! Not now—
All's fever—but when calm shall come again,
I am prepared: I have made life my own. 700
I would not be content with all the change
One frame should feel, but I have gone in thought
Thro' all conjuncture, I have lived all life
When it is most alive, where strangest fate
New-shapes it past surmise—the throes of men 705
Bit by some curse or in the grasps of doom
Half-visible and still-increasing round,
Or crowning their wide being's general aim.
These are wild fancies, but I feel, sweet friend,
As one breathing his weakness to the ear 710
Of pitying angel—dear as a winter flower,
A slight flower growing alone, and offering
Its frail cup of three leaves to the cold sun,
Yet joyous and confiding like the triumph
Of a child: and why am I not worthy thee? 715
I can live all the life of plants, and gaze
Drowsily on the bees that flit and play,
Or bare my breast for sunbeams which will kill,
Or open in the night of sounds, to look

For the dim stars; I can mount with the bird   720
Leaping airily his pyramid of leaves
And twisted boughs of some tall mountain tree,
Or rise cheerfully springing to the heavens;
Or like a fish breathe deep the morning air
In the misty sun-warm water; or with flower   725
And tree can smile in light at the sinking sun
Just as the storm comes, as a girl would look
On a departing lover—most serene.

Pauline, come with me, see how I could build
A home for us, out of the world, in thought!   730
I am uplifted: fly with me, Pauline!

Night, and one single ridge of narrow path
Between the sullen river and the woods
Waving and muttering, for the moonless night
Has shaped them into images of life,   735
Like the uprising of the giant-ghosts,
Looking on earth to know how their sons fare:
Thou art so close by me, the roughest swell
Of wind in the tree-tops hides not the panting
Of thy soft breasts. No, we will pass to morning—   740
Morning, the rocks and valleys and old woods.
How the sun brightens in the mist, and here,
Half in the air, like creatures of the place,
Trusting the element, living on high boughs
That swing in the wind—look at the silver spray   745
Flung from the foam-sheet of the cataract
Amid the broken rocks! Shall we stay here
With the wild hawks? No, ere the hot noon come,
Dive we down—safe! See this our new retreat
Walled in with a sloped mound of matted shrubs,   750
Dark, tangled, old and green, still sloping down
To a small pool whose waters lie asleep
Amid the trailing boughs turned water-plants:
And tall trees overarch to keep us in,
Breaking the sunbeams into emerald shafts,   755
And in the dreamy water one small group

Of two or three strange trees are got together
Wondering at all around, as strange beasts herd
Together far from their own land: all wildness,
No turf nor moss, for boughs and plants pave all, 760
And tongues of bank go shelving in the lymph,
Where the pale-throated snake reclines his head,
And old grey stones lie making eddies there,
The wild-mice cross them dry-shod. Deeper in!
Shut thy soft eyes—now look—still deeper in! 765
This is the very heart of the woods all round
Mountain-like heaped above us; yet even here
One pond of water gleams; far off the river
Sweeps like a sea, barred out from land; but one—
One thin clear sheet has overleaped and wound 770
Into this silent depth, which gained, it lies
Still, as but let by sufferance; the trees bend
O'er it as wild men watch a sleeping girl,
And through their roots long creeping plants out-stretch
Their twined hair, steeped and sparkling; farther on, 775
Tall rushes and thick flag-knots have combined
To narrow it; so, at length, a silver thread,
It winds, all noiselessly through the deep wood
Till thro' a cleft-way, thro' the moss and stone,
It joins its parent-river with a shout. 780

Up for the glowing day, leave the old woods!
See, they part, like a ruined arch: the sky!
Nothing but sky appears, so close the roots
And grass of the hill-top level with the air—
Blue sunny air, where a great cloud floats laden 785
With light, like a dead whale that white birds pick,
Floating away in the sun in some north sea.
Air, air, fresh life-blood, thin and searching air,
The clear, dear breath of God that loveth us,
Where small birds reel and winds take their delight! 790
Water is beautiful, but not like air:
See, where the solid azure waters lie
Made as of thickened air, and down below,
The fern-ranks like a forest spread themselves
As though each pore could feel the element; 795

Where the quick glancing serpent winds his way,
Float with me there, Pauline!—but not like air.

Down the hill! Stop—a clump of trees, see, set
On a heap of rock, which look o'er the far plain:
So, envious climbing shrubs would mount to rest   800
And peer from their spread boughs; wide they wave, looking
At the muleteers who whistle on their way,
To the merry chime of morning bells, past all
The little smoking cots, mid fields and banks
And copses bright in the sun. My spirit wanders: 805
Hedgerows for me—those living hedgerows where
The bushes close and clasp above and keep
Thought in—I am concentrated—I feel;
But my soul saddens when it looks beyond:
I cannot be immortal, taste all joy.   810

O God, where do they tend—these struggling aims?*
What would I have? What is this 'sleep' which seems
To bound all? can there be a 'waking' point

---

* Je crains bien que mon pauvre ami ne soit pas toujours parfaitement compris dans ce qui reste à lire de cet étrange fragment, mais il est moins propre que tout autre à éclaircir ce qui de sa nature ne peut jamais être que songe et confusion. D'ailleurs je ne sais trop si en cherchant à mieux co-ordonner certaines parties l'on ne courrait pas le risque de nuire au seul mérite auquel une production si singulière peut prétendre, celui de donner une idée assez précise du genre qu'elle n'a fait qu'ébaucher. Ce début sans prétention, ce remuement des passions qui va d'abord en accroissant et puis s'apaise par degrés, ces élans de l'âme, ce retour soudain sur soi-même, et par-dessus tout, la tournure d'esprit tout particulière de mon ami, rendent les changemens presque impossibles. Les raisons qu'il fait valoir ailleurs, et d'autres encore plus puissantes, ont fait trouver grâce à mes yeux pour cet écrit qu'autrement je lui eusse conseillé de jeter au feu. Je n'en crois pas moins au grand principe de toute composition—à ce principe de Shakespeare, de Rafaelle, de Beethoven, d'où il suit que la concentration des idées est due bien plus à leur conception qu'à leur mise en exécution: j'ai tout lieu de craindre que la première de ces qualités ne soit encore étrangère à mon ami, et je doute fort qu'un redoublement de travail lui fasse acquérir la seconde. Le mieux serait de brûler ceci; mais que faire?

Je crois que dans ce qui suit il fait allusion à un certain examen qu'il fit autrefois de l'âme, ou plutôt de son âme, pour découvrir la suite des objets auxquels il lui serait possible d'atteindre, et dont chacun une fois obtenu devait former une espèce de plateau d'où l'on pouvait apercevoir d'autres buts, d'autres projets, d'autres jouissances qui, à leur tour, devaient être surmontés. Il en résultait que l'oubli et le sommeil devaient tout terminer. Cette idée, que je ne saisis pas parfaitement, lui est peut-être aussi inintelligible qu'à moi.

PAULINE.

Of crowning life? The soul would never rule;
It would be first in all things, it would have   815
Its utmost pleasure filled, but, that complete,
Commanding, for commanding, sickens it.
The last point I can trace is—rest beneath
Some better essence than itself, in weakness;
This is 'myself,' not what I think should be: 820
And what is that I hunger for but God?

My God, my God, let me for once look on thee
As though nought else existed, we alone!
And as creation crumbles, my soul's spark
Expands till I can say,—Even from myself   825
I need thee and I feel thee and I love thee.
I do not plead my rapture in thy works
For love of thee, nor that I feel as one
Who cannot die: but there is that in me
Which turns to thee, which loves or which should love.   830

Why have I girt myself with this hell-dress?
Why have I laboured to put out my life?
Is it not in my nature to adore,
And e'en for all my reason do I not
Feel him, and thank him, and pray to him—now?   835
Can I forego the trust that he loves me?
Do I not feel a love which only ONE . . .
O thou pale form, so dimly seen, deep-eyed!
I have denied thee calmly—do I not
Pant when I read of thy consummate power,   840
And burn to see thy calm pure truths out-flash
The brightest gleams of earth's philosophy?
Do I not shake to hear aught question thee?
If I am erring save me, madden me,
Take from me powers and pleasures, let me die   845
Ages, so I see thee! I am knit round
As with a charm by sin and lust and pride,
Yet though my wandering dreams have seen all shapes
Of strange delight, oft have I stood by thee—
Have I been keeping lonely watch with thee   850
In the damp night by weeping Olivet,

Or leaning on thy bosom, proudly less,
Or dying with thee on the lonely cross,
Or witnessing thine outburst from the tomb.

A mortal, sin's familiar friend, doth here   855
Avow that he will give all earth's reward,
But to believe and humbly teach the faith,
In suffering and poverty and shame,
Only believing he is not unloved.

And now, my Pauline, I am thine for ever!   860
I feel the spirit which has buoyed me up
Desert me, and old shades are gathering fast;
Yet while the last light waits, I would say much,
This chiefly, it is gain that I have said
Somewhat of love I ever felt for thee   865
But seldom told; our hearts so beat together
That speech seemed mockery; but when dark hours come,
And joy departs, and thou, sweet, deem'st it strange
A sorrow moves me, thou canst not remove,
Look on this lay I dedicate to thee,   870
Which through thee I began, which thus I end,
Collecting the last gleams to strive to tell
How I am thine, and more than ever now
That I sink fast: yet though I deeplier sink,
No less song proves one word has brought me bliss,   875
Another still may win bliss surely back.
Thou knowest, dear, I could not think all calm,
For fancies followed thought and bore me off,
And left all indistinct; ere one was caught
Another glanced; so, dazzled by my wealth,   880
I knew not which to leave nor which to choose,
For all so floated, nought was fixed and firm.
And then thou said'st a perfect bard was one
Who chronicled the stages of all life,
And so thou bad'st me shadow this first stage.   885
'T is done, and even now I recognize
The shift, the change from last to past—discern
Faintly how life is truth and truth is good.
And why thou must be mine is, that e'en now

In the dim hush of night, that I have done,   890
Despite the sad forebodings, love looks through—
Whispers,—E'en at the last I have her still,
With her delicious eyes as clear as heaven
When rain in a quick shower has beat down mist,
And clouds float white above like broods of swans.   895
How the blood lies upon her cheek, outspread
As thinned by kisses! only in her lips
It wells and pulses like a living thing,
And her neck looks like marble misted o'er
With love-breath,—a Pauline from heights above,   900
Stooping beneath me, looking up—one look
As I might kill her and be loved the more.

So, love me—me, Pauline, and nought but me,
Never leave loving! Words are wild and weak,
Believe them not, Pauline! I stained myself   905
But to behold thee purer by my side,
To show thou art my breath, my life, a last
Resource, an extreme want: never believe
Aught better could so look on thee; nor seek
Again the world of good thoughts left for mine!   910
There were bright troops of undiscovered suns,
Each equal in their radiant course; there were
Clusters of far fair isles which ocean kept
For his own joy, and his waves broke on them
Without a choice; and there was a dim crowd   915
Of visions, each a part of some grand whole:
And one star left his peers and came with peace
Upon a storm, and all eyes pined for him;
And one isle harboured a sea-beaten ship,
And the crew wandered in its bowers and plucked   920
Its fruits and gave up all their hopes of home;
And one dream came to a pale poet's sleep,
And he said, 'I am singled out by God,
'No sin must touch me.' Words are wild and weak,
But what they would express is,—Leave me not,   925
Still sit by me with beating breast and hair
Loosened, be watching earnest by my side,
Turning my books or kissing me when I

Look up—like summer wind! Be still to me
A help to music's mystery which mind fails   930
To fathom, its solution, no mere clue!
O reason's pedantry, life's rule prescribed!
I hopeless, I the loveless, hope and love.
Wiser and better, know me now, not when
You loved me as I was. Smile not! I have   935
Much yet to dawn on you, to gladden you.
No more of the past! I'll look within no more.
I have too trusted my own lawless wants,
Too trusted my vain self, vague intuition—
Draining soul's wine alone in the still night,   940
And seeing how, as gathering films arose,
As by an inspiration life seemed bare
And grinning in its vanity, while ends
Foul to be dreamed of, smiled at me as fixed
And fair, while others changed from fair to foul   945
As a young witch turns an old hag at night.
No more of this! We will go hand in hand,
I with thee, even as a child—love's slave,
Looking no farther than his liege commands.

And thou hast chosen where this life shall be: 950
The land which gave me thee shall be our home,
Where nature lies all wild amid her lakes
And snow-swathed mountains and vast pines begirt
With ropes of snow—where nature lies all bare,
Suffering none to view her but a race   955
Or stinted or deformed, like the mute dwarfs
Which wait upon a naked Indian queen.
And there (the time being when the heavens are thick
With storm) I'll sit with thee while thou dost sing
Thy native songs, gay as a desert bird   960
Which crieth as it flies for perfect joy,
Or telling me old stories of dead knights;
Or I will read great lays to thee—how she,
The fair pale sister, went to her chill grave
With power to love and to be loved and live: 965
Or we will go together, like twin gods
Of the infernal world, with scented lamp

Over the dead, to call and to awake,
Over the unshaped images which lie
Within my mind's cave: only leaving all,   970
That tells of the past doubt. So, when spring comes
With sunshine back again like an old smile,
And the fresh waters and awakened birds
And budding woods await us, I shall be
Prepared, and we will question life once more,   975
Till its old sense shall come renewed by change,
Like some clear thought which harsh words veiled before,
Feeling God loves us, and that all which errs
Is but a dream which death will dissipate.
And then what need of longer exile? Seek   980
My England, and, again there, calm approach
All I once fled from, calmly look on those
The works of my past weakness, as one views
Some scene where danger met him long before.
Ah that such pleasant life should be but dreamed!   985

But whate'er come of it, and though it fade,
And though ere the cold morning all be gone,
As it may be;—tho' music wait to wile,
And strange eyes and bright wine lure, laugh like sin
Which steals back softly on a soul half saved,   990
And I the first deny, decry, despise,
With this avowal, these intents so fair,—
Still be it all my own, this moment's pride!
No less I make an end in perfect joy.
E'en in my brightest time, a lurking fear   995
Possessed me: I well knew my weak resolves,
I felt the witchery that makes mind sleep
Over its treasure, as one half afraid
To make his riches definite: but now
These feelings shall not utterly be lost,   1000
I shall not know again that nameless care
Lest, leaving all undone in youth, some new
And undreamed end reveal itself too late:
For this song shall remain to tell for ever
That when I lost all hope of such a change,   1005
Suddenly beauty rose on me again.

C

No less I make an end in perfect joy,
For I, who thus again was visited,
Shall doubt not many another bliss awaits,
And, though this weak soul sink and darkness whelm,   1010
Some little word shall light it, raise aloft,
To where I clearlier see and better love,
As I again go o'er the tracts of thought
Like one who has a right, and I shall live
With poets, calmer, purer still each time,   1015
And beauteous shapes will come for me to seize,
And unknown secrets will be trusted me
Which were denied the waverer once; but now
I shall be priest and prophet as of old.

Sun-treader, I believe in God and truth   1020
And love; and as one just escaped from death
Would bind himself in bands of friends to feel
He lives indeed, so, I would lean on thee!
Thou must be ever with me, most in gloom
If such must come, but chiefly when I die,   1025
For I seem, dying, as one going in the dark
To fight a giant: but live thou for ever,
And be to all what thou hast been to me!
All in whom this wakes pleasant thoughts of me
Know my last state is happy, free from doubt   1030
Or touch of fear. Love me and wish me well.

Richmond:
October 22, 1832.

PARACELSUS

The following preface is found only in the first edition:

I am anxious that the reader should not, at the very outset—mistaking my performance for one of a class with which it has nothing in common—judge it by principles on which it was never moulded, and subject it to a standard to which it was never meant to conform. I therefore anticipate his discovery, that it is an attempt, probably more novel than happy, to reverse the method usually adopted by writers whose aim it is to set forth any phenomenon of the mind or the passions, by the operation of persons and events; and that, instead of having recourse to an external machinery of incidents to create and evolve the crisis I desire to produce, I have ventured to display somewhat minutely the mood itself in its rise and progress, and have suffered the agency by which it is influenced and determined, to be generally discernible in its effects alone, and subordinate throughout, if not altogether excluded: and this for a reason. I have endeavoured to write a poem, not a drama; the canons of the drama are well known, and I cannot but think that, inasmuch as they have immediate regard to stage representation, the peculiar advantages they hold out are really such only so long as the purpose for which they were at first instituted is kept in view. I do not very well understand what is called a Dramatic Poem, wherein all those restrictions only submitted to on account of compensating good in the original scheme are scrupulously retained, as though for some special fitness in themselves—and all new facilities placed at an author's disposal by the vehicle he selects, as pertinaciously rejected. It is certain, however, that a work like mine depends more immediately on the intelligence and sympathy of the reader for its success—indeed were my scenes stars it must be his co-operating fancy which, supplying all chasms, shall connect the scattered lights into one constellation—a Lyre or a Crown. I trust for his indulgence towards a poem which had not been imagined six months ago; and that even should he think slightingly of the present (an experiment I am in no case likely to repeat) he will not be prejudiced against other productions which may follow in a more popular, and perhaps less difficult form.

15th March, 1835.

PARACELSUS

1835

PERSONS

AUREOLUS PARACELSUS, *a student.*
FESTUS *and* MICHAL, *his friends.*
APRILE, *an Italian poet.*

PART I

PARACELSUS ASPIRES

SCENE. *Würzburg; a garden in the environs.* 1512.

FESTUS, PARACELSUS, MICHAL

PARACELSUS. Come close to me, dear friends; still closer; thus!
　　Close to the heart which, though long time roll by
　　Ere it again beat quicker, pressed to yours,
　　As now it beats—perchance a long, long time—
　　At least henceforth your memories shall make　　　　　5
　　Quiet and fragrant as befits their home.
　　Nor shall my memory want a home in yours—
　　Alas, that it requires too well such free
　　Forgiving love as shall embalm it there!
　　For if you would remember me aright,　　　　　　10
　　As I was born to be, you must forget
　　All fitful strange and moody waywardness
　　Which e'er confused my better spirit, to dwell
　　Only on moments such as these, dear friends!
　　—My heart no truer, but my words and ways　　　　15
　　More true to it: as Michal, some months hence,
　　Will say, 'this autumn was a pleasant time,'
　　For some few sunny days; and overlook
　　Its bleak wind, hankering after pining leaves.
　　Autumn would fain be sunny; I would look　　　　20
　　Liker my nature's truth: and both are frail,
　　And both beloved, for all our frailty.
MICHAL.　　　　　　　　　　　　Aureole!
PARACELSUS. Drop by drop! she is weeping like a child!
　　Not so! I am content—more than content;

Nay, autumn wins you best by this its mute   25
Appeal to sympathy for its decay:
Look up, sweet Michal, nor esteem the less
Your stained and drooping vines their grapes bow down,
Nor blame those creaking trees bent with their fruit,
That apple-tree with a rare after-birth   30
Of peeping blooms sprinkled its wealth among!
Then for the winds—what wind that ever raved
Shall vex that ash which overlooks you both,
So proud it wears its berries? Ah, at length,
The old smile meet for her, the lady of this   35
Sequestered nest!—this kingdom, limited
Alone by one old populous green wall
Tenanted by the ever-busy flies,
Grey crickets and shy lizards and quick spiders,
Each family of the silver-threaded moss—   40
Which, look through near, this way, and it appears
A stubble-field or a cane-brake, a marsh
Of bulrush whitening in the sun: laugh now!
Fancy the crickets, each one in his house,
Looking out, wondering at the world—or best,   45
Yon painted snail with his gay shell of dew,
Travelling to see the glossy balls high up
Hung by the caterpillar, like gold lamps.
MICHAL. In truth we have lived carelessly and well.
PARACELSUS. And shall, my perfect pair!—each, trust me, born
For the other; nay, your very hair, when mixed,   51
Is of one hue. For where save in this nook
Shall you two walk, when I am far away,
And wish me prosperous fortune? Stay: that plant
Shall never wave its tangles lightly and softly,   55
As a queen's languid and imperial arm
Which scatters crowns among her lovers, but you
Shall be reminded to predict to me
Some great success! Ah see, the sun sinks broad
Behind Saint Saviour's: wholly gone, at last!   60
FESTUS. Now, Aureole, stay those wandering eyes awhile!
You are ours to-night, at least; and while you spoke
Of Michal and her tears, I thought that none
Could willing leave what he so seemed to love:

But that last look destroys my dream—that look   65
As if, where'er you gazed, there stood a star!
How far was Würzburg with its church and spire
And garden-walls and all things they contain,
From that look's far alighting?

PARACELSUS.   I but spoke
And looked alike from simple joy to see   70
The beings I love best, shut in so well
From all rude chances like to be my lot,
That, when afar, my weary spirit,—disposed
To lose awhile its care in soothing thoughts
Of them, their pleasant features, looks and words,—   75
Needs never hesitate, nor apprehend
Encroaching trouble may have reached them too,
Nor have recourse to fancy's busy aid
And fashion even a wish in their behalf
Beyond what they possess already here;   80
But, unobstructed, may at once forget
Itself in them, assured how well they fare.
Beside, this Festus knows he holds me one
Whom quiet and its charms arrest in vain,
One scarce aware of all the joys I quit,   85
Too filled with airy hopes to make account
Of soft delights his own heart garners up:
Whereas behold how much our sense of all
That's beauteous proves alike! When Festus learns
That every common pleasure of the world   90
Affects me as himself; that I have just
As varied appetite for joy derived
From common things; a stake in life, in short,
Like his; a stake which rash pursuit of aims
That life affords not, would as soon destroy;—   95
He may convince himself that, this in view,
I shall act well advised. And last, because,
Though heaven and earth and all things were at stake,
Sweet Michal must not weep, our parting eve.

FESTUS. True: and the eve is deepening, and we sit   100
As little anxious to begin our talk
As though to-morrow I could hint of it
As we paced arm-in-arm the cheerful town

At sun-dawn; or could whisper it by fits
(Trithemius busied with his class the while)   105
In that dim chamber where the noon-streaks peer
Half-frightened by the awful tomes around;
Or in some grassy lane unbosom all
From even-blush to midnight: but, to-morrow!
Have I full leave to tell my inmost mind?   110
We have been brothers, and henceforth the world
Will rise between us:—all my freest mind?
'T is the last night, dear Aureole!

PARACELSUS.   Oh, say on!
Devise some test of love, some arduous feat
To be performed for you: say on! If night   115
Be spent the while, the better! Recall how oft
My wondrous plans and dreams and hopes and fears
Have—never wearied you, oh no!—as I
Recall, and never vividly as now,
Your true affection, born when Einsiedeln   120
And its green hills were all the world to us;
And still increasing to this night which ends
My further stay at Würzburg. Oh, one day
You shall be very proud! Say on, dear friends!

FESTUS. In truth? 'T is for my proper peace, indeed,   125
Rather than yours; for vain all projects seem
To stay your course: I said my latest hope
Is fading even now. A story tells
Of some far embassy despatched to win
The favour of an eastern king, and how   130
The gifts they offered proved but dazzling dust
Shed from the ore-beds native to his clime.
Just so, the value of repose and love,
I meant should tempt you, better far than I
You seem to comprehend; and yet desist   135
No whit from projects where repose nor love
Has part.

PARACELSUS. Once more? Alas! As I foretold.
FESTUS. A solitary briar the bank puts forth
To save our swan's nest floating out to sea.
PARACELSUS. Dear Festus, hear me. What is it you wish?   140
That I should lay aside my heart's pursuit,

Abandon the sole ends for which I live,
Reject God's great commission, and so die!
You bid me listen for your true love's sake:
Yet how has grown that love? Even in a long   145
And patient cherishing of the self-same spirit
It now would quell; as though a mother hoped
To stay the lusty manhood of the child
Once weak upon her knees. I was not born
Informed and fearless from the first, but shrank   150
From aught which marked me out apart from men:
I would have lived their life, and died their death,
Lost in their ranks, eluding destiny:
But you first guided me through doubt and fear,
Taught me to know mankind and know myself;   155
And now that I am strong and full of hope,
That, from my soul, I can reject all aims
Save those your earnest words made plain to me,
Now that I touch the brink of my design,
When I would have a triumph in their eyes,   160
A glad cheer in their voices—Michal weeps,
And Festus ponders gravely!

FESTUS.   When you deign
To hear my purpose . . .

PARACELSUS.   Hear it? I can say
Beforehand all this evening's conference!
'T is this way, Michal, that he uses: first,   165
Or he declares, or I, the leading points
Of our best scheme of life, what is man's end
And what God's will; no two faiths e'er agreed
As his with mine. Next, each of us allows
Faith should be acted on as best we may;   170
Accordingly, I venture to submit
My plan, in lack of better, for pursuing
The path which God's will seems to authorize.
Well, he discerns much good in it, avows
This motive worthy, that hope plausible,   175
A danger here to be avoided, there
An oversight to be repaired: in fine
Our two minds go together—all the good
Approved by him, I gladly recognize,

All he counts bad, I thankfully discard,   180
And nought forbids my looking up at last
For some stray comfort in his cautious brow.
When, lo! I learn that, spite of all, there lurks
Some innate and inexplicable germ
Of failure in my scheme; so that at last   185
It all amounts to this—the sovereign proof
That we devote ourselves to God, is seen
In living just as though no God there were;
A life which, prompted by the sad and blind
Folly of man, Festus abhors the most;   190
But which these tenets sanctify at once,
Though to less subtle wits it seems the same,
Consider it how they may.

MICHAL.   Is it so, Festus?
He speaks so calmly and kindly: is it so?

PARACELSUS. Reject those glorious visions of God's love   195
And man's design; laugh loud that God should send
Vast longings to direct us; say how soon
Power satiates these, or lust, or gold; I know
The world's cry well, and how to answer it.
But this ambiguous warfare . . .

FESTUS.   . . . Wearies so   200
That you will grant no last leave to your friend
To urge it?—for his sake, not yours? I wish
To send my soul in good hopes after you;
Never to sorrow that uncertain words
Erringly apprehended, a new creed   205
Ill understood, begot rash trust in you,
Had share in your undoing.

PARACELSUS.   Choose your side,
Hold or renounce: but meanwhile blame me not
Because I dare to act on your own views,
Nor shrink when they point onward, nor espy   210
A peril where they most ensure success.

FESTUS. Prove that to me—but that! Prove you abide
Within their warrant, nor presumptuous boast
God's labour laid on you; prove, all you covet
A mortal may expect; and, most of all,   215
Prove the strange course you now affect, will lead

To its attainment—and I bid you speed,
Nay, count the minutes till you venture forth!
You smile; but I had gathered from slow thought—
Much musing on the fortunes of my friend—   220
Matter I deemed could not be urged in vain;
But it all leaves me at my need: in shreds
And fragments I must venture what remains.
MICHAL. Ask at once, Festus, wherefore he should scorn . . .
FESTUS. Stay, Michal: Aureole, I speak guardedly   225
And gravely, knowing well, whate'er your error,
This is no ill-considered choice of yours,
No sudden fancy of an ardent boy.
Not from your own confiding words alone
Am I aware your passionate heart long since   230
Gave birth to, nourished and at length matures
This scheme. I will not speak of Einsiedeln,
Where I was born your elder by some years
Only to watch you fully from the first:
In all beside, our mutual tasks were fixed   235
Even then—'t was mine to have you in my view
As you had your own soul and those intents
Which filled it when, to crown your dearest wish,
With a tumultuous heart, you left with me
Our childhood's home to join the favoured few   240
Whom, here, Trithemius condescends to teach
A portion of his lore: and not one youth
Of those so favoured, whom you now despise,
Came earnest as you came, resolved, like you,
To grasp all, and retain all, and deserve   245
By patient toil a wide renown like his.
Now, this new ardour which supplants the old
I watched, too; 't was significant and strange,
In one matched to his soul's content at length
With rivals in the search for wisdom's prize,   250
To see the sudden pause, the total change;
From contest, the transition to repose—
From pressing onward as his fellows pressed,
To a blank idleness, yet most unlike
The dull stagnation of a soul, content,   255
Once foiled, to leave betimes a thriveless quest.

That careless bearing, free from all pretence
Even of contempt for what it ceased to seek—
Smiling humility, praising much, yet waiving
What it professed to praise—though not so well   260
Maintained but that rare outbreaks, fierce and brief,
Revealed the hidden scorn, as quickly curbed.
That ostentatious show of past defeat,
That ready acquiescence in contempt,
I deemed no other than the letting go   265
His shivered sword, of one about to spring
Upon his foe's throat; but it was not thus:
Not that way looked your brooding purpose then.
For after-signs disclosed, what you confirmed,
That you prepared to task to the uttermost   270
Your strength, in furtherance of a certain aim
Which—while it bore the name your rivals gave
Their own most puny efforts—was so vast
In scope that it included their best flights,
Combined them, and desired to gain one prize   275
In place of many,—the secret of the world,
Of man, and man's true purpose, path and fate.
—That you, not nursing as a mere vague dream
This purpose, with the sages of the past,
Have struck upon a way to this, if all   280
You trust be true, which following, heart and soul,
You, if a man may, dare aspire to KNOW:
And that this aim shall differ from a host
Of aims alike in character and kind,
Mostly in this,—that in itself alone   285
Shall its reward be, not an alien end
Blending therewith; no hope nor fear nor joy
Nor woe, to elsewhere move you, but this pure
Devotion to sustain you or betray:
Thus you aspire.

PARACELSUS.   You shall not state it thus: 290
I should not differ from the dreamy crew
You speak of. I profess no other share
In the selection of my lot, than this
My ready answer to the will of God
Who summons me to be his organ. All   295

Whose innate strength supports them shall succeed
No better than the sages.
FESTUS.   Such the aim, then,
  God sets before you; and 't is doubtless need
  That he appoint no less the way of praise
  Than the desire to praise; for, though I hold   300
  With you, the setting forth such praise to be
  The natural end and service of a man,
  And hold such praise is best attained when man
  Attains the general welfare of his kind—
  Yet this, the end, is not the instrument.   305
  Presume not to serve God apart from such
  Appointed channel as he wills shall gather
  Imperfect tributes, for that sole obedience
  Valued perchance! He seeks not that his altars
  Blaze, careless how, so that they do but blaze.   310
  Suppose this, then; that God selected you
  To KNOW (heed well your answers, for my faith
  Shall meet implicitly what they affirm)
  I cannot think you dare annex to such
  Selection aught beyond a steadfast will,   315
  An intense hope; nor let your gifts create
  Scorn or neglect of ordinary means
  Conducive to success, make destiny
  Dispense with man's endeavour. Now, dare you search
  Your inmost heart, and candidly avow   320
  Whether you have not rather wild desire
  For this distinction than security
  Of its existence? whether you discern
  The path to the fulfilment of your purpose
  Clear as that purpose—and again, that purpose   325
  Clear as your yearning to be singled out
  For its pursuer. Dare you answer this?
PARACELSUS [after a pause]. No, I have nought to fear! Who will
      may know
  The secret'st workings of my soul. What though
  It be so?—if indeed the strong desire   330
  Eclipse the aim in me?—if splendour break
  Upon the outset of my path alone,
  And duskest shade succeed? What fairer seal

Shall I require to my authentic mission
Than this fierce energy?—this instinct striving   335
Because its nature is to strive?—enticed
By the security of no broad course,
Without success forever in its eyes!
How know I else such glorious fate my own,
But in the restless irresistible force   340
That works within me? Is it for human will
To institute such impulses?—still less,
To disregard their promptings! What should I
Do, kept among you all; your loves, your cares,
Your life—all to be mine? Be sure that God   345
Ne'er dooms to waste the strength he deigns impart!
Ask the geier-eagle why she stoops at once
Into the vast and unexplored abyss,
What full-grown power informs her from the first,
Why she not marvels, strenuously beating   350
The silent boundless regions of the sky!
Be sure they sleep not whom God needs! Nor fear
Their holding light his charge, when every hour
That finds that charge delayed, is a new death.
This for the faith in which I trust; and hence   355
I can abjure so well the idle arts
These pedants strive to learn and teach; Black Arts,
Great Works, the Secret and Sublime, forsooth—
Let others prize: too intimate a tie
Connects me with our God! A sullen fiend   360
To do my bidding, fallen and hateful sprites
To help me—what are these, at best, beside
God helping, God directing everywhere,
So that the earth shall yield her secrets up,
And every object there be charged to strike,   365
Teach, gratify her master God appoints?
And I am young, my Festus, happy and free!
I can devote myself; I have a life
To give; I, singled out for this, the One!
Think, think! the wide East, where all Wisdom sprung;   370
The bright South, where she dwelt; the hopeful North,
All are passed o'er—it lights on me! 'T is time
New hopes should animate the world, new light

Should dawn from new revealings to a race
Weighed down so long, forgotten so long; thus shall   375
The heaven reserved for us at last receive
Creatures whom no unwonted splendours blind,
But ardent to confront the unclouded blaze
Whose beams not seldom blessed their pilgrimage,
Not seldom glorified their life below.   380
FESTUS. My words have their old fate and make faint stand
Against your glowing periods. Call this, truth—
Why not pursue it in a fast retreat,
Some one of Learning's many palaces,
After approved example?—seeking there   385
Calm converse with the great dead, soul to soul,
Who laid up treasure with the like intent
—So lift yourself into their airy place,
And fill out full their unfulfilled careers,
Unravelling the knots their baffled skill   390
Pronounced inextricable, true!—but left
Far less confused. A fresh eye, a fresh hand,
Might do much at their vigour's waning-point;
Succeeding with new-breathed new-hearted force,
As at old games the runner snatched the torch   395
From runner still: this way success might be.
But you have coupled with your enterprise,
An arbitrary self-repugnant scheme
Of seeking it in strange and untried paths.
What books are in the desert? Writes the sea   400
The secret of her yearning in vast caves
Where yours will fall the first of human feet?
Has wisdom sat there and recorded aught
You press to read? Why turn aside from her
To visit, where her vesture never glanced,   405
Now—solitudes consigned to barrenness
By God's decree, which who shall dare impugn?
Now—ruins where she paused but would not stay,
Old ravaged cities that, renouncing her,
She called an endless curse on, so it came: 410
Or worst of all, now—men you visit, men,
Ignoblest troops who never heard her voice
Or hate it, men without one gift from Rome

Or Athens,—these shall Aureole's teachers be!
Rejecting past example, practice, precept,   415
Aidless 'mid these he thinks to stand alone:
Thick like a glory round the Stagirite
Your rivals throng, the sages: here stand you!
Whatever you may protest, knowledge is not
Paramount in your love; or for her sake   420
You would collect all help from every source—
Rival, assistant, friend, foe, all would merge
In the broad class of those who showed her haunts,
And those who showed them not.

PARACELSUS.   What shall I say?
Festus, from childhood I have been possessed   425
By a fire—by a true fire, or faint or fierce,
As from without some master, so it seemed,
Repressed or urged its current: this but ill
Expresses what I would convey: but rather
I will believe an angel ruled me thus,   430
Than that my soul's own workings, own high nature,
So became manifest. I knew not then
What whispered in the evening, and spoke out
At midnight. If some mortal, born too soon,
Were laid away in some great trance—the ages   435
Coming and going all the while—till dawned
His true time's advent; and could then record
The words they spoke who kept watch by his bed,—
Then I might tell more of the breath so light
Upon my eyelids, and the fingers light   440
Among my hair. Youth is confused; yet never
So dull was I but, when that spirit passed,
I turned to him, scarce consciously, as turns
A water-snake when fairies cross his sleep.
And having this within me and about me   445
While Einsiedeln, its mountains, lakes and woods
Confined me—what oppressive joy was mine
When life grew plain, and I first viewed the thronged,
The everlasting concourse of mankind!
Believe that ere I joined them, ere I knew   450
The purpose of the pageant, or the place
Consigned me in its ranks—while, just awake,

Wonder was freshest and delight most pure—
'T was then that least supportable appeared
A station with the brightest of the crowd,   455
A portion with the proudest of them all.
And from the tumult in my breast, this only
Could I collect, that I must thenceforth die
Or elevate myself far, far above
The gorgeous spectacle. I seemed to long   460
At once to trample on, yet save mankind,
To make some unexampled sacrifice
In their behalf, to wring some wondrous good
From heaven or earth for them, to perish, winning
Eternal weal in the act: as who should dare   465
Pluck out the angry thunder from its cloud,
That, all its gathered flame discharged on him,
No storm might threaten summer's azure sleep:
Yet never to be mixed with men so much
As to have part even in my own work, share   470
In my own largess. Once the feat achieved,
I would withdraw from their officious praise,
Would gently put aside their profuse thanks,
Like some knight traversing a wilderness,
Who, on his way, may chance to free a tribe   475
Of desert-people from their dragon-foe;
When all the swarthy race press round to kiss
His feet, and choose him for their king, and yield
Their poor tents, pitched among the sand-hills, for
His realm: and he points, smiling, to his scarf   480
Heavy with riveled gold, his burgonet
Gay set with twinkling stones—and to the East,
Where these must be displayed!

FESTUS.   Good: let us hear
No more about your nature, 'which first shrank
'From all that marked you out apart from men!'   485

PARACELSUS. I touch on that; these words but analyse
The first mad impulse: 't was as brief as fond,
For as I gazed again upon the show,
I soon distinguished here and there a shape
Palm-wreathed and radiant, forehead and full eye.   490
Well pleased was I their state should thus at once

Interpret my own thoughts:—'Behold the clue
'To all,' I rashly said, 'and what I pine
'To do, these have accomplished: we are peers.
'They know and therefore rule: I, too, will know!'   495
You were beside me, Festus, as you say;
You saw me plunge in their pursuits whom fame
Is lavish to attest the lords of mind,
Not pausing to make sure the prize in view
Would satiate my cravings when obtained,   500
But since they strove I strove. Then came a slow
And strangling failure. We aspired alike,
Yet not the meanest plodder, Tritheim counts
A marvel, but was all-sufficient, strong,
Or staggered only at his own vast wits;   505
While I was restless, nothing satisfied,
Distrustful, most perplexed. I would slur over
That struggle; suffice it, that I loathed myself
As weak compared with them, yet felt somehow
A mighty power was brooding, taking shape   510
Within me; and this lasted till one night
When, as I sat revolving it and more,
A still voice from without said—'Seest thou not,
'Desponding child, whence spring defeat and loss?
'Even from thy strength. Consider: hast thou gazed   515
'Presumptuously on wisdom's countenance,
'No veil between; and can thy faltering hands,
'Unguided by the brain the sight absorbs,
'Pursue their task as earnest blinkers do
'Whom radiance ne'er distracted? Live their life   520
'If thou wouldst share their fortune, choose their eyes
'Unfed by splendour. Let each task present
'Its petty good to thee. Waste not thy gifts
'In profitless waiting for the gods' descent,
'But have some idol of thine own to dress   525
'With their array. Know, not for knowing's sake,
'But to become a star to men for ever;
'Know, for the gain it gets, the praise it brings,
'The wonder it inspires, the love it breeds:
'Look one step onward, and secure that step!'   530
And I smiled as one never smiles but once,

Then first discovering my own aim's extent,
Which sought to comprehend the works of God,
And God himself, and all God's intercourse
With the human mind; I understood, no less,   535
My fellows' studies, whose true worth I saw,
But smiled not, well aware who stood by me.
And softer came the voice—'There is a way:
''T is hard for flesh to tread therein, imbued
'With frailty—hopeless, if indulgence first   540
'Have ripened inborn germs of sin to strength:
'Wilt thou adventure for my sake and man's,
'Apart from all reward?' And last it breathed—
'Be happy, my good soldier; I am by thee,
'Be sure, even to the end!'—I answered not,   545
Knowing him. As he spoke, I was endued
With comprehension and a steadfast will;
And when he ceased, my brow was sealed his own.
If there took place no special change in me,
How comes it all things wore a different hue   550
Thenceforward?—pregnant with vast consequence,
Teeming with grand result, loaded with fate?
So that when, quailing at the mighty range
Of secret truths which yearn for birth, I haste
To contemplate undazzled some one truth,   555
Its bearings and effects alone—at once
What was a speck expands into a star,
Asking a life to pass exploring thus,
Till I near craze. I go to prove my soul!
I see my way as birds their trackless way.   560
I shall arrive! what time, what circuit first,
I ask not: but unless God send his hail
Or blinding fireballs, sleet or stifling snow,
In some time, his good time, I shall arrive:
He guides me and the bird. In his good time!   565
MICHAL. Vex him no further, Festus; it is so!
FESTUS. Just thus you help me ever. This would hold
Were it the trackless air, and not a path
Inviting you, distinct with footprints yet
Of many a mighty marcher gone that way.   570
You may have purer views than theirs, perhaps,

But they were famous in their day—the proofs
Remain. At least accept the light they lend.
PARACELSUS. Their light! the sum of all is briefly this:
They laboured and grew famous, and the fruits   575
Are best seen in a dark and groaning earth
Given over to a blind and endless strife
With evils, what of all their lore abates?
No; I reject and spurn them utterly
And all they teach. Shall I still sit beside   580
Their dry wells, with a white lip and filmed eye,
While in the distance heaven is blue above
Mountains where sleep the unsunned tarns?
FESTUS.   And yet
As strong delusions have prevailed ere now.
Men have set out as gallantly to seek   585
Their ruin. I have heard of such: yourself
Avow all hitherto have failed and fallen.
MICHAL. Nay, Festus, when but as the pilgrims faint
Through the drear way, do you expect to see
Their city dawn amid the clouds afar?   590
PARACELSUS. Ay, sounds it not like some old well-known tale?
For me, I estimate their works and them
So rightly, that at times I almost dream
I too have spent a life the sages' way,
And tread once more familiar paths. Perchance   595
I perished in an arrogant self-reliance
Ages ago; and in that act, a prayer
For one more chance went up so earnest, so
Instinct with better light let in by death,
That life was blotted out—not so completely   600
But scattered wrecks enough of it remain,
Dim memories, as now, when once more seems
The goal in sight again. All which, indeed,
Is foolish, and only means—the flesh I wear,
The earth I tread, are not more clear to me   605
Than my belief, explained to you or no.
FESTUS. And who am I, to challenge and dispute
That clear belief? I will divest all fear.
MICHAL. Then Aureole is God's commissary! he shall
Be great and grand—and all for us!

PARACELSUS.   No, sweet!   610
  Not great and grand. If I can serve mankind
  'T is well; but there our intercourse must end:
  I never will be served by those I serve.
FESTUS. Look well to this; here is a plague-spot, here,
  Disguise it how you may! 'T is true, you utter   615
  This scorn while by our side and loving us;
  'T is but a spot as yet: but it will break
  Into a hideous blotch if overlooked.
  How can that course be safe which from the first
  Produces carelessness to human love?   620
  It seems you have abjured the helps which men
  Who overpass their kind, as you would do,
  Have humbly sought; I dare not thoroughly probe
  This matter, lest I learn too much. Let be
  That popular praise would little instigate   625
  Your efforts, nor particular approval
  Reward you; put reward aside; alone
  You shall go forth upon your arduous task,
  None shall assist you, none partake your toil,
  None share your triumph: still you must retain   630
  Some one to cast your glory on, to share
  Your rapture with. Were I elect like you,
  I would encircle me with love, and raise
  A rampart of my fellows; it should seem
  Impossible for me to fail, so watched   635
  By gentle friends who made my cause their own.
  They should ward off fate's envy—the great gift,
  Extravagant when claimed by me alone,
  Being so a gift to them as well as me.
  If danger daunted me or ease seduced,   640
  How calmly their sad eyes should gaze reproach!
MICHAL. O Aureole, can I sing when all alone,
  Without first calling, in my fancy, both
  To listen by my side—even I! And you?
  Do you not feel this? Say that you feel this!   645
PARACELSUS. I feel 't is pleasant that my aims, at length
  Allowed their weight, should be supposed to need
  A further strengthening in these goodly helps!
  My course allures for its own sake, its sole

Intrinsic worth; and ne'er shall boat of mine   650
Adventure forth for gold and apes at once.
Your sages say, 'if human, therefore weak:'
If weak, more need to give myself entire
To my pursuit; and by its side, all else . . .
No matter! I deny myself but little   655
In waiving all assistance save its own.
Would there were some real sacrifice to make!
Your friends the sages threw their joys away,
While I must be content with keeping mine.
FESTUS. But do not cut yourself from human weal!   660
You cannot thrive—a man that dares affect
To spend his life in service to his kind
For no reward of theirs, unbound to them
By any tie; nor do so, Aureole! No—
There are strange punishments for such. Give up   665
(Although no visible good flow thence) some part
Of the glory to another; hiding thus,
Even from yourself, that all is for yourself.
Say, say almost to God—'I have done all
'For her, not for myself!'
PARACELSUS.   And who but lately   670
Was to rejoice in my success like you?
Whom should I love but both of you?
FESTUS.   I know not:
But know this, you, that 't is no will of mine
You should abjure the lofty claims you make;
And this the cause—I can no longer seek   675
To overlook the truth, that there would be
A monstrous spectacle upon the earth,
Beneath the pleasant sun, among the trees:
—A being knowing not what love is. Hear me!
You are endowed with faculties which bear   680
Annexed to them as 't were a dispensation
To summon meaner spirits to do their will
And gather round them at their need; inspiring
Such with a love themselves can never feel,
Passionless 'mid their passionate votaries.   685
I know not if you joy in this or no,
Or ever dream that common men can live

On objects you prize lightly, but which make
Their heart's sole treasure: the affections seem
Beauteous at most to you, which we must taste   690
Or die: and this strange quality accords,
I know not how, with you; sits well upon
That luminous brow, though in another it scowls
An eating brand, a shame. I dare not judge you.
The rules of right and wrong thus set aside,   695
There's no alternative—I own you one
Of higher order, under other laws
Than bind us; therefore, curb not one bold glance!
'T is best aspire. Once mingled with us all . . .
MICHAL. Stay with us, Aureole! cast those hopes away, 700
And stay with us! An angel warns me, too,
Man should be humble; you are very proud:
And God, dethroned, has doleful plagues for such!
—Warns me to have in dread no quick repulse,
No slow defeat, but a complete success: 705
You will find all you seek, and perish so!
PARACELSUS [*after a pause*]. Are these the barren firstfruits of my
        quest?
Is love like this the natural lot of all?
How many years of pain might one such hour
O'erbalance? Dearest Michal, dearest Festus,   710
What shall I say, if not that I desire
To justify your love; and will, dear friends,
In swerving nothing from my first resolves.
See, the great moon! and ere the mottled owls
Were wide awake, I was to go. It seems   715
You acquiesce at last in all save this—
If I am like to compass what I seek
By the untried career I choose; and then,
If that career, making but small account
Of much of life's delight, will yet retain   720
Sufficient to sustain my soul: for thus
I understand these fond fears just expressed.
And first; the lore you praise and I neglect,
The labours and the precepts of old time,
I have not lightly disesteemed. But, friends,   725
Truth is within ourselves; it takes no rise

From outward things, whate'er you may believe.
There is an inmost centre in us all,
Where truth abides in fulness; and around,
Wall upon wall, the gross flesh hems it in,   730
This perfect, clear perception—which is truth.
A baffling and perverting carnal mesh
Binds it, and makes all error: and to KNOW
Rather consists in opening out a way
Whence the imprisoned splendour may escape,   735
Than in effecting entry for a light
Supposed to be without. Watch narrowly
The demonstration of a truth, its birth,
And you trace back the effluence to its spring
And source within us; where broods radiance vast,   740
To be elicited ray by ray, as chance
Shall favour: chance—for hitherto, your sage
Even as he knows not how those beams are born,
As little knows he what unlocks their fount:
And men have oft grown old among their books   745
To die case-hardened in their ignorance,
Whose careless youth had promised what long years
Of unremitted labour ne'er performed:
While, contrary, it has chanced some idle day,
To autumn loiterers just as fancy-free   750
As the midges in the sun, gives birth at last
To truth—produced mysteriously as cape
Of cloud grown out of the invisible air.
Hence, may not truth be lodged alike in all,
The lowest as the highest? some slight film   755
The interposing bar which binds a soul
And makes the idiot, just as makes the sage
Some film removed, the happy outlet whence
Truth issues proudly? See this soul of ours!
How it strives weakly in the child, is loosed   760
In manhood, clogged by sickness, back compelled
By age and waste, set free at last by death:
Why is it, flesh enthrals it or enthrones?
What is this flesh we have to penetrate?
Oh, not alone when life flows still, do truth   765
And power emerge, but also when strange chance

Ruffles its current; in unused conjuncture,
When sickness breaks the body—hunger, watching,
Excess or languor—oftenest death's approach,
Peril, deep joy or woe. One man shall crawl　　　770
Through life surrounded with all stirring things,
Unmoved; and he goes mad: and from the wreck
Of what he was, by his wild talk alone,
You first collect how great a spirit he hid.
Therefore, set free the soul alike in all,　　　775
Discovering the true laws by which the flesh
Accloys the spirit! We may not be doomed
To cope with seraphs, but at least the rest
Shall cope with us. Make no more giants, God,
But elevate the race at once! We ask　　　780
To put forth just our strength, our human strength,
All starting fairly, all equipped alike,
Gifted alike, all eagle-eyed, true-hearted—
See if we cannot beat thine angels yet!
Such is my task. I go to gather this　　　785
The sacred knowledge, here and there dispersed
About the world, long lost or never found.
And why should I be sad or lorn of hope?
Why ever make man's good distinct from God's,
Or, finding they are one, why dare mistrust?　　　790
Who shall succeed if not one pledged like me?
Mine is no mad attempt to build a world
Apart from his, like those who set themselves
To find the nature of the spirit they bore,
And, taught betimes that all their gorgeous dreams　　　795
Were only born to vanish in this life,
Refused to fit them to its narrow sphere,
But chose to figure forth another world
And other frames meet for their vast desires,—
And all a dream! Thus was life scorned; but life　　　800
Shall yet be crowned: twine amaranth! I am priest!
And all for yielding with a lively spirit
A poor existence, parting with a youth
Like those who squander every energy
Convertible to good, on painted toys,　　　805
Breath-bubbles, gilded dust! And though I spurn

All adventitious aims, from empty praise
To love's award, yet whoso deems such helps
Important, and concerns himself for me,
May know even these will follow with the rest—   810
As in the steady rolling Mayne, asleep
Yonder, is mixed its mass of schistous ore.
My own affections laid to rest awhile,
Will waken purified, subdued alone
By all I have achieved. Till then—till then . . .   815
Ah, the time-wiling loitering of a page
Through bower and over lawn, till eve shall bring
The stately lady's presence whom he loves—
The broken sleep of the fisher whose rough coat
Enwraps the queenly pearl—these are faint types!   820
See, see, they look on me: I triumph now!
But one thing, Festus, Michal! I have told
All I shall e'er disclose to mortal: say—
Do you believe I shall accomplish this?
FESTUS. I do believe!
MICHAL.   I ever did believe!   825
PARACELSUS. Those words shall never fade from out my brain!
This earnest of the end shall never fade!
Are there not, Festus, are there not, dear Michal,
Two points in the adventure of the diver,
One—when, a beggar, he prepares to plunge,   830
One—when, a prince, he rises with his pearl?
Festus, I plunge!
FESTUS.   We wait you when you rise!

PART II

PARACELSUS ATTAINS

SCENE. *Constantinople; the house of a Greek Conjurer.* 1521.

PARACELSUS

Over the waters in the vaporous West
The sun goes down as in a sphere of gold

Behind the arm of the city, which between,
With all that length of domes and minarets,
Athwart the splendour, black and crooked runs   5
Like a Turk verse along a scimitar.
There lie, sullen memorial, and no more
Possess my aching sight! 'T is done at last.
Strange—and the juggles of a sallow cheat
Have won me to this act! 'T is as yon cloud   10
Should voyage unwrecked o'er many a mountain-top
And break upon a molehill. I have dared
Come to a pause with knowledge; scan for once
The heights already reached, without regard
To the extent above; fairly compute   15
All I have clearly gained; for once excluding
A brilliant future to supply and perfect
All half-gains and conjectures and crude hopes:
And all because a fortune-teller wills
His credulous seekers should inscribe thus much   20
Their previous life's attainment, in his roll,
Before his promised secret, as he vaunts,
Make up the sum: and here amid the scrawled
Uncouth recordings of the dupes of this
Old arch-genethliac, lie my life's results!   25

A few blurred characters suffice to note
A stranger wandered long through many lands
And reaped the fruit he coveted in a few
Discoveries, as appended here and there,
The fragmentary produce of much toil,   30
In a dim heap, fact and surmise together
Confusedly massed as when acquired; he was
Intent on gain to come too much to stay
And scrutinize the little gained: the whole
Slipt in the blank space 'twixt an idiot's gibber   35
And a mad lover's ditty—there it lies.

And yet those blottings chronicle a life—
A whole life, and my life! Nothing to do,
No problem for the fancy, but a life
Spent and decided, wasted past retrieve   40

Or worthy beyond peer. Stay, what does this
Remembrancer set down concerning 'life'?
' "Time fleets, youth fades, life is an empty dream,"
'It is the echo of time; and he whose heart
'Beat first beneath a human heart, whose speech   45
'Was copied from a human tongue, can never
'Recall when he was living yet knew not this.
'Nevertheless long seasons pass o'er him
'Till some one hour's experience shows what nothing,
'It seemed, could clearer show; and ever after,   50
'An altered brow and eye and gait and speech
'Attest that now he knows the adage true
' "Time fleets, youth fades, life is an empty dream." '

Ay, my brave chronicler, and this same hour
As well as any: now, let my time be!   55

Now! I can go no farther; well or ill,
'T is done. I must desist and take my chance.
I cannot keep on the stretch: 't is no back-shrinking—
For let but some assurance beam, some close
To my toil grow visible, and I proceed   60
At any price, though closing it, I die.
Else, here I pause. The old Greek's prophecy
Is like to turn out true: 'I shall not quit
'His chamber till I know what I desire!'
Was it the light wind sang it o'er the sea?   65

An end, a rest! strange how the notion, once
Encountered, gathers strength by moments! Rest!
Where has it kept so long? this throbbing brow
To cease, this beating heart to cease, all cruel
And gnawing thoughts to cease! To dare let down   70
My strung, so high-strung brain, to dare unnerve
My harassed o'ertasked frame, to know my place,
My portion, my reward, even my failure,
Assigned, made sure for ever! To lose myself
Among the common creatures of the world,   75
To draw some gain from having been a man,
Neither to hope nor fear, to live at length!

Even in failure, rest! But rest in truth
And power and recompense . . . I hoped that once!

What, sunk insensibly so deep? Has all   80
Been undergone for this? This the request
My labour qualified me to present
With no fear of refusal? Had I gone
Slightingly through my task, and so judged fit
To moderate my hopes; nay, were it now   85
My sole concern to exculpate myself,
End things or mend them,—why, I could not choose
A humbler mood to wait for the event!
No, no, there needs not this; no, after all,
At worst I have performed my share of the task: 90
The rest is God's concern; mine, merely this,
To know that I have obstinately held
By my own work. The mortal whose brave foot
Has trod, unscathed, the temple-court so far
That he descries at length the shrine of shrines,   95
Must let no sneering of the demons' eyes,
Whom he could pass unquailing, fasten now
Upon him, fairly past their power; no, no—
He must not stagger, faint, fall down at last,
Having a charm to baffle them; behold,   100
He bares his front: a mortal ventures thus
Serene amid the echoes, beams and glooms!
If he be priest henceforth, if he wake up
The god of the place to ban and blast him there,
Both well! What's failure or success to me?   105
I have subdued my life to the one purpose
Whereto I ordained it; there alone I spy,
No doubt, that way I may be satisfied.

Yes, well have I subdued my life! beyond
The obligation of my strictest vow,   110
The contemplation of my wildest bond,
Which gave my nature freely up, in truth,
But in its actual state, consenting fully
All passionate impulses its soil was formed
To rear, should wither; but foreseeing not   115

The tract, doomed to perpetual barrenness,
Would seem one day, remembered as it was,
Beside the parched sand-waste which now it is,
Already strewn with faint blooms, viewless then.
I ne'er engaged to root up loves so frail   120
I felt them not; yet now, 't is very plain
Some soft spots had their birth in me at first,
If not love, say, like love: there was a time
When yet this wolfish hunger after knowledge
Set not remorselessly love's claims aside.   125
This heart was human once, or why recall
Einsiedeln, now, and Würzburg which the Mayne
Forsakes her course to fold as with an arm?

And Festus—my poor Festus, with his praise
And counsel and grave fears—where is he now   130
With the sweet maiden, long ago his bride?
I surely loved them—that last night, at least,
When we . . . gone! gone! the better. I am saved
The sad review of an ambitious youth
Choked by vile lusts, unnoticed in their birth,   135
But let grow up and wind around a will
Till action was destroyed. No, I have gone
Purging my path successively of aught
Wearing the distant likeness of such lusts.
I have made life consist of one idea: 140
Ere that was master, up till that was born,
I bear a memory of a pleasant life
Whose small events I treasure; till one morn
I ran o'er the seven little grassy fields,
Startling the flocks of nameless birds, to tell   145
Poor Festus, leaping all the while for joy,
To leave all trouble for my future plans,
Since I had just determined to become
The greatest and most glorious man on earth.
And since that morn all life has been forgotten;   150
All is one day, one only step between
The outset and the end: one tyrant all-
Absorbing aim fills up the interspace,
One vast unbroken chain of thought, kept up

Through a career apparently adverse   155
To its existence: life, death, light and shadow,
The shows of the world, were bare receptacles
Or indices of truth to be wrung thence,
Not ministers of sorrow or delight:
A wondrous natural robe in which she went.   160
For some one truth would dimly beacon me
From mountains rough with pines, and flit and wink
O'er dazzling wastes of frozen snow, and tremble
Into assured light in some branching mine
Where ripens, swathed in fire, the liquid gold—   165
And all the beauty, all the wonder fell
On either side the truth, as its mere robe;
I see the robe now—then I saw the form.
So far, then, I have voyaged with success,
So much is good, then, in this working sea   170
Which parts me from that happy strip of land:
But o'er that happy strip a sun shone, too!
And fainter gleams it as the waves grow rough,
And still more faint as the sea widens; last
I sicken on a dead gulf streaked with light   175
From its own putrefying depths alone.
Then, God was pledged to take me by the hand;
Now, any miserable juggle can bid
My pride depart. All is alike at length:
God may take pleasure in confounding pride   180
By hiding secrets with the scorned and base—
I am here, in short: so little have I paused
Throughout! I never glanced behind to know
If I had kept my primal light from wane,
And thus insensibly am—what I am!   185

Oh, bitter; very bitter!
                              And more bitter,
To fear a deeper curse, an inner ruin,
Plague beneath plague, the last turning the first
To light beside its darkness. Let me weep
My youth and its brave hopes, all dead and gone,   190
In tears which burn! Would I were sure to win
Some startling secret in their stead, a tincture

D

Of force to flush old age with youth, or breed
Gold, or imprison moonbeams till they change
To opal shafts!—only that, hurling it   195
Indignant back, I might convince myself
My aims remained supreme and pure as ever!
Even now, why not desire, for mankind's sake,
That if I fail, some fault may be the cause,
That, though I sink, another may succeed?   200
O God, the despicable heart of us!
Shut out this hideous mockery from my heart!

'T was politic in you, Aureole, to reject
Single rewards, and ask them in the lump;
At all events, once launched, to hold straight on: 205
For now 't is all or nothing. Mighty profit
Your gains will bring if they stop short of such
Full consummation! As a man, you had
A certain share of strength; and that is gone
Already in the getting these you boast.   210
Do not they seem to laugh, as who should say—
'Great master, we are here indeed, dragged forth
'To light; this hast thou done: be glad! Now, seek
'The strength to use which thou hast spent in getting!'

And yet 't is much, surely 't is very much,   215
Thus to have emptied youth of all its gifts,
To feed a fire meant to hold out till morn
Arrived with inexhaustible light; and lo,
I have heaped up my last, and day dawns not!
And I am left with grey hair, faded hands,   220
And furrowed brow. Ha, have I, after all,
Mistaken the wild nursling of my breast?
Knowledge it seemed, and power, and recompense!
Was she who glided through my room of nights,
Who laid my head on her soft knees and smoothed   225
The damp locks,—whose sly soothings just began
When my sick spirit craved repose awhile—
God! was I fighting sleep off for death's sake?

God! Thou art mind! Unto the master-mind

Mind should be precious. Spare my mind alone!   230
All else I will endure; if, as I stand
Here, with my gains, thy thunder smite me down,
I bow me; 't is thy will, thy righteous will;
I o'erpass life's restrictions, and I die;
And if no trace of my career remain   235
Save a thin corpse at pleasure of the wind
In these bright chambers level with the air,
See thou to it! But if my spirit fail,
My once proud spirit forsake me at the last,
Hast thou done well by me? So do not thou!   240
Crush not my mind, dear God, though I be crushed!
Hold me before the frequence of thy seraphs
And say—'I crushed him, lest he should disturb
'My law. Men must not know their strength: behold
'Weak and alone, how he had raised himself!'   245

But if delusions trouble me, and thou,
Not seldom felt with rapture in thy help
Throughout my toils and wanderings, dost intend
To work man's welfare through my weak endeavour,
To crown my mortal forehead with a beam   250
From thine own blinding crown, to smile, and guide
This puny hand and let the work so wrought
Be styled my work,—hear me! I covet not
An influx of new power, an angel's soul:
It were no marvel then—but I have reached   255
Thus far, a man; let me conclude, a man!
Give but one hour of my first energy,
Of that invincible faith, but only one!
That I may cover with an eagle-glance
The truths I have, and spy some certain way   260
To mould them, and completing them, possess!
Yet God is good: I started sure of that,
And why dispute it now? I'll not believe
But some undoubted warning long ere this
Had reached me: a fire-labarum was not deemed   265
Too much for the old founder of these walls.
Then, if my life has not been natural,
It has been monstrous: yet, till late, my course

So ardently engrossed me, that delight,
A pausing and reflecting joy, 't is plain,   270
Could find no place in it. True, I am worn;
But who clothes summer, who is life itself?
God, that created all things, can renew!
And then, though after-life to please me now
Must have no likeness to the past, what hinders   275
Reward from springing out of toil, as changed
As bursts the flower from earth and root and stalk?
What use were punishment, unless some sin
Be first detected? let me know that first!
No man could ever offend as I have done . . .   280

[*A voice from within.*]

I hear a voice, perchance I heard
Long ago, but all too low,
So that scarce a care it stirred
If the voice were real or no:
I heard it in my youth when first   285
The waters of my life outburst:
But, now their stream ebbs faint, I hear
That voice, still low, but fatal-clear—
As if all poets, God ever meant
Should save the world, and therefore lent   290
Great gifts to, but who, proud, refused
To do his work, or lightly used
Those gifts, or failed through weak endeavour,
So, mourn cast off by him for ever,—
As if these leaned in airy ring   295
To take me; this the song they sing.

'Lost, lost! yet come,
With our wan troop make thy home.
Come, come! for we
Will not breathe, so much as breathe   300
Reproach to thee,
Knowing what thou sink'st beneath.
So sank we in those old years,
We who bid thee, come! thou last

Who, living yet, hast life o'erpast.   305
And altogether we, thy peers,
Will pardon crave for thee, the last
Whose trial is done, whose lot is cast
With those who watch but work no more,
Who gaze on life but live no more.   310
Yet we trusted thou shouldst speak
The message which our lips, too weak,
Refused to utter,—shouldst redeem
Our fault: such trust, and all a dream!
Yet we chose thee a birthplace   315
Where the richness ran to flowers:
Couldst not sing one song for grace?
Not make one blossom man's and ours?
Must one more recreant to his race
Die with unexerted powers,   320
And join us, leaving as he found
The world, he was to loosen, bound?
Anguish! ever and for ever;
Still beginning, ending never.
Yet, lost and last one, come!   325
How couldst understand, alas,
What our pale ghosts strove to say,
As their shades did glance and pass
Before thee night and day?
Thou wast blind as we were dumb: 330
Once more, therefore, come, O come!
How should we clothe, how arm the spirit
Shall next thy post of life inherit—
How guard him from thy speedy ruin?
Tell us of thy sad undoing   335
Here, where we sit, ever pursuing
Our weary task, ever renewing
Sharp sorrow, far from God who gave
Our powers, and man they could not save!'

APRILE *enters.*

Ha, ha! our king that wouldst be, here at last?   340
Art thou the poet who shall save the world?

Thy hand to mine! Stay, fix thine eyes on mine!
Thou wouldst be king? Still fix thine eyes on mine!
PARACELSUS. Ha, ha! why crouchest not? Am I not king?
So torture is not wholly unavailing!   345
Have my fierce spasms compelled thee from thy lair?
Art thou the sage I only seemed to be,
Myself of after-time, my very self
With sight a little clearer, strength more firm,
Who robes him in my robe and grasps my crown   350
For just a fault, a weakness, a neglect?
I scarcely trusted God with the surmise
That such might come, and thou didst hear the while!
APRILE. Thine eyes are lustreless to mine; my hair
Is soft, nay silken soft: to talk with thee   355
Flushes my cheek, and thou art ashy-pale.
Truly, thou hast laboured, hast withstood her lips,
The siren's! Yes, 't is like thou hast attained!
Tell me, dear master, wherefore now thou comest?
I thought thy solemn songs would have their meed   360
In after-time; that I should hear the earth
Exult in thee and echo with thy praise,
While I was laid forgotten in my grave.
PARACELSUS. Ah fiend, I know thee, I am not thy dupe!
Thou art ordained to follow in my track,   365
Reaping my sowing, as I scorned to reap
The harvest sown by sages passed away.
Thou art the sober searcher, cautious striver,
As if, except through me, thou hast searched or striven!
Ay, tell the world! Degrade me after all,   370
To an aspirant after fame, not truth—
To all but envy of thy fate, be sure!
APRILE. Nay, sing them to me; I shall envy not:
Thou shalt be king! Sing thou, and I will sit
Beside, and call deep silence for thy songs,   375
And worship thee, as I had ne'er been meant
To fill thy throne: but none shall ever know!
Sing to me; for already thy wild eyes
Unlock my heart-strings, as some crystal-shaft
Reveals by some chance blaze its parent fount   380
After long time: so thou reveal'st my soul.

All will flash forth at last, with thee to hear!

PARACELSUS. (His secret! I shall get his secret—fool!)
   I am he that aspired to KNOW: and thou?

APRILE. I would LOVE infinitely, and be loved!   385

PARACELSUS. Poor slave! I am thy king indeed.

APRILE.   Thou deem'st
   That—born a spirit, dowered even as thou,
   Born for thy fate—because I could not curb
   My yearnings to possess at once the full
   Enjoyment, but neglected all the means   390
   Of realizing even the frailest joy,
   Gathering no fragments to appease my want,
   Yet nursing up that want till thus I die—
   Thou deem'st I cannot trace thy safe sure march
   O'er perils that o'erwhelm me, triumphing,   395
   Neglecting nought below for aught above,
   Despising nothing and ensuring all—
   Nor that I could (my time to come again)
   Lead thus my spirit securely as thine own.
   Listen, and thou shalt see I know thee well.   400
   I would love infinitely . . . Ah, lost! lost!
           Oh ye who armed me at such cost,
           How shall I look on all of ye
           With your gifts even yet on me?

PARACELSUS. (Ah, 't is some moonstruck creature after all!   405
   Such fond fools as are like to haunt this den:
   They spread contagion, doubtless: yet he seemed
   To echo one foreboding of my heart
   So truly, that . . . no matter! How he stands
   With eve's last sunbeam staying on his hair   410
   Which turns to it as if they were akin:
   And those clear smiling eyes of saddest blue
   Nearly set free, so far they rise above
   The painful fruitless striving of the brow
   And enforced knowledge of the lips, firm-set   415
   In slow despondency's eternal sigh!
   Has he, too, missed life's end, and learned the cause?)
   I charge thee, by thy fealty, be calm!
   Tell me what thou wouldst be, and what I am.

APRILE. I would love infinitely, and be loved.   420

First: I would carve in stone, or cast in brass,
The forms of earth. No ancient hunter lifted
Up to the gods by his renown, no nymph
Supposed the sweet soul of a woodland tree
Or sapphirine spirit of a twilight star,   425
Should be too hard for me; no shepherd-king
Regal for his white locks; no youth who stands
Silent and very calm amid the throng,
His right hand ever hid beneath his robe
Until the tyrant pass; no lawgiver,   430
No swan-soft woman rubbed with lucid oils
Given by a god for love of her—too hard!
Every passion sprung from man, conceived by man,
Would I express and clothe it in its right form,
Or blend with others struggling in one form,   435
Or show repressed by an ungainly form.
Oh, if you marvelled at some mighty spirit
With a fit frame to execute its will—
Even unconsciously to work its will—
You should be moved no less beside some strong   440
Rare spirit, fettered to a stubborn body,
Endeavouring to subdue it and inform it
With its own splendour! All this I would do:
And I would say, this done, 'His sprites created,
'God grants to each a sphere to be its world,   445
'Appointed with the various objects needed
'To satisfy its own peculiar want;
'So, I create a world for these my shapes
'Fit to sustain their beauty and their strength!'
And, at the word, I would contrive and paint   450
Woods, valleys, rocks and plains, dells, sands and wastes,
Lakes which, when morn breaks on their quivering bed,
Blaze like a wyvern flying round the sun,
And ocean isles so small, the dog-fish tracking
A dead whale, who should find them, would swim thrice   455
Around them, and fare onward—all to hold
The offspring of my brain. Nor these alone:
Bronze labyrinth, palace, pyramid and crypt,
Baths, galleries, courts, temples and terraces,
Marts, theatres and wharfs—all filled with men,   460

Men everywhere! And this performed in turn,
When those who looked on, pined to hear the hopes
And fears and hates and loves which moved the crowd,
I would throw down the pencil as the chisel,
And I would speak; no thought which ever stirred   465
A human breast should be untold; all passions,
All soft emotions, from the turbulent stir
Within a heart fed with desires like mine,
To the last comfort shutting the tired lids
Of him who sleeps the sultry noon away   470
Beneath the tent-tree by the wayside well:
And this in language as the need should be,
Now poured at once forth in a burning flow,
Now piled up in a grand array of words.
This done, to perfect and consummate all,   475
Even as a luminous haze links star to star,
I would supply all chasms with music, breathing
Mysterious motions of the soul, no way
To be defined save in strange melodies.
Last, having thus revealed all I could love,   480
Having received all love bestowed on it,
I would die: preserving so throughout my course
God full on me, as I was full on men:
He would approve my prayer, 'I have gone through
'The loveliness of life; create for me   485
'If not for men, or take me to thyself,
'Eternal, infinite love!'
                        If thou hast ne'er
Conceived this mighty aim, this full desire,
Thou hast not passed my trial, and thou art
No king of mine.
PARACELSUS.   Ah me!
APRILE.   But thou art here!   490
Thou didst not gaze like me upon that end
Till thine own powers for compassing the bliss
Were blind with glory; nor grow mad to grasp
At once the prize long patient toil should claim,
Nor spurn all granted short of that. And I   495
Would do as thou, a second time: nay, listen!
Knowing ourselves, our world, our task so great,

Our time so brief, 't is clear if we refuse
The means so limited, the tools so rude
To execute our purpose, life will fleet,   500
And we shall fade, and leave our task undone.
We will be wise in time: what though our work
Be fashioned in despite of their ill-service,
Be crippled every way? 'T were little praise
Did full resources wait on our goodwill   505
At every turn. Let all be as it is.
Some say the earth is even so contrived
That tree and flower, a vesture gay, conceal
A bare and skeleton framework. Had we means
Answering to our mind! But now I seem   510
Wrecked on a savage isle: how rear thereon
My palace? Branching palms the props shall be,
Fruit glossy mingling; gems are for the East;
Who heeds them? I can pass them. Serpents' scales,
And painted birds' down, furs and fishes' skins   515
Must help me; and a little here and there
Is all I can aspire to: still my art
Shall show its birth was in a gentler clime.
'Had I green jars of malachite, this way
'I'd range them: where those sea-shells glisten above,   520
'Cressets should hang, by right: this way we set
'The purple carpets, as these mats are laid,
'Woven of fern and rush and blossoming flag.'
Or if, by fortune, some completer grace
Be spared to me, some fragment, some slight sample   525
Of the prouder workmanship my own home boasts,
Some trifle little heeded there, but here
The place's one perfection—with what joy
Would I enshrine the relic, cheerfully
Foregoing all the marvels out of reach!   530
Could I retain one strain of all the psalm
Of the angels, one word of the fiat of God,
To let my followers know what such things are!
I would adventure nobly for their sakes:
When nights were still, and still the moaning sea,   535
And far away I could descry the land
Whence I departed, whither I return,

I would dispart the waves, and stand once more
At home, and load my bark, and hasten back,
And fling my gains to them, worthless or true.   540
'Friends,' I would say, 'I went far, far for them,
'Past the high rocks the haunt of doves, the mounds
'Of red earth from whose sides strange trees grow out,
'Past tracts of milk-white minute blinding sand,
'Till, by a mighty moon, I tremblingly   545
'Gathered these magic herbs, berry and bud,
'In haste, not pausing to reject the weeds,
'But happy plucking them at any price.
'To me, who have seen them bloom in their own soil,
'They are scarce lovely: plait and wear them, you!   550
'And guess, from what they are, the springs that fed them,
'The stars that sparkled o'er them, night by night,
'The snakes that travelled far to sip their dew!'
Thus for my higher loves; and thus even weakness
Would win me honour. But not these alone   555
Should claim my care; for common life, its wants
And ways, would I set forth in beauteous hues:
The lowest hind should not possess a hope,
A fear, but I'd be by him, saying better
Than he his own heart's language. I would live   560
For ever in the thoughts I thus explored,
As a discoverer's memory is attached
To all he finds; they should be mine henceforth,
Imbued with me, though free to all before:
For clay, once cast into my soul's rich mine,   565
Should come up crusted o'er with gems. Nor this
Would need a meaner spirit, than the first;
Nay, 't would be but the selfsame spirit, clothed
In humbler guise, but still the selfsame spirit:
As one spring wind unbinds the mountain snow   570
And comforts violets in their hermitage.

But, master, poet, who hast done all this,
How didst thou 'scape the ruin whelming me?
Didst thou, when nerving thee to this attempt,
Ne'er range thy mind's extent, as some wide hall,   575
Dazzled by shapes that filled its length with light,

Shapes clustered there to rule thee, not obey,
That will not wait thy summons, will not rise
Singly, nor when thy practised eye and hand
Can well transfer their loveliness, but crowd   580
By thee for ever, bright to thy despair?
Didst thou ne'er gaze on each by turns, and ne'er
Resolve to single out one, though the rest
Should vanish, and to give that one, entire
In beauty, to the world; forgetting, so,   585
Its peers, whose number baffles mortal power?
And, this determined, wast thou ne'er seduced
By memories and regrets and passionate love,
To glance once more farewell? and did their eyes
Fasten thee, brighter and more bright, until   590
Thou couldst but stagger back unto their feet,
And laugh that man's applause or welfare ever
Could tempt thee to forsake them? Or when years
Had passed and still their love possessed thee wholly,
When from without some murmur startled thee   595
Of darkling mortals famished for one ray
Of thy so-hoarded luxury of light,
Didst thou ne'er strive even yet to break those spells
And prove thou couldst recover and fulfil
Thy early mission, long ago renounced,   600
And to that end, select some shape once more?
And did not mist-like influences, thick films,
Faint memories of the rest that charmed so long
Thine eyes, float fast, confuse thee, bear thee off,
As whirling snow-drifts blind a man who treads   605
A mountain ridge, with guiding spear, through storm?
Say, though I fell, I had excuse to fall;
Say, I was tempted sorely: say but this,
Dear lord, Aprile's lord!
PARACELSUS.   Clasp me not thus,
Aprile! That the truth should reach me thus!   610
We are weak dust. Nay, clasp not or I faint!
APRILE. My king! and envious thoughts could outrage thee?
Lo, I forget my ruin, and rejoice
In thy success, as thou! Let our God's praise
Go bravely through the world at last! What care   615

Through me or thee? I feel thy breath. Why, tears?
Tears in the darkness, and from thee to me?
PARACELSUS. Love me henceforth, Aprile, while I learn
To love; and, merciful God, forgive us both!
We wake at length from weary dreams; but both   620
Have slept in fairy-land: though dark and drear
Appears the world before us, we no less
Wake with our wrists and ankles jewelled still.
I too have sought to KNOW as thou to LOVE—
Excluding love as thou refusedst knowledge.   625
Still thou hast beauty and I, power. We wake:
What penance canst devise for both of us?
APRILE. I hear thee faintly. The thick darkness! Even
Thine eyes are hid. 'T is as I knew: I speak,
And now I die. But I have seen thy face!   630
O poet, think of me, and sing of me!
But to have seen thee and to die so soon!
PARACELSUS. Die not, Aprile! We must never part.
Are we not halves of one dissevered world,
Whom this strange chance unites once more? Part? never!   635
Till thou the lover, know; and I, the knower,
Love—until both are saved. Aprile, hear!
We will accept our gains, and use them—now!
God, he will die upon my breast! Aprile!
APRILE. To speak but once, and die! yet by his side.   640
Hush! hush!
        Ha! go you ever girt about
With phantoms, powers? I have created such,
But these seem real as I.
PARACELSUS.   Whom can you see
Through the accursed darkness?
APRILE.   Stay; I know,
I know them: who should know them well as I?   645
White brows, lit up with glory; poets all!
PARACELSUS. Let him but live, and I have my reward!
APRILE. Yes; I see now. God is the perfect poet,
Who in his person acts his own creations.
Had you but told me this at first! Hush! hush!   650
PARACELSUS. Live! for my sake, because of my great sin,
To help my brain, oppressed by these wild words

And their deep import. Live! 't is not too late.
I have a quiet home for us, and friends.
Michal shall smile on you. Hear you? Lean thus,   655
And breathe my breath. I shall not lose one word
Of all your speech, one little word, Aprile!
APRILE. No, no. Crown me? I am not one of you!
'T is he, the king, you seek. I am not one.
PARACELSUS. Thy spirit, at least, Aprile! Let me love!   660

I have attained, and now I may depart.

PART III

PARACELSUS

SCENE.—*Basil; a chamber in the house of* PARACELSUS. 1526.

PARACELSUS, FESTUS

PARACELSUS. Heap logs and let the blaze laugh out!
FESTUS.   True, true!
'T is very fit all, time and chance and change
Have wrought since last we sat thus, face to face
And soul to soul—all cares, far-looking fears,
Vague apprehensions, all vain fancies bred   5
By your long absence, should be cast away,
Forgotten in this glad unhoped renewal
Of our affections.
PARACELSUS.   Oh, omit not aught
Which witnesses your own and Michal's own
Affection: spare not that! Only forget   10
The honours and the glories and what not,
It pleases you to tell profusely out.
FESTUS. Nay, even your honours, in a sense, I waive:
The wondrous Paracelsus, life's dispenser,
Fate's commissary, idol of the schools   15
And courts, shall be no more than Aureole still,
Still Aureole and my friend as when we parted
Some twenty years ago, and I restrained

As best I could the promptings of my spirit
Which secretly advanced you, from the first,   20
To the pre-eminent rank which, since, your own
Adventurous ardour, nobly triumphing,
Has won for you.
PARACELSUS.   Yes, yes. And Michal's face
Still wears that quiet and peculiar light
Like the dim circlet floating round a pearl?   25
FESTUS. Just so.
PARACELSUS.   And yet her calm sweet countenance,
Though saintly, was not sad; for she would sing
Alone. Does she still sing alone, bird-like,
Not dreaming you are near? Her carols dropt
In flakes through that old leafy bower built under   30
The sunny wall at Würzburg, from her lattice
Among the trees above, while I, unseen,
Sat conning some rare scroll from Tritheim's shelves
Much wondering notes so simple could divert
My mind from study. Those were happy days.   35
Respect all such as sing when all alone!
FESTUS. Scarcely alone: her children, you may guess,
Are wild beside her.
PARACELSUS.   Ah, those children quite
Unsettle the pure picture in my mind:
A girl, she was so perfect, so distinct: 40
No change, no change! Not but this added grace
May blend and harmonize with its compeers,
And Michal may become her motherhood;
But 't is a change, and I detest all change,
And most a change in aught I loved long since.   45
So, Michal—you have said she thinks of me?
FESTUS. O very proud will Michal be of you!
Imagine how we sat, long winter-nights,
Scheming and wondering, shaping your presumed
Adventure, or devising its reward;   50
Shutting out fear with all the strength of hope.
For it was strange how, even when most secure
In our domestic peace, a certain dim
And flitting shade could sadden all; it seemed
A restlessness of heart, a silent yearning,   55

A sense of something wanting, incomplete—
Not to be put in words, perhaps avoided
By mute consent—but, said or unsaid, felt
To point to one so loved and so long lost.
And then the hopes rose and shut out the fears—   60
How you would laugh should I recount them now!
I still predicted your return at last
With gifts beyond the greatest of them all,
All Tritheim's wondrous troop; did one of which
Attain renown by any chance, I smiled,   65
As well aware of who would prove his peer.
Michal was sure some woman, long ere this,
As beautiful as you were sage, had loved . . .

PARACELSUS. Far-seeing, truly, to discern so much
In the fantastic projects and day-dreams   70
Of a raw restless boy!

FESTUS.   Oh, no: the sunrise
Well warranted our faith in this full noon!
Can I forget the anxious voice which said
'Festus, have thoughts like these ere shaped themselves
'In other brains than mine? have their possessors   75
'Existed in like circumstance? were they weak
'As I, or ever constant from the first,
'Despising youth's allurements and rejecting
'As spider-films the shackles I endure?
'Is there hope for me?'—and I answered gravely   80
As an acknowledged elder, calmer, wiser,
More gifted mortal. O you must remember,
For all your glorious . . .

PARACELSUS.   Glorious? ay, this hair,
These hands—nay, touch them, they are mine! Recall
With all the said recallings, times when thus   85
To lay them by your own ne'er turned you pale
As now. Most glorious, are they not?

FESTUS.   Why—why—
Something must be subtracted from success
So wide, no doubt. He would be scrupulous, truly,
Who should object such drawbacks. Still, still, Aureole,   90
You are changed, very changed! 'T were losing nothing
To look well to it: you must not be stolen

From the enjoyment of your well-won meed.

PARACELSUS. My friend! you seek my pleasure, past a doubt:
    You will best gain your point, by talking, not   95
    Of me, but of yourself.

FESTUS.   Have I not said
    All touching Michal and my children? Sure
    You know, by this, full well how Aennchen looks
    Gravely, while one disparts her thick brown hair;
    And Aureole's glee when some stray gannet builds   100
    Amid the birch-trees by the lake. Small hope
    Have I that he will honour (the wild imp)
    His namesake. Sigh not! 't is too much to ask
    That all we love should reach the same proud fate.
    But you are very kind to humour me   105
    By showing interest in my quiet life;
    You, who of old could never tame yourself
    To tranquil pleasures, must at heart despise . . .

PARACELSUS. Festus, strange secrets are let out by death
    Who blabs so oft the follies of this world: 110
    And I am death's familiar, as you know.
    I helped a man to die, some few weeks since,
    Warped even from his go-cart to one end—
    The living on princes' smiles, reflected from
    A mighty herd of favourites. No mean trick   115
    He left untried, and truly well-nigh wormed
    All traces of God's finger out of him:
    Then died, grown old. And just an hour before,
    Having lain long with blank and soulless eyes,
    He sat up suddenly, and with natural voice   120
    Said that in spite of thick air and closed doors
    God told him it was June; and he knew well,
    Without such telling, harebells grew in June;
    And all that kings could ever give or take
    Would not be precious as those blooms to him.   125
    Just so, allowing I am passing sage,
    It seems to me much worthier argument
    Why pansies,* eyes that laugh, bear beauty's prize
    From violets, eyes that dream—(your Michal's choice)—
    Than all fools find to wonder at in me   130

     * Citrinula (flammula) herba Paracelso multum familiaris.—DORN.

Or in my fortunes. And be very sure
I say this from no prurient restlessness,
No self-complacency, itching to turn,
Vary and view its pleasure from all points,
And, in this instance, willing other men   135
May be at pains, demonstrate to itself
The realness of the very joy it tastes.
What should delight me like the news of friends
Whose memories were a solace to me oft,
As mountain-baths to wild fowls in their flight?   140
Ofter than you had wasted thought on me
Had you been wise, and rightly valued bliss.
But there's no taming nor repressing hearts:
God knows I need such!—So, you heard me speak?
FESTUS. Speak? when?
PARACELSUS.   When but this morning at my class?   145
There was noise and crowd enough. I saw you not.
Surely you know I am engaged to fill
The chair here?—that 't is part of my proud fate
To lecture to as many thick-skulled youths
As please, each day, to throng the theatre,   150
To my great reputation, and no small
Danger of Basil's benches long unused
To crack beneath such honour?
FESTUS.   I was there;
I mingled with the throng: shall I avow
Small care was mine to listen?—too intent   155
On gathering from the murmurs of the crowd
A full corroboration of my hopes!
What can I learn about your powers? but they
Know, care for nought beyond your actual state,
Your actual value; yet they worship you,   160
Those various natures whom you sway as one!
But ere I go, be sure I shall attend . . .
PARACELSUS. Stop, o' God's name: the thing's by no means yet
Past remedy! Shall I read this morning's labour
—At least in substance? Nought so worth the gaining   165
As an apt scholar! Thus then, with all due
Precision and emphasis—you, beside, are clearly
Guiltless of understanding more, a whit,

The subject than your stool—allowed to be
A notable advantage.
FESTUS.   Surely, Aureole,   170
You laugh at me!
PARACELSUS.   I laugh? Ha, ha! thank heaven,
I charge you, if 't be so! for I forget
Much, and what laughter should be like. No less,
However, I forego that luxury
Since it alarms the friend who brings it back.   175
True, laughter like my own must echo strangely
To thinking men; a smile were better far;
So, make me smile! If the exulting look
You wore but now be smiling, 't is so long
Since I have smiled! Alas, such smiles are born   180
Alone of hearts like yours, or herdsmen's souls
Of ancient time, whose eyes, calm as their flocks,
Saw in the stars mere garnishry of heaven,
And in the earth a stage for altars only.
Never change, Festus: I say, never change!   185
FESTUS. My God, if he be wretched after all!
PARACELSUS. When last we parted, Festus, you declared,
—Or Michal, yes, her soft lips whispered words
I have preserved. She told me she believed
I should succeed (meaning, that in the search   190
I then engaged in, I should meet success)
And yet be wretched: now, she augured false.
FESTUS. Thank heaven! but you spoke strangely: could I venture
To think bare apprehension lest your friend,
Dazzled by your resplendent course, might find   195
Henceforth less sweetness in his own, could move
Such earnest mood in you? Fear not, dear friend,
That I shall leave you, inwardly repining
Your lot was not my own!
PARACELSUS.   And this for ever!
For ever! gull who may, they will be gulled!   200
They will not look nor think; 't is nothing new
In them: but surely he is not of them!
My Festus, do you know, I reckoned, you—
Though all beside were sand-blind—you, my friend,
Would look at me, once close, with piercing eye   205

Untroubled by the false glare that confounds
A weaker vision: would remain serene,
Though singular amid a gaping throng.
I feared you, or I had come, sure, long ere this,
To Einsiedeln. Well, error has no end,   210
And Rhasis is a sage, and Basil boasts
A tribe of wits, and I am wise and blest
Past all dispute! 'T is vain to fret at it.
I have vowed long ago my worshippers
Shall owe to their own deep sagacity   215
All further information, good or bad.
Small risk indeed my reputation runs,
Unless perchance the glance now searching me
Be fixed much longer; for it seems to spell
Dimly the characters a simpler man   220
Might read distinct enough. Old Eastern books
Say, the fallen prince of morning some short space
Remained unchanged in semblance; nay, his brow
Was hued with triumph: every spirit then
Praising, *his* heart on flame the while:—a tale!   225
Well, Festus, what discover you, I pray?
FESTUS. Some foul deed sullies then a life which else
    Were raised supreme?
PARACELSUS.   Good: I do well, most well!
Why strive to make men hear, feel, fret themselves
With what is past their power to comprehend?   230
I should not strive now: only, having nursed
The faint surmise that one yet walked the earth,
One, at least, not the utter fool of show,
Not absolutely formed to be the dupe
Of shallow plausibilities alone: 235
One who, in youth, found wise enough to choose
The happiness his riper years approve,
Was yet so anxious for another's sake,
That, ere his friend could rush upon a mad
And ruinous course, the converse of his own,   240
His gentle spirit essayed, prejudged for him
The perilous path, foresaw its destiny,
And warned the weak one in such tender words,
Such accents—his whole heart in every tone—

That oft their memory comforted that friend　　　　245
When it by right should have increased despair:
—Having believed, I say, that this one man
Could never lose the light thus from the first
His portion—how should I refuse to grieve
At even my gain if it disturb our old　　　　　250
Relation, if it make me out more wise?
Therefore, once more reminding him how well
He prophesied, I note the single flaw
That spoils his prophet's title. In plain words,
You were deceived, and thus were you deceived—　255
I have not been successful, and yet am
Most miserable; 't is said at last; nor you
Give credit, lest you force me to concede
That common sense yet lives upon the world!

FESTUS. You surely do not mean to banter me?　　260
PARACELSUS. You know, or—if you have been wise enough
To cleanse your memory of such matters—knew,
As far as words of mine could make it clear,
That 't was my purpose to find joy or grief
Solely in the fulfilment of my plan　　　　265
Or plot or whatsoe'er it was; rejoicing
Alone as it proceeded prosperously,
Sorrowing then only when mischance retarded
Its progress. That was in those Würzburg days!
Not to prolong a theme I thoroughly hate,　　270
I have pursued this plan with all my strength;
And having failed therein most signally,
Cannot object to ruin utter and drear
As all-excelling would have been the prize
Had fortune favoured me. I scarce have right　275
To vex your frank good spirit late so glad
In my supposed prosperity, I know,
And, were I lucky in a glut of friends,
Would well agree to let your error live,
Nay, strengthen it with fables of success.　　280
But mine is no condition to refuse
The transient solace of so rare a godsend,
My solitary luxury, my one friend:
Accordingly I venture to put off

The wearisome vest of falsehood galling me,   285
Secure when he is by. I lay me bare,
Prone at his mercy—but he is my friend!
Not that he needs retain his aspect grave;
That answers not my purpose; for 't is like,
Some sunny morning—Basil being drained   290
Of its wise population, every corner
Of the amphitheatre crammed with learned clerks,
Here Œcolampadius, looking worlds of wit,
Here Castellanus, as profound as he,
Munsterus here, Frobenius there, all squeezed   295
And staring,—that the zany of the show,
Even Paracelsus, shall put off before them
His trappings with a grace but seldom judged
Expedient in such cases:—the grim smile
That will go round! Is it not therefore best   300
To venture a rehearsal like the present
In a small way? Where are the signs I seek,
The first-fruits and fair sample of the scorn
Due to all quacks? Why, this will never do!
FESTUS. These are foul vapours, Aureole; nought beside!   305
The effect of watching, study, weariness.
Were there a spark of truth in the confusion
Of these wild words, you would not outrage thus
Your youth's companion. I shall ne'er regard
These wanderings, bred of faintness and much study.   310
'T is not thus you would trust a trouble to me,
To Michal's friend.
PARACELSUS.   I have said it, dearest Festus!
For the manner, 't is ungracious probably;
You may have it told in broken sobs, one day,
And scalding tears, ere long: but I thought best   315
To keep that off as long as possible.
Do you wonder still?
EESTUS.   No; it must oft fall out
That one whose labour perfects any work,
Shall rise from it with eye so worn that he
Of all men least can measure the extent   320
Of what he has accomplished. He alone
Who, nothing tasked, is nothing weary too,

May clearly scan the little he effects:
But we, the bystanders, untouched by toil,
Estimate each aright.
PARACELSUS.   This worthy Festus   325
Is one of them, at last! 'T is so with all!
First, they set down all progress as a dream;
And next, when he whose quick discomfiture
Was counted on, accomplishes some few
And doubtful steps in his career,—behold,   330
They look for every inch of ground to vanish
Beneath his tread, so sure they spy success!
FESTUS. Few doubtful steps? when death retires before
Your presence—when the noblest of mankind,
Broken in body or subdued in soul,   335
May through your skill renew their vigour, raise
The shattered frame to pristine stateliness?
When men in racking pain may purchase dreams
Of what delights them most, swooning at once
Into a sea of bliss or rapt along   340
As in a flying sphere of turbulent light?
When we may look to you as one ordained
To free the flesh from fell disease, as frees
Our Luther's burning tongue the fettered soul?
When . . .
PARACELSUS. When and where, the devil, did you get   345
This notable news?
FESTUS.   Even from the common voice;
From those whose envy, daring not dispute
The wonders it decries, attributes them
To magic and such folly.
PARACELSUS.   Folly? Why not
To magic, pray? You find a comfort doubtless   350
In holding, God ne'er troubles him about
Us or our doings: once we were judged worth
The devil's tempting . . . I offend: forgive me,
And rest content. Your prophecy on the whole
Was fair enough as prophesyings go;   355
At fault a little in detail, but quite
Precise enough in the main; and hereupon
I pay due homage: you guessed long ago

(The prophet!) I should fail—and I have failed.

FESTUS. You mean to tell me, then, the hopes which fed   360
 Your youth have not been realized as yet?
 Some obstacle has barred them hitherto?
 Or that their innate . . .

PARACELSUS.   As I said but now,
 You have a very decent prophet's fame,
 So you but shun details here. Little matter   365
 Whether those hopes were mad,—the aims they sought,
 Safe and secure from all ambitious fools;
 Or whether my weak wits are overcome
 By what a better spirit would scorn: I fail.
 And now methinks 't were best to change a theme   370
 I am a sad fool to have stumbled on.
 I say confusedly what comes uppermost;
 But there are times when patience proves at fault,
 As now: this morning's strange encounter—you
 Beside me once again! you, whom I guessed   375
 Alive, since hitherto (with Luther's leave)
 No friend have I among the saints at peace,
 To judge by any good their prayers effect.
 I knew you would have helped me—why not he,
 My strange competitor in enterprise,   380
 Bound for the same end by another path,
 Arrived, or ill or well, before the time,
 At our disastrous journey's doubtful close?
 How goes it with Aprile? Ah, they miss
 Your lone sad sunny idleness of heaven,   385
 Our martyrs for the world's sake; heaven shuts fast:
 The poor mad poet is howling by this time!
 Since you are my sole friend then, here or there,
 I could not quite repress the varied feelings
 This meeting wakens; they have had their vent,   390
 And now forget them. Do the rear-mice still
 Hang like a fretwork on the gate (or what
 In my time was a gate) fronting the road
 From Einsiedeln to Lachen?

FESTUS.   Trifle not:
 Answer me, for my sake alone! You smiled   395
 Just now, when I supposed some deed, unworthy

Yourself, might blot the else so bright result;
Yet if your motives have continued pure,
Your will unfaltering, and in spite of this,
You have experienced a defeat, why then   400
I say not you would cheerfully withdraw
From contest—mortal hearts are not so fashioned—
But surely you would ne'ertheless withdraw.
You sought not fame nor gain nor even love,
No end distinct from knowledge,—I repeat   405
Your very words: once satisfied that knowledge
Is a mere dream, you would announce as much,
Yourself the first. But how is the event?
You are defeated—and I find you here!
PARACELSUS. As though 'here' did not signify defeat!   410
I spoke not of my little labours here,
But of the break-down of my general aims:
For you, aware of their extent and scope,
To look on these sage lecturings, approved
By beardless boys, and bearded dotards worse,   415
As a fit consummation of such aims,
Is worthy notice. A professorship
At Basil! Since you see so much in it,
And think my life was reasonably drained
Of life's delights to render me a match   420
For duties arduous as such post demands,—
Be it far from me to deny my power
To fill the petty circle lotted out
Of infinite space, or justify the host
Of honours thence accruing. So, take notice,   425
This jewel dangling from my neck preserves
The features of a prince, my skill restored
To plague his people some few years to come:
And all through a pure whim. He had eased the earth
For me, but that the droll despair which seized   430
The vermin of his household, tickled me.
I came to see. Here, drivelled the physician,
Whose most infallible nostrum was at fault;
There quaked the astrologer, whose horoscope
Had promised him interminable years;   435
Here a monk fumbled at the sick man's mouth

With some undoubted relic—a sudary
Of the Virgin; while another piebald knave
Of the same brotherhood (he loved them ever)
Was actively preparing 'neath his nose   440
Such a suffumigation as, once fired,
Had stunk the patient dead ere he could groan.
I cursed the doctor and upset the brother,
Brushed past the conjurer, vowed that the first gust
Of stench from the ingredients just alight   445
Would raise a cross-grained devil in my sword,
Not easily laid: and ere an hour the prince
Slept as he never slept since prince he was.
A day—and I was posting for my life,
Placarded through the town as one whose spite   450
Had near availed to stop the blessed effects
Of the doctor's nostrum which, well seconded
By the sudary, and most by the costly smoke—
Not leaving out the strenuous prayers sent up
Hard by in the abbey—raised the prince to life: 455
To the great reputation of the seer
Who, confident, expected all along
The glad event—the doctor's recompense—
Much largess from his highness to the monks—
And the vast solace of his loving people,   460
Whose general satisfaction to increase,
The prince was pleased no longer to defer
The burning of some dozen heretics
Remanded till God's mercy should be shown
Touching his sickness: last of all were joined   465
Ample directions to all loyal folk
To swell the complement by seizing me
Who—doubtless some rank sorcerer—endeavoured
To thwart these pious offices, obstruct
The prince's cure, and frustrate heaven by help 470
Of certain devils dwelling in his sword.
By luck, the prince in his first fit of thanks
Had forced this bauble on me as an earnest
Of further favours. This one case may serve
To give sufficient taste of many such,   475
So, let them pass. Those shelves support a pile

Of patents, licences, diplomas, titles
From Germany, France, Spain, and Italy;
They authorize some honour; ne'ertheless,
I set more store by this Erasmus sent;   480
He trusts me; our Frobenius is his friend,
And him 'I raised' (nay, read it) 'from the dead.'
I weary you, I see. I merely sought
To show, there's no great wonder after all
That, while I fill the class-room and attract   485
A crowd to Basil, I get leave to stay,
And therefore need not scruple to accept
The utmost they can offer, if I please:
For 't is but right the world should be prepared
To treat with favour e'en fantastic wants   490
Of one like me, used up in serving her.
Just as the mortal, whom the gods in part
Devoured, received in place of his lost limb
Some virtue or other—cured disease, I think;
You mind the fables we have read together.   495

FESTUS. You do not think I comprehend a word.
  The time was, Aureole, you were apt enough
To clothe the airiest thoughts in specious breath;
But surely you must feel how vague and strange
These speeches sound.

PARACELSUS.   Well, then: you know my hopes; 500
  I am assured, at length, those hopes were vain;
That truth is just as far from me as ever;
That I have thrown my life away; that sorrow
On that account is idle, and further effort
To mend and patch what's marred beyond repairing,   505
As useless: and all this was taught your friend
By the convincing good old-fashioned method
Of force—by sheer compulsion. Is that plain?

FESTUS. Dear Aureole, can it be my fears were just?
  God wills not . . .

PARACELSUS.   Now, 't is this I most admire— 510
  The constant talk men of your stamp keep up
Of God's will, as they style it; one would swear
Man had but merely to uplift his eye,
And see the will in question charactered

On the heaven's vault. 'T is hardly wise to moot   515
Such topics: doubts are many and faith is weak.
I know as much of any will of God
As knows some dumb and tortured brute what Man,
His stern lord, wills from the perplexing blows
That plague him every way; but there, of course,   520
Where least he suffers, longest he remains—
My case; and for such reasons I plod on,
Subdued but not convinced. I know as little
Why I deserve to fail, as why I hoped
Better things in my youth. I simply know   525
I am no master here, but trained and beaten
Into the path I tread; and here I stay,
Until some further intimation reach me,
Like an obedient drudge. Though I prefer
To view the whole thing as a task imposed   530
Which, whether dull or pleasant, must be done—
Yet, I deny not, there is made provision
Of joys which tastes less jaded might affect;
Nay, some which please me too, for all my pride—
Pleasures that once were pains: the iron ring   535
Festering about a slave's neck grows at length
Into the flesh it eats. I hate no longer
A host of petty vile delights, undreamed of
Or spurned before; such now supply the place
Of my dead aims: as in the autumn woods   540
Where tall trees used to flourish, from their roots
Springs up a fungous brood sickly and pale,
Chill mushrooms coloured like a corpse's cheek.
FESTUS. If I interpret well your words, I own
It troubles me but little that your aims,   545
Vast in their dawning and most likely grown
Extravagantly since, have baffled you.
Perchance I am glad; you merit greater praise;
Because they are too glorious to be gained,
You do not blindly cling to them and die;   550
You fell, but have not sullenly refused
To rise, because an angel worsted you
In wrestling, though the world holds not your peer;
And though too harsh and sudden is the change

To yield content as yet, still you pursue   555
The ungracious path as though 't were rosy-strewn.
'T is well: and your reward, or soon or late,
Will come from him whom no man serves in vain.
PARACELSUS. Ah, very fine! For my part, I conceive
The very pausing from all further toil,   560
Which you find heinous, would become a seal
To the sincerity of all my deeds.
To be consistent I should die at once;
I calculated on no after-life;
Yet (how crept in, how fostered, I know not)   565
Here am I with as passionate regret
For youth and health and love so vainly lavished,
As if their preservation had been first
And foremost in my thoughts; and this strange fact
Humbled me wondrously, and had due force   570
In rendering me the less averse to follow
A certain counsel, a mysterious warning—
You will not understand—but 't was a man
With aims not mine and yet pursued like mine,
With the same fervour and no more success,   575
Perishing in my sight; who summoned me
As I would shun the ghastly fate I saw,
To serve my race at once; to wait no longer
That God should interfere in my behalf,
But to distrust myself, put pride away,   580
And give my gains, imperfect as they were,
To men. I have not leisure to explain
How, since, a singular series of events
Has raised me to the station you behold,
Wherein I seem to turn to most account   585
The mere wreck of the past,—perhaps receive
Some feeble glimmering token that God views
And may approve my penance: therefore here
You find me, doing most good or least harm.
And if folks wonder much and profit little   590
'T is not my fault; only, I shall rejoice
When my part in the farce is shuffled through,
And the curtain falls: I must hold out till then.
FESTUS. Till when, dear Aureole?

PARACELSUS.   Till I'm fairly thrust
    From my proud eminence. Fortune is fickle   595
    And even professors fall: should that arrive,
    I see no sin in ceding to my bent.
    You little fancy what rude shocks apprise us
    We sin; God's intimations rather fail
    In clearness than in energy: 't were well   600
    Did they but indicate the course to take
    Like that to be forsaken. I would fain
    Be spared a further sample. Here I stand,
    And here I stay, be sure, till forced to flit.

FESTUS. Be you but firm on that head! long ere then   605
    All I expect will come to pass, I trust:
    The cloud that wraps you will have disappeared.
    Meantime, I see small chance of such event:
    They praise you here as one whose lore, already
    Divulged, eclipses all the past can show,   610
    But whose achievements, marvellous as they be,
    Are faint anticipations of a glory
    About to be revealed. When Basil's crowds
    Dismiss their teacher, I shall be content
    That he depart.

PARACELSUS.   This favour at their hands   615
    I look for earlier than your view of things
    Would warrant. Of the crowd you saw to-day,
    Remove the full half sheer amazement draws,
    Mere novelty, nought else; and next, the tribe
    Whose innate blockish dulness just perceives   620
    That unless miracles (as seem my works)
    Be wrought in their behalf, their chance is slight
    To puzzle the devil; next, the numerous set
    Who bitterly hate established schools, and help
    The teacher that oppugns them, till he once   625
    Have planted his own doctrine, when the teacher
    May reckon on their rancour in his turn;
    Take, too, the sprinkling of sagacious knaves
    Whose cunning runs not counter to the vogue
    But seeks, by flattery and crafty nursing,   630
    To force my system to a premature
    Short-lived development. Why swell the list?

Each has his end to serve, and his best way
Of serving it: remove all these, remains
A scantling, a poor dozen at the best,   635
Worthy to look for sympathy and service,
And likely to draw profit from my pains.
FESTUS. 'T is no encouraging picture: still these few
Redeem their fellows. Once the germ implanted,
Its growth, if slow, is sure.
PARACELSUS.   God grant it so!   640
I would make some amends: but if I fail,
The luckless rogues have this excuse to urge,
That much is in my method and my manner,
My uncouth habits, my impatient spirit,
Which hinders of reception and result   645
My doctrine: much to say, small skill to speak!
These old aims suffered not a looking-off
Though for an instant; therefore, only when
I thus renounced them and resolved to reap
Some present fruit—to teach mankind some truth   650
So dearly purchased—only then I found
Such teaching was an art requiring cares
And qualities peculiar to itself:
That to possess was one thing—to display
Another. With renown first in my thoughts,   655
Or popular praise, I had soon discovered it:
One grows but little apt to learn these things.
FESTUS. If it be so, which nowise I believe,
There needs no waiting fuller dispensation
To leave a labour of so little use.   660
Why not throw up the irksome charge at once?
PARACELSUS. A task, a task!
                       But wherefore hide the whole
Extent of degradation, once engaged
In the confessing vein? Despite of all
My fine talk of obedience and repugnance,   665
Docility and what not, 't is yet to learn
If when the task shall really be performed,
My inclination free to choose once more,
I shall do aught but slightly modify
The nature of the hated task I quit.   670

In plain words, I am spoiled; my life still tends
As first it tended; I am broken and trained
To my old habits: they are part of me.
I know, and none so well, my darling ends
Are proved impossible: no less, no less,   675
Even now what humours me, fond fool, as when
Their faint ghosts sit with me and flatter me
And send me back content to my dull round?
How can I change this soul?—this apparatus
Constructed solely for their purposes,   680
So well adapted to their every want,
To search out and discover, prove and perfect;
This intricate machine whose most minute
And meanest motions have their charm to me
Though to none else—an aptitude I seize,   685
An object I perceive, a use, a meaning,
A property, a fitness, I explain
And I alone:—how can I change my soul?
And this wronged body, worthless save when tasked
Under that soul's dominion—used to care   690
For its bright master's cares and quite subdue
Its proper cravings—not to ail nor pine
So he but prosper—whither drag this poor
Tried patient body? God! how I essayed
To live like that mad poet, for a while,   695
To love alone; and how I felt too warped
And twisted and deformed! What should I do,
Even tho' released from drudgery, but return
Faint, as you see, and halting, blind and sore,
To my old life and die as I began?   700
I cannot feed on beauty for the sake
Of beauty only, nor can drink in balm
From lovely objects for their loveliness;
My nature cannot lose her first imprint;
I still must hoard and heap and class all truths   705
With one ulterior purpose: I must know!
Would God translate me to his throne, believe
That I should only listen to his word
To further my own aim! For other men,
Beauty is prodigally strewn around,   710

And I were happy could I quench as they
　This mad and thriveless longing, and content me
With beauty for itself alone: alas,
I have addressed a frock of heavy mail
Yet may not join the troop of sacred knights;　　　　715
And now the forest-creatures fly from me,
The grass-banks cool, the sunbeams warm no more.
Best follow, dreaming that ere night arrive,
I shall o'ertake the company and ride
Glittering as they!

FESTUS.　　　　　　I think I apprehend　　　　720
What you would say: if you, in truth, design
To enter once more on the life thus left,
Seek not to hide that all this consciousness
Of failure is assumed!

PARACELSUS.　　　　　　My friend, my friend.
I toil, you listen; I explain, perhaps　　　　725
You understand: there our communion ends.
Have you learnt nothing from to-day's discourse?
When we would thoroughly know the sick man's state
We feel awhile the fluttering pulse, press soft
The hot brow, look upon the languid eye,　　　　730
And thence divine the rest. Must I lay bare
My heart, hideous and beating, or tear up
My vitals for your gaze, ere you will deem
Enough made known? You! who are you, forsooth?
That is the crowning operation claimed　　　　735
By the arch-demonstrator—heaven the hall,
And earth the audience. Let Aprile and you
Secure good places: 't will be worth the while.

FESTUS. Are you mad, Aureole? What can I have said
To call for this? I judged from your own words.　　　　740

PARACELSUS. Oh, doubtless! A sick wretch describes the ape
That mocks him from the bed-foot, and all gravely
You thither turn at once: or he recounts
The perilous journey he has late performed,
And you are puzzled much how that could be!　　　　745
You find me here, half stupid and half mad;
It makes no part of my delight to search
Into these matters, much less undergo

E

Another's scrutiny; but so it chances
That I am led to trust my state to you: 750
And the event is, you combine, contrast
And ponder on my foolish words as though
They thoroughly conveyed all hidden here—
Here, loathsome with despair and hate and rage!
Is there no fear, no shrinking and no shame?   755
Will you guess nothing? will you spare me nothing?
Must I go deeper? Ay or no?

FESTUS.   Dear friend . . .

PARACELSUS. True: I am brutal—'t is a part of it;
The plague's sign—you are not a lazar-haunter,
How should you know? Well then, you think it strange   760
I should profess to have failed utterly,
And yet propose an ultimate return
To courses void of hope: and this, because
You know not what temptation is, nor how
'T is like to ply men in the sickliest part.   765
You are to understand that we who make
Sport for the gods, are hunted to the end:
There is not one sharp volley shot at us,
Which 'scaped with life, though hurt, we slacken pace
And gather by the wayside herbs and roots   770
To staunch our wounds, secure from further harm:
We are assailed to life's extremest verge.
It will be well indeed if I return,
A harmless busy fool, to my old ways!
I would forget hints of another fate,   775
Significant enough, which silent hours
Have lately scared me with.

FESTUS.   Another! and what?

PARACELSUS. After all, Festus, you say well: I am
A man yet: I need never humble me.
I would have been—something, I know not what;   780
But though I cannot soar, I do not crawl.
There are worse portions than this one of mine.
You say well!

FESTUS.   Ah!

PARACELSUS.   And deeper degradation!
If the mean stimulants of vulgar praise,

If vanity should become the chosen food   785
Of a sunk mind, should stifle even the wish
To find its early aspirations true,
Should teach it to breathe falsehood like life-breath—
An atmosphere of craft and trick and lies;
Should make it proud to emulate, surpass   790
Base natures in the practices which woke
Its most indignant loathing once . . . No, no!
Utter damnation is reserved for hell!
I had immortal feelings; such shall never
Be wholly quenched: no, no!
                        My friend, you wear   795
A melancholy face, and certain 't is
There's little cheer in all this dismal work.
But was it my desire to set abroach
Such memories and forebodings? I foresaw
Where they would drive. 'T were better we discuss   800
News from Lucerne or Zurich; ask and tell
Of Egypt's flaring sky or Spain's cork-groves.
FESTUS. I have thought: trust me, this mood will pass away!
I know you and the lofty spirit you bear,
And easily ravel out a clue to all.   805
These are the trials meet for such as you,
Nor must you hope exemption: to be mortal
Is to be plied with trials manifold.
Look round! The obstacles which kept the rest
From your ambition, have been spurned by you;   810
Their fears, their doubts, the chains that bind them all,
Were flax before your resolute soul, which nought
Avails to awe save these delusions bred
From its own strength, its selfsame strength disguised,
Mocking itself. Be brave, dear Aureole! Since   815
The rabbit has his shade to frighten him,
The fawn a rustling bough, mortals their cares,
And higher natures yet would slight and laugh
At these entangling fantasies, as you
At trammels of a weaker intellect,—   820
Measure your mind's height by the shade it casts!
I know you.
PARACELSUS.   And I know you, dearest Festus!

And how you love unworthily; and how
All admiration renders blind.

FESTUS.   You hold
That admiration blinds?

PARACELSUS.   Ay and alas!   825

FESTUS. Nought blinds you less than admiration, friend!
Whether it be that all love renders wise
In its degree; from love which blends with love—
Heart answering heart—to love which spends itself
In silent mad idolatry of some   830
Pre-eminent mortal, some great soul of souls,
Which ne'er will know how well it is adored.
I say, such love is never blind; but rather
Alive to every the minutest spot
Which mars its object, and which hate (supposed   835
So vigilant and searching) dreams not of.
Love broods on such: what then? When first perceived
Is there no sweet strife to forget, to change,
To overflush those blemishes with all
The glow of general goodness they disturb?   840
—To make those very defects an endless source
Of new affection grown from hopes and fears?
And, when all fails, is there no gallant stand
Made even for much proved weak? no shrinking-back
Lest, since all love assimilates the soul   845
To what it loves, it should at length become
Almost a rival of its idol? Trust me,
If there be fiends who seek to work our hurt,
To ruin and drag down earth's mightiest spirits
Even at God's foot, 't will be from such as love,   850
Their zeal will gather most to serve their cause;
And least from those who hate, who most essay
By contumely and scorn to blot the light
Which forces entrance even to their hearts:
For thence will our defender tear the veil   855
And show within each heart, as in a shrine,
The giant image of perfection, grown
In hate's despite, whose calumnies were spawned
In the untroubled presence of its eyes.
True admiration blinds not; nor am I   860

So blind. I call your sin exceptional;
It springs from one whose life has passed the bounds
Prescribed to life. Compound that fault with God!
I speak of men; to common men like me
The weakness you reveal endears you more,   865
Like the far traces of decay in suns.
I bid you have good cheer!
PARACELSUS.   *Præclare! Optime!*
Think of a quiet mountain-cloistered priest
Instructing Paracelsus! yet 't is so.
Come, I will show you where my merit lies.   870
'T is in the advance of individual minds
That the slow crowd should ground their expectation
Eventually to follow; as the sea
Waits ages in its bed till some one wave
Out of the multitudinous mass, extends   875
The empire of the whole, some feet perhaps,
Over the strip of sand which could confine
Its fellows so long time: thenceforth the rest,
Even to the meanest, hurry in at once,
And so much is clear gained. I shall be glad   880
If all my labours, failing of aught else,
Suffice to make such inroad and procure
A wider range for thought: nay, they do this;
For, whatsoe'er my notions of true knowledge
And a legitimate success, may be,   885
I am not blind to my undoubted rank
When classed with others: I precede my age:
And whoso wills is very free to mount
These labours as a platform whence his own
May have a prosperous outset. But, alas!   890
My followers—they are noisy as you heard;
But, for intelligence, the best of them
So clumsily wield the weapons I supply
And they extol, that I begin to doubt
Whether their own rude clubs and pebble-stones   895
Would not do better service than my arms
Thus vilely swayed—if error will not fall
Sooner before the old awkward batterings
Than my more subtle warfare, not half learned.

FESTUS. I would supply that art, then, or withhold   900
  New arms until you teach their mystery.
PARACELSUS. Content you, 't is my wish; I have recourse
  To the simplest training. Day by day I seek
  To wake the mood, the spirit which alone
  Can make those arms of any use to men.   905
  Of course they are for swaggering forth at once
  Graced with Ulysses' bow, Achilles' shield—
  Flash on us, all in armour, thou Achilles!
  Make our hearts dance to thy resounding step!
  A proper sight to scare the crows away!   910
FESTUS. Pity you choose not then some other method
  Of coming at your point. The marvellous art
  At length established in the world bids fair
  To remedy all hindrances like these:
  Trust to Frobenius' press the precious lore   915
  Obscured by uncouth manner, or unfit
  For raw beginners; let his types secure
  A deathless monument to after-time;
  Meanwhile wait confidently and enjoy
  The ultimate effect: sooner or later   920
  You shall be all-revealed.
PARACELSUS.   The old dull question
  In a new form; no more. Thus: I possess
  Two sorts of knowledge; one,—vast, shadowy,
  Hints of the unbounded aim I once pursued:
  The other consists of many secrets, caught   925
  While bent on nobler prize,—perhaps a few
  Prime principles which may conduct to much:
  These last I offer to my followers here.
  Now, bid me chronicle the first of these,
  My ancient study, and in effect you bid   930
  Revert to the wild courses just abjured:
  I must go find them scattered through the world.
  Then, for the principles, they are so simple
  (Being chiefly of the overturning sort),
  That one time is as proper to propound them   935
  As any other—to-morrow at my class,
  Or half a century hence embalmed in print.
  For if mankind intend to learn at all,

They must begin by giving faith to them
And acting on them: and I do not see   940
But that my lectures serve indifferent well:
No doubt these dogmas fall not to the earth,
For all their novelty and rugged setting.
I think my class will not forget the day
I let them know the gods of Israel,   945
Aëtius, Oribasius, Galen, Rhasis,
Serapion, Avicenna, Averröes,
Were blocks!
FESTUS.   And that reminds me, I heard something
About your waywardness: you burned their books,
It seems, instead of answering those sages.   950
PARACELSUS. And who said that?
FESTUS.   Some I met yesternight
With Œcolampadius. As you know, the purpose
Of this short stay at Basil was to learn
His pleasure touching certain missives sent
For our Zuinglius and himself. 'T was he   955
Apprised me that the famous teacher here
Was my old friend.
PARACELSUS.   Ah, I forgot: you went . . .
FESTUS. From Zurich with advices for the ear
Of Luther, now at Wittenberg—(you know,
I make no doubt, the differences of late   960
With Carolostadius)—and returning sought
Basil and . . .
PARACELSUS.   I remember. Here's a case, now,
Will teach you why I answer not, but burn
The books you mention. Pray, does Luther dream
His arguments convince by their own force   965
The crowds that own his doctrine? No, indeed!
His plain denial of established points
Ages had sanctified and men supposed
Could never be oppugned while earth was under
And heaven above them—points which chance or time   970
Affected not—did more than the array
Of argument which followed. Boldly deny!
There is much breath-stopping, hair-stiffening
Awhile; then, amazed glances, mute awaiting

The thunderbolt which does not come: and next,   975
Reproachful wonder and inquiry: those
Who else had never stirred, are able now
To find the rest out for themselves, perhaps
To outstrip him who set the whole at work,
—As never will my wise class its instructor.   980
And you saw Luther?

FESTUS.   'T is a wondrous soul!

PARACELSUS. True: the so-heavy chain which galled mankind
Is shattered, and the noblest of us all
Must bow to the deliverer—nay, the worker
Of our own project—we who long before   985
Had burst our trammels, but forgot the crowd,
We should have taught, still groaned beneath their load:
This he has done and nobly. Speed that may!
Whatever be my chance or my mischance,
What benefits mankind must glad me too;   990
And men seem made, though not as I believed,
For something better than the times produce.
Witness these gangs of peasants your new lights
From Suabia have possessed, whom Münzer leads,
And whom the duke, the landgrave and the elector   995
Will calm in blood! Well, well; 't is not my world!

FESTUS. Hark!

PARACELSUS.   'T is the melancholy wind astir
Within the trees; the embers too are grey:
Morn must be near.

FESTUS.   Best ope the casement: see,
The night, late strewn with clouds and flying stars,   1000
Is blank and motionless: how peaceful sleep
The tree-tops altogether! Like an asp,
The wind slips whispering from bough to bough.

PARACELSUS. Ay; you would gaze on a wind-shaken tree
By the hour, nor count time lost.

FESTUS.   So you shall gaze: 1005
Those happy times will come again.

PARACELSUS.   Gone, gone,
Those pleasant times! Does not the moaning wind
Seem to bewail that we have gained such gains
And bartered sleep for them?

FESTUS.   It is our trust
   That there is yet another world to mend   1010
   All error and mischance.
PARACELSUS.   Another world!
   And why this world, this common world, to be
   A make-shift, a mere foil, how fair soever,
   To some fine life to come? Man must be fed
   With angels' food, forsooth; and some few traces   1015
   Of a diviner nature which look out
   Through his corporeal baseness, warrant him
   In a supreme contempt of all provision
   For his inferior tastes—some straggling marks
   Which constitute his essence, just as truly   1020
   As here and there a gem would constitute
   The rock, their barren bed, one diamond.
   But were it so—were man all mind—he gains
   A station little enviable. From God
   Down to the lowest spirit ministrant,   1025
   Intelligence exists which casts our mind
   Into immeasurable shade. No, no:
   Love, hope, fear, faith—these make humanity;
   These are its sign and note and character,
   And these I have lost!—gone, shut from me for ever,   1030
   Like a dead friend safe from unkindness more!
   See, morn at length. The heavy darkness seems
   Diluted, grey and clear without the stars;
   The shrubs bestir and rouse themselves as if
   Some snake, that weighed them down all night, let go   1035
   His hold; and from the East, fuller and fuller,
   Day, like a mighty river, flowing in;
   But clouded, wintry, desolate and cold.
   Yet see how that broad prickly star-shaped plant,
   Half-down in the crevice, spreads its woolly leaves   1040
   All thick and glistering with diamond dew.
   And you depart for Einsiedeln this day,
   And we have spent all night in talk like this!
   If you would have me better for your love,
   Revert no more to these sad themes.
FESTUS.   One favour,   1045
   And I have done. I leave you, deeply moved;

Unwilling to have fared so well, the while
My friend has changed so sorely. If this mood
Shall pass away, if light once more arise
Where all is darkness now, if you see fit   1050
To hope and trust again, and strive again,
You will remember—not our love alone—
But that my faith in God's desire that man
Should trust on his support, (as I must think
You trusted) is obscured and dim through you: 1055
For you are thus, and this is no reward.
Will you not call me to your side, dear Aureole?

PART IV

PARACELSUS ASPIRES

Scene.—*Colmar in Alsatia: an Inn.* 1528.

PARACELSUS, FESTUS

PARACELSUS [*to* JOHANNES OPORINUS, *his Secretary*].
   Sic itur ad astra! Dear Von Visenburg
Is scandalized, and poor Torinus paralysed,
And every honest soul that Basil holds
Aghast; and yet we live, as one may say,
Just as though Liechtenfels had never set   5
So true a value on his sorry carcass,
And learned Pütter had not frowned us dumb.
We live; and shall as surely start to-morrow
For Nuremberg, as we drink speedy scathe
To Basil in this mantling wine, suffused   10
A delicate blush, no fainter tinge is born
I' the shut heart of a bud. Pledge me, good John—
'Basil; a hot plague ravage it, and Pütter
'Oppose the plague!' Even so? Do you too share
Their panic, the reptiles? Ha, ha; faint through these,   15
Desist for these! They manage matters so
At Basil, 't is like: but others may find means
To bring the stoutest braggart of the tribe

Once more to crouch in silence—means to breed
A stupid wonder in each fool again,   20
Now big with admiration at the skill
Which stript a vain pretender of his plumes:
And, that done,—means to brand each slavish brow
So deeply, surely, ineffaceably,
That henceforth flattery shall not pucker it   25
Out of the furrow; there that stamp shall stay
To show the next they fawn on, what they are,
This Basil with its magnates,—fill my cup,—
Whom I curse soul and limb. And now despatch,
Despatch, my trusty John; and what remains   30
To do, whate'er arrangements for our trip
Are yet to be completed, see you hasten
This night; we'll weather the storm at least: to-morrow
For Nuremberg! Now leave us; this grave clerk
Has divers weighty matters for my ear: 35

                        [OPORINUS *goes out.*

And spare my lungs. At last, my gallant Festus,
I am rid of this arch-knave that dogs my heels
As a gaunt crow a gasping sheep; at last
May give a loose to my delight. How kind,
How very kind, my first best only friend!   40
Why, this looks like fidelity. Embrace me!
Not a hair silvered yet? Right! you shall live
Till I am worth your love; you shall be proud,
And I—but let time show! Did you not wonder?
I sent to you because our compact weighed   45
Upon my conscience—(you recall the night
At Basil, which the gods confound!)—because
Once more I aspire. I call you to my side:
You come. You thought my message strange?

FESTUS.   So strange
That I must hope, indeed, your messenger   50
Has mingled his own fancies with the words
Purporting to be yours.

PARACELSUS.   He said no more,
'T is probable, than the precious folk I leave
Said fiftyfold more roughly. Well-a-day,
'T is true! poor Paracelsus is exposed   55

At last; a most egregious quack he proves:
And those he overreached must spit their hate
On one who, utterly beneath contempt,
Could yet deceive their topping wits. You heard
Bare truth; and at my bidding you come here   60
To speed me on my enterprise, as once
Your lavish wishes sped me, my own friend!
FESTUS. What is your purpose, Aureole?
PARACELSUS.   Oh, for purpose,
There is no lack of precedents in a case
Like mine; at least, if not precisely mine,   65
The case of men cast off by those they sought
To benefit.
FESTUS.   They really cast you off?
I only heard a vague tale of some priest,
Cured by your skill, who wrangled at your claim,
Knowing his life's worth best; and how the judge   70
The matter was referred to, saw no cause
To interfere, nor you to hide your full
Contempt of him; nor he, again, to smother
His wrath thereat, which raised so fierce a flame
That Basil soon was made no place for you.   75
PARACELSUS. The affair of Liechtenfels? the shallowest fable,
The last and silliest outrage—mere pretence!
I knew it, I foretold it from the first,
How soon the stupid wonder you mistook
For genuine loyalty—a cheering promise   80
Of better things to come—would pall and pass;
And every word comes true. Saul is among
The prophets! Just so long as I was pleased
To play off the mere antics of my art,
Fantastic gambols leading to no end,   85
I got huge praise: but one can ne'er keep down
Our foolish nature's weakness. There they flocked,
Poor devils, jostling, swearing and perspiring,
Till the walls rang again; and all for me!
I had a kindness for them, which was right;   90
But then I stopped not till I tacked to that
A trust in them and a respect—a sort
Of sympathy for them; I must needs begin

To teach them, not amaze them, 'to impart
'The spirit which should instigate the search   95
'Of truth,' just what you bade me! I spoke out.
Forthwith a mighty squadron, in disgust,
Filed off—'the sifted chaff of the sack,' I said,
Redoubling my endeavours to secure
The rest. When lo! one man had tarried so long   100
Only to ascertain if I supported
This tenet of his, or that; another loved
To hear impartially before he judged,
And having heard, now judged; this bland disciple
Passed for my dupe, but all along, it seems,   105
Spied error where his neighbours marvelled most;
That fiery doctor who had hailed me friend,
Did it because my by-paths, once proved wrong
And beaconed properly, would commend again
The good old ways our sires jogged safely o'er,   110
Though not their squeamish sons; the other worthy
Discovered divers verses of St. John,
Which, read successively, refreshed the soul,
But, muttered backwards, cured the gout, the stone,
The colic and what not. *Quid multa?* The end   115
Was a clear class-room, and a quiet leer
From grave folk, and a sour reproachful glance
From those in chief who, cap in hand, installed
The new professor scarce a year before;
And a vast flourish about patient merit   120
Obscured awhile by flashy tricks, but sure
Sooner or later to emerge in splendour—
Of which the example was some luckless wight
Whom my arrival had discomfited,
But now, it seems, the general voice recalled   125
To fill my chair and so efface the stain
Basil had long incurred. I sought no better,
Only a quiet dismissal from my post,
And from my heart I wished them better suited
And better served. Good night to Basil, then!   130
But fast as I proposed to rid the tribe
Of my obnoxious back, I could not spare them
The pleasure of a parting kick.

FESTUS.   You smile:
  Despise them as they merit!
PARACELSUS.   If I smile,
    'T is with as very contempt as ever turned   135
    Flesh into stone. This courteous recompense,
    This grateful . . . Festus, were your nature fit
    To be defiled, your eyes the eyes to ache
    At gangrene-blotches, eating poison-blains,
    The ulcerous barky scurf of leprosy   140
    Which finds—a man, and leaves—a hideous thing
    That cannot but be mended by hell fire,
    —I would lay bare to you the human heart
    Which God cursed long ago, and devils make since
    Their pet nest and their never-tiring home.   145
    Oh, sages have discovered we are born
    For various ends—to love, to know: has ever
    One stumbled, in his search, on any signs
    Of a nature in us formed to hate? To hate?
    If that be our true object which evokes   150
    Our powers in fullest strength, be sure 't is hate!
    Yet men have doubted if the best and bravest
    Of spirits can nourish him with hate alone.
    I had not the monopoly of fools,
    It seems, at Basil.
FESTUS.   But your plans, your plans!   155
  I have yet to learn your purpose, Aureole!
PARACELSUS. Whether to sink beneath such ponderous shame,
    To shrink up like a crushed snail, undergo
    In silence and desist from further toil,
    And so subside into a monument   160
    Of one their censure blasted? or to bow
    Cheerfully as submissively, to lower
    My old pretensions even as Basil dictates,
    To drop into the rank her wits assign me
    And live as they prescribe, and make that use   165
    Of my poor knowledge which their rules allow,
    Proud to be patted now and then, and careful
    To practise the true posture for receiving
    The amplest benefit from their hoofs' appliance
    When they shall condescend to tutor me?   170

Then, one may feel resentment like a flame
Within, and deck false systems in truth's garb,
And tangle and entwine mankind with error,
And give them darkness for a dower and falsehood
For a possession, ages: or one may mope   175
Into a shade through thinking, or else drowse
Into a dreamless sleep and so die off.
But I,—now Festus shall divine!—but I
Am merely setting out once more, embracing
My earliest aims again! What thinks he now?   180
FESTUS. Your aims? the aims?—to Know? and where is found
The early trust ...
PARACELSUS.   Nay, not so fast; I say,
The aims—not the old means. You know they made me
A laughing-stock; I was a fool; you know
The when and the how: hardly those means again!   185
Not but they had their beauty; who should know
Their passing beauty, if not I? Still, dreams
They were, so let them vanish, yet in beauty
If that may be. Stay: thus they pass in song!

                                          [*He sings.*

        Heap cassia, sandal-buds and stripes   190
            Of labdanum, and aloe-balls,
        Smeared with dull nard an Indian wipes
            From out her hair: such balsam falls
            Down sea-side mountain pedestals,
        From tree-tops where tired winds are fain,   195
        Spent with the vast and howling main,
        To treasure half their island-gain.

        And strew faint sweetness from some old
            Egyptian's fine worm-eaten shroud
        Which breaks to dust when once unrolled;   200
            Or shredded perfume, like a cloud
            From closet long to quiet vowed,
        With mothed and dropping arras hung,
        Mouldering her lute and books among,
        As when a queen, long dead, was young.   205

Mine, every word! And on such pile shall die
My lovely fancies, with fair perished things,
Themselves fair and forgotten; yes, forgotten,
Or why abjure them? So, I made this rhyme
That fitting dignity might be preserved;   210
No little proud was I; though the list of drugs
Smacks of my old vocation, and the verse
Halts like the best of Luther's psalms.

FESTUS.   But, Aureole,
Talk not thus wildly and madly. I am here—
Did you know all! I have travelled far, indeed,   215
To learn your wishes. Be yourself again!
For in this mood I recognize you less
Than in the horrible despondency
I witnessed last. You may account this, joy;
But rather let me gaze on that despair   220
Than hear these incoherent words and see
This flushed cheek and intensely-sparkling eye.

PARACELSUS. Why, man, I was light-hearted in my prime,
I am light-hearted now; what would you have?
Aprile was a poet, I make songs—   225
'T is the very augury of success I want!
Why should I not be joyous now as then?

FESTUS. Joyous! and how? and what remains for joy?
You have declared the ends (which I am sick
Of naming) are impracticable.

PARACELSUS.   Ay,   230
Pursued as I pursued them—the arch-fool!
Listen: my plan will please you not, 't is like,
But you are little versed in the world's ways.
This is my plan—(first drinking its good luck)—
I will accept all helps; all I despised   235
So rashly at the outset, equally
With early impulses, late years have quenched:
I have tried each way singly: now for both!
All helps! no one sort shall exclude the rest.
I seek to know and to enjoy at once,   240
Not one without the other as before.
Suppose my labour should seem God's own cause
Once more, as first I dreamed,—it shall not baulk me

Of the meanest earthliest sensualest delight
That may be snatched; for every joy is gain,   245
And gain is gain, however small. My soul
Can die then, nor be taunted—'what was gained?'
Nor, on the other hand, should pleasure follow
As though I had not spurned her hitherto,
Shall she o'ercloud my spirit's rapt communion   250
With the tumultuous past, the teeming future,
Glorious with visions of a full success.

FESTUS. Success!

PARACELSUS.   And wherefore not? Why not prefer
Results obtained in my best state of being,
To those derived alone from seasons dark   255
As the thoughts they bred? When I was best, my youth
Unwasted, seemed success not surest too?
It is the nature of darkness to obscure.
I am a wanderer: I remember well
One journey, how I feared the track was missed,   260
So long the city I desired to reach
Lay hid; when suddenly its spires afar
Flashed through the circling clouds; you may conceive
My transport. Soon the vapours closed again,
But I had seen the city, and one such glance   265
No darkness could obscure: nor shall the present—
A few dull hours, a passing shame or two,
Destroy the vivid memories of the past.
I will fight the battle out; a little spent
Perhaps, but still an able combatant.   270
You look at my grey hair and furrowed brow?
But I can turn even weakness to account:
Of many tricks I know, 't is not the least
To push the ruins of my frame, whereon
The fire of vigour trembles scarce alive,   275
Into a heap, and send the flame aloft.
What should I do with age? So, sickness lends
An aid; it being, I fear, the source of all
We boast of: mind is nothing but disease,
And natural health is ignorance.

FESTUS.   I see   280
But one good symptom in this notable scheme.

I feared your sudden journey had in view
To wreak immediate vengeance on your foes;
'T is not so: I am glad.

PARACELSUS.   And if I please
To spit on them, to trample them, what then?   285
'T is sorry warfare truly, but the fools
Provoke it. I would spare their self-conceit
But if they must provoke me, cannot suffer
Forbearance on my part, if I may keep
No quality in the shade, must needs put forth   290
Power to match power, my strength against their strength,
And teach them their own game with their own arms—
Why, be it so and let them take their chance!
I am above them like a god, there's no
Hiding the fact: what idle scruples, then,   295
Were those that ever bade me soften it,
Communicate it gently to the world,
Instead of proving my supremacy,
Taking my natural station o'er their head,
Then owning all the glory was a man's!   300
—And in my elevation man's would be.
But live and learn, though life's short, learning, hard!
And therefore, though the wreck of my past self,
I fear, dear Pütter, that your lecture-room
Must wait awhile for its best ornament,   305
The penitent empiric, who set up
For somebody, but soon was taught his place;
Now, but too happy to be let confess
His error, snuff the candles, and illustrate
(*Fiat experientia corpore vili*)   310
Your medicine's soundness in his person. Wait,
Good Pütter!

FESTUS.   He who sneers thus, is a god!

PARACELSUS. Ay, ay, laugh at me! I am very glad
You are not gulled by all this swaggering; you
Can see the root of the matter!—how I strive   315
To put a good face on the overthrow
I have experienced, and to bury and hide
My degradation in its length and breadth;
How the mean motives I would make you think

Just mingle as is due with nobler aims,   320
The appetites I modestly allow
May influence me as being mortal still—
Do goad me, drive me on, and fast supplant
My youth's desires. You are no stupid dupe:
You find me out! Yes, I had sent for you   325
To palm these childish lies upon you, Festus!
Laugh—you shall laugh at me!
FESTUS.   The past, then, Aureole,
Proves nothing? Is our interchange of love
Yet to begin? Have I to swear I mean
No flattery in this speech or that? For you,   330
Whate'er you say, there is no degradation;
These low thoughts are no inmates of your mind,
Or wherefore this disorder? You are vexed
As much by the intrusion of base views,
Familiar to your adversaries, as they   335
Were troubled should your qualities alight
Amid their murky souls; not otherwise,
A stray wolf which the winter forces down
From our bleak hills, suffices to affright
A village in the vales—while foresters   340
Sleep calm, though all night long the famished troop
Snuff round and scratch against their crazy huts.
These evil thoughts are monsters, and will flee.
PARACELSUS. May you be happy, Festus, my own friend!
FESTUS. Nay, further; the delights you fain would think   345
The superseders of your nobler aims,
Though ordinary and harmless stimulants,
Will ne'er content you. . . .
PARACELSUS.   Hush! I once despised them,
But that soon passes. We are high at first
In our demand, nor will abate a jot   350
Of toil's strict value; but time passes o'er,
And humbler spirits accept what we refuse:
In short, when some such comfort is doled out
As these delights, we cannot long retain
Bitter contempt which urges us at first   355
To hurl it back, but hug it to our breast
And thankfully retire. This life of mine

Must be lived out and a grave thoroughly earned:
I am just fit for that and nought beside.
I told you once, I cannot now enjoy,   360
Unless I deem my knowledge gains through joy;
Nor can I know, but straight warm tears reveal
My need of linking also joy to knowledge:
So, on I drive, enjoying all I can,
And knowing all I can. I speak, of course,   365
Confusedly; this will better explain—feel here!
Quick beating, is it not?—a fire of the heart
To work off some way, this as well as any.
So, Festus sees me fairly launched; his calm
Compassionate look might have disturbed me once,   370
But now, far from rejecting, I invite
What bids me press the closer, lay myself
Open before him, and be soothed with pity;
I hope, if he command hope, and believe
As he directs me—satiating myself   375
With his enduring love. And Festus quits me
To give place to some credulous disciple
Who holds that God is wise, but Paracelsus
Has his peculiar merits: I suck in
That homage, chuckle o'er that admiration,   380
And then dismiss the fool; for night is come,
And I betake myself to study again,
Till patient searchings after hidden lore
Half wring some bright truth from its prison; my frame
Trembles, my forehead's veins swell out, my hair   385
Tingles for triumph. Slow and sure the morn
Shall break on my pent room and dwindling lamp
And furnace dead, and scattered earths and ores;
When, with a failing heart and throbbing brow,
I must review my captured truth, sum up   390
Its value, trace what ends to what begins,
Its present power with its eventual bearings,
Latent affinities, the views it opens,
And its full length in perfecting my scheme.
I view it sternly circumscribed, cast down   395
From the high place my fond hopes yielded it,
Proved worthless—which, in getting, yet had cost

Another wrench to this fast-falling frame.
Then, quick, the cup to quaff, that chases sorrow!
I lapse back into youth, and take again   400
My fluttering pulse for evidence that God
Means good to me, will make my cause his own.
See! I have cast off this remorseless care
Which clogged a spirit born to soar so free,
And my dim chamber has become a tent,   405
Festus is sitting by me, and his Michal . . .
Why do you start? I say, she listening here,
(For yonder—Würzburg through the orchard-bough!)
Motions as though such ardent words should find
No echo in a maiden's quiet soul,   410
But her pure bosom heaves, her eyes fill fast
With tears, her sweet lips tremble all the while!
Ha, ha!
FESTUS.   It seems, then, you expect to reap
No unreal joy from this your present course,
But rather . . .
PARACELSUS.   Death! To die! I owe that much   415
To what, at least, I was. I should be sad
To live contented after such a fall,
To thrive and fatten after such reverse!
The whole plan is a makeshift, but will last
My time.
FESTUS.   And you have never mused and said,   420
'I had a noble purpose, and the strength
'To compass it; but I have stopped half-way,
'And wrongly given the first-fruits of my toil
'To objects little worthy of the gift.
'Why linger round them still? why clench my fault?   425
'Why seek for consolation in defeat,
'In vain endeavours to derive a beauty
'From ugliness? why seek to make the most
'Of what no power can change, nor strive instead
'With mighty effort to redeem the past   430
'And, gathering up the treasures thus cast down,
'To hold a steadfast course till I arrive
'At their fit destination and my own?'
You have never pondered thus?

PARACELSUS.   Have I, you ask?
   Often at midnight, when most fancies come,   435
   Would some such airy project visit me:
   But ever at the end . . . or will you hear
   The same thing in a tale, a parable?
   You and I, wandering over the world wide,
   Chance to set foot upon a desert coast.   440
   Just as we cry, 'No human voice before
   'Broke the inveterate silence of these rocks!'
   —Their querulous echo startles us; we turn:
   What ravaged structure still looks o'er the sea?
   Some characters remain, too! While we read,   445
   The sharp salt wind, impatient for the last
   Of even this record, wistfully comes and goes,
   Or sings what we recover, mocking it.
   This is the record; and my voice, the wind's.

                                                   [*He sings.*
                                                               450
         Over the sea our galleys went,
      With cleaving prows in order brave
      To a speeding wind and a bounding wave,
         A gallant armament:
      Each bark built out of a forest-tree
         Left leafy and rough as first it grew,   455
      And nailed all over the gaping sides,
      Within and without, with black bull-hides,
      Seethed in fat and suppled in flame,
      To bear the playful billows' game:
      So, each good ship was rude to see,   460
      Rude and bare to the outward view,
         But each upbore a stately tent
      Where cedar pales in scented row
      Kept out the flakes of the dancing brine,
      And an awning drooped the mast below,   465
      In fold on fold of the purple fine,
      That neither noontide nor starshine
      Nor moonlight cold which maketh mad,
         Might pierce the regal tenement.
      When the sun dawned, oh, gay and glad   470
      We set the sail and plied the oar;
      But when the night-wind blew like breath,

For joy of one day's voyage more,
We sang together on the wide sea,
Like men at peace on a peaceful shore;   475
Each sail was loosed to the wind so free,
Each helm made sure by the twilight star,
And in a sleep as calm as death,
We, the voyagers from afar,
    Lay stretched along, each weary crew   480
In a circle round its wondrous tent
Whence gleamed soft light and curled rich scent,
    And with light and perfume, music too:
So the stars wheeled round, and the darkness past,
And at morn we started beside the mast,   485
And still each ship was sailing fast.

Now, one morn, land appeared—a speck
Dim trembling betwixt sea and sky:
'Avoid it,' cried our pilot, 'check
    'The shout, restrain the eager eye!'   490
But the heaving sea was black behind
For many a night and many a day,
And land, though but a rock, drew nigh;
So, we broke the cedar pales away,
Let the purple awning flap in the wind,   495
    And a statue bright was on every deck!
We shouted, every man of us,
And steered right into the harbour thus,
With pomp and pæan glorious.

A hundred shapes of lucid stone!   500
    All day we built its shrine for each,
A shrine of rock for every one,
Nor paused till in the westering sun
    We sat together on the beach
To sing because our task was done.   505
When lo! what shouts and merry songs!
What laughter all the distance stirs!
A loaded raft with happy throngs
Of gentle islanders!
'Our isles are just at hand,' they cried,   510

'Like cloudlets faint in even sleeping;
'Our temple-gates are opened wide,
    'Our olive-groves thick shade are keeping
'For these majestic forms'—they cried.
Oh, then we awoke with sudden start   515
From our deep dream, and knew, too late,
How bare the rock, how desolate,
Which had received our precious freight:
    Yet we called out—'Depart!
'Our gifts, once given, must here abide.   520
    'Our work is done; we have no heart
'To mar our work,'—we cried.

FESTUS. In truth?
PARACELSUS.   Nay, wait: all this in tracings faint
  On rugged stones strewn here and there, but piled
  In order once: then follows—mark what follows!   525
  'The sad rhyme of the men who proudly clung
  'To their first fault, and withered in their pride.'
FESTUS. Come back then, Aureole; as you fear God, come!
  This is foul sin; come back! Renounce the past,
  Forswear the future; look for joy no more,   530
  But wait death's summons amid holy sights,
  And trust me for the event—peace, if not joy.
  Return with me to Einsiedeln, dear Aureole!
PARACELSUS. No way, no way! it would not turn to good.
  A spotless child sleeps on the flowering moss—   535
  'T is well for him; but when a sinful man,
  Envying such slumber, may desire to put
  His guilt away, shall he return at once
  To rest by lying there? Our sires knew well
  (Spite of the grave discoveries of their sons)   540
  The fitting course for such: dark cells, dim lamps,
  A stone floor one may writhe on like a worm:
  No mossy pillow blue with violets!
FESTUS. I see no symptom of these absolute
  And tyrannous passions. You are calmer now.   545
  This verse-making can purge you well enough
  Without the terrible penance you describe.
  You love me still: the lusts you fear will never

Outrage your friend. To Einsiedeln, once more!
Say but the word!

PARACELSUS.   No, no; those lusts forbid: 550
They crouch, I know, cowering with half-shut eye
Beside you; 't is their nature. Thrust yourself
Between them and their prey; let some fool style me
Or king or quack, it matters not—then try
Your wisdom, urge them to forego their treat!   555
No, no; learn better and look deeper, Festus!
If you knew how a devil sneers within me
While you are talking now of this, now that,
As though we differed scarcely save in trifles!

FESTUS. Do we so differ? True, change must proceed,   560
Whether for good or ill; keep from me, which!
Do not confide all secrets: I was born
To hope, and you . . .

PARACELSUS.   To trust: you know the fruits!

FESTUS. Listen: I do believe, what you call trust
Was self-delusion at the best: for, see!   565
So long as God would kindly pioneer
A path for you, and screen you from the world,
Procure you full exemption from man's lot,
Man's common hopes and fears, on the mere pretext
Of your engagement in his service—yield you   570
A limitless licence, make you God, in fact,
And turn your slave—you were content to say
Most courtly praises! What is it, at last,
But selfishness without example? None
Could trace God's will so plain as you, while yours   575
Remained implied in it; but now you fail,
And we, who prate about that will, are fools!
In short, God's service is established here
As he determines fit, and not your way,
And this you cannot brook. Such discontent   580
Is weak. Renounce all creatureship at once!
Affirm an absolute right to have and use
Your energies; as though the rivers should say—
'We rush to the ocean; what have we to do
'With feeding streamlets, lingering in the vales,   585
'Sleeping in lazy pools?' Set up that plea,

That will be bold at least!

PARACELSUS.   'T is like enough.
The serviceable spirits are those, no doubt,
The East produces: lo, the master bids,—
They wake, raise terraces and garden-grounds   590
In one night's space; and, this done, straight begin
Another century's sleep, to the great praise
Of him that framed them wise and beautiful,
Till a lamp's rubbing, or some chance akin,
Wake them again. I am of different mould.   595
I would have soothed my lord, and slaved for him
And done him service past my narrow bond,
And thus I get rewarded for my pains!
Beside, 't is vain to talk of forwarding
God's glory otherwise; this is alone   600
The sphere of its increase, as far as men
Increase it; why, then, look beyond this sphere?
We are his glory; and if we be glorious,
Is not the thing achieved?

FESTUS.   Shall one like me
Judge hearts like yours? Though years have changed you
          much,   605
And you have left your first love, and retain
Its empty shade to veil your crooked ways,
Yet I still hold that you have honoured God.
And who shall call your course without reward?
For, wherefore this repining at defeat   610
Had triumph ne'er inured you to high hopes?
I urge you to forsake the life you curse,
And what success attends me?—simply talk
Of passion, weakness and remorse; in short,
Anything but the naked truth—you choose   615
This so-despised career, and cheaply hold
My happiness, or rather other men's.
Once more, return!

PARACELSUS.   And quickly. John the thief
Has pilfered half my secrets by this time:
And we depart by daybreak. I am weary,   620
I know not how; not even the wine-cup soothes
My brain to-night . . .

Do you not thoroughly despise me, Festus?
No flattery! One like you needs not be told
We live and breathe deceiving and deceived.   625
Do you not scorn me from your heart of hearts,
Me and my cant, each petty subterfuge,
My rhymes and all this frothy shower of words,
My glozing self-deceit, my outward crust
Of lies which wrap, as tetter, morphew, furfair   630
Wrapt the sound flesh?—so, see you flatter not!
Even God flatters: but my friend, at least,
Is true. I would depart, secure henceforth
Against all further insult, hate and wrong
From puny foes; my one friend's scorn shall brand me: 635
No fear of sinking deeper!
FESTUS.   No, dear Aureole!
No, no; I came to counsel faithfully.
There are old rules, made long ere we were born,
By which I judge you. I, so fallible,
So infinitely low beside your mighty   640
Majestic spirit!—even I can see
You own some higher law than ours which call
Sin, what is no sin—weakness, what is strength.
But I have only these, such as they are,
To guide me; and I blame you where they bid,   645
Only so long as blaming promises
To win peace for your soul: the more, that sorrow
Has fallen on me of late, and they have helped me
So that I faint not under my distress.
But wherefore should I scruple to avow   650
In spite of all, as brother judging brother,
Your fate is most inexplicable to me?
And should you perish without recompense
And satisfaction yet—too hastily
I have relied on love: you may have sinned,   655
But you have loved. As a mere human matter—
As I would have God deal with fragile men
In the end—I say that you will triumph yet!
PARACELSUS. Have you felt sorrow, Festus?—'t is because
You love me. Sorrow, and sweet Michal yours!   660
Well thought on: never let her know this last

Dull winding-up of all: these miscreants dared
Insult me—me she loved:—so, grieve her not!

FESTUS. Your ill success can little grieve her now.

PARACELSUS. Michal is dead! pray Christ we do not craze!   665

FESTUS. Aureole, dear Aureole, look not on me thus!
Fool, fool! this is the heart grown sorrow-proof—
I cannot bear those eyes.

PARACELSUS.   Nay, really dead?

FESTUS. 'T is scarce a month.

PARACELSUS.   Stone dead!—then you have laid her
Among the flowers ere this. Now, do you know,   670
I can reveal a secret which shall comfort
Even you. I have no julep, as men think,
To cheat the grave; but a far better secret.
Know, then, you did not ill to trust your love
To the cold earth: I have thought much of it: 675
For I believe we do not wholly die.

FESTUS. Aureole!

PARACELSUS.   Nay, do not laugh; there is a reason
For what I say: I think the soul can never
Taste death. I am, just now, as you may see,
Very unfit to put so strange a thought   680
In an intelligible dress of words;
But take it as my trust, she is not dead.

FESTUS. But not on this account alone? you surely,
—Aureole, you have believed this all along?

PARACELSUS. And Michal sleeps among the roots and dews,   685
While I am moved at Basil, and full of schemes
For Nuremberg, and hoping and despairing,
As though it mattered how the farce plays out,
So it be quickly played. Away, away!
Have your will, rabble! while we fight the prize,   690
Troop you in safety to the snug back-seats
And leave a clear arena for the brave
About to perish for your sport!—Behold!

PART V

PARACELSUS ATTAINS

SCENE.—*Salzburg; a cell in the Hospital of St. Sebastian.* 1541.

FESTUS, PARACELSUS

FESTUS. No change! The weary night is well-nigh spent,
　The lamp burns low, and through the casement-bars
　Grey morning glimmers feebly: yet no change!
　Another night, and still no sigh has stirred
　That fallen discoloured mouth, no pang relit　　　　5
　Those fixed eyes, quenched by the decaying body,
　Like torch-flame choked in dust. While all beside
　Was breaking, to the last they held out bright,
　As a stronghold where life intrenched itself;
　But they are dead now—very blind and dead:　　　10
　He will drowse into death without a groan.

　My Aureole—my forgotten, ruined Aureole!
　The days are gone, are gone! How grand thou wast!
　And now not one of those who struck thee down—
　Poor glorious spirit—concerns him even to stay　　15
　And satisfy himself his little hand
　Could turn God's image to a livid thing.

　Another night, and yet no change! 'T is much
　That I should sit by him, and bathe his brow,
　And chafe his hands; 't is much: but he will sure　20
　Know me, and look on me, and speak to me
　Once more—but only once! His hollow cheek
　Looked all night long as though a creeping laugh
　At his own state were just about to break
　From the dying man: my brain swam, my throat swelled,　25
　And yet I could not turn away. In truth,
　They told me how, when first brought here, he seemed
　Resolved to live, to lose no faculty;
　Thus striving to keep up his shattered strength,

Until they bore him to this stifling cell: 30
When straight his features fell, an hour made white
The flushed face, and relaxed the quivering limb,
Only the eye remained intense awhile
As though it recognized the tomb-like place,
And then he lay as here he lies.
                        Ay, here!   35
Here is earth's noblest, nobly garlanded—
Her bravest champion with his well-won prize—
Her best achievement, her sublime amends
For countless generations fleeting fast
And followed by no trace;—the creature-god   40
She instances when angels would dispute
The title of her brood to rank with them.
Angels, this is our angel! Those bright forms
We clothe with purple, crown and call to thrones,
Are human, but not his; those are but men   45
Whom other men press round and kneel before;
Those palaces are dwelt in by mankind;
Higher provision is for him you seek
Amid our pomps and glories: see it here!
Behold earth's paragon! Now, raise thee, clay!   50

God! Thou art love! I build my faith on that.
Even as I watch beside thy tortured child
Unconscious whose hot tears fall fast by him,
So doth thy right hand guide us through the world
Wherein we stumble. God! what shall we say?   55
How has he sinned? How else should he have done?
Surely he sought thy praise—thy praise, for all
He might be busied by the task so much
As half forget awhile its proper end.
Dost thou well, Lord? Thou canst not but prefer   60
That I should range myself upon his side—
How could he stop at every step to set
Thy glory forth? Hadst thou but granted him
Success, thy honour would have crowned success,
A halo round a star. Or, say he erred,—   65
Save him, dear God; it will be like thee: bathe him
In light and life! Thou art not made like us;

We should be wroth in such a case; but thou
Forgivest—so, forgive these passionate thoughts
Which come unsought and will not pass away!   70
I know thee, who hast kept my path, and made
Light for me in the darkness, tempering sorrow
So that it reached me like a solemn joy;
It were too strange that I should doubt thy love.
But what am I? Thou madest him and knowest   75
How he was fashioned. I could never err
That way: the quiet place beside thy feet,
Reserved for me, was ever in my thoughts:
But he—thou shouldst have favoured him as well!

Ah! he wakens! Aureole, I am here! 't is Festus!   80
I cast away all wishes save one wish—
Let him but know me, only speak to me!
He mutters; louder and louder; any other
Than I, with brain less laden, could collect
What he pours forth. Dear Aureole, do but look!   85
Is it talking or singing, this he utters fast?
Misery that he should fix me with his eye,
Quick talking to some other all the while!
If he would husband this wild vehemence
Which frustrates its intent!—I heard, I know   90
I heard my name amid those rapid words.
Oh, he will know me yet! Could I divert
This current, lead it somehow gently back
Into the channels of the past!—His eye
Brighter than ever! It must recognize me!   95

I am Erasmus: I am here to pray
That Paracelsus use his skill for me.
The schools of Paris and of Padua send
These questions for your learning to resolve.
We are your students, noble master: leave   100
This wretched cell, what business have you here?
Our class awaits you; come to us once more!
(O agony! the utmost I can do
Touches him not; how else arrest his ear?)
I am commissioned . . . I shall craze like him.   105

Better be mute and see what God shall send.
PARACELSUS. Stay, stay with me!
FESTUS.   I will; I am come here
To stay with you—Festus, you loved of old;
Festus, you know, you must know!
PARACELSUS.   Festus! Where's
Aprile, then? Has he not chanted softly   110
The melodies I heard all night? I could not
Get to him for a cold hand on my breast,
But I made out his music well enough,
O well enough! If they have filled him full
With magical music, as they freight a star   115
With light, and have remitted all his sin,
They will forgive me too, I too shall know!
FESTUS. Festus, your Festus!
PARACELSUS   Ask him if Aprile
Knows as he Loves—if I shall Love and Know?
I try; but that cold hand, like lead—so cold!   120
FESTUS. My hand, see!
PARACELSUS.   Ah, the curse, Aprile, Aprile!
We get so near—so very, very near!
'T is an old tale: Jove strikes the Titans down,
Not when they set about their mountain-piling
But when another rock would crown the work.   125
And Phaeton—doubtless his first radiant plunge
Astonished mortals, though the gods were calm,
And Jove prepared his thunder: all old tales!
FESTUS. And what are these to you?
PARACELSUS.   Ay, fiends must laugh
So cruelly, so well! most like I never   130
Could tread a single pleasure underfoot,
But they were grinning by my side, were chuckling
To see me toil and drop away by flakes!
Hell-spawn! I am glad, most glad, that thus I fail!
Your cunning has o'ershot its aim. One year,   135
One month, perhaps, and I had served your turn!
You should have curbed your spite awhile. But now,
Who will believe 't was you that held me back?
Listen: there's shame and hissing and contempt,
And none but laughs who names me, none but spits   140

Measureless scorn upon me, me alone,
The quack, the cheat, the liar,—all on me!
And thus your famous plan to sink mankind
In silence and despair, by teaching them
One of their race had probed the inmost truth,   145
Had done all man could do, yet failed no less—
Your wise plan proves abortive. Men despair?
Ha, ha! why, they are hooting the empiric,
The ignorant and incapable fool who rushed
Madly upon a work beyond his wits;   150
Nor doubt they but the simplest of themselves
Could bring the matter to triumphant issue.
So, pick and choose among them all, accursed!
Try now, persuade some other to slave for you,
To ruin body and soul to work your ends!   155
No, no; I am the first and last, I think.
FESTUS. Dear friend, who are accursed? who has done . . .
PARACELSUS. What have I done? Fiends dare ask that? or you,
Brave men? Oh, you can chime in boldly, backed
By the others! What had you to do, sage peers?   160
Here stand my rivals; Latin, Arab, Jew,
Greek, join dead hands against me: all I ask
Is, that the world enrol my name with theirs,
And even this poor privilege, it seems,
They range themselves, prepared to disallow.   165
Only observe! why, fiends may learn from them!
How they talk calmly of my throes, my fierce
Aspirings, terrible watchings, each one claiming
Its price of blood and brain; how they dissect
And sneeringly disparage the few truths   170
Got at a life's cost; they too hanging the while
About my neck, their lies misleading me
And their dead names browbeating me! Grey crew,
Yet steeped in fresh malevolence from hell,
Is there a reason for your hate? My truths   175
Have shaken a little the palm about each prince?
Just think, Aprile, all these leering dotards
Were bent on nothing less than to be crowned
As we! That yellow blear-eyed wretch in chief
To whom the rest cringe low with feigned respect,   180

Galen of Pergamos and hell—nay speak
The tale, old man! We met there face to face:
I said the crown should fall from thee. Once more
We meet as in that ghastly vestibule:
Look to my brow! Have I redeemed my pledge?   185
FESTUS. Peace, peace; ah, see!
PARACELSUS.   Oh, emptiness of fame!
Oh Persic Zoroaster, lord of stars!
—Who said these old renowns, dead long ago,
Could make me overlook the living world
To gaze through gloom at where they stood, indeed,   190
But stand no longer? What a warm light life
After the shade! In truth, my delicate witch,
My serpent-queen, you did but well to hide
The juggles I had else detected. Fire
May well run harmless o'er a breast like yours!   195
The cave was not so darkened by the smoke
But that your white limbs dazzled me: oh, white,
And panting as they twinkled, wildly dancing!
I cared not for your passionate gestures then,
But now I have forgotten the charm of charms,   200
The foolish knowledge which I came to seek,
While I remember that quaint dance; and thus
I am come back, not for those mummeries,
But to love you, and to kiss your little feet
Soft as an ermine's winter coat!
FESTUS.   A light   205
Will struggle through these thronging words at last.
As in the angry and tumultuous West
A soft star trembles through the drifting clouds.
These are the strivings of a spirit which hates
So sad a vault should coop it, and calls up   210
The past to stand between it and its fate.
Were he at Einsiedeln—or Michal here!
PARACELSUS. Cruel! I seek her now—I kneel—I shriek—
I clasp her vesture—but she fades, still fades;
And she is gone; sweet human love is gone!   215
'T is only when they spring to heaven that angels
Reveal themselves to you; they sit all day
Beside you, and lie down at night by you

Who care not for their presence, muse or sleep,
And all at once they leave you, and you know them!   220
We are so fooled, so cheated! Why, even now
I am not too secure against foul play;
The shadows deepen and the walls contract:
No doubt some treachery is going on.
'T is very dusk. Where are we put, Aprile?   225
Have they left us in the lurch? This murky loathsome
Death-trap, this slaughter-house, is not the hall
In the golden city! Keep by me, Aprile!
There is a hand groping amid the blackness
To catch us. Have the spider-fingers got you,   230
Poet? Hold on me for your life! If once
They pull you!—Hold!
                        'Tis but a dream—no more!
I have you still; the sun comes out again;
Let us be happy: all will yet go well!
Let us confer: is it not like, Aprile,   235
That spite of trouble, this ordeal passed,
The value of my labours ascertained,
Just as some stream foams long among the rocks
But after glideth glassy to the sea,
So, full content shall henceforth be my lot?   240
What think you, poet? Louder! Your clear voice
Vibrates too like a harp-string. Do you ask
How could I still remain on earth, should God
Grant me the great approval which I seek?
I, you, and God can comprehend each other,   245
But men would murmur, and with cause enough;
For when they saw me, stainless of all sin,
Preserved and sanctified by inward light,
They would complain that comfort, shut from them,
I drank thus unespied; that they live on,   250
Nor taste the quiet of a constant joy,
For ache and care and doubt and weariness,
While I am calm; help being vouchsafed to me,
And hid from them.—'T were best consider that!
You reason well, Aprile; but at least   255
Let me know this, and die! Is this too much?
I will learn this, if God so please, and die!

If thou shalt please, dear God, if thou shalt please!
We are so weak, we know our motives least
In their confused beginning. If at first   260
I sought . . . but wherefore bare my heart to thee?
I know thy mercy; and already thoughts
Flock fast about my soul to comfort it,
And intimate I cannot wholly fail,
For love and praise would clasp me willingly   265
Could I resolve to seek them. Thou art good,
And I should be content. Yet—yet first show
I have done wrong in daring! Rather give
The supernatural consciousness of strength
Which fed my youth! Only one hour of that   270
With thee to help—O what should bar me then!

Lost, lost! Thus things are ordered here! God's creatures,
And yet he takes no pride in us!—none, none!
Truly there needs another life to come!
If this be all—(I must tell Festus that)   275
And other life await us not—for one,
I say 't is a poor cheat, a stupid bungle,
A wretched failure. I, for one, protest
Against it, and I hurl it back with scorn.

Well, onward though alone! Small time remains,   280
And much to do: I must have fruit, must reap
Some profit from my toils. I doubt my body
Will hardly serve me through; while I have laboured
It has decayed; and now that I demand
Its best assistance, it will crumble fast: 285
A sad thought, a sad fate! How very full
Of wormwood 't is, that just at altar-service,
The rapt hymn rising with the rolling smoke,
When glory dawns and all is at the best,
The sacred fire may flicker and grow faint   290
And die for want of a wood-piler's help!
Thus fades the flagging body, and the soul
Is pulled down in the overthrow. Well, well—
Let men catch every word, let them lose nought
Of what I say; something may yet be done.   295

They are ruins! Trust me who am one of you!
All ruins, glorious once, but lonely now.
It makes my heart sick to behold you crouch
Beside your desolate fane: the arches dim,
The crumbling columns grand against the moon,   300
Could I but rear them up once more—but that
May never be, so leave them! Trust me, friends,
Why should you linger here when I have built
A far resplendent temple, all your own?
Trust me, they are but ruins! See, Aprile,   305
Men will not heed! Yet were I not prepared
With better refuge for them, tongue of mine
Should ne'er reveal how blank their dwelling is:
I would sit down in silence with the rest.

Ha, what? you spit at me, you grin and shriek   310
Contempt into my ear—my ear which drank
God's accents once? you curse me? Why men, men,
I am not formed for it! Those hideous eyes
Will be before me sleeping, waking, praying,
They will not let me even die. Spare, spare me,   315
Sinning or no, forget that, only spare me
The horrible scorn! You thought I could support it.
But now you see what silly fragile creature
Cowers thus. I am not good nor bad enough,
Not Christ nor Cain, yet even Cain was saved   320
From Hate like this. Let me but totter back!
Perhaps I shall elude those jeers which creep
Into my very brain, and shut these scorched
Eyelids and keep those mocking faces out.

Listen, Aprile! I am very calm: 325
Be not deceived, there is no passion here
Where the blood leaps like an imprisoned thing:
I am calm: I will exterminate the race!
Enough of that: 't is said and it shall be.
And now be merry: safe and sound am I   330
Who broke through their best ranks to get at you.
And such a havoc, such a rout, Aprile!
FESTUS. Have you no thought, no memory for me,

Aureole? I am so wretched—my pure Michal
Is gone, and you alone are left me now,   335
And even you forget me. Take my hand—
Lean on me thus. Do you not know me, Aureole?
PARACELSUS. Festus, my own friend, you are come at last?
As you say, 't is an awful enterprise;
But you believe I shall go through with it: 340
'T is like you, and I thank you. Thank him for me,
Dear Michal! See how bright St. Saviour's spire
Flames in the sunset; all its figures quaint
Gay in the glancing light: you might conceive them
A troop of yellow-vested white-haired Jews   345
Bound for their own land where redemption dawns.
FESTUS. Not that blest time—not our youth's time, dear God!
PARACELSUS. Ha—stay! true, I forget—all is done since,
And he is come to judge me. How he speaks,
How calm, how well! yes, it is true, all true;   350
All quackery; all deceit; myself can laugh
The first at it, if you desire: but still
You know the obstacles which taught me tricks
So foreign to my nature—envy and hate,
Blind opposition, brutal prejudice,   355
Bald ignorance—what wonder if I sunk
To humour men the way they most approved?
My cheats were never palmed on such as you,
Dear Festus! I will kneel if you require me,
Impart the meagre knowledge I possess,   360
Explain its bounded nature, and avow
My insufficiency—whate'er you will:
I give the fight up: let there be an end,
A privacy, an obscure nook for me.
I want to be forgotten even by God.   365
But if that cannot be, dear Festus, lay me,
When I shall die, within some narrow grave,
Not by itself—for that would be too proud—
But where such graves are thickest; let it look
Nowise distinguished from the hillocks round,   370
So that the peasant at his brother's bed
May tread upon my own and know it not;
And we shall all be equal at the last,

Or classed according to life's natural ranks,
Fathers, sons, brothers, friends—not rich, nor wise,   375
Nor gifted: lay me thus, then say, 'He lived
'Too much advanced before his brother men;
'They kept him still in front: 't was for their good
'But yet a dangerous station. It were strange
'That he should tell God he had never ranked   380
'With men: so, here at least he is a man.'
FESTUS. That God shall take thee to his breast, dear spirit,
    Unto his breast, be sure! and here on earth
    Shall splendour sit upon thy name for ever.
    Sun! all the heaven is glad for thee: what care   385
    If lower mountains light their snowy phares
    At thine effulgence, yet acknowledge not
    The source of day? Their theft shall be their bale:
    For after-ages shall retrack thy beams,
    And put aside the crowd of busy ones   390
    And worship thee alone—the master-mind,
    The thinker, the explorer, the creator!
    Then, who should sneer at the convulsive throes
    With which thy deeds were born, would scorn as well
    The sheet of winding subterraneous fire   395
    Which, pent and writhing, sends no less at last
    Huge islands up amid the simmering sea.
    Behold thy might in me! thou hast infused
    Thy soul in mine; and I am grand as thou,
    Seeing I comprehend thee—I so simple,   400
    Thou so august. I recognize thee first;
    I saw thee rise, I watched thee early and late,
    And though no glance reveal thou dost accept
    My homage—thus no less I proffer it,
    And bid thee enter gloriously thy rest.   405
PARACELSUS. Festus!
FESTUS.   I am for noble Aureole, God!
    I am upon his side, come weal or woe.
    His portion shall be mine. He has done well.
    I would have sinned, had I been strong enough,
    As he has sinned. Reward him or I waive   410
    Reward! If thou canst find no place for him,
    He shall be king elsewhere, and I will be

His slave for ever. There are two of us.

PARACELSUS. Dear Festus!

FESTUS.   Here, dear Aureole! ever by you!

PARACELSUS. Nay, speak on, or I dream again. Speak on!   415
  Some story, anything—only your voice.
  I shall dream else. Speak on! ay, leaning so!

FESTUS.   Thus the Mayne glideth
        Where my Love abideth.
        Sleep's no softer: it proceeds   420
        On through lawns, on through meads,
        On and on, whate'er befall,
        Meandering and musical,
        Though the niggard pasturage
        Bears not on its shaven ledge   425
        Aught but weeds and waving grasses
        To view the river as it passes,
        Save here and there a scanty patch
        Of primroses too faint to catch
        A weary bee.   430

PARACELSUS. More, more; say on!

FESTUS.   And scarce it pushes
        Its gentle way through strangling rushes
        Where the glossy kingfisher
        Flutters when noon-heats are near,
        Glad the shelving banks to shun,   435
        Red and steaming in the sun,
        Where the shrew-mouse with pale throat
        Burrows, and the speckled stoat;
        Where the quick sandpipers flit
        In and out the marl and grit   440
        That seems to breed them, brown as they:
        Nought disturbs its quiet way,
        Save some lazy stork that springs,
        Trailing it with legs and wings,
        Whom the shy fox from the hill   445
        Rouses, creep he ne'er so still.

PARACELSUS. My heart! they loose my heart, those simple words;
  Its darkness passes, which nought else could touch:
  Like some dark snake that force may not expel,
  Which glideth out to music sweet and low.   450

What were you doing when your voice broke through
A chaos of ugly images? You, indeed!
Are you alone here?

FESTUS.   All alone: you know me?
This cell?

PARACELSUS. An unexceptionable vault:
  Good brick and stone: the bats kept out, the rats   455
  Kept in: a snug nook: how should I mistake it?

FESTUS. But wherefore am I here?

PARACELSUS.   Ah, well remembered!
  Why, for a purpose—for a purpose, Festus!
  'T is like me: here I trifle while time fleets,
  And this occasion, lost, will ne'er return.   460
  You are here to be instructed. I will tell
  God's message; but I have so much to say,
  I fear to leave half out. All is confused
  No doubt; but doubtless you will learn in time.
  He would not else have brought you here: no doubt   465
  I shall see clearer soon.

FESTUS.   Tell me but this—
  You are not in despair?

PARACELSUS.   I? and for what?

FESTUS. Alas, alas! he knows not, as I feared!

PARACELSUS. What is it you would ask me with that earnest
  Dear searching face?

FESTUS.   How feel you, Aureole?

PARACELSUS.   Well: 470
  Well. 'T is a strange thing: I am dying, Festus,
  And now that fast the storm of life subsides,
  I first perceive how great the whirl has been.
  I was calm then, who am so dizzy now—
  Calm in the thick of the tempest, but no less   475
  A partner of its motion and mixed up
  With its career. The hurricane is spent,
  And the good boat speeds through the brightening weather;
  But is it earth or sea that heaves below?
  The gulf rolls like a meadow-swell, o'erstrewn   480
  With ravaged boughs and remnants of the shore;
  And now some islet, loosened from the land,
  Swims past with all its trees, sailing to ocean;

And now the air is full of uptorn canes,
Light strippings from the fan-trees, tamarisks   485
Unrooted, with their birds still clinging to them,
All high in the wind. Even so my varied life
Drifts by me; I am young, old, happy, sad,
Hoping, desponding, acting, taking rest,
And all at once: that is, those past conditions   490
Float back at once on me. If I select
Some special epoch from the crowd, 't is but
To will, and straight the rest dissolve away,
And only that particular state is present
With all its long-forgotten circumstance   495
Distinct and vivid as at first—myself
A careless looker-on and nothing more,
Indifferent and amused, but nothing more.
And this is death: I understand it all.
New being waits me; new perceptions must   500
Be born in me before I plunge therein;
Which last is Death's affair; and while I speak,
Minute by minute he is filling me
With power; and while my foot is on the threshold
Of boundless life—the doors unopened yet,   505
All preparations not complete within—
I turn new knowledge upon old events,
And the effect is . . . but I must not tell;
It is not lawful. Your own turn will come
One day. Wait, Festus! You will die like me.   510
FESTUS. 'T is of that past life that I burn to hear.
PARACELSUS. You wonder it engages me just now?
In truth, I wonder too. What's life to me?
Where'er I look is fire, where'er I listen
Music, and where I tend bliss evermore.   515
Yet how can I refrain? 'T is a refined
Delight to view those chances,—one last view.
I am so near the perils I escape,
That I must play with them and turn them over,
To feel how fully they are past and gone.   520
Still, it is like, some further cause exists
For this peculiar mood—some hidden purpose;
Did I not tell you something of it, Festus?

 I had it fast, but it has somehow slipt
 Away from me; it will return anon.   525
FESTUS. (Indeed his cheek seems young again, his voice
 Complete with its old tones: that little laugh
 Concluding every phrase, with upturned eye,
 As though one stooped above his head to whom
 He looked for confirmation and approval,   530
 Where was it gone so long, so well preserved?
 Then, the fore-finger pointing as he speaks,
 Like one who traces in an open book
 The matter he declares; 't is many a year
 Since I remarked it last: and this in him,   535
 But now a ghastly wreck!)
          And can it be,
 Dear Aureole, you have then found out at last
 That worldly things are utter vanity?
 That man is made for weakness, and should wait
 In patient ignorance, till God appoint . . .   540
PARACELSUS. Ha, the purpose: the true purpose: that is it!
 How could I fail to apprehend! You here,
 I thus! But no more trifling: I see all,
 I know all: my last mission shall be done
 If strength suffice. No trifling! Stay; this posture 545
 Hardly befits one thus about to speak:
 I will arise.
FESTUS.   Nay, Aureole, are you wild?
 You cannot leave your couch.
PARACELSUS.   No help; no help;
 Not even your hand. So! there, I stand once more!
 Speak from a couch? I never lectured thus.   550
 My gown—the scarlet lined with fur; now put
 The chain about my neck; my signet-ring
 Is still upon my hand, I think—even so;
 Last, my good sword; ah, trusty Azoth, leapest
 Beneath thy master's grasp for the last time? 555
 This couch shall be my throne: I bid these walls
 Be consecrate, this wretched cell become
 A shrine, for here God speaks to men through me.
 Now, Festus, I am ready to begin.
FESTUS. I am dumb with wonder.   560

PARACELSUS.   Listen, therefore, Festus!
   There will be time enough, but none to spare.
   I must content myself with telling only
   The most important points. You doubtless feel
   That I am happy, Festus; very happy.
FESTUS. 'T is no delusion which uplifts him thus!   565
   Then you are pardoned, Aureole, all your sin?
PARACELSUS. Ay, pardoned: yet why pardoned?
FESTUS.   'T is God's praise
   That man is bound to seek, and you . . .
PARACELSUS.   Have lived!
   We have to live alone to set forth well
   God's praise. 'T is true, I sinned much, as I thought,   570
   And in effect need mercy, for I strove
   To do that very thing; but, do your best
   Or worst, praise rises, and will rise for ever.
   Pardon from him, because of praise denied—
   Who calls me to himself to exalt himself?   575
   He might laugh as I laugh!
FESTUS.   But all comes
   To the same thing. 'T is fruitless for mankind
   To fret themselves with what concerns them not;
   They are no use that way: they should lie down
   Content as God has made them, nor go mad   580
   In thriveless cares to better what is ill.
PARACELSUS. No, no; mistake me not; let me not work
   More harm than I have worked! This is my case:
   If I go joyous back to God, yet bring
   No offering, if I render up my soul   585
   Without the fruits it was ordained to bear,
   If I appear the better to love God
   For sin, as one who has no claim on him,—
   Be not deceived! It may be surely thus
   With me, while higher prizes still await   590
   The mortal persevering to the end.
   Beside I am not all so valueless:
   I have been something, though too soon I left
   Following the instincts of that happy time.
FESTUS. What happy time? For God's sake, for man's sake,   595
   What time was happy? All I hope to know

That answer will decide. What happy time?
PARACELSUS. When but the time I vowed myself to man?
FESTUS. Great God, thy judgments are inscrutable!
PARACELSUS. Yes, it was in me; I was born for it—   600
   I, Paracelsus: it was mine by right.
   Doubtless a searching and impetuous soul
   Might learn from its own motions that some task
   Like this awaited it about the world;
   Might seek somewhere in this blank life of ours   605
   For fit delights to stay its longings vast;
   And, grappling Nature, so prevail on her
   To fill the creature full she dared thus frame
   Hungry for joy; and, bravely tyrannous,
   Grow in demand, still craving more and more,   610
   And make each joy conceded prove a pledge
   Of other joy to follow—bating nought
   Of its desires, still seizing fresh pretence
   To turn the knowledge and the rapture wrung
   As an extreme, last boon, from destiny,   615
   Into occasion for new covetings,
   New strifes, new triumphs:—doubtless a strong soul,
   Alone, unaided might attain to this,
   So glorious is our nature, so august
   Man's inborn uninstructed impulses,   620
   His naked spirit so majestical!
   But this was born in me; I was made so;
   Thus much time saved: the feverish appetites,
   The tumult of unproved desire, the unaimed
   Uncertain yearnings, aspirations blind,   625
   Distrust, mistake, and all that ends in tears
   Were saved me; thus I entered on my course.
   You may be sure I was not all exempt
   From human trouble; just so much of doubt
   As bade me plant a surer foot upon   630
   The sun-road, kept my eye unruined 'mid
   The fierce and flashing splendour, set my heart
   Trembling so much as warned me I stood there
   On sufferance—not to idly gaze, but cast
   Light on a darkling race; save for that doubt,   635
   I stood at first where all aspire at last

To stand: the secret of the world was mine.
I knew, I felt, (perception unexpressed,
Uncomprehended by our narrow thought,
But somehow felt and known in every shift   640
And change in the spirit,—nay, in every pore
Of the body, even,)—what God is, what we are,
What life is—how God tastes an infinite joy
In infinite ways—one everlasting bliss,
From whom all being emanates, all power   645
Proceeds; in whom is life for evermore,
Yet whom existence in its lowest form
Includes; where dwells enjoyment there is he:
With still a flying point of bliss remote,
A happiness in store afar, a sphere   650
Of distant glory in full view; thus climbs
Pleasure its heights for ever and for ever.
The centre-fire heaves underneath the earth,
And the earth changes like a human face;
The molten ore bursts up among the rocks,   655
Winds into the stone's heart, outbranches bright
In hidden mines, spots barren river-beds,
Crumbles into fine sand where sunbeams bask—
God joys therein. The wroth sea's waves are edged
With foam, white as the bitten lip of hate,   660
When, in the solitary waste, strange groups
Of young volcanos come up, cyclops-like,
Staring together with their eyes on flame—
God tastes a pleasure in their uncouth pride.
Then all is still; earth is a wintry clod: 665
But spring-wind, like a dancing psaltress, passes
Over its breast to waken it, rare verdure
Buds tenderly upon rough banks, between
The withered tree-roots and the cracks of frost,
Like a smile striving with a wrinkled face;   670
The grass grows bright, the boughs are swoln with blooms
Like chrysalids impatient for the air,
The shining dorrs are busy, beetles run
Along the furrows, ants make their ado;
Above, birds fly in merry flocks, the lark   675
Soars up and up, shivering for very joy;

Afar the ocean sleeps; white fishing-gulls
Flit where the strand is purple with its tribe
Of nested limpets; savage creatures seek
Their loves in wood and plain—and God renews   680
His ancient rapture. Thus he dwells in all,
From life's minute beginnings, up at last
To man—the consummation of this scheme
Of being, the completion of this sphere
Of life: whose attributes had here and there   685
Been scattered o'er the visible world before,
Asking to be combined, dim fragments meant
To be united in some wondrous whole,
Imperfect qualities throughout creation,
Suggesting some one creature yet to make,   690
Some point where all those scattered rays should meet
Convergent in the faculties of man.
Power—neither put forth blindly, nor controlled
Calmly by perfect knowledge; to be used
At risk, inspired or checked by hope and fear: 695
Knowledge—not intuition, but the slow
Uncertain fruit of an enhancing toil,
Strengthened by love: love—not serenely pure,
But strong from weakness, like a chance-sown plant
Which, cast on stubborn soil, puts forth changed buds 700
And softer stains, unknown in happier climes;
Love which endures and doubts and is oppressed
And cherished, suffering much and much sustained,
And blind, oft-failing, yet believing love,
A half-enlightened, often-chequered trust:—   705
Hints and previsions of which faculties,
Are strewn confusedly everywhere about
The inferior natures, and all lead up higher,
All shape out dimly the superior race,
The heir of hopes too fair to turn out false,   710
And man appears at last. So far the seal
Is put on life; one stage of being complete,
One scheme wound up: and from the grand result
A supplementary reflux of light,
Illustrates all the inferior grades, explains   715
Each back step in the circle. Not alone

For their possessor dawn those qualities,
But the new glory mixes with the heaven
And earth; man, once descried, imprints for ever
His presence on all lifeless things: the winds   720
Are henceforth voices, wailing or a shout,
A querulous mutter or a quick gay laugh,
Never a senseless gust now man is born.
The herded pines commune and have deep thoughts,
A secret they assemble to discuss   725
When the sun drops behind their trunks which glare
Like grates of hell: the peerless cup afloat
Of the lake-lily is an urn, some nymph
Swims bearing high above her head: no bird
Whistles unseen, but through the gaps above   730
That let light in upon the gloomy woods,
A shape peeps from the breezy forest-top,
Arch with small puckered mouth and mocking eye.
The morn has enterprise, deep quiet droops
With evening, triumph takes the sunset hour,   735
Voluptuous transport ripens with the corn
Beneath a warm moon like a happy face:
—And this to fill us with regard for man,
With apprehension of his passing worth,
Desire to work his proper nature out,   740
And ascertain his rank and final place,
For these things tend still upward, progress is
The law of life, man is not Man as yet.
Nor shall I deem his object served, his end
Attained, his genuine strength put fairly forth,   745
While only here and there a star dispels
The darkness, here and there a towering mind
O'erlooks its prostrate fellows: when the host
Is out at once to the despair of night,
When all mankind alike is perfected,   750
Equal in full-blown powers—then, not till then,
I say, begins man's general infancy.
For wherefore make account of feverish starts
Of restless members of a dormant whole,
Impatient nerves which quiver while the body   755
Slumbers as in a grave? Oh long ago

The brow was twitched, the tremulous lids astir,
The peaceful mouth disturbed; half-uttered speech
Ruffled the lip, and then the teeth were set,
The breath drawn sharp, the strong right-hand clenched stronger,
As it would pluck a lion by the jaw;　　　　761
The glorious creature laughed out even in sleep!
But when full roused, each giant-limb awake,
Each sinew strung, the great heart pulsing fast,
He shall start up and stand on his own earth,　　　　765
Then shall his long triumphant march begin,
Thence shall his being date,—thus wholly roused,
What he achieves shall be set down to him.
When all the race is perfected alike
As man, that is; all tended to mankind,　　　　770
And, man produced, all has its end thus far:
But in completed man begins anew
A tendency to God. Prognostics told
Man's near approach; so in man's self arise
August anticipations, symbols, types　　　　775
Of a dim splendour ever on before
In that eternal circle life pursues.
For men begin to pass their nature's bound,
And find new hopes and cares which fast supplant
Their proper joys and griefs; they grow too great　　　　780
For narrow creeds of right and wrong, which fade
Before the unmeasured thirst for good: while peace
Rises within them ever more and more.
Such men are even now upon the earth,
Serene amid the half-formed creatures round　　　　785
Who should be saved by them and joined with them.
Such was my task, and I was born to it—
Free, as I said but now, from much that chains
Spirits, high-dowered but limited and vexed
By a divided and delusive aim,　　　　790
A shadow mocking a reality
Whose truth avails not wholly to disperse
The flitting mimic called up by itself,
And so remains perplexed and nigh put out
By its fantastic fellow's wavering gleam.　　　　795
I, from the first, was never cheated thus;

I never fashioned out a fancied good
Distinct from man's; a service to be done,
A glory to be ministered unto
With powers put forth at man's expense, withdrawn   800
From labouring in his behalf; a strength
Denied that might avail him. I cared not
Lest his success ran counter to success
Elsewhere: for God is glorified in man,
And to man's glory vowed I soul and limb.   805
Yet, constituted thus, and thus endowed,
I failed: I gazed on power till I grew blind.
Power; I could not take my eyes from that:
That only, I thought, should be preserved, increased
At any risk, displayed, struck out at once—   810
The sign and note and character of man.
I saw no use in the past: only a scene
Of degradation, ugliness and tears,
The record of disgraces best forgotten,
A sullen page in human chronicles   815
Fit to erase. I saw no cause why man
Should not stand all-sufficient even now,
Or why his annals should be forced to tell
That once the tide of light, about to break
Upon the world, was sealed within its spring: 820
I would have had one day, one moment's space,
Change man's condition, push each slumbering claim
Of mastery o'er the elemental world
At once to full maturity, then roll
Oblivion o'er the work, and hide from man   825
What night had ushered morn. Not so, dear child
Of after-days, wilt thou reject the past
Big with deep warnings of the proper tenure
By which thou hast the earth: for thee the present
Shall have distinct and trembling beauty, seen   830
Beside that past's own shade when, in relief,
Its brightness shall stand out: nor yet on thee
Shall burst the future, as successive zones
Of several wonder open on some spirit
Flying secure and glad from heaven to heaven: 835
But thou shalt painfully attain to joy,

While hope and fear and love shall keep thee man!
All this was hid from me: as one by one
My dreams grew dim, my wide aims circumscribed,
As actual good within my reach decreased,   840
While obstacles sprung up this way and that
To keep me from effecting half the sum,
Small as it proved; as objects, mean within
The primal aggregate, seemed, even the least,
Itself a match for my concentred strength—   845
What wonder if I saw no way to shun
Despair? The power I sought for man, seemed God's.
In this conjuncture, as I prayed to die,
A strange adventure made me know, one sin
Had spotted my career from its uprise;   850
I saw Aprile—my Aprile there!
And as the poor melodious wretch disburthened
His heart, and moaned his weakness in my ear,
I learned my own deep error; love's undoing
Taught me the worth of love in man's estate,   855
And what proportion love should hold with power
In his right constitution; love preceding
Power, and with much power, always much more love;
Love still too straitened in his present means,
And earnest for new power to set love free.   860
I learned this, and supposed the whole was learned:
And thus, when men received with stupid wonder
My first revealings, would have worshipped me,
And I despised and loathed their proffered praise—
When, with awakened eyes, they took revenge   865
For past credulity in casting shame
On my real knowledge, and I hated them—
It was not strange I saw no good in man,
To overbalance all the wear and waste
Of faculties, displayed in vain, but born   870
To prosper in some better sphere: and why?
In my own heart love had not been made wise
To trace love's faint beginnings in mankind,
To know even hate is but a mask of love's,
To see a good in evil, and a hope   875
In ill-success; to sympathize, be proud

Of their half-reasons, faint aspirings, dim
Struggles for truth, their poorest fallacies,
Their prejudice and fears and cares and doubts;
All with a touch of nobleness, despite   880
Their error, upward tending all though weak,
Like plants in mines which never saw the sun,
But dream of him, and guess where he may be,
And do their best to climb and get to him.
All this I knew not, and I failed. Let men   885
Regard me, and the poet dead long ago
Who loved too rashly; and shape forth a third
And better-tempered spirit, warned by both:
As from the over-radiant star too mad
To drink the life-springs, beamless thence itself—   890
And the dark orb which borders the abyss,
Ingulfed in icy night,—might have its course
A temperate and equidistant world.
Meanwhile, I have done well, though not all well.
As yet men cannot do without contempt;   895
'T is for their good, and therefore fit awhile
That they reject the weak, and scorn the false,
Rather than praise the strong and true, in me:
But after, they will know me. If I stoop
Into a dark tremendous sea of cloud,   900
It is but for a time; I press God's lamp
Close to my breast; its splendour, soon or late,
Will pierce the gloom: I shall emerge one day.
You understand me? I have said enough?
FESTUS. Now die, dear Aureole!
PARACELSUS.   Festus, let my hand—   905
This hand, lie in your own, my own true friend!
Aprile! Hand in hand with you, Aprile!

FESTUS. And this was Paracelsus!

NOTE

The liberties I have taken with my subject are very trifling; and the reader may slip the foregoing scenes between the leaves of any memoir of Paracelsus he pleases, by way of commentary. To prove this, I subjoin a popular account, translated from the 'Biographie Universelle, Paris,' 1822, which I select, not as the best, certainly, but as being at hand, and sufficiently concise for my purpose. I also append a few notes, in order to correct those parts which do not bear out my own view of the character of Paracelsus; and have incorporated with them a notice or two, illustrative of the poem itself.

'Paracelsus (Philippus Aureolus Theophrastus Bombastus ab Hohenheim) was born in 1493 at Einsiedeln, (¹) a little town in the canton of Schwyz, some leagues distant from Zurich. His father, who exercised the profession of medicine at Villach in Carinthia, was nearly related to George Bombast de Hohenheim, who became afterward Grand Prior of the Order of Malta: consequently Paracelsus could not spring from the dregs of the people, as Thomas Erastus, his sworn enemy, pretends.* It appears that his elementary education was much neglected, and that he spent part of his youth in pursuing the life common to the travelling *literati* of the age; that is to say, in wandering from country to country, predicting the future by astrology and cheiromancy, evoking apparitions, and practising the different operations of magic and alchemy, in which he had been initiated whether by his father or by various ecclesiastics, among the number of whom he particularizes the Abbot Tritheim, (²) and many German bishops.

'As Paracelsus displays everywhere an ignorance of the rudiments of the most ordinary knowledge, it is not probable that he ever studied seriously in the schools: he contented himself with visiting the Universities of Germany, France and Italy; and in spite of his boasting himself to have been the ornament of those institutions, there is no proof of his having legally acquired the title of Doctor, which he assumes. It is only known that he applied himself long, under the direction of the wealthy Sigismond Fugger of Schwatz, to the discovery of the Magnum Opus.

'Paracelsus travelled among the mountains of Bohemia, in the East, and in Sweden, in order to inspect the labours of the miners, to be initiated in the mysteries of the oriental adepts, and to observe the secrets of nature and the famous mountain of loadstone. (³) He professes also to have visited Spain, Portugal, Prussia, Poland, and Transylvania; everywhere communicating freely, not merely with the physicians, but the old women, charlatans and conjurers of these several lands. It is even believed that he extended his journeyings as far as Egypt and Tartary, and that he accompanied the son of the Khan of the Tartars to Constantinople, for the purpose of obtaining the secret of the tincture of Trismegistus from a Greek who inhabited that capital.

'The period of his return to Germany is unknown: it is only certain that, at

---

* I shall disguise M. Renauldin's next sentence a little. 'Hic (Erastus sc.) Paracelsum trimum a milite quodam, alii a sue exectum ferunt: constat imberbem illum, mulierumque osorem fuisse.' A standing High-Dutch joke in those days at the expense of a number of learned men, as may be seen by referring to such rubbish at Melander's 'Jocoseria,' etc. In the prints from his portrait by Tintoretto, painted a year before his death, Paracelsus is *barbatulus*, at all events. But Erastus was never without a good reason for his faith—*e.g.* 'Helvetium fuisse (Paracelsum) vix credo, vix enim ea regio tale monstrum ediderit.' (De Medicina Nova.)

about the age of thirty-three, many astonishing cures which he wrought on eminent personages procured him such a celebrity, that he was called in 1526, on the recommendation of Œcolampadius, (⁴) to fill a chair of physic and surgery at the University of Basil. There Paracelsus began by burning publicly in the amphitheatre the works of Avicenna and Galen, assuring his auditors that the latchets of his shoes were more instructed than those two physicians; that all Universities, all writers put together, were less gifted than the hairs of his beard and of the crown of his head; and that, in a word, he was to be regarded as the legitimate monarch of medicine. 'You shall follow me,' cried he, 'you, Avicenna, Galen, Rhasis, Montagnana, Mesues, you, gentlemen of Paris, Montpellier, Germany, Cologne, Vienna,* and whomsoever the Rhine and Danube nourish; you who inhabit the isles of the sea; you, likewise, Dalmatians, Athenians; thou, Arab; thou, Greek; thou, Jew: all shall follow me, and the monarchy shall be mine.'**

'But at Basil it was speedily perceived that the new Professor was no better than an egregious quack. Scarcely a year elapsed before his lectures had fairly driven away an audience incapable of comprehending their emphatic jargon. That which above all contributed to sully his reputation was the debauched life he led. According to the testimony of Oporinus, who lived two years in his intimacy, Paracelsus scarcely ever ascended the lecture-desk unless half drunk, and only dictated to his secretaries when in a state of intoxication: if summoned to attend the sick, he rarely proceeded thither without previously drenching himself with wine. He was accustomed to retire to bed without changing his clothes; sometimes he spent the night in pot-houses with peasants, and in the morning knew no longer what he was about; and, nevertheless, up to the age of twenty-five his only drink had been water. (⁵)

'At length, fearful of being punished for a serious outrage on a magistrate, (⁶) he fled from Basil towards the end of the year 1527, and took refuge in Alsatia, whither he caused Oporinus to follow with his chemical apparatus.

'He then entered once more upon the career of ambulatory theosophist.† Accordingly we find him at Colmar in 1528; at Nuremberg in 1529; at St. Gall

---

* Erastus, who relates this, here oddly remarks, 'mirum quod non et Garamantos, Indos et *Anglos* adjunxit.' Not so wonderful neither, if we believe what another adversary 'had heard somewhere,'—that all Paracelsus' system came of his pillaging 'Anglum, quendam, Rogerium Bacchonem.'

** See his works *passim*. I must give one specimen:—Somebody had been styling him 'Luther alter.' 'And why not?' (he asks, as he well might). 'Luther is abundantly learned, therefore you hate him and me; but we are at least a match for you.—Nam et contra vos et vestros universos principes Avicennam, Galenum, Aristotelem, etc. me satis superque munitum esse novi. Et vertex iste meus calvus ac depilis multo plura et sublimiora novit quam vester vel Avicenna vel universæ academiæ. Prodite, et signum date, qui viri sitis, quid roboris habeatis? quid autem sitis? Doctores et magistri, pediculos pectentes et fricantes podicem.' (Frag. Med.)

† 'So migratory a life could afford Paracelsus but little leisure for application to books, and accordingly he informs us that for the space of ten years he never opened a single volume, and that his whole medical library was not composed of six sheets: in effect, the inventory drawn up after his death states that the only books which he left were the Bible, the New Testament, the Commentaries of St. Jerome on the Gospels, a printed volume on Medicine, and seven manuscripts.'

in 1531; at Pfeffers in 1535; and at Augsburg in 1536: he next made some stay in Moravia, where he still further compromised his reputation by the loss of many distinguished patients, which compelled him to betake himself to Vienna; from thence he passed into Hungary; and in 1538 was at Villach, where he dedicated his "Chronicle" to the States of Carinthia, in gratitude for the many kindnesses with which they had honoured his father. Finally, from Mindelheim, which he visited in 1540, Paracelsus proceeded to Salzburg, where he died in the Hospital of St. Stephen (*Sebastian* is meant), Sept. 24, 1541.'—(Here follows a criticism on his writings, which I omit.)

(1) *Paracelsus* would seem to be a fantastic version of *Von Hohenheim*; Einsiedeln is the Latinized Eremus, whence Paracelsus is sometimes called, as in the correspondence of Erasmus, Eremita; Bombast, his proper name, probably acquired, from the characteristic phraseology of his lectures, that unlucky signification which it has ever since retained.

(2) Then Bishop of Spanheim, and residing at Würzburg in Franconia; a town situated in a grassy fertile country, whence its name, Herbipolis. He was much visited there by learned men, as may be seen by his 'Epistolæ Familiares,' Hag. 1536: among others, by his staunch friend Cornelius Agrippa, to whom he dates thence, in 1510, a letter in answer to the dedicatory epistle prefixed to the treatise De Occult. Philosoph., which last contains the following ominous allusion to Agrippa's sojourn: 'Quum nuper tecum, R. P. in cœnobio tuo apud Herbipolim aliquamdiu conversatus, multa de chymicis, multa de magicis, multa de cabalisticis, cæterisque quæ adhuc in occulto delitescunt, arcanis scientiis atque artibus una contulissemus,' etc.

(3) 'Inexplebilis illa aviditas naturæ perscrutandi secreta et reconditarum supellectile scientiarum animum locupletandi, uno eodemque loco diu persistere non patiebatur, sed Mercurii instar, omnes terras, nationes et urbes perlustrandi igniculos supponebat, ut cum viris naturæ scrutatoribus, chymicis præsertim, ore tenus conferret, et quæ diuturnis laboribus nocturnisque vigiliis invenerant una vel altera communicatione obtineret.' (Bitiskius in Præfat.) 'Patris auxilio primum, deinde propria industria doctissimos viros in Germania, Italia, Gallia, Hispania, aliisque Europæ regionibus, nactus est præceptores; quorum liberali doctrina, et potissimum propria inquisitione ut qui esset ingenio acutissimo ac fere divino, tantum profecit, ut multi testati sint, in universa philosophia, tam ardua, tam arcana et abdita eruisse mortalium neminem.' (Melch. Adam. in Vit. Germ. Medic.) 'Paracelsus qui in intima naturæ viscera sic penitus introierit, metallorum stirpiumque vires et facultates tam incredibili ingenii acumine exploraverit ac perviderit, ad morbos omnes vel desperatos et opinione hominum insanabiles percurandum; ut cum Theophrasto nata primum medicina perfectaque videatur.' (Petri Rami Orat. de Basilea.) His passion for wandering is best described in his own words: 'Ecce amatorem adolescentem difficillimi itineris haud piget, ut venustam saltem puellam vel fœminam aspiciat: quanto minus nobilissimarum artium amore laboris ac cujuslibet tædii pigebit?' etc. ('Defensiones Septem adversus æmulos suos.' 1573. Def. 4ta. 'De peregrinationibus et exilio.')

(4) The reader may remember that it was in conjunction with Œcolampadius,

then Divinity Professor at Basil, that Zuinglius published in 1528 an answer to
Luther's Confession of Faith; and that both proceeded in company to the sub-
sequent conference with Luther and Melanchthon at Marpurg. Their letters fill
a large volume.—'D.D. Johannis Œcolampadii et Huldrichi Zuinglii Episto-
larum lib. quatuor.' Bas. 1536. It must be also observed that Zuinglius began to
preach in 1516, and at Zurich in 1519, and that in 1525 the Mass was abolished
in the cantons. The tenets of Œcolampadius were supposed to be more evangeli-
cal than those up to that period maintained by the glorious German, and our
brave Bishop Fisher attacked them as the fouler heresy:—'About this time arose
out of Luther's school one Œcolampadius, like a mighty and fierce giant; who,
as his master had gone beyond the Church, went beyond his master (or else it
had been impossible he could have been reputed the better scholar), who denied
the real presence; him, this worthy champion (the Bishop) sets upon, and with
five books (like so many smooth stones taken out of the river that doth always run
with living water) slays the Philistine; which five books were written in the year
of our Lord 1526, at which time he had governed the see of Rochester twenty
years.' (Life of Bishop Fisher, 1655.) Now, there is no doubt of the Protestantism
of Paracelsus, Erasmus, Agrippa, etc., but the nonconformity of Paracelsus was
always scandalous. L. Crasso ('Elogj d'Huomini Letterati,' Ven. 1666) informs
us that his books were excommunicated by the Church. Quenstedt (de Patr.
Doct.) affirms 'nec tantum novæ medicinæ, verum etiam novæ theologiæ autor
est.' Delrio, in his Disquisit. Magicar., classes him among those 'partim atheos,
partim hæreticos' (lib. i. cap. 3). 'Omnino tamen multa theologica in ejusdem
scriptis plane atheismum olent, ac duriuscule sonant in auribus vere Christiani.'
(D. Gabrielis Clauderi Schediasma de Tinct. Univ. Norimb. 1736.) I shall only
add one more authority:—'Oporinus dicit se (Paracelsum) aliquando Lutherum
et Papam, non minus quam nunc Galenum et Hippocratem redacturum in
ordinem minabatur, neque enim eorum qui hactenus in scripturam sacram
scripsissent, sive veteres, sive recentiores, quenquam scripturæ nucleum recte
eruisse, sed circa corticem et quasi membranam tantum hærere.' (Th. Erastus,
Disputat. de Med. Nova.) These and similar notions had their due effect on
Oporinus, who, says Zuingerus, in his 'Theatrum,' 'longum vale dixit ei (Para-
celso), ne ob præceptoris, alioqui amicissimi, horrendas blasphemias ipse quoque
aliquando pœnas Deo Opt. Max. lueret.'

(5) His defenders allow the drunkenness. Take a sample of their excuses:
'Gentis hoc, non viri vitiolum est, a Taciti seculo ad nostrum usque non inter-
rupto filo devolutum, sinceritati forte Germanæ coævum, et nescio an aliquo
consanguinitatis vinculo junctum.' (Bitiskius.) The other charges were chiefly
trumped up by Oporinus: 'Domi, quod Oporinus amanuensis ejus sæpe narravit,
nunquam nisi potus ad explicanda sua accessit, atque in medio conclavi ad
columnam τετυφωμένος adsistens, apprehenso manibus capulo ensis, cujus κοίλωμα
hospitium præbuit, ut aiunt, spiritui familiari, imaginationes aut concepta sua
protulit:—alii illud quod in capulo habuit, ab ipso Azoth appellatum, medicinam
fuisse præstantissimam aut lapidem Philosophicum putant.' (Melch. Adam.)
This famous sword was no laughing-matter in those days, and it is now a material
feature in the popular idea of Paracelsus. I recollect a couple of allusions to it in
our own literature, at the moment.

Ne had been known the Danish Gonswart,
Or Paracelsus with his long sword.

'Volpone,' act ii. scene 2.

Bumbastus kept a devil's bird
Shut in the pummel of his sword,
That taught him all the cunning pranks
Of past and future mountebanks.

'Hudibras,' part ii. cant. 3.

This Azoth was simply '*laudanum suum.*' But in his time he was commonly
believed to possess the double tincture—the power of curing diseases and trans-
muting metals. Oporinus often witnessed, as he declares, both these effects, as
did also Franciscus, the servant of Paracelsus, who describes, in a letter to
Neander, a successful projection at which he was present, and the results of
which, good golden ingots, were confided to his keeping. For the other quality,
let the following notice vouch among many others:—'Degebat Theophrastus
Norimbergæ procitus a medentibus illius urbis, et vaniloquus deceptorque
proclamatus, qui, ut laboranti famæ subveniat, viros quosdam authoritatis
summæ in Republica illa adit, et infamiæ amoliendæ, artique suæ asserendæ,
specimen ejus pollicetur editurum, nullo stipendio vel accepto pretio, horum
faciles præbentium aures jussu elephantiacos aliquot, a communione hominum
cæterorum segregatos, et in valetudinarium detrusos, alieno arbitrio eliguntur,
quos virtute singulari remediorum suorum Theophrastus a fœda Græcorum lepra
mundat, pristinæque sanitati restituit; conservat illustre harum curationum urbs
in archivis suis testimonium.' (Bitiskius.)* It is to be remarked that Oporinus
afterwards repented of his treachery: 'Sed resipuit tandem, et quem vivum con-
vitiis insectatus fuerat defunctum veneratione prosequutus, infames famæ præ-
ceptoris morsus in remorsus conscientiæ conversi pœnitentia, heu nimis tarda,
vulnera clausere exanimi quæ spiranti inflixerant.' For these 'bites' of Oporinus,
see Disputat. Erasti, and Andreæ Jocisci 'Oratio de Vit. ob. Opor[i];' for the
'remorse,' Mic. Toxita in pref. Testamenti, and Conringius (otherwise an enemy
of Paracelsus), who says it was contained in a letter from Oporinus to Doctor
Vegerus.†

Whatever the moderns may think of these marvellous attributes, the title of
Paracelsus to be considered the father of modern chemistry is indisputable.
Gerardus Vossius, 'De Philos[a] et Philos[um] sectis,' thus prefaces the ninth section
of cap. 9, 'De Chymia'—'Nobilem hanc medicinæ partem, diu sepultam avorum

---

* The premature death of Paracelsus casts no manner of doubt on the fact of his
having possessed the Elixir Vitæ: the alchemists have abundant reasons to adduce, from
which I select the following, as explanatory of a property of the Tincture not calculated
on by its votaries:—'Objectionem illam, quod Paracelsus non fuerit longævus, nonnulli
quoque solvunt per rationes physicas: vitæ nimirum abbreviationem fortasse talibus
accidere posse, ob Tincturam frequentiore ac largiore dosi sumtam, dum a summe
efficaci et penetrabili hujus virtute calor innatus quasi suffocatur.' (Gabrielis Clauderi
Schediasma.)

† For a good defence of Paracelsus I refer the reader to Olaus Borrichius' treatise—
'Hermetis etc. Sapientia vindicata,' 1674. Or, if he is no more learned than myself in
such matters, I mention simply that Paracelsus introduced the use of Mercury and
Laudanum.

ætate, quasi ab orco revocavit Th. Paracelsus.' I suppose many hints lie scattered in his neglected books, which clever appropriators have since developed with applause. Thus, it appears from his treatise 'De Phlebotomia,' and elsewhere, that he had discovered the circulation of the blood and the sanguification of the heart; as did after him Realdo Colombo, and still more perfectly Andrea Cesalpino of Arezzo, as Bayle and Bartoli observe. Even Lavater quotes a passage from his work 'De Natura Rerum,' on practical Physiognomy, in which the definitions and axioms are precise enough: he adds, 'though an astrological enthusiast, a man of prodigious genius.' See Holcroft's translation, vol. iii. p. 179—'The Eyes.' While on the subject of the writings of Paracelsus, I may explain a passage in the third part of the Poem. He was, as I have said, unwilling to publish his works, but in effect did publish a vast number. Valentius (in Præfat. in Paramyr.) declares 'quod ad librorum Paracelsi copiam attinet, audio, a Germanis prope trecentos recenseri.' 'O fœcunditas ingenii!' adds he, appositely. Many of these, were, however, spurious; and Fred. Bitiskius gives his good edition (3 vols. fol. Gen. 1658) 'rejectis suppositis solo ipsius nomine superbientibus quorum ingens circumfertur numerus.' The rest were 'charissimum et pretiosissimum authoris pignus, extorsum potius ab illo quam obtentum.' 'Jam minime eo volente atque jubente hæc ipsius scripta in lucem prodisse videntur; quippe quæ muro inclusa ipso absente, servi cujusdam indicio, furto surrepta atque sublata sunt,' says Valentius. These have been the study of a host of commentators, amongst whose labours are most notable, Petri Severini, 'Idea Medicinæ Philosophiæ. Bas. 1571;' Mic. Toxetis, 'Onomastica. Arg. 1574;' Dornei, 'Dict. Parac. Franc. 1584;' and 'P[i] Philos[ae] Compendium cum scholiis auctore Leone Suavio. Paris.' (This last, a good book.)

(6) A disgraceful affair. One Liechtenfels, a canon, having been rescued *in extremis* by the '*laudanum*' of Paracelsus, refused the stipulated fee, and was supported in his meanness by the authorities, whose interference Paracelsus would not brook. His own liberality was allowed by his bitterest foes, who found a ready solution of his indifference to profit in the aforesaid sword-handle and its guest. His freedom from the besetting sin of a profession he abhorred—(as he curiously says somewhere, 'Quis quæso deinceps honorem deferat professioni tali, quæ a tam facinorosis nebulonibus obitur et administratur?')—is recorded in his epitaph, which affirms—'Bona sua in pauperes distribuenda collocandaque erogavit,' *honoravit*, or *ordinavit*—for accounts differ.

SORDELLO

TO J. MILSAND, OF DIJON

DEAR FRIEND.—Let the next poem be introduced by your name, therefore remembered along with one of the deepest of my affections, and so repay all trouble it ever cost me. I wrote it twenty-five years ago for only a few, counting even in these on somewhat more care about its subject than they really had. My own faults of expression were many; but with care for a man or book such would be surmounted, and without it what avails the faultlessness of either? I blame nobody, least of all myself, who did my best then and since; for I lately gave time and pains to turn my work into what the many might,—instead of what the few must,—like: but after all, I imagined another thing at first, and therefore leave as I find it. The historical decoration was purposely of no more importance than a background requires; and my stress lay on the incidents in the development of a soul: little else is worth study. I, at least, always thought so—you, with many known and unknown to me, think so—others may one day think so; and whether my attempt remain for them or not, I trust, though away and past it, to continue ever yours,

R. B.

London: *June* 9, 1863.

SORDELLO

1840

[*Omitted in 1849. Reprinted in 1863, 1868 and 1888-9. Although the final text is given here, the helpful running-titles printed only in 1863 and 1868 have been retained.*]

BOOK THE FIRST

WHO will, may hear Sordello's story told:
His story? Who believes me shall behold
The man, pursue his fortunes to the end,
Like me: for as the friendless-people's friend
Spied from his hill-top once, despite the din   5
And dust of multitudes, Pentapolin
Named o' the Naked Arm, I single out
Sordello, compassed murkily about
With ravage of six long sad hundred years.
Only believe me. Ye believe?   10
       Appears
Verona . . . Never,—I should warn you first,—
Of my own choice had this, if not the worst
Yet not the best expedient, served to tell
A story I could body forth so well
By making speak, myself kept out of view,   15
The very man as he was wont to do,
And leaving you to say the rest for him.
Since, though I might be proud to see the dim
Abysmal past divide its hateful surge,
Letting of all men this one man emerge   20
Because it pleased me, yet, that moment past,
I should delight in watching first to last
His progress as you watch it, not a whit
More in the secret than yourselves who sit
Fresh-chapleted to listen. But it seems   25
Your setters-forth of unexampled themes,
Makers of quite new men, producing them,

A Quixotic attempt.

Why the poet himself ad-dresses

Would best chalk broadly on each vesture's hem
The wearer's quality; or take their stand,
Motley on back and pointing-pole in hand,   30
Beside him. So, for once I face ye, friends,
Summoned together from the world's four ends,
Dropped down from heaven or cast up from hell,
To hear the story I propose to tell.
Confess now, poets know the dragnet's trick,   35
Catching the dead, if fate denies the quick,
And shaming her; 't is not for fate to choose
Silence or song because she can refuse
Real eyes to glisten more, real hearts to ache
Less oft, real brows turn smoother for our sake: 40
I have experienced something of her spite;
But there's a realm wherein she has no right
And I have many lovers. Say, but few
Friends fate accords me? Here they are: now view
The host I muster! Many a lighted face   45
Foul with no vestige of the grave's disgrace;

his audience—
few living,
many dead.

What else should tempt them back to taste our air
Except to see how their successors fare?
My audience! and they sit, each ghostly man
Striving to look as living as he can,   50
Brother by breathing brother; thou art set,
Clear-witted critic, by . . . but I'll not fret
A wondrous soul of them, nor move death's spleen
Who loves not to unlock them. Friends! I mean
The living in good earnest—ye elect   55
Chiefly for love—suppose not I reject
Judicious praise, who contrary shall peep,
Some fit occasion, forth, for fear ye sleep,
To glean your bland approvals. Then, appear,
Verona! stay—thou, spirit, come not near   60
Now—not this time desert thy cloudy place
To scare me, thus employed, with that pure face!
I need not fear this audience, I make free
With them, but then this is no place for thee!
The thunder-phrase of the Athenian, grown   65
Up out of memories of Marathon,
Would echo like his own sword's griding screech

Braying a Persian shield,—the silver speech
Of Sidney's self, the starry paladin,
Turn intense as a trumpet sounding in   70
The knights to tilt,—wert thou to hear! What heart
Have I to play my puppets, bear my part
Before these worthies?
                           Lo, the past is hurled
In twain: up-thrust, out-staggering on the world,
Subsiding into shape, a darkness rears   75
Its outline, kindles at the core, appears
Verona. 'T is six hundred years and more
Since an event. The Second Friedrich wore
The purple, and the Third Honorius filled
The holy chair. That autumn eve was stilled: 80
A last remains of sunset dimly burned
O'er the far forests, like a torch-flame turned
By the wind back upon its bearer's hand
In one long flare of crimson; as a brand,
The woods beneath lay black. A single eye   85
From all Verona cared for the soft sky.
But, gathering in its ancient market-place,
Talked group with restless group; and not a face
But wrath made livid, for among them were
Death's staunch purveyors, such as have in care   90
To feast him. Fear had long since taken root
In every breast, and now these crushed its fruit,
The ripe hate, like a wine: to note the way
It worked while each grew drunk! Men grave and grey
Stood, with shut eyelids, rocking to and fro,   95
Letting the silent luxury trickle slow
About the hollows where a heart should be;
But the young gulped with a delirious glee
Some foretaste of their first debauch in blood
At the fierce news: for, be it understood,   100
Envoys apprised Verona that her prince
Count Richard of Saint Boniface, joined since
A year with Azzo, Este's Lord, to thrust
Taurello Salinguerra, prime in trust
With Ecelin Romano, from his seat   105
Ferrara,—over zealous in the feat

Shelley departing, Verona appears.

How her Guelfs are discomfited.

And stumbling on a peril unaware,
Was captive, trammelled in his proper snare,
They phrase it, taken by his own intrigue.
Immediate succour from the Lombard League   110
Of fifteen cities that affect the Pope,
For Azzo, therefore, and his fellow-hope
Of the Guelf cause, a glory overcast!
Men's faces, late agape, are now aghast.
'Prone is the purple pavis; Este makes   115
'Mirth for the devil when he undertakes
'To play the Ecelin; as if it cost
'Merely your pushing-by to gain a post
'Like his! The patron tells ye, once for all,
'There be sound reasons that preferment fall   120
'On our beloved' . . .
                    'Duke o' the Rood, why not?'
Shouted an Estian, 'grudge ye such a lot?
'The hill-cat boasts some cunning of her own,
'Some stealthy trick to better beasts unknown,
'That quick with prey enough her hunger blunts,   125
'And feeds her fat while gaunt the lion hunts.'
    'Taurello,' quoth an envoy, 'as in wane
'Dwelt at Ferrara. Like an osprey fain
'To fly but forced the earth his couch to make
'Far inland, till his friend the tempest wake,   130
'Waits he the Kaiser's coming; and as yet
'That fast friend sleeps, and he too sleeps: but let
'Only the billow freshen, and he snuffs
'The aroused hurricane ere it enroughs
'The sea it means to cross because of him.   135
'Sinketh the breeze? His hope-sick eye grows dim;
'Creep closer on the creature! Every day
'Strengthens the Pontiff; Ecelin, they say,
'Dozes now at Oliero, with dry lips
'Telling upon his perished finger-tips   140
'How many ancestors are to depose
'Ere he be Satan's Viceroy when the doze
'Deposits him in hell. So, Guelfs rebuilt
'Their houses; not a drop of blood was spilt
'When Cino Bocchimpane chanced to meet   145

*Why they
entreat the
Lombard
League,*

'Buccio Virtù—God's wafer, and the street
'Is narrow! Tutti Santi, think, a-swarm
'With Ghibellins, and yet he took no harm!
'This could not last. Off Salinguerra went
'To Padua, Podestà, "with pure intent,"   150
'Said he, "my presence, judged the single bar
' "To permanent tranquillity, may jar
' "No longer"—so! his back is fairly turned?
'The pair of goodly palaces are burned,
'The gardens ravaged, and our Guelfs laugh, drunk   155
'A week with joy. The next, their laughter sunk
'In sobs of blood, for they found, some strange way,
'Old Salinguerra back again—I say,
'Old Salinguerra in the town once more
'Uprooting, overturning, flame before,   160   in their
'Blood fetlock-high beneath him. Azzo fled;   changed
'Who 'scaped the carnage followed; then the dead   fortune at
'Were pushed aside from Salinguerra's throne,   Ferrara:
'He ruled once more Ferrara, all alone,
'Till Azzo, stunned awhile, revived, would pounce   165
'Coupled with Boniface, like lynx and ounce,
'On the gorged bird. The burghers ground their teeth
'To see troop after troop encamp beneath
'I' the standing corn thick o'er the scanty patch
'It took so many patient months to snatch   170
'Out of the marsh; while just within their walls
'Men fed on men. At length Taurello calls
'A parley: "let the Count wind up the war!"
'Richard, light-hearted as a plunging star,
'Agrees to enter for the kindest ends   175
'Ferrara, flanked with fifty chosen friends,
'No horse-boy more, for fear your timid sort
'Should fly Ferrara at the bare report.
'Quietly through the town they rode, jog-jog,
' "Ten, twenty, thirty,—curse the catalogue   180
' "Of burnt Guelf houses! Strange, Taurello shows
' "Not the least sign of life"—whereat arose
'A general growl: "How? With his victors by?
' "I and my Veronese? My troops and I?
' "Receive us, was your word?" So jogged they on,   185

'Nor laughed their host too openly: once gone
'Into the trap!—'
           Six hundred years ago!

For the times
grow stormy
again.
Such the time's aspect and peculiar woe
(Yourselves may spell it yet in chronicles,
Albeit the worm, our busy brother, drills   190
His sprawling path through letters anciently
Made fine and large to suit some abbot's eye)
When the new Hohenstauffen dropped the mask,
Flung John of Brienne's favour from his casque,
Forswore crusading, had no mind to leave   195
Saint Peter's proxy leisure to retrieve
Losses to Otho and to Barbaross,
Or make the Alps less easy to recross;
And, thus confirming Pope Honorius' fear,
Was excommunicate that very year.   200
'The triple-bearded Teuton come to life!'
Groaned the Great League; and, arming for the strife,
Wide Lombardy, on tiptoe to begin,
Took up, as it was Guelf or Ghibellin,
Its cry: what cry?
           'The Emperor to come!'   205
His crowd of feudatories, all and some,
That leapt down with a crash of swords, spears, shields,
One fighter on his fellow, to our fields,
Scattered anon, took station here and there,
And carried it, till now, with little care—   210
Cannot but cry for him; how else rebut
Us longer?—cliffs, an earthquake suffered jut
In the mid-sea, each domineering crest
Which nought save such another throe can wrest
From out (conceive) a certain chokeweed grown   215

The
Ghibbelins'
wish: the
Guelfs' wish.
Since o'er the waters, twine and tangle thrown
Too thick, too fast accumulating round,
Too sure to over-riot and confound
Ere long each brilliant islet with itself,
Unless a second shock save shoal and shelf,   220
Whirling the sea-drift wide: alas, the bruised
And sullen wreck! Sunlight to be diffused
For that!—sunlight, 'neath which, a scum at first,

The million fibres of our chokeweed nurst
Dispread themselves, mantling the troubled main,   225
And, shattered by those rocks, took hold again,
So kindly blazed it—that same blaze to brood
O'er every cluster of the multitude
Still hazarding new clasps, ties, filaments,
An emulous exchange of pulses, vents   230
Of nature into nature; till some growth
Unfancied yet, exuberantly clothe
A surface solid now, continuous, one:
'The Pope, for us the People, who begun
'The People, carried on the People thus,   235
'To keep that Kaiser off and dwell with us!'
See you?
          Or say, Two Principles that live
Each fitly by its Representative.
'Hill-cat'—who called him so?—the gracefullest
Adventurer, the ambiguous stranger-guest   240
Of Lombardy (sleek but that ruffling fur,
Those talons to their sheath!) whose velvet purr
Soothes jealous neighbours when a Saxon scout
—Arpo or Yoland, is it?—one without   *How Ecelo's*
A country or a name, presumes to couch   245 *house grew*
Beside their noblest; until men avouch   *head of those,*
That, of all Houses in the Trevisan,
Conrad descries no fitter, rear or van,
Than Ecelo! They laughed as they enrolled
That name at Milan on the page of gold,   250
Godego's lord,—Ramon, Marostica,
Cartiglion, Bassano, Loria,
And every sheep-cote on the Suabian's fief!
No laughter when his son, 'the Lombard Chief'
Forsooth, as Barbarossa's path was bent   255
To Italy along the Vale of Trent,
Welcomed him at Roncaglia! Sadness now—
The hamlets nested on the Tyrol's brow,
The Asolan and Euganean hills,
The Rhetian and the Julian, sadness fills   260
Them all, for Ecelin vouchsafes to stay
Among and care about them; day by day

Choosing this pinnacle, the other spot,
A castle building to defend a cot,
A cot built for a castle to defend,   265
Nothing but castles, castles, nor an end
To boasts how mountain ridge may join with ridge
By sunken gallery and soaring bridge.
He takes, in brief, a figure that beseems
The griesliest nightmare of the Church's dreams,   270
—A Signory firm-rooted, unestranged
From its old interests, and nowise changed
By its new neighbourhood: perchance the vaunt
Of Otho, 'my own Este shall supplant
'Your Este,' come to pass. The sire led in   275
A son as cruel; and this Ecelin
Had sons, in turn, and daughters sly and tall
And curling and compliant; but for all
Romano (so they styled him) throve, that neck
Of his so pinched and white, that hungry cheek   280
Proved 't was some fiend, not him, the man's-flesh went
To feed: whereas Romano's instrument,
Famous Taurello Salinguerra, sole
I' the world, a tree whose boughs were slipt the bole
Successively, why should not he shed blood   285
To further a design? Men understood
Living was pleasant to him as he wore
His careless surcoat, glanced some missive o'er,
Propped on his truncheon in the public way,
While his lord lifted writhen hands to pray,   290
Lost at Oliero's convent.

as Azzo Lord
of Este heads
these.
                                        Hill-cats, face
Our Azzo, our Guelf Lion! Why disgrace
A worthiness conspicuous near and far
(Atii at Rome while free and consular,
Este at Padua who repulsed the Hun)   295
By trumpeting the Church's princely son?
—Styled Patron of Rovigo's Polesine,
Ancona's march, Ferrara's . . . ask, in fine,
Our chronicles, commenced when some old monk
Found it intolerable to be sunk   300
(Vexed to the quick by his revolting cell)

Quite out of summer while alive and well:
Ended when by his mat the Prior stood,
'Mid busy promptings of the brotherhood,
Striving to coax from his decrepit brains　　　　305
The reason Father Porphyry took pains
To blot those ten lines out which used to stand
First on their charter drawn by Hildebrand.
　　The same night wears. Verona's rule of yore
Was vested in a certain Twenty-four;　　　　310
And while within his palace these debate
Concerning Richard and Ferrara's fate,
Glide we by clapping doors, with sudden glare
Of cressets vented on the dark, nor care
For aught that's seen or heard until we shut　　　　315
The smother in, the lights, all noises but
The carroch's booming: safe at last! Why strange
Such a recess should lurk behind a range
Of banquet-rooms? Your finger—thus—you push
A spring, and the wall opens, would you rush　　　　320
Upon the banqueters, select your prey,
Waiting (the slaughter-weapons in the way
Strewing this very bench) with sharpened ear
A preconcerted signal to appear;
Or if you simply crouch with beating heart,　　　　325
Bearing in some voluptuous pageant part
To startle them. Nor mutes nor masquers now;
Nor any . . . does that one man sleep whose brow
The dying lamp-flame sinks and rises o'er?
What woman stood beside him? not the more　　　　330
Is he unfastened from the earnest eyes
Because that arras fell between! Her wise
And lulling words are yet about the room,
Her presence wholly poured upon the gloom
Down even to her vesture's creeping stir.　　　　335
And so reclines he, saturate with her,
Until an outcry from the square beneath
Pierces the charm: he springs up, glad to breathe,
Above the cunning element, and shakes
The stupor off as (look you) morning breaks　　　　340
On the gay dress, and, near concealed by it,

Count Richard's Palace at Verona.

Of the couple found therein,

The lean frame like a half-burnt taper, lit
Erst at some marriage-feast, then laid away
Till the Armenian bridegroom's dying day,
In his wool wedding-robe.

                    For he—for he,   345
Gate-vein of this hearts' blood of Lombardy,
(If I should falter now)—for he is thine!
Sordello, thy forerunner, Florentine!
A herald-star I know thou didst absorb
Relentless into the consummate orb   350
That scared it from its right to roll along
A sempiternal path with dance and song
Fulfilling its allotted period,
Serenest of the progeny of God—
Who yet resigns it not! His darling stoops   355
With no quenched lights, desponds with no blank troops
Of disenfranchised brilliances, for, blent
Utterly with thee, its shy element
Like thine upburneth prosperous and clear.
Still, what if I approach the august sphere   360
Named now with only one name, disentwine
That under-current soft and argentine
From its fierce mate in the majestic mass
Leavened as the sea whose fire was mixt with glass
In John's transcendent vision,—launch once more   365
That lustre? Dante, pacer of the shore
Where glutted hell disgorgeth filthiest gloom,
Unbitten by its whirring sulphur-spume—
Or whence the grieved and obscure waters slope
Into a darkness quieted by hope;   370
Plucker of amaranths grown beneath God's eye
In gracious twilights where his chosen lie,—
I would do this! If I should falter now!

    In Mantua territory half is slough,
Half pine-tree forest; maples, scarlet oaks   375
Breed o'er the river-beds; even Mincio chokes
With sand the summer through: but 't is morass
In winter up to Mantua walls. There was,
Some thirty years before this evening's coil,
One spot reclaimed from the surrounding spoil,   380

one belongs to
Dante; his
birthplace.

Goito; just a castle built amid
A few low mountains; firs and larches hid
Their main defiles, and rings of vineyard bound
The rest. Some captured creature in a pound,
Whose artless wonder quite precludes distress,   385
Secure beside in its own loveliness,
So peered with airy head, below, above,
The castle at its toils, the lapwings love
To glean among at grape-time. Pass within.
A maze of corridors contrived for sin,   390
Dusk winding-stairs, dim galleries got past,
You gain the inmost chambers, gain at last
A maple-panelled room: that haze which seems
Floating about the panel, if there gleams
A sunbeam over it, will turn to gold   395
And in light-graven characters unfold
The Arab's wisdom everywhere; what shade
Marred them a moment, those slim pillars made,
Cut like a company of palms to prop
The roof, each kissing top entwined with top,   400
Leaning together; in the carver's mind
Some knot of bacchanals, flushed cheek combined
With straining forehead, shoulders purpled, hair
Diffused between, who in a goat-skin bear
A vintage; graceful sister-palms! But quick   405
To the main wonder, now. A vault, see; thick
Black shade about the ceiling, though fine slits
Across the buttress suffer light by fits
Upon a marvel in the midst. Nay, stoop—
A dullish grey-streaked cumbrous font, a group   410
Round it,—each side of it, where'er one sees,—
Upholds it; shrinking Caryatides
Of just-tinged marble like Eve's lilied flesh
Beneath her maker's finger when the fresh
First pulse of life shot brightening the snow.   415
The font's edge burthens every shoulder, so
They muse upon the ground, eyelids half closed;
Some, with meek arms behind their backs disposed,
Some, crossed above their bosoms, some, to veil
Their eyes, some, propping chin and cheek so pale,   420

A vault inside
the castle at
Goito,

and what
Sordello
would see
there.

Some, hanging slack an utter helpless length
Dead as a buried vestal whose whole strength
Goes when the grate above shuts heavily.
So dwell these noiseless girls, patient to see,
Like priestesses because of sin impure   425
Penanced for ever, who resigned endure,
Having that once drunk sweetness to the dregs.
And every eve, Sordello's visit begs
Pardon for them: constant as eve he came
To sit beside each in her turn, the same   430
As one of them, a certain space: and awe
Made a great indistinctness till he saw
Sunset slant cheerful through the buttress-chinks,
Gold seven times globed; surely our maiden shrinks
And a smile stirs her as if one faint grain   435
Her load were lightened, one shade less the stain
Obscured her forehead, yet one more bead slipt
From off the rosary whereby the crypt
Keeps count of the contritions of its charge?
Then with a step more light, a heart more large,   440
He may depart, leave her and every one
To linger out the penance in mute stone.
Ah, but Sordello? 'T is the tale I mean
To tell you.

His boyhood
in the domain
of Ecelin.

              In this castle may be seen,
On the hill tops, or underneath the vines,   445
Or eastward by the mound of firs and pines
That shuts out Mantua, still in loneliness,
A slender boy in a loose page's dress,
Sordello: do but look on him awhile
Watching ('t is autumn) with an earnest smile   450
The noisy flock of thievish birds at work
Among the yellowing vineyards; see him lurk
('T is winter with its sullenest of storms)
Beside that arras-length of broidered forms,
On tiptoe, lifting in both hands a light   455
Which makes yon warrior's visage flutter bright
—Ecelo, dismal father of the brood,
And Ecelin, close to the girl he wooed,
Auria, and their Child, with all his wives

From Agnes to the Tuscan that survives,　　　460
Lady of the castle, Adelaide. His face
—Look, now he turns away! Yourselves shall trace
(The delicate nostril swerving wide and fine,
A sharp and restless lip, so well combine
With that calm brow) a soul fit to receive　　　465
Delight at every sense; you can believe
Sordello foremost in the regal class
Nature has broadly severed from her mass
Of men, and framed for pleasure, as she frames
Some happy lands, that have luxurious names,　　　470
For loose fertility; a footfall there
Suffices to upturn to the warm air

How a poet's
soul comes
into play.

Half-germinating spices; mere decay
Produces richer life; and day by day
New pollen on the lily-petal grows,　　　475
And still more labyrinthine buds the rose.
You recognise at once the finer dress
Of flesh that amply lets in loveliness
At eye and ear, while round the rest is furled
(As though she would not trust them with her world)　　　480
A veil that shows a sky not near so blue,
And lets but half the sun look fervid through.
How can such love?—like souls on each full-fraught
Discovery brooding, blind at first to aught
Beyond its beauty, till exceeding love　　　485
Becomes an aching weight; and, to remove
A curse that haunts such natures—to preclude
Their finding out themselves can work no good
To what they love nor make it very blest
By their endeavour,—they are fain invest　　　490
The lifeless thing with life from their own soul,
Availing it to purpose, to control,
To dwell distinct and have peculiar joy
And separate interests that may employ
That beauty fitly, for its proper sake.　　　495
Nor rest they here; fresh births of beauty wake
Fresh homage, every grade of love is past,
With every mode of loveliness: then cast
Inferior idols off their borrowed crown

Before a coming glory. Up and down   500
Runs arrowy fire, while earthly forms combine
To throb the secret forth; a touch divine—
And the scaled eyeball owns the mystic rod;
Visibly through his garden walketh God.

What denotes
such a soul's
progress.

    So fare they. Now revert. One character   505
Denotes them through the progress and the stir,—
A need to blend with each external charm,
Bury themselves, the whole heart wide and warm,—
In something not themselves; they would belong
To what they worship—stronger and more strong   510
Thus prodigally fed—which gathers shape
And feature, soon imprisons past escape
The votary framed to love and to submit
Nor ask, as passionate he kneels to it,
Whence grew the idol's empery. So runs   515
A legend; light had birth ere moons and suns,
Flowing through space a river and alone,
Till chaos burst and blank the spheres were strown
Hither and thither, foundering and blind:
When into each of them rushed light—to find   520
Itself no place, foiled of its radiant chance.
Let such forego their just inheritance!

How poets
class at length
—for honour,

For there's a class that eagerly looks, too,
On beauty, but, unlike the gentler crew,
Proclaims each new revealment born a twin   525
With a distinctest consciousness within,
Referring still the quality, now first
Revealed, to their own soul—its instinct nursed
In silence, now remembered better, shown
More thoroughly, but not the less their own;   530
A dream come true; the special exercise
Of any special function that implies
The being fair, or good, or wise, or strong,
Dormant within their nature all along—
Whose fault? So, homage, other souls direct   535
Without, turns inward. 'How should this deject
'Thee, soul?' they murmur; 'wherefore strength be
    quelled
'Because, its trivial accidents withheld,

'Organs are missed that clog the world, inert,
'Wanting a will, to quicken and exert,   540
'Like thine—existence cannot satiate,
'Cannot surprise? Laugh thou at envious fate,
'Who, from earth's simplest combination stampt
'With individuality—uncrampt
'By living its faint elemental life,   545
'Dost soar to heaven's complexest essence, rife
'With grandeurs, unaffronted to the last,
'Equal to being all!'
       In truth? Thou hast
Life, then—wilt challenge life for us: our race
Is vindicated so, obtains its place   550
In thy ascent, the first of us; whom we
May follow, to the meanest, finally,
With our more bounded wills?
        Ah, but to find
A certain mood enervate such a mind,
Counsel it slumber in the solitude   555
Thus reached nor, stooping, task for mankind's good
Its nature just as life and time accord   *or shame—*
'—Too narrow an arena to reward   *which may the*
'Emprize—the world's occasion worthless since *gods avert*
'Not absolutely fitted to evince   560
'Its mastery!' Or if yet worse befall,
And a desire possess it to put all
That nature forth, forcing our straitened sphere
Contain it,—to display completely here
The mastery another life should learn,   565
Thrusting in time eternity's concern,—
So that Sordello. . . .
      Fool, who spied the mark
Of leprosy upon him, violet-dark
Already as he loiters? Born just now,
With the new century, beside the glow   570
And efflorescence out of barbarism;
Witness a Greek or two from the abysm
That stray through Florence-town with studious air,
Calming the chisel of that Pisan pair:
If Nicolo should carve a Christus yet!   575

While at Siena is Guidone set,
Forehead on hand; a painful birth must be
Matured ere Saint Eufemia's sacristy
Or transept gather fruits of one great gaze
At the moon: look you! The same orange haze,—   580
The same blue stripe round that—and, in the midst,
Thy spectral whiteness, Mother-maid, who didst
Pursue the dizzy painter!
                                        Woe, then, worth
Any officious babble letting forth
The leprosy confirmed and ruinous   585
To spirit lodged in a contracted house!
Go back to the beginning, rather; blend
It gently with Sordello's life; the end
Is piteous, you may see, but much between
Pleasant enough. Meantime, some pyx to screen   590
The full-grown pest, some lid to shut upon
The goblin! So they found at Babylon,
(Colleagues, mad Lucius and sage Antonine)
Sacking the city, by Apollo's shrine,
In rummaging among the rarities,   595
A certain coffer; he who made the prize
Opened it greedily; and out there curled
Just such another plague, for half the world
Was stung. Crawl in then, hag, and couch asquat,
Keeping that blotchy bosom thick in spot   600
Until your time is ripe! The coffer-lid
Is fastened, and the coffer safely hid
Under the Loxian's choicest gifts of gold.

from
Sordello, now
in childhood.
            Who will may hear Sordello's story told,
And how he never could remember when   605
He dwelt not at Goito. Calmly, then,
About this secret lodge of Adelaide's
Glided his youth away; beyond the glades
On the fir-forest border, and the rim
Of the low range of mountain, was for him   610
No other world: but this appeared his own
To wander through at pleasure and alone.
The delights
of his childish
fancy,
The castle too seemed empty; far and wide
Might he disport; only the northern side

Lay under a mysterious interdict—   615
Slight, just enough remembered to restrict
His roaming to the corridors, the vault
Where those font-bearers expiate their fault,
The maple-chamber, and the little nooks
And nests, and breezy parapet that looks   620
Over the woods to Mantua: there he strolled.
Some foreign women-servants, very old,
Tended and crept about him—all his clue
To the world's business and embroiled ado
Distant a dozen hill-tops at the most.   625
And first a simple sense of life engrossed
Sordello in his drowsy Paradise;
The day's adventures for the day suffice—
Its constant tribute of perceptions strange,
With sleep and stir in healthy interchange,   630
Suffice, and leave him for the next at ease
Like the great palmer-worm that strips the trees,
Eats the life out of every luscious plant,
And, when September finds them sere or scant,
Puts forth two wondrous winglets, alters quite, 635
And hies him after unforeseen delight.
So fed Sordello, not a shard dissheathed;
As ever, round each new discovery, wreathed
Luxuriantly the fancies infantine
His admiration, bent on making fine   640
Its novel friend at any risk, would fling
In gay profusion forth: a ficklest king,   which could
Confessed those minions!—eager to dispense   blow out a
So much from his own stock of thought and sense   great bubble,
As might enable each to stand alone   645
And serve him for a fellow; with his own,
Joining the qualities that just before
Had graced some older favourite. Thus they wore
A fluctuating halo, yesterday
Set flicker and to-morrow filched away,—   650
Those upland objects each of separate name,
Each with an aspect never twice the same,
Waxing and waning as the new-born host
Of fancies, like a single night's hoar-frost,

Gave to familiar things a face grotesque;   655
Only, preserving through the mad burlesque
A grave regard. Conceive! the orpine patch
Blossoming earliest on the log-house thatch
The day those archers wound along the vines—
Related to the Chief that left their lines   660
To climb with clinking step the northern stair
Up to the solitary chambers where
Sordello never came. Thus thrall reached thrall:
He o'er-festooning every interval,
As the adventurous spider, making light   665
Of distance, shoots her threads from depth to height,
From barbican to battlement: so flung
Fantasies forth and in their centre swung
Our architect,—the breezy morning fresh
Above, and merry,—all his waving mesh   670
Laughing with lucid dew-drops rainbow-edged.

    This world of ours by tacit pact is pledged
To laying such a spangled fabric low
Whether by gradual brush or gallant blow.
But its abundant will was baulked here: doubt   675
Rose tardily in one so fenced about
From most that nurtures judgment,—care and pain:
Judgment, that dull expedient we are fain,
Less favoured, to adopt betimes and force
Stead us, diverted from our natural course   680
Of joys—contrive some yet amid the dearth,
Vary and render them, it may be, worth
Most we forego. Suppose Sordello hence
Selfish enough, without a moral sense
However feeble; what informed the boy   685
Others desired a portion in his joy?
Or say a ruthful chance broke woof and warp—
A heron's nest beat down by March winds sharp,
A fawn breathless beneath the precipice,
A bird with unsoiled breast and unfilmed eyes   690
Warm in the brake—could these undo the trance
Lapping Sordello? Not a circumstance
That makes for you, friend Naddo! Eat fern-seed
And peer beside us and report indeed

If (your word) 'genius' dawned with throes and stings 695
And the whole fiery catalogue, while springs,
Summers, and winters quietly came and went.
    Time put at length that period to content,
By right the world should have imposed: bereft
Of its good offices, Sordello, left   700
To study his companions, managed rip
Their fringe off, learn the true relationship,
Core with its crust, their nature with his own:
Amid his wild-wood sights he lived alone.
As if the poppy felt with him! Though he   705
Partook the poppy's red effrontery
Till Autumn spoiled their fleering quite with rain,
And, turbanless, a coarse brown rattling crane
Lay bare. That's gone: yet why renounce, for that,
His disenchanted tributaries—flat   710
Perhaps, but scarce so utterly forlorn,
Their simple presence might not well be borne
Whose parley was a transport once: recall
The poppy's gifts, it flaunts you, after all,
A poppy:—why distrust the evidence   715
Of each soon satisfied and healthy sense?
The new-born judgment answered, 'little boots
'Beholding other creatures' attributes
'And having none!' or, say that it sufficed,
'Yet, could one but possess, oneself,' (enticed   720
Judgment) 'some special office!' Nought beside
Serves you? 'Well then, be somehow justified
'For this ignoble wish to circumscribe
'And concentrate, rather than swell, the tribe
'Of actual pleasures: what, now, from without   725
'Effects it?—proves, despite a lurking doubt,
'Mere sympathy sufficient, trouble spared?
'That, tasting joys by proxy thus, you fared
'The better for them?' Thus much craved his soul.
Alas, from the beginning love is whole   730
And true; if sure of nought beside, most sure
Of its own truth at least; nor may endure
A crowd to see its face, that cannot know
How hot the pulses throb its heart below:

But it comes;
and new-born
judgment

decides that
he needs
sympathizers.

While its own helplessness and utter want   735
Of means to worthily be ministrant
To what it worships, do but fan the more
Its flame, exalt the idol far before
Itself as it would have it ever be.
Souls like Sordello, on the contrary,   740
Coerced and put to shame, retaining will,
Care little, take mysterious comfort still,
But look forth tremblingly to ascertain
If others judge their claims not urged in vain,
And say for them their stifled thoughts aloud.   745
So, they must ever live before a crowd:
—'Vanity,' Naddo tells you.
                          Whence contrive
A crowd, now? From these women just alive,
That archer-troop? Forth glided—not alone
Each painted warrior, every girl of stone,   750
Nor Adelaide (bent double o'er a scroll,
One maiden at her knees, that eve, his soul
Shook as he stumbled through the arras'd glooms
On them, for, 'mid quaint robes and weird perfumes,
Started the meagre Tuscan up,—her eyes,   755
The maiden's, also, bluer with surprise)

He therefore
creates such a
company;

—But the entire out-world: whatever, scraps
And snatches, song and story, dreams perhaps,
Conceited the world's offices, and he
Had hitherto transferred to flower or tree,   760
Not counted a befitting heritage
Each, of its own right, singly to engage
Some man, no other,—such now dared to stand
Alone. Strength, wisdom, grace on every hand
Soon disengaged themselves, and he discerned   765
A sort of human life: at least, was turned
A stream of lifelike figures through his brain.
Lord, liegeman, valvassor and suzerain,
Ere he could choose, surrounded him; a stuff
To work his pleasure on; there, sure enough: 770
But as for gazing, what shall fix that gaze?
Are they to simply testify the ways
He who convoked them sends his soul along

With the cloud's thunder or a dove's brood-song?
—While they live each his life, boast each his own   775   each of which,
leading its
own life,
Peculiar dower of bliss, stand each alone
In some one point where something dearest loved
Is easiest gained—far worthier to be proved
Than aught he envies in the forest-wights!
No simple and self-evident delights,   780
But mixed desires of unimagined range,
Contrasts or combinations, new and strange,
Irksome perhaps, yet plainly recognized
By this, the sudden company—loves prized
By those who are to prize his own amount   785
Of loves. Once care because such make account,
Allow that foreign recognitions stamp
The current value, and his crowd shall vamp
Him counterfeits enough; and so their print
Be on the piece, 't is gold, attests the mint,   790
And 'good,' pronounce they whom his new appeal
Is made to: if their casual print conceal—
This arbitrary good of theirs o'ergloss
What he has lived without, nor felt the loss—
Qualities strange, ungainly, wearisome,   795
—What matter? So must speech expand the dumb
Part-sigh, part-smile with which Sordello, late
Whom no poor woodland-sights could satiate,
Betakes himself to study hungrily
Just what the puppets his crude phantasy   800
Supposes notablest,—popes, kings, priests, knights,—
May please to promulgate for appetites;
Accepting all their artificial joys
Not as he views them, but as he employs
Each shape to estimate the other's stock   805
Of attributes, whereon—a marshalled flock
Of authorized enjoyments—he may spend
Himself, be men, now, as he used to blend
With tree and flower—nay more entirely, else
'T were mockery: for instance, 'How excels   810
'My life that chieftain's?' (who apprised the youth
Ecelin, here, becomes this month, in truth,
Imperial Vicar?) 'Turns he in his tent

has qualities
impossible to
a boy,

'Remissly? Be it so—my head is bent
'Deliciously amid my girls to sleep.   815
'What if he stalks the Trentine-pass? Yon steep
'I climbed an hour ago with little toil:
'We are alike there. But can I, too, foil
'The Guelf's paid stabber, carelessly afford
'Saint Mark's a spectacle, the sleight o' the sword   820
'Baffling the treason in a moment?' Here
No rescue! Poppy he is none, but peer
To Ecelin, assuredly: his hand,
Fashioned no otherwise, should wield a brand
With Ecelin's success—try, now! He soon   825
Was satisfied, returned as to the moon
From earth; left each abortive boy's-attempt
For feats, from failure happily exempt,
In fancy at his beck. 'One day I will
'Accomplish it! Are they not older still   830
'—Not grown-up men and women? 'T is beside
'Only a dream; and though I must abide
'With dreams now, I may find a thorough vent
'For all myself, acquire an instrument
'For acting what these people act; my soul   835
'Hunting a body out may gain its whole
'Desire some day!' How else express chagrin
And resignation, show the hope steal in
With which he let sink from an aching wrist
The rough-hewn ash-bow? Straight, a gold shaft
          hissed   840
Into the Syrian air, struck Malek down
Superbly! 'Crosses to the breach! God's Town
'Is gained him back!' Why bend rough ash-bows more?

so, only to be
appropriated
in fancy,

     Thus lives he: if not careless as before,
Comforted: for one may anticipate,   845
Rehearse the future, be prepared when fate
Shall have prepared in turn real men whose names
Startle, real places of enormous fames,
Este abroad and Ecelin at home
To worship him,—Mantua, Verona, Rome   850
To witness it. Who grudges time so spent?
Rather test qualities to heart's content—

Summon them, thrice selected, near and far—
Compress the starriest into one star,
And grasp the whole at once!
                              The pageant thinned 855
Accordingly; from rank to rank, like wind
His spirit passed to winnow and divide;
Back fell the simpler phantasms; every side
The strong clave to the wise; with either classed
The beauteous; so, till two or three amassed   860
Mankind's beseemingnesses, and reduced
Themselves eventually,—graces loosed,
Strengths lavished,—all to heighten up One Shape
Whose potency no creature should escape.
Can it be Friedrich of the bowmen's talk?   865
Surely that grape-juice, bubbling at the stalk,
Is some grey scorching Saracenic wine
The Kaiser quaffs with the Miramoline—
Those swarthy hazel-clusters, seamed and chapped,
Or filberts russet-sheathed and velvet-capped,   870
Are dates plucked from the bough John Brienne sent   and practised
To keep in mind his sluggish armament   on till the real
Of Canaan:—Friedrich's, all the pomp and fierce   come.
Demeanour! But harsh sounds and sights transpierce
So rarely the serene cloud where he dwells   875
Whose looks enjoin, whose lightest words are spells
On the obdurate! That right arm indeed
Has thunder for its slave; but where's the need
Of thunder if the stricken multitude
Hearkens, arrested in its angriest mood,   880
While songs go up exulting, then dispread,
Dispart, disperse, lingering overhead
Like an escape of angels? 'T is the tune,
Nor much unlike the words his women croon
Smilingly, colourless and faint-designed   885
Each, as a worn-out queen's face some remind
Of her extreme youth's love-tales. 'Eglamor
'Made that!' Half minstrel and half emperor,
What but ill objects vexed him? Such he slew.
The kinder sort were easy to subdue   890
By those ambrosial glances, dulcet tones;

And these a gracious hand advanced to thrones
Beneath him. Wherefore twist and torture this,
Striving to name afresh the antique bliss,
Instead of saying, neither less nor more,   895
He had discovered, as our world before,

He means to
be perfect—
say, Apollo:

Apollo? That shall be the name; nor bid
Me rag by rag expose how patchwork hid
The youth—what thefts of every clime and day
Contributed to purfle the array   900
He climbed with (June at deep) some close ravine
Mid clatter of its million pebbles sheen,
Over which, singing soft, the runnel slipped
Elate with rains: into whose streamlet dipped
He foot, yet trod, you thought, with unwet sock—   905
Though really on the stubs of living rock
Ages ago it crenelled; vines for roof,
Lindens for wall; before him, aye aloof,
Flittered in the cool some azure damsel-fly,
Born of the simmering quiet, there to die.   910
Emerging whence, Apollo still, he spied
Mighty descents of forest; multiplied
Tuft on tuft, here, the frolic myrtle-trees,
There gendered the grave maple stocks at ease.
And, proud of its observer, straight the wood   915
Tried old surprises on him; black it stood
A sudden barrier ('twas a cloud passed o'er)
So dead and dense, the tiniest brute no more
Must pass; yet presently (the cloud dispatched)
Each clump, behold, was glistering detached   920
A shrub, oak-boles shrunk into ilex-stems!
Yet could not he denounce the stratagems
He saw thro', till, hours thence, aloft would hang
White summer-lightnings; as it sank and sprang
To measure, that whole palpitating breast   925
Of heaven, 't was Apollo, nature prest
At eve to worship.
                     Time stole: by degrees
The Pythons perish off; his votaries
Sink to respectful distance; songs redeem
Their pains, but briefer; their dismissals seem   930

Emphatic; only girls are very slow
To disappear—his Delians! Some that glow
O' the instant, more with earlier loves to wrench
Away, reserves to quell, disdains to quench;
Alike in one material circumstance—　　　　935
All soon or late adore Apollo! Glance
The bevy through, divine Apollo's choice,
His Daphne! 'We secure Count Richard's voice
'In Este's counsels, good for Este's ends
'As our Taurello,' say his faded friends,　　　940
'By granting him our Palma!'—the sole child,
They mean, of Agnes Este who beguiled
Ecelin, years before this Adelaide
Wedded and turned him wicked: 'but the maid
'Rejects his suit,' those sleepy women boast.　　945
She, scorning all beside, deserves the most
Sordello: so, conspicuous in his world
Of dreams sat Palma. How the tresses curled
Into a sumptuous swell of gold and wound
About her like a glory! even the ground　　　950
Was bright as with spilt sunbeams; breathe not, breathe
Not!—poised, see, one leg doubled underneath,
Its small foot buried in the dimpling snow,
Rests, but the other, listlessly below,
O'er the couch-side swings feeling for cool air,　　955
The vein-streaks swollen a richer violet where
The languid blood lies heavily; yet calm
On her slight prop, each flat and outspread palm,
As but suspended in the act to rise
By consciousness of beauty, whence her eyes　　960
Turn with so frank a triumph, for she meets
Apollo's gaze in the pine glooms.

Time fleets:

That's worst! Because the pre-appointed age
Approaches. Fate is tardy with the stage
And crowd she promised. Lean he grows and pale,　965
Though restlessly at rest. Hardly avail
Fancies to soothe him. Time steals, yet alone
He tarries here! The earnest smile is gone.
How long this might continue matters not;

Margin notes:

and Apollo must one day find Daphne.

But when will this dream turn truth?

—For ever, possibly; since to the spot   970
None come: our lingering Taurello quits
Mantua at last, and light our lady flits
Back to her place disburthened of a care.
Strange—to be constant here if he is there!
Is it distrust? Oh, never! for they both   975
Goad Ecelin alike, Romano's growth
Is daily manifest, with Azzo dumb
And Richard wavering: let but Friedrich come,
Find matter for the minstrelsy's report
—Lured from the Isle and its young Kaiser's court   980
To sing us a Messina morning up,
And, double rillet of a drinking cup,
Sparkle along to ease the land of drouth,
Northward to Provence that, and thus far south
The other! What a method to apprise   985
Neighbours of births, espousals, obsequies,
Which in their very tongue the Troubadour
Records! and his performance makes a tour,
For Trouveres bear the miracle about,
Explain its cunning to the vulgar rout,   990
Until the Formidable House is famed
Over the country—as Taurello aimed,
Who introduced, although the rest adopt,
The novelty. Such games, her absence stopped,
Begin afresh now Adelaide, recluse   995
No longer, in the light of day pursues
Her plans at Mantua: whence an accident

For the time is
ripe, and he
ready.

Which, breaking on Sordello's mixed content
Opened, like any flash that cures the blind,
The veritable business of mankind.   1000

BOOK THE SECOND

This bubble
of fancy,

THE woods were long austere with snow: at last
Pink leaflets budded on the beech, and fast
Larches, scattered through pine-tree solitudes,
Brightened, 'as in the slumbrous heart o' the woods
'Our buried year, a witch, grew young again   5

'To placid incantations, and that stain
'About were from her cauldron, green smoke blent
'With those black pines'—so Eglamor gave vent
To a chance fancy. Whence a just rebuke
From his companion; brother Naddo shook   10
The solemnest of brows: 'Beware,' he said,
'Of setting up conceits in nature's stead!'
Forth wandered our Sordello. Nought so sure
As that to-day's adventure will secure
Palma, the visioned lady—only pass   15
O'er yon damp mound and its exhausted grass,
Under that brake where sundawn feeds the stalks
Of withered fern with gold, into those walks
Of pine and take her! Buoyantly he went.
Again his stooping forehead was besprent   20
With dew-drops from the skirting ferns. Then wide
Opened the great morass, shot every side
With flashing water through and through; a-shine,
Thick-steaming, all-alive. Whose shape divine,
Quivered i' the farthest rainbow-vapour, glanced   25   when greatest
Athwart the flying herons? He advanced,   and brightest,
But warily; though Mincio leaped no more,   bursts.
Each foot-fall burst up in the marish-floor
A diamond jet: and if he stopped to pick
Rose-lichen, or molest the leeches quick,   30
And circling blood-worms, minnow, newt or loach,
A sudden pond would silently encroach
This way and that. On Palma passed. The verge
Of a new wood was gained. She will emerge
Flushed, now, and panting,—crowds to see,—will own 35
She loves him—Boniface to hear, to groan,
To leave his suit! One screen of pine-trees still
Opposes: but—the startling spectacle—
Mantua, this time! Under the walls—a crowd
Indeed, real men and women, gay and loud   40
Round a pavilion. How he stood!
                              In truth
No prophecy had come to pass: his youth
In its prime now—and where was homage poured
Upon Sordello?—born to be adored,

And suddenly discovered weak, scarce made   45
To cope with any, cast into the shade
By this and this. Yet something seemed to prick
And tingle in his blood; a sleight—a trick—
And much would be explained. It went for nought—
The best of their endowments were ill bought   50
With his identity: nay, the conceit,
That this day's roving led to Palma's feet
Was not so vain—list! The word, 'Palma!' Steal
Aside, and die, Sordello; this is real,
And this—abjure!
                    What next? The curtains see   55
Dividing! She is there; and presently
He will be there—the proper You, at length—
In your own cherished dress of grace and strength:
Most like, the very Boniface!
                              Not so.

At a court of
love, a min-
strel sings.

It was a showy man advanced; but though   60
A glad cry welcomed him, then every sound
Sank and the crowd disposed themselves around,
—'This is not he,' Sordello felt; while, 'Place
'For the best Troubadour of Boniface!'
Hollaed the Jongleurs,—'Eglamor, whose lay   65
'Concludes his patron's Court of Love to-day!'
Obsequious Naddo strung the master's lute
With the new lute-string, 'Elys,' named to suit
The song: he stealthily at watch, the while,
Biting his lip to keep down a great smile   70
Of pride: then up he struck. Sordello's brain
Swam; for he knew a sometime deed again;
So, could supply each foolish gap and chasm
The minstrel left in his enthusiasm,
Mistaking its true version—was the tale   75
Not of Apollo? Only, what avail
Luring her down, that Elys an he pleased,
If the man dared no further? Has he ceased?

Sordello,
before Palma,
conquers him,

And, lo, the people's frank applause half done,
Sordello was beside him, had begun   80
(Spite of indignant twitchings from his friend
The Trouvere) the true lay with the true end,

Taking the other's names and time and place
For his. On flew the song, a giddy race,
After the flying story; word made leap   85
Out word, rhyme—rhyme; the lay could barely keep
Pace with the action visibly rushing past:
Both ended. Back fell Naddo more aghast
Than some Egyptian from the harassed bull
That wheeled abrupt and, bellowing, fronted full   90
His plague, who spied a scarab 'neath the tongue,
And found 't was Apis' flank his hasty prong
Insulted. But the people—but the cries,
The crowding round, and proffering the prize!
—For he had gained some prize. He seemed to
       shrink   95
Into a sleepy cloud, just at whose brink
One sight withheld him. There sat Adelaide,
Silent; but at her knees the very maid
Of the North Chamber, her red lips as rich,
The same pure fleecy hair; one weft of which,   100
Golden and great, quite touched his cheek as o'er
She leant, speaking some six words and no more.
He answered something, anything; and she
Unbound a scarf and laid it heavily
Upon him, her neck's warmth and all. Again   105
Moved the arrested magic; in his brain
Noises grew, and a light that turned to glare,
And greater glare, until the intense flare
Engulfed him, shut the whole scene from his sense.   *receives the*
And when he woke 't was many a furlong thence,   110   *prize, and*
At home; the sun shining his ruddy wont;   *ruminates.*
The customary birds'-chirp; but his front
Was crowned—was crowned! Her scented scarf around
His neck! Whose gorgeous vesture heaps the ground?
A prize? He turned, and peeringly on him   115
Brooded the women-faces, kind and dim,
Ready to talk—'The Jongleurs in a troop
'Had brought him back, Naddo and Squarcialupe
'And Tagliafer; how strange! a childhood spent
'In taking, well for him, so brave a bent!   120
'Since Eglamor,' they heard, 'was dead with spite,

'And Palma chose him for her minstrel.'

                                          Light
Sordello rose—to think, now; hitherto
He had perceived. Sure, a discovery grew
Out of it all! Best live from first to last   125
The transport o'er again. A week he passed,
Sucking the sweet out of each circumstance,
From the bard's outbreak to the luscious trance
Bounding his own achievement. Strange! A man
Recounted an adventure, but began   130
Imperfectly; his own task was to fill
The frame-work up, sing well what he sung ill,
Supply the necessary points, set loose
As many incidents of little use
—More imbecile the other, not to see   135
Their relative importance clear as he!
But, for a special pleasure in the act
Of singing—had he ever turned, in fact,
From Elys, to sing Elys?—from each fit
Of rapture to contrive a song of it?   140
True, this snatch or the other seemed to wind
Into a treasure, helped himself to find
A beauty in himself; for, see, he soared
By means of that mere snatch, to many a hoard
Of fancies; as some falling cone bears soft   145
The eye along the fir-tree-spire, aloft

How had he been superior to Eglamor?

To a dove's nest. Then, how divine the cause
Why such performance should exact applause
From men, if they had fancies too? Did fate
Decree they found a beauty separate   150
In the poor snatch itself?—'Take Elys, there,
'—"Her head that's sharp and perfect like a pear,
' "So close and smooth are laid the few fine locks
' "Coloured like honey oozed from topmost rocks
' "Sun-blanched the livelong summer"—if they heard 155
'Just those two rhymes, assented at my word,
'And loved them as I love them who have run
'These fingers through those pale locks, let the sun
'Into the white cool skin—who first could clutch,
'Then praise—I needs must be a god to such.   160

'Or what if some, above themselves, and yet
'Beneath me, like their Eglamor, have set
'An impress on our gift? So, men believe
'And worship what they know not, nor receive
'Delight from. Have they fancies—slow, perchance,   165
'Not at their beck, which indistinctly glance
'Until, by song, each floating part be linked
'To each, and all grow palpable, distinct?'
He pondered this.

           Meanwhile, sounds low and drear
Stole on him, and a noise of footsteps, near   170
And nearer, while the underwood was pushed
Aside, the larches grazed, the dead leaves crushed
At the approach of men. The wind seemed laid;
Only, the trees shrunk slightly and a shade
Came o'er the sky although 't was midday yet: 175
You saw each half-shut downcast floweret
Flutter—'a Roman bride, when they'd dispart
'Her unbound tresses with the Sabine dart,
'Holding that famous rape in memory still,
'Felt creep into her curls the iron chill,   180
'And looked thus,' Eglamor would say—indeed
'T is Eglamor, no other, these precede
Home hither in the woods. ' 'T were surely sweet
'Far from the scene of one's forlorn defeat
'To sleep!' judged Naddo, who in person led   185
Jongleurs and Trouveres, chanting at their head,
A scanty company; for, sooth to say,
Our beaten Troubadour had seen his day.
Old worshippers were something shamed, old friends
Nigh weary; still the death proposed amends.   190
'Let us but get them safely through my song
'And home again!' quoth Naddo.

                All along,
This man (they rest the bier upon the sand)
—This calm corpse with the loose flowers in his hand,
Eglamor, lived Sordello's opposite.   195
For him indeed was Naddo's notion right,
And verse a temple-worship vague and vast,
A ceremony that withdrew the last

Marginal notes:

This is answered by Eglamor himself:

one who belonged to what he loved,

Opposing bolt, looped back the lingering veil
Which hid the holy place: should one so frail   200
Stand there without such effort? or repine
If much was blank, uncertain at the shrine
He knelt before, till, soothed by many a rite,
The power responded, and some sound or sight
Grew up, his own forever, to be fixed,   205
In rhyme, the beautiful, forever!—mixed
With his own life, unloosed when he should please,
Having it safe at hand, ready to ease
All pain, remove all trouble; every time
He loosed that fancy from its bonds of rhyme,   210
(Like Perseus when he loosed his naked love)
Faltering; so distinct and far above
Himself, these fancies! He, no genius rare,
Transfiguring in fire or wave or air
At will, but a poor gnome that, cloistered up   215
In some rock-chamber with his agate cup,
His topaz rod, his seed-pearl, in these few
And their arrangement finds enough to do
For his best art. Then, how he loved that art!
The calling marking him a man apart   220

loving his art
and rewarded
by it,

From men—one not to care, take counsel for
Cold hearts, comfortless faces—(Eglamor
Was neediest of his tribe)—since verse, the gift,
Was his, and men, the whole of them, must shift
Without it, e'en content themselves with wealth   225
And pomp and power, snatching a life by stealth.
So, Eglamor was not without his pride!
The sorriest bat which cowers throughout noontide
While other birds are jocund, has one time
When moon and stars are blinded, and the prime   230
Of earth is his to claim, nor find a peer;
And Eglamor was noblest poet here—
He well knew, 'mid those April woods he cast
Conceits upon in plenty as he passed,
That Naddo might suppose him not to think   235
Entirely on the coming triumph: wink
At the one weakness! 'T was a fervid child,
That song of his; no brother of the guild

Had e'er conceived its like. The rest you know,
The exaltation and the overthrow: 240
Our poet lost his purpose, lost his rank,
His life—to that it came. Yet envy sank
Within him, as he heard Sordello out,
And, for the first time, shouted—tried to shout
Like others, not from any zeal to show   245
Pleasure that way: the common sort did so,
What else was Eglamor? who, bending down
As they, placed his beneath Sordello's crown,
Printed a kiss on his successor's hand,
Left one great tear on it, then joined his band   250
—In time; for some were watching at the door:
Who knows what envy may effect? 'Give o'er,
'Nor charm his lips, nor craze him!' (here one spied
And disengaged the withered crown)—'Beside
'His crown? How prompt and clear those verses rang   255
'To answer yours! nay, sing them!' And he sang
Them calmly. Home he went; friends used to wait
His coming, zealous to congratulate;
But, to a man—so quickly runs report—
Could do no less than leave him, and escort   260
His rival. That eve, then, bred many a thought: ending with
What must his future life be? was he brought   what had
So low, who stood so lofty this Spring morn?   possessed
At length he said, 'Best sleep now with my scorn,   him.
'And by to-morrow I devise some plain   265
'Expedient!' So, he slept, nor woke again.
They found as much, those friends, when they returned
O'erflowing with the marvels they had learned
About Sordello's paradise, his roves
Among the hills and vales and plains and groves,   270
Wherein, no doubt, this lay was roughly cast,
Polished by slow degrees, completed last
To Eglamor's discomfiture and death.
    Such form the chanters now, and, out of breath,
They lay the beaten man in his abode,   275
Naddo reciting that same luckless ode,
Doleful to hear. Sordello could explore
By means of it, however, one step more

Eglamor done
with, Sordello
begins.

In joy; and, mastering the round at length,
Learnt how to live in weakness as in strength,   280
When from his covert forth he stood, addressed
Eglamor, bade the tender ferns invest,
Primæval pines o'ercanopy his couch,
And, most of all, his fame—(shall I avouch
Eglamor heard it, dead though he might look,   285
And laughed as from his brow Sordello took
The crown, and laid on the bard's breast, and said
It was a crown, now, fit for poet's head?)
—Continue. Nor the prayer quite fruitless fell.
A plant they have, yielding a three-leaved bell   290
Which whitens at the heart ere noon, and ails
Till evening; evening gives it to her gales
To clear away with such forgotten things
As are an eyesore to the morn: this brings
Him to their mind, and bears his very name.   295
　　So much for Eglamor. My own month came;
'T was a sunrise of blossoming and May.
Beneath a flowering laurel thicket lay
Sordello; each new sprinkle of white stars
That smell fainter of wine than Massic jars   300
Dug up at Baiæ, when the south wind shed
The ripest, made him happier; filleted
And robed the same, only a lute beside
Lay on the turf. Before him far and wide
The country stretched: Goito slept behind   305
—The castle and its covert, which confined
Him with his hopes and fears; so fain of old

Who he really
was, and why
at Goito.

To leave the story of his birth untold.
At intervals, 'spite the fantastic glow
Of his Apollo-life, a certain low   310
And wretched whisper, winding through the bliss,
Admonished, no such fortune could be his,
All was quite false and sure to fade one day:
The closelier drew he round him his array
Of brilliance to expel the truth. But when   315
A reason for his difference from men
Surprised him at the grave, he took no rest
While aught of that old life, superbly dressed

Down to its meanest incident, remained
A mystery: alas, they soon explained   320
Away Apollo! and the tale amounts
To this: when at Vicenza both her counts
Banished the Vivaresi kith and kin,
Those Maltraversi hung on Ecelin,
Reviled him as he followed; he for spite   325
Must fire their quarter, though that self-same night
Among the flames young Ecelin was born
Of Adelaide, there too, and barely torn
From the roused populace hard on the rear,
By a poor archer when his chieftain's fear   330
Grew high; into the thick Elcorte leapt,
Saved her, and died; no creature left except
His child to thank. And when the full escape
Was known—how men impaled from chine to nape
Unlucky Prata, all to pieces spurned   335
Bishop Pistore's concubines, and burned
Taurello's entire household, flesh and fell,
Missing the sweeter prey—such courage well
Might claim reward. The orphan, ever since,
Sordello, had been nurtured by his prince   340
Within a blind retreat where Adelaide—
(For, once this notable discovery made,
The past at every point was understood)
—Might harbour easily when times were rude,
When Azzo schemed for Palma, to retrieve   345
That pledge of Agnes Este—loth to leave
Mantua unguarded with a vigilant eye,
While there Taurello bode ambiguously—
He who could have no motive now to moil
For his own fortunes since their utter spoil—   350
As it were worth while yet (went the report)
To disengage himself from her. In short,   He, so little,
Apollo vanished; a mean youth, just named   would fain be
His lady's minstrel, was to be proclaimed   so much:
—How shall I phrase it?—Monarch of the World!   355
For, on the day when that array was furled
Forever, and in place of one a slave
To longings, wild indeed, but longings save

In dreams as wild, suppressed—one daring not
Assume the mastery such dreams allot,   360
Until a magical equipment, strength,
Grace, wisdom, decked him too,—he chose at length,
Content with unproved wits and failing frame,
In virtue of his simple will, to claim
That mastery, no less—to do his best   365
With means so limited, and let the rest
Go by,—the seal was set: never again
Sordello could in his own sight remain
One of the many, one with hopes and cares
And interests nowise distinct from theirs,   370
Only peculiar in a thriveless store
Of fancies, which were fancies and no more;
Never again for him and for the crowd
A common law was challenged and allowed
If calmly reasoned of, howe'er denied   375
By a mad impulse nothing justified
Short of Apollo's presence. The divorce
Is clear: why needs Sordello square his course
By any known example? Men no more
Compete with him than tree and flower before.   380
Himself, inactive, yet is greater far
Than such as act, each stooping to his star,
Acquiring thence his function; he has gained
The same result with meaner mortals trained
To strength or beauty, moulded to express   385
Each the idea that rules him; since no less
He comprehends that function, but can still
Embrace the others, take of might his fill
With Richard as of grace with Palma, mix
Their qualities, or for a moment fix   390
On one; abiding free meantime, uncramped
By any partial organ, never stamped
Strong, and to strength turning all energies—
Wise, and restricted to becoming wise—
That is, he loves not, nor possesses One   395
Idea that, star-like over, lures him on
To its exclusive purpose. 'Fortunate!
'This flesh of mine ne'er strove to emulate

leaves the dream he may be something, (margin, lines 366–369)

for the fact that he can do nothing, (margin, lines 395–397)

'A soul so various—took no casual mould
'Of the first fancy and, contracted, cold,   400
'Clogged her forever—soul averse to change
'As flesh: whereas flesh leaves soul free to range,
'Remains itself a blank, cast into shade,
'Encumbers little, if it cannot aid.
'So, range, free soul!—who, by self-consciousness,   405
'The last drop of all beauty dost express—
'The grace of seeing grace, a quintessence
'For thee: while for the world, that can dispense
'Wonder on men who, themselves, wonder—make
'A shift to love at second-hand, and take   410
'For idols those who do but idolize,
'Themselves,—the world that counts men strong or
        wise,
'Who, themselves, court strength, wisdom,—it shall
        bow
'Surely in unexampled worship now,
'Discerning me!'—

                (Dear monarch, I beseech,   415
Notice how lamentably wide a breach
Is here: discovering this, discover too
What our poor world has possibly to do
With it! As pigmy natures as you please—
So much the better for you; take your ease,   420
Look on, and laugh; style yourself God alone;
Strangle some day with a cross olive-stone!
All that is right enough: but why want us
To know that you yourself know thus and thus?)
'The world shall bow to me conceiving all   425   yet is able to
'Man's life, who see its blisses, great and small,   imagine
'Afar—not tasting any; no machine   everything,
'To exercise my utmost will is mine:
'Be mine mere consciousness! Let men perceive
'What I could do, a mastery believe,   430
'Asserted and established to the throng
'By their selected evidence of song
'Which now shall prove, whate'er they are, or seek
'To be, I am—whose words, not actions speak,
'Who change no standards of perfection, vex   435

                            H

'With no strange forms created to perplex,
'But just perform their bidding and no more,
'At their own satiating-point give o'er,
'While each shall love in me the love that leads
'His soul to power's perfection.' Song, not deeds,   440
(For we get tired) was chosen. Fate would brook
Mankind no other organ; he would look
For not another channel to dispense
His own volition by, receive men's sense
Of its supremacy—would live content,   445
Obstructed else, with merely verse for vent.
Nor should, for instance, strength an outlet seek
And, striving, be admired: nor grace bespeak
Wonder, displayed in gracious attitudes:
Nor wisdom, poured forth, change unseemly moods; 450
But he would give and take on song's one point.
Like some huge throbbing stone that, poised a-joint,
Sounds, to affect on its basaltic bed,
Must sue in just one accent; tempests shed
Thunder, and raves the windstorm: only let   455
That key by any little noise be set—
The far benighted hunter's halloo pitch
On that, the hungry curlew chance to scritch
Or serpent hiss it, rustling through the rift,
However loud, however low—all lift   460
The groaning monster, stricken to the heart.

if the world
esteem this
equivalent.

        Lo ye, the world's concernment, for its part,
And this, for his, will hardly interfere!
Its businesses in blood and blaze this year
But wile the hour away—a pastime slight   465
Till he shall step upon the platform: right!
And, now thus much is settled, cast in rough,
Proved feasible, be counselled! thought enough,—
Slumber, Sordello! any day will serve:
Were it a less digested plan! how swerve   470
To-morrow? Meanwhile eat these sun-dried grapes,
And watch the soaring hawk there! Life escapes
Merrily thus.
                    He thoroughly read o'er
His truchman Naddo's missive six times more,

Praying him visit Mantua and supply   475
A famished world.
                    The evening star was high
When he reached Mantua, but his fame arrived
Before him: friends applauded, foes connived,
And Naddo looked an angel, and the rest
Angels, and all these angels would be blest   480
Supremely by a song—the thrice-renowned
Goito-manufacture. Then he found
(Casting about to satisfy the crowd)
That happy vehicle, so late allowed,
A sore annoyance; 't was the song's effect   485   He has loved
He cared for, scarce the song itself: reflect!   song's results,
In the past life, what might be singing's use?   not song;
Just to delight his Delians, whose profuse
Praise, not the toilsome process which procured
That praise, enticed Apollo: dreams abjured,   490
No overleaping means for ends—take both
For granted or take neither! I am loth
To say the rhymes at last were Eglamor's;
But Naddo, chuckling, bade competitors
Go pine; 'the master certes meant to waste   495
'No effort, cautiously had probed the taste
'He'd please anon: true bard, in short,—disturb
'His title if they could; nor spur nor curb,
'Fancy nor reason, wanting in him; whence
'The staple of his verses, common sense: 500
'He built on man's broad nature—gift of gifts,
'That power to build! The world contented shifts
'With counterfeits enough, a dreary sort
'Of warriors, statesmen, ere it can extort
'Its poet-soul—that's, after all, a freak   505
'(The having eyes to see and tongue to speak)
'With our herd's stupid sterling happiness
'So plainly incompatible that—yes—   so, must effect
'Yes—should a son of his improve the breed   this to obtain
'And turn out poet, he were cursed indeed!'   510   those.
'Well, there's Goito and its woods anon,
'If the worst happen; best go stoutly on
'Now!' thought Sordello.

Ay, and goes on yet!
You pother with your glossaries to get
A notion of the Troubadour's intent   515
In rondel, tenzon, virlai or sirvent—
Much as you study arras how to twirl
His angelot, plaything of page and girl
Once; but you surely reach, at last,—or, no!
Never quite reach what struck the people so,   520
As from the welter of their time he drew
Its elements successively to view,
Followed all actions backward on their course,
And catching up, unmingled at the source,
Such a strength, such a weakness, added then   525
A touch or two, and turned them into men.
Virtue took form, nor vice refused a shape;
Here heaven opened, there was hell agape,
As Saint this simpered past in sanctity,
Sinner the other flared portentous by   530
A greedy people. Then why stop, surprised
At his success? The scheme was realized
Too suddenly in one respect: a crowd
Praising, eyes quick to see, and lips as loud
To speak, delicious homage to receive,   535

He succeeds a
little, but fails
more;

The woman's breath to feel upon his sleeve,
Who said, 'But Anafest—why asks he less
'Than Lucio, in your verses? how confess,
'It seemed too much but yestereve!'—the youth,
Who bade him earnestly, 'Avow the truth!   540
'You love Bianca, surely, from your song;
'I knew I was unworthy!'—soft or strong,
In poured such tributes ere he had arranged
Ethereal ways to take them, sorted, changed,
Digested. Courted thus at unawares,   545
In spite of his pretensions and his cares,
He caught himself shamefully hankering
After the obvious petty joys that spring
From true life, fain relinquish pedestal
And condescend with pleasures—one and all   550
To be renounced, no doubt; for, thus to chain
Himself to single joys and so refrain

From tasting their quintessence, frustrates, sure,
His prime design; each joy must he abjure
Even for love of it.
              He laughed: what sage   555
But perishes if from his magic page
He look because, at the first line, a proof
'T was heard salutes him from the cavern roof?
'On! Give yourself, excluding aught beside,
'To the day's task; compel your slave provide   560
'Its utmost at the soonest; turn the leaf
'Thoroughly conned. These lays of yours, in brief—
'Cannot men bear, now, something better?—fly
'A pitch beyond this unreal pageantry
'Of essences? the period sure has ceased   565
'For such: present us with ourselves, at least,
'Not portions of ourselves, mere loves and hates
'Made flesh: wait not!'
              Awhile the poet waits
However. The first trial was enough: *tries again, is*
He left imagining, to try the stuff   570   *no better*
That held the imaged thing, and, let it writhe   *satisfied,*
Never so fiercely, scarce allowed a tithe
To reach the light—his Language. How he sought
The cause, conceived a cure, and slow re-wrought
That Language,—welding words into the crude   575
Mass from the new speech round him, till a rude
Armour was hammered out, in time to be
Approved beyond the Roman panoply
Melted to make it,—boots not. This obtained
With some ado, no obstacle remained   580
To using it; accordingly he took
An action with its actors, quite forsook
Himself to live in each, returned anon
With the result—a creature, and, by one
And one, proceeded leisurely to equip   585
Its limbs in harness of his workmanship.
'Accomplished! Listen, Mantuans!' Fond essay!
Piece after piece that armour broke away,
Because perceptions whole, like that he sought
To clothe, reject so pure a work of thought   590

As language: thought may take perception's place
and declines
from the ideal
of song.
But hardly co-exist in any case,
Being its mere presentment—of the whole
By parts, the simultaneous and the sole
By the successive and the many. Lacks   595
The crowd perception? painfully it tacks
Thought to thought, which Sordello, needing such,
Has rent perception into: its to clutch
And reconstruct—his office to diffuse,
Destroy: as hard, then, to obtain a Muse   600
As to become Apollo. 'For the rest,
'E'en if some wondrous vehicle expressed
'The whole dream, what impertinence in me
'So to express it, who myself can be
'The dream! nor, on the other hand, are those   605
'I sing to, over-likely to suppose
'A higher than the highest I present
'Now, which they praise already: be content
'Both parties, rather—they with the old verse,
'And I with the old praise—far go, fare worse!'   610
A few adhering rivets loosed, upsprings
The angel, sparkles off his mail, which rings
Whirled from each delicatest limb it warps;
So might Apollo from the sudden corpse
Of Hyacinth have cast his luckless quoits.   615
He set to celebrating the exploits
Of Montfort o'er the Mountaineers.
                                        Then came
The world's revenge: their pleasure, now his aim
Merely,—what was it? 'Not to play the fool
What is the
world's
recognition
worth?
'So much as learn our lesson in your school!'   620
Replied the world. He found that, every time
He gained applause by any ballad-rhyme,
His auditory recognized no jot
As he intended, and, mistaking not
Him for his meanest hero, ne'er was dunce   625
Sufficient to believe him—all, at once.
His will . . . conceive it caring for his will!
—Mantuans, the main of them, admiring still
How a mere singer, ugly, stunted, weak,

Had Montfort at completely (so to speak)   630
His fingers' ends; while past the praise-tide swept
To Montfort, either's share distinctly kept:
The true meed for true merit!—his abates
Into a sort he most repudiates,
And on them angrily he turns. Who were   635
The Mantuans, after all, that he should care
About their recognition, ay or no?
In spite of the convention months ago,
(Why blink the truth?) was not he forced to help
This same ungrateful audience, every whelp   640
Of Naddo's litter, make them pass for peers
With the bright band of old Goito years,
As erst he toiled for flower or tree? Why, there
Sat Palma! Adelaide's funereal hair
Ennobled the next corner. Ay, he strewed   645
A fairy dust upon that multitude,
Although he feigned to take them by themselves;
His giants dignified those puny elves,
Sublimed their faint applause. In short, he found
Himself still footing a delusive round,   650
Remote as ever from the self-display
He meant to compass, hampered every way
By what he hoped assistance. Wherefore then
Continue, make believe to find in men
A use he found not?

            Weeks, months, years went by;   655   How, poet no
And lo, Sordello vanished utterly,   longer in unity
Sundered in twain; each spectral part at strife   with man,
With each; one jarred against another life;
The Poet thwarting hopelessly the Man—
Who, fooled no longer, free in fancy ran   660
Here, there: let slip no opportunities
As pitiful, forsooth, beside the prize
To drop on him some no-time and acquit
His constant faith (the Poet-half's to wit—
That waiving any compromise between   665
No joy and all joy kept the hunger keen
Beyond most methods)—of incurring scoff
From the Man-portion—not to be put off

With self-reflectings by the Poet's scheme,
Though ne'er so bright. Who sauntered forth in
    dream,   670

the whole
visible
Sordello goes
wrong

Dressed any how, nor waited mystic frames,
Immeasurable gifts, astounding claims,
But just his sorry self?—who yet might be
Sorrier for aught he in reality
Achieved, so pinioned Man's the Poet-part,   675
Fondling, in turn of fancy, verse; the Art
Developing his soul a thousand ways—
Potent, by its assistance, to amaze
The multitude with majesties, convince
Each sort of nature that the nature's prince   680
Accosted it. Language, the makeshift, grew
Into a bravest of expedients, too;
Apollo, seemed it now, perverse had thrown
Quiver and bow away, the lyre alone
Sufficed. While, out of dream, his day's work went   685
To tune a crazy tenzon or sirvent—
So hampered him the Man-part, thrust to judge
Between the bard and the bard's audience, grudge
A minute's toil that missed its due reward!
But the complete Sordello, Man and Bard,   690
John's cloud-girt angel, this foot on the land,
That on the sea, with, open in his hand,
A bitter-sweetling of a book—was gone.
    Then, if internal struggles to be one,
Which frittered him incessantly piecemeal,   695
Referred, ne'er so obliquely, to the real
Intruding Mantuans! ever with some call
To action while he pondered, once for all,
Which looked the easier effort—to pursue
This course, still leap o'er paltry joys, yearn through 700
The present ill-appreciated stage
Of self-revealment, and compel the age
Know him—or else, forswearing bard-craft, wake
From out his lethargy and nobly shake
Off timid habits of denial, mix   705

with those too
hard for half
of him,

With men, enjoy like men. Ere he could fix
On aught, in rushed the Mantuans; much they cared

For his perplexity! Thus unprepared,
The obvious if not only shelter lay
In deeds, the dull conventions of his day   710
Prescribed the like of him: why not be glad
'T is settled Palma's minstrel, good or bad,
Submits to this and that established rule?
Let Vidal change, or any other fool,
His murrey-coloured robe for filamot,   715
And crop his hair; too skin-deep, is it not,
Such vigour? Then, a sorrow to the heart,
His talk! Whatever topics they might start
Had to be groped for in his consciousness
Straight, and as straight delivered them by guess.   720
Only obliged to ask himself, 'What was,'
A speedy answer followed; but, alas,
One of God's large ones, tardy to condense
Itself into a period; answers whence
A tangle of conclusions must be stripped   725
At any risk ere, trim to pattern clipped,
They matched rare specimens the Mantuan flock
Regaled him with, each talker from his stock
Of sorted-o'er opinions, every stage,
Juicy in youth or desiccate with age,   730
Fruits like the fig-tree's, rathe-ripe, rotten-rich,
Sweet-sour, all tastes to take: a practice which
He too had not impossibly attained,
Once either of those fancy-flights restrained;
(For, at conjecture how might words appear   735 of whom he is
To others, playing there what happened here,   also too con-
And occupied abroad by what he spurned   temptuous.
At home, 't was slipped, the occasion he returned
To seize:) he'd strike that lyre adroitly—speech,
Would but a twenty-cubit plectre reach;   740
A clever hand, consummate instrument,
Were both brought close; each excellency went
For nothing, else. The question Naddo asked,
Had just a lifetime moderately tasked
To answer, Naddo's fashion. More disgust   745
And more: why move his soul, since move it must
At minute's notice or as good it failed

To move at all? The end was, he retailed
Some ready-made opinion, put to use
This quip, that maxim, ventured reproduce   750
Gestures and tones—at any folly caught
Serving to finish with, nor too much sought
If false or true 't was spoken; praise and blame
Of what he said grew pretty nigh the same
—Meantime awards to meantime acts: his soul,   755
Unequal to the compassing a whole,
Saw, in a tenth part, less and less to strive
About. And as for men in turn . . . contrive
Who could to take eternal interest
In them, so hate the worst, so love the best!   760
Though, in pursuance of his passive plan,
He hailed, decried, the proper way.

                                        As Man

He pleases
neither
himself nor
them:

So figured he; and how as Poet? Verse
Came only not to a stand-still. The worse,
That his poor piece of daily work to do   765
Was—not sink under any rivals; who
Loudly and long enough, without these qualms,
Turned, from Bocafoli's stark-naked psalms,
To Plara's sonnets spoilt by toying with,
'As knops that stud some almug to the pith   770
'Prickèd for gum, wry thence, and crinklèd worse
'Than pursèd eyelids of a river-horse
'Sunning himself o' the slime when whirrs the breese'—
Gad-fly, that is. He might compete with these!
But—but—
                    'Observe a pompion-twine afloat;   775
'Pluck me one cup from off the castle-moat!
'Along with cup you raise leaf, stalk and root,
'The entire surface of the pool to boot.
'So could I pluck a cup, put in one song
'A single sight, did not my hand, too strong,   780
'Twitch in the least the root-strings of the whole.
'How should externals satisfy my soul?'
'Why that's precise the error Squarcialupe'
(Hazarded Naddo) 'finds; "the man can't stoop
' "To sing us out," quoth he, "a mere romance;   785

' "He'd fain do better than the best, enhance
' "The subjects' rarity, work problems out
' "Therewith." Now, you're a bard, a bard past doubt,
'And no philosopher; why introduce
'Crotchets like these? fine, surely, but no use   790
'In poetry—which still must be, to strike,
'Based upon common sense; there's nothing like
'Appealing to our nature! what beside
'Was your first poetry? No tricks were tried
'In that, no hollow thrills, affected throes!   795
' "The man," said we, "tells his own joys and woes:
' "We'll trust him." Would you have your songs endure?
'Build on the human heart!—why, to be sure
'Yours is one sort of heart—but I mean theirs,
'Ours, every one's, the healthy heart one cares   800
'To build on! Central peace, mother of strength,
'That's father of . . . nay, go yourself that length,
'Ask those calm-hearted doers what they do
'When they have got their calm! And is it true,
'Fire rankles at the heart of every globe?   805
'Perhaps. But these are matters one may probe
'Too deeply for poetic purposes:
'Rather select a theory that . . . yes,
'Laugh! what does that prove?—stations you midway
'And saves some little o'er-refining. Nay,   810
'That's rank injustice done me! I restrict
'The poet? Don't I hold the poet picked
'Out of a host of warriors, statesmen . . . did
'I tell you? Very like! As well you hid
'That sense of power, you have! True bards believe   815
'All able to achieve what they achieve—
'That is, just nothing—in one point abide
'Profounder simpletons than all beside.
'Oh, ay! The knowledge that you are a bard
'Must constitute your prime, nay sole, reward!'   820
So prattled Naddo, busiest of the tribe
Of genius-haunters—how shall I describe
What grubs or nips or rubs or rips—your louse
For love, your flea for hate, magnanimous,
Malignant, Pappacoda, Tagliafer,   825

which the best
judges account
for.

Their
criticisms
give small
comfort:

Picking a sustenance from wear and tear
By implements it sedulous employs
To undertake, lay down, mete out, o'er-toise
Sordello? Fifty creepers to elude
At once! They settled staunchly; shame ensued: 830
Behold the monarch of mankind succumb
To the last fool who turned him round his thumb,
As Naddo styled it! 'T was not worth oppose
The matter of a moment, gainsay those
He aimed at getting rid of; better think   835
Their thoughts and speak their speech, secure to slink
Back expeditiously to his safe place,
And chew the cud—what he and what his race
Were really, each of them. Yet even this
Conformity was partial. He would miss   840
Some point, brought into contact with them ere
Assured in what small segment of the sphere
Of his existence they attended him;
Whence blunders, falsehoods rectified—a grim
List—slur it over! How? If dreams were tried,   845
His will swayed sicklily from side to side,
Nor merely neutralized his waking act
But tended e'en in fancy to distract

and his own
degradation is
complete.

The intermediate will, the choice of means.
He lost the art of dreaming: Mantuan scenes   850
Supplied a baron, say, he sang before,
Handsomely reckless, full to running-o'er
Of gallantries; 'abjure the soul, content
'With body, therefore!' Scarcely had he bent
Himself in dream thus low, when matter fast   855
Cried out, he found, for spirit to contrast
And task it duly; by advances slight,
The simple stuff becoming composite,
Count Lori grew Apollo: best recall
His fancy! Then would some rough peasant-Paul,   860
Like those old Ecelin confers with, glance
His gay apparel o'er; that countenance
Gathered his shattered fancies into one,
And, body clean abolished, soul alone
Sufficed the grey Paulician: by and by,   865

To balance the ethereality,
Passions were needed; foiled he sank again.
    Meanwhile the world rejoiced ('t is time explain)   Adelaide's
death: what
happens on it:
Because a sudden sickness set it free
From Adelaide. Missing the mother-bee,   870
Her mountain-hive Romano swarmed; at once
A rustle-forth of daughters and of sons
Blackened the valley. 'I am sick too, old,
'Half-crazed I think; what good's the Kaiser's gold
'To such an one? God help me! for I catch   875
'My children's greedy sparkling eyes at watch—
' "He bears that double breastplate on," they say,
' "So many minutes less than yesterday!"
'Beside, Monk Hilary is on his knees
'Now, sworn to kneel and pray till God shall please   880
'Exact a punishment for many things
'You know, and some you never knew; which brings
'To memory, Azzo's sister Beatrix
'And Richard's Giglia are my Alberic's
'And Ecelin's betrothed; the Count himself   885
'Must get my Palma; Ghibellin and Guelf
'Mean to embrace each other.' So began
Romano's missive to his fighting man
Taurello—on the Tuscan's death, away
With Friedrich sworn to sail from Naples' bay   890
Next month for Syria. Never thunder-clap
Out of Vesuvius' throat, like this mishap
Startled him. 'That accursed Vicenza! I
'Absent, and she selects this time to die!
'Ho, fellows, for Vicenza!' Half a score   895
Of horses ridden dead, he stood before
Romano in his reeking spurs: too late—
'Boniface urged me, Este could not wait,'
The chieftain stammered; 'let me die in peace—
'Forget me! Was it I who craved increase   900
'Of rule? Do you and Friedrich plot your worst
'Against the Father: as you found me first
'So leave me now. Forgive me! Palma, sure,
'Is at Goito still. Retain that lure—
'Only be pacified!'

and a trouble
it occasions
Sordello.

                              The country rung   905
With such a piece of news: on every tongue,
How Ecelin's great servant, congeed off,
Had done a long day's service, so, might doff
The green and yellow, and recover breath
At Mantua, whither,—since Retrude's death,   910
(The girlish slip of a Sicilian bride
From Otho's house, he carried to reside
At Mantua till the Ferrarese should pile
A structure worthy her imperial style,
The gardens raise, the statues there enshrine,   915
She never lived to see)—although his line
Was ancient in her archives and she took
A pride in him, that city, nor forsook
Her child when he forsook himself and spent
A prowess on Romano surely meant   920
For his own growth—whither he ne'er resorts
If wholly satisfied (to trust reports)
With Ecelin. So, forward in a trice
Were shows to greet him. 'Take a friend's advice,'
Quoth Naddo to Sordello, 'nor be rash   925
'Because your rivals (nothing can abash
'Some folks) demur that we pronounced you best
'To sound the great man's welcome; 't is a test,
'Remember! Strojavacca looks asquint,
'The rough fat sloven; and there's plenty hint   930
'Your pinions have received of late a shock—
'Outsoar them, cobswan of the silver flock!
'Sing well!' A signal wonder, song's no whit
Facilitated.

He chances
upon his old
environment,
                    Fast the minutes flit;
Another day, Sordello finds, will bring   935
The soldier, and he cannot choose but sing;
So, a last shift, quits Mantua—slow, alone:
Out of that aching brain, a very stone,
Song must be struck. What occupies that front?
Just how he was more awkward than his wont   940
The night before, when Naddo, who had seen
Taurello on his progress, praised the mien
For dignity no crosses could affect—

Such was a joy, and might not he detect
A satisfaction if established joys   945
Were proved imposture? Poetry annoys
Its utmost: wherefore fret? Verses may come
Or keep away! And thus he wandered, dumb
Till evening, when he paused, thoroughly spent,
On a blind hill-top: down the gorge he went,   950
Yielding himself up as to an embrace.
The moon came out; like features of a face,
A querulous fraternity of pines,
Sad blackthorn clumps, leafless and grovelling vines
Also came out, made gradually up   955
The picture; 't was Goito's mountain-cup
And castle. He had dropped through one defile
He never dared explore, the Chief erewhile
Had vanished by. Back rushed the dream, enwrapped
Him wholly. 'T was Apollo now they lapped,   960
Those mountains, not a pettish minstrel meant
To wear his soul away in discontent,
Brooding on fortune's malice. Heart and brain
Swelled; he expanded to himself again,
As some thin seedling spice-tree starved and frail,   965
Pushing between cat's head and ibis' tail
Crusted into the porphyry pavement smooth,
—Suffered remain just as it sprung, to soothe
The Soldan's pining daughter, never yet
Well in her chilly green-glazed minaret,—   970
When rooted up, the sunny day she died,
And flung into the common court beside
Its parent tree. Come home, Sordello! Soon
Was he low muttering, beneath the moon,
Of sorrow saved, of quiet evermore,—   975
Since from the purpose, he maintained before,
Only resulted wailing and hot tears.
Ah, the slim castle! dwindled of late years,
But more mysterious; gone to ruin—trails
Of vine through every loop-hole. Nought avails   980
The night as, torch in hand, he must explore
The maple chamber: did I say, its floor
Was made of intersecting cedar beams?

*sees but
failure in all
done since,*

Worn now with gaps so large, there blew cold streams
Of air quite from the dungeon; lay your ear   985
Close and 't is like, one after one, you hear
In the blind darkness water drop. The nests
And nooks retain their long ranged vesture-chests
Empty and smelling of the iris root
The Tuscan grated o'er them to recruit   990
Her wasted wits. Palma was gone that day,
Said the remaining women. Last, he lay
Beside the Carian group reserved and still.
    The Body, the Machine for Acting Will,
Had been at the commencement proved unfit;   995
That for Demonstrating, Reflecting it,
Mankind—no fitter: was the Will Itself
In fault?

and resolves to
desist from
the like.
          His forehead pressed the moonlit shelf
Beside the youngest marble maid awhile;
Then, raising it, he thought, with a long smile,   1000
'I shall be king again!' as he withdrew
The envied scarf; into the font he threw
His crown.
        Next day, no poet! 'Wherefore?' asked
Taurello, when the dance of Jongleurs, masked
As devils, ended; 'don't a song come next?'   1005
The master of the pageant looked perplexed
Till Naddo's whisper came to his relief.
'His Highness knew what poets were: in brief,
'Had not the tetchy race prescriptive right
'To peevishness, caprice? or, call it spite,   1010
'One must receive their nature in its length
'And breadth, expect the weakness with the strength!'
—So phrasing, till, his stock of phrases spent,
The easy-natured soldier smiled assent,
Settled his portly person, smoothed his chin,   1015
And nodded that the bull-bait might begin.

BOOK THE THIRD

Nature may tri-
umph therefore;
AND the font took them: let our laurels lie!
Braid moonfern now with mystic trifoly

Because once more Goito gets, once more,
Sordello to itself! A dream is o'er,
And the suspended life begins anew;   5
Quiet those throbbing temples, then, subdue
That cheek's distortion! Nature's strict embrace,
Putting aside the past, shall soon efface
Its print as well—factitious humours grown
Over the true—loves, hatreds not his own—   10
And turn him pure as some forgotten vest
Woven of painted byssus, silkiest
Tufting the Tyrrhene whelk's pearl-sheeted lip,
Left welter where a trireme let it slip
I' the sea, and vexed a satrap; so the stain   15
O' the world forsakes Sordello, with its pain,
Its pleasure: how the tinct loosening escapes,
Cloud after cloud! Mantua's familiar shapes
Die, fair and foul die, fading as they flit,
Men, women, and the pathos and the wit,   20
Wise speech and foolish, deeds to smile or sigh
For, good, bad, seemly or ignoble, die.
The last face glances through the eglantines,
The last voice murmurs, 'twixt the blossomed   *for her son,*
    vines,   *lately alive,*
                                           dies again,
Of Men, of that machine supplied by thought   25
To compass self-perception with, he sought
By forcing half himself—an insane pulse
Of a god's blood, on clay it could convulse,
Never transmute—on human sights and sounds,
To watch the other half with; irksome bounds   30
It ebbs from to its source, a fountain sealed
Forever. Better sure be unrevealed
Than part revealed: Sordello well or ill
Is finished: then what further use of Will,
Point in the prime idea not realized,   35
An oversight? inordinately prized,
No less, and pampered with enough of each
Delight to prove the whole above its reach.
'To need become all natures, yet retain
'The law of my own nature—to remain   40
'Myself, yet yearn . . . as if that chestnut, think,

'Should yearn for this first larch-bloom crisp and
        pink,
'Or those pale fragrant tears where zephyrs stanch
'March wounds along the fretted pine-tree branch!
'Will and the means to show will, great and small,   45
'Material, spiritual,—abjure them all
'Save any so distinct, they may be left
'To amuse, not tempt become! and, thus bereft,
'Just as I first was fashioned would I be!
'Nor, moon, is it Apollo now, but me   50
'Thou visitest to comfort and befriend!
'Swim thou into my heart, and there an end,
'Since I possess thee!—nay, thus shut mine eyes
'And know, quite know, by this heart's fall and rise,
'When thou dost bury thee in clouds, and when   55
'Out-standest: wherefore practise upon men
'To make that plainer to myself?'
                                        Slide here
Over a sweet and solitary year
Wasted; or simply notice change in him—
How eyes, once with exploring bright, grew dim   60
And satiate with receiving. Some distress
Was caused, too, by a sort of consciousness
Under the imbecility,—nought kept
That down; he slept, but was aware he slept,
So, frustrated: as who brainsick made pact   65
Erst with the overhanging cataract
To deafen him, yet still distinguished plain
His own blood's measured clicking at his brain.
    To finish. One declining Autumn day—
Few birds about the heaven chill and grey,   70
No wind that cared trouble the tacit woods—
He sauntered home complacently, their moods
According, his and nature's. Every spark
Of Mantua life was trodden out; so dark
The embers, that the Troubadour, who sung   75
Hundreds of songs, forgot, its trick his tongue,
Its craft his brain, how either brought to pass
Singing at all; that faculty might class
With any of Apollo's now. The year

—was found
and is lost.

Began to find its early promise sere   80
As well. Thus beauty vanishes; thus stone
Outlingers flesh: nature's and his youth gone,
They left the world to you, and wished you joy.
When, stopping his benevolent employ,
A presage shuddered through the welkin; harsh   85
The earth's remonstrance followed. 'T was the marsh
Gone of a sudden. Mincio, in its place,
Laughed, a broad water, in next morning's face,
And, where the mists broke up immense and white
I' the steady wind, burned like a spilth of light   90
Out of the crashing of a myriad stars.
And here was nature, bound by the same bars
Of fate with him!
                          'No! youth once gone is gone: *But nature is
'Deeds, let escape, are never to be done.   one thing,
                                                             man another—*
'Leaf-fall and grass-spring for the year; for us—   95
'Oh forfeit I unalterably thus
'My chance? nor two lives wait me, this to spend,
'Learning save that? Nature has time, may mend
'Mistake, she knows occasion will recur;
'Landslip or seabreach, how affects it her   100
'With her magnificent resources?—I
'Must perish once and perish utterly.
'Not any strollings now at even-close
'Down the field-path, Sordello! by thorn-rows
'Alive with lamp-flies, swimming spots of fire   105
'And dew, outlining the black cypress' spire
'She waits you at, Elys, who heard you first
'Woo her, the snow-month through, but ere she durst
'Answer 't was April. Linden-flower-time-long   *having multi-*
'Her eyes were on the ground; 't is July, strong   110 *farious*
'Now; and because white dust-clouds overwhelm   *sympathies,*
'The woodside, here or by the village elm
'That holds the moon, she meets you, somewhat pale,
'But letting you lift up her coarse flax veil
'And whisper (the damp little hand in yours)   115
'Of love, heart's love, your heart's love that endures
'Till death. Tush! No mad mixing with the rout
'Of haggard ribalds wandering about

'The hot torchlit wine-scented island-house
'Where Friedrich holds his wickedest carouse,   120
'Parading,—to the gay Palermitans,
'Soft Messinese, dusk Saracenic clans
'Nuocera holds,—those tall grave dazzling Norse,
'High-cheeked, lank-haired, toothed whiter than the
          morse,
'Queens of the caves of jet stalactites,   125
'He sent his barks to fetch through icy seas,
'The blind night seas without a saving star,
'And here in snowy birdskin robes they are,
'Sordello!—here, mollitious alcoves gilt
'Superb as Byzant domes that devils built!   130
'—Ah, Byzant, there again! no chance to go
'Ever like august cheery Dandolo,
'Worshipping hearts about him for a wall,
'Conducted, blind eyes, hundred years and all,
'Through vanquished Byzant where friends note for
          him   135
'What pillar, marble massive, sardius slim,
' 'T were fittest he transport to Venice' Square—
'Flattered and promised life to touch them there
'Soon, by those fervid sons of senators!
'No more lifes, deaths, loves, hatreds, peaces, wars!   140
'Ah, fragments of a whole ordained to be,
'Points in the life I waited! what are ye
'But roundels of a ladder which appeared
'Awhile the very platform it was reared
'To lift me on?—that happiness I find   145
'Proofs of my faith in, even in the blind
'Instinct which bade forego you all unless
'Ye led me past yourselves. Ay, happiness
'Awaited me; the way life should be used
'Was to acquire, and deeds like you conduced   150
'To teach it by a self-revealment, deemed
he may neither
renounce nor
satisfy;
'Life's very use, so long! Whatever seemed
'Progress to that, was pleasure; aught that stayed
'My reaching it—no pleasure. I have laid
'The ladder down; I climb not; still, aloft   155
'The platform stretches! Blisses strong and soft,

'I dared not entertain, elude me; yet
'Never of what they promised could I get
'A glimpse till now! The common sort, the crowd,
'Exist, perceive; with Being are endowed,　　160
'However slight, distinct from what they See,
'However bounded; Happiness must be,
'To feed the first by gleanings from the last,
'Attain its qualities, and slow or fast
'Become what they behold; such peace-in-strife,　　165　in the process
'By transmutation, is the Use of Life,　　　　　　　to which is
'The Alien turning Native to the soul　　　　　　　pleasure,
'Or body—which instructs me; I am whole
'There and demand a Palma; had the world
'Been from my soul to a like distance hurled,　　170
' 'T were Happiness to make it one with me:
'Whereas I must, ere I begin to Be,
'Include a world, in flesh, I comprehend
'In spirit now; and this done, what's to blend
'With? Nought is Alien in the world—my Will　　175
'Owns all already; yet can turn it—still
'Less—Native, since my Means to correspond
'With Will are so unworthy, 't was my bond
'To tread the very joys that tantalize
'Most now, into a grave, never to rise.　　180
'I die then! Will the rest agree to die?
'Next Age or no? Shall its Sordello try
'Clue after clue, and catch at last the clue
'I miss?—that's underneath my finger too,
'Twice, thrice a day, perhaps,—some yearning traced　185
'Deeper, some petty consequence embraced
'Closer! Why fled I Mantua, then?—complained
'So much my Will was fettered, yet remained
'Content within a tether half the range
'I could assign it?—able to exchange　　190
'My ignorance (I felt) for knowledge, and
'Idle because I could thus understand—
'Could e'en have penetrated to its core
'Our mortal mystery, yet—fool—forbore,
'Preferred elaborating in the dark　　195　while renun-
'My casual stuff, by any wretched spark　　　ciation ensures
　　　　　　　　　　　　　　　　　　　　　　　despair.

'Born of my predecessors, though one stroke
'Of mine had brought the flame forth! Mantua's yoke,
'My minstrel's-trade, was to behold mankind,—
'My own concern was just to bring my mind   200
'Behold, just extricate, for my acquist,
'Each object suffered stifle in the mist
'Which hazard, custom, blindness interpose
'Betwixt things and myself.'
                                        Whereat he rose.
The level wind carried above the firs   205
Clouds, the irrevocable travellers,
Onward.
              'Pushed thus into a drowsy copse,
'Arms twine about my neck, each eyelid drops
'Under a humid finger; while there fleets,
'Outside the screen, a pageant time repeats   210
'Never again! To be deposed, immured
'Clandestinely—still petted, still assured
'To govern were fatiguing work—the Sight
'Fleeting meanwhile! 'T is noontide: wreak ere night
'Somehow my will upon it, rather! Slake   215
'This thirst somehow, the poorest impress take
'That serves! A blasted bud displays you, torn,
'Faint rudiments of the full flower unborn;
'But who divines what glory coats o'erclasp
'Of the bulb dormant in the mummy's grasp   220
'Taurello sent?' . . .

There is yet a
way of escap-
ing this;
                              'Taurello? Palma sent
'Your Trouvere,' (Naddo interposing leant
Over the lost bard's shoulder)—'and, believe,
'You cannot more reluctantly receive
'Than I pronounce her message: we depart   225
'Together. What avail a poet's heart
'Verona's pomps and gauds? five blades of grass
'Suffice him. News? Why, where your marish was,
'On its mud-banks smoke rises after smoke
'I' the valley, like a spout of hell new-broke.   230
'Oh, the world's tidings! small your thanks, I guess,
'For them. The father of our Patroness,
'Has played Taurello an astounding trick,

'Parts between Ecelin and Alberic
'His wealth and goes into a convent: both   235
'Wed Guelfs: the Count and Palma plighted troth
'A week since at Verona: and they want
'You doubtless to contrive the marriage-chant
'Ere Richard storms Ferrara.' Then was told
The tale from the beginning—how, made bold   240
By Salinguerra's absence, Guelfs had burned
And pillaged till he unawares returned
To take revenge: how Azzo and his friend
Were doing their endeavour, how the end
O' the siege was nigh, and how the Count, released   245
From further care, would with his marriage-feast
Inaugurate a new and better rule,
Absorbing thus Romano.
                              'Shall I school
'My master,' added Naddo, 'and suggest   which he now
'How you may clothe in a poetic vest   250   takes by obey-
'These doings, at Verona? Your response   ing Palma:
'To Palma! Wherefore jest? "Depart at once?"'
'A good resolve! In truth, I hardly hoped
'So prompt an acquiescence. Have you groped
'Out wisdom in the wilds here?—thoughts may be   255
'Over-poetical for poetry.
'Pearl-white, you poets liken Palma's neck;
'And yet what spoils an orient like some speck
'Of genuine white, turning its own white grey?
'You take me? Curse the cicala!'
                              One more day,   260
One eve—appears Verona! Many a group,
(You mind) instructed of the osprey's swoop
On lynx and ounce, was gathering—Christendom
Sure to receive, whate'er the end was, from
The evening's purpose cheer or detriment,   265
Since Friedrich only waited some event
Like this, of Ghibellins establishing
Themselves within Ferrara, ere, as King
Of Lombardy, he'd glad descend there, wage
Old warfare with the Pontiff, disengage   270
His barons from the burghers, and restore

The rule of Charlemagne, broken of yore
By Hildebrand.

            I' the palace, each by each,
Sordello sat and Palma: little speech
At first in that dim closet, face with face   275
(Despite the tumult in the market-place)

who there-
upon becomes
his associate,

Exchanging quick low laughters: now would rush
Word upon word to meet a sudden flush,
A look left off, a shifting lips' surmise—
But for the most part their two histories   280
Ran best thro' the locked fingers and linked arms.
And so the night flew on with its alarms
Till in burst one of Palma's retinue;
'Now, Lady!' gasped he. Then arose the two
And leaned into Verona's air, dead-still.   285
A balcony lay black beneath until
Out, 'mid a gush of torchfire, grey-haired men
Came on it and harangued the people: then
Sea-like that people surging to and fro
Shouted, 'Hale forth the carroch—trumpets, ho,   290
'A flourish! Run it in the ancient grooves!
'Back from the bell! Hammer—that whom behoves
'May hear the League is up! Peal—learn who list,
'Verona means not first of towns break tryst
'To-morrow with the League!'

                      Enough. Now turn—   295
Over the eastern cypresses: discern!
Is any beacon set a-glimmer?

                    Rang
The air with shouts that overpowered the clang
Of the incessant carroch, even: 'Haste—
'The candle's at the gateway! ere it waste,   300
'Each soldier stand beside it, armed to march
'With Tiso Sampier through the eastern arch!'
Ferrara's succoured, Palma!

                    Once again

as her own
history will
account for,

They sat together; some strange thing in train
To say, so difficult was Palma's place   305
In taking, with a coy fastidious grace
Like the bird's flutter ere it fix and feed.

But when she felt she held her friend indeed
Safe, she threw back her curls, began implant
Her lessons; telling of another want   310
Goito's quiet nourished than his own;
Palma—to serve him—to be served, alone
Importing; Agnes' milk so neutralized
The blood of Ecelin. Nor be surprised
If, while Sordello fain had captive led   315
Nature, in dream was Palma subjected
To some out-soul, which dawned not though she pined
Delaying, till its advent, heart and mind
Their life. 'How dared I let expand the force
'Within me, till some out-soul, whose resource   320
'It grew for, should direct it? Every law
'Of life, its every fitness, every flaw,
'Must One determine whose corporeal shape
'Would be no other than the prime escape
'And revelation to me of a Will   325
'Orb-like o'ershrouded and inscrutable
'Above, save at the point which, I should know,
'Shone that myself, my powers, might overflow
'So far, so much; as now it signified
'Which earthly shape it henceforth chose my guide,   330   —a reverse to,
'Whose mortal lip selected to declare   and comple-
'Its oracles, what fleshly garb would wear   tion of, his.
'—The first of intimations, whom to love;
'The next, how love him. Seemed that orb, above
'The castle-covert and the mountain-close,   335
'Slow in appearing?—if beneath it rose
'Cravings, aversions,—did our green precinct
'Take pride in me, at unawares distinct
'With this or that endowment,—how, repressed
'At once, such jetting power shrank to the rest!   340
'Was I to have a chance touch spoil me, leave
'My spirit thence unfitted to receive
'The consummating spell?—that spell so near
'Moreover! "Waits he not the waking year?
' "His almond-blossoms must be honey-ripe   345
' "By this; to welcome him, fresh runnels stripe
' "The thawed ravines; because of him, the wind

' "Walks like a herald. I shall surely find
' "Him now!"
                        'And chief, that earnest April morn
'Of Richard's Love-court, was it time, so worn   350
'And white my cheek, so idly my blood beat,
'Sitting that morn beside the Lady's feet
'And saying as she prompted; till outburst
'One face from all the faces. Not then first
'I knew it; where in maple chamber glooms,   355
'Crowned with what sanguine-heart pomegranate blooms,
'Advanced it ever? Men's acknowledgement
'Sanctioned my own: 't was taken, Palma's bent,—
'Sordello,—recognized, accepted.
                                    'Dumb

How she ever
aspired for his
sake,

'Sat she still scheming. Ecelin would come   360
'Gaunt, scared, "Cesano baffles me," he'd say:
' "Better I fought it out, my father's way!
' "Strangle Ferrara in its drowning flats,
' "And you and your Taurello yonder!—what's
' "Romano's business there?" An hour's concern   365
'To cure the froward Chief!—induce return
'As heartened from those overmeaning eyes,
'Wound up to persevere,—his enterprise
'Marked out anew, its exigent of wit
'Apportioned,—she at liberty to sit   370
'And scheme against the next emergence, I—
'To covet her Taurello-sprite, made fly
'Or fold the wing—to con your horoscope
'For leave command those steely shafts shoot ope,
'Or straight assuage their blinding eagerness   375
'In blank smooth snow. What semblance of success
'To any of my plans for making you
'Mine and Romano's? Break the first wall through,
'Tread o'er the ruins of the Chief, supplant
'His sons beside, still, vainest were the vaunt: 380
'There, Salinguerra would obstruct me sheer,
'And the insuperable Tuscan, here,
'Stay me! But one wild eve that Lady died
'In her lone chamber: only I beside:
'Taurello far at Naples, and my sire   385

'At Padua, Ecelin away in ire

circumstances
helping or
hindering.

'With Alberic. She held me thus—a clutch
'To make our spirits as our bodies touch—
'And so began flinging the past up, heaps
'Of uncouth treasure from their sunless sleeps 390
'Within her soul; deeds rose along with dreams,
'Fragments of many miserable schemes,
'Secrets, more secrets, then—no, not the last—
' 'Mongst others, like a casual trick o' the past,
'How . . . ay, she told me, gathering up her face, 395
'All left of it, into one arch-grimace
'To die with . . .
     'Friend, 't is gone! but not the fear
'Of that fell laughing, heard as now I hear.
'Nor faltered voice, nor seemed her heart grow weak
'When i' the midst abrupt she ceased to speak 400
'—Dead, as to serve a purpose, mark!—for in
'Rushed o' the very instant Ecelin
'(How summoned, who divines?)—looking as if
'He understood why Adelaide lay stiff
'Already in my arms; for "Girl, how must 405
' "I manage Este in the matter thrust
' "Upon me, how unravel your bad coil?—
' "Since" (he declared) " 't is on your brow—a soil
' "Like hers there!" then in the same breath, "he lacked
' "No counsel after all, had signed no pact 410
' "With devils, nor was treason here or there,
' "Goito or Vicenza, his affair:
' "He buried it in Adelaide's deep grave,
' "Would begin life afresh, now,—would not slave
' "For any Friedrich's nor Taurello's sake! 415
' "What booted him to meddle or to make
' "In Lombardy?" And afterward I knew
'The meaning of his promise to undo
'All she had done—why marriages were made,
'New friendships entered on, old followers paid 420
'With curses for their pains,—new friends' amaze
'At height, when, passing out by Gate Saint Blaise,
'He stopped short in Vicenza, bent his head
'Over a friar's neck,—"had vowed," he said,

' "Long since, nigh thirty years, because his wife   425
' "And child were saved there, to bestow his life
' "On God, his gettings on the Church."

'Exiled

'Within Goito, still one dream beguiled
'My days and nights; 't was found, the orb I sought
'To serve, those glimpses came of Fomalhaut,   430
'No other: but how serve it?—authorize
'You and Romano mingle destinies?
'And straight Romano's angel stood beside
'Me who had else been Boniface's bride,

'For Salinguerra 't was, with neck low bent,   435
'And voice lightened to music, (as he meant
'To learn, not teach me,) who withdrew the pall
'From the dead past and straight revived it all,
'Making me see how first Romano waxed,
'Wherefore he waned now, why, if I relaxed   440
'My grasp (even I!) would drop a thing effete,
'Frayed by itself, unequal to complete
'Its course, and counting every step astray
'A gain so much. Romano, every way
'Stable, a Lombard House now—why start back   445
'Into the very outset of its track?
'This patching principle which late allied
'Our House with other Houses—what beside
'Concerned the apparition, the first Knight
'Who followed Conrad hither in such plight   450
'His utmost wealth was summed in his one steed?
'For Ecelo, that prowler, was decreed
'A task, in the beginning hazardous
'To him as ever task can be to us;
'But did the weather-beaten thief despair   455
'When first our crystal cincture of warm air
'That binds the Trevisan,—as its spice-belt
'(Crusaders say) the tract where Jesus dwelt,—
'Furtive he pierced, and Este was to face—
'Despaired Saponian strength of Lombard grace?   460
'Tried he at making surer aught made sure,
'Maturing what already was mature?
'No; his heart prompted Ecelo, "Confront

' "Este, inspect yourself. What's nature? Wont.
' "Discard three-parts your nature, and adopt　　　465
' "The rest as an advantage!" Old strength propped
'The man who first grew Podestà among
'The Vicentines, no less than, while there sprung
'His palace up in Padua like a threat,
'Their noblest spied a grace, unnoticed yet　　　470
'In Conrad's crew. Thus far the object gained,
'Romano was established—has remained—
' "For are you not Italian, truly peers
' "With Este? *Azzo* better soothes our ears
' "Than *Alberic*? or is this lion's-crine　　　475
' "From over-mounts" (this yellow hair of mine)
' "So weak a graft on Agnes Este's stock?"
'(Thus went he on with something of a mock)
' "Wherefore recoil, then, from the very fate
' "Conceded you, refuse to imitate　　　480
' "Your model farther? Este long since left

who remedied
ill wrought by
Ecelin,

' "Being mere Este: as a blade its heft,
' "Este required the Pope to further him:
' "And you, the Kaiser—whom your father's whim
' "Foregoes or, better, never shall forego　　　485
' "If Palma dare pursue what Ecelo
' "Commenced, but Ecelin desists from: just
' "As Adelaide of Susa could intrust
' "Her donative,—her Piedmont given the Pope,
' "Her Alpine-pass for him to shut or ope　　　490
' " 'Twixt France and Italy,—to the superb
' "Matilda's perfecting,—so, lest aught curb
' "Our Adelaide's great counter-project for
' "Giving her Trentine to the Emperor
' "With passage here from Germany,—shall you　　　495
' "Take it,—my slender plodding talent, too!"
'—Urged me Taurello with his half-smile.
　　　　　　　　　　　　　　　　　'He
'As Patron of the scattered family
'Conveyed me to his Mantua, kept in bruit

and had a
project for her
own glory,

'Azzo's alliances and Richard's suit　　　500
'Until, the Kaiser excommunicate,
' "Nothing remains," Taurello said, "but wait

' "Some rash procedure: Palma was the link,
' "As Agnes' child, between us, and they shrink
' "From losing Palma: judge if we advance,   505
' "Your father's method, your inheritance!"
'The day I was betrothed to Boniface
'At Padua by Taurello's self, took place
'The outrage of the Ferrarese: again,
'The day I sought Verona with the train   510
'Agreed for,—by Taurello's policy
'Convicting Richard of the fault, since we
'Were present to annul or to confirm,—
'Richard, whose patience had outstayed its term,
'Quitted Verona for the siege.

which she
would change
to Sordello's.

                       'And now   515
'What glory may engird Sordello's brow
'Through this? A month since at Oliero slunk
'All that was Ecelin into a monk;
'But how could Salinguerra so forget
'His liege of thirty years as grudge even yet   520
'One effort to recover him? He sent
'Forthwith the tidings of this last event
'To Ecelin—declared that he, despite
'The recent folly, recognized his right
'To order Salinguerra: "Should he wring   525
' "Its uttermost advantage out, or fling
' "This chance away? Or were his sons now Head
' "O' the House?" Through me Taurello's missive sped;
'My father's answer will by me return.
'Behold! "For him," he writes, "no more concern   530
' "With strife than, for his children, with fresh plots
' "Of Friedrich. Old engagements out he blots
' "For aye: Taurello shall no more subserve,
' "Nor Ecelin impose." Lest this unnerve
'Taurello at this juncture, slack his grip   535
'Of Richard, suffer the occasion slip,—
'I, in his sons' default (who, mating with
'Este, forsake Romano as the frith
'Its mainsea for that firmland, sea makes head
'Against) I stand, Romano,—in their stead   540
'Assume the station they desert, and give

'Still, as the Kaiser's representative,
'Taurello licence he demands. Midnight—
'Morning—by noon to-morrow, making light
'Of the League's issue, we, in some gay weed   545
'Like yours, disguised together, may precede
'The arbitrators to Ferrara: reach
'Him, let Taurello's noble accents teach
'The rest! Then say if I have misconceived
'Your destiny, too readily believed   550
'The Kaiser's cause your own!'
                              And Palma's fled.
Though no affirmative disturbs the head,
A dying lamp-flame sinks and rises o'er,
Like the alighted planet Pollux wore,
Until, morn breaking, he resolves to be   555
Gate-vein of this heart's blood of Lombardy,
Soul of this body—to wield this aggregate
Of souls and bodies, and so conquer fate
Though he should live—a centre of disgust
Even—apart, core of the outward crust   560
He vivifies, assimilates. For thus
I bring Sordello to the rapturous
Exclaim at the crowd's cry, because one round
Of life was quite accomplished; and he found
Not only that a soul, whate'er its might,   565
Is insufficient to its own delight,
Both in corporeal organs and in skill
By means of such to body forth its Will—
And, after, insufficient to apprise
Men of that Will, oblige them recognize   570
The Hid by the Revealed—but that,—the last
Nor lightest of the struggles overpast,—
Will, he bade abdicate, which would not void
The throne, might sit there, suffer he enjoyed
Mankind, a varied and divine array   575
Incapable of homage, the first way,
Nor fit to render incidentally
Tribute connived at, taken by the by,
In joys. If thus with warrant to rescind
The ignominious exile of mankind—   580

Thus then, having completed a circle,

Whose proper service, ascertained intact
As yet, (to be by him themselves made act,
Not watch Sordello acting each of them)
Was to secure—if the true diadem
Seemed imminent while our Sordello drank   585
The wisdom of that golden Palma,—thank
Verona's Lady in her citadel
Founded by Gaulish Brennus, legends tell:
And truly when she left him, the sun reared
A head like the first clamberer's who peered   590
A-top the Capitol, his face on flame
With triumph, triumphing till Manlius came,
Nor slight too much my rhymes—that spring, dispread,
Dispart, disperse, lingering over head
Like an escape of angels! Rather say,   595
My transcendental platan! mounting gay
(An archimage so courts a novice-queen)
With tremulous silvered trunk, whence branches sheen
Laugh out, thick-foliaged next, a-shiver soon
With coloured buds, then glowing like the moon   600

the poet may pause and breathe,

One mild flame,—last a pause, a burst, and all
Her ivory limbs are smothered by a fall,
Bloom-flinders and fruit-sparkles and leaf-dust,
Ending the weird work prosecuted just
For her amusement; he decrepit, stark,   605
Dozes; her uncontrolled delight may mark
Apart—
              Yet not so, surely never so
Only, as good my soul were suffered go
O'er the lagune: forth fare thee, put aside—
Entrance thy synod, as a god may glide   610
Out of the world he fills, and leave it mute
For myriad ages as we men compute,
Returning into it without a break
O' the consciousness! They sleep, and I awake

being really in the flesh at Venice,

O'er the lagune, being at Venice.
                                   Note,   615
In just such songs as Eglamor (say) wrote
With heart and soul and strength, for he believed
Himself achieving all to be achieved

By, singer—in such songs you find alone
Completeness, judge the song and singer one,   620
And either purpose answered, his in it
Or its in him: while from true works (to wit
Sordello's dream-performances that will
Never be more than dreamed) escapes there still
Some proof, the singer's proper life was 'neath   625
The life his song exhibits, this a sheath
To that; a passion and a knowledge far
Transcending these, majestic as they are,
Smouldered; his lay was but an episode
In the bard's life: which evidence you owed   630
To some slight weariness, some looking-off
Or start-away. The childish skit or scoff
In 'Charlemagne,' (his poem, dreamed divine
In every point except one silly line
About the restiff daughters)—what may lurk   635
In that? 'My life commenced before this work,'
(So I interpret the significance
Of the bard's start aside and look askance)
'My life continues after: on I fare
'With no more stopping, possibly, no care   640   and watching
'To note the undercurrent, the why and how,   his own life
'Where, when, o' the deeper life, as thus just now.   sometimes,
'But, silent, shall I cease to live? Alas
'For you! who sigh, "When shall it come to pass
' "We read that story? How will he compress   645
' "The future gains, his life's true business,
' "Into the better lay which—that one flout,
' "Howe'er inopportune it be, lets out—
' "Engrosses him already, though professed
' "To meditate with us eternal rest,   650
' "And partnership in all his life has found?" '
'T is but a sailor's promise, weather-bound:
'Strike sail, slip cable, here the bark be moored
'For once, the awning stretched, the poles assured!
'Noontide above; except the wave's crisp dash,   655
'Or buzz of colibri, or tortoise' splash,
'The margin's silent: out with every spoil
'Made in our tracking, coil by mighty coil,

I

'This serpent of a river to his head
'I' the midst! Admire each treasure, as we spread   660
'The bank, to help us tell our history
'Aright: give ear, endeavour to descry
'The groves of giant rushes, how they grew
'Like demons' endlong tresses we sailed through,
'What mountains yawned, forests to give us vent   665
'Opened, each doleful side, yet on we went
'Till . . . may that beetle (shake your cap) attest
'The springing of a land-wind from the West!'
          —Wherefore? Ah yes, you frolic it to-day!
To-morrow, and, the pageant moved away   670
Down to the poorest tent-pole, we and you
Part company: no other may pursue
Eastward your voyage, be informed what fate
Intends, if triumph or decline await
The tempter of the everlasting steppe.   675
          I muse this on a ruined palace-step
At Venice: why should I break off, nor sit
Longer upon my step, exhaust the fit
England gave birth to? Who's adorable
Enough reclaim a —— no Sordello's Will   680
Alack!—be queen to me? That Bassanese
Busied among her smoking fruit-boats? These
Perhaps from our delicious Asolo
Who twinkle, pigeons o'er the portico
Not prettier, bind June lilies into sheaves   685
To deck the bridge-side chapel, dropping leaves
Soiled by their own loose gold-meal? Ah, beneath
The cool arch stoops she, brownest cheek! Her wreath
Endures a month—a half-month—if I make
A queen of her, continue for her sake   690
Sordello's story? Nay, that Paduan girl
Splashes with barer legs where a live whirl
In the dead black Giudecca proves sea-weed
Drifting has sucked down three, four, all indeed
Save one pale-red striped, pale-blue turbaned post   695
For gondolas.
          You sad dishevelled ghost
That pluck at me and point, are you advised

because it is
pleasant to be
young,

I breathe? Let stay those girls (e'en her disguised
—Jewels i' the locks that love no crownet like
Their native field-buds and the green wheat-spike,   700
So fair!—who left this end of June's turmoil,
Shook off, as might a lily its gold soil,
Pomp, save a foolish gem or two, and free
In dream, came join the peasants o'er the sea.)
Look they too happy, too tricked out? Confess   705
There is such niggard stock of happiness
To share, that, do one's uttermost, dear wretch,
One labours ineffectually to stretch
It o'er you so that mother and children, both
May equitably flaunt the sumpter-cloth!   710
Divide the robe yet farther: be content
With seeing just a score pre-eminent
Through shreds of it, acknowledged happy wights,
Engrossing what should furnish all, by rights!
For, these in evidence, you clearlier claim   715
A like garb for the rest,—grace all, the same
As these my peasants. I ask youth and strength
And health for each of you, not more—at length
Grown wise, who asked at home that the whole race
Might add the spirit's to the body's grace,   720
And all be dizened out as chiefs and bards.
But in this magic weather one discards
Much old requirement. Venice seems a type
Of Life—'twixt blue and blue extends, a stripe,
As Life, the somewhat, hangs 'twixt nought and
        nought: 725
'T is Venice, and 't is Life—as good you sought
To spare me the Piazza's slippery stone
Or keep me to the unchoked canals alone,
As hinder Life the evil with the good
Which make up Living, rightly understood.   730
Only, do finish something! Peasants, queens,
Take them, made happy by whatever means,
Parade them for the common credit, vouch
That a luckless residue, we send to crouch
In corners out of sight, was just as framed   735
For happiness, its portion might have claimed

705 would but
suffering
humanity
allow!

—which
instigates to
tasks like this,

As well, and so, obtaining joy, had stalked
Fastuous as any!—such my project, baulked
Already; I hardly venture to adjust
The first rags, when you find me. To mistrust   740
Me!—nor unreasonably. You, no doubt,
Have the true knack of tiring suitors out
With those thin lips on tremble, lashless eyes
Inveterately tear-shot: there, be wise,
Mistress of mine, there, there, as if I meant   745
You insult!—shall your friend (not slave) be shent
For speaking home? Beside, care-bit erased
Broken-up beauties ever took my taste
Supremely; and I love you more, far more
Than her I looked should foot Life's temple-floor.   750
Years ago, leagues at distance, when and where
A whisper came, 'Let others seek!—thy care
'Is found, thy life's provision; if thy race
'Should be thy mistress, and into one face
'The many faces crowd?' Ah, had I, judge,   755
Or no, your secret? Rough apparel—grudge
All ornaments save tag or tassel worn
To hint we are not thoroughly forlorn—
Slouch bonnet, unloop mantle, careless go
Alone (that's saddest, but it must be so)   760
Through Venice, sing now and now glance aside,
Aught desultory or undignified,—
Then, ravishingest lady, will you pass
Or not each formidable group, the mass
Before the Basilic (that feast gone by,   765
God's great day of the Corpus Domini)
And, wistfully foregoing proper men,
Come timid up to me for alms? And then
The luxury to hesitate, feign do
Some unexampled grace!—when, whom but you   770
Dare I bestow your own upon? And hear
Further before you say, it is to sneer
I call you ravishing; for I regret
Little that she, whose early foot was set
Forth as she'd plant it on a pedestal,   775
Now, i' the silent city, seems to fall

and doubt-
lessly compen-
sates them,

Toward me—no wreath, only a lip's unrest
To quiet, surcharged eyelids to be pressed
Dry of their tears upon my bosom. Strange
Such sad chance should produce in thee such change, 780
My love! Warped souls and bodies! yet God spoke
Of right-hand, foot and eye—selects our yoke,
Sordello, as your poetship may find!
So, sleep upon my shoulder, child, nor mind
Their foolish talk; we'll manage reinstate   785
Your old worth; ask moreover, when they prate
Of evil men past hope, 'Don't each contrive,
'Despite the evil you abuse, to live?—
'Keeping, each losel, through a maze of lies,
'His own conceit of truth? to which he hies   790
'By obscure windings, tortuous, if you will,
'But to himself not inaccessible;
'He sees truth, and his lies are for the crowd
'Who cannot see; some fancied right allowed
'His vilest wrong, empowered the losel clutch   795
'One pleasure from a multitude of such
'Denied him.' Then assert, 'All men appear
'To think all better than themselves, by here
'Trusting a crowd they wrong; but really,' say,
'All men think all men stupider than they,   800
'Since, save themselves, no other comprehends
'The complicated scheme to make amends
'—Evil, the scheme by which, thro' Ignorance,
'Good labours to exist.' A slight advance,—
Merely to find the sickness you die through,   805
And nought beside! but if one can't eschew
One's portion in the common lot, at least
One can avoid an ignorance increased
Tenfold by dealing out hint after hint
How nought were like dispensing without stint   810
The water of life—so easy to dispense
Beside, when one has probed the centre whence
Commotion's born—could tell you of it all!
'—Meantime, just meditate my madrigal
'O' the mugwort that conceals a dewdrop safe!'   815
What, dullard? we and you in smothery chafe,

as those who
desist should
remember.

Let the poet
take his own
part, then,

Babes, baldheads, stumbled thus far into Zin
The Horrid, getting neither out nor in,
A hungry sun above us, sands that bung
Our throats,—each dromedary lolls a tongue,   820
Each camel churns a sick and frothy chap,
And you, 'twixt tales of Potiphar's mishap,
And sonnets on the earliest ass that spoke,
—Remark, you wonder any one needs choke
With founts about! Potsherd him, Gibeonites!   825
While awkwardly enough your Moses smites
The rock, though he forego his Promised Land
Thereby, have Satan claim his carcass, and
Figure as Metaphysic Poet . . . ah,
Mark ye the dim first oozings? Meribah!   830
Then, quaffing at the fount my courage gained,
Recall—not that I prompt ye—who explained . . .
     'Presumptuous!' interrupts one. You, not I
'T is brother, marvel at and magnify
Such office: 'office,' quotha? can we get   835
To the beginning of the office yet?
What do we here? simply experiment
Each on the other's power and its intent
When elsewhere tasked,—if this of mine were trucked
For yours to either's good,—we watch construct,   840
In short, an engine: with a finished one,
What it can do, is all,—nought, how 't is done.
But this of ours yet in probation, dusk
A kernel of strange wheelwork through its husk
Grows into shape by quarters and by halves;   845
Remark this tooth's spring, wonder what that valve's
Fall bodes, presume each faculty's device,
Make out each other more or less precise—
The scope of the whole engine's to be proved;
We die: which means to say, the whole's removed,   850
Dismounted wheel by wheel, this complex gin,—
To be set up anew elsewhere, begin
A task indeed, but with a clearer clime
Than the murk lodgment of our building-time.
And then, I grant you, it behoves forget   855
How 't is done—all that must amuse us yet

should any
object that he
was dull

So long: and, while you turn upon your heel,
Pray that I be not busy slitting steel
Or shredding brass, camped on some virgin shore
Under a cluster of fresh stars, before   860
I name a tithe o' the wheels I trust to do!
  So occupied, then, are we: hitherto,
At present, and a weary while to come,
The office of ourselves,—nor blind nor dumb,
And seeing somewhat of man's state,—has been,   865
For the worst of us, to say they so have seen;
For the better, what it was they saw; the best
Impart the gift of seeing to the rest:
'So that I glance,' says such an one, 'around,
'And there's no face but I can read profound   870
'Disclosures in; this stands for hope, that—fear,   *beside his*
'And for a speech, a deed in proof, look here!   *sprightlier*
' "Stoop, else the strings of blossom, where the nuts   *predecessors.*
' "O'erarch, will blind thee! Said I not? She shuts
' "Both eyes this time, so close the hazels meet!   875
' "Thus, prisoned in the Piombi, I repeat
' "Events one rove occasioned, o'er and o'er,
' "Putting 'twixt me and madness evermore
' "Thy sweet shape, Zanze! Therefore stoop!"
                            ' "That's truth!"   880
'(Adjudge you) "the incarcerated youth
' "Would say that!"
                    'Youth? Plara the bard? Set down
'That Plara spent his youth in a grim town
'Whose cramped ill-featured streets huddled about
'The minster for protection, never out   885
'Of its black belfry's shade and its bells' roar.
'The brighter shone the suburb,—all the more
'Ugly and absolute that shade's reproof
'Of any chance escape of joy,—some roof,
'Taller than they, allowed the rest detect,—   890
'Before the sole permitted laugh (suspect
'Who could, 't was meant for laughter, that ploughed cheek's
'Repulsive gleam!) when the sun stopped both peaks
'Of the cleft belfry like a fiery wedge,
'Then sank, a huge flame on its socket edge,   895

'With leavings on the grey glass oriel-pane
'Ghastly some minutes more. No fear of rain—
'The minster minded that! in heaps the dust
'Lay everywhere. This town, the minster's trust,
'Held Plara; who, its denizen, bade hail   900
'In twice twelve sonnets, Tempe's dewy vale.'
    ' "Exact the town, the minster and the street!" '
    'As all mirth triumphs, sadness means defeat:
'Lust triumphs and is gay, Love's triumphed o'er
'And sad: but Lucio's sad. I said before,   905
'Love's sad, not Lucio; one who loves may be
'As gay his love has leave to hope, as he
'Downcast that lusts' desire escapes the springe:
' 'T is of the mood itself I speak, what tinge
'Determines it, else colourless,—or mirth,   910
'Or melancholy, as from heaven or earth.'
    ' "Ay, that's the variation's gist!"
                        'Indeed?
'Thus far advanced in safety then, proceed!
'And having seen too what I saw, be bold
'And next encounter what I do behold   915
'(That's sure) but bid you take on trust!'
                              Attack

One ought not blame but praise this; The use and purpose of such sights! Alack,
Not so unwisely does the crowd dispense
On Salinguerras praise in preference
To the Sordellos: men of action, these!   920
Who, seeing just as little as you please,
Yet turn that little to account,—engage
With, do not gaze at,—carry on, a stage,
The work o' the world, not merely make report
The work existed ere their day! In short,   925
at all events, his own audience may: When at some future no-time a brave band
Sees, using what it sees, then shake my hand
In heaven, my brother! Meanwhile where's the hurt
Of keeping the Makers-see on the alert,
At whose defection mortals stare aghast   930
As though heaven's bounteous windows were slammed fast
Incontinent? Whereas all you, beneath,
Should scowl at, bruise their lips and break their teeth

Who ply the pullies, for neglecting you:
And therefore have I moulded, made anew   935
A Man, and give him to be turned and tried,
Be angry with or pleased at. On your side,
Have ye times, places, actors of your own?
Try them upon Sordello when full-grown,
And then—ah then! If Hercules first parched   940
His foot in Egypt only to be marched
A sacrifice for Jove with pomp to suit,
What chance have I? The demigod was mute
Till, at the altar, where time out of mind
Such guests became oblations, chaplets twined   945
His forehead long enough, and he began
Slaying the slayers, nor escaped a man.
Take not affront, my gentle audience! whom
No Hercules shall make his hecatomb,
Believe, nor from his brows your chaplet rend—   950
That's your kind suffrage, yours, my patron-friend,
Whose great verse blares unintermittent on
Like your own trumpeter at Marathon,—
You who, Platæa and Salamis being scant,
Put up with Ætna for a stimulant—   955   *what if things brighten, who knows?*
And did well, I acknowledged, as he loomed
Over the midland sea last month, presumed
Long, lay demolished in the blazing West
At eve, while towards him tilting cloudlets pressed
Like Persian ships at Salamis. Friend, wear   960
A crest proud as desert while I declare
Had I a flawless ruby fit to wring
Tears of its colour from that painted king
Who lost it, I would, for that smile which went
To my heart, fling it in the sea, content,   965
Wearing your verse in place, an amulet
Sovereign against all passion, wear and fret!
My English Eyebright, if you are not glad
That, as I stopped my task awhile, the sad
Dishevelled form, wherein I put mankind   970
To come at times and keep my pact in mind,
Renewed me,—hear no crickets in the hedge,
Nor let a glowworm spot the river's edge

At home, and may the summer showers gush
Without a warning from the missel thrush!   975
So, to our business, now—the fate of such
As find our common nature—overmuch
Despised because restricted and unfit
To bear the burthen they impose on it—
Cling when they would discard it; craving strength   980
To leap from the allotted world, at length
They do leap,—flounder on without a term,
Each a god's germ, doomed to remain a germ
In unexpanded infancy, unless . . .
But that's the story—dull enough, confess!   985
There might be fitter subjects to allure;
Still, neither misconceive my portraiture
Nor undervalue its adornments quaint:
What seems a fiend perchance may prove a saint.

Whereupon,
with a story to
the point,

Ponder a story ancient pens transmit,   990
Then say if you condemn me or acquit.
   John the Beloved, banished Antioch
For Patmos, bade collectively his flock
Farewell, but set apart the closing eve
To comfort those his exile most would grieve,   995
He knew: a touching spectacle, that house
In motion to receive him! Xanthus' spouse
You missed, made panther's meat a month since; but
Xanthus himself (his nephew 't was, they shut
'Twixt boards and sawed asunder) Polycarp,   1000
Soft Charicle, next year no wheel could warp
To swear by Cæsar's fortune, with the rest
Were ranged; thro' whom the grey disciple pressed,
Busily blessing right and left, just stopped
To pat one infant's curls, the hangman cropped   1005
Soon after, reached the portal. On its hinge
The door turns and he enters: what quick twinge
Ruins the smiling mouth, those wide eyes fix
Whereon, why like some spectral candlestick's
Branch the disciple's arms? Dead swooned he, woke   1010
Anon, heaved sigh, made shift to gasp, heart-broke,
'Get thee behind me, Satan! Have I toiled
'To no more purpose? Is the gospel foiled

'Here too, and o'er my son's, my Xanthus' hearth,
'Portrayed with sooty garb and features swarth—   1015
'Ah Xanthus, am I to thy roof beguiled
'To see the—the—the Devil domiciled?'
Whereto sobbed Xanthus, 'Father, 't is yourself
'Installed, a limning which our utmost pelf
'Went to procure against to-morrow's loss;   1020
'And that's no twy-prong, but a pastoral cross,
'You're painted with!'
                              His puckered brows unfold—   *he takes up the*
And you shall hear Sordello's story told.   *thread of*
                                                                  discourse.

BOOK THE FOURTH

MEANTIME Ferrara lay in rueful case;   *Men suffered*
The lady-city, for whose sole embrace   *much,*
Her pair of suitors struggled, felt their arms
A brawny mischief to the fragile charms
They tugged for—one discovering that to twist   5
Her tresses twice or thrice about his wrist
Secured a point of vantage—one, how best
He'd parry that by planting in her breast
His elbow spike—each party too intent
For noticing, howe'er the battle went,   10
The conqueror would but have a corpse to kiss.
'May Boniface be duly damned for this!'
—Howled some old Ghibellin, as up he turned,
From the wet heap of rubbish where they burned
His house, a little skull with dazzling teeth: 15
'A boon, sweet Christ—let Salinguerra seethe
'In hell for ever, Christ, and let myself
'Be there to laugh at him!'—moaned some young
          Guelf
Stumbling upon a shrivelled hand nailed fast
To the charred lintel of the doorway, last   20
His father stood within to bid him speed.
The thoroughfares were overrun with weed
—Docks, quitchgrass, loathy mallows no man plants.

whichever of
the parties was
victor.

The stranger, none of its inhabitants
Crept out of doors to taste fresh air again,   25
And ask the purpose of a splendid train
Admitted on a morning; every town
Of the East League was come by envoy down
To treat for Richard's ransom: here you saw
The Vicentine, here snowy oxen draw   30
The Paduan carroch, its vermilion cross
On its white field. A-tiptoe o'er the fosse
Looked Legate Montelungo wistfully
After the flock of steeples he might spy
In Este's time, gone (doubts he) long ago   35
To mend the ramparts: sure the laggards know
The Pope's as good as here! They paced the streets
More soberly. At last, 'Taurello greets
'The League,' announced a pursuivant,—'will match
'Its courtesy, and labours to dispatch   40
'At earliest Tito, Friedrich's Pretor, sent
'On pressing matters from his post at Trent,
'With Mainard Count of Tyrol,—simply waits
'Their going to receive the delegates.'
'Tito!' Our delegates exchanged a glance,   45
And, keeping the main way, admired askance
The lazy engines of outlandish birth,
Couched like a king each on its bank of earth—
Arbalist, manganel and catapult;
While stationed by, as waiting a result,   50
Lean silent gangs of mercenaries ceased
Working to watch the strangers. 'This, at least,

How Guelfs
criticize
Ghibellin
work

'Were better spared; he scarce presumes gainsay
'The League's decision! Get our friend away
'And profit for the future: how else teach   55
'Fools 't is not safe to stray within claw's reach
'Ere Salinguerra's final gasp be blown?
'Those mere convulsive scratches find the bone.
'Who bade him bloody the spent osprey's nare?'
The carrochs halted in the public square.   60
Pennons of every blazon once a-flaunt,
Men prattled, freelier that the crested gaunt
White ostrich with a horse-shoe in her beak

Was missing, and whoever chose might speak
'Ecelin' boldly out: so,—'Ecelin   65
'Needed his wife to swallow half the sin
'And sickens by himself: the devil's whelp,
'He styles his son, dwindles away, no help
'From conserves, your fine triple-curded froth
'Of virgin's blood, your Venice viper-broth—   70
'Eh? Jubilate!'—'Peace! no little word
'You utter here that's not distinctly heard
'Up at Oliero: he was absent sick
'When we besieged Bassano—who, i' the thick
'O' the work, perceived the progress Azzo made,   75
'Like Ecelin, through his witch Adelaide?
'She managed it so well that, night by night
'At their bed-foot stood up a soldier-sprite,
'First fresh, pale by-and-by without a wound,
'And, when it came with eyes filmed as in swound,   80
'They knew the place was taken.'—'Ominous
'That Ghibellins should get what cautelous   as unusually
'Old Redbeard sought from Azzo's sire to wrench   energetic in
'Vainly; Saint George contrived his town a trench   this case.
'O' the marshes, an impermeable bar.'   85
'—Young Ecelin is meant the tutelar
'Of Padua, rather; veins embrace upon
'His hand like Brenta and Bacchiglion.'
What now?—'The founts! God's bread, touch not a
        plank!
'A crawling hell of carrion—every tank   90
'Choke-full!—found out just now to Cino's cost—
'The same who gave Taurello up for lost,
'And, making no account of fortune's freaks,
'Refused to budge from Padua then, but sneaks
'Back now with Concorezzi: 'faith! they drag   95
'Their carroch to San Vitale, plant the flag
'On his own palace, so adroitly razed
'He knew it not; a sort of Guelf folk gazed
'And laughed apart; Cino disliked their air—
'Must pluck up spirit, show he does not care—   100
'Seats himself on the tank's edge—will begin
'To hum, *za, za, Cavaler Ecelin*—

'A silence; he gets warmer, clinks to chime,
'Now both feet plough the ground, deeper each time,
'At last, *za*, *za* and up with a fierce kick   105
'Comes his own mother's face caught by the thick
'Grey hair about his spur!'
                              Which means, they lift
The covering, Salinguerra made a shift
To stretch upon the truth; as well avoid
Further disclosures; leave them thus employed.   110
Our dropping Autumn morning clears apace,
And poor Ferrara puts a softened face

How, passing
through the
rare garden,

On her misfortunes. Let us scale this tall
Huge foursquare line of red brick garden-wall
Bastioned within by trees of every sort   115
On three sides, slender, spreading, long and short;
Each grew as it contrived, the poplar ramped,
The fig-tree reared itself,—but stark and cramped,
Made fools of, like tamed lions: whence, on the edge,
Running 'twixt trunk and trunk to smooth one ledge   120
Of shade, were shrubs inserted, warp and woof,
Which smothered up that variance. Scale the roof
Of solid tops, and o'er the slope you slide
Down to a grassy space level and wide,
Here and there dotted with a tree, but trees   125
Of rarer leaf, each foreigner at ease,
Set by itself: and in the centre spreads,
Borne upon three uneasy leopards' heads,
A laver, broad and shallow, one bright spirt
Of water bubbles in. The walls begirt   130
With trees leave off on either hand; pursue
Your path along a wondrous avenue
Those walls abut on, heaped of gleamy stone,
With aloes leering everywhere, grey-grown
From many a Moorish summer: how they wind   135
Out of the fissures! likelier to bind
The building than those rusted cramps which drop

Salinguerra
contrived for a
purpose,

Already in the eating sunshine. Stop,
You fleeting shapes above there! Ah, the pride
Or else despair of the whole country-side!   140
A range of statues, swarming o'er with wasps,

God, goddess, woman, man, the Greek rough-rasps
In crumbling Naples marble—meant to look
Like those Messina marbles Constance took
Delight in, or Taurello's self conveyed   145
To Mantua for his mistress, Adelaide,—
A certain font with caryatides
Since cloistered at Goito; only, these
Are up and doing, not abashed, a troop
Able to right themselves—who see you, stoop   150
Their arms o' the instant after you! Unplucked
By this or that, you pass; for they conduct
To terrace raised on terrace, and, between,
Creatures of brighter mould and braver mien
Than any yet, the choicest of the Isle   155
No doubt. Here, left a sullen breathing-while,
Up-gathered on himself the Fighter stood
For his last fight, and, wiping treacherous blood
Out of the eyelids just held ope beneath
Those shading fingers in their iron sheath,   160
Steadied his strengths amid the buzz and stir
Of the dusk hideous amphitheatre
At the announcement of his over-match
To wind the day's diversion up, dispatch
The pertinacious Gaul: while, limbs one heap,   165
The Slave, no breath in her round mouth, watched
    leap
Dart after dart forth, as her hero's car
Clove dizzily the solid of the war
—Let coil about his knees for pride in him.
We reach the farthest terrace, and the grim   170
San Pietro Palace stops us.
                   Such the state
Of Salinguerra's plan to emulate
Sicilian marvels, that his girlish wife
Retrude still might lead her ancient life
In her new home: whereat enlarged so much   175
Neighbours upon the novel princely touch
He took,—who here imprisons Boniface.
Here must the Envoys come to sue for grace;
And here, emerging from the labyrinth

Sordello
ponders all
seen and
heard,

Below, Sordello paused beside the plinth   180
Of the door-pillar.
            He had really left
Verona for the cornfields (a poor theft
From the morass) where Este's camp was made;
The Envoys' march, the Legate's cavalcade—
All had been seen by him, but scarce as when,—   185
Eager for cause to stand aloof from men
At every point save the fantastic tie
Acknowledged in his boyish sophistry,—
He made account of such. A crowd,—he meant
To task the whole of it; each part's intent   190
Concerned him therefore: and, the more he pried,
The less became Sordello satisfied
With his own figure at the moment. Sought

finds in men
no machine
for his sake,

He respite from his task? Descried he aught
Novel in the anticipated sight   195
Of all these livers upon all delight?
This phalanx, as of myriad points combined,
Whereby he still had imaged the mankind
His youth was passed in dreams of rivalling,
His age—in plans to prove at least such thing   200
Had been so dreamed,—which now he must impress
With his own will, effect a happiness
By theirs,—supply a body to his soul
Thence, and become eventually whole
With them as he had hoped to be without—   205
Made these the mankind he once raved about?
Because a few of them were notable,
Should all be figured worthy note? As well
Expect to find Taurello's triple line
Of trees a single and prodigious pine.   210
Real pines rose here and there; but, close among,
Thrust into and mixed up with pines, a throng
Of shrubs, he saw,—a nameless common sort
O'erpast in dreams, left out of the report
And hurried into corners, or at best   215
Admitted to be fancied like the rest.
Reckon that morning's proper chiefs—how few!
And yet the people grew, the people grew,

Grew ever, as if the many there indeed,
More left behind and most who should succeed,—   220
Simply in virtue of their mouths and eyes,
Petty enjoyments and huge miseries,—
Mingled with, and made veritably great
Those chiefs: he overlooked not Mainard's state
Nor Concorezzi's station, but instead   225
Of stopping there, each dwindled to be head
Of infinite and absent Tyrolese
Or Paduans; startling all the more, that these
Seemed passive and disposed of, uncared for,
Yet doubtless on the whole (like Eglamor)   230
Smiling; for if a wealthy man decays
And out of store of robes must wear, all days,
One tattered suit, alike in sun and shade,
'T is commonly some tarnished gay brocade
Fit for a feast-night's flourish and no more: 235
Nor otherwise poor Misery from her store
Of looks is fain upgather, keep unfurled
For common wear as she goes through the world,
The faint remainder of some worn-out smile
Meant for a feast-night's service merely. While   240
Crowd upon crowd rose on Sordello thus,—
(Crowds no way interfering to discuss,
Much less dispute, life's joys with one employed
In envying them,—or, if they aught enjoyed,
Where lingered something indefinable   245
In every look and tone, the mirth as well
As woe, that fixed at once his estimate
Of the result, their good or bad estate)—
Old memories returned with new effect:
And the new body, ere he could suspect,   250
Cohered, mankind and he were really fused,
The new self seemed impatient to be used
By him, but utterly another way
Than that anticipated: strange to say,
They were too much below him, more in thrall   255
Than he, the adjunct than the principal.
What booted scattered units?—here a mind
And there, which might repay his own to find,

but a thing with a life of its own,

and rights hitherto ignored by him,

And stamp, and use?—a few, howe'er august,
If all the rest were grovelling in the dust?   260
No: first a mighty equilibrium, sure,
Should he establish, privilege procure
For all, the few had long possessed! He felt
An error, an exceeding error melt:
While he was occupied with Mantuan chants,   265
Behoved him think of men, and take their wants,
Such as he now distinguished every side,
As his own want which might be satisfied,—
And, after that, think of rare qualities
Of his own soul demanding exercise.   270
It followed naturally, through no claim
On their part, which made virtue of the aim
At serving them, on his,—that, past retrieve,
He felt now in their toils, theirs—nor could leave
Wonder how, in the eagerness to rule,   275
Impress his will on mankind, he (the fool!)
Had never even entertained the thought
That this his last arrangement might be fraught
With incidental good to them as well,
And that mankind's delight would help to swell   280
His own. So, if he sighed, as formerly
Because the merry time of life must fleet,
'T was deeplier now,—for could the crowds repeat
Their poor experiences? His hand that shook
Was twice to be deplored. 'The Legate, look!   285
'With eyes, like fresh-blown thrush-eggs on a thread,
'Faint-blue and loosely floating in his head,
'Large tongue, moist open mouth; and this long while
'That owner of the idiotic smile
'Serves them!'

—a fault he is
now anxious to
repair,
                    He fortunately saw in time   290
His fault however, and since the office prime
Includes the secondary—best accept
Both offices; Taurello, its adept,
Could teach him the preparatory one,
And how to do what he had fancied done   295
Long previously, ere take the greater task.
How render first these people happy? Ask

The people's friends: for there must be one good
One way to it—the Cause! He understood
The meaning now of Palma; why the jar   300
Else, the ado, the trouble wide and far
Of Guelfs and Ghibellins, the Lombard hope
And Rome's despair?—'twixt Emperor and Pope
The confused shifting sort of Eden tale—
Hardihood still recurring, still to fail—   305
That foreign interloping fiend, this free
And native overbrooding deity:
Yet a dire fascination o'er the palms
The Kaiser ruined, troubling even the calms
Of paradise; or, on the other hand,   310
The Pontiff, as the Kaisers understand,
One snake-like cursed of God to love the ground,
Whose heavy length breaks in the noon profound
Some saving tree—which needs the Kaiser, dressed
As the dislodging angel of that pest: 315
Yet flames that pest bedropped, flat head, full fold,
With coruscating dower of dyes. 'Behold
'The secret, so to speak, and master-spring
'O' the contest!—which of the two Powers shall
      bring
'Men good, perchance the most good: ay, it may   320
'Be that!—the question, which best knows the way.'
   And hereupon Count Mainard strutted past
Out of San Pietro; never seemed the last
Of archers, slingers: and our friend began
To recollect strange modes of serving man—   325
Arbalist, catapult, brake, manganel,
And more. 'This way of theirs may,—who can tell?—
'Need perfecting,' said he: 'let all be solved
'At once! Taurello 't is, the task devolved
'On late: confront Taurello!'

                        And at last   330   since he
He did confront him. Scarce an hour had past   apprehends its
When forth Sordello came, older by years   full extent,
Than at his entry. Unexampled fears
Oppressed him, and he staggered off, blind, mute
And deaf, like some fresh-mutilated brute,   335

and would
fain have
helped some
way.

Into Ferrara—not the empty town
That morning witnessed: he went up and down
Streets whence the veil had been stript shred by shred,
So that, in place of huddling with their dead
Indoors, to answer Salinguerra's ends,   340
Townsfolk make shift to crawl forth, sit like friends
With any one. A woman gave him choice
Of her two daughters, the infantile voice
Or the dimpled knee, for half a chain, his throat
Was clasped with; but an archer knew the coat—   345
Its blue cross and eight lilies,—bade beware
One dogging him in concert with the pair
Though thrumming on the sleeve that hid his knife.
Night set in early, autumn dews were rife,
They kindled great fires while the Leaguers' mass   350
Began at every carroch: he must pass
Between the kneeling people. Presently
The carroch of Verona caught his eye
With purple trappings; silently he bent
Over its fire, when voices violent   355
Began, 'Affirm not whom the youth was like
'That struck me from the porch: I did not strike
'Again: I too have chestnut hair; my kin
'Hate Azzo and stand up for Ecelin.
'Here, minstrel, drive bad thoughts away! Sing! Take 360
'My glove for guerdon!' And for that man's sake
He turned: 'A song of Eglamor's!'—scarce named,
When, 'Our Sordello's rather!'—all exclaimed;
'Is not Sordello famousest for rhyme?'
He had been happy to deny, this time,—   365
Profess as heretofore the aching head
And failing heart,—suspect that in his stead
Some true Apollo had the charge of them,
Was champion to reward or to condemn,
So his intolerable risk might shift   370
Or share itself; but Naddo's precious gift
Of gifts, he owned, be certain! At the close—
'I made that,' said he to a youth who rose
As if to hear: 't was Palma through the band
Conducted him in silence by her hand.   375

Back now for Salinguerra. Tito of Trent
Gave place to Palma and her friend, who went
In turn at Montelungo's visit: one
After the other were they come and gone,—
These spokesmen for the Kaiser and the Pope,   380
This incarnation of the People's hope,
Sordello,—all the say of each was said;
And Salinguerra sat,—himself instead
Of these to talk with, lingered musing yet.
'T was a drear vast presence-chamber roughly set   385
In order for the morning's use; full face,
The Kaiser's ominous sign-mark had first place,
The crowned grim twy-necked eagle, coarsely-blacked
With ochre on the naked wall; nor lacked
Romano's green and yellow either side;   390
But the new token Tito brought had tried
The Legate's patience—nay, if Palma knew
What Salinguerra almost meant to do
Until the sight of her restored his lip
A certain half-smile, three months' chieftainship   395
Had banished! Afterward, the Legate found
No change in him, nor asked what badge he wound
And unwound carelessly. Now sat the Chief
Silent as when our couple left, whose brief
Encounter wrought so opportune effect   400
In thoughts he summoned not, nor would reject,
Though time 't was now if ever, to pause—fix
On any sort of ending: wiles and tricks
Exhausted, judge! his charge, the crazy town,
Just managed to be hindered crashing down—   405
His last sound troops ranged—care observed to post
His best of the maimed soldiers innermost—
So much was plain enough, but somehow struck
Him not before. And now with this strange luck
Of Tito's news, rewarding his address   410
So well, what thought he of?—how the success
With Friedrich's rescript there, would either hush
Old Ecelin's scruples, bring the manly flush
To his young son's white cheek, or, last, exempt
Himself from telling what there was to tempt?   415

But
Salinguerra
is also pre-
occupied;

resembling
Sordello in
nothing else.

No: that this minstrel was Romano's last
Servant—himself the first! Could he contrast
The whole!—that minstrel's thirty years just spent
In doing nought, their notablest event
This morning's journey hither, as I told—   420
Who yet was lean, outworn and really old,
A stammering awkward man that scarce dared raise
His eye before the magisterial gaze—

How he was
made in body
and spirit,

And Salinguerra with his fears and hopes
Of sixty years, his Emperors and Popes,   425
Cares and contrivances, yet, you would say,
'T was a youth nonchalantly looked away
Through the embrasure northward o'er the sick
Expostulating trees—so agile, quick
And graceful turned the head on the broad chest   430
Encased in pliant steel, his constant vest,
Whence split the sun off in a spray of fire
Across the room; and, loosened of its tire
Of steel, that head let breathe the comely brown
Large massive locks discoloured as if a crown   435
Encircled them, so frayed the basnet where
A sharp white line divided clean the hair;
Glossy above, glossy below, it swept
Curling and fine about a brow thus kept
Calm, laid coat upon coat, marble and sound: 440
This was the mystic mark the Tuscan found,
Mused of, turned over books about. Square-faced,
No lion more; two vivid eyes, enchased
In hollows filled with many a shade and streak
Settling from the bold nose and bearded cheek.   445
Nor might the half-smile reach them that deformed
A lip supremely perfect else—unwarmed,
Unwidened, less or more; indifferent
Whether on trees or men his thoughts were bent,
Thoughts rarely, after all, in trim and train   450
As now a period was fulfilled again:
Of such, a series made his life, compressed

and what had
been his career
of old.

In each, one story serving for the rest—
How his life-streams rolling arrived at last
At the barrier, whence, were it once overpast,   455

They would emerge, a river to the end,—
Gathered themselves up, paused, bade fate befriend,
Took the leap, hung a minute at the height,
Then fell back to oblivion infinite:
Therefore he smiled. Beyond stretched garden-grounds 460
Where late the adversary, breaking bounds,
Had gained him an occasion, That above,
That eagle, testified he could improve
Effectually. The Kaiser's symbol lay
Beside his rescript, a new badge by way 465
Of baldric; while,—another thing that marred
Alike emprise, achievement and reward,—
Ecelin's missive was conspicuous too.
What past life did those flying thoughts pursue?
As his, few names in Mantua half so old; 470
But at Ferrara, where his sires enrolled
It latterly, the Adelardi spared
No pains to rival them: both factions shared
Ferrara, so that, counted out, 't would yield
A product very like the city's shield, 475
Half black and white, or Ghibellin and Guelf
As after Salinguerra styled himself
And Este who, till Marchesalla died,
(Last of the Adelardi)—never tried
His fortune there: with Marchesalla's child 480
Would pass,—could Blacks and Whites be reconciled
And young Taurello wed Linguetta,—wealth
And sway to a sole grasp. Each treats by stealth
Already: when the Guelfs, the Ravennese   The original
Arrive, assault the Pietro quarter, seize 485 check to his
Linguetta, and are gone! Men's first dismay   fortunes,
Abated somewhat, hurries down, to lay
The after indignation, Boniface,
This Richard's father. 'Learn the full disgrace
'Averted, ere you blame us Guelfs, who rate 490
'Your Salinguerra, your sole potentate
'That might have been, 'mongst Este's valvassors—
'Ay, Azzo's—who, not privy to, abhors
'Our step; but we were zealous.' Azzo then
To do with! Straight a meeting of old men: 495

'Old Salinguerra dead, his heir a boy,
'What if we change our ruler and decoy
'The Lombard Eagle of the azure sphere
'With Italy to build in, fix him here,
'Settle the city's troubles in a trice?   500
'For private wrong, let public good suffice!'
In fine, young Salinguerra's staunchest friends
Talked of the townsmen making him amends,
Gave him a goshawk, and affirmed there was
Rare sport, one morning, over the green grass   505
A mile or so. He sauntered through the plain,
Was restless, fell to thinking, turned again
In time for Azzo's entry with the bride;
Count Boniface rode smirking at their side;
'She brings him half Ferrara,' whispers flew,   510
'And all Ancona! If the stripling knew!'

which he was
in the way to
retrieve,

   Anon the stripling was in Sicily
Where Heinrich ruled in right of Constance; he
Was gracious nor his guest incapable;
Each understood the other. So it fell,   515
One Spring, when Azzo, thoroughly at ease,
Had near forgotten by what precise degrees
He crept at first to such a downy seat,
The Count trudged over in a special heat
To bid him of God's love dislodge from each   520
Of Salinguerra's palaces,—a breach
Might yawn else, not so readily to shut,
For who was just arrived at Mantua but
The youngster, sword on thigh and tuft on chin,
With tokens for Celano, Ecelin,   525
Pistore, and the like! Next news,—no whit
Do any of Ferrara's domes befit
His wife of Heinrich's very blood: a band
Of foreigners assemble, understand
Garden-constructing, level and surround,   530
Build up and bury in. A last news crowned
The consternation: since his infant's birth,
He only waits they end his wondrous girth
Of trees that link San Pietro with Tomà,
To visit Mantua. When the Podestà   535

Ecelin, at Vicenza, called his friend
Taurello thither, what could be their end
But to restore the Ghibellins' late Head,
The Kaiser helping? He with most to dread
From vengeance and reprisal, Azzo, there   540
With Boniface beforehand, as aware
Of plots in progress, gave alarm, expelled
Both plotters: but the Guelfs in triumph yelled
Too hastily. The burning and the flight,   *when a fresh*
And how Taurello, occupied that night   *calamity*
With Ecelin, lost wife and son, I told: 545   *destroyed all.*
—Not how he bore the blow, retained his hold,
Got friends safe through, left enemies the worst
O' the fray, and hardly seemed to care at first:
But afterward men heard not constantly   550
Of Salinguerra's House so sure to be!
Though Azzo simply gained by the event
A shifting of his plagues—the first, content
To fall behind the second and estrange
So far his nature, suffer such a change   555
That in Romano sought he wife and child,
And for Romano's sake seemed reconciled
To losing individual life, which shrunk
As the other prospered—mortised in his trunk;
Like a dwarf palm which wanton Arabs foil   560
Of bearing its own proper wine and oil,
By grafting into it the stranger-vine,
Which sucks its heart out, sly and serpentine,
Till forth one vine-palm feathers to the root,
And red drops moisten the insipid fruit.   565
Once Adelaide set on,—the subtle mate
Of the weak soldier, urged to emulate
The Church's valiant women deed for deed,
And paragon her namesake, win the meed
O' the great Matilda,—soon they overbore   570
The rest of Lombardy,—not as before
By an instinctive truculence, but patched
The Kaiser's strategy until it matched
The Pontiff's, sought old ends by novel means.
'Only, why is it Salinguerra screens   575

He sank into a
secondary
personage,

'Himself behind Romano?—him we bade
'Enjoy our shine i' the front, not seek the shade!'
—Asked Heinrich, somewhat of the tardiest
To comprehend. Nor Philip acquiesced
At once in the arrangement; reasoned, plied   580
His friend with offers of another bride,
A statelier function—fruitlessly: 't was plain
Taurello through some weakness must remain
Obscure. And Otho, free to judge of both
—Ecelin the unready, harsh and loth,   585
And this more plausible and facile wight
With every point a-sparkle—chose the right,
Admiring how his predecessors harped
On the wrong man: 'thus,' quoth he, 'wits are warped
'By outsides!' Carelessly, meanwhile, his life   590
Suffered its many turns of peace and strife
In many lands—you hardly could surprise
The man; who shamed Sordello (recognize!)
In this as much beside, that, unconcerned
What qualities were natural or earned,   595
With no ideal of graces, as they came
He took them, singularly well the same—

with the
appropriate
graces of such.

Speaking the Greek's own language, just because
Your Greek eludes you, leave the least of flaws
In contracts with him; while, since Arab lore   600
Holds the stars' secret—take one trouble more
And master it! 'T is done, and now deter
Who may the Tuscan, once Jove trined for her,
From Friedrich's path!—Friedrich, whose pilgrimage
The same man puts aside, whom he'll engage   605
To leave next year John Brienne in the lurch,
Come to Bassano, see Saint Francis' church
And judge of Guido the Bolognian's piece
Which,—lend Taurello credit,—rivals Greece—
Angels, with aureoles like golden quoits   610
Pitched home, applauding Ecelin's exploits.
For elegance, he strung the angelot,
Made rhymes thereto; for prowess, clove he not
Tiso, last siege, from crest to crupper? Why
Detail you thus a varied mastery   615

But to show how Taurello, on the watch
For men, to read their hearts and thereby catch
Their capabilities and purposes,
Displayed himself so far as displayed these:
While our Sordello only cared to know   620
About men as a means whereby he'd show
Himself, and men had much or little worth
According as they kept in or drew forth
That self; the other's choicest instruments
Surmised him shallow.

                  Meantime, malcontents   625
Dropped off, town after town grew wiser. 'How
'Change the world's face?' asked people; 'as 't is now
'It has been, will be ever: very fine
'Subjecting things profane to things divine,
'In talk! This contumacy will fatigue   630
'The vigilance of Este and the League!
'The Ghibellins gain on us!'—as it happed.
Old Azzo and old Boniface, entrapped
By Ponte Alto, both in one month's space
Slept at Verona: either left a brace   635
Of sons—but, three years after, either's pair
Lost Guglielm and Aldobrand its heir:
Azzo remained and Richard—all the stay
Of Este and Saint Boniface, at bay
As 't were. Then, either Ecelin grew old   640   But Ecelin, he
Or his brain altered—not o' the proper mould   set in front,
For new appliances—his old palm-stock   falling,
Endured no influx of strange strengths. He'd rock
As in a drunkenness, or chuckle low
As proud of the completeness of his woe,   645
Then weep real tears;—now make some mad onslaught
On Este, heedless of the lesson taught
So painfully,—now cringe for peace, sue peace
At price of past gain, bar of fresh increase
To the fortunes of Romano. Up at last   650
Rose Este, down Romano sank as fast.
And men remarked these freaks of peace and war
Happened while Salinguerra was afar:
Whence every friend besought him, all in vain,

To use his old adherent's wits again.   655
Not he!—'who had advisers in his sons,
'Could plot himself, nor needed any one's
'Advice.' 'T was Adelaide's remaining staunch
Prevented his destruction root and branch
Forthwith; but when she died, doom fell, for gay   660
He made alliances, gave lands away
To whom it pleased accept them, and withdrew

Salinguerra
must again
come forward,

For ever from the world. Taurello, who
Was summoned to the convent, then refused
A word at the wicket, patience thus abused,   665
Promptly threw off alike his imbecile
Ally's yoke, and his own frank, foolish smile.
Soon a few movements of the happier sort
Changed matters, put himself in men's report
As heretofore; he had to fight, beside,   670
And that became him ever. So, in pride
And flushing of this kind of second youth,
He dealt a good-will blow. Este in truth
Lay prone—and men remembered, somewhat late,
A laughing old outrageous stifled hate   675
He bore to Este—how it would outbreak
At times spite of disguise, like an earthquake
In sunny weather—as that noted day
When with his hundred friends he tried to slay
Azzo before the Kaiser's face: and how,   680
On Azzo's calm refusal to allow
A liegeman's challenge, straight he too was calmed:
As if his hate could bear to lie embalmed,
Bricked up, the moody Pharaoh, and survive
All intermediate crumblings, to arrive   685
At earth's catastrophe—'t was Este's crash
Not Azzo's he demanded, so, no rash
Procedure! Este's true antagonist
Rose out of Ecelin: all voices whist,
All eyes were sharpened, wits predicted. He   690
'T was, leaned in the embrasure absently,
Amused with his own efforts, now, to trace
With his steel-sheathed forefinger Friedrich's face
I' the dust: but as the trees waved sere, his smile

Deepened, and words expressed its thought erewhile. 695
  'Ay, fairly housed at last, my old compeer?
'That we should stick together, all the year
'I kept Vicenza!—How old Boniface,
'Old Azzo caught us in its market-place,
'He by that pillar, I at this,—caught each   700
'In mid swing, more than fury of his speech,
'Egging the rabble on to disavow
'Allegiance to their Marquis—Bacchus, how
'They boasted! Ecelin must turn their drudge,
'Nor, if released, will Salinguerra grudge   705
'Paying arrears of tribute due long since—
'Bacchus! My man could promise then, nor wince:
'The bones-and-muscles! Sound of wind and limb,
'Spoke he the set excuse I framed for him:
'And now he sits me, slavering and mute,   710
'Intent on chafing each starved purple foot
'Benumbed past aching with the altar slab:
'Will no vein throb there when some monk shall blab
'Spitefully to the circle of bald scalps,
' "Friedrich's affirmed to be our side the Alps"   715
'—Eh, brother Lactance, brother Anaclet?
'Sworn to abjure the world, its fume and fret,
'God's own now? Drop the dormitory bar,
'Enfold the scanty grey serge scapular
'Twice o'er the cowl to muffle memories out!   720
'So! But the midnight whisper turns a shout,
'Eyes wink, mouths open, pulses circulate
'In the stone walls: the past, the world you hate
'Is with you, ambush, open field—or see
'The surging flame—we fire Vicenza—glee!   725
'Follow, let Pilio and Bernardo chafe!
'Bring up the Mantuans—through San Biagio—safe!
'Ah, the mad people waken? Ah, they writhe
'And reach us? If they block the gate? No tithe
'Can pass—keep back, you Bassanese! The edge, 730
'Use the edge—shear, thrust, hew, melt down the wedge,
'Let out the black of those black upturned eyes!
'Hell—are they sprinkling fire too? The blood fries
'And hisses on your brass gloves as they tear

—why and
how, is let out
in soliloquy.

Ecelin, he did
all for, is a
monk now,

'Those upturned faces choking with despair.   735
'Brave! Slidder through the reeking gate! "How now?
' "You six had charge of her?" And then the vow
'Comes, and the foam spirts, hair's plucked, till one
    shriek
'(I hear it) and you fling—you cannot speak—
'Your gold-flowered basnet to a man who haled   740
'The Adelaide he dared scarce view unveiled
'This morn, naked across the fire: how crown
'The archer that exhausted lays you down
'Your infant, smiling at the flame, and dies?
'While one, while mine . . .
                    'Bacchus! I think there lies   745
'More than one corpse there' (and he paced the room)
'—Another cinder somewhere: 't was my doom

just when the
prize awaits
somebody

'Beside, my doom! If Adelaide is dead,
'I live the same, this Azzo lives instead
'Of that to me, and we pull, any how,   750
'Este into a heap: the matter's now
'At the true juncture slipping us so oft.
'Ay, Heinrich died and Otho, please you, doffed
'His crown at such a juncture! Still, if holds
'Our Friedrich's purpose, if this chain enfolds   755
'The neck of . . . who but this same Ecelin
'That must recoil when the best days begin!
'Recoil? that's nought; if the recoiler leaves
'His name for me to fight with, no one grieves:
'But he must interfere, forsooth, unlock   760
'His cloister to become my stumbling-block
'Just as of old! Ay, ay, there 't is again—
'The land's inevitable Head—explain
'The reverences that subject us! Count
'These Ecelins now! Not to say as fount,   765
'Originating power of thought,—from twelve
'That drop i' the trenches they joined hands to delve,
'Six shall surpass him, but . . . why men must twine
'Somehow with something! Ecelin's a fine
'Clear name! 'Twere simpler, doubtless, twine with
    me   770
'At once: our cloistered friend's capacity

'Was of a sort! I had to share myself
'In fifty portions, like an o'ertasked elf
'That's forced illume in fifty points the vast
'Rare vapour he's environed by. At last   775
'My strengths, though sorely frittered, e'en converge
'And crown . . . no, Bacchus, they have yet to urge
'The man be crowned!

                              'That aloe, an he durst,
'Would climb! Just such a bloated sprawler first
'I noted in Messina's castle-court   780
'The day I came, when Heinrich asked in sport
'If I would pledge my faith to win him back
'His right in Lombardy: "for, once bid pack
' "Marauders," he continued, "in my stead
' "You rule, Taurello!" and upon this head   785
'Laid the silk glove of Constance—I see her
'Too, mantled head to foot in miniver,
'Retrude following!

                    'I am absolved
'From further toil: the empery devolved
'On me, 't was Tito's word: I have to lay   790
'For once my plan, pursue my plan my way,
'Prompt nobody, and render an account
'Taurello to Taurello! Nay, I mount
'To Friedrich: he conceives the post I kept,
'—Who did true service, able or inept,   795
'Who's worthy guerdon, Ecelin or I.
'Me guerdoned, counsel follows: would he vie
'With the Pope really? Azzo, Boniface
'Compose a right-arm Hohenstauffen's race
'Must break ere govern Lombardy. I point   800
'How easy 't were to twist, once out of joint,
'The socket from the bone: my Azzo's stare
'Meanwhile! for I, this idle strap to wear,
'Shall—fret myself abundantly, what end
'To serve? There's left me twenty years to spend   805
'—How better than my old way? Had I one
'Who laboured to o'erthrow my work—a son
'Hatching with Azzo superb treachery,
'To root my pines up and then poison me,

—himself, if
it were only
worth while,

as it may be—
but also, as it
may not be

'Suppose—'t were worth while frustrate that! Beside, 810
'Another life's ordained me: the world's tide
'Rolls, and what hope of parting from the press
'Of waves, a single wave through weariness
'Gently lifted aside, laid upon shore?
'My life must be lived out in foam and roar,   815
'No question. Fifty years the province held
'Taurello; troubles raised, and troubles quelled,
'He in the midst—who leaves this quaint stone place,
'These trees a year or two, then not a trace
'Of him! How obtain hold, fetter men's tongues   820
'Like this poor minstrel with the foolish songs—
'To which, despite our bustle, he is linked?
'—Flowers one may teaze, that never grow extinct.
'Ay, that patch, surely, green as ever, where
'I set Her Moorish lentisk, by the stair,   825
'To overawe the aloes; and we trod
'Those flowers, how call you such?—into the sod;
'A stately foreigner—a world of pain
'To make it thrive, arrest rough winds—all vain!
'It would decline; these would not be destroyed: 830
'And now, where is it? where can you avoid
'The flowers? I frighten children twenty years
'Longer!—which way, too, Ecelin appears
'To thwart me, for his son's besotted youth
'Gives promise of the proper tiger-tooth: 835
'The feel it at Vicenza! Fate, fate, fate,
'My fine Taurello! Go you, promulgate
'Friedrich's decree, and here's shall aggrandise
'Young Ecelin—your Prefect's badge! a prize
'Too precious, certainly.

                          'How now? Compete   840
'With my old comrade? shuffle from their seat
'His children? Paltry dealing! Don't I know
'Ecelin? now, I think, and years ago!
'What's changed—the weakness? did not I compound
'For that, and undertake to keep him sound   845
'Despite it? Here's Taurello hankering
'After a boy's preferment—this plaything
'To carry, Bacchus!' And he laughed.

—the suppos-
ition he most
    inclines to;

Remark
Why schemes wherein cold-blooded men embark
Prosper, when your enthusiastic sort   850
Fail: while these last are ever stopping short—
(So much they should—so little they can do!)
The careless tribe see nothing to pursue
If they desist; meantime their scheme succeeds.

  Thoughts were caprices in the course of deeds   855
Methodic with Taurello; so, he turned,—
Enough amused by fancies fairly earned
Of Este's horror-struck submitted neck,
And Richard, the cowed braggart, at his beck,—
To his own petty but immediate doubt   860
If he could pacify the League without
Conceding Richard; just to this was brought
That interval of vain discursive thought!
As, shall I say, some Ethiop, past pursuit
Of all enslavers, dips a shackled foot   865
Burnt to the blood, into the drowsy black
Enormous watercourse which guides him back
To his own tribe again, where he is king;
And laughs because he guesses, numbering
The yellower poison-wattles on the pouch   870
Of the first lizard wrested from its couch
Under the slime (whose skin, the while, he strips
To cure his nostril with, and festered lips,
And eyeballs bloodshot through the desert-blast)
That he has reached its boundary, at last   875
May breathe;—thinks o'er enchantments of the South
Sovereign to plague his enemies, their mouth,
Eyes, nails, and hair; but, these enchantments tried
In fancy, puts them soberly aside
For truth, projects a cool return with friends,   880
The likelihood of winning mere amends
Ere long; thinks that, takes comfort silently,
Then, from the river's brink, his wrongs and he,
Hugging revenge close to their hearts, are soon
Off-striding for the Mountains of the Moon.   885
  Midnight: the watcher nodded on his spear,
Since clouds dispersing left a passage clear

*being con-
tented with
mere
vengeance.*

K

For any meagre and discoloured moon
To venture forth; and such was peering soon
Above the harassed city—her close lanes   890
Closer, not half so tapering her fanes,
As though she shrunk into herself to keep
What little life was saved, more safely. Heap
By heap the watch-fires mouldered, and beside
The blackest spoke Sordello and replied   895
Palma with none to listen. ' 'T is your cause:
'What makes a Ghibellin? There should be laws—

Sordello,
taught what
Ghibellins
are,

'(Remember how my youth escaped! I trust
'To you for manhood, Palma! tell me just
'As any child)—there must be laws at work   900
'Explaining this. Assure me, good may lurk
'Under the bad,—my multitude has part
'In your designs, their welfare is at heart
'With Salinguerra, to their interest
'Refer the deeds he dwelt on,—so divest   905
'Our conference of much that scared me. Why
'Affect that heartless tone to Tito? I
'Esteemed myself, yes, in my inmost mind
'This morn, a recreant to my race—mankind
'O'erlooked till now: why boast my spirit's force,   910
'—Such force denied its object? why divorce
'These, then admire my spirit's flight the same
'As though it bore up, helped some half-orbed flame
'Else quenched in the dead void, to living space?
'That orb cast off to chaos and disgrace,   915
'Why vaunt so much my unencumbered dance,
'Making a feat's facilities enhance
'Its marvel? But I front Taurello, one
'Of happier fate, and all I should have done,
'He does; the people's good being paramount   920
'With him, their progress may perhaps account
'For his abiding still; whereas you heard
'The talk with Tito—the excuse preferred
'For burning those five hostages,—and broached
'By way of blind, as you and I approached,   925
'I do believe.'
                    She spoke: then he, 'My thought

'Plainlier expressed! All to your profit—nought
'Meantime of these, of conquests to achieve
'For them, of wretchedness he might relieve
'While profiting your party. Azzo, too,   930
'Supports a cause: what cause? Do Guelfs pursue
'Their ends by means like yours, or better?'

                          When

The Guelfs were proved alike, men weighed with men,
And deed with deed, blaze, blood, with blood and blaze,
Morn broke: 'Once more, Sordello, meet its gaze   935
'Proudly—the people's charge against thee fails
'In every point, while either party quails!
'These are the busy ones: be silent thou!
'Two parties take the world up, and allow
'No third, yet have one principle, subsist   940
'By the same injustice; whoso shall enlist
'With either, ranks with man's inveterate foes.
'So there is one less quarrel to compose:
'The Guelf, the Ghibellin may be to curse—
'I have done nothing, but both sides do worse   945
'Than nothing. Nay, to me, forgotten, reft
'Of insight, lapped by trees and flowers, was left
'The notion of a service—ha? What lured
'Me here, what mighty aim was I assured
'Must move Taurello? What if there remained   950
'A cause, intact, distinct from these, ordained
'For me, its true discoverer?'

                            Some one pressed
Before them here, a watcher, to suggest
The subject for a ballad: 'They must know
'The tale of the dead worthy, long ago   955
'Consul of Rome—that's long ago for us,
'Minstrels and bowmen, idly squabbling thus
'In the world's corner—but too late no doubt,
'For the brave time he sought to bring about.
'—Not know Crescentius Nomentanus?' Then   960
He cast about for terms to tell him, when
Sordello disavowed it, how they used
Whenever their Superior introduced
A novice to the Brotherhood—('for I

Marginal notes:

and what Guelfs, approves of neither.

Have men a cause distinct from both?

'Was just a brown-sleeve brother, merrily   965
'Appointed too,' quoth he, 'till Innocent
'Bade me relinquish, to my small content,
'My wife or my brown sleeves')—some brother spoke
Ere nocturns of Crescentius, to revoke
The edict issued, after his demise,   970
Which blotted fame alike and effigies,
All out except a floating power, a name
Including, tending to produce the same
Great act. Rome, dead, forgotten, lived at least
Within that brain, though to a vulgar priest   975
And a vile stranger,—two not worth a slave
Of Rome's, Pope John, King Otho,—fortune gave
The rule there: so, Crescentius, haply dressed
In white, called Roman Consul for a jest,
Taking the people at their word, forth stepped   980
As upon Brutus' heel, nor ever kept
Rome waiting,—stood erect, and from his brain
Gave Rome out on its ancient place again,
Ay, bade proceed with Brutus' Rome, Kings styled
Themselves mere citizens of, and, beguiled   985
Into great thoughts thereby, would choose the gem
Out of a lapfull, spoil their diadem
—The Senate's cypher was so hard to scratch!
He flashes like a phanal, all men catch
The flame, Rome's just accomplished! when returned   990
Otho, with John, the Consul's step had spurned,
And Hugo Lord of Este, to redress
The wrongs of each. Crescentius in the stress
Of adverse fortune bent. 'They crucified
'Their Consul in the Forum; and abide   995
'E'er since such slaves at Rome, that I—(for I
'Was once a brown-sleeve brother, merrily
'Appointed)—I had option to keep wife
'Or keep brown sleeves, and managed in the strife
'Lose both. A song of Rome!'

                                        And Rome, indeed,   1000
Robed at Goito in fantastic weed,
The Mother-City of his Mantuan days,
Looked an established point of light whence rays

Who was the
famed
Roman
Crescentius?

Traversed the world; for, all the clustered homes
Beside of men, seemed bent on being Romes   1005
In their degree; the question was, how each
Should most resemble Rome, clean out of reach.
Nor, of the Two, did either principle
Struggle to change, but to possess Rome,—still
Guelf Rome or Ghibellin Rome.

                     Let Rome advance!   1010
Rome, as she struck Sordello's ignorance—
How could he doubt one moment? Rome's the
    Cause!
Rome of the Pandects, all the world's new laws—
Of the Capitol, of Castle Angelo;
New structures, that inordinately glow,   1015
Subdued, brought back to harmony, made ripe
By many a relic of the archetype
Extant for wonder; every upstart church
That hoped to leave old temples in the lurch,
Corrected by the Theatre forlorn   1020
That,—as a mundane shell, its world late born,—
Lay and o'ershadowed it. These hints combined,
Rome typifies the scheme to put mankind
Once more in full possession of their rights.
'Let us have Rome again! On me it lights   1025
'To build up Rome—on me, the first and last:
'For such a future was endured the past!'
And thus, in the grey twilight, forth he sprung
To give his thought consistency among
The very People—let their facts avail   1030
Finish the dream grown from the archer's tale.

BOOK THE FIFTH

Is it the same Sordello in the dusk
As at the dawn?—merely a perished husk
Now, that arose a power fit to build
Up Rome again? The proud conception chilled
So soon? Ay, watch that latest dream of thine   5
—A Rome indebted to no Palatine—

How if, in the
re-integration
of Rome,

be typified the
triumph of
mankind?

Mankind
triumph of a
sudden?

Drop arch by arch, Sordello! Art possessed
Of thy wish now, rewarded for thy quest
To-day among Ferrara's squalid sons?
Are this and this and this the shining ones   10
Meet for the Shining City? Sooth to say,
Your favoured tenantry pursue their way
After a fashion! This companion slips
On the smooth causey, t' other blinkard trips
At his mooned sandal. 'Leave to lead the brawls   15
'Here i' the atria?' No, friend! He that sprawls
On aught but a stibadium . . . what his dues
Who puts the lustral vase to such an use?
Oh, huddle up the day's disasters! March,
Ye runagates, and drop thou, arch by arch,   20
Rome!
                    Yet before they quite disband—a whim—
Study mere shelter, now, for him, and him,

Why, the work
should be one
of ages,
Nay, even the worst,—just house them! Any cave
Suffices: throw out earth! A loophole? Brave!
They ask to feel the sun shine, see the grass   25
Grow, hear the larks sing? Dead art thou, alas,
And I am dead! But here's our son excels
At hurdle-weaving any Scythian, fells
Oak and devises rafters, dreams and shapes
His dream into a door-post, just escapes   30
The mystery of hinges. Lie we both
Perdue another age. The goodly growth
Of brick and stone! Our building-pelt was rough,
But that descendant's garb suits well enough
A portico-contriver. Speed the years—   35
What's time to us? At last, a city rears
Itself! nay, enter—what's the grave to us?
Lo, our forlorn acquaintance carry thus
The head! Successively sewer, forum, cirque—
Last age, an aqueduct was counted work,   40
But now they tire the artificer upon
Blank alabaster, black obsidion,
—Careful, Jove's face be duly fulgurant,
And mother Venus' kiss-creased nipples pant
Back into pristine pulpiness, ere fixed   45

Above the baths. What difference betwixt
This Rome and ours—resemblance what, between
That scurvy dumb-show and this pageant sheen—
These Romans and our rabble? Use thy wit!
The work marched: step by step,—a workman fit   50
Took each, nor too fit,—to one task, one time,—
No leaping o'er the petty to the prime,
When just the substituting osier lithe
For brittle bulrush, sound wood for soft withe,
To further loam-and-roughcast-work a stage,—   55
Exacts an architect, exacts an age:
No tables of the Mauritanian tree
For men whose maple log's their luxury!
That way was Rome built. 'Better' (say you) 'merge
'At once all workmen in the demiurge,   60
'All epochs in a lifetime, every task
'In one!' So should the sudden city bask
I' the day—while those we'd feast there, want the knack
Of keeping fresh-chalked gowns from speck and brack,
Distinguish not rare peacock from vile swan,   65
Nor Mareotic juice from Cæcuban.
'Enough of Rome! 'T was happy to conceive
'Rome on a sudden, nor shall fate bereave
'Me of that credit: for the rest, her spite
'Is an old story—serves my folly right   70
'By adding yet another to the dull
'List of abortions—things proved beautiful
'Could they be done, Sordello cannot do.'
    He sat upon the terrace, plucked and threw
The powdery aloe-cusps away, saw shift   75
Rome's walls, and drop arch after arch, and drift
Mist-like afar those pillars of all stripe,
Mounds of all majesty. 'Thou archetype,
'Last of my dreams and loveliest, depart!'
    And then a low voice wound into his heart: 80
'Sordello!' (low as some old Pythoness
Conceding to a Lydian King's distress
The cause of his long error—one mistake
Of her past oracle) 'Sordello, wake!
'God has conceded two sights to a man—   85

*if performed
equally and
thoroughly;*

*and a man can
but do a man's
portion.*

'One, of men's whole work, time's completed plan,
'The other, of the minute's work, man's first
'Step to the plan's completeness: what's dispersed
'Save hope of that supreme step which, descried
'Earliest, was meant still to remain untried   90
'Only to give you heart to take your own
'Step, and there stay, leaving the rest alone?
'Where is the vanity? Why count as one
'The first step, with the last step? What is gone
'Except Rome's aëry magnificence,   95
'That last step you'd take first?—an evidence
'You were God: be man now! Let those glances fall!
'The basis, the beginning step of all,
'Which proves you just a man—is that gone too?
'Pity to disconcert one versed as you   100
'In fate's ill-nature! but its full extent
'Eludes Sordello, even: the veil rent,
'Read the black writing—that collective man
'Outstrips the individual. Who began
'The acknowledged greatnesses? Ay, your own art   105
'Shall serve us: put the poet's mimes apart—
'Close with the poet's self, and lo, a dim
'Yet too plain form divides itself from him!
'Alcamo's song enmeshes the lulled Isle,

The last of
each series of
workmen

'Woven into the echoes left erewhile   110
'By Nina, one soft web of song: no more
'Turning his name, then, flower-like o'er and o'er!
'An elder poet in the younger's place;
'Nina's the strength, but Alcamo's the grace:
'Each neutralizes each then! Search your fill;   115
'You get no whole and perfect Poet—still
'New Ninas, Alcamos, till time's mid-night
'Shrouds all—or better say, the shutting light
'Of a forgotten yesterday. Dissect
'Every ideal workman—(to reject   120
'In favour of your fearful ignorance
'The thousand phantasms eager to advance,
'And point you but to those within your reach)—
'Were you the first who brought—(in modern speech)
'The Multitude to be materialized?   125

'That loose eternal unrest—who devised
'An apparition i' the midst? The rout
'Was checked, a breathless ring was formed about
'That sudden flower: get round at any risk
'The gold-rough pointel, silver-blazing disk 13c
'O' the lily! Swords across it! Reign thy reign
'And serve thy frolic service, Charlemagne!
'—The very child of over-joyousness,
'Unfeeling thence, strong therefore: Strength by stress
'Of Strength comes of that forehead confident, 135
'Those widened eyes expecting heart's content,
'A calm as out of just-quelled noise; nor swerves
'For doubt, the ample cheek in gracious curves
'Abutting on the upthrust nether lip:
'He wills, how should he doubt then? Ages slip: 140
'Was it Sordello pried into the work
'So far accomplished, and discovered lurk
'A company amid the other clans,
'Only distinct in priests for castellans
'And popes for suzerains (their rule confessed 145
'Its rule, their interest its interest,
'Living for sake of living—there an end,—
'Wrapt in itself, no energy to spend
'In making adversaries or allies)—
'Dived you into its capabilities 150
'And dared create, out of that sect, a soul
'Should turn a multitude, already whole,
'Into its body? Speak plainer! Is 't so sure
'God's church lives by a King's investiture?
'Look to last step! A staggering—a shock— 155   sums up in
'What's mere sand is demolished, while the rock   himself all
'Endures: a column of black fiery dust   predecessors.
'Blots heaven—that help was prematurely thrust
'Aside, perchance!—but air clears, nought's erased
'Of the true outline. Thus much being firm based, 160
'The other was a scaffold. See him stand   We just see
'Buttressed upon his mattock, Hildebrand   Charlemagne,
'Of the huge brain-mask welded ply o'er ply   Hildebrand,
'As in a forge; it buries either eye
'White and extinct, that stupid brow; teeth clenched, 165

'The neck tight-corded, too, the chin deep-trenched,
'As if a cloud enveloped him while fought
'Under its shade, grim prizers, thought with thought
'At dead-lock, agonizing he, until
'The victor thought leap radiant up, and Will,   170
'The slave with folded arms and drooping lids
'They fought for, lean forth flame-like as it bids.
'Call him no flower—a mandrake of the earth,
Thwarted and dwarfed and blasted in its birth,
'Rather,—a fruit of suffering's excess,   175
'Thence feeling, therefore stronger: still by stress
'Of Strength, work Knowledge! Full three hundred years
'Have men to wear away in smiles and tears
'Between the two that nearly seemed to touch,
'Observe you! quit one workman and you clutch   180
'Another, letting both their trains go by—
'The actors-out of either's policy,
'Heinrich, on this hand, Otho, Barbaross,
'Carry the three Imperial crowns across,
'Aix' Iron, Milan's Silver, and Rome's Gold—   185
'While Alexander, Innocent uphold
'On that, each Papal key—but, link on link,
'Why is it neither chain betrays a chink?
'How coalesce the small and great? Alack,
'For one thrust forward, fifty such fall back!   190
'Do the popes coupled there help Gregory
'Alone? Hark—from the hermit Peter's cry
'At Claremont, down to the first serf that says
'Friedrich's no liege of his while he delays
'Getting the Pope's curse off him! The Crusade—   195

in composite
work they end
and name.

'Or trick of breeding Strength by other aid
'Than Strength, is safe. Hark—from the wild harangue
'Of Vimmercato, to the carroch's clang
'Yonder! The League—or trick of turning Strength
'Against Pernicious Strength, is safe at length.   200
'Yet hark—from Mantuan Albert making cease
'The fierce ones, to Saint Francis preaching peace
'Yonder! God's Truce—or trick to supersede
'The very Use of Strength, is safe. Indeed
'We trench upon the future. Who is found   205

'To take next step, next age—trail o'er the ground—
'Shall I say, gourd-like?—not the flower's display
'Nor the root's prowess, but the plenteous way
'O' the plant—produced by joy and sorrow, whence
'Unfeeling and yet feeling, strongest thence?   210
'Knowledge by stress of merely Knowledge? No—
'E'en were Sordello ready to forego
'His life for this, 't were overleaping work
'Some one has first to do, howe'er it irk,
'Nor stray a foot's breadth from the beaten road.   215
'Who means to help must still support the load
'Hildebrand lifted—"why hast Thou," he groaned,
' "Imposed on me a burthen, Paul had moaned,
' "And Moses dropped beneath?" Much done—and yet
'Doubtless that grandest task God ever set   220
'On man, left much to do: at his arm's wrench,
'Charlemagne's scaffold fell; but pillars blench
'Merely, start back again—perchance have been
'Taken for buttresses: crash every screen,
'Hammer the tenons better, and engage   225
'A gang about your work, for the next age
'Or two, of Knowledge, part by Strength and part
'By Knowledge! Then, indeed, perchance may start
'Sordello on his race—would time divulge
'Such secrets! If one step's awry, one bulge   230
'Calls for correction by a step we thought
'Got over long since, why, till that is wrought,
'No progress! And the scaffold in its turn
'Becomes, its service o'er, a thing to spurn.
'Meanwhile, if your half-dozen years of life   235   If associates
'In store dispose you to forego the strife,   trouble you,
'Who takes exception? Only bear in mind   stand off!
'Ferrara's reached, Goito's left behind:
'As you then were, as half yourself, desist!
'—The warrior-part of you may, an it list,   240
'Finding real faulchions difficult to poise,
'Fling them afar and taste the cream of joys
'By wielding such in fancy,—what is bard
'Of you may spurn the vehicle that marred
'Elys so much, and in free fancy glut   245

'His sense, yet write no verses—you have but
'To please yourself for law, and once could please
'What once appeared yourself, by dreaming these
'Rather than doing these, in days gone by.
'But all is changed the moment you descry   250
'Mankind as half yourself,—then, fancy's trade
'Ends once and always: how may half evade

—should the
new sym-
pathies allow
you.

'The other half? men are found half of you.
'Out of a thousand helps, just one or two
'Can be accomplished presently: but flinch   255
'From these (as from the faulchion, raised an inch,
'Elys, described a couplet) and make proof
'Of fancy,—then, while one half lolls aloof
'I' the vines, completing Rome to the tip-top—
'See if, for that, your other half will stop   260
'A tear, begin a smile! The rabble's woes,
'Ludicrous in their patience as they chose
'To sit about their town and quietly
'Be slaughtered,—the poor reckless soldiery,
'With their ignoble rhymes on Richard, how   265
' "Polt-foot," sang they, "was in a pitfall now,"
'Cheering each other from the engine-mounts,—
'That crippled spawling idiot who recounts
'How, lopped of limbs, he lay, stupid as stone,
'Till the pains crept from out him one by one,   270
'And wriggles round the archers on his head
'To earn a morsel of their chestnut bread,—
'And Cino, always in the self-same place
'Weeping; beside that other wretch's case,
'Eyepits to ear, one gangrene since he plied   275
'The engine in his coat of raw sheep's hide
'A double watch in the noon sun; and see
'Lucchino, beauty, with the favours free,
'Trim hacqueton, spruce beard and scented hair,
'Campaigning it for the first time—cut there   280
'In two already, boy enough to crawl
'For latter orpine round the southern wall,
'Tomà, where Richard's kept, because that whore
'Marfisa, the fool never saw before,
'Sickened for flowers this wearisomest siege: 285

'And Tiso's wife—men liked their pretty liege,
'Cared for her least of whims once,—Berta, wed
'A twelvemonth gone, and, now poor Tiso's dead,
'Delivering herself of his first child
'On that chance heap of wet filth, reconciled   290
'To fifty gazers!'—(Here a wind below
Made moody music augural of woe
From the pine barrier)—'What if, now the scene
'Draws to a close, yourself have really been
'—You, plucking purples in Goito's moss   295
'Like edges of a trabea (not to cross
'Your consul-humour) or dry aloe-shafts
'For fasces, at Ferrara—he, fate wafts,
'This very age, her whole inheritance
'Of opportunities? Yet you advance   300
'Upon the last! Since talking is your trade,
'There's Salinguerra left you to persuade:
'Fail! then'—

         'No—no—which latest chance secure!'
Leaped up and cried Sordello: 'this made sure,
'The past were yet redeemable; its work   305
'Was—help the Guelfs, whom I, howe'er it irk,
'Thus help!' He shook the foolish aloe-haulm
Out of his doublet, paused, proceeded calm
To the appointed presence. The large head
Turned on its socket; 'And your spokesman,' said   310
The large voice, 'is Elcorte's happy sprout?
'Few such'—(so finishing a speech no doubt
Addressed to Palma, silent at his side)
'—My sober councils have diversified.
'Elcorte's son! good: forward as you may,   315
'Our lady's minstrel with so much to say!'
The hesitating sunset floated back,
Rosily traversed in the wonted track
The chamber, from the lattice o'er the girth
Of pines, to the huge eagle blacked in earth   320
Opposite,—outlined sudden, spur to crest,
That solid Salinguerra, and caressed
Palma's contour; 't was day looped back night's pall;
Sordello had a chance left spite of all.

Time having
been lost,
choose quick!

He takes his
first step as a
Guelf;

And much he made of the convincing speech   325
Meant to compensate for the past and reach
Through his youth's daybreak of unprofit, quite
To his noon's labour, so proceed till night
Leisurely! The great argument to bind
Taurello with the Guelf Cause, body and mind,   330
—Came the consummate rhetoric to that?
Yet most Sordello's argument dropped flat
Through his accustomed fault of breaking yoke,
Disjoining him who felt from him who spoke.
Was't not a touching incident—so prompt   335
A rendering the world its just accompt,
Once proved its debtor? Who'd suppose, before
This proof, that he, Goito's god of yore,
At duty's instance could demean himself

but to will and
to do are
different:

So memorably, dwindle to a Guelf?   340
Be sure, in such delicious flattery steeped,
His inmost self at the out-portion peeped,
Thus occupied; then stole a glance at those
Appealed to, curious if her colour rose
Or his lip moved, while he discreetly urged   345
The need of Lombardy becoming purged
At soonest of her barons; the poor part
Abandoned thus, missing the blood at heart
And spirit in brain, unseasonably off
Elsewhere! But, though his speech was worthy scoff,   350
Good-humoured Salinguerra, famed for tact
And tongue, who, careless of his phrase, ne'er lacked
The right phrase, and harangued Honorius dumb
At his accession,—looked as all fell plumb
To purpose and himself found interest   355
In every point his new instructor pressed
—Left playing with the rescript's white wax seal
To scrutinize Sordello head and heel.
He means to yield assent sure? No, alas!
All he replied was, 'What, it comes to pass   360
'That poesy, sooner than politics,
'Makes fade young hair?' To think such speech could
        fix
Taurello!

Then a flash of bitter truth:
So fantasies could break and fritter youth
That he had long ago lost earnestness,   365
Lost will to work, lost power to even express
The need of working! Earth was turned a grave:
No more occasions now, though he should crave
Just one, in right of superhuman toil,
To do what was undone, repair such spoil,   370
Alter the past—nothing would give the chance!
Not that he was to die; he saw askance
Protract the ignominious years beyond
To dream in—time to hope and time despond,
Remember and forget, be sad, rejoice   375
As saved a trouble; he might, at his choice,
One way or other, idle life out, drop
No few smooth verses by the way—for prop,
A thyrsus, these sad people, all the same,
Should pick up, and set store by,—far from blame,   380
Plant o'er his hearse, convinced his better part
Survived him. 'Rather tear men out the heart
'O' the truth!'—Sordello muttered, and renewed
His propositions for the Multitude.

> But Salinguerra, who at this attack   385
Had thrown great breast and ruffling corslet back
To hear the better, smilingly resumed
His task; beneath, the carroch's warning boomed;
He must decide with Tito; courteously
He turned then, even seeming to agree   390
With his admonisher—'Assist the Pope,
'Extend Guelf domination, fill the scope
'O' the Church, thus based on All, by All, for All—
'Change Secular to Evangelical'—
Echoing his very sentence: all seemed lost,   395
When suddenly he looked up, laughingly almost,
To Palma: 'This opinion of your friend's—
'For instance, would it answer Palma's ends?
'Best, were it not, turn Guelf, submit our Strength'—
(Here he drew out his baldric to its length)   400
—'To the Pope's Knowledge—let our captive slip,
'Wide to the walls throw ope our gates, equip

he may sleep
on the bed he
has made.

'Azzo with . . . what I hold here! Who'll subscribe
'To a trite censure of the minstrel tribe

Scorn flings
cold water in
his face,

'Henceforward? or pronounce, as Heinrich used,   405
' "Spear-heads for battle, burr-heads for the joust!"
'—When Constance, for his couplets, would promote
'Alcamo, from a parti-coloured coat,
'To holding her lord's stirrup in the wars.
'Not that I see where couplet-making jars   410
'With common sense: at Mantua I had borne
'This chanted, better than their most forlorn
'Of bull-baits,—that's indisputable!'
                                        Brave!
Whom vanity nigh slew, contempt shall save!
All's at an end: a Troubadour suppose   415
Mankind will class him with their friends or foes?
A puny uncouth ailing vassal think
The world and him bound in some special link?
Abrupt the visionary tether burst.
What were rewarded here, or what amerced   420
If a poor drudge, solicitous to dream
Deservingly, got tangled by his theme
So far as to conceit the knack or gift
Or whatsoe'er it be, of verse, might lift
The globe, a lever like the hand and head   425
Of—'Men of Action,' as the Jongleurs said,
—'The Great Men,' in the people's dialect?

arouses him at
last, to some
purpose,

    And not a moment did this scorn affect
Sordello: scorn the poet? They, for once,
Asking 'what was,' obtained a full response.   430
Bid Naddo think at Mantua—he had but
To look into his promptuary, put
Finger on a set thought in a set speech:
But was Sordello fitted thus for each
Conjecture? Nowise; since within his soul,   435
Perception brooded unexpressed and whole.
A healthy spirit like a healthy frame
Craves aliment in plenty—all the same,
Changes, assimilates its aliment.
Perceived Sordello, on a truth intent?   440
Next day no formularies more you saw

Than figs or olives in a sated maw.
'T is Knowledge, whither such perceptions tend;
They lose themselves in that, means to an end,
The many old producing some one new,   445
A last unlike the first. If lies are true,
The Caliph's wheel-work man of brass receives
A meal, munched millet grains and lettuce leaves
Together in his stomach rattle loose;
You find them perfect next day to produce: 450
But ne'er expect the man, on strength of that,
Can roll an iron camel-collar flat
Like Haroun's self! I tell you, what was stored
Bit by bit through Sordello's life, outpoured
That eve, was, for that age, a novel thing: 455
And round those three the People formed a ring,
Of visionary judges whose award
He recognised in full—faces that barred
Henceforth return to the old careless life,
In whose great presence, therefore, his first strife   460
For their sake must not be ignobly fought;
All these, for once, approved of him, he thought,
Suspended their own vengeance, chose await
The issue of this strife to reinstate
Them in the right of taking it—in fact   465
He must be proved king ere they could exact
Vengeance for such king's defalcation. Last,
A reason why the phrases flowed so fast
Was in his quite forgetting for a time
Himself in his amazement that the rhyme   470
Disguised the royalty so much: he there—
And Salinguerra yet all-unaware
Who was the lord, who liegeman!

                              'Thus I lay
'On thine my spirit and compel obey
'His lord,—my liegeman,—impotent to build   475
'Another Rome, but hardly so unskilled
'In what such builder should have been, as brook
'One shame beyond the charge that I forsook
'His function! Free me from that shame, I bend
'A brow before, suppose new years to spend,—   480

*and thus gets
the utmost out
of him.*

He asserts the
poet's rank
and right,

'Allow each chance, nor fruitlessly, recur—
'Measure thee with the Minstrel, then, demur
'At any crowd he claims! That I must cede
'Shamed now, my right to my especial meed—
'Confess thee fitter help the world than I   485
'Ordained its champion from eternity,
'Is much: but to behold thee scorn the post
'I quit in thy behalf—to hear thee boast
'What makes my own despair!' And while he rung
The changes on this theme, the roof up-sprung,   490
The sad walls of the presence-chamber died
Into the distance, or embowering vied
With far-away Goito's vine-frontier;
And crowds of faces—(only keeping clear
The rose-light in the midst, his vantage-ground   495
To fight their battle from)—deep clustered round
Sordello, with good wishes no mere breath,
Kind prayers for him no vapour, since, come death
Come life, he was fresh-sinewed every joint,
Each bone new-marrowed as whom gods anoint   500
Though mortal to their rescue. Now let sprawl
The snaky volumes hither! Is Typhon all
For Hercules to trample—good report
From Salinguerra only to extort?
'So was I' (closed he his inculcating   505
A poet must be earth's essential king)
'So was I, royal so, and if I fail,
' 'T is not the royalty, ye witness quail,
'But one deposed who, caring not exert
'Its proper essence, trifled malapert   510
'With accidents instead—good things assigned
'As heralds of a better thing behind—
'And, worthy through display of these, put forth
'Never the inmost all-surpassing worth
'That constitutes him king precisely since   515
'As yet no other spirit may evince
'Its like: the power he took most pride to test,
'Whereby all forms of life had been professed
'At pleasure, forms already on the earth,
'Was but a means to power beyond, whose birth   520

'Should, in its novelty, be kingship's proof.
'Now, whether he came near or kept aloof
'The several forms he longed to imitate,
'Not there the kingship lay, he sees too late.
'Those forms, unalterable first as last,   525
'Proved him her copier, not the protoplast
'Of nature: what would come of being free,
'By action to exhibit tree for tree,
'Bird, beast, for beast and bird, or prove earth bore
'One veritable man or woman more?   530
'Means to an end, such proofs are: what the end?
'Let essence, whatsoe'er it be, extend—
'Never contract. Already you include
'The multitude; then let the multitude
'Include yourself; and the result were new: 535
'Themselves before, the multitude turn you.
This were to live and move and have, in them,
'Your being, and secure a diadem
'You should transmit (because no cycle yearns
'Beyond itself, but on itself returns)   540
'When, the full sphere in wane, the world o'erlaid
'Long since with you, shall have in turn obeyed
'Some orb still prouder, some displayer, still
'More potent than the last, of human will,
'And some new king depose the old. Of such   545
'Am I—whom pride of this elates too much?
'Safe, rather say, 'mid troops of peers again;
'I, with my words, hailed brother of the train
'Deeds once sufficed: for, let the world roll back,
'Who fails, through deeds howe'er diverse, retrack   550
'My purpose still, my task? A teeming crust—
'Air, flame, earth, wave at conflict! Then, needs must
'Emerge some Calm embodied, these refer
'The brawl to—yellow-bearded Jupiter?
'No! Saturn; some existence like a pact   555
'And protest against Chaos, some first fact
'I' the faint of time. My deep of life, I know
'Is unavailing e'en to poorly show' . . .
(For here the Chief immeasurably yawned)
. . . 'Deeds in their due gradation till Song dawned—   560

basing these
on their
proper
ground,

recognizing
true dignity in
service,

'The fullest effluence of the finest mind,
'All in degree, no way diverse in kind
'From minds about it, minds which, more or less,
'Lofty or low, move seeking to impress
'Themselves on somewhat; but one mind has climbed 565
'Step after step, by just ascent sublimed.
'Thought is the soul of act, and, stage by stage,
'Soul is from body still to disengage
'As tending to a freedom which rejects
'Such help and incorporeally affects   570
'The world, producing deeds but not by deeds,
'Swaying, in others, frames itself exceeds,
'Assigning them the simpler tasks it used
'To patiently perform till Song produced
'Acts, by thoughts only, for the mind: divest   575
'Mind of e'en Thought, and, lo, God's unexpressed
'Will draws above us! All then is to win
'Save that. How much for me, then? where begin

whether
successively
that of epoist,

'My work? About me, faces! and they flock,
'The earnest faces. What shall I unlock   580
'By song? behold me prompt, whate'er it be,
'To minister: how much can mortals see
'Of Life? No more than so? I take the task
'And marshal you Life's elemental masque,
'Show Men, on evil or on good lay stress,   585
'This light, this shade make prominent, suppress
'All ordinary hues that softening blend
'Such natures with the level. Apprehend
'Which sinner is, which saint, if I allot
'Hell, Purgatory, Heaven, a blaze or blot,   590
'To those you doubt concerning! I enwomb
'Some wretched Friedrich with his red-hot tomb;
'Some dubious spirit, Lombard Agilulph
'With the black chastening river I engulph!
'Some unapproached Matilda I enshrine   595
'With languors of the planet of decline—

dramatist, or,
so to call him,
analyst,

'These, fail to recognize, to arbitrate
'Between henceforth, to rightly estimate
'Thus marshalled in the masque! Myself, the while,
'As one of you, am witness, shrink or smile   600

'At my own showing! Next age—what's to do?
'The men and women stationed hitherto
'Will I unstation, good and bad, conduct
'Each nature to its farthest, or obstruct
'At soonest, in the world: light, thwarted, breaks   605
'A limpid purity to rainbow flakes,
'Or shadow, massed, freezes to gloom: behold
'How such, with fit assistance to unfold,
'Or obstacles to crush them, disengage
'Their forms, love, hate, hope, fear, peace make, war
     wage,   610
'In presence of you all! Myself, implied
'Superior now, as, by the platform's side,
'I bade them do and suffer,—would last content
'The world . . . no—that's too far! I circumvent
'A few, my masque contented, and to these   615
'Offer unveil the last of mysteries—
'Man's inmost life shall have yet freer play:
'Once more I cast external things away,
'And natures composite, so decompose
'That' . . . Why, he writes *Sordello*!

                              'How I rose,   620
'And how have you advanced! since evermore
'Yourselves effect what I was fain before
'Effect, what I supplied yourselves suggest,
'What I leave bare yourselves can now invest.
'How we attain to talk as brothers talk,   625   who turns in
'In half-words, call things by half-names, no balk   due course
'From discontinuing old aids. To-day   synthetist.
'Takes in account the work of Yesterday:
'Has not the world a Past now, its adept
'Consults ere he dispense with or accept   630
'New aids? a single touch more may enhance,
'A touch less turn to insignificance
'Those structures' symmetry the past has strewed
'The world with, once so bare. Leave the mere rude
'Explicit details! 't is but brother's speech   635
'We need, speech where an accent's change gives each
'The other's soul—no speech to understand
'By former audience: need was then to expand,

'Expatiate—hardly were we brothers! true—
'Nor I lament my small remove from you,   640
'Nor reconstruct what stands already. Ends
'Accomplished turn to means: my art intends
'New structure from the ancient: as they changed
'The spoils of every clime at Venice, ranged
'The horned and snouted Libyan god, upright   645
'As in his desert, by some simple bright
'Clay cinerary pitcher—Thebes as Rome,
'Athens as Byzant rifled, till their Dome
'From earth's reputed consummations razed
'A seal, the all-transmuting Triad blazed   650
'Above. Ah, whose that fortune? Ne'erthe-
        less
'E'en he must stoop contented to express
'No tithe of what's to say—the vehicle
'Never sufficient: but his work is still
'For faces like the faces that select   655
'The single service I am bound effect,—
'That bid me cast aside such fancies, bow
'Taurello to the Guelf cause, disallow
'The Kaiser's coming—which with heart, soul,
        strength,
'I labour for, this eve, who feel at length   660
'My past career's outrageous vanity,
'And would, as its amends, die, even die
'Now I first estimate the boon of life,
'If death might win compliance—sure, this strife
'Is right for once—the People my support.'   665
    My poor Sordello! what may we extort
By this, I wonder? Palma's lighted eyes
Turned to Taurello who, long past surprise,
Began, 'You love him—what you'd say at large
'Let me say briefly. First, your father's charge   670
'To me, his friend, peruse: I guessed indeed
'You were no stranger to the course decreed.
'He bids me leave his children to the saints:
'As for a certain project, he acquaints
'The Pope with that, and offers him the best   675
'Of your possessions to permit the rest

This for one
day: now,
serve as
Guelf!

'Go peaceably—to Ecelin, a stripe
'Of soil the cursed Vicentines will gripe,
'—To Alberic, a patch the Trevisan
'Clutches already; extricate, who can,   680
'Treville, Villarazzi, Puissolo,
'Loria and Cartiglione!—all must go,
'And with them go my hopes. 'T is lost, then! Lost
'This eve, our crisis, and some pains it cost
'Procuring; thirty years—as good I'd spent   685
'Like our admonisher! But each his bent
'Pursues: no question, one might live absurd
'Oneself this while, by deed as he by word
'Persisting to obtrude an influence where
' 'T is made account of, much as . . . nay, you fare   690
'With twice the fortune, youngster!—I submit,
'Happy to parallel my waste of wit
'With the renowned Sordello's: you decide
'A course for me. Romano may abide
'Romano,—Bacchus! After all, what dearth   695
'Of Ecelins and Alberics on earth?
'Say there's a prize in prospect, must disgrace
'Betide competitors, unless they style
'Themselves Romano? Were it worth my while
'To try my own luck! But an obscure place   700
'Suits me—there wants a youth to bustle, stalk
'And attitudinize—some fight, more talk,
'Most flaunting badges—how, I might make clear
'Since Friedrich's very purposes lie here
'—Here, pity they are like to lie! For me,   705
'With station fixed unceremoniously
'Long since, small use contesting; I am but
'The liegeman—you are born the lieges: shut
'That gentle mouth now! or resume your kin
'In your sweet self; were Palma Ecelin   710
'For me to work with! Could that neck endure
'This bauble for a cumbrous garniture,
'She should . . . or might one bear it for her? Stay—
'I have not been so flattered many a day
'As by your pale friend—Bacchus! The least help   715
'Would lick the hind's fawn to a lion's whelp:

Salinguerra,
dislodged
from his post,

'His neck is broad enough—a ready tongue
'Beside: too writhled—but, the main thing, young—
'I could . . . why, look ye!'
                         And the badge was thrown

in moving,
opens a door
to Sordello,

Across Sordello's neck: 'This badge alone   720
'Makes you Romano's Head—becomes superb
'On your bare neck, which would, on mine, disturb
'The pauldron,' said Taurello. A mad act,
Nor even dreamed about before—in fact,
Not when his sportive arm rose for the nonce—   725
But he had dallied overmuch, this once,
With power: the thing was done, and he, aware
The thing was done, proceeded to declare—
(So like a nature made to serve, excel
In serving, only feel by service well!)   730
—That he would make Sordello that and more.
'As good a scheme as any. What's to pore
'At in my face?' he asked—'ponder instead
'This piece of news; you are Romano's Head!
'One cannot slacken pace so near the goal,   735
'Suffer my Azzo to escape heart-whole
'This time! For you there's Palma to espouse—
'For me, one crowning trouble ere I house
'Like my compeer.'
                    On which ensued a strange

who is
declared
Salinguerra's
son,

And solemn visitation; there came change   740
O'er every one of them; each looked on each:
Up in the midst a truth grew, without speech.
And when the giddiness sank and the haze
Subsided, they were sitting, no amaze,
Sordello with the baldric on, his sire   745
Silent, though his proportions seemed aspire
Momently; and, interpreting the thrill,—
Night at its ebb,—Palma was found there still
Relating somewhat Adelaide confessed
A year ago, while dying on her breast,—   750
Of a contrivance, that Vicenza night
When Ecelin had birth. 'Their convoy's flight,
'Cut off a moment, coiled inside the flame
'That wallowed like a dragon at his game

'The toppling city through—San Biagio rocks!　　755
'And wounded lies in her delicious locks
'Retrude, the frail mother, on her face,
'None of her wasted, just in one embrace
'Covering her child: when, as they lifted her,
'Cleaving the tumult, mighty, mightier　　760
'And mightiest Taurello's cry outbroke,
'Leapt like a tongue of fire that cleaves the smoke,
'Midmost to cheer his Mantuans onward—drown
'His colleague Ecelin's clamour, up and down
'The disarray: failed Adelaide see then　　765
'Who was the natural chief, the man of men?
'Outstripping time, her infant there burst swathe,
'Stood up with eyes haggard beyond the scathe
'From wandering after his heritage
'Lost once and lost for aye: and why that rage,　　770
'That deprecating glance? A new shape leant
'On a familiar shape—gloatingly bent
'O'er his discomfiture; 'mid wreaths it wore,
'Still one outflamed the rest—her child's before
' 'T was Salinguerra's for his child: scorn, hate,　　775
'Rage now might startle her when all too late!
'Then was the moment!—rival's foot had spurned
'Never that House to earth else! Sense returned—
'The act conceived, adventured and complete,
'They bore away to an obscure retreat　　780
'Mother and child—Retrude's self not slain'
(Nor even here Taurello moved) 'though pain
'Was fled; and what assured them most 't was fled,
'All pain, was, if they raised the pale hushed head
' 'T would turn this way and that, waver awhile,　　785
'And only settle into its old smile—
'(Graceful as the disquieted water-flag
'Steadying itself, remarked they, in the quag
'On either side their path)—when suffered look
'Down on her child. They marched: no sign once
　　　shook　　790
'The company's close litter of crossed spears
'Till, as they reached Goito, a few tears
'Slipped in the sunset from her long black lash,

hidden hither-
to by
Adelaide's
policy.

'And she was gone. So far the action rash;
'No crime. They laid Retrude in the font,   795
'Taurello's very gift, her child was wont
'To sit beneath—constant as eve he came
'To sit by its attendant girls the same
'As one of them. For Palma, she would blend
'With this magnific spirit to the end,   800
'That ruled her first; but scarcely had she dared
'To disobey the Adelaide who scared
'Her into vowing never to disclose
'A secret to her husband, which so froze
'His blood at half-recital, she contrived   805
'To hide from him Taurello's infant lived,
'Lest, by revealing that, himself should mar
'Romano's fortunes. And, a crime so far,
'Palma received that action: she was told
'Of Salinguerra's nature, of his cold   810
'Calm acquiescence in his lot! But free
'To impart the secret to Romano, she
'Engaged to repossess Sordello of
'His heritage, and hers, and that way doff
'The mask, but after years, long years: while now,   815
'Was not Romano's sign-mark on that brow?'

How the
discovery
moves
Salinguerra,
                    Across Taurello's heart his arms were locked:
And when he did speak 't was as if he mocked
The minstrel, 'who had not to move,' he said,
'Nor stir—should fate defraud him of a shred   820
'Of his son's infancy? much less his youth!'
(Laughingly all this)—'which to aid, in truth,
'Himself, reserved on purpose, had not grown
'Old, not too old—'t was best they kept alone
'Till now, and never idly met till now;'   825
—Then, in the same breath, told Sordello how
All intimations of this eve's event
Were lies, for Friedrich must advance to Trent,
Thence to Verona, then to Rome, there stop,
Tumble the Church down, institute a-top   830
The Alps a Prefecture of Lombardy:
—'That's now!—no prophesying what may be
'Anon, with a new monarch of the clime,

'Native of Gesi, passing his youth's prime
'At Naples. Tito bids my choice decide   835
'On whom . . .'
         'Embrace him, madman!' Palma cried,
Who through the laugh saw sweat-drops burst apace,
And his lips blanching: he did not embrace
Sordello, but he laid Sordello's hand
On his own eyes, mouth, forehead.
                 Understand,   840   and Sordello
This while Sordello was becoming flushed   the finally-
Out of his whiteness; thoughts rushed, fancies rushed;   determined,
He pressed his hand upon his head and signed
Both should forbear him. 'Nay, the best's behind!'
Taurello laughed—not quite with the same laugh: 845
'The truth is, thus we scatter, ay, like chaff
'These Guelfs, a despicable monk recoils
'From: nor expect a fickle Kaiser spoils
'Our triumph!—Friedrich? Think you, I intend
'Friedrich shall reap the fruits of blood I spend   850   —the Devil
'And brain I waste? Think you, the people clap   putting forth
'Their hands at my out-hewing this wild gap   his potency:
'For any Friedrich to fill up? 'T is mine—
'That's yours: I tell you, towards some such design
'Have I worked blindly, yes, and idly, yes,   855
'And for another, yes—but worked no less
'With instinct at my heart; I else had swerved,
'While now—look round! My cunning has preserved
'Samminiato—that's a central place
'Secures us Florence, boy,—in Pisa's case.   860
'By land as she by sea; with Pisa ours,
'And Florence, and Pistoia, one devours
'The land at leisure! Gloriously dispersed—
'Brescia, observe, Milan, Piacenza first
'That flanked us (ah, you know not!) in the March;   865
'On these we pile, as keystone of our arch,
'Romagna and Bologna, whose first span
'Covered the Trentine and the Valsugan;
'Sofia's Egna by Bolgiano's sure!' . . .
So he proceeded: half of all this, pure   870
Delusion, doubtless, nor the rest too true,

But what was undone he felt sure to do,
As ring by ring he wrung off, flung away
The pauldron-rings to give his sword-arm play—
Need of the sword now! That would soon adjust   875
Aught wrong at present; to the sword intrust
Sordello's whiteness, undersize: 't was plain

Since
Sordello, who
began by
rhyming,

He hardly rendered right to his own brain—
Like a brave hound, men educate to pride
Himself on speed or scent nor aught beside,   880
As though he could not, gift by gift, match men!
Palma had listened patiently: but when
'T was time expostulate, attempt withdraw
Taurello from his child, she, without awe
Took off his iron arms from, one by one,   885
Sordello's shrinking shoulders, and, that done,
Made him avert his visage and relieve
Sordello (you might see his corslet heave
The while) who, loose, rose—tried to speak, then sank:
They left him in the chamber. All was blank.   890
And even reeling down the narrow stair
Taurello kept up, as though unaware
Palma was by to guide him, the old device
—Something of Milan—'how we muster thrice
'The Torriani's strength there; all along   895
'Our own Visconti cowed them'—thus the song
Continued even while she bade him stoop,
Thrid somehow, by some glimpse of arrow-loop,
The turnings to the gallery below,
Where he stopped short as Palma let him go.   900
When he had sat in silence long enough
Splintering the stone bench, braving a rebuff
She stopped the truncheon; only to commence
One of Sordello's poems, a pretence
For speaking, some poor rhyme of 'Elys' hair   905
'And head that's sharp and perfect like a pear,
'So smooth and close are laid the few fine locks

may, even
from the
depths of
failure,

'Stained like pale honey oozed from topmost rocks
'Sun-blanched the livelong summer'—from his worst
Performance, the Goito, as his first: 910
And that at end, conceiving from the brow

And open mouth no silence would serve now,
Went on to say the whole world loved that man
And, for that matter, thought his face, tho' wan,
Eclipsed the Count's—he sucking in each phrase   915
As if an angel spoke. The foolish praise
Ended, he drew her on his mailed knees, made
Her face a framework with his hands, a shade,
A crown, an aureole: there must she remain
(Her little mouth compressed with smiling pain   920
As in his gloves she felt her tresses twitch)
To get the best look at, in fittest niche
Dispose his saint. That done, he kissed her brow,
—'Lauded her father for his treason now,'
He told her, 'only, how could one suspect   925
'The wit in him?—whose clansman, recollect,
'Was ever Salinguerra—she, the same,
'Romano and his lady—so, might claim
'To know all, as she should'—and thus begun
Schemes with a vengeance, schemes on schemes,
          'not one   930
'Fit to be told that foolish boy,' he said,
'But only let Sordello Palma wed,
'—Then!'

          'T was a dim long narrow place at best:
Midway a sole grate showed the fiery West,
As shows its corpse the world's end some split tomb—   935   yet spring to
A gloom, a rift of fire, another gloom,   the summit of
Faced Palma—but at length Taurello set   success,
Her free; the grating held one ragged jet
Of fierce gold fire: he lifted her within
The hollow underneath—how else begin   940
Fate's second marvellous cycle, else renew
The ages than with Palma plain in view?
Then paced the passage, hands clenched, head erect,
Pursuing his discourse; a grand unchecked
Monotony made out from his quick talk   945
And the recurring noises of his walk;
—Somewhat too much like the o'ercharged assent
Of two resolved friends in one danger blent,
Who hearten each the other against heart;

Boasting there's nought to care for, when, apart   950
The boaster, all's to care for. He, beside
Some shape not visible, in power and pride
Approached, out of the dark, ginglingly near,
Nearer, passed close in the broad light, his ear
Crimson, eyeballs suffused, temples full-fraught,   955
Just a snatch of the rapid speech you caught,
And on he strode into the opposite dark,
Till presently the harsh heel's turn, a spark
I' the stone, and whirl of some loose embossed thong
That crashed against the angle aye so long   960
After the last, punctual to an amount
Of mailed great paces you could not but count,—
Prepared you for the pacing back again.
And by the snatches you might ascertain

if he consent
to oppress the
world.

That, Friedrich's Prefecture surmounted, left   965
By this alone in Italy, they cleft
Asunder, crushed together, at command
Of none, were free to break up Hildebrand,
Rebuild, he and Sordello, Charlemagne—
But garnished, Strength with Knowledge, 'if we deign   970
'Accept that compromise and stoop to give
'Rome law, the Cæsar's Representative.'
Enough, that the illimitable flood
Of triumphs after triumphs, understood
In its faint reflux (you shall hear) sufficed   975
Young Ecelin for appanage, enticed
Him on till, these long quiet in their graves,
He found 't was looked for that a whole life's braves
Should somehow be made good; so, weak and worn,
Must stagger up at Milan, one grey morn   980
Of the to-come, and fight his latest fight.
But, Salinguerra's prophecy at height—
He voluble with a raised arm and stiff,
A blaring voice, a blazing eye, as if
He had our very Italy to keep   985
Or cast away, or gather in a heap
To garrison the better—ay, his word
Was, 'run the cucumber into a gourd,
'Drive Trent upon Apulia'—at their pitch

Who spied the continents and islands which   990
Grew mulberry leaves and sickles, in the map—
(Strange that three such confessions so should hap
To Palma, Dante spoke with in the clear   Just this
decided, as it
now may be,
Amorous silence of the Swooning-sphere,—
Cunizza, as he called her! Never ask   995
Of Palma more! She sat, knowing her task
Was done, the labour of it,—for, success
Concerned not Palma, passion's votaress.)
Triumph at height, and thus Sordello crowned—
Above the passage suddenly a sound   1000
Stops speech, stops walk: back shrinks Taurello, bids
With large involuntary asking lids,
Palma interpret. ' 'T is his own foot-stamp—
'Your hand! His summons! Nay, this idle damp
'Befits not!' Out they two reeled dizzily.   1005
'Visconti's strong at Milan,' resumed he,
In the old, somewhat insignificant way—
(Was Palma wont, years afterward, to say)
As though the spirit's flight, sustained thus far,
Dropped at that very instant.
                  Gone they are—   1010
Palma, Taurello; Eglamor anon,
Ecelin,—only Naddo's never gone!
—Labours, this moonrise, what the Master meant:
'Is Squarcialupo speckled?—purulent,
'I'd say, but when was Providence put out?   1015
'He carries somehow handily about
'His spite nor fouls himself!' Goito's vines
Stand like a cheat detected—stark rough lines,
The moon breaks through, a grey mean scale against
The vault where, this eve's Maiden, thou remain'st 1020
Like some fresh martyr, eyes fixed—who can tell?
As Heaven, now all's at end, did not so well,
Spite of the faith and victory, to leave
Its virgin quite to death in the lone eve.
While the persisting hermit-bee . . . ha! wait   1025   and we have
done.
No longer: these in compass, forward fate!

BOOK THE SIXTH

At the close of
a day or a life,

THE thought of Eglamor's least like a thought,
And yet a false one, was, 'Man shrinks to nought
'If matched with symbols of immensity;
'Must quail, forsooth, before a quiet sky
'Or sea, too little for their quietude:'   5
And, truly, somewhat in Sordello's mood
Confirmed its speciousness, while eve slow sank
Down the near terrace to the farther bank,
And only one spot left from out the night
Glimmered upon the river opposite—   10
A breadth of watery heaven like a bay,
A sky-like space of water, ray for ray,
And star for star, one richness where they mixed
As this and that wing of an angel, fixed,
Tumultuary splendours folded in   15
To die. Nor turned he till Ferrara's din
(Say, the monotonous speech from a man's lip
Who lets some first and eager purpose slip
In a new fancy's birth—the speech keeps on
Though elsewhere its informing soul be gone)   20
—Aroused him, surely offered succour. Fate
Paused with this eve; ere she precipitate
Herself,—best put off new strange thoughts awhile,
That voice, those large hands, that portentous smile,—
What help to pierce the future as the past   25
Lay in the plaining city?

past procedure
is fitliest
reviewed,
                              And at last
The main discovery and prime concern,
All that just now imported him to learn,
Truth's self, like yonder slow moon to complete
Heaven, rose again, and, naked at his feet,   30
Lighted his old life's every shift and change,
Effort with counter-effort; nor the range
Of each looked wrong except wherein it checked,
Some other—which of these could he suspect,
Prying into them by the sudden blaze?   35
The real way seemed made up of all the ways—

Mood after mood of the one mind in him;
Tokens of the existence, bright or dim,
Of a transcendent all-embracing sense
Demanding only outward influence,   40
A soul, in Palma's phrase, above his soul,
Power to uplift his power,—such moon's control
Over such sea-depths,—and their mass had swept
Onward from the beginning and still kept
Its course: but years and years the sky above   45
Held none, and so, untasked of any love,
His sensitiveness idled, now amort,
Alive now, and, to sullenness or sport
Given wholly up, disposed itself anew
At every passing instigation, grew   50
And dwindled at caprice, in foam-showers spilt,
Wedge-like insisting, quivered now a gilt
Shield in the sunshine, now a blinding race
Of whitest ripples o'er the reef—found place
For much display; not gathered up and, hurled   55
Right from its heart, encompassing the world.
So had Sordello been, by consequence,
Without a function: others made pretence
To strength not half his own, yet had some core
Within, submitted to some moon, before   60
Them still, superior still whate'er their force,—
Were able therefore to fulfil a course,
Nor missed life's crown, authentic attribute.
To each who lives must be a certain fruit   ·as more
Of having lived in his degree,—a stage,   65 appreciable in
Earlier or later in men's pilgrimage,   its entirety.
To stop at; and to this the spirits tend
Who, still discovering beauty without end,
Amass the scintillations, make one star
—Something unlike them, self-sustained, afar,—   70
And meanwhile nurse the dream of being blest
By winning it to notice and invest
Their souls with alien glory, some one day
Whene'er the nucleus, gathering shape alway,
Round to the perfect circle—soon or late,   75
According as themselves are formed to wait;

Whether mere human beauty will suffice
—The yellow hair and the luxurious eyes,
Or human intellect seem best, or each
Combine in some ideal form past reach   80
On earth, or else some shade of these, some aim,
Some love, hate even, take their place, the same,
So to be served—all this they do not lose,
Waiting for death to live, nor idly choose
What must be Hell—a progress thus pursued   85
Through all existence, still above the food
That's offered them, still fain to reach beyond
The widened range, in virtue of their bond

Strong, he
needed exter-
nal strength:

Of sovereignty. Not that a Palma's Love,
A Salinguerra's Hate, would equal prove   90
To swaying all Sordello: but why doubt
Some love meet for such strength, some moon without
Would match his sea?—or fear, Good manifest,
Only the Best breaks faith?—Ah but the Best
Somehow eludes us ever, still might be   95
And is not! Crave we gems? No penury
Of their material round us! Pliant earth
And plastic flame—what balks the mage his birth
—Jacinth in balls or lodestone by the block?
Flinders enrich the strand, veins swell the rock;   100
Nought more! Seek creatures? Life's i' the tempest,
        thought
Clothes the keen hill-top, mid-day woods are fraught
With fervours: human forms are well enough!
But we had hoped, encouraged by the stuff
Profuse at nature's pleasure, men beyond   105
These actual men!—and thus are over-fond
In arguing, from Good—the Best, from force
Divided—force combined, an ocean's course
From this our sea whose mere intestine pants
Might seem at times sufficient to our wants.   110

even now,
where can he
perceive such?

        External power! If none be adequate,
And he stand forth ordained (a prouder fate)
Himself a law to his own sphere? 'Remove
'All incompleteness!' for that law, that love?
Nay, if all other laws be feints,—truth veiled   115

Helpfully to weak vision that had failed
To grasp aught but its special want,—for lure,
Embodied? Stronger vision could endure
The unbodied want: no part—the whole of truth!
The People were himself; nor, by the ruth   120
At their condition, was he less impelled
To alter the discrepancy beheld,
Than if, from the sound whole, a sickly part
Subtracted were transformed, decked out with art,
Then palmed on him as alien woe—the Guelf   125
To succour, proud that he forsook himself.
All is himself; all service, therefore, rates
Alike, nor serving one part, immolates
The rest: but all in time! 'That lance of yours
'Makes havoc soon with Malek and his Moors,   130
'That buckler's lined with many a giant's beard
'Ere long, our champion, be the lance upreared,
'The buckler wielded handsomely as now!
'But view your escort, bear in mind your vow,
'Count the pale tracts of sand to pass ere that,   135
'And, if you hope we struggle through the flat,
'Put lance and buckler by! Next half-month lacks
'Mere sturdy exercise of mace and axe
'To cleave this dismal brake of prickly-pear
'Which bristling holds Cydippe by the hair,   140
'Lames barefoot Agathon: this felled, we'll try
'The picturesque achievements by and by—
'Next life!'

        Ay, rally, mock, O People, urge
Your claims!—for thus he ventured, to the verge,
Push a vain mummery which perchance distrust   145
Of his fast-slipping resolution thrust
Likewise: accordingly the Crowd—(as yet
He had unconsciously contrived forget
I' the whole, to dwell o' the points . . . one might assuage
The signal horrors easier than engage   150
With a dim vulgar vast unobvious grief
Not to be fancied off, nor gained relief
In brilliant fits, cured by a happy quirk,
But by dim vulgar vast unobvious work

Internal
strength must
suffice then,

To correspond . . .) this Crowd then, forth they stood. 155
'And now content thy stronger vision, brood
'On thy bare want; uncovered, turf by turf,
'Study the corpse-face thro' the taint-worms' scurf!'
  Down sank the People's Then; uprose their Now.
These sad ones render service to! And how   160
Piteously little must that service prove
—Had surely proved in any case! for, move
Each other obstacle away, let youth
Become aware it had surprised a truth
'T were service to impart—can truth be seized,   165
his sympathy
with the
people, to wit;
Settled forthwith, and, of the captive eased,
Its captor find fresh prey, since this alit
So happily, no gesture luring it,
The earnest of a flock to follow? Vain,
Most vain! a life to spend ere this he chain   170
To the poor crowd's complacence: ere the crowd
Pronounce it captured, he descries a cloud
Its kin of twice the plume; which he, in turn,
If he shall live as many lives, may learn
How to secure: not else. Then Mantua called   175
Back to his mind how certain bards were thralled
—Buds blasted, but of breath more like perfume
Than Naddo's staring nosegay's carrion bloom;
Some insane rose that burnt heart out in sweets,
A spendthrift in the spring, no summer greets;   180
Some Dularete, drunk with truths and wine,
Grown bestial, dreaming how become divine.
Yet to surmount this obstacle, commence
With the commencement, merits crowning! Hence
Must truth be casual truth, elicited   185
In sparks so mean, at intervals dispread
So rarely, that 't is like at no one time
Of the world's story has not truth, the prime
Of truth, the very truth which, loosed, had hurled
The world's course right, been really in the world   190
—Content the while with some mean spark by dint
Of some chance-blow, the solitary hint
Of buried fire, which, rip earth's breast, would stream
Sky-ward!

Sordello's miserable gleam

Was looked for at the moment: he would dash   195 of which, try
now the
inherent
force!
This badge, and all it brought, to earth,—abash
Taurello thus, perhaps persuade him wrest
The Kaiser from his purpose,—would attest
His own belief, in any case. Before
He dashes it however, think once more!   200
For, were that little, truly service? 'Ay,
'I' the end, no doubt; but meantime? Plain you spy
'Its ultimate effect, but many flaws
'Of vision blur each intervening cause.
'Were the day's fraction clear as the life's sum   205
'Of service, Now as filled as teems To-come
'With evidence of good—nor too minute
'A share to vie with evil! No dispute,
' 'T were fitliest maintain the Guelfs in rule:
'That makes your life's work: but you have to school 210
'Your day's work on these natures circumstanced
'Thus variously, which yet, as each advanced
'Or might impede the Guelf rule, must be moved
'Now, for the Then's sake,—hating what you loved,
'Loving old hatreds! Nor if one man bore   215
'Brand upon temples while his fellow wore
'The aureole, would it task you to decide:
'But, portioned duly out, the future vied
'Never with the unparcelled present! Smite
'Or spare so much on warrant all so slight?   220
'The present's complete sympathies to break,
'Aversions bear with, for a future's sake
'So feeble? Tito ruined through one speck,
'The Legate saved by his sole lightish fleck?
'This were work, true, but work performed at cost 225
'Of other work; aught gained here, elsewhere lost.
'For a new segment spoil an orb half-done?
'Rise with the People one step, and sink—one? How much of
man's ill may
be removed?
'Were it but one step, less than the whole face
'Of things, your novel duty bids erase!   230
'Harms to abolish! What, the prophet saith,
'The minstrel singeth vainly then? Old faith,
'Old courage, only born because of harms,

'Were not, from highest to the lowest, charms?
'Flame may persist; but is not glare as staunch?   235
'Where the salt marshes stagnate, crystals branch;
'Blood dries to crimson; Evil's beautified
'In every shape. Thrust Beauty then aside
'And banish Evil! Wherefore? After all,
'Is Evil a result less natural   240
'Than Good? For overlook the seasons' strife
'With tree and flower,—the hideous animal life,
'(Of which who seeks shall find a grinning taunt
'For his solution, and endure the vaunt
'Of nature's angel, as a child that knows   245
'Himself befooled, unable to propose
'Aught better than the fooling)—and but care
'For men, for the mere People then and there,—
'In these, could you but see that Good and Ill
'Claimed you alike! Whence rose their claim but still   250
'From Ill, as fruit of Ill? What else could knit
'You theirs but Sorrow? Any free from it
'Were also free from you! Whose happiness
'Could be distinguished in this morning's press
'Of miseries?—the fool's who passed a gibe   255
' "On thee," jeered he, "so wedded to thy tribe,
' "Thou carriest green and yellow tokens in
' "Thy very face that thou art Ghibellin!"

How much of
ill ought to be
removed?

'Much hold on you that fool obtained! Nay mount
'Yet higher—and upon men's own account   260
'Must Evil stay: for, what is joy?—to heave
'Up one obstruction more, and common leave
'What was peculiar, by such act destroy
'Itself; a partial death is every joy;
'The sensible escape, enfranchisement   265
'Of a sphere's essence: once the vexed—content,
'The cramped—at large, the growing circle—round,
'All's to begin again—some novel bound
'To break, some new enlargement to entreat;
'The sphere though larger is not more complete.   270
'Now for Mankind's experience: who alone
'Might style the unobstructed world his own?
'Whom palled Goito with its perfect things?

'Sordello's self: whereas for Mankind springs
'Salvation by each hindrance interposed.   275
'They climb; life's view is not at once disclosed
'To creatures caught up, on the summit left,
'Heaven plain above them, yet of wings bereft:
'But lower laid, as at the mountain's foot.
'So, range on range, the girdling forests shoot   280
' 'Twixt your plain prospect and the throngs who scale
'Height after height, and pierce mists, veil by veil,
'Heartened with each discovery; in their soul,
'The Whole they seek by Parts—but, found that Whole,
'Could they revert, enjoy past gains? The space   285
'Of time you judge so meagre to embrace
'The Parts were more than plenty, once attained
'The Whole, to quite exhaust it: nought were gained
'But leave to look—not leave to do: Beneath
'Soon sates the looker—look Above, and Death   290
'Tempts ere a tithe of Life be tasted. Live
'First, and die soon enough, Sordello! Give
'Body and spirit the first right they claim,
'And pasture soul on a voluptuous shame
'That you, a pageant-city's denizen,   295
'Are neither vilely lodged midst Lombard men—
'Can force joy out of sorrow, seem to truck
'Bright attributes away for sordid muck,
'Yet manage from that very muck educe
'Gold; then subject, nor scruple, to your cruce   300
'The world's discardings! Though real ingots pay
'Your pains, the clods that yielded them are clay
'To all beside,—would clay remain, though quenched
'Your purging-fire; who's robbed then? Had you
          wrenched
'An ampler treasure forth!—As 't is, they crave   305
'A share that ruins you and will not save
'Them. Why should sympathy command you quit
'The course that makes your joy, nor will remit
'Their woe? Would all arrive at joy? Reverse
'The order (time instructs you) nor coerce   310
'Each unit till, some predetermined mode,
'The total be emancipate; men's road

—if removed,
at what cost to
Sordello?

Men win
little thereby;
he loses all:

'Is one, men's times of travel many; thwart
'No enterprising soul's precocious start
'Before the general march! If slow or fast   315
'All straggle up to the same point at last,
'Why grudge your having gained, a month ago,
'The brakes at balm-shed, asphodels in blow,
'While they were landlocked? Speed their Then, but
          how
'This badge would suffer you improve your Now!'   320
    His time of action for, against, or with
Our world (I labour to extract the pith
Of this his problem) grew, that even-tide,
Gigantic with its power of joy, beside
The world's eternity of impotence   325
To profit though at his whole joy's expense.
'Make nothing of my day because so brief?
'Rather make more: instead of joy, use grief
'Before its novelty have time subside!
'Wait not for the late savour, leave untried   330
'Virtue, the creaming honey-wine, quick squeeze
'Vice like a biting spirit from the lees
'Of life! Together let wrath, hatred, lust,
'All tyrannies in every shape, be thrust
'Upon this Now, which time may reason out   335
'As mischiefs, far from benefits, no doubt;

for he can
infinitely
enjoy himself,

'But long ere then Sordello will have slipt
'Away; you teach him at Goito's crypt,
'There's a blank issue to that fiery thrill.
'Stirring, the few cope with the many, still: 340
'So much of sand as, quiet, makes a mass
'Unable to produce three tufts of grass,
'Shall, troubled by the whirlwind, render void
'The whole calm glebe's endeavour: be employed!
'And e'en though somewhat smart the Crowd for this,   345
'Contribute each his pang to make your bliss,
' 'T is but one pang—one blood-drop to the bowl
'Which brimful tempts the sluggish asp uncowl
'At last, stains ruddily the dull red cape,
'And, kindling orbs grey as the unripe grape   350
'Before, avails forthwith to disentrance

'The portent, soon to lead a mystic dance
'Among you! For, who sits alone in Rome?
'Have those great hands indeed hewn out a home,
'And set me there to live? Oh life, life-breath,   355
'Life-blood,—ere sleep, come travail, life ere death!
'This life stream on my soul, direct, oblique,
'But always streaming! Hindrances? They pique:
'Helps? such . . . but why repeat, my soul o'ertops
'Each height, then every depth profoundlier drops?   360
'Enough that I can live, and would live! Wait
'For some transcendent life reserved by Fate
'To follow this? Oh, never! Fate, I trust
'The same, my soul to; for, as who flings dust,
'Perchance (so facile was the deed) she chequed   365
'The void with these materials to affect
'My soul diversely: these consigned anew
'To nought by death, what marvel if she threw
'A second and superber spectacle
'Before me? What may serve for sun, what still   370
'Wander a moon above me? What else wind
'About me like the pleasures left behind,
'And how shall some new flesh that is not flesh
'Cling to me? What's new laughter? Soothes the fresh
'Sleep like sleep? Fate's exhaustless for my sake   375   freed from a
'In brave resource: but whether bids she slake   problematic
'My thirst at this first rivulet, or count   obligation,
'No draught worth lip save from some rocky fount
'Above i' the clouds, while here she's provident
'Of pure loquacious pearl, the soft tree-tent   380
'Guards, with its face of reate and sedge, nor fail
'The silver globules and gold-sparkling grail
'At bottom? Oh, 't were too absurd to slight
'For the hereafter the to-day's delight!
'Quench thirst at this, then seek next well-spring:
        wear   385
'Home-lilies ere strange lotus in my hair!
'Here is the Crowd, whom I with freest heart
'Offer to serve, contented for my part
'To give life up in service,—only grant
'That I do serve; if otherwise, why want   390

'Aught further of me? If men cannot choose
'But set aside life, why should I refuse
'The gift? I take it—I, for one, engage
'Never to falter through my pilgrimage—
'Nor end it howling that the stock or stone   395
'Were enviable, truly: I, for one,
'Will praise the world, you style mere anteroom
'To palace—be it so! shall I assume
'—My foot the courtly gait, my tongue the trope,
'My mouth the smirk, before the doors fly ope   400
'One moment? What? with guarders row on row,
'Gay swarms of varletry that come and go,
'Pages to dice with, waiting-girls unlace
'The plackets of, pert claimants help displace,
'Heart-heavy suitors get a rank for,—laugh   405
'At yon sleek parasite, break his own staff
' 'Cross Beetle-brows the Usher's shoulder,—why
'Admitted to the presence by and by,
'Should thought of having lost these make me grieve
'Among new joys I reach, for joys I leave?   410
'Cool citrine-crystals, fierce pyropus-stone,
'Are floor-work there! But do I let alone
'That black-eyed peasant in the vestibule
'Once and for ever?—Floor-work? No such fool!
'Rather, were heaven to forestall earth, I'd say   415
'I, is it, must be blest? Then, my own way
'Bless me! Giver firmer arm and fleeter foot,
'I'll thank you: but to no mad wings transmute
'These limbs of mine—our greensward was so soft!
'Nor camp I on the thunder-cloud aloft: 420
'We feel the bliss distinctlier, having thus
'Engines subservient, not mixed up with us.
'Better move palpably through heaven: nor, freed
'Of flesh, forsooth, from space to space proceed
' 'Mid flying synods of worlds! No: in heaven's marge 425
'Show Titan still, recumbent o'er his targe
'Solid with stars—the Centaur at his game,
'Made tremulously out in hoary flame!
    'Life! Yet the very cup whose extreme dull
'Dregs, even, I would quaff, was dashed, at full,   430

'Aside so oft; the death I fly, revealed
'So oft a better life this life concealed,
'And which sage, champion, martyr, through each path
'Have hunted fearlessly—the horrid bath,
'The crippling-irons and the fiery chair.   435
' 'T was well for them; let me become aware
'As they, and I relinquish life, too! Let
'What masters life disclose itself! Forget
'Vain ordinances, I have one appeal—
'I feel, am what I feel, know what I feel;   440
'So much is truth to me. What Is, then? Since
'One object, viewed diversely, may evince
'Beauty and ugliness—this way attract,
'That way repel,—why gloze upon the fact?
'Why must a single of the sides be right?   445
'What bids choose this and leave the opposite?
'Where's abstract Right for me?—in youth endued
'With Right still present, still to be pursued,
'Thro' all the interchange of circles, rife
'Each with its proper law and mode of life,   450
'Each to be dwelt at ease in: where, to sway
'Absolute with the Kaiser, or obey
'Implicit with his serf of fluttering heart,
'Or, like a sudden thought of God's, to start
'Up, Brutus in the presence, then go shout   455
'That some should pick the unstrung jewels out—
'Each, well!'

        And, as in moments when the past
Gave partially enfranchisement, he cast
Himself quite through mere secondary states
Of his soul's essence, little loves and hates,   460
Into the mid deep yearnings overlaid
By these; as who should pierce hill, plain, grove, glade,
And on into the very nucleus probe
That first determined there exist a globe.
As that were easiest, half the globe dissolved,   465
So seemed Sordello's closing-truth evolved
By his flesh-half's break-up; the sudden swell
Of his expanding soul showed Ill and Well,
Sorrow and Joy, Beauty and Ugliness,

which, yet,
others have
renounced:
how?

Because there
is a life
beyond life,

Virtue and Vice, the Larger and the Less,   470
All qualities, in fine, recorded here,
Might be but modes of Time and this one sphere,
Urgent on these, but not of force to bind
Eternity, as Time—as Matter—Mind,
If Mind, Eternity, should choose assert   475
Their attributes within a Life: thus girt
With circumstance, next change beholds them cinct
Quite otherwise—with Good and Ill distinct,
Joys, sorrows, tending to a like result—
Contrived to render easy, difficult,   480

and with new
conditions of
success,

This or the other course of . . . what new bond
In place of flesh may stop their flight beyond
Its new sphere, as that course does harm or good
To its arrangements. Once this understood,
As suddenly he felt himself alone,   485
Quite out of Time and this world: all was known.
What made the secret of his past despair?
—Most imminent when he seemed most aware
Of his own self-sufficiency: made mad
By craving to expand the power he had,   490
And not new power to be expanded?—just
This made it; Soul on Matter being thrust,
Joy comes when so much Soul is wreaked in Time
On Matter: let the Soul's attempt sublime
Matter beyond the scheme and so prevent   495
By more or less that deed's accomplishment,
And Sorrow follows: Sorrow how avoid?
Let the employer match the thing employed,
Fit to the finite his infinity,
And thus proceed for ever, in degree   500
Changed but in kind the same, still limited
To the appointed circumstance and dead
To all beyond. A sphere is but a sphere;
Small, Great, are merely terms we bandy here;
Since to the spirit's absoluteness all   505
Are like. Now, of the present sphere we call
Life, are conditions; take but this among
Many; the body was to be so long
Youthful, no longer: but, since no control

Tied to that body's purposes his soul,　　　510
She chose to understand the body's trade
More than the body's self—had fain conveyed
Her boundless to the body's bounded lot.
Hence, the soul permanent, the body not,—
Scarcely its minute for enjoying here,—　　　515
The soul must needs instruct her weak compeer,
Run o'er its capabilities and wring
A joy thence, she held worth experiencing:
Which, far from half discovered even,—lo,
The minute gone, the body's power let go　　　520
Apportioned to that joy's acquirement! Broke
Morning o'er earth, he yearned for all it woke—
From the volcano's vapour-flag, winds hoist
Black o'er the spread of sea,—down to the moist
Dale's silken barley-spikes sullied with rain,　　　525
Swayed earthwards, heavily to rise again—
The Small, a sphere as perfect as the Great
To the soul's absoluteness. Meditate
Too long on such a morning's cluster-chord
And the whole music it was framed afford,—　　　530
The chord's might half discovered, what should pluck
One string, his finger, was found palsy-struck.
And then no marvel if the spirit, shown
A saddest sight—the body lost alone
Through her officious proffered help, deprived　　　535
Of this and that enjoyment Fate contrived,—
Virtue, Good, Beauty, each allowed slip hence,—
Vain-gloriously were fain, for recompense,
To stem the ruin even yet, protract
The body's term, supply the power it lacked　　　540
From her infinity, compel it learn
These qualities were only Time's concern,
And body may, with spirit helping, barred—
Advance the same, vanquished—obtain reward,
Reap joy where sorrow was intended grow,　　　545
Of Wrong make Right, and turn Ill Good below.
And the result is, the poor body soon
Sinks under what was meant a wondrous boon,
Leaving its bright accomplice all aghast.

nor such as, in this, produce failure.

But, even
here, is failure
inevitable?

So much was plain then, proper in the past;   550
To be complete for, satisfy the whole
Series of spheres—Eternity, his soul
Needs must exceed, prove incomplete for, each
Single sphere—Time. But does our knowledge reach
No farther? Is the cloud of hindrance broke   555
But by the failing of the fleshly yoke,
Its loves and hates, as now when death lets soar
Sordello, self-sufficient as before,
Though during the mere space that shall elapse
'Twixt his enthralment in new bonds perhaps?   560
Must life be ever just escaped, which should
Have been enjoyed?—nay, might have been and would,
Each purpose ordered right—the soul's no whit
Beyond the body's purpose under it.
Like yonder breadth of watery heaven, a bay,   565
And that sky-space of water, ray for ray
And star for star, one richness where they mixed
As this and that wing of an angel, fixed,
Tumultuary splendours folded in
To die—would soul, proportioned thus, begin   570
Exciting discontent, or surelier quell
The body if, aspiring, it rebel?

Or may failure
here be
success also

But how so order life? Still brutalize
The soul, the sad world's way, with muffled eyes
To all that was before, all that shall be   575
After this sphere—all and each quality
Save some sole and immutable Great, Good
And Beauteous whither fate has loosed its hood
To follow? Never may some soul see All
—The Great Before and After, and the Small   580
Now, yet be saved by this the simplest lore,
And take the single course prescribed before,
As the king-bird with ages on his plumes
Travels to die in his ancestral glooms?
But where descry the Love that shall select   585
That course? Here is a soul whom, to affect,
Nature has plied with all her means, from trees
And flowers e'en to the Multitude!—and these,
Decides he save or no? One word to end!

Ah my Sordello, I this once befriend 590
And speak for you. Of a Power above you still
Which, utterly incomprehensible,
Is out of rivalry, which thus you can
Love, tho' unloving all conceived by man—
What need! And of—none the minutest duct 595
To that out-nature, nought that would instruct
And so let rivalry begin to live—
But of a Power its representative
Who, being for authority the same,
Communication different, should claim 600
A course, the first chose but this last revealed—
This Human clear, as that Divine concealed—
What utter need!

            What has Sordello found?
Or can his spirit go the mighty round,
End where poor Eglamor begun? So, says 605
Old fable, the two eagles went two ways
About the world: where, in the midst, they met,
Though on a shifting waste of sand, men set
Jove's temple. Quick, what has Sordello found?
For they approach—approach—that foot's rebound 610
Palma? No, Salinguerra though in mail;
They mount, have reached the threshold, dash the veil
Aside—and you divine who sat there dead,
Under his foot the badge: still, Palma said,
A triumph lingering in the wide eyes, 615
Wider than some spent swimmer's if he spies
Help from above in his extreme despair,
And, head far back on shoulder thrust, turns there
With short quick passionate cry: as Palma pressed
In one great kiss, her lips upon his breast, 620
It beat.

          By this, the hermit-bee has stopped
His day's toil at Goito: the new-cropped
Dead vine-leaf answers, now 't is eve, he bit,
Twirled so, and filed all day: the mansion's fit,
God counselled for. As easy guess the word 625
That passed betwixt them, and become the third
To the soft small unfrighted bee, as tax

Marginal notes:

when induced
by love?
Sordello
605 knows:

625 but too late:
an insect
knows sooner.

Him with one fault—so, no remembrance racks
Of the stone maidens and the font of stone
He, creeping through the crevice, leaves alone.   630
Alas, my friend, alas Sordello, whom
Anon they laid within that old font-tomb,
And, yet again, alas!

On his dis-
appearance
from the
stage,

                              And now is 't worth
Our while bring back to mind, much less set forth
How Salinguerra extricates himself   635
Without Sordello? Ghibellin and Guelf
May fight their fiercest out? If Richard sulked
In durance or the Marquis paid his mulct,
Who cares, Sordello gone? The upshot, sure,
Was peace; our chief made some frank overture   640
That prospered; compliment fell thick and fast
On its disposer, and Taurello passed
With foe and friend for an outstripping soul,
Nine days at least. Then,—fairly reached the goal,—
He, by one effort, blotted the great hope   645
Out of his mind, nor further tried to cope
With Este, that mad evening's style, but sent
Away the Legate and the League, content
No blame at least the brothers had incurred,
—Dispatched a message to the Monk, he heard   650
Patiently first to last, scarce shivered at,
Then curled his limbs up on his wolfskin mat
And ne'er spoke more,—informed the Ferrarese
He but retained their rule so long as these
Lingered in pupilage,—and last, no mode   655
Apparent else of keeping safe the road
From Germany direct to Lombardy
For Friedrich,—none, that is, to guarantee
The faith and promptitude of who should next
Obtain Sofia's dowry,—sore perplexed—   660
(Sofia being youngest of the tribe
Of daughters, Ecelin was wont to bribe
The envious magnates with—nor, since he sent
Henry of Egna this fair child, had Trent
Once failed the Kaiser's purposes—'we lost   665
'Egna last year, and who takes Egna's post—

'Opens the Lombard gate if Friedrich knock?')
Himself espoused the Lady of the Rock
In pure necessity, and, so destroyed
His slender last of chances, quite made void   670
Old prophecy, and spite of all the schemes
Overt and covert, youth's deeds, age's dreams,
Was sucked into Romano. And so hushed
He up this evening's work that, when 't was brushed
Somehow against by a blind chronicle   675
Which, chronicling whatever woe befell
Ferrara, noted this the obscure woe
Of 'Salinguerra's sole son Giacomo
'Deceased, fatuous and doting, ere his sire,'
The townsfolk rubbed their eyes, could but admire   680
Which of Sofia's five was meant.
                             The chaps
Of earth's dead hope were tardy to collapse,
Obliterated not the beautiful
Distinctive features at a crash: but dull
And duller these, next year, as Guelfs withdrew   685
Each to his stronghold. Then (securely too
Ecelin at Campese slept; close by,
Who likes may see him in Solagna lie,
With cushioned head and gloved hand to denote
The cavalier he was)—then his heart smote   690
Young Ecelin at last; long since adult.
And, save Vicenza's business, what result
In blood and blaze? (So hard to intercept
Sordello till his plain withdrawal!) Stepped   *the next*
Then its new lord on Lombardy. I' the nick   695 *aspirant can*
Of time when Ecelin and Alberic   *press forward;*
Closed with Taurello, come precisely news
That in Verona half the souls refuse
Allegiance to the Marquis and the Count—
Have cast them from a throne they bid him mount,   700
Their Podestà, thro' his ancestral worth.
Ecelin flew there, and the town henceforth
Was wholly his—Taurello sinking back
From temporary station to a track
That suited. News received of this acquist,   705

Friedrich did come to Lombardy: who missed
Taurello then? Another year: they took
Vicenza, left the Marquis scarce a nook
For refuge, and, when hundreds two or three
Of Guelfs conspired to call themselves 'The Free,'   710
Opposing Alberic,—vile Bassanese,—

Salinguerra's
part lapsing to
Ecelin,

(Without Sordello!)—Ecelin at ease
Slaughtered them so observably, that oft
A little Salinguerra looked with soft
Blue eyes up, asked his sire the proper age   715
To get appointed his proud uncle's page.
More years passed, and that sire had dwindled down
To a mere showy turbulent soldier, grown
Better through age, his parts still in repute,
Subtle—how else?—but hardly so astute   720
As his contemporaneous friends professed;
Undoubtedly a brawler: for the rest,
Known by each neighbour, and allowed for, let
Keep his incorrigible ways, nor fret
Men who would miss their boyhood's bugbear: 'trap   725
'The ostrich, suffer our bald osprey flap
'A battered pinion!'—was the word. In fine,
One flap too much and Venice's marine
Was meddled with; no overlooking that!
She captured him in his Ferrara, fat   730
And florid at a banquet, more by fraud
Than force, to speak the truth; there's slender laud
Ascribed you for assisting eighty years
To pull his death on such a man; fate shears
The life-cord prompt enough whose last fine thread   735
You fritter: so, presiding his board-head,
The old smile, your assurance all went well

who, with his
brother,
played it out,

With Friedrich (as if he were like to tell!)
In rushed (a plan contrived before) our friends,
Made some pretence at fighting, some amends   740
For the shame done his eighty years—(apart
The principle, none found it in his heart
To be much angry with Taurello)—gained
Their galleys with the prize, and what remained
But carry him to Venice for a show?   745

—Set him, as 't were, down gently—free to go
His gait, inspect our square, pretend observe
The swallows soaring their eternal curve
'Twixt Theodore and Mark, if citizens
Gathered importunately, fives and tens, 　　　　750
To point their children the Magnifico,
All but a monarch once in firm-land, go'
His gait among them now—'it took, indeed,
'Fully this Ecelin to supersede
'That man,' remarked the seniors. Singular! 　　　755
Sordello's inability to bar
Rivals the stage, that evening, mainly brought
About by his strange disbelief that aught
Was ever to be done,—this thrust the Twain
Under Taurello's tutelage,—whom, brain 　　　760
And heart and hand, he forthwith in one rod
Indissolubly bound to baffle God
Who loves the world—and thus allowed the thin
Grey wizened dwarfish devil Ecelin,
And massy-muscled big-boned Alberic 　　　765
(Mere man, alas!) to put his problem quick
To demonstration—prove wherever's will
To do, there's plenty to be done, or ill
Or good. Anointed, then, to rend and rip— 　and went
Kings of the gag and flesh-hook, screw and whip, 　home duly to
They plagued the world: a touch of Hildebrand 　their reward.
(So far from obsolete!) made Lombards band 　　　770
Together, cross their coats as for Christ's cause,
And saving Milan win the world's applause.
Ecelin perished: and I think grass grew 　　　775
Never so pleasant as in Valley Rù
By San Zenon where Alberic in turn
Saw his exasperated captors burn
Seven children and their mother; then, regaled
So far, tied on to a wild horse, was trailed 　　　780
To death through raunce and bramble-bush. I take
God's part and testify that 'mid the brake
Wild o'er his castle on the pleasant knoll,
You hear its one tower left, a belfry, toll—
The earthquake spared it last year, laying flat 　　　785

The modern church beneath,—no harm in that!
Chirrups the contumacious grasshopper,
Rustles the lizard and the cushats chirre
Above the ravage: there, at deep of day
A week since, heard I the old Canon say   790
He saw with his own eyes a barrow burst
And Alberic's huge skeleton unhearsed
Only five years ago. He added, 'June's
'The month for carding off our first cocoons
'The silkworms fabricate'—a double news,   795
Nor he nor I could tell the worthier. Choose!
        And Naddo gone, all's gone; not Eglamor!
Believe, I knew the face I waited for,
A guest my spirit of the golden courts!
Oh strange to see how, despite ill-reports,   800
Disuse, some wear of years, that face retained
Its joyous look of love! Suns waxed and waned,
And still my spirit held an upward flight,
Spiral on spiral, gyres of life and light
More and more gorgeous—ever that face there   805
The last admitted! crossed, too, with some care
As perfect triumph were not sure for all,
But, on a few, enduring damp must fall,
—A transient struggle, haply a painful sense
Of the inferior nature's clinging—whence   810
Slight starting tears easily wiped away,
Fine jealousies soon stifled in the play
Of irrepressible admiration—not
Aspiring, all considered, to their lot
Who ever, just as they prepare ascend   815
Spiral on spiral, wish thee well, impend
Thy frank delight at their exclusive track,
That upturned fervid face and hair put back!
        Is there no more to say? He of the rhymes—
Many a tale, of this retreat betimes,   820
Was born: Sordello die at once for men?
The Chroniclers of Mantua tired their pen
Telling how *Sordello Prince Visconti* saved
Mantua, and elsewhere notably behaved—
Who thus, by fortune ordering events,   825

Good will—
ill luck, get
second prize:

Passed with posterity, to all intents,
For just the god he never could become.
As Knight, Bard, Gallant, men were never dumb
In praise of him: while what he should have been,
Could be, and was not—the one step too mean   830
For him to take,—we suffer at this day
Because of: Ecelin had pushed away
Its chance ere Dante could arrive and take
That step Sordello spurned, for the world's sake:
He did much—but Sordello's chance was gone.   835
Thus, had Sordello dared that step alone,
Apollo had been compassed: 't was a fit
He wished should go to him, not he to it
—As one content to merely be supposed
Singing or fighting elsewhere, while he dozed   840
Really at home—one who was chiefly glad
To have achieved the few real deeds he had,
Because that way assured they were not worth
Doing, so spared from doing them henceforth—
A tree that covets fruitage and yet tastes   845
Never itself, itself. Had he embraced
Their cause then, men had plucked Hesperian fruit
And, praising that, just thrown him in to boot
All he was anxious to appear, but scarce
Solicitous to be. A sorry farce   850
Such life is, after all! Cannot I say

What least one may I award Sordello?

He lived for some one better thing? this way.—
Lo, on a heathy brown and nameless hill
By sparkling Asolo, in mist and chill,
Morning just up, higher and higher runs   855
A child barefoot and rosy. See! the sun's
On the square castle's inner-court's low wall
Like the chine of some extinct animal
Half turned to earth and flowers; and through the
      haze
(Save where some slender patches of grey maize   860
Are to be overleaped) that boy has crossed
The whole hill-side of dew and powder-frost
Matting the balm and mountain camomile.
Up and up goes he, singing all the while

Some unintelligible words to beat   865
The lark, God's poet, swooning at his feet,

This—that
must perforce
content him,

So worsted is he at 'the few fine locks
'Stained like pale honey oozed from topmost rocks
'Sun-blanched the livelong summer,'—all that's left
Of the Goito lay! And thus bereft,   870
Sleep and forget, Sordello! In effect
He sleeps, the feverish poet—I suspect
Not utterly companionless; but, friends,
Wake up! The ghost's gone, and the story ends
I'd fain hope, sweetly; seeing, peri or ghoul,   875
That spirits are conjectured fair or foul,
Evil or good, judicious authors think,
According as they vanish in a stink
Or in a perfume. Friends, be frank! ye snuff
Civet, I warrant. Really? Like enough!   880
Merely the savour's rareness; any nose
May ravage with impunity a rose:
Rifle a musk-pod and 't will ache like yours!

as no prize at
all, has
contented me.

I'd tell you that same pungency ensures
An after-gust, but that were overbold.   885
Who would has heard Sordello's story told.

PIPPA PASSES

A DRAMA

I DEDICATE MY BEST INTENTIONS, IN THIS POEM,
ADMIRINGLY TO THE AUTHOR OF 'ION,'
AFFECTIONATELY TO MR. SERGEANT TALFOURD.

R. B.

LONDON: 1841.

PERSONS

PIPPA.

OTTIMA.

SEBALD.

Foreign Students.

GOTTLIEB.

SCHRAMM.

JULES.

PHENE.

Austrian Police.

BLUPHOCKS.

LUIGI *and his* Mother.

Poor Girls.

MONSIGNOR *and his Attendants.*

PIPPA PASSES

1841

[*Between 1841 and 1846 Browning published eight pamphlets with the general title* Bells and Pomegranates. *Only the first* (Pippa Passes), *third* (Dramatic Lyrics), *and seventh* (Dramatic Romances and Lyrics) *are reprinted here. For the contents of the others, see Chronology, pp. xiii–xiv above.*]

INTRODUCTION

NEW YEAR'S DAY AT ASOLO IN THE TREVISAN

SCENE.—*A large mean airy chamber. A girl,* PIPPA, *from the Silk-mills, springing out of bed.*

DAY!
Faster and more fast,
O'er night's brim, day boils at last:
Boils, pure gold, o'er the cloud-cup's brim
Where spurting and suppressed it lay,   5
For not a froth-flake touched the rim
Of yonder gap in the solid gray
Of the eastern cloud, an hour away;
But forth one wavelet, then another, curled,
Till the whole sunrise, not to be suppressed,   10
Rose, reddened, and its seething breast
Flickered in bounds, grew gold, then overflowed the world.
Oh, Day, if I squander a wavelet of thee,
A mite of my twelve hours' treasure,
The least of thy gazes or glances,   15
(Be they grants thou art bound to or gifts above measure)
One of thy choices or one of thy chances,
(Be they tasks God imposed thee or freaks at thy pleasure)
—My Day, if I squander such labour or leisure,
Then shame fall on Asolo, mischief on me!   20

Thy long blue solemn hours serenely flowing,
Whence earth, we feel, gets steady help and good—

Thy fitful sunshine-minutes, coming, going,
As if earth turned from work in gamesome mood—
All shall be mine! But thou must treat me not   25
As prosperous ones are treated, those who live
At hand here, and enjoy the higher lot,
In readiness to take what thou wilt give,
And free to let alone what thou refusest;
For, Day, my holiday, if thou ill-usest   30
Me, who am only Pippa,—old-year's sorrow,
Cast off last night, will come again to-morrow:
Whereas, if thou prove gentle, I shall borrow
Sufficient strength of thee for new-year's sorrow.
All other men and women that this earth   35
Belongs to, who all days alike possess,
Make general plenty cure particular dearth,
Get more joy one way, if another, less:
Thou art my single day, God lends to leaven
What were all earth else, with a feel of heaven,—   40
Sole light that helps me through the year, thy sun's!
Try now! Take Asolo's Four Happiest Ones—
And let thy morning rain on that superb
Great haughty Ottima; can rain disturb
Her Sebald's homage? All the while thy rain   45
Beats fiercest on her shrub-house window-pane,
He will but press the closer, breathe more warm
Against her cheek; how should she mind the storm?
And, morning past, if mid-day shed a gloom
O'er Jules and Phene,—what care bride and groom   50
Save for their dear selves? 'T is their marriage-day;
And while they leave church and go home their way,
Hand clasping hand, within each breast would be
Sunbeams and pleasant weather spite of thee.
Then, for another trial, obscure thy eve   55
With mist,—will Luigi and his mother grieve—
The lady and her child, unmatched, forsooth,
She in her age, as Luigi in his youth,
For true content? The cheerful town, warm, close
And safe, the sooner that thou art morose,   60
Receives them. And yet once again, outbreak
In storm at night on Monsignor, they make

Such stir about,—whom they expect from Rome
To visit Asolo, his brothers' home,
And say here masses proper to release   65
A soul from pain,—what storm dares hurt his peace?
Calm would he pray, with his own thoughts to ward
Thy thunder off, nor want the angels' guard.
But Pippa—just one such mischance would spoil
Her day that lightens the next twelvemonth's toil   70
At wearisome silk-winding, coil on coil!
    And here I let time slip for nought!
Aha, you foolhardy sunbeam, caught
With a single splash from my ewer!
You that would mock the best pursuer,   75
Was my basin over-deep?
One splash of water ruins you asleep,
And up, up, fleet your brilliant bits
Wheeling and counterwheeling,
Reeling, broken beyond healing: 80
Now grow together on the ceiling!
That will task your wits.
Whoever it was quenched fire first, hoped to see
Morsel after morsel flee
As merrily, as giddily . . .   85
Meantime, what lights my sunbeam on,
Where settles by degrees the radiant cripple?
Oh, is it surely blown, my martagon?
New-blown and ruddy as St. Agnes' nipple,
Plump as the flesh-bunch on some Turk bird's poll!   90
Be sure if corals, branching 'neath the ripple
Of ocean, bud there,—fairies watch unroll
Such turban-flowers; I say, such lamps disperse
Thick red flame through that dusk green universe!
I am queen of thee, floweret!   95
And each fleshy blossom
Preserve I not—(safer
Than leaves that embower it,
Or shells that embosom)
—From weevil and chafer?   100
Laugh through my pane then; solicit the bee;
Gibe him, be sure; and, in midst of thy glee,

Love thy queen, worship me!

—Worship whom else? For am I not, this day,
Whate'er I please? What shall I please to-day?   105
My morn, noon, eve and night—how spend my day?
To-morrow I must be Pippa who winds silk,
The whole year round, to earn just bread and milk:
But, this one day, I have leave to go,
And play out my fancy's fullest games;   110
I may fancy all day—and it shall be so—
That I taste of the pleasures, am called by the names
Of the Happiest Four in our Asolo!
See! Up the hill-side yonder, through the morning,
Some one shall love me, as the world calls love: 115
I am no less than Ottima, take warning!
The gardens, and the great stone house above,
And other house for shrubs, all glass in front,
Are mine; where Sebald steals, as he is wont,
To court me, while old Luca yet reposes: 120
And therefore, till the shrub-house door uncloses,
I . . . what now?—give abundant cause for prate
About me—Ottima, I mean—of late,
Too bold, too confident she'll still face down
The spitefullest of talkers in our town.   125
How we talk in the little town below!
    But love, love, love—there's better love, I know!
This foolish love was only day's first offer;
I choose my next love to defy the scoffer:
For do not our Bride and Bridegroom sally   130
Out of Possagno church at noon?
Their house looks over Orcana valley:
Why should not I be the bride as soon
As Ottima? For I saw, beside,
Arrive last night that little bride—   135
Saw, if you call it seeing her, one flash
Of the pale snow-pure cheek and black bright tresses,
Blacker than all except the black eyelash;
I wonder she contrives those lids no dresses!
—So strict was she, the veil   140
Should cover close her pale

Pure cheeks—a bride to look at and scarce touch,
Scarce touch, remember, Jules! For are not such
Used to be tended, flower-like, every feature,
As if one's breath would fray the lily of a creature?   145
A soft and easy life these ladies lead:
Whiteness in us were wonderful indeed.
Oh, save that brow its virgin dimness,
Keep that foot its lady primness,
Let those ankles never swerve   150
From their exquisite reserve,
Yet have to trip along the streets like me,
All but naked to the knee!
How will she ever grant her Jules a bliss
So startling as her real first infant kiss?   155
Oh, no—not envy, this!

—Not envy, sure!—for if you gave me
Leave to take or to refuse,
In earnest, do you think I'd choose
That sort of new love to enslave me?   160
Mine should have lapped me round from the beginning;
As little fear of losing it as winning:
Lovers grow cold, men learn to hate their wives,
And only parents' love can last our lives.
At eve the Son and Mother, gentle pair,   165
Commune inside our turret: what prevents
My being Luigi? While that mossy lair
Of lizards through the winter-time is stirred
With each to each imparting sweet intents
For this new-year, as brooding bird to bird—   170
(For I observe of late, the evening walk
Of Luigi and his mother, always ends
Inside our ruined turret, where they talk,
Calmer than lovers, yet more kind than friends)
—Let me be cared about, kept out of harm,   175
And schemed for, safe in love as with a charm;
Let me be Luigi! If I only knew
What was my mother's face—my father, too!
    Nay, if you come to that, best love of all
Is God's; then why not have God's love befall   180

Myself as, in the palace by the Dome,
Monsignor?—who to-night will bless the home
Of his dead brother; and God bless in turn
That heart which beats, those eyes which mildly burn
With love for all men! I, to-night at least,   185
Would be that holy and beloved priest.

Now wait!—even I already seem to share
In God's love: what does New-year's hymn declare?
What other meaning do these verses bear?

> *All service ranks the same with God:*   190
> *If now, as formerly he trod*
> *Paradise, his presence fills*
> *Our earth, each only as God wills*
> *Can work—God's puppets, best and worst,*
> *Are we; there is no last nor first.*   195

> *Say not 'a small event!' Why 'small'?*
> *Costs it more pain that this, ye call*
> *A 'great event,' should come to pass,*
> *Than that? Untwine me from the mass*
> *Of deeds which make up life, one deed*   200
> *Power shall fall short in or exceed!*

And more of it, and more of it!—oh yes—
I will pass each, and see their happiness,
And envy none—being just as great, no doubt,
Useful to men, and dear to God, as they!   205
A pretty thing to care about
So mightily, this single holiday!
But let the sun shine! Wherefore repine?
—With thee to lead me, O Day of mine,
Down the grass path grey with dew,   210
Under the pine-wood, blind with boughs,
Where the swallow never flew
Nor yet cicala dared carouse—
No, dared carouse!   [*She enters the street.*

PART I

MORNING

SCENE.— *Up the Hill-side, inside the Shrub-house.* LUCA'S *wife,*
   OTTIMA, *and her paramour, the German* SEBALD.

SEBALD [*sings*].

> Let the watching lids wink!
> Day's a-blaze with eyes, think!
> Deep into the night, drink!

OTTIMA. Night? Such may be your Rhine-land nights perhaps;
  But this blood-red beam through the shutter's chink   5
  —We call such light, the morning: let us see!
  Mind how you grope your way, though! How these tall
  Naked geraniums straggle! Push the lattice
  Behind that frame!—Nay, do I bid you!—Sebald,
  It shakes the dust down on me! Why, of course   10
  The slide-bolt catches. Well, are you content,
  Or must I find you something else to spoil?
  Kiss and be friends, my Sebald! Is 't full morning?
  Oh, don't speak then!
SEBALD.   Ay, thus it used to be.
  Ever your house was, I remember, shut   15
  Till mid-day; I observed that, as I strolled
  On mornings through the vale here; country girls
  Were noisy, washing garments in the brook,
  Hinds drove the slow white oxen up the hills:
  But no, your house was mute, would ope no eye.   20
  And wisely: you were plotting one thing there,
  Nature, another outside. I looked up—
  Rough white wood shutters, rusty iron bars,
  Silent as death, blind in a flood of light.
  Oh, I remember!—and the peasants laughed   25
  And said, 'The old man sleeps with the young wife.'
  This house was his, this chair, this window—his.
OTTIMA. Ah, the clear morning! I can see St. Mark's;
  That black streak is the belfry. Stop: Vicenza

M

Should lie . . . there's Padua, plain enough, that blue!　　30
Look o'er my shoulder, follow my finger!

SEBALD.　　　　　　　　　　　　　Morning?
It seems to me a night with a sun added.
Where's dew, where's freshness? That bruised plant, I bruised
In getting through the lattice yestereve,
Droops as it did. See, here's my elbow's mark　　35
I' the dust o' the sill.

OTTIMA.　　　　　　Oh, shut the lattice, pray!

SEBALD. Let me lean out. I cannot scent blood here,
Foul as the morn may be.
　　　　　　　　　　There, shut the world out!
How do you feel now, Ottima? There, curse
The world and all outside! Let us throw off　　40
This mask: how do you bear yourself? Let's out
With all of it.

OTTIMA.　　　　Best never speak of it.

SEBALD. Best speak again and yet again of it,
Till words cease to be more than words. 'His blood,'
For instance—let those two words mean 'His blood'　　45
And nothing more. Notice, I'll say them now,
'His blood.'

OTTIMA.　　　　Assuredly if I repented
The deed—

SEBALD.　　　Repent? Who should repent, or why?
What puts that in your head? Did I once say
That I repented?

OTTIMA.　　　　No, I said the deed . . .　　50

SEBALD. 'The deed' and 'the event'—just now it was
'Our passion's fruit'—the devil take such cant!
Say, once and always, Luca was a wittol,
I am his cut-throat, you are . . .

OTTIMA　　　　　　　　　　Here's the wine;
I brought it when we left the house above,　　55
And glasses too—wine of both sorts. Black? White then?

SEBALD. But am not I his cut-throat? What are you?

OTTIMA. There trudges on his business from the Duomo
Benet the Capuchin, with his brown hood
And bare feet; always in one place at church,　　60
Close under the stone wall by the south entry.

I used to take him for a brown cold piece
Of the wall's self, as out of it he rose
To let me pass—at first, I say, I used:
Now, so has that dumb figure fastened on me,   65
I rather should account the plastered wall
A piece of him, so chilly does it strike.
This, Sebald?

SEBALD.   No, the white wine—the white wine!
Well, Ottima, I promised no new year
Should rise on us the ancient shameful way;   70
Nor does it rise. Pour on! To your black eyes!
Do you remember last damned New Year's day?

OTTIMA. You brought those foreign prints. We looked at them
Over the wine and fruit. I had to scheme
To get him from the fire. Nothing but saying   75
His own set wants the proof-mark, roused him up
To hunt them out.

SEBALD.   'Faith, he is not alive
To fondle you before my face.

OTTIMA.   Do you
Fondle me then! Who means to take your life
For that, my Sebald?

SEBALD.   Hark you, Ottima!   80
One thing to guard against. We'll not make much
One of the other—that is, not make more
Parade of warmth, childish officious coil,
Than yesterday: as if, sweet, I supposed
Proof upon proof were needed now, now first,   85
To show I love you—yes, still love you—love you
In spite of Luca and what's come to him
—Sure sign we had him ever in our thoughts,
White sneering old reproachful face and all!
We'll even quarrel, love, at times, as if   90
We still could lose each other, were not tied
By this: conceive you?

OTTIMA.   Love!

SEBALD.   Not tied so sure.
Because though I was wrought upon, have struck
His insolence back into him—am I
So surely yours?—therefore forever yours?   95

OTTIMA. Love, to be wise, (one counsel pays another)
    Should we have—months ago, when first we loved,
    For instance that May morning we two stole
    Under the green ascent of sycamores—
    If we had come upon a thing like that   100
    Suddenly . . .

SEBALD.   'A thing'—there again—'a thing!'

OTTIMA. Then, Venus' body, had we come upon
    My husband Luca Gaddi's murdered corpse
    Within there, at his couch-foot, covered close—
    Would you have pored upon it? Why persist   105
    In poring now upon it? For 't is here
    As much as there in the deserted house:
    You cannot rid your eyes of it. For me,
    Now he is dead I hate him worse: I hate . . .
    Dare you stay here? I would go back and hold   110
    His two dead hands, and say, 'I hate you worse,
    'Luca, than . . .'

SEBALD.   Off, off—take your hands off mine,
    'T is the hot evening—off! oh, morning is it?

OTTIMA. There's one thing must be done; you know what thing.
    Come in and help to carry. We may sleep   115
    Anywhere in the whole wide house to-night.

SEBALD. What would come, think you, if we let him lie
    Just as he is? Let him lie there until
    The angels take him! He is turned by this
    Off from his face beside, as you will see.   120

OTTIMA. This dusty pane might serve for looking glass.
    Three, four—four grey hairs! Is it so you said
    A plait of hair should wave across my neck?
    No—this way.

SEBALD.   Ottima, I would give your neck,
    Each splendid shoulder, both those breasts of yours,   125
    That this were undone! Killing! Kill the world,
    So Luca lives again!—ay, lives to sputter
    His fulsome dotage on you—yes, and feign
    Surprise that I return at eve to sup,
    When all the morning I was loitering here—   130
    Bid me despatch my business and begone.

I would . . .

OTTIMA.   See!

SEBALD.   No, I'll finish. Do you think
   I fear to speak the bare truth once for all?
   All we have talked of, is, at bottom, fine
   To suffer; there's a recompense in guilt;   135
   One must be venturous and fortunate:
   What is one young for, else? In age we'll sigh
   O'er the wild reckless wicked days flown over;
   Still, we have lived: the vice was in its place.
   But to have eaten Luca's bread, have worn   140
   His clothes, have felt his money swell my purse—
   Do lovers in romances sin that way?
   Why, I was starving when I used to call
   And teach you music, starving while you plucked me
   These flowers to smell!

OTTIMA.   My poor lost friend!

SEBALD.   He gave me 145
   Life, nothing less: what if he did reproach
   My perfidy, and threaten, and do more—
   Had he no right? What was to wonder at?
   He sat by us at table quietly:
   Why must you lean across till our cheeks touched?   150
   Could he do less than make pretence to strike?
   'T is not the crime's sake—I'd commit ten crimes
   Greater, to have this crime wiped out, undone!
   And you—O how feel you? Feel you for me?

OTTIMA. Well then, I love you better now than ever,   155
   And best (look at me while I speak to you)—
   Best for the crime; nor do I grieve, in truth,
   This mask, this simulated ignorance,
   This affectation of simplicity,
   Falls off our crime; this naked crime of ours   160
   May not now be looked over: look it down!
   Great? let it be great; but the joys it brought,
   Pay they or no its price? Come: they or it!
   Speak not! The past, would you give up the past
   Such as it is, pleasure and crime together?   165
   Give up that noon I owned my love for you?
   The garden's silence: even the single bee

Persisting in his toil, suddenly stopped,
And where he hid you only could surmise
By some campanula chalice set a-swing.   170
Who stammered—'Yes, I love you?'

SEBALD.   And I drew
Back; put far back your face with both my hands
Lest you should grow too full of me—your face
So seemed athirst for my whole soul and body!

OTTIMA. And when I ventured to receive you here,   175
Made you steal hither in the mornings—

SEBALD.   When
I used to look up 'neath the shrub-house here,
Till the red fire on its glazed windows spread
To a yellow haze?

OTTIMA.   Ah—my sign was, the sun
Inflamed the sere side of yon chestnut-tree   180
Nipped by the first frost.

SEBALD.   You would always laugh
At my wet boots: I had to stride thro' grass
Over my ankles.

OTTIMA.   Then our crowning night!

SEBALD. The July night?

OTTIMA.   The day of it too, Sebald!
When heaven's pillars seemed o'erbowed with heat,   185
Its black-blue canopy suffered descend
Close on us both, to weigh down each to each,
And smother up all life except our life.
So lay we till the storm came.

SEBALD.   How it came!

OTTIMA. Buried in woods we lay, you recollect;   190
Swift ran the searching tempest overhead;
And ever and anon some bright white shaft
Burned thro' the pine-tree roof, here burned and there,
As if God's messenger thro' the close wood screen
Plunged and replunged his weapon at a venture,   195
Feeling for guilty thee and me: then broke
The thunder like a whole sea overhead—

SEBALD. Yes!

OTTIMA. —While I stretched myself upon you, hands
To hands, my mouth to your hot mouth, and shook   200

All my locks loose, and covered you with them—
You, Sebald, the same you!

SEBALD.   Slower, Ottima!

OTTIMA. And as we lay—

SEBALD.   Less vehemently! Love me!
Forgive me! Take not words, mere words, to heart!
Your breath is worse than wine! Breathe slow, speak slow!   205
Do not lean on me!

OTTIMA.   Sebald, as we lay,
Rising and falling only with our pants,
Who said, 'Let death come now! 'Tis right to die!
'Right to be punished! Nought completes such bliss
'But woe!' Who said that?

SEBALD.   How did we ever rise?   210
Was't that we slept? Why did it end?

OTTIMA.   I felt you
Taper into a point the ruffled ends
Of my loose locks 'twixt both your humid lips.
My hair is fallen now: knot it again!

SEBALD. I kiss you now, dear Ottima, now and now!   215
This way? Will you forgive me—be once more
My great queen?

OTTIMA.   Bind it thrice about my brow;
Crown me your queen, your spirit's arbitress,
Magnificent in sin. Say that!

SEBALD.   I crown you
My great white queen, my spirit's arbitress,   220
Magnificent . . .

              [From without is heard the voice of PIPPA, *singing*—
                    The year's at the spring
                    And day's at the morn;
                    Morning's at seven;
                    The hill-side's dew-pearled;   225
                    The lark's on the wing;
                    The snail's on the thorn:
                    God's in his heaven—
                    All's right with the world!

                            *[*PIPPA *passes.*

SEBALD. God's in his heaven! Do you hear that? Who spoke?   230
You, you spoke!

OTTIMA.   Oh—that little ragged girl!
  She must have rested on the step: we give them
  But this one holiday the whole year round.
  Did you ever see our silk-mills—their inside?
  There are ten silk-mills now belong to you.   235
  She stoops to pick my double heartsease . . . Sh!
  She does not hear: call you out louder!
SEBALD.   Leave me!
  Go, get your clothes on—dress those shoulders!
OTTIMA.   Sebald?
SEBALD. Wipe off that paint! I hate you.
OTTIMA.   Miserable!
SEBALD. My God, and she is emptied of it now!   240
  Outright now!—how miraculously gone
  All of the grace—had she not strange grace once?
  Why, the blank cheek hangs listless as it likes,
  No purpose holds the features up together,
  Only the cloven brow and puckered chin   245
  Stay in their places: and the very hair,
  That seemed to have a sort of life in it,
  Drops, a dead web!
OTTIMA.   Speak to me—not of me!
SEBALD. —That round great full-orbed face, where not an angle
  Broke the delicious indolence—all broken!   250
OTTIMA. To me—not of me! Ungrateful, perjured cheat!
  A coward too: but ingrate's worse than all.
  Beggar—my slave—a fawning, cringing lie!
  Leave me! Betray me! I can see your drift!
  A lie that walks and eats and drinks!
SEBALD.   My God!   255
  Those morbid olive faultless shoulder-blades—
  I should have known there was no blood beneath!
OTTIMA. You hate me then? You hate me then?
SEBALD.   To think
  She would succeed in her absurd attempt,
  And fascinate by sinning, show herself   260
  Superior—guilt from its excess superior
  To innocence! That little peasant's voice
  Has righted all again. Though I be lost,

I know which is the better, never fear,
Of vice or virtue, purity or lust,   265
Nature or trick! I see what I have done,
Entirely now! Oh I am proud to feel
Such torments—let the world take credit thence—
I, having done my deed, pay too its price!
I hate, hate—curse you! God's in his heaven!

OTTIMA.   —Me!   270
Me? no, no, Sebald, not yourself—kill me!
Mine is the whole crime. Do but kill me—then
Yourself—then—presently—first hear me speak!
I always meant to kill myself—wait, you!
Lean on my breast—not as a breast; don't love me   275
The more because you lean on me, my own
Heart's Sebald! There, there, both deaths presently!

SEBALD. My brain is drowned now—quite drowned: all I feel
Is . . . is, at swift-recurring intervals,
A hurry-down within me, as of waters   280
Loosened to smother up some ghastly pit:
There they go—whirls from a black fiery sea!

OTTIMA. Not me—to him, O God, be merciful!

Talk by the way, while PIPPA *is passing from the hill-side to Orcana.
Foreign* Students *of painting and sculpture, from Venice,
assembled opposite the house of* JULES, *a young French statuary,
at Possagno.*

1ST STUDENT. Attention! My own post is beneath this window,
but the pomegranate clump yonder will hide three or four of you
with a little squeezing, and Schramm and his pipe must lie flat in the
balcony. Four, five—who's a defaulter? We want everybody, for
Jules must not be suffered to hurt his bride when the jest's found
out.

2ND STUDENT. All here! Only our poet's away—never having
much meant to be present, moonstrike him! The airs of that
fellow, that Giovacchino! He was in violent love with himself,
and had a fair prospect of thriving in his suit, so unmolested was
it,—when suddenly a woman falls in love with him, too; and out
of pure jealousy he takes himself off to Trieste, immortal poem
and all: whereto is this prophetical epitaph appended already, as

Bluphocks assures me,—'*Here a mammoth-poem lies, Fouled to death by butterflies.*' His own fault, the simpleton! Instead of cramp couplets, each like a knife in your entrails, he should write, says Bluphocks, both classically and intelligibly.—*Æsculapius, an Epic. Catalogue of the drugs: Hebe's plaister—One strip Cools your lip. Phœbus' emulsion—One bottle Clears your throttle. Mercury's bolus—One box Cures . . .*

3RD STUDENT. Subside, my fine fellow! If the marriage was over by ten o'clock, Jules will certainly be here in a minute with his bride.

2ND STUDENT. Good!—only, so should the poet's muse have been universally acceptable, says Bluphocks, *et canibus nostris . . .* and Delia not better known to our literary dogs than the boy Giovacchino!

1ST STUDENT. To the point, now. Where's Gottlieb, the newcomer? Oh,—listen, Gottlieb, to what has called down this piece of friendly vengeance on Jules, of which we now assemble to witness the winding-up. We are all agreed, all in a tale, observe, when Jules shall burst out on us in a fury by and by: I am spokesman—the verses that are to undeceive Jules bear my name of Lutwyche—but each professes himself alike insulted by this strutting stone-squarer, who came alone from Paris to Munich, and thence with a crowd of us to Venice and Possagno here, but proceeds in a day or two alone again—oh, alone indubitably!— to Rome and Florence. He, forsooth, take up his portion with these dissolute, brutalized, heartless bunglers!—so he was heard to call us all: now, is Schramm brutalized, I should like to know? Am I heartless?

GOTTLIEB. Why, somewhat heartless; for, suppose Jules a coxcomb as much as you choose, still, for this mere coxcombry, you will have brushed off—what do folks style it?—the bloom of his life. Is it too late to alter? These love-letters now, you call his— I can't laugh at them.

4TH STUDENT. Because you never read the sham letters of our inditing which drew forth these.

GOTTLIEB. His discovery of the truth will be frightful.

4TH STUDENT. That's the joke. But you should have joined us at the beginning: there's no doubt he loves the girl—loves a model he might hire by the hour!

GOTTLIEB. See here! 'He has been accustomed,' he writes, 'to have Canova's women about him, in stone, and the world's women beside him, in flesh; these being as much below, as those above, his soul's aspiration: but now he is to have the reality.' There you laugh again! I say, you wipe off the very dew of his youth.

1ST STUDENT. Schramm! (Take the pipe out of his mouth, somebody!) Will Jules lose the bloom of his youth?

SCHRAMM. Nothing worth keeping is ever lost in this world: look at a blossom—it drops presently, having done its service and lasted its time; but fruits succeed, and where would be the blossom's place could it continue? As well affirm that your eye is no longer in your body, because its earliest favourite, whatever it may have first loved to look on, is dead and done with—as that any affection is lost to the soul when its first object, whatever happened first to satisfy it, is superseded in due course. Keep but ever looking, whether with the body's eye or the mind's, and you will soon find something to look on! Has a man done wondering at women?—there follow men, dead and alive, to wonder at. Has he done wondering at men?—there's God to wonder at: and the faculty of wonder may be, at the same time, old and tired enough with respect to its first object, and yet young and fresh sufficiently, so far as concerns its novel one. Thus . . .

1ST STUDENT. Put Schramm's pipe into his mouth again! There, you see! Well, this Jules . . . a wretched fribble—oh, I watched his disportings at Possagno, the other day! Canova's gallery—you know: there he marches first resolvedly past great works by the dozen without vouchsafing an eye: all at once he stops full at the *Psiche-fanciulla*—cannot pass that old acquaintance without a nod of encouragement—'In your new place, beauty? Then behave yourself as well here as at Munich—I see you!' Next he posts himself deliberately before the unfinished *Pietà* for half an hour without moving, till up he starts of a sudden, and thrusts his very nose into—I say, into—the group; by which gesture you are informed that precisely the sole point he had not fully mastered in Canova's practice was a certain method of using the drill in the articulation of the knee-joint—and that, likewise, has he mastered at length! Good-bye, therefore, to poor Canova—whose gallery no longer needs detain his successor Jules, the predestinated novel thinker in marble!

5TH STUDENT. Tell him about the women: go on to the women!

1ST STUDENT. Why, on that matter he could never be supercilious enough. How should we be other (he said) than the poor devils

you see, with those debasing habits we cherish? He was not to
wallow in that mire, at least: he would wait, and love only at the
proper time, and meanwhile put up with the *Psiche-fanciulla*. Now,
I happened to hear of a young Greek—real Greek girl at Mala-
mocco; a true Islander, do you see, with Alciphron's 'hair like
sea-moss'—Schramm knows!—white and quiet as an apparition,
and fourteen years old at farthest,—a daughter of Natalia, so she
swears—that hag Natalia, who helps us to models at three *lire* an
hour. We selected this girl for the heroine of our jest. So first, Jules
received a scented letter—somebody had seen his Tydeus at the
Academy, and my picture was nothing to it: a profound admirer
bade him persevere—would make herself known to him ere long.
(Paolina, my little friend of the *Fenice*, transcribes divinely.) And
in due time, the mysterious correspondent gave certain hints of
her peculiar charms—the pale cheeks, the black hair—whatever,
in short, had struck us in our Malamocco model: we retained her
name, too—Phene, which is, by interpretation, sea-eagle. Now,
think of Jules finding himself distinguished from the herd of us
by such a creature! In his very first answer he proposed marrying
his monitress: and fancy us over these letters, two, three times a
day, to receive and despatch! I concocted the main of it: relations
were in the way—secrecy must be observed—in fine, would he wed
her on trust, and only speak to her when they were indissolubly
united? St—st—Here they come!

6TH STUDENT. Both of them! Heaven's love, speak softly, speak
within yourselves!

5TH STUDENT. Look at the bridegroom! Half his hair in storm and
half in calm,—patted down over the left temple,—like a frothy
cup one blows on to cool it: and the same old blouse that he
murders the marble in.

2ND STUDENT. Not a rich vest like yours, Hannibal Scratchy!—
rich, that your face may the better set it off.

6TH STUDENT. And the bride! Yes, sure enough, our Phene!
Should you have known her in her clothes? How magnificently
pale!

GOTTLIEB. She does not also take it for earnest, I hope?

1ST STUDENT. Oh, Natalia's concern, that is! We settle with
Natalia.

6TH STUDENT. She does not speak—has evidently let out no word.
The only thing is, will she equally remember the rest of her

lesson, and repeat correctly all those verses which are to break the
secret to Jules?

GOTTLIEB. How he gazes on her! Pity—pity!

1ST STUDENT. They go in: now, silence! You three,—not nearer
the window, mind, than that pomegranate: just where the little
girl, who a few minutes ago passed us singing, is seated!

PART II

NOON

SCENE.— *Over Orcana. The house of* JULES, *who crosses its
threshold with* PHENE: *she is silent, on which* JULES *begins—*

Do not die, Phene! I am yours now, you
Are mine now; let fate reach me how she likes,
If you'll not die: so, never die! Sit here—
My work-room's single seat. I over-lean
This length of hair and lustrous front; they turn   5
Like an entire flower upward: eyes, lips, last
Your chin—no, last your throat turns: 't is their scent
Pulls down my face upon you. Nay, look ever
This one way till I change, grow you—I could
Change into you, beloved!
                              You by me,   10
And I by you; this is your hand in mine,
And side by side we sit: all's true. Thank God!
I have spoken: speak you!
                              O my life to come!
My Tydeus must be carved that's there in clay;
Yet how be carved, with you about the room?   15
Where must I place you? When I think that once
This room-full of rough block-work seemed my heaven
Without you! Shall I ever work again,
Get fairly into my old ways again,
Bid each conception stand while, trait by trait,   20
My hand transfers its lineaments to stone?
Will my mere fancies live near you, their truth—

The live truth, passing and repassing me,
Sitting beside me?
>Now speak!
>>>Only first,
See, all your letters! Was 't not well contrived?   25
Their hiding-place is Psyche's robe; she keeps
Your letters next her skin: which drops out foremost?
Ah,—this that swam down like a first moonbeam
Into my world!
>>>Again those eyes complete
Their melancholy survey, sweet and slow,   30
Of all my room holds; to return and rest
On me, with pity, yet some wonder too:
As if God bade some spirit plague a world,
And this were the one moment of surprise
And sorrow while she took her station, pausing   35
O'er what she sees, finds good, and must destroy!
What gaze you at? Those? Books, I told you of;
Let your first word to me rejoice them, too:
This minion, a Coluthus, writ in red
Bistre and azure by Bessarion's scribe—   40
Read this line . . . no, shame—Homer's be the Greek
First breathed me from the lips of my Greek girl!
This Odyssey in coarse black vivid type
With faded yellow blossoms 'twixt page and page,
To mark great places with due gratitude;   45
'He said, *and on Antinous directed*
'A bitter shaft' . . . a flower blots out the rest!
Again upon your search? My statues, then!
—Ah, do not mind that—better that will look
When cast in bronze—an Almaign Kaiser, that,   50
Swart-green and gold, with truncheon based on hip.
This, rather, turn to! What, unrecognized?
I thought you would have seen that here you sit
As I imagined you,—Hippolyta,
Naked upon her bright Numidian horse.   55
Recall you this then? 'Carve in bold relief'—
So you commanded—'carve, against I come,
'A Greek, in Athens, as our fashion was,
'Feasting, bay-filleted and thunder-free,

'Who rises 'neath the lifted myrtle-branch.   60
' "Praise those who slew Hipparchus!" cry the guests,
' "While o'er thy head the singer's myrtle waves
' "As erst above our champion: stand up, all!" '
See, I have laboured to express your thought.
Quite round, a cluster of mere hands and arms,   65
(Thrust in all senses, all ways, from all sides,
Only consenting at the branch's end
They strain toward) serves for frame to a sole face,
The Praiser's, in the centre: who with eyes
Sightless, so bend they back to light inside   70
His brain where visionary forms throng up,
Sings, minding not that palpitating arch
Of hands and arms, nor the quick drip of wine
From the drenched leaves o'erhead, nor crowns cast off,
Violet and parsley crowns to trample on—   75
Sings, pausing as the patron-ghosts approve,
Devoutly their unconquerable hymn.
But you must say a 'well' to that—say 'well!'
Because you gaze—am I fantastic, sweet?
Gaze like my very life's-stuff, marble—marbly   80
Even to the silence! Why, before I found
The real flesh Phene, I inured myself
To see, throughout all nature, varied stuff
For better nature's birth by means of art:
With me, each substance tended to one form   85
Of beauty—to the human archetype.
On every side occurred suggestive germs
Of that—the tree, the flower—or take the fruit,—
Some rosy shape, continuing the peach,
Curved beewise o'er its bough; as rosy limbs,   90
Depending, nestled in the leaves; and just
From a cleft rose-peach the whole Dryad sprang.
But of the stuffs one can be master of,
How I divined their capabilities!
From the soft-rinded smoothening facile chalk   95
That yields your outline to the air's embrace,
Half-softened by a halo's pearly gloom;
Down to the crisp imperious steel, so sure
To cut its one confided thought clean out

Of all the world. But marble!—'neath my tools   100
More pliable than jelly—as it were
Some clear primordial creature dug from depths
In the earth's heart, where itself breeds itself,
And whence all baser substance may be worked;
Refine it off to air, you may,—condense it   105
Down to the diamond;—is not metal there,
When o'er the sudden speck my chisel trips?
—Not flesh, as flake off flake I scale, approach,
Lay bare those bluish veins of blood asleep?
Lurks flame in no strange windings where, surprised   110
By the swift implement sent home at once,
Flushes and glowings radiate and hover
About its track?
                    Phene? what—why is this?
That whitening cheek, those still dilating eyes!
Ah, you will die—I knew that you would die!   115

PHENE *begins, on his having long remained silent.*

Now the end's coming; to be sure, it must
Have ended sometime! Tush, why need I speak
Their foolish speech? I cannot bring to mind
One half of it, beside; and do not care
For old Natalia now, nor any of them.   120
Oh, you—what are you?—if I do not try
To say the words Natalia made me learn,
To please your friends,—it is to keep myself
Where your voice lifted me, by letting that
Proceed: but can it? Even you, perhaps,   125
Cannot take up, now you have once let fall,
The music's life, and me along with that—
No, or you would! We'll stay then, as we are:
Above the world.
                    You creature with the eyes!
If I could look for ever up to them,   130
As now you let me,—I believe, all sin,
All memory of wrong done, suffering borne,
Would drop down, low and lower, to the earth
Whence all that's low comes, and there touch and stay
—Never to overtake the rest of me,   135

All that, unspotted, reaches up to you,
Drawn by those eyes! What rises is myself,
Not me the shame and suffering; but they sink,
Are left, I rise above them. Keep me so,
Above the world!
                But you sink, for your eyes   140
Are altering—altered! Stay—'I love you, love' . . .
I could prevent it if I understood:
More of your words to me: was 't in the tone
Or the words, your power?
                Or stay—I will repeat
Their speech, if that contents you! Only change   145
No more, and I shall find it presently
Far back here, in the brain yourself filled up.
Natalia threatened me that harm should follow
Unless I spoke their lesson to the end,
But harm to me, I thought she meant, not you.   150
Your friends,—Natalia said they were your friends
And meant you well,—because, I doubted it,
Observing (what was very strange to see)
On every face, so different in all else,
The same smile girls like me are used to bear,   155
But never men, men cannot stoop so low;
Yet your friends, speaking of you, used that smile,
That hateful smirk of boundless self-conceit
Which seems to take possession of the world
And make of God a tame confederate,   160
Purveyor to their appetites . . . you know!
But still Natalia said they were your friends,
And they assented though they smiled the more,
And all came round me,—that thin Englishman
With light lank hair seemed leader of the rest;   165
He held a paper—'What we want,' said he,
Ending some explanation to his friends—
'Is something slow, involved and mystical,
'To hold Jules long in doubt, yet take his taste
'And lure him on until, at innermost   170
'Where he seeks sweetness' soul, he may find—this!
'—As in the apple's core, the noisome fly:
'For insects on the rind are seen at once,

'And brushed aside as soon, but this is found
'Only when on the lips or loathing tongue.'   175
And so he read what I have got by heart:
I'll speak it,—'Do not die, love! I am yours.'
No—is not that, or like that, part of words
Yourself began by speaking? Strange to lose
What cost such pains to learn! Is this more right?   180

> *I am a painter who cannot paint;*
> *In my life, a devil rather than saint;*
> *In my brain, as poor a creature too:*
> *No end to all I cannot do!*
> *Yet do one thing at least I can—*   185
> *Love a man or hate a man*
> *Supremely: thus my lore began.*
> *Through the Valley of Love I went,*
> *In the lovingest spot to abide,*
> *And just on the verge where I pitched my tent,*   190
> *I found Hate dwelling beside.*
> *(Let the Bridegroom ask what the painter meant,*
> *Of his bride, of the peerless Bride!)*
> *And further, I traversed Hate's grove,*
> *In the hatefullest nook to dwell;*   195
> *But lo, where I flung myself prone, couched Love*
> *Where the shadow threefold fell.*
> *(The meaning—those black bride's-eyes above,*
> *Not a painter's lips should tell!)*

'And here,' said he, 'Jules probably will ask,   200
' "You have black eyes, Love,—you are, sure enough,
' "My peerless bride,—then do you tell indeed
' "What needs some explanation! What means this?" '
—And I am to go on, without a word—

> *So, I grew wise in Love and Hate,*   205
> *From simple that I was of late.*
> *Once, when I loved, I would enlace*
> *Breast, eyelids, hands, feet, form and face*
> *Of her I loved, in one embrace—*
> *As if by mere love I could love immensely!*   210
> *Once, when I hated, I would plunge*
> *My sword, and wipe with the first lunge*

My foe's whole life out like a sponge—
As if by mere hate I could hate intensely!
But now I am wiser, know better the fashion   215
How passion seeks aid from its opposite passion:
And if I see cause to love more, hate more
Than ever man loved, ever hated before—
And seek in the Valley of Love,
The nest, or the nook in Hate's Grove,   220
Where my soul may surely reach
The essence, nought less, of each,
The Hate of all Hates, the Love
Of all Loves, in the Valley or Grove,—
I find them the very warders   225
Each of the other's borders.
When I love most, Love is disguised
In Hate; and when Hate is surprised
In Love, then I hate most: ask
How Love smiles through Hate's iron casque,   230
Hate grins through Love's rose-braided mask,—
And how, having hated thee,
I sought long and painfully
To reach thy heart, nor prick
The skin but pierce to the quick—   235
Ask this, my Jules, and be answered straight
By thy bride—how the painter Lutwyche can hate!

JULES *interposes.*

Lutwyche! Who else? But all of them, no doubt,
Hated me: they at Venice—presently
Their turn, however! You I shall not meet: 240
If I dreamed, saying this would wake me.

                                        Keep
What's here, the gold—we cannot meet again,
Consider! and the money was but meant
For two years' travel, which is over now,
All chance or hope or care or need of it.   245
This—and what comes from selling these, my casts
And books and medals, except . . . let them go
Together, so the produce keeps you safe
Out of Natalia's clutches! If by chance

(For all's chance here) I should survive the gang   250
At Venice, root out all fifteen of them,
We might meet somewhere, since the world is wide.
            [*From without is heard the voice of* PIPPA, *singing*—

> *Give her but a least excuse to love me!*
> *When—where—*
> *How—can this arm establish her above me,*   255
> *If fortune fixed her as my lady there,*
> *There already, to eternally reprove me?*
>   (*'Hist!'—said Kate the Queen;*
>   *But 'Oh!'—cried the maiden, binding her tresses,*
>   *' 'T is only a page that carols unseen,*   260
>   *'Crumbling your hounds their messes!'*)
>
> *Is she wronged?—To the rescue of her honour,*
> *My heart!*
> *Is she poor?—What costs it to be styled a donor?*
> *Merely an earth to cleave, a sea to part.*   265
> *But that fortune should have thrust all this upon her!*
>   (*'Nay, list!'—bade Kate the Queen;*
>   *And still cried the maiden, binding her tresses,*
>   *' 'T is only a page that carols unseen,*
>   *'Fitting your hawks their jesses!'*)   270
>   [PIPPA *passes.*

JULES *resumes.*

What name was that the little girl sang forth?
Kate? The Cornaro, doubtless, who renounced
The crown of Cyprus to be lady here
At Asolo, where still her memory stays,
And peasants sing how once a certain page   275
Pined for the grace of her so far above
His power of doing good to, 'Kate the Queen—
'She never could be wronged, be poor,' he sighed,
'Need him to help her!'
                Yes, a bitter thing
To see our lady above all need of us;   280
Yet so we look ere we will love; not I,
But the world looks so. If whoever loves
Must be, in some sort, god or worshipper,

The blessing or the blest one, queen or page,
Why should we always choose the page's part?   285
Here is a woman with utter need of me,—
I find myself queen here, it seems!
                                How strange!
Look at the woman here with the new soul,
Like my own Psyche,—fresh upon her lips
Alit, the visionary butterfly,   290
Waiting my word to enter and make bright,
Or flutter off and leave all blank as first.
This body had no soul before, but slept
Or stirred, was beauteous or ungainly, free
From taint or foul with stain, as outward things   295
Fastened their image on its passiveness:
Now, it will wake, feel, live—or die again!
Shall to produce form out of unshaped stuff
Be Art—and further, to evoke a soul
From form be nothing? This new soul is mine!   300

Now, to kill Lutwyche, what would that do?—save
A wretched dauber, men will hoot to death
Without me, from their hooting. Oh, to hear
God's voice plain as I heard it first, before
They broke in with their laughter! I heard them   305
Henceforth, not God.
                    To Ancona—Greece—some isle!
I wanted silence only; there is clay
Everywhere. One may do whate'er one likes
In Art: the only thing is, to make sure
That one does like it—which takes pains to know.   310
   Scatter all this, my Phene—this mad dream!
Who, what is Lutwyche, what Natalia's friends,
What the whole world except our love—my own,
Own Phene? But I told you, did I not,
Ere night we travel for your land—some isle   315
With the sea's silence on it? Stand aside—
I do but break these paltry models up
To begin Art afresh. Meet Lutwyche, I—
And save him from my statue meeting him?
Some unsuspected isle in the far seas!   320

Like a god going through his world, there stands
One mountain for a moment in the dusk,
Whole brotherhoods of cedars on its brow:
And you are ever by me while I gaze
—Are in my arms as now—as now—as now!   325
Some unsuspected isle in the far seas!
Some unsuspected isle in far-off seas!

Talk by the way, while PIPPA *is passing from Orcana to the Turret.
Two or three of the Austrian Police loitering with* BLUPHOCKS,
an English vagabond, just in view of the Turret.

BLUPHOCKS.* So, that is your Pippa, the little girl who passed us
singing? Well, your Bishop's Intendant's money shall be honestly
earned:—now, don't make me that sour face because I bring the
Bishop's name into the business; we know he can have nothing to
do with such horrors: we know that he is a saint and all that a
bishop should be, who is a great man beside. *Oh were but every
worm a maggot, Every fly a grig, Every bough a Christmas faggot,
Every tune a jig!* In fact, I have abjured all religions; but the last
I inclined to, was the Armenian: for I have travelled, do you see,
and at Koenigsberg, Prussia Improper (so styled because there's
a sort of bleak hungry sun there), you might remark over a
venerable house-porch, a certain Chaldee inscription; and brief
as it is, a mere glance at it used absolutely to change the mood of
every bearded passenger. In they turned one and all; the young
and lightsome, with no irreverent pause, the aged and decrepit,
with a sensible alacrity: 't was the Grand Rabbi's abode, in short.
Struck with curiosity, I lost no time in learning Syriac—(these
are vowels, you dogs,—follow my stick's end in the mud—
Celarent, Darii, Ferio!) and one morning presented myself,
spelling-book in hand, a, b, c,—I picked it out letter by letter, and
what was the purport of this miraculous posy? Some cherished
legend of the past, you'll say—'*How Moses hocus-pocussed Egypt's
land with fly and locust,*'—or, '*How to Jonah sounded harshish, Get
thee up and go to Tarshish,*'—or, '*How the angel meeting Balaam,
Straight his ass returned a salaam.*' In no wise! '*Shackabrack—
Boach—somebody or other—Isaach, Re-cei-ver, Pur-cha-ser and*

---

* 'He maketh his sun to rise on the evil and on the good, and sendeth rain on the
just and on the unjust.'

Ex-chan-ger of—Stolen Goods!' So, talk to me of the religion of a bishop! I have renounced all bishops save Bishop Beveridge—mean to live so—and die—*As some Greek dog-sage, dead and merry, Hellward bound in Charon's wherry, With food for both worlds, under and upper, Lupine-seed and Hecate's supper, And never an obolus . . .* (Though thanks to you, or this Intendant through you, or this Bishop through his Intendant—I possess a burning pocketful of *zwanzigers*) . . . *To pay the Stygian Ferry!*

IST POLICEMAN. There is the girl, then; go and deserve them the moment you have pointed out to us Signor Luigi and his mother. [*To the rest*]. I have been noticing a house yonder, this long while: not a shutter unclosed since morning!

2ND POLICEMAN. Old Luca Gaddi's, that owns the silk-mills here: he dozes by the hour, wakes up, sighs deeply, says he should like to be Prince Metternich, and then dozes again, after having bidden young Sebald, the foreigner, set his wife to playing draughts. Never molest such a household, they mean well.

BLUPHOCKS. Only, cannot you tell me something of this little Pippa, I must have to do with? One could make something of that name. Pippa—that is, short for Felippa—rhyming to *Panurge consults Hertrippa—Believest thou, King Agrippa?* Something might be done with that name.

2ND POLICEMAN. Put into rhyme that your head and a ripe musk-melon would not be dear at half a *zwanziger!* Leave this fooling, and look out; the afternoon's over or nearly so.

3RD POLICEMAN. Where in this passport of Signor Luigi does our Principal instruct you to watch him so narrowly? There? What's there beside a simple signature? (That English fool's busy watching.)

2ND POLICEMAN. Flourish all round—'Put all possible obstacles in his way;' oblong dot at the end—'Detain him till further advices reach you;' scratch at bottom—'Send him back on pretence of some informality in the above;' ink-spirt on right-hand side (which is the case here)—'Arrest him at once.' Why and wherefore, I don't concern myself, but my instructions amount to this: if Signor Luigi leaves home to-night for Vienna—well and good, the passport deposed with us for our *visa* is really for his own use, they have misinformed the Office, and he means well; but let him stay over to-night—there has been the pretence we suspect, the accounts of his corresponding and holding intelligence with

the Carbonari are correct, we arrest him at once, to-morrow
comes Venice, and presently Spielberg. Bluphocks makes the
signal, sure enough! That is he, entering the turret with his
mother, no doubt.

PART III

EVENING

SCENE.— *Inside the Turret on the Hill above Asolo.*
LUIGI *and his* Mother *entering.*

MOTHER. If there blew wind, you'd hear a long sigh, easing
    The utmost heaviness of music's heart.
LUIGI. Here in the archway?
MOTHER.   Oh no, no—in farther,
    Where the echo is made, on the ridge.
LUIGI.   Here surely, then.
    How plain the tap of my heel as I leaped up!   5
    Hark—'Lucius Junius!' The very ghost of a voice
    Whose body is caught and kept by . . . what are those?
    Mere withered wallflowers, waving overhead?
    They seem an elvish group with thin bleached hair
    That lean out of their topmost fortress—look   10
    And listen, mountain men, to what we say,
    Hand under chin of each grave earthy face.
    Up and show faces all of you!—'All of you!'
    That's the king dwarf with the scarlet comb; old Franz,
    Come down and meet your fate? Hark—'Meet your fate!' 15
MOTHER. Let him not meet it, my Luigi—do not
    Go to his City! Putting crime aside,
    Half of these ills of Italy are feigned:
    Your Pellicos and writers for effect,
    Write for effect.
LUIGI.   Hush! Say A. writes, and B.   20
MOTHER. These A.s and B.s write for effect, I say.
    Then, evil is in its nature loud, while good
    Is silent; you hear each petty injury,

None of his virtues; he is old beside,
Quiet and kind, and densely stupid. Why   25
Do A. and B. not kill him themselves?

LUIGI.   They teach
Others to kill him—me—and, if I fail,
Others to succeed; now, if A. tried and failed,
I could not teach that: mine's the lesser task.
Mother, they visit night by night . . .

MOTHER.   —You, Luigi?   30
Ah, will you let me tell you what you are?

LUIGI. Why not? Oh, the one thing you fear to hint,
You may assure yourself I say and say
Ever to myself! At times—nay, even as now
We sit—I think my mind is touched, suspect   35
All is not sound: but is not knowing that,
What constitutes one sane or otherwise?
I know I am thus—so, all is right again.
I laugh at myself as through the town I walk,
And see men merry as if no Italy   40
Were suffering; then I ponder—'I am rich,
'Young, healthy; why should this fact trouble me,
'More than it troubles these?' But it does trouble.
No, trouble's a bad word: for as I walk
There's springing and melody and giddiness,   45
And old quaint turns and passages of my youth,
Dreams long forgotten, little in themselves,
Return to me—whatever may amuse me:
And earth seems in a truce with me, and heaven
Accords with me, all things suspend their strife,   50
The very cicala laughs 'There goes he, and there!
'Feast him, the time is short; he is on his way
'For the world's sake: feast him this once, our friend!'
And in return for all this, I can trip
Cheerfully up the scaffold-steps. I go   55
This evening, mother!

MOTHER.   But mistrust yourself—
Mistrust the judgment you pronounce on him!

LUIGI. Oh, there I feel—am sure that I am right!

MOTHER. Mistrust your judgment then, of the mere means
To this wild enterprise. Say, you are right,—   60

How should one in your state e'er bring to pass
What would require a cool head, a cold heart,
And a calm hand? You never will escape.
LUIGI. Escape? To even wish that, would spoil all.
The dying is best part of it. Too much   65
Have I enjoyed these fifteen years of mine,
To leave myself excuse for longer life:
Was not life pressed down, running o'er with joy,
That I might finish with it ere my fellows
Who, sparelier feasted, make a longer stay?   70
I was put at the board-head, helped to all
At first; I rise up happy and content.
God must be glad one loves his world so much.
I can give news of earth to all the dead
Who ask me:—last year's sunsets, and great stars   75
Which had a right to come first and see ebb
The crimson wave that drifts the sun away—
Those crescent moons with notched and burning rims
That strengthened into sharp fire, and there stood,
Impatient of the azure—and that day   80
In March, a double rainbow stopped the storm—
May's warm slow yellow moonlit summer nights—
Gone are they, but I have them in my soul!
MOTHER. (He will not go!)
LUIGI.   You smile at me? 'T is true,—
Voluptuousness, grotesqueness, ghastliness,   85
Environ my devotedness as quaintly
As round about some antique altar wreathe
The rose festoons, goats' horns, and oxen's skulls.
MOTHER. See now: you reach the city, you must cross
His threshold—how?
LUIGI.   Oh, that's if we conspired!   90
Then would come pains in plenty, as you guess—
But guess not how the qualities most fit
For such an office, qualities I have,
Would little stead me, otherwise employed,
Yet prove of rarest merit only here.   95
Every one knows for what his excellence
Will serve, but no one ever will consider
For what his worst defect might serve: and yet

Have you not seen me range our coppice yonder
In search of a distorted ash?—I find   100
The wry spoilt branch a natural perfect bow.
Fancy the thrice-sage, thrice-precautioned man
Arriving at the palace on my errand!
No, no! I have a handsome dress packed up—
White satin here, to set off my black hair;   105
In I shall march—for you may watch your life out
Behind thick walls, make friends there to betray you;
More than one man spoils everything. March straight—
Only, no clumsy knife to fumble for.
Take the great gate, and walk (not saunter) on   110
Thro' guards and guards——I have rehearsed it all
Inside the turret here a hundred times.
Don't ask the way of whom you meet, observe!
But where they cluster thickliest is the door
Of doors; they'll let you pass—they'll never blab   115
Each to the other, he knows not the favourite,
Whence he is bound and what's his business now.
Walk in—straight up to him; you have no knife:
Be prompt, how should he scream? Then, out with you!
Italy, Italy, my Italy!   120
You're free, you're free! Oh mother, I could dream
They got about me—Andrea from his exile,
Pier from his dungeon, Gualtier from his grave!
MOTHER. Well, you shall go. Yet seems this patriotism
The easiest virtue for a selfish man   125
To acquire: he loves himself—and next, the world—
If he must love beyond,—but nought between:
As a short-sighted man sees nought midway
His body and the sun above. But you
Are my adored Luigi, ever obedient   130
To my least wish, and running o'er with love:
I could not call you cruel or unkind.
Once more, your ground for killing him!—then go!
LUIGI. Now do you try me, or make sport of me?
How first the Austrians got these provinces . . .   135
(If that is all, I 'll satisfy you soon)
—Never by conquest but by cunning, for
That treaty whereby . . .

MOTHER.   Well?
LUIGI.   (Sure, he's arrived,
    The tell-tale cuckoo: spring 's his confidant,
    And he lets out her April purposes!)   140
    Or . . . better go at once to modern time,
    He has . . . they have . . . in fact, I understand
    But can't restate the matter; that's my boast:
    Others could reason it out to you, and prove
    Things they have made me feel.
MOTHER.   Why go to-night?   145
    Morn's for adventure. Jupiter is now
    A morning star. I cannot hear you, Luigi!
LUIGI. 'I am the bright and morning star,' saith God—
    And, 'to such an one I give the morning-star.'
    The gift of the morning star! Have I God's gift   150
    Of the morning-star?
MOTHER.   Chiara will love to see
    That Jupiter an evening-star next June.
LUIGI. True, mother. Well for those who live through June!
    Great noontides, thunder-storms, all glaring pomps
    That triumph at the heels of June the god   155
    Leading his revel through our leafy world.
    Yes, Chiara will be here.
MOTHER.   In June: remember,
    Yourself appointed that month for her coming.
LUIGI. Was that low noise the echo?
MOTHER.   The night-wind.
    She must be grown—with her blue eyes upturned   160
    As if life were one long and sweet surprise:
    In June she comes.
LUIGI.   We were to see together
    The Titian at Treviso. There, again!
        [From without is heard the voice of PIPPA, *singing—*

        A king lived long ago,
        In the morning of the world,   165
        When earth was nigher heaven than now:
        And the king's locks curled,
        Disparting o'er a forehead full
        As the milk-white space 'twixt horn and horn

Of some sacrificial bull—   170
Only calm as a babe new-born:
For he was got to a sleepy mood,
So safe from all decrepitude,
Age with its bane, so sure gone by,
(The gods so loved him while he dreamed)   175
That, having lived thus long, there seemed
No need the king should ever die.

LUIGI. No need that sort of king should ever die!

Among the rocks his city was:
Before his palace, in the sun,   180
He sat to see his people pass,
And judge them every one
From its threshold of smooth stone.
They haled him many a valley-thief
Caught in the sheep-pens, robber-chief   185
Swarthy and shameless, beggar-cheat,
Spy-prowler, or rough pirate found
On the sea-sand left aground;
And sometimes clung about his feet,
With bleeding lip and burning cheek,   190
A woman, bitterest wrong to speak
Of one with sullen thickset brows:
And sometimes from the prison-house
The angry priests a pale wretch brought,
Who through some chink had pushed and pressed   195
On knees and elbows, belly and breast,
Worm-like into the temple,—caught
He was by the very god,
Who ever in the darkness strode
Backward and forward, keeping watch   200
O'er his brazen bowls, such rogues to catch!
These, all and every one,
The king judged, sitting in the sun.

LUIGI. That king should still judge sitting in the sun!

His councillors, on left and right,   205
Looked anxious up,—but no surprise

Disturbed the king's old smiling eyes
Where the very blue had turned to white.
'T is said, a Python scared one day
The breathless city, till he came,   210
With forky tongue and eyes on flame,
Where the old king sat to judge alway;
But when he saw the sweepy hair
Girt with a crown of berries rare
Which the god will hardly give to wear   215
To the maiden who singeth, dancing bare
In the altar-smoke by the pine-torch lights,
At his wondrous forest rites,—
Seeing this, he did not dare
Approach that threshold in the sun,   220
Assault the old king smiling there.
Such grace had kings when the world begun![1]

[PIPPA *passes.*

LUIGI. And such grace have they, now that the world ends!
    The Python at the city, on the throne,
    And brave men, God would crown for slaying him,   225
    Lurk in bye-corners lest they fall his prey.
    Are crowns yet to be won in this late time,
    Which weakness makes me hesitate to reach?
    'T is God's voice calls: how could I stay? Farewell!

Talk by the way, while PIPPA *is passing from the Turret to the Bishop's*
    Brother's House, close to the Duomo S. Maria. Poor Girls *sitting*
    on the steps.

1ST GIRL. There goes a swallow to Venice—the stout
    seafarer!   230
    Seeing those birds fly, makes one wish for wings.
    Let us all wish; you wish first!
2ND GIRL.   I? This sunset
    To finish.
3RD GIRL. That old—somebody I know,
    Greyer and older than my grandfather,   235
    To give me the same treat he gave last week—

   [1] An earlier version of this lyric was published in the *Monthly Repository*, November
1835.

Feeding me on his knee with fig-peckers,
Lampreys and red Breganze-wine, and mumbling
The while some folly about how well I fare,
Let sit and eat my supper quietly: 240
Since had he not himself been late this morning
Detained at—never mind where,—had he not . . .
'Eh, baggage, had I not!'—

2ND GIRL.   How she can lie!

3RD GIRL. Look there—by the nails!

2ND GIRL.   What makes your fingers red?

3RD GIRL. Dipping them into wine to write bad words with   245
  On the bright table: how he laughed!

1ST GIRL.   My turn.
  Spring's come and summer's coming. I would wear
  A long loose gown, down to the feet and hands,
  With plaits here, close about the throat, all day;
  And all night lie, the cool long nights, in bed;   250
  And have new milk to drink, apples to eat,
  Deuzans and junetings, leather-coats . . ah, I should say,
  This is away in the fields—miles!

3RD GIRL.   Say at once
  You'd be at home: she'd always be at home!
  Now comes the story of the farm among   255
  The cherry orchards, and how April snowed
  White blossoms on her as she ran. Why, fool,
  They've rubbed the chalk-mark out, how tall you were,
  Twisted your starling's neck, broken his cage,
  Made a dung-hill of your garden!

1ST GIRL.   They, destroy   260
  My garden since I left them? well—perhaps!
  I would have done so: so I hope they have!
  A fig-tree curled out of our cottage wall;
  They called it mine, I have forgotten why,
  It must have been there long ere I was born: 265
  Cric—cric—I think I hear the wasps o'erhead
  Pricking the papers strung to flutter there
  And keep off birds in fruit-time—coarse long papers,
  And the wasps eat them, prick them through and through.

3RD GIRL. How her mouth twitches! Where was I?—   270
    before

She broke in with her wishes and long gowns
And wasps—would I be such a fool!—Oh, here!
This is my way: I answer every one
Who asks me why I make so much of him—
(If you say, 'you love him'—straight 'he'll not be gulled!')   275
'He that seduced me when I was a girl
'Thus high—had eyes like yours, or hair like yours,
'Brown, red, white,'—as the case may be: that pleases!
See how that beetle burnishes in the path!
There sparkles he along the dust: and, there—   280
Your journey to that maize-tuft spoiled at least!

1ST GIRL. When I was young, they said if you killed one
Of those sunshiny beetles, that his friend
Up there, would shine no more that day nor next.

2ND GIRL. When you were young? Nor are you young, that's
    true.   285
How your plump arms, that were, have dropped away!
Why, I can span them. Cecco beats you still?
No matter, so you keep your curious hair.
I wish they'd find a way to dye our hair
Your colour—any lighter tint, indeed,   290
Than black: the men say they are sick of black,
Black eyes, black hair!

4TH GIRL.   Sick of yours, like enough.
Do you pretend you ever tasted lampreys
And ortolans? Giovita, of the palace,
Engaged (but there's no trusting him) to slice me   295
Polenta with a knife that had cut up
An ortolan.

2ND GIRL. Why, there! Is not that Pippa
We are to talk to, under the window,—quick,—
Where the lights are?

1ST GIRL.   That she? No, or she would sing.   300
For the Intendant said . . .

3RD GIRL.   Oh, you sing first!
Then, if she listens and comes close . . I'll tell you,—
Sing that song the young English noble made,
Who took you for the purest of the pure,
And meant to leave the world for you—what fun!   305

2ND GIRL [*sings*].

> You'll love me yet!—and I can tarry
> 　Your love's protracted growing:
> June reared that bunch of flowers you carry,
> 　From seeds of April's sowing.

> I plant a heartful now: some seed　　　　　　　310
> 　At least is sure to strike,
> And yield—what you'll not pluck indeed,
> 　Not love, but, may be, like.

> You'll look at least on love's remains,
> 　A grave's one violet:　　　　　　　　　　315
> Your look?—that pays a thousand pains.
> 　What's death? You'll love me yet!

3RD GIRL [*to* PIPPA *who approaches*]. Oh, you may come closer—
we shall not eat you! Why, you seem the very person that the
great rich handsome Englishman has fallen so violently in love
with. I'll tell you all about it.

PART IV

NIGHT

SCENE.—*Inside the Palace by the Duomo.* MONSIGNOR, *dismissing
his* Attendants.

MONSIGNOR. Thanks, friends, many thanks! I chiefly desire life
now, that I may recompense every one of you. Most I know
something of already. What, a repast prepared? *Benedicto bene-
dicatur* . . . ugh, ugh! Where was I? Oh, as you were remarking,
Ugo, the weather is mild, very unlike winter-weather: but I am a
Sicilian, you know, and shiver in your Julys here. To be sure,
when 't was full summer at Messina, as we priests used to cross in
procession the great square on Assumption Day, you might see our
thickest yellow tapers twist suddenly in two, each like a falling star,
or sink down on themselves in a gore of wax. But go, my friends,
but go! [*To the* Intendant.] Not you, Ugo! [*The others leave the
apartment.*] I have long wanted to converse with you, Ugo.

INTENDANT. Uguccio—

MONSIGNOR. . . . 'guccio Stefani, man! of Ascoli, Fermo and Fossombruno;—what I do need instructing about, are these accounts of your administration of my poor brother's affairs. Ugh! I shall never get through a third part of your accounts: take some of these dainties before we attempt it, however. Are you bashful to that degree? For me, a crust and water suffice.

INTENDANT. Do you choose this especial night to question me?

MONSIGNOR. This night, Ugo. You have managed my late brother's affairs since the death of our elder brother: fourteen years and a month, all but three days. On the Third of December, I find him . . .

INTENDANT. If you have so intimate an acquaintance with your brother's affairs, you will be tender of turning so far back: they will hardly bear looking into, so far back.

MONSIGNOR. Ay, ay, ugh, ugh,—nothing but disappointments here below! I remark a considerable payment made to yourself on this Third of December. Talk of disappointments! There was a young fellow here, Jules, a foreign sculptor I did my utmost to advance, that the Church might be a gainer by us both: he was going on hopefully enough, and of a sudden he notifies to me some marvellous change that has happened in his notions of Art. Here's his letter,—'He never had a clearly conceived Ideal within his brain till to-day. Yet since his hand could manage a chisel, he has practised expressing other men's Ideals; and, in the very perfection he has attained to, he foresees an ultimate failure: his unconscious hand will pursue its prescribed course of old years, and will reproduce with a fatal expertness the ancient types, let the novel one appear never so palpably to his spirit. There is but one method of escape: confiding the virgin type to as chaste a hand, he will turn painter instead of sculptor, and paint, not carve, its characteristics,'—strike out, I dare say, a school like Correggio: how think you, Ugo?

INTENDANT. Is Correggio a painter?

MONSIGNOR. Foolish Jules! and yet, after all, why foolish? He may —probably will—fail egregiously; but if there should arise a new painter, will it not be in some such way, by a poet now, or a musician (spirits who have conceived and perfected an Ideal through some other channel), transferring it to this, and escaping our conventional roads by pure ignorance of them; eh, Ugo? If you have no appetite, talk at least, Ugo!

INTENDANT. Sir, I can submit no longer to this course of yours. First, you select the group of which I formed one,—next you thin it gradually,—always retaining me with your smile,—and so do you proceed till you have fairly got me alone with you between four stone walls. And now then? Let this farce, this chatter end now: what is it you want with me?

MONSIGNOR. Ugo!

INTENDANT. From the instant you arrived, I felt your smile on me as you questioned me about this and the other article in those papers—why your brother should have given me this villa, that *podere*,—and your nod at the end meant,—what?

MONSIGNOR. Possibly that I wished for no loud talk here. If once you set me coughing, Ugo!—

INTENDANT. I have your brother's hand and seal to all I possess: now ask me what for! what service I did him—ask me!

MONSIGNOR. I would better not: I should rip up old disgraces, let out my poor brother's weaknesses. By the way, Maffeo of Forli (which, I forgot to observe, is your true name), was the interdict ever taken off you, for robbing that church at Cesena?

INTENDANT. No, nor needs be: for when I murdered your brother's friend, Pasquale, for him . . .

MONSIGNOR. Ah, he employed you in that business, did he? Well, I must let you keep, as you say, this villa and that *podere*, for fear the world should find out my relations were of so indifferent a stamp? Maffeo, my family is the oldest in Messina, and century after century have my progenitors gone on polluting themselves with every wickedness under heaven: my own father . . . rest his soul!—I have, I know, a chapel to support that it may rest: my dear two dead brothers were,—what you know tolerably well; I, the youngest, might have rivalled them in vice, if not in wealth: but from my boyhood I came out from among them, and so am not partaker of their plagues. My glory springs from another source; or if from this, by contrast only,—for I, the bishop, am the brother of your employers, Ugo. I hope to repair some of their wrong, however; so far as my brother's ill-gotten treasure reverts to me, I can stop the consequences of his crime: and not one *soldo* shall escape me. Maffeo, the sword we quiet men spurn away, you shrewd knaves pick up and commit murders with; what opportunities the virtuous forego, the villanous seize. Because, to pleasure myself apart from other considerations, my food would

be millet-cake, my dress sackcloth, and my couch straw,—am
I therefore to let you, the offscouring of the earth, seduce the
poor and ignorant by appropriating a pomp these will be sure to
think lessens the abominations so unaccountably and exclusively
associated with it? Must I let villas and *poderi* go to you, a
murderer and thief, that you may beget by means of them other
murderers and thieves? No—if my cough would but allow me to
speak!

INTENDANT. What am I to expect? You are going to punish me?

MONSIGNOR. —Must punish you, Maffeo. I cannot afford to cast
away a chance. I have whole centuries of sin to redeem, and only
a month or two of life to do it in. How should I dare to say . . .

INTENDANT. 'Forgive us our trespasses'?

MONSIGNOR. My friend, it is because I avow myself a very worm,
sinful beyond measure, that I reject a line of conduct you would
applaud perhaps. Shall I proceed, as it were, a-pardoning?—I?—
who have no symptom of reason to assume that aught less than my
strenuousest efforts will keep myself out of mortal sin, much less
keep others out. No: I do trespass, but will not double that by
allowing you to trespass.

INTENDANT. And suppose the villas are not your brother's to give,
nor yours to take? Oh, you are hasty enough just now!

MONSIGNOR. 1, 2—N° 3!—ay, can you read the substance of a
letter, N° 3, I have received from Rome? It is precisely on the
ground there mentioned, of the suspicion I have that a certain
child of my late elder brother, who would have succeeded to his
estates, was murdered in infancy by you, Maffeo, at the instigation
of my late younger brother—that the Pontiff enjoins on me not
merely the bringing that Maffeo to condign punishment, but the
taking all pains, as guardian of the infant's heritage for the
Church, to recover it parcel by parcel, howsoever, whensoever,
and wheresoever. While you are now gnawing those fingers, the
police are engaged in sealing up your papers, Maffeo, and the
mere raising my voice brings my people from the next room to
dispose of yourself. But I want you to confess quietly, and save
me raising my voice. Why, man, do I not know the old story?
The heir between the succeeding heir, and this heir's ruffianly
instrument, and their complot's effect, and the life of fear and
bribes and ominous smiling silence? Did you throttle or stab my
brother's infant? Come now!

INTENDANT. So old a story, and tell it no better? When did such an instrument ever produce such an effect? Either the child smiles in his face; or, most likely, he is not fool enough to put himself in the employer's power so thoroughly: the child is always ready to produce—as you say—howsoever, wheresoever, and whensoever.

MONSIGNOR. Liar!

INTENDANT. Strike me? Ah, so might a father chastise! I shall sleep soundly to-night at least, though the gallows await me to-morrow; for what a life did I lead! Carlo of Cesena reminds me of his connivance, every time I pay his annuity; which happens commonly thrice a year. If I remonstrate, he will confess all to the good bishop—you!

MONSIGNOR. I see through the trick, caitiff! I would you spoke truth for once. All shall be sifted, however—seven times sifted.

INTENDANT. And how my absurd riches encumbered me! I dared not lay claim to above half my possessions. Let me but once unbosom myself, glorify Heaven, and die!

Sir, you are no brutal dastardly idiot like your brother I frightened to death: let us understand one another. Sir, I will make away with her for you—the girl—here close at hand; not the stupid obvious kind of killing; do not speak—know nothing of her nor of me! I see her every day—saw her this morning: of course there is to be no killing; but at Rome the courtesans perish off every three years, and I can entice her thither—have indeed begun operations already. There's a certain lusty blue-eyed florid-complexioned English knave, I and the Police employ occasionally. You assent, I perceive—no, that's not it—assent I do not say—but you will let me convert my present havings and holdings into cash, and give me time to cross the Alps? 'T is but a little black-eyed pretty singing Felippa, gay silk-winding girl. I have kept her out of harm's way up to this present; for I always intended to make your life a plague to you with her. 'T is as well settled once and for ever. Some women I have procured will pass Bluphocks, my handsome scoundrel, off for somebody; and once Pippa entangled!—you conceive? Through her singing? Is it a bargain?

[*From without is heard the voice of* PIPPA, *singing*—

Overhead the tree-tops meet,
Flowers and grass spring 'neath one's feet;

There was nought above me, nought below,
My childhood had not learned to know:
For, what are the voices of birds
—Ay, and of beasts,—but words, our words,
Only so much more sweet?
The knowledge of that with my life begun.
But I had so near made out the sun,
And counted your stars, the seven and one,
Like the fingers of my hand:
Nay, I could all but understand
Wherefore through heaven the white moon ranges;
And just when out of her soft fifty changes
No unfamiliar face might overlook me—
Suddenly God took me.

[PIPPA *passes.*

MONSIGNOR [*springing up*]. My people—one and all—all—within
there! Gag this villain—tie him hand and foot! He dares . . . I
know not half he dares—but remove him—quick! *Miserere mei,*
Domine! Quick, I say!

SCENE.—PIPPA'S *chamber again. She enters it.*

The bee with his comb,
The mouse at her dray,
The grub in his tomb,
Wile winter away;
But the fire-fly and hedge-shrew and lob-worm, I pray,   5
How fare they?
Ha, ha, thanks for your counsel, my Zanze!
'Feast upon lampreys, quaff Breganze'—
The summer of life so easy to spend,
And care for to-morrow so soon put away!   10
But winter hastens at summer's end,
And fire-fly, hedge-shrew, lob-worm, pray,
How fare they?
No bidding me then to . . . what did Zanze say?
'Pare your nails pearlwise, get your small feet shoes   15
'More like' . . (what said she?)—'and less like canoes!'
How pert that girl was!—would I be those pert

Impudent staring women! It had done me,
However, surely no such mighty hurt
To learn his name who passed that jest upon me:　　　20
No foreigner, that I can recollect,
Came, as she says, a month since, to inspect
Our silk-mills—none with blue eyes and thick rings
Of raw-silk-coloured hair, at all events.
Well, if old Luca keep his good intents,　　　25
We shall do better, see what next year brings.
I may buy shoes, my Zanze, not appear
More destitute than you perhaps next year!
Bluph . . . something! I had caught the uncouth name
But for Monsignor's people's sudden clatter　　　30
Above us—bound to spoil such idle chatter
As ours: it were indeed a serious matter
If silly talk like ours should put to shame
The pious man, the man devoid of blame,
The . . . ah but—ah but, all the same,　　　35
No mere mortal has a right
To carry that exalted air;
Best people are not angels quite:
While—not the worst of people's doings scare
The devil; so there's that proud look to spare!　　　40
　　Which is mere counsel to myself, mind! for
I have just been the holy Monsignor:
And I was you too, Luigi's gentle mother,
And you too, Luigi!—how that Luigi started
Out of the turret—doubtlessly departed　　　45
On some good errand or another,
For he passed just now in a traveller's trim,
And the sullen company that prowled
About his path, I noticed, scowled
As if they had lost a prey in him.　　　50
And I was Jules the sculptor's bride,
And I was Ottima beside,
And now what am I?—tired of fooling.
Day for folly, night for schooling!
New year's day is over and spent,　　　55
Ill or well, I must be content.
　　Even my lily's asleep, I vow:

Wake up—here's a friend I've plucked you:
Call this flower a heart's-ease now!
Something rare, let me instruct you,   60
Is this, with petals triply swollen,
Three times spotted, thrice the pollen;
While the leaves and parts that witness
Old proportions and their fitness,
Here remain unchanged, unmoved now;   65
Call this pampered thing improved now!
Suppose there's a king of the flowers
And a girl-show held in his bowers—
'Look ye, buds, this growth of ours,'
Says he, 'Zanze from the Brenta,   70
'I have made her gorge polenta
'Till both cheeks are near as bouncing
'As her . . . name there's no pronouncing!
'See this heightened colour too,
'For she swilled Breganze wine   75
'Till her nose turned deep carmine;
' 'T was but white when wild she grew.
'And only by this Zanze's eyes
'Of which we could not change the size,
'The magnitude of all achieved   80
'Otherwise, may be perceived.'

Oh what a drear dark close to my poor day!
How could that red sun drop in that black cloud?
Ah Pippa, morning's rule is moved away,
Dispensed with, never more to be allowed!   85
Day's turn is over, now arrives the night's.
Oh lark, be day's apostle
To mavis, merle and throstle,
Bid them their betters jostle
From day and its delights!   90
But at night, brother howlet, over the woods,
Toll the world to thy chantry;
Sing to the bats' sleek sisterhoods
Full complines with gallantry:
Then, owls and bats,   95
Cowls and twats,

Monks and nuns, in a cloister's moods,
Adjourn to the oak-stump pantry!
                    [*After she has begun to undress herself.*
Now, one thing I should like to really know:
How near I ever might approach all these   100
I only fancied being, this long day:
—Approach, I mean, so as to touch them, so
As to . . . in some way . . . move them—if you please,
Do good or evil to them some slight way.
For instance, if I wind   105
Silk to-morrow, my silk may bind
                    [*Sitting on the bedside.*
And border Ottima's cloak's hem.
Ah me, and my important part with them,
This morning's hymn half promised when I rose!
True in some sense or other, I suppose.   110
                    [*As she lies down.*
God bless me! I can pray no more to-night.
No doubt, some way or other, hymns say right.

        All service ranks the same with God—
        With God, whose puppets, best and worst,
        Are we: there is no last nor first.   115
                    [*She sleeps.*

DRAMATIC LYRICS

DRAMATIC LYRICS

[*First published as* Bells and Pomegranates, No. III, *in 1842. Although Browning's final text is given here, the arrangement of the poems remains that of 1842. For Browning's later arrangement and classification of these poems, see Appendix D below.*]

CAVALIER TUNES[1]

I. MARCHING ALONG

I

KENTISH Sir Byng stood for his King,
Bidding the crop-headed Parliament swing:
And, pressing a troop unable to stoop
And see the rogues flourish and honest folk droop,
Marched them along, fifty-score strong,   5
Great-hearted gentlemen, singing this song.

II

God for King Charles! Pym and such carles
To the Devil that prompts 'em their treasonous parles!
Cavaliers, up! Lips from the cup,
Hands from the pasty, nor bite take nor sup   10
Till you're—

CHORUS. *Marching along, fifty-score strong,*
         Great-hearted gentlemen, singing this song.

III

Hampden to hell, and his obsequies' knell
Serve Hazelrig, Fiennes, and young Harry as well!
England, good cheer! Rupert is near!

[1] In 1842 the following 'ADVERTISEMENT' was printed opposite the first page of the text: 'Such Poems as the following come properly enough, I suppose, under the head of "Dramatic Pieces;" being, though for the most part Lyric in expression, always Dramatic in principle, and so many utterances of so many imaginary persons, not mine.   R.B.' Browning here refers to his original intention of including only dramatic poetry in the *Bells and Pomegranates*. In 1849 the 'ADVERTISEMENT' became a footnote, and in 1863 and subsequently the footnote was reworded as follows: 'Such Poems as the majority in this volume might also come properly enough, I suppose, under the head of "Dramatic Pieces;" being, though often Lyric in expression, always Dramatic in principle, and so many utterances of so many imaginary persons, not mine.—*R.B.*'

Kentish and loyalists, keep we not here   15
CHORUS. *Marching along, fifty-score strong,*
          Great-hearted gentlemen, singing this song?

IV

Then, God for King Charles! Pym and his snarls
To the Devil that pricks on such pestilent carles!
Hold by the right, you double your might;
So, onward to Nottingham, fresh for the fight,

CHORUS. *March we along, fifty-score strong,*
          Great-hearted gentlemen, singing this song!

II. GIVE A ROUSE

I

King Charles, and who'll do him right now?   20
King Charles, and who's ripe for fight now?
Give a rouse: here's, in hell's despite now,
King Charles!

II

Who gave me the goods that went since?
Who raised me the house that sank once?   25
Who helped me to gold I spent since?
Who found me in wine you drank once?

CHORUS. *King Charles, and who'll do him right now?*
          King Charles, and who's ripe for fight now?
          Give a rouse: here's, in hell's despite now,
          King Charles!

III

To whom used my boy George quaff else,
By the old fool's side that begot him?
For whom did he cheer and laugh else,
While Noll's damned troopers shot him?   30

CHORUS. *King Charles, and who'll do him right now?*
          King Charles, and who's ripe for fight now?
          Give a rouse: here's, in hell's despite now,
          King Charles!

III. BOOT AND SADDLE[1]

I

Boot, saddle, to horse, and away!
Rescue my castle before the hot day
Brightens to blue from its silvery grey,
CHORUS. *Boot, saddle, to horse, and away!*

II

Ride past the suburbs, asleep as you 'd say;   35
Many's the friend there, will listen and pray
'God's luck to gallants that strike up the lay—
CHORUS. *'Boot, saddle, to horse, and away!'*

III

Forty miles off, like a roebuck at bay,
Flouts Castle Brancepeth the Roundheads' array:
Who laughs, 'Good fellows ere this, by my fay,   40
CHORUS. *'Boot, saddle, to horse, and away!'*

IV

Who? My wife Gertrude; that, honest and gay,
Laughs when you talk of surrendering, 'Nay!
'I've better counsellors; what counsel they?
CHORUS. *'Boot, saddle, to horse, and away!'*

MY LAST DUCHESS

FERRARA[2]

THAT'S my last Duchess painted on the wall,
Looking as if she were alive. I call
That piece a wonder, now: Frà Pandolf's hands
Worked busily a day, and there she stands.
Will 't please you sit and look at her? I said   5
'Frà Pandolf' by design, for never read
Strangers like you that pictured countenance,

---

[1] In 1842 the title was 'My Wife Gertrude'.
[2] In 1842 this and the following poem were entitled 'Italy and France, I.—Italy,' and 'II.—France'.

The depth and passion of its earnest glance,
But to myself they turned (since none puts by
The curtain I have drawn for you, but I)   10
And seemed as they would ask me, if they durst,
How such a glance came there; so, not the first
Are you to turn and ask thus. Sir, 't was not
Her husband's presence only, called that spot
Of joy into the Duchess' cheek: perhaps   15
Frà Pandolf chanced to say 'Her mantle laps
'Over my lady's wrist too much,' or 'Paint
'Must never hope to reproduce the faint
'Half-flush that dies along her throat:' such stuff
Was courtesy, she thought, and cause enough   20
For calling up that spot of joy. She had
A heart—how shall I say?—too soon made glad,
Too easily impressed; she liked whate'er
She looked on, and her looks went everywhere.
Sir, 't was all one! My favour at her breast,   25
The dropping of the daylight in the West,
The bough of cherries some officious fool
Broke in the orchard for her, the white mule
She rode with round the terrace—all and each
Would draw from her alike the approving speech,   30
Or blush, at least. She thanked men,—good! but thanked
Somehow—I know not how—as if she ranked
My gift of a nine-hundred-years-old name
With anybody's gift. Who'd stoop to blame
This sort of trifling? Even had you skill   35
In speech—(which I have not)—to make your will
Quite clear to such an one, and say, 'Just this
'Or that in you disgusts me; here you miss,
'Or there exceed the mark'—and if she let
Herself be lessoned so, nor plainly set   40
Her wits to yours, forsooth, and made excuse,
—E'en then would be some stooping; and I choose
Never to stoop. Oh sir, she smiled, no doubt,
Whene'er I passed her; but who passed without
Much the same smile? This grew; I gave commands;   45
Then all smiles stopped together. There she stands
As if alive. Will 't please you rise? We'll meet

The company below, then. I repeat,
The Count your master's known munificence
Is ample warrant that no just pretence 50
Of mine for dowry will be disallowed;
Though his fair daughter's self, as I avowed
At starting, is my object. Nay, we'll go
Together down, sir. Notice Neptune, though,
Taming a sea-horse, thought a rarity, 55
Which Claus of Innsbruck cast in bronze for me!

COUNT GISMOND

AIX IN PROVENCE

I

CHRIST God who savest man, save most
   Of men Count Gismond who saved me! .
Count Gauthier, when he chose his post,
   Chose time and place and company
To suit it; when he struck at length 5
My honour, 't was with all his strength.

II

And doubtlessly ere he could draw
   All points to one, he must have schemed!
That miserable morning saw
   Few half so happy as I seemed, 10
While being dressed in queen's array
To give our tourney prize away.

III

I thought they loved me, did me grace
   To please themselves; 't was all their deed;
God makes, or fair or foul, our face; 15
   If showing mine so caused to bleed
My cousins' hearts, they should have dropped
A word, and straight the play had stopped.

IV

They, too, so beauteous! Each a queen
   By virtue of her brow and breast; 20

Not needing to be crowned, I mean,
  As I do. E'en when I was dressed,
Had either of them spoke, instead
Of glancing sideways with still head!

V

But no: they let me laugh, and sing   25
  My birthday song quite through, adjust
The last rose in my garland, fling
  A last look on the mirror, trust
My arms to each an arm of theirs,
And so descend the castle-stairs—   30

VI

And come out on the morning-troop
  Of merry friends who kissed my cheek,
And called me queen, and made me stoop
  Under the canopy—(a streak
That pierced it, of the outside sun,   35
Powdered with gold its gloom's soft dun)—

VII

And they could let me take my state
  And foolish throne amid applause
Of all come there to celebrate
  My queen's-day—Oh I think the cause   40
Of much was, they forgot no crowd
Makes up for parents in their shroud!

VIII

However that be, all eyes were bent
  Upon me, when my cousins cast
Theirs down; 't was time I should present   45
  The victor's crown, but . . . there, 't will last
No long time . . . the old mist again
Blinds me as then it did. How vain!

IX

See! Gismond's at the gate, in talk
  With his two boys: I can proceed.   50
Well, at that moment, who should stalk

Forth boldly—to my face, indeed—
But Gauthier, and he thundered 'Stay!'
And all stayed. 'Bring no crowns, I say!

X

'Bring torches! Wind the penance-sheet   55
   'About her! Let her shun the chaste,
'Or lay herself before their feet!
   'Shall she whose body I embraced
'A night long, queen it in the day?
'For honour's sake no crowns, I say!'   60

XI

I? What I answered? As I live,
   I never fancied such a thing
As answer possible to give.
   What says the body when they spring
Some monstrous torture-engine's whole   65
Strength on it? No more says the soul.

XII

Till out strode Gismond; then I knew
   That I was saved. I never met
His face before, but, at first view,
   I felt quite sure that God had set   70
Himself to Satan; who would spend
A minute's mistrust on the end?

XIII

He strode to Gauthier, in his throat
   Gave him the lie, then struck his mouth
With one back-handed blow that wrote   75
   In blood men's verdict there. North, South,
East, West, I looked. The lie was dead,
And damned, and truth stood up instead.

XIV

This glads me most, that I enjoyed
   The heart of the joy, with my content   80
In watching Gismond unalloyed
   By any doubt of the event:

God took that on him—I was bid
Watch Gismond for my part: I did.

XV

Did I not watch him while he let   85
  His armourer just brace his greaves,
Rivet his hauberk, on the fret
  The while! His foot . . . my memory leaves
No least stamp out, nor how anon
He pulled his ringing gauntlets on.   90

XVI

And e'en before the trumpet's sound
  Was finished, prone lay the false knight,
Prone as his lie, upon the ground:
  Gismond flew at him, used no sleight
O' the sword, but open-breasted drove,   95
Cleaving till out the truth he clove.

XVII

Which done, he dragged him to my feet
  And said 'Here die, but end thy breath
'In full confession, lest thou fleet
  'From my first, to God's second death!   100
'Say, hast thou lied?' And, 'I have lied
'To God and her,' he said, and died.

XVIII

Then Gismond, kneeling to me, asked
  —What safe my heart holds, though no word
Could I repeat now, if I tasked   105
  My powers for ever, to a third
Dear even as you are. Pass the rest
Until I sank upon his breast.

XIX

Over my head his arm he flung
  Against the world; and scarce I felt   110
His sword (that dripped by me and swung)
  A little shifted in its belt:
For he began to say the while
How South our home lay many a mile.

XX

So 'mid the shouting multitude   115
   We two walked forth to never more
Return. My cousins have pursued
   Their life, untroubled as before
I vexed them. Gauthier's dwelling-place
God lighten! May his soul find grace!   120

XXI

Our elder boy has got the clear
   Great brow; tho' when his brother's black
Full eye shows scorn, it . . . Gismond here?
   And have you brought my tercel back?
I just was telling Adela   125
How many birds it struck since May.

INCIDENT OF THE FRENCH CAMP[1]

I

You know, we French stormed Ratisbon:
   A mile or so away,
On a little mound, Napoleon
   Stood on our storming-day;
With neck out-thrust, you fancy how,   5
   Legs wide, arms locked behind,
As if to balance the prone brow
   Oppressive with its mind.

II

Just as perhaps he mused 'My plans
   'That soar, to earth may fall,   10
'Let once my army-leader Lannes
   'Waver at yonder wall,'—
Out 'twixt the battery-smokes there flew
   A rider, bound on bound
Full-galloping; nor bridle drew   15
   Until he reached the mound.

[1] In 1842 this and the following poem were entitled 'Camp and Cloister. I.—Camp (*French*)' and 'II.—Cloister (*Spanish*)'.

III

Then off there flung in smiling joy,
   And held himself erect
By just his horse's mane, a boy:
   You hardly could suspect—   20
(So tight he kept his lips compressed,
   Scarce any blood came through)
You looked twice ere you saw his breast
   Was all but shot in two.

IV

'Well,' cried he, 'Emperor, by God's grace   25
   'We've got you Ratisbon!
'The Marshal's in the market-place,
   'And you'll be there anon
'To see your flag-bird flap his vans
   'Where I, to heart's desire,   30
'Perched him!' The chief's eye flashed; his plans
   Soared up again like fire.

V

The chief's eye flashed; but presently
   Softened itself, as sheathes
A film the mother-eagle's eye   35
   When her bruised eaglet breathes;
'You're wounded!' 'Nay,' the soldier's pride
   Touched to the quick, he said:
'I'm killed, Sire!' And his chief beside
   Smiling the boy fell dead.   40

SOLILOQUY OF THE SPANISH CLOISTER

I

GR-R-R—there go, my heart's abhorrence!
   Water your damned flower-pots, do!
If hate killed men, Brother Lawrence,
   God's blood, would not mine kill you!
What? your myrtle-bush wants trimming?   5
   Oh, that rose has prior claims—
Needs its leaden vase filled brimming?
   Hell dry you up with its flames!

II

At the meal we sit together:
  Salve tibi! I must hear   10
Wise talk of the kind of weather,
  Sort of season, time of year:
Not a plenteous cork-crop: scarcely
  Dare we hope oak-galls, I doubt:
What's the Latin name for 'parsley'?   15
  What's the Greek name for Swine's Snout?

III

Whew! We'll have our platter burnished,
  Laid with care on our own shelf!
With a fire-new spoon we're furnished,
  And a goblet for ourself,   20
Rinsed like something sacrificial
  Ere 't is fit to touch our chaps—
Marked with L. for our initial!
  (He-he! There his lily snaps!)

IV

Saint, forsooth! While brown Dolores   25
  Squats outside the Convent bank
With Sanchicha, telling stories,
  Steeping tresses in the tank,
Blue-black, lustrous, thick like horsehairs,
  —Can't I see his dead eye glow,   30
Bright as 't were a Barbary corsair's?
  (That is, if he'd let it show!)

V

When he finishes refection,
  Knife and fork he never lays
Cross-wise, to my recollection,   35
  As do I, in Jesu's praise.
I the Trinity illustrate,
  Drinking watered orange-pulp—
In three sips the Arian frustrate;
  While he drains his at one gulp.   40

VI

Oh, those melons? If he's able
 We're to have a feast! so nice!
One goes to the Abbot's table,
 All of us get each a slice.
How go on your flowers? None double? 45
 Not one fruit-sort can you spy?
Strange!—And I, too, at such trouble,
 Keep them close-nipped on the sly!

VII

There's a great text in Galatians,
 Once you trip on it, entails 50
Twenty-nine distinct damnations,
 One sure, if another fails:
If I trip him just a-dying,
 Sure of heaven as sure can be,
Spin him round and send him flying 55
 Off to hell, a Manichee?

VIII

Or, my scrofulous French novel
 On grey paper with blunt type!
Simply glance at it, you grovel
 Hand and foot in Belial's gripe: 60
If I double down its pages
 At the woeful sixteenth print,
When he gathers his greengages,
 Ope a sieve and slip it in 't?

IX

Or, there's Satan!—one might venture 65
 Pledge one's soul to him, yet leave
Such a flaw in the indenture
 As he'd miss till, past retrieve,
Blasted lay that rose-acacia
 We're so proud of! *Hy, Zy, Hine* . . . 70
'St, there's Vespers! *Plena gratiâ*
 Ave, Virgo! Gr-r-r—you swine!

IN A GONDOLA

He sings.

I SEND my heart up to thee, all my heart
  In this my singing.
For the stars help me, and the sea bears part;
  The very night is clinging
Closer to Venice' streets to leave one space   5
  Above me, whence thy face
May light my joyous heart to thee its dwelling-place.

She speaks.

Say after me, and try to say
My very words, as if each word
Came from you of your own accord,   10
In your own voice, in your own way:
'This woman's heart and soul and brain
'Are mine as much as this gold chain
'She bids me wear; which' (say again)
'I choose to make by cherishing   15
'A precious thing, or choose to fling
'Over the boat-side, ring by ring.'
And yet once more say . . . no word more!
Since words are only words. Give o'er!

Unless you call me, all the same,   20
Familiarly by my pet name,
Which if the Three should hear you call,
And me reply to, would proclaim
At once our secret to them all.
Ask of me, too, command me, blame—   25
Do, break down the partition-wall
'Twixt us, the daylight world beholds
Curtained in dusk and splendid folds!
What's left but—all of me to take?
I am the Three's: prevent them, slake   30

Your thirst! 'T is said, the Arab sage,
In practising with gems, can loose
Their subtle spirit in his cruce
And leave but ashes: so, sweet mage,
Leave them my ashes when thy use　　　　　35
Sucks out my soul, thy heritage!

He sings.

I

Past we glide, and past, and past!
　What's that poor Agnese doing
Where they make the shutters fast?
　Grey Zanobi's just a-wooing　　　　　40
To his couch the purchased bride:
　Past we glide!

II

Past we glide, and past, and past!
　Why's the Pucci Palace flaring
Like a beacon to the blast?　　　　　45
　Guests by hundreds, not one caring
If the dear host's neck were wried:
　Past we glide!

She sings.

I

The moth's kiss, first!
Kiss me as if you made believe　　　　　50
You were not sure, this eve,
How my face, your flower, had pursed
Its petals up; so, here and there
You brush it, till I grow aware
Who wants me, and wide ope I burst.　　　　　55

II

The bee's kiss, now!
Kiss me as if you entered gay
My heart at some noonday,
A bud that dares not disallow
The claim, so all is rendered up,　　　　　60
And passively its shattered cup
Over your head to sleep I bow.

He sings.

I

What are we two?
I am a Jew,
And carry thee, farther than friends can pursue,   65
To a feast of our tribe;
Where they need thee to bribe
The devil that blasts them unless he imbibe
Thy . . . Scatter the vision for ever! And now,
As of old, I am I, thou art thou!   70

II

Say again, what we are?
The sprite of a star,
I lure thee above where the destinies bar
My plumes their full play
Till a ruddier ray   75
Than my pale one announce there is withering
    away
Some . . . Scatter the vision for ever! And now,
As of old, I am I, thou art thou!

He muses.

Oh, which were best, to roam or rest?
The land's lap or the water's breast?   80
To sleep on yellow millet-sheaves,
Or swim in lucid shallows just
Eluding water-lily leaves,
An inch from Death's black fingers, thrust
To lock you, whom release he must;   85
Which life were best on Summer eves?

He speaks, musing.

Lie back; could thought of mine improve you?
From this shoulder let there spring
A wing; from this, another wing;
Wings, not legs and feet, shall move you!   90
Snow-white must they spring, to blend
With your flesh, but I intend
They shall deepen to the end,

Broader, into burning gold,
Till both wings crescent-wise enfold   95
Your perfect self, from 'neath your feet
To o'er your head, where, lo, they meet
As if a million sword-blades hurled
Defiance from you to the world!

Rescue me thou, the only real!   100
And scare away this mad ideal
That came, nor motions to depart!
Thanks! Now, stay ever as thou art!

Still he muses.

I

What if the Three should catch at last
Thy serenader? While there's cast   105
Paul's cloak about my head, and fast
Gian pinions me, Himself has past
His stylet thro' my back; I reel;
And . . . is it thou I feel?

II

They trail me, these three godless knaves,   110
Past every church that saints and saves,
Nor stop till, where the cold sea raves
By Lido's wet accursed graves,
They scoop mine, roll me to its brink,
And . . . on thy breast I sink!   115

She replies, musing.

Dip your arm o'er the boat-side, elbow-deep,
As I do: thus: were death so unlike sleep,
Caught this way? Death's to fear from flame or steel,
Or poison doubtless; but from water—feel!

Go find the bottom! Would you stay me? There!   120
Now pluck a great blade of that ribbon-grass
To plait in where the foolish jewel was,
I flung away: since you have praised my hair,
'T is proper to be choice in what I wear.

He speaks.

Row home? must we row home? Too surely 125
Know I where its front's demurely
Cver the Giudecca piled;
Window just with window mating,
Door on door exactly waiting,
All's the set face of a child: 130
But behind it, where's a trace
Of the staidness and reserve,
And formal lines without a curve,
In the same child's playing-face?
No two windows look one way 135
O'er the small sea-water thread
Below them. Ah, the autumn day
I, passing, saw you overhead!
First, out a cloud of curtain blew,
Then a sweet cry, and last came you— 140
To catch your lory that must needs
Escape just then, of all times then,
To peck a tall plant's fleecy seeds,
And make me happiest of men.
I scarce could breathe to see you reach 145
So far back o'er the balcony
To catch him ere he climbed too high
Above you in the Smyrna peach
That quick the round smooth cord of gold,
This coiled hair on your head, unrolled, 150
Fell down you like a gorgeous snake
The Roman girls were wont, of old,
When Rome there was, for coolness' sake
To let lie curling o'er their bosoms.
Dear lory, may his beak retain 155
Ever its delicate rose stain
As if the wounded lotus-blossoms
Had marked their thief to know again!

Stay longer yet, for others' sake
Than mine! What should your chamber do? 160
—With all its rarities that ache
In silence while day lasts, but wake

At night-time and their life renew,
Suspended just to pleasure you
Who brought against their will together   165
These objects, and, while day lasts, weave
Around them such a magic tether
That dumb they look: your harp, believe,
With all the sensitive tight strings
Which dare not speak, now to itself   170
Breathes slumberously, as if some elf
Went in and out the chords, his wings
Make murmur wheresoe'er they graze,
As an angel may, between the maze
Of midnight palace-pillars, on   175
And on, to sow God's plagues, have gone
Through guilty glorious Babylon.
And while such murmurs flow, the nymph
Bends o'er the harp-top from her shell
As the dry limpet for the lymph   180
Come with a tune he knows so well.
And how your statues' hearts must swell!
And how your pictures must descend
To see each other, friend with friend!
Oh, could you take them by surprise,   185
You'd find Schidone's eager Duke
Doing the quaintest courtesies
To that prim saint by Haste-thee-Luke!
And, deeper into her rock den,
Bold Castelfranco's Magdalen   190
You'd find retreated from the ken
Of that robed counsel-keeping Ser—
As if the Tizian thinks of her,
And is not, rather, gravely bent
On seeing for himself what toys   195
Are these, his progeny invent,
What litter now the board employs
Whereon he signed a document
That got him murdered! Each enjoys
Its night so well, you cannot break   200
The sport up, so, indeed must make
More stay with me, for others' sake.

She speaks.

I

To-morrow, if a harp-string, say,
Is used to tie the jasmine back
That overfloods my room with sweets,   205
Contrive your Zorzi somehow meets
My Zanze! If the ribbon's black,
The Three are watching: keep away!

II

Your gondola—let Zorzi wreathe
A mesh of water-weeds about   210
Its prow, as if he unaware
Had struck some quay or bridge-foot stair!
That I may throw a paper out
As you and he go underneath.

There's Zanze's vigilant taper; safe are we.   215
Only one minute more to-night with me?
Resume your past self of a month ago!
Be you the bashful gallant, I will be
The lady with the colder breast than snow.
Now bow you, as becomes, nor touch my hand   220
More than I touch yours when I step to land,
And say, 'All thanks, Siora!'—
                              Heart to heart
And lips to lips! Yet once more, ere we part,
Clasp me and make me thine, as mine thou art!
                    [He is surprised, and stabbed.
It was ordained to be so, sweet!—and best   225
Comes now, beneath thine eyes, upon thy breast.
Still kiss me! Care not for the cowards! Care
Only to put aside thy beauteous hair
My blood will hurt! The Three, I do not scorn
To death, because they never lived: but I   230
Have lived indeed, and so—(yet one more kiss)—can
    die!

ARTEMIS PROLOGIZES

I AM a goddess of the ambrosial courts,
And save by Here, Queen of Pride, surpassed
By none whose temples whiten this the world.
Through heaven I roll my lucid moon along;
I shed in hell o'er my pale people peace;   5
On earth I, caring for the creatures, guard
Each pregnant yellow wolf and fox-bitch sleek,
And every feathered mother's callow brood,
And all that love green haunts and loneliness.
Of men, the chaste adore me, hanging crowns   10
Of poppies red to blackness, bell and stem,
Upon my image at Athenai here;
And this dead Youth, Asclepios bends above,
Was dearest to me. He, my buskined step
To follow through the wild-wood leafy ways,   15
And chase the panting stag, or swift with darts
Stop the swift ounce, or lay the leopard low,
Neglected homage to another god:
Whence Aphrodite, by no midnight smoke
Of tapers lulled, in jealousy despatched   20
A noisome lust that, as the gadbee stings,
Possessed his stepdame Phaidra for himself
The son of Theseus her great absent spouse.
Hippolutos exclaiming in his rage
Against the fury of the Queen, she judged   25
Life insupportable; and, pricked at heart
An Amazonian stranger's race should dare
To scorn her, perished by the murderous cord:
Yet, ere she perished, blasted in a scroll
The fame of him her swerving made not swerve.   30
And Theseus, read, returning, and believed,
And exiled, in the blindness of his wrath,
The man without a crime who, last as first,
Loyal, divulged not to his sire the truth.
Now Theseus from Poseidon had obtained   35
That of his wishes should be granted three,
And one he imprecated straight—'Alive
'May ne'er Hippolutos reach other lands!'

Poseidon heard, ai ai! And scarce the prince
Had stepped into the fixed boots of the car   40
That give the feet a stay against the strength
Of the Henetian horses, and around
His body flung the rein, and urged their speed
Along the rocks and shingles of the shore,
When from the gaping wave a monster flung   45
His obscene body in the coursers' path.
These, mad with terror, as the sea-bull sprawled
Wallowing about their feet, lost care of him
That reared them; and the master-chariot-pole
Snapping beneath their plunges like a reed,   50
Hippolutos, whose feet were trammelled fast,
Was yet dragged forward by the circling rein
Which either hand directed; nor they quenched
The frenzy of their flight before each trace,
Wheel-spoke and splinter of the woeful car,   55
Each boulder-stone, sharp stub and spiny shell,
Huge fish-bone wrecked and wreathed amid the sands
On that detested beach, was bright with blood
And morsels of his flesh: then fell the steeds
Head-foremost, crashing in their mooned fronts,   60
Shivering with sweat, each white eye horror-fixed.
His people, who had witnessed all afar,
Bore back the ruins of Hippolutos.
But when his sire, too swoln with pride, rejoiced
(Indomitable as a man foredoomed)   65
That vast Poseidon had fulfilled his prayer,
I, in a flood of glory visible,
Stood o'er my dying votary and, deed
By deed, revealed, as all took place, the truth.
Then Theseus lay the woefullest of men,   70
And worthily; but ere the death-veils hid
His face, the murdered prince full pardon breathed
To his rash sire. Whereat Athenai wails.

    So I, who ne'er forsake my votaries,
Lest in the cross-way none the honey-cake   75
Should tender, nor pour out the dog's hot life;
Lest at my fane the priests disconsolate

Should dress my image with some faded poor
Few crowns, made favours of, nor dare object
Such slackness to my worshippers who turn   80
Elsewhere the trusting heart and loaded hand,
As they had climbed Olumpos to report
Of Artemis and nowhere found her throne—
I interposed: and, this eventful night,—
(While round the funeral pyre the populace   85
Stood with fierce light on their black robes which bound
Each sobbing head, while yet their hair they clipped
O'er the dead body of their withered prince,
And, in his palace, Theseus prostrated
On the cold hearth, his brow cold as the slab   90
'T was bruised on, groaned away the heavy grief—
As the pyre fell, and down the cross-logs crashed,
Sending a crowd of sparkles through the night,
And the gay fire, elate with mastery,
Towered like a serpent o'er the clotted jars   95
Of wine, dissolving oils and frankincense,
And splendid gums like gold),—my potency
Conveyed the perished man to my retreat
In the thrice-venerable forest here.
And this white-bearded sage who squeezes now   100
The berried plant, is Phoibos' son of fame,
Asclepios, whom my radiant brother taught
The doctrine of each herb and flower and root,
To know their secret'st virtue and express
The saving soul of all: who so has soothed   105
With lavers the torn brow and murdered cheeks,
Composed the hair and brought its gloss again,
And called the red bloom to the pale skin back,
And laid the strips and jagged ends of flesh
Even once more, and slacked the sinew's knot   110
Of every tortured limb—that now he lies
As if mere sleep possessed him underneath
These interwoven oaks and pines. Oh cheer,
Divine presenter of the healing rod,
Thy snake, with ardent throat and lulling eye,   115
Twines his lithe spires around! I say, much cheer!
Proceed thou with thy wisest pharmacies!

And ye, white crowd of woodland sister-nymphs,
Ply, as the sage directs, these buds and leaves
That strew the turf around the twain! While I   120
Await, in fitting silence, the event.

WARING

I

1

WHAT'S become of Waring
Since he gave us all the slip,
Chose land-travel or seafaring,
Boots and chest or staff and scrip,
Rather than pace up and down   5
Any longer London town?

II

Who'd have guessed it from his lip
Or his brow's accustomed bearing,
On the night he thus took ship
Or started landward?—little caring   10
For us, it seems, who supped together
(Friends of his too, I remember)
And walked home thro' the merry weather,
The snowiest in all December.
I left his arm that night myself   15
For what's-his-name's, the new prose-poet
Who wrote the book there, on the shelf—
How, forsooth, was I to know it
If Waring meant to glide away
Like a ghost at break of day?   20
Never looked he half so gay!

III

He was prouder than the devil:
How he must have cursed our revel!
Ay and many other meetings,
Indoor visits, outdoor greetings,   25
As up and down he paced this London,
With no work done, but great works undone,
Where scarce twenty knew his name.
Why not, then, have earlier spoken,

Written, bustled? Who's to blame   30
If your silence kept unbroken?
'True, but there were sundry jottings,
'Stray-leaves, fragments, blurrs and blottings,
'Certain first steps were achieved
'Already which'—(is that your meaning?)   35
'Had well borne out whoe'er believed
'In more to come!' But who goes gleaning
Hedgeside chance-blades, while full-sheaved
Stand cornfields by him? Pride, o'erweening
Pride alone, puts forth such claims   40
O'er the day's distinguished names.

IV

Meantime, how much I loved him,
I find out now I've lost him.
I who cared not if I moved him,
Who could so carelessly accost him,   45
Henceforth never shall get free
Of his ghostly company,
His eyes that just a little wink
As deep I go into the merit
Of this and that distinguished spirit—   50
His cheeks' raised colour, soon to sink,
As long I dwell on some stupendous
And tremendous (Heaven defend us!)
Monstr'-inform'-ingens-horrend-ous
Demoniaco-seraphic   55
Penman's latest piece of graphic.
Nay, my very wrist grows warm
With his dragging weight of arm.
E'en so, swimmingly appears,
Through one's after-supper musings,   60
Some lost lady of old years
With her beauteous vain endeavour
And goodness unrepaid as ever;
The face, accustomed to refusings,
We, puppies that we were . . . Oh never   65
Surely, nice of conscience, scrupled
Being aught like false, forsooth, to?

Telling aught but honest truth to?
What a sin, had we centupled
Its possessor's grace and sweetness!   70
No! she heard in its completeness
Truth, for truth's a weighty matter,
And truth, at issue, we can't flatter!
Well, 't is done with; she's exempt
From damning us thro' such a sally;   75
And so she glides, as down a valley,
Taking up with her contempt,
Past our reach; and in, the flowers
Shut her unregarded hours.

V

Oh, could I have him back once more,   80
This Waring, but one half-day more!
Back, with the quiet face of yore,
So hungry for acknowledgment
Like mine! I'd fool him to his bent.
Feed, should not he, to heart's content?   85
I'd say, 'to only have conceived,
'Planned your great works, apart from progress,
'Surpasses little works achieved!'
I'd lie so, I should be believed.
I'd make such havoc of the claims   90
Of the day's distinguished names
To feast him with, as feasts an ogress
Her feverish sharp-toothed gold-crowned child!
Or as one feasts a creature rarely
Captured here, unreconciled   95
To capture; and completely gives
Its pettish humours license, barely
Requiring that it lives.

VI

Ichabod, Ichabod,
The glory is departed!   100
Travels Waring East away?
Who, of knowledge, by hearsay,
Reports a man upstarted

Somewhere as a god,
Hordes grown European-hearted,   105
Millions of the wild made tame
On a sudden at his fame?
In Vishnu-land what Avatar?
Or who in Moscow, toward the Czar,
With the demurest of footfalls   110
Over the Kremlin's pavement bright
With serpentine and syenite,
Steps, with five other Generals
That simultaneously take snuff,
For each to have pretext enough   115
And kerchiefwise unfold his sash
Which, softness' self, is yet the stuff
To hold fast where a steel chain snaps,
And leave the grand white neck no gash?
Waring in Moscow, to those rough   120
Cold northern natures born perhaps,
Like the lambwhite maiden dear
From the circle of mute kings
Unable to repress the tear,
Each as his sceptre down he flings,   125
To Dian's fane at Taurica,
Where now a captive priestess, she alway
Mingles her tender grave Hellenic speech
With theirs, tuned to the hailstone-beaten beach
As pours some pigeon, from the myrrhy lands   130
Rapt by the whirlblast to fierce Scythian strands
Where breed the swallows, her melodious cry
Amid their barbarous twitter!
In Russia? Never! Spain were fitter!
Ay, most likely 't is in Spain   135
That we and Waring meet again
Now, while he turns down that cool narrow lane
Into the blackness, out of grave Madrid
All fire and shine, abrupt as when there's slid
Its stiff gold blazing pall   140
From some black coffin-lid.
Or, best of all,
I love to think

The leaving us was just a feint;
Back here to London did he slink,   145
And now works on without a wink
Of sleep, and we are on the brink
Of something great in fresco-paint:
Some garret's ceiling, walls and floor,
Up and down and o'er and o'er   150
He splashes, as none splashed before
Since great Caldara Polidore.
Or Music means this land of ours
Some favour yet, to pity won
By Purcell from his Rosy Bowers,—   155
'Give me my so-long promised son,
'Let Waring end what I begun!'
Then down he creeps and out he steals
Only when the night conceals
His face; in Kent 't is cherry-time,   160
Or hops are picking: or at prime
Of March he wanders as, too happy,
Years ago when he was young,
Some mild eve when woods grew sappy
And the early moths had sprung   165
To life from many a trembling sheath
Woven the warm boughs beneath;
While small birds said to themselves
What should soon be actual song,
And young gnats, by tens and twelves,   170
Made as if they were the throng
That crowd around and carry aloft
The sound they have nursed, so sweet and pure,
Out of a myriad noises soft,
Into a tone that can endure   175
Amid the noise of a July noon
When all God's creatures crave their boon,
All at once and all in tune,
And get it, happy as Waring then,
Having first within his ken   180
What a man might do with men:
And far too glad, in the even-glow,
To mix with the world he meant to take

Into his hand, he told you, so—
And out of it his world to make,   185
To contract and to expand
As he shut or oped his hand.
Oh Waring, what's to really be?
A clear stage and a crowd to see!
Some Garrick, say, out shall not he   190
The heart of Hamlet's mystery pluck?
Or, where most unclean beasts are rife,
Some Junius—am I right?—shall tuck
His sleeve, and forth with flaying-knife!
Some Chatterton shall have the luck   195
Of calling Rowley into life!
Some one shall somehow run a muck
With this old world for want of strife
Sound asleep. Contrive, contrive
To rouse us, Waring! Who's alive?   200
Our men scarce seem in earnest now.
Distinguished names!—but 't is, somehow,
As if they played at being names
Still more distinguished, like the games
Of children. Turn our sport to earnest   205
With a visage of the sternest!
Bring the real times back, confessed
Still better than our very best!

II

I

'WHEN I last saw Waring . . .'
(How all turned to him who spoke!
You saw Waring? Truth or joke?
In land-travel or sea-faring?)

II

'We were sailing by Triest   5
'Where a day or two we harboured:
'A sunset was in the West,
'When, looking over the vessel's side,
'One of our company espied
'A sudden speck to larboard.   10

'And as a sea-duck flies and swims
'At once, so came the light craft up,
'With its sole lateen sail that trims
'And turns (the water round its rims
'Dancing, as round a sinking cup)   15
'And by us like a fish it curled,
'And drew itself up close beside,
'Its great sail on the instant furled,
'And o'er its thwarts a shrill voice cried,
'(A neck as bronzed as a Lascar's)   20
' "Buy wine of us, you English Brig?
' "Or fruit, tobacco and cigars?
' "A pilot for you to Triest?
' "Without one, look you ne'er so big,
' "They'll never let you up the bay!   25
' "We natives should know best."
'I turned, and "just those fellows' way,"
'Our captain said, "The 'long-shore thieves
' "Are laughing at us in their sleeves."

III

'In truth, the boy leaned laughing back;   30
'And one, half-hidden by his side
'Under the furled sail, soon I spied,
'With great grass hat and kerchief black,
'Who looked up with his kingly throat,
'Said somewhat, while the other shook   35
'His hair back from his eyes to look
'Their longest at us; then the boat,
'I know not how, turned sharply round,
'Laying her whole side on the sea
'As a leaping fish does; from the lee   40
'Into the weather, cut somehow
'Her sparkling path beneath our bow
'And so went off, as with a bound,
'Into the rosy and golden half
'O' the sky, to overtake the sun   45
'And reach the shore, like the sea-calf
'Its singing cave; yet I caught one
'Glance ere away the boat quite passed,

'And neither time nor toil could mar
'Those features: so I saw the last   50
'Of Waring!'—You? Oh, never star
Was lost here but it rose afar!
Look East, where whole new thousands are!
In Vishnu-land what Avatar?

RUDEL TO THE LADY OF TRIPOLI[1]

I

I KNOW a Mount, the gracious Sun perceives
First, when he visits, last, too, when he leaves
The world; and, vainly favoured, it repays
The day-long glory of his steadfast gaze
By no change of its large calm front of snow.   5
And underneath the Mount, a Flower I know,
He cannot have perceived, that changes ever
At his approach; and, in the lost endeavour
To live his life, has parted, one by one,
With all a flower's true graces, for the grace   10
Of being but a foolish mimic sun,
With ray-like florets round a disk-like face.
Men nobly call by many a name the Mount
As over many a land of theirs its large
Calm front of snow like a triumphal targe   15
Is reared, and still with old names, fresh names vie,
Each to its proper praise and own account:
Men call the Flower, the Sunflower, sportively.

II

Oh, Angel of the East, one, one gold look
Across the waters to this twilight nook,   20
—The far sad waters, Angel, to this nook!

III

Dear Pilgrim, art thou for the East indeed?
Go!—saying ever as thou dost proceed,
That I, French Rudel, choose for my device
A sunflower outspread like a sacrifice   25

---

[1] In 1842 this and the following poem were entitled 'Queen Worship. I.—Rudel and the Lady of Tripoli' and 'II.—Cristina'.

Before its idol. See! These inexpert
And hurried fingers could not fail to hurt
The woven picture; 't is a woman's skill
Indeed; but nothing baffled me, so, ill
Or well, the work is finished. Say, men feed   30
On songs I sing, and therefore bask the bees
On my flower's breast as on a platform broad:
But, as the flower's concern is not for these
But solely for the sun, so men applaud
In vain this Rudel, he not looking here   35
But to the East—the East! Go, say this, Pilgrim dear!

CRISTINA

I

SHE should never have looked at me
   If she meant I should not love her!
There are plenty . . . men, you call such,
   I suppose . . . she may discover
All her soul to, if she pleases,   5
   And yet leave much as she found them:
But I'm not so, and she knew it
   When she fixed me, glancing round them.

II

What? To fix me thus meant nothing?
   But I can't tell (there's my weakness)   10
What her look said!—no vile cant, sure,
   About 'need to strew the bleakness
'Of some lone shore with its pearl-seed,
   'That the sea feels'—no 'strange yearning
'That such souls have, most to lavish   15
   'Where there's chance of least returning.'

III

Oh, we're sunk enough here, God knows!
   But not quite so sunk that moments,
Sure tho' seldom, are denied us,
   When the spirit's true endowments   20
Stand out plainly from its false ones,
   And apprise it if pursuing

Or the right way or the wrong way,
  To its triumph or undoing.

IV

There are flashes struck from midnights,   25
  There are fire-flames noondays kindle,
Whereby piled-up honours perish,
  Whereby swollen ambitions dwindle,
While just this or that poor impulse,
  Which for once had play unstifled,   30
Seems the sole work of a life-time
  That away the rest have trifled.

V

Doubt you if, in some such moment,
  As she fixed me, she felt clearly,
Ages past the soul existed,   35
  Here an age 't is resting merely,
And hence fleets again for ages,
  While the true end, sole and single,
It stops here for is, this love-way,
  With some other soul to mingle?   40

VI

Else it loses what it lived for,
  And eternally must lose it;
Better ends may be in prospect,
  Deeper blisses (if you choose it),
But this life's end and this love-bliss   45
  Have been lost here. Doubt you whether
This she felt as, looking at me,
  Mine and her souls rushed together?

VII

Oh, observe! Of course, next moment,
  The world's honours, in derision,   50
Trampled out the light for ever:
  Never fear but there's provision
Of the devil's to quench knowledge
  Lest we walk the earth in rapture!

—Making those who catch God's secret   55
Just so much more prize their capture!

VIII

Such am I: the secret's mine now!
    She has lost me, I have gained her;
Her soul's mine: and thus, grown perfect,
    I shall pass my life's remainder.   60
Life will just hold out the proving
    Both our powers, alone and blended:
And then, come the next life quickly!
    This world's use will have been ended.

JOHANNES AGRICOLA IN MEDITATION[1]

THERE'S heaven above, and night by night
    I look right through its gorgeous roof;
No suns and moons though e'er so bright
    Avail to stop me; splendour-proof
    I keep the broods of stars aloof: 5
For I intend to get to God,
    For 't is to God I speed so fast,
For in God's breast, my own abode,
    Those shoals of dazzling glory, passed,
    I lay my spirit down at last.   10
I lie where I have always lain,
    God smiles as he has always smiled;
Ere suns and moons could wax and wane,
    Ere stars were thundergirt, or piled
    The heavens, God thought on me his child;   15
Ordained a life for me, arrayed
    Its circumstances every one
To the minutest; ay, God said
    This head this hand should rest upon
    Thus, ere he fashioned star or sun.   20

---

[1] First published in the *Monthly Repository*, January 1836. In 1842 this and the
following poem were entitled 'Madhouse Cells. I' and 'II'. In 1849 the title of this
poem became 'I.—Madhouse Cell. Johannes Agricola in Meditation'. In 1863 and
subsequently the two poems were dissociated.

And having thus created me,
   Thus rooted me, he bade me grow,
Guiltless for ever, like a tree
   That buds and blooms, nor seeks to know
   The law by which it prospers so: 25
But sure that thought and word and deed
   All go to swell his love for me,
Me, made because that love had need
   Of something irreversibly
   Pledged solely its content to be.   30
Yes, yes, a tree which must ascend,
   No poison-gourd foredoomed to stoop!
I have God's warrant, could I blend
   All hideous sins, as in a cup,
   To drink the mingled venoms up;   35
Secure my nature will convert
   The draught to blossoming gladness fast:
While sweet dews turn to the gourd's hurt,
   And bloat, and while they bloat it, blast,
   As from the first its lot was cast.   40
For as I lie, smiled on, full-fed
   By unexhausted power to bless,
I gaze below on hell's fierce bed,
   And those its waves of flame oppress,
   Swarming in ghastly wretchedness;   45
Whose life on earth aspired to be
   One altar-smoke, so pure!—to win
If not love like God's love for me,
   At least to keep his anger in;
   And all their striving turned to sin.   50
Priest, doctor, hermit, monk grown white
   With prayer, the broken-hearted nun,
The martyr, the wan acolyte,
   The incense-swinging child,—undone
   Before God fashioned star or sun!   55
God, whom I praise; how could I praise,
   If such as I might understand,
Make out and reckon on his ways,
   And bargain for his love, and stand,
   Paying a price, at his right hand?   60

PORPHYRIA'S LOVER[1]

THE rain set early in to-night,
   The sullen wind was soon awake,
It tore the elm-tops down for spite,
   And did its worst to vex the lake:
   I listened with heart fit to break.   5
When glided in Porphyria; straight
   She shut the cold out and the storm,
And kneeled and made the cheerless grate
   Blaze up, and all the cottage warm;
   Which done, she rose, and from her form   10
Withdrew the dripping cloak and shawl,
   And laid her soiled gloves by, untied
Her hat and let the damp hair fall,
   And, last, she sat down by my side
   And called me. When no voice replied,   15
She put my arm about her waist,
   And made her smooth white shoulder bare,
And all her yellow hair displaced,
   And, stooping, made my cheek lie there,
   And spread, o'er all, her yellow hair,   20
Murmuring how she loved me—she
   Too weak, for all her heart's endeavour,
To set its struggling passion free
   From pride, and vainer ties dissever,
   And give herself to me for ever.   25
But passion sometimes would prevail,
   Nor could to-night's gay feast restrain
A sudden thought of one so pale
   For love of her, and all in vain:
   So, she was come through wind and rain.   30
Be sure I looked up at her eyes
   Happy and proud; at last I knew
Porphyria worshipped me; surprise
   Made my heart swell, and still it grew
   While I debated what to do.   35

[1] First printed in the *Monthly Repository*, January 1836. In 1842 this and the preceding poem were entitled 'Madhouse Cells. I' and 'II'. In 1849 the title of this poem became 'II.—Madhouse Cell. Porphyria's Lover'. In 1863 and subsequently the two poems were dissociated.

That moment she was mine, mine, fair,
  Perfectly pure and good: I found
A thing to do, and all her hair
  In one long yellow string I wound
  Three times her little throat around,   40
And strangled her. No pain felt she;
  I am quite sure she felt no pain.
As a shut bud that holds a bee,
  I warily oped her lids: again
  Laughed the blue eyes without a stain.   45
And I untightened next the tress
  About her neck; her cheek once more
Blushed bright beneath my burning kiss:
  I propped her head up as before,
  Only, this time my shoulder bore   50
Her head, which droops upon it still:
  The smiling rosy little head,
So glad it has its utmost will,
  That all it scorned at once is fled,
  And I, its love, am gained instead!   55
Porphyria's love: she guessed not how
  Her darling one wish would be heard.
And thus we sit together now,
  And all night long we have not stirred,
  And yet God has not said a word!   60

THROUGH THE METIDJA TO
ABD-EL-KADR

I

As I ride, as I ride,
With a full heart for my guide,
So its tide rocks my side,
As I ride, as I ride,
That, as I were double-eyed,   5
He, in whom our Tribes confide,
Is descried, ways untried
As I ride, as I ride.

II

As I ride, as I ride
To our Chief and his Allied,   10
Who dares chide my heart's pride
As I ride, as I ride?
Or are witnesses denied—
Through the desert waste and wide
Do I glide unespied   15
As I ride, as I ride?

III

As I ride, as I ride,
When an inner voice has cried,
The sands slide, nor abide
(As I ride, as I ride)   20
O'er each visioned homicide
That came vaunting (has he lied?)
To reside—where he died,
As I ride, as I ride.

IV

As I ride, as I ride,   25
Ne'er has spur my swift horse plied,
Yet his hide, streaked and pied,
As I ride, as I ride,
Shows where sweat has sprung and dried,
—Zebra-footed, ostrich-thighed—   30
How has vied stride with stride
As I ride, as I ride!

V

As I ride, as I ride,
Could I loose what Fate has tied,
Ere I pried, she should hide   35
(As I ride, as I ride)
All that's meant me—satisfied
When the Prophet and the Bride
Stop veins I'd have subside
As I ride, as I ride!   40

THE PIED PIPER OF HAMELIN;

A CHILD'S STORY

(WRITTEN FOR, AND INSCRIBED TO, W. M. THE YOUNGER)

I

HAMELIN Town's in Brunswick,
   By famous Hanover city;
The river Weser, deep and wide,
Washes its wall on the southern side;
A pleasanter spot you never spied;   5
   But, when begins my ditty,
Almost five hundred years ago,
To see the townsfolk suffer so
   From vermin, was a pity.

II

Rats!   10
They fought the dogs and killed the cats,
   And bit the babies in the cradles,
And ate the cheeses out of the vats,
   And licked the soup from the cooks' own ladles,
Split open the kegs of salted sprats,   15
Made nests inside men's Sunday hats,
And even spoiled the women's chats
      By drowning their speaking
      With shrieking and squeaking
In fifty different sharps and flats.   20

III

At last the people in a body
   To the Town Hall came flocking:
' 'T is clear,' cried they, 'our Mayor's a noddy;
   'And as for our Corporation—shocking
'To think we buy gowns lined with ermine   25
'For dolts that can't or won't determine
'What's best to rid us of our vermin!
'You hope, because you're old and obese,
'To find in the furry civic robe ease?
'Rouse up, sirs! Give your brains a racking   30

'To find the remedy we're lacking,
'Or, sure as fate, we'll send you packing!'
At this the Mayor and Corporation
Quaked with a mighty consternation.

IV

An hour they sat in council,   35
    At length the Mayor broke silence:
'For a guilder I'd my ermine gown sell,
    'I wish I were a mile hence!
'It's easy to bid one rack one's brain—
'I'm sure my poor head aches again,   40
'I've scratched it so, and all in vain.
'Oh for a trap, a trap, a trap!'
Just as he said this, what should hap
At the chamber door but a gentle tap?
'Bless us,' cried the Mayor, 'what's that?'   45
(With the Corporation as he sat,
Looking little though wondrous fat;
Nor brighter was his eye, nor moister
Than a too-long-opened oyster,
Save when at noon his paunch grew mutinous   50
For a plate of turtle green and glutinous)
'Only a scraping of shoes on the mat?
'Anything like the sound of a rat
'Makes my heart go pit-a-pat!'

V

'Come in!'—the Mayor cried, looking bigger: 55
And in did come the strangest figure!
His queer long coat from heel to head
Was half of yellow and half of red,
And he himself was tall and thin,
With sharp blue eyes, each like a pin,   60
And light loose hair, yet swarthy skin,
No tuft on cheek nor beard on chin,
But lips where smiles went out and in;
There was no guessing his kith and kin:
And nobody could enough admire   65
The tall man and his quaint attire.

Quoth one: 'It's as my great-grandsire,
'Starting up at the Trump of Doom's tone,
'Had walked this way from his painted tomb-stone!'

VI

He advanced to the council-table: 70
And, 'Please your honours,' said he, 'I'm able,
'By means of a secret charm, to draw
    'All creatures living beneath the sun,
    'That creep or swim or fly or run,
'After me so as you never saw!   75
'And I chiefly use my charm
'On creatures that do people harm,
'The mole and toad and newt and viper;
'And people call me the Pied Piper.'
(And here they noticed round his neck   80
    A scarf of red and yellow stripe,
To match with his coat of the self-same cheque;
    And at the scarf's end hung a pipe;
And his fingers, they noticed, were ever straying
As if impatient to be playing   85
Upon this pipe, as low it dangled
Over his vesture so old-fangled.)
'Yet,' said he, 'poor piper as I am,
'In Tartary I freed the Cham,
    'Last June, from his huge swarms of gnats;   90
'I eased in Asia the Nizam
    'Of a monstrous brood of vampyre-bats:
'And as for what your brain bewilders,
    'If I can rid your town of rats
'Will you give me a thousand guilders?'   95
'One? fifty thousand!'—was the exclamation
Of the astonished Mayor and Corporation.

VII

Into the street the Piper stept,
    Smiling first a little smile,
As if he knew what magic slept   100
    In his quiet pipe the while;

Then, like a musical adept,
To blow the pipe his lips he wrinkled,
And green and blue his sharp eyes twinkled,
Like a candle-flame where salt is sprinkled;   105
And ere three shrill notes the pipe uttered,
You heard as if an army muttered;
And the muttering grew to a grumbling;
And the grumbling grew to a mighty rumbling;
And out of the houses the rats came tumbling.   110
Great rats, small rats, lean rats, brawny rats,
Brown rats, black rats, grey rats, tawny rats,
Grave old plodders, gay young friskers,
    Fathers, mothers, uncles, cousins,
Cocking tails and pricking whiskers,   115
    Families by tens and dozens,
Brothers, sisters, husbands, wives—
Followed the Piper for their lives.
From street to street he piped advancing,
And step for step they followed dancing,   120
Until they came to the river Weser,
    Wherein all plunged and perished!
—Save one who, stout as Julius Cæsar,
Swam across and lived to carry
    (As he, the manuscript he cherished)   125
To Rat-land home his commentary:
Which was, 'At the first shrill notes of the pipe,
'I heard a sound as of scraping tripe,
'And putting apples, wondrous ripe,
'Into a cider-press's gripe: 130
'And a moving away of pickle-tub-boards,
'And a leaving ajar of conserve-cupboards,
'And a drawing the corks of train-oil-flasks,
'And a breaking the hoops of butter-casks:
'And it seemed as if a voice   135
    '(Sweeter far than bý harp or bý psaltery
'Is breathed) called out, "Oh rats, rejoice!
    ' "The world is grown to one vast drysaltery!
' "So munch on, crunch on, take your nuncheon,
' "Breakfast, supper, dinner, luncheon!"   140
'And just as a bulky sugar-puncheon,

'All ready staved, like a great sun shone
'Glorious scarce an inch before me,
'Just as methought it said, "Come, bore me!"
'—I found the Weser rolling o'er me.'   145

VIII

You should have heard the Hamelin people
Ringing the bells till they rocked the steeple.
'Go,' cried the Mayor, 'and get long poles,
'Poke out the nests and block up the holes!
'Consult with carpenters and builders,   150
'And leave in our town not even a trace
'Of the rats!'—when suddenly, up the face
Of the Piper perked in the market-place,
With a, 'First, if you please, my thousand guilders!'

IX

A thousand guilders! The Mayor looked blue;   155
So did the Corporation too.
For council dinners made rare havoc
With Claret, Moselle, Vin-de-Grave, Hock;
And half the money would replenish
Their cellar's biggest butt with Rhenish.   160
To pay this sum to a wandering fellow
With a gipsy coat of red and yellow!
'Beside,' quoth the Mayor with a knowing wink,
'Our business was done at the river's brink;
'We saw with our eyes the vermin sink,   165
'And what's dead can't come to life, I think.
'So, friend, we're not the folks to shrink
'From the duty of giving you something for drink,
'And a matter of money to put in your poke;
'But as for the guilders, what we spoke   170
'Of them, as you very well know, was in joke.
'Beside, our losses have made us thrifty.
'A thousand guilders! Come, take fifty!'

X

The Piper's face fell, and he cried
'No trifling! I can't wait, beside!   175

'I've promised to visit by dinnertime
'Bagdat, and accept the prime
'Of the Head-Cook's pottage, all he's rich in,
'For having left, in the Caliph's kitchen,
'Of a nest of scorpions no survivor: 180
'With him I proved no bargain-driver,
'With you, don't think I'll bate a stiver!
'And folks who put me in a passion
'May find me pipe after another fashion.'

XI

'How?' cried the Mayor, 'd'ye think I brook   185
'Being worse treated than a Cook?
'Insulted by a lazy ribald
'With idle pipe and vesture piebald?
'You threaten us, fellow? Do your worst,
'Blow your pipe there till you burst!'   190

XII

Once more he stept into the street
     And to his lips again
     Laid his long pipe of smooth straight cane;
And ere he blew three notes (such sweet
Soft notes as yet musician's cunning   195
     Never gave the enraptured air)
There was a rustling that seemed like a bustling
Of merry crowds justling at pitching and hustling,
Small feet were pattering, wooden shoes clattering,
Little hands clapping and little tongues chattering,
And, like fowls in a farm-yard when barley is scattering,
Out came the children running.
All the little boys and girls,
With rosy cheeks and flaxen curls,
And sparkling eyes and teeth like pearls,   205
Tripping and skipping, ran merrily after
The wonderful music with shouting and laughter.

XIII

The Mayor was dumb, and the Council stood
As if they were changed into blocks of wood,

Unable to move a step, or cry   210
To the children merrily skipping by,
—Could only follow with the eye
That joyous crowd at the Piper's back.
But how the Mayor was on the rack,
And the wretched Council's bosoms beat,   215
As the Piper turned from the High Street
To where the Weser rolled its waters
Right in the way of their sons and daughters!
However he turned from South to West,
And to Koppelberg Hill his steps addressed,   220
And after him the children pressed;
Great was the joy in every breast.
'He never can cross that mighty top!
'He's forced to let the piping drop,
'And we shall see our children stop!'   225
When, lo, as they reached the mountain-side,
A wondrous portal opened wide,
As if a cavern was suddenly hollowed;
And the Piper advanced and the children followed,
And when all were in to the very last,   230
The door in the mountain-side shut fast.
Did I say, all? No! One was lame,
    And could not dance the whole of the way;
And in after years, if you would blame
    His sadness, he was used to say,—   235
'It's dull in our town since my playmates left!
'I can't forget that I'm bereft
'Of all the pleasant sights they see,
'Which the Piper also promised me.
'For he led us, he said, to a joyous land,   240
'Joining the town and just at hand,
'Where waters gushed and fruit-trees grew
'And flowers put forth a fairer hue,
'And everything was strange and new;
'The sparrows were brighter than peacocks here, 245
'And their dogs outran our fallow deer,
'And honey-bees had lost their stings,
'And horses were born with eagles' wings:
'And just as I became assured

'My lame foot would be speedily cured,   250
'The music stopped and I stood still,
'And found myself outside the hill.
'Left alone against my will,
'To go now limping as before,
'And never hear of that country more!'   255

XIV

Alas, alas for Hamelin!
    There came into many a burgher's pate
    A text which says that heaven's gate
    Opes to the rich at as easy rate
As the needle's eye takes a camel in!   260
The mayor sent East, West, North and South,
To offer the Piper, by word of mouth,
    Wherever it was men's lot to find him,
Silver and gold to his heart's content,
If he'd only return the way he went,   265
    And bring the children behind him.
But when they saw 't was a lost endeavour,
And Piper and dancers were gone for ever,
They made a decree that lawyers never
    Should think their records dated duly   270
If, after the day of the month and year,
These words did not as well appear,
'And so long after what happened here
    'On the Twenty-second of July,
'Thirteen hundred and seventy-six:'   275
And the better in memory to fix
The place of the children's last retreat,
They called it, the Pied Piper's Street—
Where any one playing on pipe or tabor
Was sure for the future to lose his labour.   280
Nor suffered they hostelry or tavern
    To shock with mirth a street so solemn;
But opposite the place of the cavern
    They wrote the story on a column,
And on the great church-window painted   285
The same, to make the world acquainted
How their children were stolen away,

And there it stands to this very day.
And I must not omit to say
That in Transylvania there's a tribe   290
Of alien people who ascribe
The outlandish ways and dress
On which their neighbours lay such stress,
To their fathers and mothers having risen
Out of some subterraneous prison   295
Into which they were trepanned
Long time ago in a mighty band
Out of Hamelin town in Brunswick land,
But how or why, they don't understand.

XV

So, Willy, let me and you be wipers   300
Of scores out with all men—especially pipers!
And, whether they pipe us free fróm rats or fróm mice,
If we've promised them aught, let us keep our promise!

DRAMATIC ROMANCES
AND LYRICS[1]

---

[1] The pamphlet containing the *Dramatic Romances and Lyrics* bore the following dedication: 'Inscribed to John Kenyon, Esq., in the hope that a recollection of his own successful "Rhymed Plea for Tolerance" may induce him to admit good-naturedly this humbler prose one of his very sincere friend, R. B.   *Nov.* 1845.'

DRAMATIC ROMANCES
AND LYRICS

First published as Bells and Pomegranates, No. VII, *in 1845. Although Browning's final text is given here, the arrangement of the poems remains that of 1845. For Browning's later arrangement and classification see Appendix D below.*]

'HOW THEY BROUGHT THE GOOD NEWS
FROM GHENT TO AIX'

(16—)

I

I SPRANG to the stirrup, and Joris, and he;
I galloped, Dirck galloped, we galloped all three;
'Good speed!' cried the watch, as the gate-bolts undrew;
'Speed!' echoed the wall to us galloping through;
Behind shut the postern, the lights sank to rest,   5
And into the midnight we galloped abreast.

II

Not a word to each other; we kept the great pace
Neck by neck, stride by stride, never changing our place;
I turned in my saddle and made its girths tight,
Then shortened each stirrup, and set the pique right,   10
Rebuckled the cheek-strap, chained slacker the bit,
Nor galloped less steadily Roland a whit.

III

'T was moonset at starting; but while we drew near
Lokeren, the cocks crew and twilight dawned clear;
At Boom, a great yellow star came out to see;   15
At Düffeld, 't was morning as plain as could be;
And from Mecheln church-steeple we heard the half-chime,
So, Joris broke silence with, 'Yet there is time!'

IV

At Aershot, up leaped of a sudden the sun,
And against him the cattle stood black every one,   20

To stare thro' the mist at us galloping past,
And I saw my stout galloper Roland at last,
With resolute shoulders, each butting away
The haze, as some bluff river headland its spray:

V

And his low head and crest, just one sharp ear bent back   25
For my voice, and the other pricked out on his track;
And one eye's black intelligence,—ever that glance
O'er its white edge at me, his own master, askance!
And the thick heavy spume-flakes which aye and anon
His fierce lips shook upwards in galloping on.   30

VI

By Hasselt, Dirck groaned; and cried Joris, 'Stay spur!
'Your Roos galloped bravely, the fault's not in her,
'We'll remember at Aix'—for one heard the quick wheeze
Of her chest, saw the stretched neck and staggering knees,
And sunk tail, and horrible heave of the flank,   35
As down on her haunches she shuddered and sank.

VII

So, we were left galloping, Joris and I,
Past Looz and past Tongres, no cloud in the sky;
The broad sun above laughed a pitiless laugh,
'Neath our feet broke the brittle bright stubble like chaff;   40
Till over by Dalhem a dome-spire sprang white,
And 'Gallop,' gasped Joris, 'for Aix is in sight!'

VIII

'How they'll greet us!'—and all in a moment his roan
Rolled neck and croup over, lay dead as a stone;
And there was my Roland to bear the whole weight   45
Of the news which alone could save Aix from her fate,
With his nostrils like pits full of blood to the brim,
And with circles of red for his eye-sockets' rim.

IX

Then I cast loose my buffcoat, each holster let fall,
Shook off both my jack-boots, let go belt and all,   50

Stood up in the stirrup, leaned, patted his ear,
Called my Roland his pet-name, my horse without peer;
Clapped my hands, laughed and sang, any noise, bad or good,
Till at length into Aix Roland galloped and stood.

X

And all I remember is—friends flocking round   55
As I sat with his head 'twixt my knees on the ground;
And no voice but was praising this Roland of mine,
As I poured down his throat our last measure of wine,
Which (the burgesses voted by common consent)
Was no more than his due who brought good news from
        Ghent.   60

PICTOR IGNOTUS

FLORENCE, 15—

I COULD have painted pictures like that youth's
    Ye praise so. How my soul springs up! No bar
Stayed me—ah, thought which saddens while it soothes!
    —Never did fate forbid me, star by star,
To outburst on your night with all my gift   5
    Of fires from God: nor would my flesh have shrunk
From seconding my soul, with eyes uplift
    And wide to heaven, or, straight like thunder, sunk
To the centre, of an instant; or around
    Turned calmly and inquisitive, to scan   10
The licence and the limit, space and bound,
    Allowed to truth made visible in man.
And, like that youth ye praise so, all I saw,
    Over the canvas could my hand have flung,
Each face obedient to its passion's law,   15
    Each passion clear proclaimed without a tongue;
Whether Hope rose at once in all the blood,
    A-tiptoe for the blessing of embrace,
Or Rapture drooped the eyes, as when her brood
    Pull down the nesting dove's heart to its place;   20
Or Confidence lit swift the forehead up,
    And locked the mouth fast, like a castle braved,—

O human faces, hath it spilt, my cup?
  What did ye give me that I have not saved?
Nor will I say I have not dreamed (how well!)   25
  Of going—I, in each new picture,—forth,
As, making new hearts beat and bosoms swell,
  To Pope or Kaiser, East, West, South, or North,
Bound for the calmly-satisfied great State,
  Or glad aspiring little burgh, it went,   30
Flowers cast upon the car which bore the freight,
  Through old streets named afresh from the event,
Till it reached home, where learned age should greet
  My face, and youth, the star not yet distinct
Above his hair, lie learning at my feet!—   35
  Oh, thus to live, I and my picture, linked
With love about, and praise, till life should end,
  And then not go to heaven, but linger here,
Here on my earth, earth's every man my friend,—
  The thought grew frightful, 't was so wildly dear!   40
But a voice changed it. Glimpses of such sights
  Have scared me, like the revels through a door
Of some strange house of idols at its rites!
  This world seemed not the world it was before:
Mixed with my loving trusting ones, there trooped   45
  . . . Who summoned those cold faces that begun
To press on me and judge me? Though I stooped
  Shrinking, as from the soldiery a nun,
They drew me forth, and spite of me . . . enough!
  These buy and sell our pictures, take and give,   50
Count them for garniture and household-stuff,
  And where they live needs must our pictures live
And see their faces, listen to their prate,
  Partakers of their daily pettiness,
Discussed of,—'This I love, or this I hate,   55
  'This likes me more, and this affects me less!'
Wherefore I chose my portion. If at whiles
  My heart sinks, as monotonous I paint
These endless cloisters and eternal aisles
  With the same series, Virgin, Babe and Saint,   60
With the same cold calm beautiful regard,—
  At least no merchant traffics in my heart;

The sanctuary's gloom at least shall ward
  Vain tongues from where my pictures stand apart:
Only prayer breaks the silence of the shrine   65
  While, blackening in the daily candle-smoke,
They moulder on the damp wall's travertine,
  'Mid echoes the light footstep never woke.
So, die my pictures! surely, gently die!
  O youth, men praise so,—holds their praise its worth?   70
Blown harshly, keeps the trump its golden cry?
  Tastes sweet the water with such specks of earth?

THE ITALIAN IN ENGLAND[1]

THAT second time they hunted me
From hill to plain, from shore to sea,
And Austria, hounding far and wide
Her blood-hounds thro' the country-side,
Breathed hot and instant on my trace,—   5
I made six days a hiding-place
Of that dry green old aqueduct
Where I and Charles, when boys, have plucked
The fire-flies from the roof above,
Bright creeping thro' the moss they love: 10
—How long it seems since Charles was lost!
Six days the soldiers crossed and crossed
The country in my very sight;
And when that peril ceased at night,
The sky broke out in red dismay   15
With signal fires; well, there I lay
Close covered o'er in my recess,
Up to the neck in ferns and cress,
Thinking on Metternich our friend,
And Charles's miserable end,   20
And much beside, two days; the third,
Hunger o'ercame me when I heard
The peasants from the village go
To work among the maize; you know,
With us in Lombardy, they bring   25

---

[1] In 1845 the title was 'Italy in England'.

P

Provisions packed on mules, a string
With little bells that cheer their task,
And casks, and boughs on every cask
To keep the sun's heat from the wine;
These I let pass in jingling line,   30
And, close on them, dear noisy crew,
The peasants from the village, too;
For at the very rear would troop
Their wives and sisters in a group
To help, I knew. When these had passed,   35
I threw my glove to strike the last,
Taking the chance: she did not start,
Much less cry out, but stooped apart,
One instant rapidly glanced round,
And saw me beckon from the ground.   40
A wild bush grows and hides my crypt;
She picked my glove up while she stripped
A branch off, then rejoined the rest
With that; my glove lay in her breast.
Then I drew breath; they disappeared: 45
It was for Italy I feared.

   An hour, and she returned alone
Exactly where my glove was thrown.
Meanwhile came many thoughts: on me
Rested the hopes of Italy.   50
I had devised a certain tale
Which, when 't was told her, could not fail
Persuade a peasant of its truth;
I meant to call a freak of youth
This hiding, and give hopes of pay,   55
And no temptation to betray.
But when I saw that woman's face,
Its calm simplicity of grace,
Our Italy's own attitude
In which she walked thus far, and stood,   60
Planting each naked foot so firm,
To crush the snake and spare the worm—
At first sight of her eyes, I said,
'I am that man upon whose head

'They fix the price, because I hate   65
'The Austrians over us: the State
'Will give you gold—oh, gold so much!—
'If you betray me to their clutch,
'And be your death, for aught I know,
'If once they find you saved their foe.   70
'Now, you must bring me food and drink,
'And also paper, pen and ink,
'And carry safe what I shall write
'To Padua, which you'll reach at night
'Before the duomo shuts; go in,   75
'And wait till Tenebræ begin;
'Walk to the third confessional,
'Between the pillar and the wall,
'And kneeling whisper, *Whence comes peace?*
'Say it a second time, then cease;   80
'And if the voice inside returns,
'*From Christ and Freedom; what concerns*
'*The cause of Peace?*—for answer, slip
'My letter where you placed your lip;
'Then come back happy we have done   85
'Our mother service—I, the son,
'As you the daughter of our land!'

   Three mornings more, she took her stand
In the same place, with the same eyes:
I was no surer of sun-rise   90
Than of her coming. We conferred
Of her own prospects, and I heard
She had a lover—stout and tall,
She said—then let her eyelids fall,
'He could do much'—as if some doubt   95
Entered her heart,—then, passing out,
'She could not speak for others, who
'Had other thoughts; herself she knew:'
And so she brought me drink and food.
After four days, the scouts pursued   100
Another path; at last arrived
The help my Paduan friends contrived
To furnish me: she brought the news.

For the first time I could not choose
But kiss her hand, and lay my own   105
Upon her head—'This faith was shown
'To Italy, our mother; she
'Uses my hand and blesses thee.'
She followed down to the sea-shore;
I left and never saw her more.   110

How very long since I have thought
Concerning—much less wished for—aught
Beside the good of Italy,
For which I live and mean to die!
I never was in love; and since   115
Charles proved false, what shall now convince
My inmost heart I have a friend?
However, if I pleased to spend
Real wishes on myself—say, three—
I know at least what one should be.   120
I would grasp Metternich until
I felt his red wet throat distil
In blood thro' these two hands. And next,
—Nor much for that am I perplexed—
Charles, perjured traitor, for his part,   125
Should die slow of a broken heart
Under his new employers. Last
—Ah, there, what should I wish? For fast
Do I grow old and out of strength.
If I resolved to seek at length   130
My father's house again, how scared
They all would look, and unprepared!
My brothers live in Austria's pay
—Disowned me long ago, men say;
And all my early mates who used   135
To praise me so—perhaps induced
More than one early step of mine—
Are turning wise: while some opine
'Freedom grows license,' some suspect
'Haste breeds delay,' and recollect   140
They always said, such premature
Beginnings never could endure!

So, with a sullen 'All 's for best,'
The land seems settling to its rest.
I think then, I should wish to stand   145
This evening in that dear, lost land,
Over the sea the thousand miles,
And know if yet that woman smiles
With the calm smile; some little farm
She lives in there, no doubt: what harm   150
If I sat on the door-side bench,
And, while her spindle made a trench
Fantastically in the dust,
Inquired of all her fortunes—just
Her children's ages and their names,   155
And what may be the husband's aims
For each of them. I'd talk this out,
And sit there, for an hour about,
Then kiss her hand once more, and lay
Mine on her head, and go my way.   160

    So much for idle wishing—how
It steals the time! To business now.

THE ENGLISHMAN IN ITALY[1]

PIANO DI SORRENTO

FORTÙ, Fortù, my beloved one,
    Sit here by my side,
On my knees put up both little feet!
    I was sure, if I tried,
I could make you laugh spite of Scirocco.   5
    Now, open your eyes,
Let me keep you amused till he vanish
    In black from the skies,
With telling my memories over
    As you tell your beads;   10
All the Plain saw me gather, I garland
    —The flowers or the weeds.

    [1] In 1845 the title was 'England in Italy'.

Time for rain! for your long hot dry Autumn
    Had net-worked with brown
The white skin of each grape on the bunches,   15
    Marked like a quail's crown,
Those creatures you make such account of,
    Whose heads,—speckled white
Over brown like a great spider's back,
    As I told you last night,—   20
Your mother bites off for her supper.
    Red-ripe as could be,
Pomegranates were chapping and splitting
    In halves on the tree:
And betwixt the loose walls of great flintstone,   25
    Or in the thick dust
On the path, or straight out of the rock-side,
    Wherever could thrust
Some burnt sprig of bold hardy rock-flower
    Its yellow face up,   30
For the prize were great butterflies fighting,
    Some five for one cup.
So, I guessed, ere I got up this morning,
    What change was in store,
By the quick rustle-down of the quail-nets   35
    Which woke me before
I could open my shutter, made fast
    With a bough and a stone,
And look thro' the twisted dead vine-twigs,
    Sole lattice that's known.   40
Quick and sharp rang the rings down the net-poles,
    While, busy beneath,
Your priest and his brother tugged at them,
    The rain in their teeth.
And out upon all the flat house-roofs   45
    Where split figs lay drying,
The girls took the frails under cover:
    Nor use seemed in trying
To get out the boats and go fishing,
    For, under the cliff,   50
Fierce the black water frothed o'er the blind-rock.
    No seeing our skiff

Arrive about noon from Amalfi,
 —Our fisher arrive,
And pitch down his basket before us,   55
 All trembling alive
With pink and grey jellies, your sea-fruit;
 You touch the strange lumps,
And mouths gape there, eyes open, all manner
 Of horns and of humps,   60
Which only the fisher looks grave at,
 While round him like imps
Cling screaming the children as naked
 And brown as his shrimps;
Himself too as bare to the middle   65
 —You see round his neck
The string and its brass coin suspended,
 That saves him from wreck.
But to-day not a boat reached Salerno,
 So back, to a man,   70
Came our friends, with whose help in the vineyards
 Grape-harvest began.
In the vat, halfway up in our house-side,
 Like blood the juice spins,
While your brother all bare-legged is dancing   75
 Till breathless he grins
Dead-beaten in effort on effort
 To keep the grapes under,
Since still when he seems all but master,
 In pours the fresh plunder   80
From girls who keep coming and going
 With basket on shoulder,
And eyes shut against the rain's driving,
 Your girls that are older,—
For under the hedges of aloe,   85
 And where, on its bed
Of the orchard's black mould, the love-apple
 Lies pulpy and red,
All the young ones are kneeling and filling
 Their laps with the snails   90
Tempted out by this first rainy weather,—
 Your best of regales,

As to-night will be proved to my sorrow,
　　When, supping in state,
We shall feast our grape-gleaners (two dozen,　　95
　　Three over one plate)
With lasagne so tempting to swallow
　　In slippery ropes,
And gourds fried in great purple slices,
　　That colour of popes.　　100
Meantime, see the grape bunch they've brought you:
　　The rain-water slips
O'er the heavy blue bloom on each globe
　　Which the wasp to your lips
Still follows with fretful persistence:　　105
　　Nay, taste, while awake,
This half of a curd-white smooth cheese-ball
　　That peels, flake by flake,
Like an onion, each smoother and whiter;
　　Next, sip this weak wine　　110
From the thin green glass flask, with its stopper,
　　A leaf of the vine;
And end with the prickly-pear's red flesh
　　That leaves thro' its juice
The stony black seeds on your pearl-teeth.　　115
　　Scirocco is loose!
Hark, the quick, whistling pelt of the olives
　　Which, thick in one's track,
Tempt the stranger to pick up and bite them,
　　Tho' not yet half black!　　120
How the old twisted olive trunks shudder,
　　The medlars let fall
Their hard fruit, and the brittle great fig-trees
　　Snap off, figs and all,
For here comes the whole of the tempest!　　125
　　No refuge, but creep
Back again to my side and my shoulder,
　　And listen or sleep.

O how will your country show next week,
　　When all the vine-boughs　　130

Have been stripped of their foliage to pasture
    The mules and the cows?
Last eve, I rode over the mountains;
    Your brother, my guide,
Soon left me, to feast on the myrtles 135
    That offered, each side,
Their fruit-balls, black, glossy and luscious,—
    Or strip from the sorbs
A treasure, or, rosy and wondrous,
    Those hairy gold orbs! 140
But my mule picked his sure sober path out,
    Just stopping to neigh
When he recognized down in the valley
    His mates on their way
With the faggots and barrels of water; 145
    And soon we emerged
From the plain, where the woods could scarce follow;
    And still as we urged
Our way, the woods wondered, and left us,
    As up still we trudged 150
Though the wild path grew wilder each instant,
    And place was e'en grudged
'Mid the rock-chasms and piles of loose stones
    Like the loose broken teeth
Of some monster which climbed there to die 155
    From the ocean beneath—
Place was grudged to the silver-grey fume-weed
    That clung to the path,
And dark rosemary ever a-dying
    That, 'spite the wind's wrath, 160
So loves the salt rock's face to seaward,
    And lentisks as staunch
To the stone where they root and bear berries,
    And . . . what shows a branch
Coral-coloured, transparent, with circlets 165
    Of pale seagreen leaves;
Over all trod my mule with the caution
    Of gleaners o'er sheaves,
Still, foot after foot like a lady,
    Till, round after round, 170

He climbed to the top of Calvano,
    And God's own profound
Was above me, and round me the mountains,
    And under, the sea,
And within me my heart to bear witness   175
    What was and shall be.
Oh, heaven and the terrible crystal!
    No rampart excludes
Your eye from the life to be lived
    In the blue solitudes.   180
Oh, those mountains, their infinite movement!
    Still moving with you;
For, ever some new head and breast of them
    Thrusts into view
To observe the intruder; you see it   185
    If quickly you turn
And, before they escape you surprise them.
    They grudge you should learn
How the soft plains they look on, lean over
    And love (they pretend)   190
—Cower beneath them, the flat sea-pine crouches,
    The wild fruit-trees bend,
E'en the myrtle-leaves curl, shrink and shut:
    All is silent and grave:
'T is a sensual and timorous beauty,   195
    How fair! but a slave.
So, I turned to the sea; and there slumbered
    As greenly as ever
Those isles of the siren, your Galli;
    No ages can sever   200
The Three, nor enable their sister
    To join them,—halfway
On the voyage, she looked at Ulysses—
    No farther to-day,
Tho' the small one, just launched in the wave,   205
    Watches breast-high and steady
From under the rock, her bold sister
    Swum halfway already.
Fortù, shall we sail there together
    And see from the sides   210

Quite new rocks show their faces, new haunts
    Where the siren abides?
Shall we sail round and round them, close over
    The rocks, tho' unseen,
That ruffle the grey glassy water   215
    To glorious green?
Then scramble from splinter to splinter,
    Reach land and explore,
On the largest, the strange square black turret
    With never a door,   220
Just a loop to admit the quick lizards;
    Then, stand there and hear
The birds' quiet singing, that tells us
    What life is, so clear?
—The secret they sang to Ulysses   225
    When, ages ago,
He heard and he knew this life's secret
    I hear and I know.

Ah, see! The sun breaks o'er Calvano;
    He strikes the great gloom   230
And flutters it o'er the mount's summit
    In airy gold fume.
All is over. Look out, see the gipsy,
    Our tinker and smith,
Has arrived, set up bellows and forge,   235
    And down-squatted forthwith
To his hammering, under the wall there;
    One eye keeps aloof
The urchins that itch to be putting
    His jews'-harps to proof,   240
While the other, thro' locks of curled wire,
    Is watching how sleek
Shines the hog, come to share in the windfall
    —Chew, abbot's own cheek!
All is over. Wake up and come out now,   245
    And down let us go,
And see the fine things got in order
    At church for the show

Of the Sacrament, set forth this evening.
    To-morrow's the Feast   250
Of the Rosary's Virgin, by no means
    Of Virgins the least,
As you'll hear in the off-hand discourse
    Which (all nature, no art)
The Dominican brother, these three weeks,   255
    Was getting by heart.
Not a pillar nor post but is dizened
    With red and blue papers;
All the roof waves with ribbons, each altar
    A-blaze with long tapers;   260
But the great masterpiece is the scaffold
    Rigged glorious to hold
All the fiddlers and fifers and drummers
    And trumpeters bold,
Not afraid of Bellini nor Auber,   265
    Who, when the priest's hoarse,
Will strike us up something that's brisk
    For the feast's second course.
And then will the flaxen-wigged Image
    Be carried in pomp   270
Thro' the plain, while in gallant procession
    The priests mean to stomp.
All round the glad church lie old bottles
    With gunpowder stopped,
Which will be, when the Image re-enters,   275
    Religiously popped;
And at night from the crest of Calvano
    Great bonfires will hang,
On the plain will the trumpets join chorus,
    And more poppers bang.   280
At all events, come—to the garden
    As far as the wall;
See me tap with a hoe on the plaster
    Till out there shall fall
A scorpion with wide angry nippers!   285

    —'Such trifles!' you say?
Fortù, in my England at home,

    Men meet gravely to-day
And debate, if abolishing Corn-laws
    Be righteous and wise   290
—If 't were proper, Scirocco should vanish
    In black from the skies!

THE LOST LEADER

I

JUST for a handful of silver he left us,
    Just for a riband to stick in his coat—
Found the one gift of which fortune bereft us,
    Lost all the others she lets us devote;
They, with the gold to give, doled him out silver,   5
    So much was theirs who so little allowed:
How all our copper had gone for his service!
    Rags—were they purple, his heart had been proud!
We that had loved him so, followed him, honoured him,
    Lived in his mild and magnificent eye,   10
Learned his great language, caught his clear accents,
    Made him our pattern to live and to die!
Shakespeare was of us, Milton was for us,
    Burns, Shelley, were with us,—they watch from their
        graves!
He alone breaks from the van and the freemen,   15
    —He alone sinks to the rear and the slaves!

II

We shall march prospering,—not thro' his presence;
    Songs may inspirit us,—not from his lyre;
Deeds will be done,—while he boasts his quiescence,
    Still bidding crouch whom the rest bade aspire: 20
Blot out his name, then, record one lost soul more,
    One task more declined, one more footpath untrod,
One more devils'-triumph and sorrow for angels,
    One wrong more to man, one more insult to God!
Life's night begins: let him never come back to us!   25
    There would be doubt, hesitation and pain,

Forced praise on our part—the glimmer of twilight,
    Never glad confident morning again!
Best fight on well, for we taught him—strike gallantly,
    Menace our heart ere we master his own;   30
Then let him receive the new knowledge and wait us,
    Pardoned in heaven, the first by the throne!

THE LOST MISTRESS

I

ALL'S over, then: does truth sound bitter
    As one at first believes?
Hark, 't is the sparrows' good-night twitter
    About your cottage eaves!

II

And the leaf-buds on the vine are woolly,   5
    I noticed that, to-day;
One day more bursts them open fully
    —You know the red turns grey.

III

To-morrow we meet the same then, dearest?
    May I take your hand in mine?   10
Mere friends are we,—well, friends the merest
    Keep much that I resign:

IV

For each glance of the eye so bright and black,
    Though I keep with heart's endeavour,—
Your voice, when you wish the snowdrops back,   15
    Though it stay in my soul for ever!—

V

Yet I will but say what mere friends say,
    Or only a thought stronger;
I will hold your hand but as long as all may,
    Or so very little longer!   20

HOME-THOUGHTS, FROM ABROAD[1]

I

OH, to be in England
Now that April 's there,
And whoever wakes in England
Sees, some morning, unaware,
That the lowest boughs and the brushwood sheaf   5
Round the elm-tree bole are in tiny leaf,
While the chaffinch sings on the orchard bough
In England—now!

II

And after April, when May follows,
And the whitethroat builds, and all the swallows!   10
Hark, where my blossomed pear-tree in the hedge
Leans to the field and scatters on the clover
Blossoms and dewdrops—at the bent spray's edge—
That's the wise thrush; he sings each song twice over,
Lest you should think he never could recapture   15
The first fine careless rapture!
And though the fields look rough with hoary dew
All will be gay when noontide wakes anew
The buttercups, the little children's dower
—Far brighter than this gaudy melon-flower!   20

HOME-THOUGHTS, FROM ABROAD: II

HERE 'S to Nelson's memory!
'T is the second time that I, at sea,
Right off Cape Trafalgar here,
Have drunk it deep in British Beer.

[1] In 1845 the title 'Home-Thoughts, from Abroad' applied to three successive poems, the second and third of these, headed simply 'II' and 'III', being 'Here's to Nelson's memory!' and 'Nobly Cape Saint Vincent'. In 1849 and subsequently the title 'Home-Thoughts, from Abroad' is appropriated to the first of these poems, while the third is entitled 'Home-Thoughts, from the Sea'. 'Here's to Nelson's memory!' was dropped altogether in 1849, but restored in 1863 as the third poem in the group called 'Nationality in Drinks', as 'Beer (Nelson.)'. It remained in 1868 and subsequently, though without these last two words.

Nelson for ever—any time   5
Am I his to command in prose or rhyme!
Give me of Nelson only a touch,
And I save it, be it little or much:
Here's one our Captain gives, and so
Down at the word, by George, shall it go!   10
He says that at Greenwich they point the beholder
To Nelson's coat, 'still with tar on the shoulder:
'For he used to lean with one shoulder digging,
'Jigging, as it were, and zig-zag-zigging
'Up against the mizen-rigging!'   15

HOME-THOUGHTS, FROM THE SEA

NOBLY, nobly Cape Saint Vincent to the North-west
      died away;
Sunset ran, one glorious blood-red, reeking into Cadiz
      Bay;
Bluish 'mid the burning water, full in face Trafalgar lay;
In the dimmest North-east distance dawned Gibraltar
      grand and gray;
'Here and here did England help me: how can I help
      England?'—say,   5
Whoso turns as I, this evening, turn to God to praise and
      pray,
While Jove's planet rises yonder, silent over Africa.

THE BISHOP ORDERS HIS TOMB AT
SAINT PRAXED'S CHURCH[1]

ROME, 15—

VANITY, saith the preacher, vanity!
Draw round my bed: is Anselm keeping back?
Nephews—sons mine . . . ah, God, I know not! Well—
She, men would have to be your mother once,
Old Gandolf envied me, so fair she was!   5

---

[1] First published in *Hood's Magazine*, March 1845, as 'The Tomb at St. Praxed's'.
In 1849 the title was changed, as above.

What's done is done, and she is dead beside,
Dead long ago, and I am Bishop since,
And as she died so must we die ourselves,
And thence ye may perceive the world's a dream.
Life, how and what is it? As here I lie   10
In this state-chamber, dying by degrees,
Hours and long hours in the dead night, I ask
'Do I live, am I dead?' Peace, peace seems all.
Saint Praxed's ever was the church for peace;
And so, about this tomb of mine. I fought   15
With tooth and nail to save my niche, ye know:
—Old Gandolf cozened me, despite my care;
Shrewd was that snatch from out the corner South
He graced his carrion with, God curse the same!
Yet still my niche is not so cramped but thence   20
One sees the pulpit o' the epistle-side,
And somewhat of the choir, those silent seats,
And up into the aery dome where live
The angels, and a sunbeam's sure to lurk:
And I shall fill my slab of basalt there,   25
And 'neath my tabernacle take my rest,
With those nine columns round me, two and two,
The odd one at my feet where Anselm stands:
Peach-blossom marble all, the rare, the ripe
As fresh-poured red wine of a mighty pulse.   30
—Old Gandolf with his paltry onion-stone,
Put me where I may look at him! True peach,
Rosy and flawless: how I earned the prize!
Draw close: that conflagration of my church
—What then? So much was saved if aught were missed!   35
My sons, ye would not be my death? Go dig
The white-grape vineyard where the oil-press stood,
Drop water gently till the surface sink,
And if ye find . . . Ah God, I know not, I! . . .
Bedded in store of rotten fig-leaves soft,   40
And corded up in a tight olive-frail,
Some lump, ah God, of *lapis lazuli*,
Big as a Jew's head cut off at the nape,
Blue as a vein o'er the Madonna's breast . . .
Sons, all have I bequeathed you, villas, all,   45

That brave Frascati villa with its bath,
So, let the blue lump poise between my knees,
Like God the Father's globe on both his hands
Ye worship in the Jesu Church so gay,
For Gandolf shall not choose but see and burst!   50
Swift as a weaver's shuttle fleet our years:
Man goeth to the grave, and where is he?
Did I say basalt for my slab, sons? Black—
'T was ever antique-black I meant! How else
Shall ye contrast my frieze to come beneath?   55
The bas-relief in bronze ye promised me,
Those Pans and Nymphs ye wot of, and perchance
Some tripod, thyrsus, with a vase or so,
The Saviour at his sermon on the mount,
Saint Praxed in a glory, and one Pan   60
Ready to twitch the Nymph's last garment off,
And Moses with the tables . . . but I know
Ye mark me not! What do they whisper thee,
Child of my bowels, Anselm? Ah, ye hope
To revel down my villas while I gasp   65
Bricked o'er with beggar's mouldy travertine
Which Gandolf from his tomb-top chuckles at!
Nay, boys, ye love me—all of jasper, then!
'T is jasper ye stand pledged to, lest I grieve
My bath must needs be left behind, alas!   70
One block, pure green as a pistachio-nut,
There's plenty jasper somewhere in the world—
And have I not Saint Praxed's ear to pray
Horses for ye, and brown Greek manuscripts,
And mistresses with great smooth marbly limbs?   75
—That's if ye carve my epitaph aright,
Choice Latin, picked phrase, Tully's every word,
No gaudy ware like Gandolf's second line—
Tully, my masters? Ulpian serves his need!
And then how I shall lie through centuries,   80
And hear the blessed mutter of the mass,
And see God made and eaten all day long,
And feel the steady candle-flame, and taste
Good strong thick stupefying incense-smoke!
For as I lie here, hours of the dead night,   85

Dying in state and by such slow degrees,
I fold my arms as if they clasped a crook,
And stretch my feet forth straight as stone can point,
And let the bedclothes, for a mortcloth, drop
Into great laps and folds of sculptor's-work:　　90
And as yon tapers dwindle, and strange thoughts
Grow, with a certain humming in my ears,
About the life before I lived this life,
And this life too, popes, cardinals and priests,
Saint Praxed at his sermon on the mount,　　95
Your tall pale mother with her talking eyes,
And new-found agate urns as fresh as day,
And marble's language, Latin pure, discreet,
—Aha, ELUCESCEBAT quoth our friend?
No Tully, said I, Ulpian at the best!　　100
Evil and brief hath been my pilgrimage.
All *lapis*, all, sons! Else I give the Pope
My villas! Will ye ever eat my heart?
Ever your eyes were as a lizard's quick,
They glitter like your mother's for my soul,　　105
Or ye would heighten my impoverished frieze,
Piece out its starved design, and fill my vase
With grapes, and add a vizor and a Term,
And to the tripod ye would tie a lynx
That in his struggle throws the thyrsus down,　　110
To comfort me on my entablature
Whereon I am to lie till I must ask
'Do I live, am I dead?' There, leave me, there!
For ye have stabbed me with ingratitude
To death—ye wish it—God, ye wish it! Stone—　　115
Gritstone, a-crumble! Clammy squares which sweat
As if the corpse they keep were oozing through—
And no more *lapis* to delight the world!
Well go! I bless ye. Fewer tapers there,
But in a row: and, going, turn your backs　　120
—Ay, like departing altar-ministrants,
And leave me in my church, the church for peace,
That I may watch at leisure if he leers—
Old Gandolf, at me, from his onion-stone,
As still he envied me, so fair she was!　　125

GARDEN FANCIES[1]

I: THE FLOWER'S NAME

I

HERE 'S the garden she walked across,
    Arm in my arm, such a short while since:
Hark, now I push its wicket, the moss
    Hinders the hinges and makes them wince!
She must have reached this shrub ere she turned,   5
    As back with that murmur the wicket swung;
For she laid the poor snail, my chance foot spurned,
    To feed and forget it the leaves among.

II

Down this side of the gravel-walk
    She went while her robe's edge brushed the box: 10
And here she paused in her gracious talk
    To point me a moth on the milk-white phlox.
Roses, ranged in valiant row,
    I will never think that she passed you by!
She loves you noble roses, I know;   15
    But yonder, see, where the rock-plants lie!

III

This flower she stopped at, finger on lip,
    Stooped over, in doubt, as settling its claim;
Till she gave me, with pride to make no slip,
    Its soft meandering Spanish name: 20
What a name! Was it love or praise?
    Speech half-asleep or song half-awake?
I must learn Spanish, one of these days,
    Only for that slow sweet name's sake.

IV

Roses, if I live and do well,   25
    I may bring her, one of these days,
To fix you fast with as fine a spell,
    Fit you each with his Spanish phrase;

---

[1] These two poems were first published in *Hood's Magazine* for July 1844. In 1863 (only) 'Soliloquy of the Spanish Cloister' was entitled 'Garden Fancies III'.

But do not detain me now; for she lingers
  There, like sunshine over the ground,   30
And ever I see her soft white fingers
  Searching after the bud she found.

V

Flower, you Spaniard, look that you grow not,
  Stay as you are and be loved for ever!
Bud, if I kiss you 't is that you blow not: 35
  Mind, the shut pink mouth opens never!
For while it pouts, her fingers wrestle,
  Twinkling the audacious leaves between,
Till round they turn and down they nestle—
  Is not the dear mark still to be seen?   40

VI

Where I find her not, beauties vanish;
  Whither I follow her, beauties flee;
Is there no method to tell her in Spanish
  June's twice June since she breathed it with me?
Come, bud, show me the least of her traces,   45
  Treasure my lady's lightest footfall!
—Ah, you may flout and turn up your faces—
  Roses, you are not so fair after all!

II: SIBRANDUS SCHAFNABURGENSIS

I

PLAGUE take all your pedants, say I!
  He who wrote what I hold in my hand,
Centuries back was so good as to die,
  Leaving this rubbish to cumber the land;
This, that was a book in its time,   5
  Printed on paper and bound in leather,
Last month in the white of a matin-prime
  Just when the birds sang all together.

II

Into the garden I brought it to read,
  And under the arbute and laurustine   10

Read it, so help me grace in my need,
  From title-page to closing line.
Chapter on chapter did I count,
  As a curious traveller counts Stonehenge;
Added up the mortal amount;   15
  And then proceeded to my revenge.

III

Yonder 's a plum-tree with a crevice
  An owl would build in, were he but sage;
For a lap of moss, like a fine pont-levis
  In a castle of the Middle Age,   20
Joins to a lip of gum, pure amber;
  When he'd be private, there might he spend
Hours alone in his lady's chamber:
  Into this crevice I dropped our friend.

IV

Splash, went he, as under he ducked,   25
  —At the bottom, I knew, rain-drippings stagnate:
Next, a handful of blossoms I plucked
  To bury him with, my bookshelf's magnate;
Then I went in-doors, brought out a loaf,
  Half a cheese, and a bottle of Chablis;   30
Lay on the grass and forgot the oaf
  Over a jolly chapter of Rabelais.

V

Now, this morning, betwixt the moss
  And gum that locked our friend in limbo,
A spider had spun his web across,   35
  And sat in the midst with arms akimbo:
So, I took pity, for learning's sake,
  And, *de profundis, accentibus lætis,*
Cantate! quoth I, as I got a rake;
  And up I fished his delectable treatise.   40

VI

Here you have it, dry in the sun,
  With all the binding all of a blister,

And great blue spots where the ink has run,
    And reddish streaks that wink and glister
O'er the page so beautifully yellow: 45
    Oh, well have the droppings played their tricks!
Did he guess how toadstools grow, this fellow?
    Here's one stuck in his chapter six!

VII

How did he like it when the live creatures
    Tickled and toused and browsed him all over,   50
And worm, slug, eft, with serious features,
    Came in, each one, for his right of trover?
—When the water-beetle with great blind deaf face
    Made of her eggs the stately deposit,
And the newt borrowed just so much of the preface   55
    As tiled in the top of his black wife's closet?

VIII

All that life and fun and romping,
    All that frisking and twisting and coupling,
While slowly our poor friend's leaves were swamping
    And clasps were cracking and covers suppling!   60
As if you had carried sour John Knox
    To the play-house at Paris, Vienna or Munich,
Fastened him into a front-row box,
    And danced off the ballet with trousers and tunic.

IX

Come, old martyr! What, torment enough is it?   65
    Back to my room shall you take your sweet self.
Good-bye, mother-beetle; husband-eft, *sufficit!*
    See the snug niche I have made on my shelf!
A.'s book shall prop you up, B.'s shall cover you,
    Here's C. to be grave with, or D. to be gay,   70
And with E. on each side, and F. right over you,
    Dry-rot at ease till the Judgment-day!

THE LABORATORY[1]

ANCIEN RÉGIME

I

Now that I, tying thy glass mask tightly,
May gaze thro' these faint smokes curling whitely,
As thou pliest thy trade in this devil's-smithy—
Which is the poison to poison her, prithee?

II

He is with her, and they know that I know   5
Where they are, what they do: they believe my tears flow
While they laugh, laugh at me, at me fled to the drear
Empty church, to pray God in, for them!—I am here.

III

Grind away, moisten and mash up thy paste,
Pound at thy powder,—I am not in haste!   10
Better sit thus, and observe thy strange things,
Than go where men wait me and dance at the King's.

IV

That in the mortar—you call it a gum?
Ah, the brave tree whence such gold oozings come!
And yonder soft phial, the exquisite blue,   15
Sure to taste sweetly,—is that poison too?

V

Had I but all of them, thee and thy treasures,
What a wild crowd of invisible pleasures!
To carry pure death in an earring, a casket,
A signet, a fan-mount, a filigree basket!   20

VI

Soon, at the King's, a mere lozenge to give,
And Pauline should have just thirty minutes to live!

[1] First published in *Hood's Magazine*, June 1844. In 1845 (only) this and the following poem were yoked together as 'France and Spain. I.—The Laboratory (*Ancien Régime*.)' and 'II.—Spain—The Confessional'.

But to light a pastile, and Elise, with her head
And her breast and her arms and her hands, should
  drop dead!

VII

Quick—is it finished? The colour's too grim!   25
Why not soft like the phial's, enticing and dim?
Let it brighten her drink, let her turn it and stir,
And try it and taste, ere she fix and prefer!

VIII

What a drop! She's not little, no minion like me!
That's why she ensnared him: this never will free   30
The soul from those masculine eyes,—say, 'no!'
To that pulse's magnificent come-and-go.

IX

For only last night, as they whispered, I brought
My own eyes to bear on her so, that I thought
Could I keep them one half minute fixed, she would
  fall   35
Shrivelled; she fell not; yet this does it all!

X

Not that I bid you spare her the pain;
Let death be felt and the proof remain:
Brand, burn up, bite into its grace—
He is sure to remember her dying face!   40

XI

Is it done? Take my mask off! Nay, be not morose;
It kills her, and this prevents seeing it close:
The delicate droplet, my whole fortune's fee!
If it hurts her, beside, can it ever hurt me?

XII

Now, take all my jewels, gorge gold to your fill,   45
You may kiss me, old man, on my mouth if you will!
But brush this dust off me, lest horror it brings
Ere I know it—next moment I dance at the King's!

THE CONFESSIONAL

[SPAIN]

I

IT is a lie—their Priests, their Pope,
Their Saints, their . . . all they fear or hope
Are lies, and lies—there! through my door
And ceiling, there! and walls and floor,
There, lies, they lie—shall still be hurled   5
Till spite of them I reach the world!

II

You think Priests just and holy men!
Before they put me in this den
I was a human creature too,
With flesh and blood like one of you,   10
A girl that laughed in beauty's pride
Like lilies in your world outside.

III

I had a lover—shame avaunt!
This poor wrenched body, grim and gaunt,
Was kissed all over till it burned,   15
By lips the truest love e'er turned
His heart's own tint: one night they kissed
My soul out in a burning mist.

IV

So, next day when the accustomed train
Of things grew round my sense again,   20
'That is a sin,' I said: and slow
With downcast eyes to church I go,
And pass to the confession-chair,
And tell the old mild father there.

V

But when I falter Beltran's name,   25
'Ha?' quoth the father; 'much I blame
'The sin; yet wherefore idly grieve?

'Despair not—strenuously retrieve!
'Nay, I will turn this love of thine
'To lawful love, almost divine;   30

VI

'For he is young, and led astray,
'This Beltran, and he schemes, men say,
'To change the laws of church and state;
'So, thine shall be an angel's fate,
'Who, ere the thunder breaks, should roll   35
'Its cloud away and save his soul.

VII

'For, when he lies upon thy breast,
'Thou mayst demand and be possessed
'Of all his plans, and next day steal
'To me, and all those plans reveal,   40
'That I and every priest, to purge
'His soul, may fast and use the scourge.'

VIII

That father's beard was long and white,
With love and truth his brow seemed bright;
I went back, all on fire with joy,   45
And, that same evening, bade the boy
Tell me, as lovers should, heart-free,
Something to prove his love of me.

IX

He told me what he would not tell
For hope of heaven or fear of hell;   50
And I lay listening in such pride!
And, soon as he had left my side,
Tripped to the church by morning-light
To save his soul in his despite.

X

I told the father all his schemes,   55
Who were his comrades, what their dreams;
'And now make haste,' I said, 'to pray

'The one spot from his soul away;
'To-night he comes, but not the same
'Will look!' At night he never came. 60

XI

Nor next night: on the after-morn,
I went forth with a strength new-born.
The church was empty; something drew
My steps into the street; I knew
It led me to the market-place: 65
Where, lo, on high, the father's face!

XII

That horrible black scaffold dressed,
That stapled block . . . God sink the rest!
That head strapped back, that blinding vest,
Those knotted hands and naked breast, 70
Till near one busy hangman pressed,
And, on the neck these arms caressed . . .

XIII

No part in aught they hope or fear!
No heaven with them, no hell!—and here,
No earth, not so much space as pens 75
My body in their worst of dens
But shall bear God and man my cry,
Lies—lies, again—and still, they lie!

THE FLIGHT OF THE DUCHESS[1]

I

You 're my friend:
    I was the man the Duke spoke to;
    I helped the Duchess to cast off his yoke, too;
So here's the tale from beginning to end,
My friend! 5

II

Ours is a great wild country:
    If you climb to our castle's top,

[1] The first nine sections were published in *Hood's Magazine* in April 1845.

I don't see where your eye can stop;
For when you've passed the cornfield country,
Where vineyards leave off, flocks are packed,   10
And sheep-range leads to cattle-tract,
And cattle-tract to open-chase,
And open-chase to the very base
Of the mountain where, at a funeral pace,
Round about, solemn and slow,   15
One by one, row after row,
Up and up the pine-trees go,
So, like black priests up, and so
Down the other side again
   To another greater, wilder country,   20
That's one vast red drear burnt-up plain,
Branched through and through with many a vein
Whence iron's dug, and copper's dealt;
   Look right, look left, look straight before,—
Beneath they mine, above they smelt,   25
   Copper-ore and iron-ore,
And forge and furnace mould and melt,
   And so on, more and ever more,
Till at the last, for a bounding belt,
   Comes the salt sand hoar of the great sea-shore, 30
—And the whole is our Duke's country.

III

I was born the day this present Duke was—
   (And O, says the song, ere I was old!)
In the castle where the other Duke was—
   (When I was happy and young, not old!)   35
I in the kennel, he in the bower:
We are of like age to an hour.
My father was huntsman in that day;
Who has not heard my father say
That, when a boar was brought to bay,   40
Three times, four times out of five,
With his huntspear he'd contrive
To get the killing-place transfixed,
And pin him true, both eyes betwixt?
And that's why the old Duke would rather   45

He lost a salt-pit than my father,
And loved to have him ever in call;
That 's why my father stood in the hall
When the old Duke brought his infant out
   To show the people, and while they passed   50
The wondrous bantling round about,
   Was first to start at the outside blast
As the Kaiser's courier blew his horn
Just a month after the babe was born.
'And,' quoth the Kaiser's courier, 'since   55
'The Duke has got an heir, our Prince
   'Needs the Duke's self at his side:'
The Duke looked down and seemed to wince,
   But he thought of wars o'er the world wide,
Castles a-fire, men on their march,   60
The toppling tower, the crashing arch;
   And up he looked, and awhile he eyed
The row of crests and shields and banners
Of all achievements after all manners,
   And 'ay,' said the Duke with a surly pride.   65
   The more was his comfort when he died
At next year's end, in a velvet suit,
With a gilt glove on his hand, his foot
In a silken shoe for a leather boot,
Petticoated like a herald,   70
   In a chamber next to an ante-room,
   Where he breathed the breath of page and groom,
   What he called stink, and they, perfume:
—They should have set him on red Berold
Mad with pride, like fire to manage!   75
They should have got his cheek fresh tannage
Such a day as to-day in the merry sunshine!
Had they stuck on his fist a rough-foot merlin!
(Hark, the wind 's on the heath at its game!
Oh for a noble falcon-lanner   80
To flap each broad wing like a banner,
And turn in the wind, and dance like flame!)
Had they broached a white-beer cask from Berlin
—Or if you incline to prescribe mere wine
Put to his lips, when they saw him pine,   85

A cup of our own Moldavia fine,
Cotnar for instance, green as May sorrel
And ropy with sweet,—we shall not quarrel.

IV

So, at home, the sick tall yellow Duchess
Was left with the infant in her clutches,   90
She being the daughter of God knows who:
    And now was the time to revisit her tribe.
Abroad and afar they went, the two,
    And let our people rail and gibe
At the empty hall and extinguished fire,   95
    As loud as we liked, but ever in vain,
Till after long years we had our desire,
    And back came the Duke and his mother again.

V

And he came back the pertest little ape
That ever affronted human shape;   100
Full of his travel, struck at himself.
    You'd say, he despised our bluff old ways?
—Not he! For in Paris they told the elf
    Our rough North land was the Land of Lays,
    The one good thing left in evil days;   105
Since the Mid-Age was the Heroic Time,
    And only in wild nooks like ours
Could you taste of it yet as in its prime,
    And see true castles, with proper towers,
Young-hearted women, old-minded men,   110
And manners now as manners were then.
So, all that the old Dukes had been, without knowing it,
This Duke would fain know he was, without being it;
'T was not for the joy's self, but the joy of his showing it,
Nor for the pride's self, but the pride of our seeing it,   115
He revived all usages thoroughly worn-out,
The souls of them fumed-forth, the hearts of them torn-out:
And chief in the chase his neck he perilled
On a lathy horse, all legs and length,
With blood for bone, all speed, no strength;   120
—They should have set him on red Berold

With the red eye slow consuming in fire,
And the thin stiff ear like an abbey-spire!

VI

Well, such as he was, he must marry, we heard:
And out of a convent, at the word, 125
Came the lady, in time of spring.
—Oh, old thoughts they cling, they cling!
That day, I know, with a dozen oaths
I clad myself in thick hunting-clothes
Fit for the chase of urochs or buffle 130
In winter-time when you need to muffle.
But the Duke had a mind we should cut a figure,
    And so we saw the lady arrive:
My friend, I have seen a white crane bigger!
    She was the smallest lady alive, 135
Made in a piece of nature's madness,
Too small, almost, for the life and gladness
    That over-filled her, as some hive
Out of the bears' reach on the high trees
Is crowded with its safe merry bees: 140
In truth, she was not hard to please!
Up she looked, down she looked, round at the mead,
Straight at the castle, that's best indeed
To look at from outside the walls:
As for us, styled the 'serfs and thralls,' 145
She as much thanked me as if she had said it,
    (With her eyes, do you understand?)
Because I patted her horse while I led it;
    And Max, who rode on her other hand,
Said, no bird flew past but she inquired 150
What its true name was, nor ever seemed tired—
If that was an eagle she saw hover,
And the green and grey bird on the field was the plover.
When suddenly appeared the Duke:
    And as down she sprung, the small foot pointed 155
On to my hand,—as with a rebuke,
    And as if his backbone were not jointed,
The Duke stepped rather aside than forward,
    And welcomed her with his grandest smile;

And, mind you, his mother all the while   160
Chilled in the rear, like a wind to Nor'ward;
And up, like a weary yawn, with its pullies
Went, in a shriek, the rusty portcullis;
And, like a glad sky the north-wind sullies,
The lady's face stopped its play,   165
As if her first hair had grown grey;
For such things must begin some one day.

VII

In a day or two she was well again;
As who should say, 'You labour in vain!
'This is all a jest against God, who meant   170
'I should ever be, as I am, content
'And glad in his sight; therefore, glad I will be.'
So, smiling as at first went she.

VIII

She was active, stirring, all fire—
Could not rest, could not tire—   175
To a stone she might have given life!
    (I myself loved once, in my day)
—For a shepherd's, miner's, huntsman's wife,
    (I had a wife, I know what I say)
Never in all the world such an one!   180
And here was plenty to be done,
And she that could do it, great or small,
She was to do nothing at all.
There was already this man in his post,
    This in his station, and that in his office,   185
And the Duke's plan admitted a wife, at most,
    To meet his eye, with the other trophies,
Now outside the hall, now in it,
    To sit thus, stand thus, see and be seen,
At the proper place in the proper minute,   190
    And die away the life between.
And it was amusing enough, each infraction
    Of rule—(but for after-sadness that came)
To hear the consummate self-satisfaction
    With which the young Duke and the old dame   195

Q

Would let her advise, and criticise,
And, being a fool, instruct the wise,
    And, child-like, parcel out praise or blame:
They bore it all in complacent guise,
As though an artificer, after contriving   200
A wheel-work image as if it were living,
Should find with delight it could motion to strike him!
So found the Duke, and his mother like him:
The lady hardly got a rebuff—
That had not been contemptuous enough,   205
With his cursed smirk, as he nodded applause,
And kept off the old mother-cat's claws.

IX

So, the little lady grew silent and thin,
    Paling and ever paling,
As the way is with a hid chagrin;   210
    And the Duke perceived that she was ailing,
And said in his heart, ' 'Tis done to spite me,
'But I shall find in my power to right me!'
Don't swear, friend! The old one, many a year,
Is in hell, and the Duke's self . . . you shall hear.   215

X

Well, early in autumn, at first winter-warning,
When the stag had to break with his foot, of a morning,
A drinking-hole out of the fresh tender ice
That covered the pond till the sun, in a trice,
Loosening it, let out a ripple of gold,   220
    And another and another, and faster and faster,
Till, dimpling to blindness, the wide water rolled:
    Then it so chanced that the Duke our master
Asked himself what were the pleasures in season,
    And found, since the calendar bade him be hearty,   225
He should do the Middle Age no treason
    In resolving on a hunting-party.
Always provided, old books showed the way of it!
    What meant old poets by their strictures?
And when old poets had said their say of it,   230
    How taught old painters in their pictures?

We must revert to the proper channels,
Workings in tapestry, paintings on panels,
And gather up woodcraft's authentic traditions:
Here was food for our various ambitions,   235
As on each case, exactly stated—
   To encourage your dog, now, the properest chirrup,
   Or best prayer to Saint Hubert on mounting your
      stirrup—
We of the household took thought and debated.
Blessed was he whose back ached with the jerkin   240
His sire was wont to do forest-work in;
Blesseder he who nobly sunk 'ohs'
And 'ahs' while he tugged on his grandsire's trunk-hose;
What signified hats if they had no rims on,
   Each slouching before and behind like the scallop, 245
   And able to serve at sea for a shallop,
Loaded with lacquer and looped with crimson!
So that the deer now, to make a short rhyme on 't,
   What with our Venerers, Prickers and Verderers,
   Might hope for real hunters at length and not
      murderers,   250
And oh the Duke's tailor, he had a hot time on 't!

XI

Now you must know that when the first dizziness
   Of flap-hats and buff-coats and jack-boots subsided,
   The Duke put this question, 'The Duke's part provided,
'Had not the Duchess some share in the business?'   255
For out of the mouth of two or three witnesses
Did he establish all fit-or-unfitnesses:
And, after much laying of heads together,
Somebody's cap got a notable feather
By the announcement with proper unction   260
That he had discovered the lady's function;
Since ancient authors gave this tenet,
   'When horns wind a mort and the deer is at siege,
'Let the dame of the castle prick forth on her jennet,
   'And, with water to wash the hands of her liege   265
'In a clean ewer with a fair toweling,
'Let her preside at the disemboweling.'

Now, my friend, if you had so little religion
　　As to catch a hawk, some falcon-lanner,
　　And thrust her broad wings like a banner   270
Into a coop for a vulgar pigeon;
And if day by day and week by week
　　You cut her claws, and sealed her eyes,
And clipped her wings, and tied her beak,
　　Would it cause you any great surprise   275
If, when you decided to give her an airing,
You found she needed a little preparing?
—I say, should you be such a curmudgeon,
If she clung to the perch, as to take it in dudgeon?
Yet when the Duke to his lady signified,   280
Just a day before, as he judged most dignified,
In what a pleasure she was to participate,—
　　And, instead of leaping wide in flashes,
　　Her eyes just lifted their long lashes,
As if pressed by fatigue even he could not dissipate,   285
And duly acknowledged the Duke's forethought,
But spoke of her health, if her health were worth aught,
Of the weight by day and the watch by night,
And much wrong now that used to be right,
So, thanking him, declined the hunting,—   290
Was conduct ever more affronting?
With all the ceremony settled—
　　With the towel ready, and the sewer
　　Polishing up his oldest ewer,
　　And the jennet pitched upon, a piebald,   295
　　Black-barred, cream-coated and pink eye-balled,—
No wonder if the Duke was nettled!
And when she persisted nevertheless,—
Well, I suppose here's the time to confess
That there ran half round our lady's chamber   300
A balcony none of the hardest to clamber;
And that Jacynth the tire-woman, ready in waiting,
Stayed in call outside, what need of relating?
And since Jacynth was like a June rose, why, a fervent
Adorer of Jacynth of course was your servant;   305
And if she had the habit to peep through the casement,
　　How could I keep at any vast distance?

And so, as I say, on the lady's persistence,
The Duke, dumb-stricken with amazement,
Stood for a while in a sultry smother,   310
    And then, with a smile that partook of the awful,
Turned her over to his yellow mother
    To learn what was held decorous and lawful;
And the mother smelt blood with a cat-like instinct,
As her cheek quick whitened thro' all its quince-tint.   315
Oh, but the lady heard the whole truth at once!
    What meant she?—Who was she?—Her duty and
        station,
The wisdom of age and the folly of youth, at once,
    Its decent regard and its fitting relation—
In brief, my friend, set all the devils in hell free   320
And turn them out to carouse in a belfry
And treat the priests to a fifty-part canon,
And then you may guess how that tongue of hers ran on!
Well, somehow or other it ended at last
And, licking her whiskers, out she passed;   325
And after her,—making (he hoped) a face
    Like Emperor Nero or Sultan Saladin,
Stalked the Duke's self with the austere grace
    Of ancient hero or modern paladin,
From door to staircase—oh such a solemn   330
Unbending of the vertebral column!

XII

However, at sunrise our company mustered;
    And here was the huntsman bidding unkennel,
And there 'neath his bonnet the pricker blustered,
    With feather dank as a bough of wet fennel;   335
For the court-yard walls were filled with fog
You might have cut as an axe chops a log—
Like so much wool for colour and bulkiness;
And out rode the Duke in a perfect sulkiness,
Since, before breakfast, a man feels but queasily,   340
    And a sinking at the lower abdomen
    Begins the day with indifferent omen.
And lo, as he looked around uneasily,
The sun ploughed the fog up and drove it asunder

This way and that from the valley under;   345
  And, looking through the court-yard arch,
Down in the valley, what should meet him
  But a troop of Gipsies on their march?
No doubt with the annual gifts to greet him.

XIII

Now, in your land, Gipsies reach you, only   350
  After reaching all lands beside;
North they go, South they go, trooping or lonely,
  And still, as they travel far and wide,
Catch they and keep now a trace here, a trace there,
That puts you in mind of a place here, a place there.   355
But with us, I believe they rise out of the ground,
And nowhere else, I take it, are found
With the earth-tint yet so freshly embrowned:
Born, no doubt, like insects which breed on
The very fruit they are meant to feed on.   360
For the earth—not a use to which they don't turn it,
  The ore that grows in the mountain's womb,
  Or the sand in the pits like a honeycomb,
They sift and soften it, bake it and burn it—
Whether they weld you, for instance, a snaffle   365
With side-bars never a brute can baffle;
Or a lock that's a puzzle of wards within wards;
Or, if your colt's fore-foot inclines to curve inwards,
Horseshoes they hammer which turn on a swivel
And won't allow the hoof to shrivel.   370
Then they cast bells like the shell of the winkle
That keep a stout heart in the ram with their tinkle;
But the sand—they pinch and pound it like otters;
Commend me to Gipsy glass-makers and potters!
Glasses they'll blow you, crystal-clear,   375
Where just a faint cloud of rose shall appear,
As if in pure water you dropped and let die
A bruised black-blooded mulberry;
And that other sort, their crowning pride,
With long white threads distinct inside,   380
Like the lake-flower's fibrous roots which dangle
Loose such a length and never tangle,

Where the bold sword-lily cuts the clear waters,
And the cup-lily couches with all the white daughters:
Such are the works they put their hand to,   385
The uses they turn and twist iron and sand to.
And these made the troop, which our Duke saw sally
Toward his castle from out of the valley,
Men and women, like new-hatched spiders,
Come out with the morning to greet our riders.   390
And up they wound till they reached the ditch,
Whereat all stopped save one, a witch
That I knew, as she hobbled from the group,
By her gait directly and her stoop,
I, whom Jacynth was used to importune   395
To let that same witch tell us our fortune,
The oldest Gipsy then above ground;
And, sure as the autumn season came round,
She paid us a visit for profit or pastime,
And every time, as she swore, for the last time.   400
And presently she was seen to sidle
Up to the Duke till she touched his bridle,
So that the horse of a sudden reared up
As under its nose the old witch peered up
With her worn-out eyes, or rather eye-holes   405
    Of no use now but to gather brine,
    And began a kind of level whine
Such as they used to sing to their viols
When their ditties they go grinding
Up and down with nobody minding: 410
And then, as of old, at the end of the humming
Her usual presents were forthcoming
—A dog-whistle blowing the fiercest of trebles,
(Just a sea-shore stone holding a dozen fine pebbles,)
Or a porcelain mouth-piece to screw on a pipe-end,—   415
And so she awaited her annual stipend.
But this time, the Duke would scarcely vouchsafe
    A word in reply; and in vain she felt
    With twitching fingers at her belt
    For the purse of sleek pine-martin pelt,   420
Ready to put what he gave in her pouch safe,—
Till, either to quicken his apprehension,

Or possibly with an after-intention,
She was come, she said, to pay her duty
To the new Duchess, the youthful beauty.   425
No sooner had she named his lady,
Than a shine lit up the face so shady,
And its smirk returned with a novel meaning—
For it struck him, the babe just wanted weaning;
If one gave her a taste of what life was and sorrow,   430
She, foolish to-day, would be wiser to-morrow;
And who so fit a teacher of trouble
As this sordid crone bent well-nigh double?
So, glancing at her wolf-skin vesture,
    (If such it was, for they grow so hirsute   435
    That their own fleece serves for natural fur-suit)
He was contrasting, 't was plain from his gesture,
The life of the lady so flower-like and delicate
With the loathsome squalor of this helicat.
I, in brief, was the man the Duke beckoned   440
    From out of the throng, and while I drew near
He told the crone—as I since have reckoned
    By the way he bent and spoke into her ear
With circumspection and mystery—
The main of the lady's history,   445
Her frowardness and ingratitude:
And for all the crone's submissive attitude
I could see round her mouth the loose plaits tightening,
And her brow with assenting intelligence brightening,
    As though she engaged with hearty goodwill   450
    Whatever he now might enjoin to fulfil,
And promised the lady a thorough frightening.
And so, just giving her a glimpse
Of a purse, with the air of a man who imps
The wing of the hawk that shall fetch the hernshaw,   455
    He bade me take the Gipsy mother
    And set her telling some story or other
Of hill or dale, oak-wood or fernshaw,
To wile away a weary hour
For the lady left alone in her bower,   460
Whose mind and body craved exertion
And yet shrank from all better diversion.

XIV

Then clapping heel to his horse, the mere curveter,
    Out rode the Duke, and after his hollo
Horses and hounds swept, huntsman and servitor,   465
    And back I turned and bade the crone follow.
And what makes me confident what's to be told you
    Had all along been of this crone's devising,
Is, that, on looking round sharply, behold you,
    There was a novelty quick as surprising: 470
For first, she had shot up a full head in stature,
    And her step kept pace with mine nor faltered,
As if age had foregone its usurpature,
    And the ignoble mien was wholly altered,
And the face looked quite of another nature,   475
And the change reached too, whatever the change meant,
Her shaggy wolf-skin cloak's arrangement:
For where its tatters hung loose like sedges,
Gold coins were glittering on the edges,
Like the band-roll strung with tomans   480
Which proves the veil a Persian woman's:
And under her brow, like a snail's horns newly
    Come out as after the rain he paces,
Two unmistakeable eye-points duly
    Live and aware looked out of their places.   485
So, we went and found Jacynth at the entry
Of the lady's chamber standing sentry;
I told the command and produced my companion,
And Jacynth rejoiced to admit any one,
For since last night, by the same token,   490
Not a single word had the lady spoken:
They went in both to the presence together,
While I in the balcony watched the weather.

XV

And now, what took place at the very first of all,
I cannot tell, as I never could learn it: 495
Jacynth constantly wished a curse to fall
On that little head of hers and burn it
If she knew how she came to drop so soundly
    Asleep of a sudden and there continue

The whole time sleeping as profoundly   500
   As one of the boars my father would pin you
'Twixt the eyes where life holds garrison,
—Jacynth forgive me the comparison!
But where I begin my own narration
Is a little after I took my station   505
To breathe the fresh air from the balcony,
And, having in those days a falcon eye,
To follow the hunt thro' the open country,
   From where the bushes thinlier crested
The hillocks, to a plain where's not one tree.   510
   When, in a moment, my ear was arrested
By—was it singing, or was it saying,
Or a strange musical instrument playing
In the chamber?—and to be certain
I pushed the lattice, pulled the curtain,   515
And there lay Jacynth asleep,
Yet as if a watch she tried to keep,
In a rosy sleep along the floor
With her head against the door;
While in the midst, on the seat of state,   520
Was a queen—the Gipsy woman late,
With head and face downbent
On the lady's head and face intent:
For, coiled at her feet like a child at ease,
The lady sat between her knees   525
And o'er them the lady's clasped hands met,
And on those hands her chin was set,
And her upturned face met the face of the crone
Wherein the eyes had grown and grown
As if she could double and quadruple   530
At pleasure the play of either pupil
   —Very like, by her hands' slow fanning,
As up and down like a gor-crow's flappers
They moved to measure, or bell-clappers.
   I said 'Is it blessing, is it banning,   535
'Do they applaud you or burlesque you—
   'Those hands and fingers with no flesh on?'
But, just as I thought to spring in to the rescue,
   At once I was stopped by the lady's expression:

For it was life her eyes were drinking   540
From the crone's wide pair above unwinking,
—Life's pure fire received without shrinking,
Into the heart and breast whose heaving
Told you no single drop they were leaving,
—Life, that filling her, passed redundant   545
  Into her very hair, back swerving
Over each shoulder, loose and abundant,
  As her head thrown back showed the white throat curving;
And the very tresses shared in the pleasure,
Moving to the mystic measure,   550
Bounding as the bosom bounded.
I stopped short, more and more confounded,
As still her cheeks burned and eyes glistened,
As she listened and she listened:
When all at once a hand detained me,   555
The selfsame contagion gained me,
And I kept time to the wondrous chime,
Making out words and prose and rhyme,
Till it seemed that the music furled
  Its wings like a task fulfilled, and dropped   560
  From under the words it first had propped,
And left them midway in the world:
Word took word as hand takes hand,
I could hear at last, and understand,
And when I held the unbroken thread,   565
The Gipsy said:—

'And so at last we find my tribe.
  'And so I set thee in the midst,
'And to one and all of them describe
'What thou saidst and what thou didst,   570
'Our long and terrible journey through,
'And all thou art ready to say and do
'In the trials that remain:
'I trace them the vein and the other vein
'That meet on thy brow and part again,   575
'Making our rapid mystic mark;
  'And I bid my people prove and probe
  'Each eye's profound and glorious globe

'Till they detect the kindred spark
'In those depths so dear and dark,   580
'Like the spots that snap and burst and flee,
'Circling over the midnight sea.
'And on that round young cheek of thine
   'I make them recognize the tinge,
'As when of the costly scarlet wine   585
   'They drip so much as will impinge
'And spread in a thinnest scale afloat
'One thick gold drop from the olive's coat
'Over a silver plate whose sheen
'Still thro' the mixture shall be seen.   590
'For so I prove thee, to one and all,
   'Fit, when my people ope their breast,
'To see the sign, and hear the call,
   'And take the vow, and stand the test
   'Which adds one more child to the rest—   595
'When the breast is bare and the arms are wide,
'And the world is left outside.
'For there is probation to decree,
'And many and long must the trials be
'Thou shalt victoriously endure,   600
'If that brow is true and those eyes are sure;
'Like a jewel-finder's fierce assay
   'Of the prize he dug from its mountain-tomb—
'Let once the vindicating ray
   'Leap out amid the anxious gloom,   605
'And steel and fire have done their part
'And the prize falls on its finder's heart;
'So, trial after trial past,
'Wilt thou fall at the very last
'Breathless, half in trance   610
'With the thrill of the great deliverance,
   'Into our arms for evermore;
'And thou shalt know, those arms once curled
   'About thee, what we knew before,
'How love is the only good in the world.   615
'Henceforth be loved as heart can love,
'Or brain devise, or hand approve!
'Stand up, look below,

'It is our life at thy feet we throw
'To step with into light and joy;   620
'Not a power of life but we employ
'To satisfy thy nature's want;
'Art thou the tree that props the plant,
'Or the climbing plant that seeks the tree—
'Canst thou help us, must we help thee?   625
'If any two creatures grew into one,
'They would do more than the world has done:
'Though each apart were never so weak,
'Ye vainly through the world should seek
'For the knowledge and the might   630
'Which in such union grew their right:
'So, to approach at least that end,
'And blend,—as much as may be, blend
'Thee with us or us with thee,—
'As climbing plant or propping tree,   635
'Shall some one deck thee, over and down
     'Up and about, with blossoms and leaves?
'Fix his heart's fruit for thy garland-crown,
     'Cling with his soul as the gourd-vine cleaves,
'Die on thy boughs and disappear   640
'While not a leaf of thine is sere?
'Or is the other fate in store,
'And art thou fitted to adore,
'To give thy wondrous self away,
'And take a stronger nature's sway?   645
'I foresee and could foretell
'Thy future portion, sure and well:
'But those passionate eyes speak true, speak true,
'Let them say what thou shalt do!
'Only be sure thy daily life,   650
'In its peace or in its strife,
'Never shall be unobserved;
     'We pursue thy whole career,
     'And hope for it, or doubt, or fear,—
'Lo, hast thou kept thy path or swerved,   655
'We are beside thee in all thy ways,
'With our blame, with our praise,
'Our shame to feel, our pride to show,

'Glad, angry—but indifferent, no!
'Whether it be thy lot to go,   660
'For the good of us all, where the haters meet
'In the crowded city's horrible street;
'Or thou step alone through the morass
'Where never sound yet was
'Save the dry quick clap of the stork's bill,   665
'For the air is still, and the water still,
'When the blue breast of the dipping coot
'Dives under, and all is mute.
'So, at the last shall come old age,
'Decrepit as befits that stage;   670
'How else wouldst thou retire apart
'With the hoarded memories of thy heart,
'And gather all to the very least
'Of the fragments of life's earlier feast,
'Let fall through eagerness to find   675
'The crowning dainties yet behind?
'Ponder on the entire past
'Laid together thus at last,
'When the twilight helps to fuse
'The first fresh with the faded hues,   680
'And the outline of the whole,
'As round eve's shades their framework roll,
'Grandly fronts for once thy soul.
'And then as, 'mid the dark, a gleam
    'Of yet another morning breaks,   685
'And like the hand which ends a dream,
'Death, with the might of his sunbeam,
    'Touches the flesh and the soul awakes,
'Then——'
        Ay, then indeed something would happen!   690
    But what? For here her voice changed like a bird's;
    There grew more of the music and less of the words;
Had Jacynth only been by me to clap pen
To paper and put you down every syllable
    With those clever clerkly fingers,   695
    All I've forgotten as well as what lingers
In this old brain of mine that's but ill able
To give you even this poor version

Of the speech I spoil, as it were, with stammering
—More fault of those who had the hammering 700
Of prosody into me and syntax,
And did it, not with hobnails but tintacks!
But to return from this excursion,—
Just, do you mark, when the song was sweetest,
The peace most deep and the charm completest, 705
There came, shall I say, a snap—
　And the charm vanished!
And my sense returned, so strangely banished,
And, starting as from a nap,
I knew the crone was bewitching my lady, 710
With Jacynth asleep; and but one spring made I
Down from the casement, round to the portal,
　Another minute and I had entered,—
When the door opened, and more than mortal
　Stood, with a face where to my mind centred 715
All beauties I ever saw or shall see,
The Duchess: I stopped as if struck by palsy.
She was so different, happy and beautiful,
　I felt at once that all was best,
　And that I had nothing to do, for the rest, 720
But wait her commands, obey and be dutiful.
Not that, in fact, there was any commanding;
　I saw the glory of her eye,
And the brow's height and the breast's expanding,
　And I was hers to live or to die. 725
As for finding what she wanted,
You know God Almighty granted
Such little signs should serve wild creatures
　To tell one another all their desires,
　So that each knows what its friend requires, 730
And does its bidding without teachers.
I preceded her; the crone
Followed silent and alone;
I spoke to her, but she merely jabbered
　In the old style; both her eyes had slunk 735
　Back to their pits; her stature shrunk;
　In short, the soul in its body sunk
Like a blade sent home to its scabbard.

We descended, I preceding;
Crossed the court with nobody heeding;   740
All the world was at the chase,
The courtyard like a desert-place,
The stable emptied of its small fry;
I saddled myself the very palfrey
I remember patting while it carried her,   745
The day she arrived and the Duke married her.
And, do you know, though it's easy deceiving
Oneself in such matters, I can't help believing
The lady had not forgotten it either,
And knew the poor devil so much beneath her   750
Would have been only too glad for her service
To dance on hot ploughshares like a Turk dervise,
But, unable to pay proper duty where owing it,
Was reduced to that pitiful method of showing it:
For though the moment I began setting   755
His saddle on my own nag of Berold's begetting,
(Not that I meant to be obtrusive)
    She stopped me, while his rug was shifting,
    By a single rapid finger's lifting,
And, with a gesture kind but conclusive,   760
And a little shake of the head, refused me,—
I say, although she never used me,
Yet when she was mounted, the Gipsy behind her,
And I ventured to remind her,
I suppose with a voice of less steadiness   765
    Than usual, for my feeling exceeded me,
—Something to the effect that I was in readiness
    Whenever God should please she needed me,—
Then, do you know, her face looked down on me
With a look that placed a crown on me,   770
And she felt in her bosom,—mark, her bosom—
And, as a flower-tree drops its blossom,
Dropped me . . . ah, had it been a purse
Of silver, my friend, or gold that's worse,
Why, you see, as soon as I found myself   775
    So understood,—that a true heart so may gain
    Such a reward,—I should have gone home again,
Kissed Jacynth, and soberly drowned myself!

It was a little plait of hair
    Such as friends in a convent make   780
    To wear, each for the other's sake,—
This, see, which at my breast I wear,
Ever did (rather to Jacynth's grudgment),
And ever shall, till the Day of Judgment.
And then,—and then,—to cut short,—this is idle,   785
    These are feelings it is not good to foster,—
I pushed the gate wide, she shook the bridle,
    And the palfrey bounded,—and so we lost her.

XVI

When the liquor's out why clink the cannikin?
I did think to describe you the panic in   790
The redoubtable breast of our master the mannikin,
And what was the pitch of his mother's yellowness,
    How she turned as a shark to snap the spare-rib
    Clean off, sailors say, from a pearl-diving Carib,
When she heard, what she called the flight of the feloness   795
—But it seems such child's play,
What they said and did with the lady away!
And to dance on, when we've lost the music,
Always made me—and no doubt makes you—sick.
Nay, to my mind, the world's face looked so stern   800
As that sweet form disappeared through the postern,
She that kept it in constant good humour,
It ought to have stopped; there seemed nothing to do more.
But the world thought otherwise and went on,
And my head's one that its spite was spent on: 805
Thirty years are fled since that morning,
And with them all my head's adorning.
Nor did the old Duchess die outright,
As you expect, of suppressed spite,
The natural end of every adder   810
Not suffered to empty its poison-bladder:
But she and her son agreed, I take it,
That no one should touch on the story to wake it,
For the wound in the Duke's pride rankled fiery,
So, they made no search and small inquiry—   815
And when fresh Gipsies have paid us a visit, I've

Noticed the couple were never inquisitive,
But told them they're folks the Duke don't want here,
And bade them make haste and cross the frontier.
Brief, the Duchess was gone and the Duke was glad of it,   820
    And the old one was in the young one's stead,
    And took, in her place, the household's head,
And a blessed time the household had of it!
And were I not, as a man may say, cautious
How I trench, more than needs, on the nauseous,   825
I could favour you with sundry touches
Of the paint-smutches with which the Duchess
Heightened the mellowness of her cheek's yellowness
(To get on faster) until at last her
Cheek grew to be one master-plaster   830
Of mucus and fucus from mere use of ceruse:
In short, she grew from scalp to udder
Just the object to make you shudder.

XVII

You're my friend—
What a thing friendship is, world without end!   835
How it gives the heart and soul a stir-up
    As if somebody broached you a glorious runlet,
    And poured out, all lovelily, sparklingly, sunlit,
Our green Moldavia, the streaky syrup,
Cotnar as old as the time of the Druids—   840
Friendship may match with that monarch of fluids;
Each supples a dry brain, fills you its ins-and-outs,
Gives your life's hour-glass a shake when the thin sand doubts
Whether to run on or stop short, and guarantees
Age is not all made of stark sloth and arrant ease.   845
I have seen my little lady once more,
    Jacynth, the Gipsy, Berold, and the rest of it,
For to me spoke the Duke, as I told you before;
    I always wanted to make a clean breast of it:
And now it is made—why, my heart's blood, that went
      trickle,   850
    Trickle, but anon, in such muddy driblets,
Is pumped up brisk now, through the main ventricle,
    And genially floats me about the giblets.

I'll tell you what I intend to do:
I must see this fellow his sad life through—   855
He is our Duke, after all,
And I, as he says, but a serf and thrall.
My father was born here, and I inherit
    His fame, a chain he bound his son with;
Could I pay in a lump I should prefer it,   860
    But there's no mine to blow up and get done with:
So, I must stay till the end of the chapter.
For, as to our middle-age-manners-adapter,
Be it a thing to be glad on or sorry on,
Some day or other, his head in a morion   865
And breast in a hauberk, his heels he'll kick up,
Slain by an onslaught fierce of hiccup.
And then, when red doth the sword of our Duke rust,
And its leathern sheath lie o'ergrown with a blue crust,
Then I shall scrape together my earnings;   870
    For, you see, in the churchyard Jacynth reposes,
    And our children all went the way of the roses:
It's a long lane that knows no turnings.
One needs but little tackle to travel in;
    So, just one stout cloak shall I indue: 875
And for a staff, what beats the javelin
    With which his boars my father pinned you?
And then, for a purpose you shall hear presently,
    Taking some Cotnar, a tight plump skinful,
I shall go journeying, who but I, pleasantly!   880
    Sorrow is vain and despondency sinful.
What's a man's age? He must hurry more, that's all;
    Cram in a day, what his youth took a year to hold:
    When we mind labour, then only, we're too old—
What age had Methusalem when he begat Saul?   885
And at last, as its haven some buffeted ship sees,
    (Come all the way from the north-parts with sperm oil)
    I hope to get safely out of the turmoil
And arrive one day at the land of the Gipsies,
And find my lady, or hear the last news of her   890
From some old thief and son of Lucifer,
His forehead chapleted green with wreathy hop,
Sunburned all over like an Æthiop.

And when my Cotnar begins to operate
And the tongue of the rogue to run at a proper rate,   895
And our wine-skin, tight once, shows each flaccid dent,
I shall drop in with—as if by accident—
'You never knew, then, how it all ended,
'What fortune good or bad attended
'The little lady your Queen befriended?'   900
—And when that's told me, what's remaining?
This world's too hard for my explaining.
The same wise judge of matters equine
   Who still preferred some slim four-year-old
   To the big-boned stock of mighty Berold,   905
And, for strong Cotnar, drank French weak wine,
He also must be such a lady's scorner!
   Smooth Jacob still robs homely Esau:
   Now up, now down, the world's one see-saw.
—So, I shall find out some snug corner   910
Under a hedge, like Orson the wood-knight,
Turn myself round and bid the world good night;
And sleep a sound sleep till the trumpet's blowing
   Wakes me (unless priests cheat us laymen)
To a world where will be no further throwing   915
   Pearls before swine that can't value them. Amen!

EARTH'S IMMORTALITIES[1]

FAME

SEE, as the prettiest graves will do in time,
Our poet's wants the freshness of its prime;
Spite of the sexton's browsing horse, the sods
Have struggled through its binding osier rods;
Headstone and half-sunk footstone lean awry,   5
Wanting the brick-work promised by-and-by;
How the minute grey lichens, plate o'er plate,
Have softened down the crisp-cut name and date!

LOVE

So, the year's done with!
(*Love me for ever!*)

[1] The sub-titles of these two poems were added in 1849.

All March begun with,
  April's endeavour;
May-wreaths that bound me   5
  June needs must sever;
Now snow falls round me,
  Quenching June's fever—
(*Love me for ever!*)

SONG

I

NAY but you, who do not love her,
  Is she not pure gold, my mistress?
Holds earth aught—speak truth—above her?
  Aught like this tress, see, and this tress,
And this last fairest tress of all,   5
So fair, see, ere I let it fall?

II

Because, you spend your lives in praising;
  To praise, you search the wide world over:
Then why not witness, calmly gazing,
  If earth holds aught—speak truth—above her?   10
Above this tress, and this, I touch
But cannot praise, I love so much!

THE BOY AND THE ANGEL[1]

MORNING, evening, noon and night,
'Praise God!' sang Theocrite.

Then to his poor trade he turned,
Whereby the daily meal was earned.

Hard he laboured, long and well;   5
O'er his work the boy's curls fell.

[1] First published in *Hood's Magazine*, August 1844.

But ever, at each period,
He stopped and sang, 'Praise God!'

Then back again his curls he threw,
And cheerful turned to work anew.   10

Said Blaise, the listening monk, 'Well done;
'I doubt not thou art heard, my son:

'As well as if thy voice to-day
'Were praising God, the Pope's great way.

'This Easter Day, the Pope at Rome   15
'Praises God from Peter's dome.'

Said Theocrite, 'Would God that I
'Might praise him, that great way, and die!'

Night passed, day shone,
And Theocrite was gone.   20

With God a day endures alway,
A thousand years are but a day.

God said in heaven, 'Nor day nor night
'Now brings the voice of my delight.'

Then Gabriel, like a rainbow's birth,   25
Spread his wings and sank to earth;

Entered, in flesh, the empty cell,
Lived there, and played the craftsman well;

And morning, evening, noon and night,
Praised God in place of Theocrite.   30

And from a boy, to youth he grew:
The man put off the stripling's hue:

The man matured and fell away
Into the season of decay:

And ever o'er the trade he bent,   35
And ever lived on earth content.

(He did God's will; to him, all one
If on the earth or in the sun.)

God said, 'A praise is in mine ear;
'There is no doubt in it, no fear: 40

'So sing old worlds, and so
'New worlds that from my footstool go.

'Clearer loves sound other ways:
'I miss my little human praise.'

Then forth sprang Gabriel's wings, off fell   45
The flesh disguise, remained the cell.

'T was Easter Day: he flew to Rome,
And paused above Saint Peter's dome.

In the tiring-room close by
The great outer gallery,   50

With his holy vestments dight,
Stood the new Pope, Theocrite:

And all his past career
Came back upon him clear,

Since when, a boy, he plied his trade,   55
Till on his life the sickness weighed;

And in his cell, when death drew near,
An angel in a dream brought cheer:

And rising from the sickness drear
He grew a priest, and now stood here.   60

To the East with praise he turned,
And on his sight the angel burned.

'I bore thee from thy craftsman's cell
'And set thee here; I did not well.

'Vainly I left my angel-sphere,   65
'Vain was thy dream of many a year.

'Thy voice's praise seemed weak; it dropped—
'Creation's chorus stopped!

'Go back and praise again
'The early way, while I remain.   70

'With that weak voice of our disdain,
'Take up creation's pausing strain.

'Back to the cell and poor employ:
'Resume the craftsman and the boy!'

Theocrite grew old at home;   75
A new Pope dwelt in Peter's dome.

One vanished as the other died:
They sought God side by side.

MEETING AT NIGHT[1]

I

THE grey sea and the long black land;
And the yellow half-moon large and low;
And the startled little waves that leap
In fiery ringlets from their sleep,
As I gain the cove with pushing prow,   5
And quench its speed i' the slushy sand.

II

Then a mile of warm sea-scented beach;
Three fields to cross till a farm appears;
A tap at the pane, the quick sharp scratch
And blue spurt of a lighted match,   10
And a voice less loud, thro' its joys and fears,
Than the two hearts beating each to each!

---

[1] In 1845 these two poems appeared under the general title 'Night and Morning':
the first was 'I.— Night', and the second 'II.—Morning'.

PARTING AT MORNING

ROUND the cape of a sudden came the sea,
And the sun looked over the mountain's rim:
And straight was a path of gold for him,
And the need of a world of men for me.

NATIONALITY IN DRINKS[1]

I

MY heart sank with our Claret-flask,
    Just now, beneath the heavy sedges
That serve this pond's black face for mask;
    And still at yonder broken edges
O' the hole, where up the bubbles glisten,   5
After my heart I look and listen.

II

Our laughing little flask, compelled
    Thro' depth to depth more bleak and shady;
As when, both arms beside her held,
    Feet straightened out, some gay French lady   10
Is caught up from life's light and motion,
And dropped into death's silent ocean!

Up jumped Tokay on our table,
Like a pygmy castle-warder,
Dwarfish to see, but stout and able,   15
Arms and accoutrements all in order;
And fierce he looked North, then, wheeling South,
Blew with his bugle a challenge to Drouth,
Cocked his flap-hat with the tosspot-feather,
Twisted his thumb in his red moustache,   20

[1] 'Claret and Tokay', as the first two of these poems were entitled in 1845, had first appeared in *Hood's Magazine* for June 1844. They were omitted in 1849. In 1863 the lines 'Here's to Nelson's memory!' became the third poem in the group (see pp. 431–2 above): the general title 'Nationality in Drinks' was then added. The sub-titles *Claret*, *Tokay*, and *Beer* (*Nelson*) are found only in 1863.

Jingled his huge brass spurs together,
Tightened his waist with its Buda sash,
And then, with an impudence nought could abash,
Shrugged his hump-shoulder, to tell the beholder,
For twenty such knaves he should laugh but the
    bolder: 25
And so, with his sword-hilt gallantly jutting,
And dexter-hand on his haunch abutting,
Went the little man, Sir Ausbruch, strutting!

SAUL[1]

SAID Abner, 'At last thou art come!
  'Ere I tell, ere thou speak,—
'Kiss my cheek, wish me well!' Then I wished it,
  And did kiss his cheek:
And he, 'Since the King, oh my friend,   5
  'For thy countenance sent,
Nor drunken nor eaten have we;
  Nor, until from his tent
Thou return with the joyful assurance
  The king liveth yet,   10
Shall our lip with the honey be brightened,
  —The water, be wet.

'For out of the black mid-tent's silence,
  A space of three days,
No sound hath escaped to thy servants,   15
  Of prayer nor of praise,
To betoken that Saul and the Spirit
  Have gone their dread ways.

'Yet now my heart leaps, O beloved!
  God's child, with his dew   20
On thy gracious gold hair, and those lilies
  Still living and blue
As thou brak'st them to twine round thy harp-strings,
  As if no wild heat
Were raging to torture the desert!'   25

[1] So printed in 1845 and 1849. The above text is that of 1845. For the completed version of the poem, in long lines, see pp. 719–30 below.

Then I, as was meet,
Knelt down to the God of my fathers,
　　And rose on my feet,
And ran o'er the sand burnt to powder.
　　The tent was unlooped;　　　　　　　30
I pulled up the spear that obstructed,
　　And under I stooped;
Hands and knees o'er the slippery grass-patch—
　　All withered and gone—
That leads to the second enclosure,　　　35
　　I groped my way on,
Till I felt where the foldskirts fly open;
　　Then once more I prayed,
And opened the foldskirts and entered,
　　And was not afraid;　　　　　　　　40
And spoke, 'Here is David, thy servant!'
　　And no voice replied;
And first I saw nought but the blackness;
　　But soon I descried
A something more black than the blackness　45
　　—The vast, the upright
Main-prop which sustains the pavilion,—
　　And slow into sight
Grew a figure, gigantic, against it,
　　And blackest of all;—　　　　　　　50
Then a sunbeam, that burst thro' the tent-roof,
　　Showed Saul.

He stood as erect as that tent-prop;
　　Both arms stretched out wide
On the great cross-support in the centre　　55
　　That goes to each side:
So he bent not a muscle but hung there
　　As, caught in his pangs
And waiting his change the king-serpent
　　All heavily hangs,　　　　　　　　60
Far away from his kind, in the Pine,
　　Till deliverance come
With the Spring-time,—so agonized Saul,
　　Drear and black, blind and dumb.

Then I tuned my harp,—took off the lilies   65
    We twine round its chords
Lest they snap 'neath the stress of the noontide
    —Those sunbeams like swords!
And I first played the tune all our sheep know,
    As, one after one,   70
So docile they come to the pen-door
    Till folding be done
—They are white and untorn by the bushes
    For lo, they have fed
Where the long grasses stifle the water   75
    Within the stream's bed;
How one after one seeks its lodging,
    As star follows star
Into eve and the blue far above us,
    —So blue and so far!   80

Then the tune for which quails on the cornland
    Will leave each his mate
To follow the player; then, what makes
    The crickets elate
Till for boldness they fight one another: 85
    And then, what has weight
To set the quick jerboa a-musing
    Outside his sand house
—There are none such as he for a wonder—
    Half bird and half mouse!   90
—God made all the creatures and gave them
    Our love and our fear,
To show, we and they are his children,
    One family here.

Then I played the help-tune of our Reapers,   95
    Their wine-song, when hand
Grasps hand, eye lights eye in good friendship,
    And great hearts expand,
And grow one in the sense of this world's life;
    And then, the low song   100
When the dead man is praised on his journey—
    'Bear, bear him along

'With his few faults shut up like dead flowrets;
   'Are balm-seeds not here
'To console us? The land has got none such   105
   'As he on the bier—
'Oh, would we might keep thee, my brother!'
   And then, the glad chaunt
Of the marriage,—first go the young maidens—
   Next, she whom we vaunt   110
As the beauty, the pride of our dwelling:
   And then, the great march
When man runs to man to assist him
   And buttress an arch
Nought can break . . . who shall harm them, our
     brothers?   115
   Then, the chorus intoned
As the Levites go up to the altar
   In glory enthroned—
But I stopped here—for here, in the darkness,
   Saul groaned: 120

And I paused, held my breath in such silence!
   And listened apart—
And the tent shook, for mighty Saul shuddered,—
   And sparkles 'gan dart
From the jewels that woke in his turban   125
   —At once with a start
All the lordly male-sapphires, and rubies
   Courageous at heart;
So the head, but the body still moved not,—
   Still hung there erect.   130
And I bent once again to my playing,
   Pursued it unchecked,
As I sang, 'Oh, our manhood's prime vigour!
   —No spirit feels waste,
No muscle is stopped in its playing   135
   No sinew unbraced,—
And the wild joys of living! The leaping
   From rock up to rock—
The rending their boughs from the palm-trees,—
   The cool silver shock   140

Of a plunge in the pool's living water—
   The hunt of the bear,
And the sultriness showing the lion
   Is couched in his lair:
And the meal—the rich dates—yellowed over   145
   With gold dust divine,
And the locust's-flesh steeped in the pitcher—
   The full draught of wine,
And the sleep in the dried river channel
   Where tall rushes tell   150
The water was wont to go warbling
   So softly and well,—
How good is man's life here, mere living!
   How fit to employ
The heart and the soul and the senses   155
   For ever in joy!
Hast thou loved the white locks of thy father
   Whose sword thou didst guard
When he trusted thee forth to the wolf hunt
   For glorious reward?   160
Didst thou see the thin hands of thy mother
   Held up, as men sung
The song of the nearly-departed,
   And heard her faint tongue
Joining in while it could to the witness   165
   "Let one more attest,
"I have lived, seen God's hand thro' that life-time,
   "And all was for best . . ."
Then they sung thro' their tears, in strong triumph,
   Not much,—but the rest!   170
And thy brothers—the help and the contest,
   The working whence grew
Such result, as from seething grape-bundles
   The spirit so true—
And the friends of thy boyhood—that boyhood   175
   With wonder and hope,
And the promise and wealth in the future,—
   The eye's eagle scope,—
Till lo, thou art grown to a monarch,
   A people is thine!   180

Oh all, all the world offers singly,
　　On one head combine,
On one head the joy and the pride,
　　Even rage like the throe
That opes the rock, helps its glad labour,   185
　　And lets the gold go—
And ambition that sees a sun lead it
　　Oh, all of these—all
Combine to unite in one creature
　　—Saul!   190
　　　　　(*End of Part the First.*)

TIME'S REVENGES

I'VE a Friend, over the sea;
I like him, but he loves me.
It all grew out of the books I write;
They find such favour in his sight
That he slaughters you with savage looks   5
Because you don't admire my books.
He does himself though,—and if some vein
Were to snap to-night in this heavy brain,
To-morrow month, if I lived to try,
Round should I just turn quietly,   10
Or out of the bedclothes stretch my hand
Till I found him, come from his foreign land
To be my nurse in this poor place,
And make my broth and wash my face
And light my fire and, all the while,   15
Bear with his old good-humoured smile
That I told him 'Better have kept away
'Than come and kill me, night and day,
'With, worse than fever throbs and shoots,
'The creaking of his clumsy boots.'   20
I am as sure that this he would do,
As that Saint Paul's is striking two.
And I think I rather . . . woe is me!
—Yes, rather would see him than not see,

If lifting a hand could seat him there   25
Before me in the empty chair
To-night, when my head aches indeed,
And I can neither think nor read
Nor make these purple fingers hold
The pen; this garret's freezing cold!   30

And I've a Lady—there he wakes,
The laughing fiend and prince of snakes
Within me, at her name, to pray
Fate send some creature in the way
Of my love for her, to be down-torn,   35
Upthrust and outward-borne,
So I might prove myself that sea
Of passion which I needs must be!
Call my thoughts false and my fancies quaint
And my style infirm and its figures faint,   40
All the critics say, and more blame yet,
And not one angry word you get.
But, please you, wonder I would put
My cheek beneath that lady's foot
Rather than trample under mine   45
The laurels of the Florentine,
And you shall see how the devil spends
A fire God gave for other ends!
I tell you, I stride up and down
This garret, crowned with love's best crown,   50
And feasted with love's perfect feast,
To think I kill for her, at least,
Body and soul and peace and fame,
Alike youth's end and manhood's aim,
—So is my spirit, as flesh with sin,   55
Filled full, eaten out and in
With the face of her, the eyes of her,
The lips, the little chin, the stir
Of shadow round her mouth; and she
—I'll tell you,—calmly would decree   60
That I should roast at a slow fire,
If that would compass her desire
And make her one whom they invite

To the famous ball to-morrow night.
There may be heaven; there must be hell;   65
Meantime, there is our earth here—well!

THE GLOVE

(PETER RONSARD *loquitur*.)

'HEIGHO!' yawned one day King Francis,
'Distance all value enhances!
'When a man's busy, why, leisure
'Strikes him as wonderful pleasure:
' 'Faith, and at leisure once is he?   5
'Straightway he wants to be busy.
'Here we've got peace; and aghast I'm
'Caught thinking war the true pastime.
'Is there a reason in metre?
'Give us your speech, master Peter!'   10
I who, if mortal dare say so,
Ne'er am at loss with my Naso,
'Sire,' I replied, 'joys prove cloudlets:
'Men are the merest Ixions'—
Here the King whistled aloud, 'Let's   15
'—Heigho—go look at our lions!'
Such are the sorrowful chances
If you talk fine to King Francis.

And so, to the courtyard proceeding,
Our company, Francis was leading,   20
Increased by new followers tenfold
Before he arrived at the penfold;
Lords, ladies, like clouds which bedizen
At sunset the western horizon.
And Sir De Lorge pressed 'mid the foremost   25
With the dame he professed to adore most.
Oh, what a face! One by fits eyed
Her, and the horrible pitside;
For the penfold surrounded a hollow
Which led where the eye scarce dared follow,   30
And shelved to the chamber secluded
Where Bluebeard, the great lion, brooded.

R

The King hailed his keeper, an Arab
As glossy and black as a scarab,
And bade him make sport and at once stir   35
Up and out of his den the old monster.
They opened a hole in the wire-work
Across it, and dropped there a firework,
And fled: one's heart's beating redoubled;
A pause, while the pit's mouth was troubled,   40
The blackness and silence so utter,
By the firework's slow sparkling and sputter;
Then earth in a sudden contortion
Gave out to our gaze her abortion.
Such a brute! Were I friend Clement Marot   45
(Whose experience of nature's but narrow,
And whose faculties move in no small mist
When he versifies David the Psalmist)
I should study that brute to describe you
Illum Juda Leonem de Tribu.   50
One's whole blood grew curdling and creepy
To see the black mane, vast and heapy,
The tail in the air stiff and straining,
The wide eyes, nor waxing nor waning,
As over the barrier which bounded   55
His platform, and us who surrounded
The barrier, they reached and they rested
On space that might stand him in best stead:
For who knew, he thought, what the amazement,
The eruption of clatter and blaze meant,   60
And if, in this minute of wonder,
No outlet, 'mid lightning and thunder,
Lay broad, and, his shackles all shivered,
The lion at last was delivered?
Ay, that was the open sky o'erhead!   65
And you saw by the flash on his forehead,
By the hope in those eyes wide and steady,
He was leagues in the desert already,
Driving the flocks up the mountain,
Or catlike couched hard by the fountain   70
To waylay the date-gathering negress:
So guarded he entrance or egress.

'How he stands!' quoth the King: 'we may well swear,
('No novice, we've won our spurs elsewhere
'And so can afford the confession,)   75
'We exercise wholesome discretion
'In keeping aloof from his threshold,
'Once hold you, those jaws want no fresh hold,
'Their first would too pleasantly purloin
'The visitor's brisket or surloin: 80
'But who's he would prove so fool-hardy?
'Not the best man of Marignan, pardie!'

The sentence no sooner was uttered,
Than over the rails a glove fluttered,
Fell close to the lion, and rested: 85
The dame 't was, who flung it and jested
With life so, De Lorge had been wooing
For months past; he sat there pursuing
His suit, weighing out with nonchalance
Fine speeches like gold from a balance.   90

Sound the trumpet, no true knight's a tarrier!
De Lorge made one leap at the barrier,
Walked straight to the glove,—while the lion
Ne'er moved, kept his far-reaching eye on
The palm-tree-edged desert-spring's sapphire,   95
And the musky oiled skin of the Kaffir,—
Picked it up, and as calmly retreated,
Leaped back where the lady was seated,
And full in the face of its owner
Flung the glove.

'Your heart's queen, you dethrone her?   100
'So should I!'—cried the King—' 't was mere vanity,
'Not love, set that task to humanity!'
Lords and ladies alike turned with loathing
From such a proved wolf in sheep's clothing.

Not so, I; for I caught an expression   105
In her brow's undisturbed self-possession
Amid the Court's scoffing and merriment,—

As if from no pleasing experiment
She rose, yet of pain not much heedful
So long as the process was needful,—   110
As if she had tried in a crucible,
To what 'speeches like gold' were reducible,
And, finding the finest prove copper,
Felt the smoke in her face was but proper;
To know what she had *not* to trust to,   115
Was worth all the ashes and dust too.
She went out 'mid hooting and laughter;
Clement Marot stayed; I followed after,
And asked, as a grace, what it all meant?
If she wished not the rash deed's recalment?   120
'For I'—so I spoke—'am a poet:
'Human nature,—behoves that I know it!'

She told me, 'Too long had I heard
'Of the deed proved alone by the word:
'For my love—what De Lorge would not dare!   125
'With my scorn—what De Lorge could compare!
'And the endless descriptions of death
'He would brave when my lip formed a breath,
'I must reckon as braved, or, of course,
'Doubt his word—and moreover, perforce,   130
'For such gifts as no lady could spurn,
'Must offer my love in return.
'When I looked on your lion, it brought
'All the dangers at once to my thought,
'Encountered by all sorts of men,   135
'Before he was lodged in his den,—
'From the poor slave whose club or bare hands
'Dug the trap, set the snare on the sands,
'With no King and no Court to applaud,
'By no shame, should he shrink, overawed,   140
'Yet to capture the creature made shift,
'That his rude boys might laugh at the gift,
'—To the page who last leaped o'er the fence
'Of the pit, on no greater pretence
'Than to get back the bonnet he dropped,   145
'Lest his pay for a week should be stopped.

'So, wiser I judged it to make
'One trial what "death for my sake"
'Really meant, while the power was yet mine,
'Than to wait until time should define   150
'Such a phrase not so simply as I,
'Who took it to mean just "to die."
'The blow a glove gives is but weak:
'Does the mark yet discolour my cheek?
'But when the heart suffers a blow,   155
'Will the pain pass so soon, do you know?'

I looked, as away she was sweeping,
And saw a youth eagerly keeping
As close as he dared to the doorway.
No doubt that a noble should more weigh   160
His life than befits a plebeian;
And yet, had our brute been Nemean—
(I judge by a certain calm fervour
The youth stepped with, forward to serve her)   164
—He'd have scarce thought you did him the worst turn
If you whispered 'Friend, what you'd get, first earn!'
And when, shortly after, she carried
Her shame from the Court, and they married,
To that marriage some happiness, maugre
The voice of the Court, I dared augur.   170

For De Lorge, he made women with men vie,
Those in wonder and praise, these in envy;
And in short stood so plain a head taller
That he wooed and won . . . how do you call her?
The beauty, that rose in the sequel   175
To the King's love, who loved her a week well.
And 't was noticed he never would honour
De Lorge (who looked daggers upon her)
With the easy commission of stretching
His legs in the service, and fetching   180
His wife, from her chamber, those straying
Sad gloves she was always mislaying,
While the King took the closet to chat in,—
But of course this adventure came pat in.

And never the King told the story,   185
How bringing a glove brought such glory,
But the wife smiled—'His nerves are grown firmer:
'Mine he brings now and utters no murmur.'

Venienti occurrite morbo!
With which moral I drop my theorbo.   190

CHRISTMAS-EVE AND
EASTER-DAY

CHRISTMAS-EVE AND EASTER-DAY

1850

CHRISTMAS-EVE

I

OUT of the little chapel I burst
　　Into the fresh night-air again.
Five minutes full, I waited first
　　In the doorway, to escape the rain
That drove in gusts down the common's centre　　　5
　　At the edge of which the chapel stands,
Before I plucked up heart to enter.
　　Heaven knows how many sorts of hands
Reached past me, groping for the latch
Of the inner door that hung on catch　　　10
More obstinate the more they fumbled,
　　Till, giving way at last with a scold
Of the crazy hinge, in squeezed or tumbled
　　One sheep more to the rest in fold,
And left me irresolute, standing sentry　　　15
In the sheepfold's lath-and-plaster entry,
Six feet long by three feet wide,
Partitioned off from the vast inside—
　　I blocked up half of it at least.
No remedy; the rain kept driving.　　　20
　　They eyed me much as some wild beast,
That congregation, still arriving,
Some of them by the main road, white
A long way past me into the night,
Skirting the common, then diverging;　　　25
Not a few suddenly emerging
From the common's self thro' the paling-gaps,
—They house in the gravel pits perhaps,
Where the road stops short with its safeguard border
Of lamps, as tired of such disorder;—　　　30

But the most turned in yet more abruptly
   From a certain squalid knot of alleys,
Where the town's bad blood once slept corruptly,
   Which now the little chapel rallies
And leads into day again,—its priestliness   35
Lending itself to hide their beastliness
So cleverly (thanks in part to the mason),
And putting so cheery a whitewashed face on
Those neophytes too much in lack of it,
   That, where you cross the common as I did,   40
   And meet the party thus presided,
'Mount Zion' with Love-lane at the back of it,
They front you as little disconcerted
As, bound for the hills, her fate averted,
And her wicked people made to mind him,   45
Lot might have marched with Gomorrah behind him.

II

Well, from the road, the lanes or the common,
In came the flock: the fat weary woman,
Panting and bewildered, down-clapping
   Her umbrella with a mighty report,   50
Grounded it by me, wry and flapping,
   A wreck of whalebones; then, with a snort,
Like a startled horse, at the interloper
(Who humbly knew himself improper,
But could not shrink up small enough)   55
—Round to the door, and in,—the gruff
Hinge's invariable scold
Making my very blood run cold.
Prompt in the wake of her, up-pattered
On broken clogs, the many-tattered   60
Little old-faced peaking sister-turned-mother
Of the sickly babe she tried to smother
Somehow up, with its spotted face,
From the cold, on her breast, the one warm place;
She too must stop, wring the poor ends dry   65
Of a draggled shawl, and add thereby
Her tribute to the door-mat, sopping
Already from my own clothes' dropping,

Which yet she seemed to grudge I should stand on:
   Then, stooping down to take off her pattens,   70
She bore them defiantly, in each hand one,
Planted together before her breast
And its babe, as good as a lance in rest.
   Close on her heels, the dingy satins
Of a female something, past me flitted,   75
   With lips as much too white, as a streak
    Lay far too red on each hollow cheek;
And it seemed the very door-hinge pitied
All that was left of a woman once,
Holding at least its tongue for the nonce.   80
Then a tall yellow man, like the Penitent Thief,
With his jaw bound up in a handkerchief,
And eyelids screwed together tight,
Led himself in by some inner light.
And, except from him, from each that entered,   85
   I got the same interrogation—
'What, you the alien, you have ventured
   'To take with us, the elect, your station?
'A carer for none of it, a Gallio!'—
   Thus, plain as print, I read the glance   90
At a common prey, in each countenance
   As of huntsman giving his hounds the tallyho.
And, when the door's cry drowned their wonder,
   The draught, it always sent in shutting,
Made the flame of the single tallow candle   95
In the cracked square lantern I stood under,
   Shoot its blue lip at me, rebutting
As it were, the luckless cause of scandal:
I verily fancied the zealous light
(In the chapel's secret, too!) for spite   100
Would shudder itself clean off the wick,
With the airs of a Saint John's Candlestick.
There was no standing it much longer.
'Good folks,' thought I, as resolve grew stronger,
'This way you perform the Grand-Inquisitor   105
'When the weather sends you a chance visitor?
'You are the men, and wisdom shall die with you,
'And none of the old Seven Churches vie with you!

'But still, despite the pretty perfection
　'To which you carry your trick of exclusiveness,　110
'And, taking God's word under wise protection,
　'Correct its tendency to diffusiveness,
'And bid one reach it over hot ploughshares,—
　'Still, as I say, though you've found salvation,
'If I should choose to cry, as now, "Shares!"—　115
　'See if the best of you bars me my ration!
'I prefer, if you please, for my expounder
'Of the laws of the feast, the feast's own Founder;
'Mine's the same right with your poorest and sickliest
　'Supposing I don the marriage vestiment:　120
　'So, shut your mouth and open your Testament,
'And carve me my portion at your quickliest!'
Accordingly, as a shoemaker's lad
　With wizened face in want of soap,
　And wet apron wound round his waist like a rope,　125
(After stopping outside, for his cough was bad,
To get the fit over, poor gentle creature,
And so avoid disturbing the preacher)
—Passed in, I sent my elbow spikewise
At the shutting door, and entered likewise,　130
Received the hinge's accustomed greeting,
　And crossed the threshold's magic pentacle,
　And found myself in full conventicle,
—To wit, in Zion Chapel Meeting,
On the Christmas-Eve of 'Forty-nine,　135
　Which, calling its flock to their special clover,
　Found all assembled and one sheep over,
Whose lot, as the weather pleased, was mine.

III

I very soon had enough of it.
　The hot smell and the human noises,　140
And my neighbour's coat, the greasy cuff of it,
　Were a pebble-stone that a child's hand poises,
Compared with the pig-of-lead-like pressure
　Of the preaching man's immense stupidity,
As he poured his doctrine forth, full measure,　145
　To meet his audience's avidity.

You needed not the wit of the Sibyl
   To guess the cause of it all, in a twinkling:
   No sooner our friend had got an inkling
Of treasure hid in the Holy Bible,   150
(Whene'er 't was the thought first struck him,
How death, at unawares, might duck him
Deeper than the grave, and quench
The gin-shop's light in hell's grim drench)
Than he handled it so, in fine irreverence,   155
   As to hug the book of books to pieces:
And, a patchwork of chapters and texts in severance,
   Not improved by the private dog's-ears and
      creases,
Having clothed his own soul with, he'd fain see equipt
     yours,—
So tossed you again your Holy Scriptures.   160
And you picked them up, in a sense, no doubt:
   Nay, had but a single face of my neighbours
   Appeared to suspect that the preacher's labours
Were help which the world could be saved without,
'T is odds but I might have borne in quiet   165
A qualm or two at my spiritual diet,
Or (who can tell?) perchance even mustered
   Somewhat to urge in behalf of the sermon:
But the flock sat on, divinely flustered,
   Sniffing, methought, its dew of Hermon   170
With such content in every snuffle,
As the devil inside us loves to ruffle.
My old fat woman purred with pleasure,
   And thumb round thumb went twirling faster,
While she, to his periods keeping measure,   175
   Maternally devoured the pastor.
The man with the handkerchief untied it,
Showed us a horrible wen inside it,
Gave his eyelids yet another screwing,
And rocked himself as the woman was doing.   180
The shoemaker's lad, discreetly choking,
Kept down his cough. 'T was too provoking!
My gorge rose at the nonsense and stuff of it;
   So, saying like Eve when she plucked the apple,

'I wanted a taste, and now there's enough of it,'   185
I flung out of the little chapel.

IV

There was a lull in the rain, a lull
   In the wind too; the moon was risen,
And would have shone out pure and full,
   But for the ramparted cloud-prison,   190
Block on block built up in the West,
For what purpose the wind knows best,
Who changes his mind continually.
And the empty other half of the sky
Seemed in its silence as if it knew   195
What, any moment, might look through
A chance gap in that fortress massy:—
   Through its fissures you got hints
   Of the flying moon, by the shifting tints,
Now, a dull lion-colour, now, brassy   200
Burning to yellow, and whitest yellow,
Like furnace-smoke just ere flames bellow,
All a-simmer with intense strain
To let her through,—then blank again,
At the hope of her appearance failing.   205
Just by the chapel, a break in the railing
Shows a narrow path directly across;
'T is ever dry walking there, on the moss—
Besides, you go gently all the way uphill.
   I stooped under and soon felt better;   210
My head grew lighter, my limbs more supple,
   As I walked on, glad to have slipt the fetter.
My mind was full of the scene I had left,
   That placid flock, that pastor vociferant,
   —How this outside was pure and different!   215
The sermon, now—what a mingled weft
Of good and ill! Were either less,
   Its fellow had coloured the whole distinctly;
But alas for the excellent earnestness,
   And the truths, quite true if stated succinctly,   220
But as surely false, in their quaint presentment,
However to pastor and flock's contentment!

Say rather, such truths looked false to your eyes,
  With his provings and parallels twisted and twined,
Till how could you know them, grown double their size   225
  In the natural fog of the good man's mind,
Like yonder spots of our roadside lamps,
Haloed about with the common's damps?
Truth remains true, the fault's in the prover;
  The zeal was good, and the aspiration;   230
And yet, and yet, yet, fifty times over,
  Pharaoh received no demonstration,
By his Baker's dream of Baskets Three,
Of the doctrine of the Trinity,—
Although, as our preacher thus embellished it,   235
Apparently his hearers relished it
With so unfeigned a gust—who knows if
They did not prefer our friend to Joseph?
But so it is everywhere, one way with all of them!
  These people have really felt, no doubt,   240
A something, the motion they style the Call of them;
  And this is their method of bringing about,
By a mechanism of words and tones,
(So many texts in so many groans)
A sort of reviving and reproducing,   245
  More or less perfectly, (who can tell?)
The mood itself, which strengthens by using;
  And how that happens, I understand well.
A tune was born in my head last week,
Out of the thump-thump and shriek-shriek   250
  Of the train, as I came by it, up from Manchester;
And when, next week, I take it back again,
My head will sing to the engine's clack again,
  While it only makes my neighbour's haunches stir,
—Finding no dormant musical sprout   255
In him, as in me, to be jolted out.
'T is the taught already that profits by teaching;
He gets no more from the railway's preaching
  Than, from this preacher who does the rail's office, I:
Whom therefore the flock cast a jealous eye on.   260
Still, why paint over their door 'Mount Zion,'
  To which all flesh shall come, saith the prophecy?

V

But wherefore be harsh on a single case?
 After how many modes, this Christmas-Eve,
Does the self-same weary thing take place?   265
 The same endeavour to make you believe,
And with much the same effect, no more:
 Each method abundantly convincing,
As I say, to those convinced before,
 But scarce to be swallowed without wincing   270
By the not-as-yet-convinced. For me,
I have my own church equally:
And in this church my faith sprang first!
 (I said, as I reached the rising ground,
And the wind began again, with a burst   275
 Of rain in my face, and a glad rebound
From the heart beneath, as if, God speeding me,
I entered his church-door, nature leading me)
—In youth I looked to these very skies,
And probing their immensities,   280
I found God there, his visible power;
 Yet felt in my heart, amid all its sense
 Of the power, an equal evidence
That his love, there too, was the nobler dower.
For the loving worm within its clod,   285
Were diviner than a loveless god
Amid his worlds, I will dare to say.
 You know what I mean: God's all, man's nought:
 But also, God, whose pleasure brought
Man into being, stands away   290
 As it were a handbreadth off, to give
Room for the newly-made to live,
And look at him from a place apart,
And use his gifts of brain and heart,
Given, indeed, but to keep for ever.   295
Who speaks of man, then, must not sever
Man's very elements from man,
Saying, 'But all is God's'—whose plan
Was to create man and then leave him
Able, his own word saith, to grieve him,   300
But able to glorify him too,

As a mere machine could never do,
That prayed or praised, all unaware
Of its fitness for aught but praise and prayer,
Made perfect as a thing of course.   305
Man, therefore, stands on his own stock
Of love and power as a pin-point rock:
And, looking to God who ordained divorce
Of the rock from his boundless continent,
Sees, in his power made evident,   310
Only excess by a million-fold
O'er the power God gave man in the mould.
For, note: man's hand, first formed to carry
A few pounds' weight, when taught to marry
Its strength with an engine's, lifts a mountain,   315
    —Advancing in power by one degree;
    And why count steps through eternity?
But love is the ever-springing fountain:
Man may enlarge or narrow his bed
For the water's play, but the water-head—   320
How can he multiply or reduce it?
    As easy create it, as cause it to cease;
He may profit by it, or abuse it,
    But 't is not a thing to bear increase
As power does: be love less or more   325
    In the heart of man, he keeps it shut
    Or opes it wide, as he pleases, but
Love's sum remains what it was before.
So, gazing up, in my youth, at love
As seen through power, ever above   330
All modes which make it manifest,
My soul brought all to a single test—
That he, the Eternal First and Last,
Who, in his power, had so surpassed
All man conceives of what is might,—   335
Whose wisdom, too, showed infinite,
—Would prove as infinitely good;
Would never, (my soul understood,)
With power to work all love desires,
Bestow e'en less than man requires;   340
That he who endlessly was teaching,

Above my spirit's utmost reaching,
What love can do in the leaf or stone,
(So that to master this alone,
This done in the stone or leaf for me,   345
I must go on learning endlessly)
Would never need that I, in turn,
 Should point him out defect unheeded,
And show that God had yet to learn
 What the meanest human creature needed,   350
—Not life, to wit, for a few short years,
Tracking his way through doubts and fears,
While the stupid earth on which I stay
 Suffers no change, but passive adds
 Its myriad years to myriads,   355
Though I, he gave it to, decay,
Seeing death come and choose about me,
And my dearest ones depart without me.
No: love which, on earth, amid all the shows of it,
 Has ever been seen the sole good of life in it,   360
The love, ever growing there, spite of the strife in it,
 Shall arise, made perfect, from death's repose of it.
And I shall behold thee, face to face,
O God, and in thy light retrace
How in all I loved here, still wast thou!   365
Whom pressing to, then, as I fain would now,
I shall find as able to satiate
 The love, thy gift, as my spirit's wonder
Thou art able to quicken and sublimate,
 With this sky of thine, that I now walk under,   370
And glory in thee for, as I gaze
Thus, thus! Oh, let men keep their ways
Of seeking thee in a narrow shrine—
Be this my way! And this is mine!

VI

For lo, what think you? suddenly   375
The rain and the wind ceased, and the sky
Received at once the full fruition
Of the moon's consummate apparition.
The black cloud-barricade was riven,

Ruined beneath her feet, and driven 380
Deep in the West; while, bare and breathless,
  North and South and East lay ready
For a glorious thing that, dauntless, deathless,
  Sprang across them and stood steady.
'T was a moon-rainbow, vast and perfect, 385
From heaven to heaven extending, perfect
As the mother-moon's self, full in face.
It rose, distinctly at the base
  With its seven proper colours chorded,
Which still, in the rising, were compressed, 390
Until at last they coalesced,
  And supreme the spectral creature lorded
In a triumph of whitest white,—
Above which intervened the night.
But above night too, like only the next, 395
  The second of a wondrous sequence,
  Reaching in rare and rarer frequence,
Till the heaven of heavens were circumflexed,
Another rainbow rose, a mightier,
Fainter, flushier and flightier,— 400
Rapture dying along its verge.
Oh, whose foot shall I see emerge,
Whose, from the straining topmost dark,
On to the keystone of that arc?

VII

This sight was shown me, there and then,— 405
Me, one out of a world of men,
Singled forth, as the chance might hap
To another if, in a thunderclap
Where I heard noise and you saw flame,
Some one man knew God called his name. 410
For me, I think I said, 'Appear!
'Good were it to be ever here.
'If thou wilt, let me build to thee
'Service-tabernacles three,
'Where, forever in thy presence, 415
'In ecstatic acquiescence,
'Far alike from thriftless learning

'And ignorance's undiscerning,
'I may worship and remain!'
   Thus at the show above me, gazing   420
With upturned eyes, I felt my brain
   Glutted with the glory, blazing
Throughout its whole mass, over and under
Until at length it burst asunder
And out of it bodily there streamed,   425
The too-much glory, as it seemed,
Passing from out me to the ground,
Then palely serpentining round
Into the dark with mazy error.

VIII

All at once I looked up with terror.   430
He was there.
He himself with his human air.
On the narrow pathway, just before.
I saw the back of him, no more—
He had left the chapel, then, as I.   435
I forgot all about the sky.
No face: only the sight
Of a sweepy garment, vast and white,
With a hem that I could recognize.
I felt terror, no surprise;   440
My mind filled with the cataract,
At one bound of the mighty fact.
'I remember, he did say
   'Doubtless that, to this world's end,
'Where two or three should meet and pray,   445
   'He would be in the midst, their friend;
'Certainly he was there with them!'
   And my pulses leaped for joy
   Of the golden thought without alloy,
That I saw his very vesture's hem.   450
Then rushed the blood back, cold and clear,
With a fresh enhancing shiver of fear;
And I hastened, cried out while I pressed
To the salvation of the vest,
'But not so, Lord! It cannot be   455

'That thou, indeed, art leaving me—
'Me, that have despised thy friends!
'Did my heart make no amends?
'Thou art the love of God—above
'His power, didst hear me place his love,   460
'And that was leaving the world for thee.
'Therefore thou must not turn from me
'As I had chosen the other part!
'Folly and pride o'ercame my heart.
'Our best is bad, nor bears thy test;   465
'Still, it should be our very best.
'I thought it best that thou, the spirit,
    'Be worshipped in spirit and in truth,
'And in beauty, as even we require it—
    'Not in the forms burlesque, uncouth,   470
'I left but now, as scarcely fitted
'For thee: I knew not what I pitied.
'But, all I felt there, right or wrong,
    'What is it to thee, who curest sinning?
'Am I not weak as thou art strong?   475
    'I have looked to thee from the beginning,
'Straight up to thee through all the world
'Which, like an idle scroll, lay furled
'To nothingness on either side:
'And since the time thou wast descried,   480
'Spite of the weak heart, so have I
'Lived ever, and so fain would die,
'Living and dying, thee before!
'But if thou leavest me——'

IX

Less or more,
I suppose that I spoke thus.   485
When,—have mercy, Lord, on us!
The whole face turned upon me full.
    And I spread myself beneath it,
    As when the bleacher spreads, to seethe it
In the cleansing sun, his wool,—   490
Steeps in the flood of noontide whiteness
    Some defiled, discoloured web—

So lay I, saturate with brightness.
　And when the flood appeared to ebb,
Lo, I was walking, light and swift,　　　　　　　　495
　With my senses settling fast and steadying,
But my body caught up in the whirl and drift
　Of the vesture's amplitude, still eddying
On, just before me, still to be followed,
　As it carried me after with its motion:　　　　500
What shall I say?—as a path were hollowed
　And a man went weltering through the ocean,
Sucked along in the flying wake
Of the luminous water-snake.

Darkness and cold were cloven, as through　　　505
I passed, upborne yet walking too.
And I turned to myself at intervals,—
'So he said, so it befalls.
'God who registers the cup
　'Of mere cold water, for his sake　　　　　　510
'To a disciple rendered up,
　'Disdains not his own thirst to slake
'At the poorest love was ever offered:
'And because my heart I proffered,
'With true love trembling at the brim,　　　　　515
'He suffers me to follow him
'For ever, my own way,—dispensed
'From seeking to be influenced
'By all the less immediate ways
　'That earth, in worships manifold,　　　　　　520
'Adopts to reach, by prayer and praise,
　'The garment's hem, which, lo, I hold!'

X

And so we crossed the world and stopped.
　For where am I, in city or plain,
　Since I am 'ware of the world again?　　　　　525
And what is this that rises propped
With pillars of prodigious girth?
Is it really on the earth,
This miraculous Dome of God?
Has the angel's measuring-rod　　　　　　　　530

Which numbered cubits, gem from gem,
'Twixt the gates of the New Jerusalem,
Meted it out,—and what he meted,
Have the sons of men completed?
—Binding, ever as he bade,   535
Columns in the colonnade
With arms wide open to embrace
The entry of the human race
To the breast of . . . what is it, yon building,
Ablaze in front, all paint and gilding,   540
With marble for brick, and stones of price
For garniture of the edifice?
Now I see; it is no dream;
It stands there and it does not seem:
For ever, in pictures, thus it looks,   545
And thus I have read of it in books
Often in England, leagues away,
And wondered how these fountains play,
Growing up eternally
Each to a musical water-tree,   550
Whose blossoms drop, a glittering boon,
Before my eyes, in the light of the moon,
To the granite lavers underneath.
Liar and dreamer in your teeth!
I, the sinner that speak to you,   555
Was in Rome this night, and stood, and knew
Both this and more. For see, for see,
The dark is rent, mine eye is free
To pierce the crust of the outer wall,
And I view inside, and all there, all,   560
As the swarming hollow of a hive,
The whole Basilica alive!
Men in the chancel, body and nave,
Men on the pillars' architrave,
Men on the statues, men on the tombs   565
With popes and kings in their porphyry wombs,
All famishing in expectation
Of the main-altar's consummation.
For see, for see, the rapturous moment
Approaches, and earth's best endowment   570

Blends with heaven's; the taper-fires
Pant up, the winding brazen spires
Heave loftier yet the baldachin;
The incense-gaspings, long kept in,
Suspire in clouds; the organ blatant   575
Holds his breath and grovels latent,
As if God's hushing finger grazed him,
(Like Behemoth when he praised him)
At the silver bell's shrill tinkling,
Quick cold drops of terror sprinkling   580
On the sudden pavement strewed
With faces of the multitude.
Earth breaks up, time drops away,
In flows heaven, with its new day
Of endless life, when He who trod,   585
Very man and very God,
This earth in weakness, shame and pain,
Dying the death whose signs remain
Up yonder on the accursed tree,—
Shall come again, no more to be   590
Of captivity the thrall,
But the one God, All in all,
King of kings, Lord of lords,
As His servant John received the words,
'I died, and live for evermore!'   595

XI

Yet I was left outside the door.
'Why sit I here on the threshold-stone
'Left till He return, alone
'Save for the garment's extreme fold
'Abandoned still to bless my hold?'   600
My reason, to my doubt, replied,
As if a book were opened wide,
And at a certain page I traced
Every record undefaced,
Added by successive years,—   605
The harvestings of truth's stray ears
Singly gleaned, and in one sheaf
Bound together for belief.

Yes, I said—that he will go
And sit with these in turn, I know.   610
Their faith's heart beats, though her head swims
Too giddily to guide her limbs,
Disabled by their palsy-stroke
From propping mine. Though Rome's gross yoke
Drops off, no more to be endured,   615
Her teaching is not so obscured
By errors and perversities,
That no truth shines athwart the lies:
And he, whose eye detects a spark
Even where, to man's, the whole seems dark,   620
May well see flame where each beholder
Acknowledges the embers smoulder.
But I, a mere man, fear to quit
The clue God gave me as most fit
To guide my footsteps through life's maze,   625
Because himself discerns all ways
Open to reach him: I, a man
Able to mark where faith began
To swerve aside, till from its summit
Judgment drops her damning plummet,   630
Pronouncing such a fatal space
Departed from the founder's base:
He will not bid me enter too,
But rather sit, as now I do,
Awaiting his return outside.   635
—'T was thus my reason straight replied
And joyously I turned, and pressed
The garment's skirt upon my breast,
Until, afresh its light suffusing me,
My heart cried—What has been abusing me   640
That I should wait here lonely and coldly,
Instead of rising, entering boldly,
Baring truth's face, and letting drift
Her veils of lies as they choose to shift?
Do these men praise him? I will raise   645
My voice up to their point of praise!
I see the error; but above
The scope of error, see the love.—

Oh, love of those first Christian days!
—Fanned so soon into a blaze,   650
From the spark preserved by the trampled sect,
That the antique sovereign Intellect
Which then sat ruling in the world,
Like a change in dreams, was hurled
From the throne he reigned upon: 655
You looked up and he was gone.
Gone, his glory of the pen!
—Love, with Greece and Rome in ken,
Bade her scribes abhor the trick
Of poetry and rhetoric,   660
And exult with hearts set free,
In blessed imbecility
Scrawled, perchance, on some torn sheet
Leaving Sallust incomplete.
Gone, his pride of sculptor, painter!   665
—Love, while able to acquaint her
While the thousand statues yet
Fresh from chisel, pictures wet
From brush, she saw on every side,
Chose rather with an infant's pride   670
To frame those portents which impart
Such unction to true Christian Art.
Gone, music too! The air was stirred
By happy wings: Terpander's bird
(That, when the cold came, fled away)   675
Would tarry not the wintry day,—
As more-enduring sculpture must,
Till filthy saints rebuked the gust
With which they chanced to get a sight
Of some dear naked Aphrodite   680
They glanced a thought above the toes of,
By breaking zealously her nose off.
Love, surely, from that music's lingering,
Might have filched her organ-fingering,
Nor chosen rather to set prayings   685
To hog-grunts, praises to horse-neighings.
Love was the startling thing, the new:
Love was the all-sufficient too;

And seeing that, you see the rest:
As a babe can find its mother's breast   690
As well in darkness as in light,
Love shut our eyes, and all seemed right.
True, the world's eyes are open now:
—Less need for me to disallow
Some few that keep Love's zone unbuckled,   695
Peevish as ever to be suckled,
Lulled by the same old baby-prattle
With intermixture of the rattle,
When she would have them creep, stand steady
Upon their feet, or walk already,   700
Not to speak of trying to climb.
I will be wise another time,
And not desire a wall between us,
    When next I see a church-roof cover
So many species of one genus,   705
    All with foreheads bearing *lover*
Written above the earnest eyes of them;
    All with breasts that beat for beauty,
Whether sublimed, to the surprise of them,
    In noble daring, steadfast duty,   710
The heroic in passion, or in action,—
Or, lowered for sense's satisfaction,
To the mere outside of human creatures,
Mere perfect form and faultless features.
What? with all Rome here, whence to levy   715
    Such contributions to their appetite,
With women and men in a gorgeous bevy,
    They take, as it were, a padlock, clap it tight
On their southern eyes, restrained from feeding
On the glories of their ancient reading,   720
On the beauties of their modern singing,
On the wonders of the builder's bringing,
On the majesties of Art around them,—
    And, all these loves, late struggling incessant,
When faith has at last united and bound them,   725
    They offer up to God for a present?
Why, I will, on the whole, be rather proud of it,—
    And, only taking the act in reference

To the other recipients who might have allowed of it
  I will rejoice that God had the preference.   730

XII

So I summed up my new resolves:
  Too much love there can never be.
And where the intellect devolves
  Its function on love exclusively,
I, a man who possesses both,   735
Will accept the provision, nothing loth,
—Will feast my love, then depart elsewhere,
That my intellect may find its share.
And ponder, O soul, the while thou departest,
And see thou applaud the great heart of the artist,   740
Who, examining the capabilities
  Of the block of marble he has to fashion
  Into a type of thought or passion,—
Not always, using obvious facilities,
Shapes it, as any artist can,   745
Into a perfect symmetrical man,
Complete from head to foot of the life-size,
Such as old Adam stood in his wife's eyes,—
But, now and then, bravely aspires to consummate
A Colossus by no means so easy to come at,   750
And uses the whole of his block for the bust,
  Leaving the mind of the public to finish it,
Since cut it ruefully short he must:
On the face alone he expends his devotion,
  He rather would mar than resolve to diminish it,   755
—Saying, 'Applaud me for this grand notion
'Of what a face may be! As for completing it
  'In breast and body and limbs, do that, you!'
All hail! I fancy how, happily meeting it,
  A trunk and legs would perfect the statue,   760
Could man carve so as to answer volition.
  And how much nobler than petty cavils,
  Were a hope to find, in my spirit-travels,
Some artist of another ambition,
Who having a block to carve, no bigger,   765
  Has spent his power on the opposite quest,

And believed to begin at the feet was best—
For so may I see, ere I die, the whole figure!

XIII

No sooner said than out in the night!
My heart beat lighter and more light: 770
And still, as before, I was walking swift,
    With my senses settling fast and steadying,
But my body caught up in the whirl and drift
    Of the vesture's amplitude, still eddying
On just before me, still to be followed,   775
    As it carried me after with its motion,
—What shall I say?—as a path were hollowed,
    And a man went weltering through the ocean,
Sucked along in the flying wake
Of the luminous water-snake.   780

XIV

Alone! I am left alone once more—
    (Save for the garment's extreme fold
    Abandoned still to bless my hold)
Alone, beside the entrance-door
Of a sort of temple,—perhaps a college,   785
—Like nothing I ever saw before
At home in England, to my knowledge.
The tall old quaint irregular town!
    It may be . . . though which, I can't affirm . . . any
    Of the famous middle-age towns of Germany;   790
And this flight of stairs where I sit down,
Is it Halle, Weimar, Cassel, Frankfort
Or Göttingen, I have to thank for 't?
It may be Göttingen,—most likely.
Through the open door I catch obliquely   795
Glimpses of a lecture-hall;
    And not a bad assembly neither,
Ranged decent and symmetrical
    On benches, waiting what 's to see there;
Which, holding still by the vesture's hem,   800
I also resolve to see with them,
Cautious this time how I suffer to slip

The chance of joining in fellowship
With any that call themselves his friends;
   As these folk do, I have a notion.   805
   But hist—a buzzing and emotion!
All settle themselves, the while ascends
By the creaking rail to the lecture-desk,
   Step by step, deliberate
   Because of his cranium's over-freight,   810
Three parts sublime to one grotesque,
If I have proved an accurate guesser,
The hawk-nosed high-cheek-boned Professor.
I felt at once as if there ran
A shoot of love from my heart to the man—   815
That sallow virgin-minded studious
   Martyr to mild enthusiasm,
As he uttered a kind of cough-preludious
   That woke my sympathetic spasm,
(Beside some spitting that made me sorry)   820
And stood, surveying his auditory
With a wan pure look, well nigh celestial,—
   Those blue eyes had survived so much!
   While, under the foot they could not smutch,
Lay all the fleshly and the bestial.   825
Over he bowed, and arranged his notes,
Till the auditory's clearing of throats
Was done with, died into a silence;
   And, when each glance was upward sent,
   Each bearded mouth composed intent,   830
And a pin might be heard drop half a mile hence,—
He pushed back higher his spectacles,
Let the eyes stream out like lamps from cells,
And giving his head of hair—a hake
   Of undressed tow, for colour and quantity—   835
One rapid and impatient shake,
   (As our own Young England adjusts a jaunty tie
When about to impart, on mature digestion,
Some thrilling view of the surplice-question)
—The Professor's grave voice, sweet though
    hoarse,   840
Broke into his Christmas-Eve discourse.

XV

And he began it by observing
  How reason dictated that men
Should rectify the natural swerving,
  By a reversion, now and then,   845
To the well-heads of knowledge, few
And far away, whence rolling grew
The life-stream wide whereat we drink,
Commingled, as we needs must think,
With waters alien to the source;   850
To do which, aimed this eve's discourse;
Since, where could be a fitter time
For tracing backward to its prime
This Christianity, this lake,
This reservoir, whereat we slake,   855
From one or other bank, our thirst?
So, he proposed inquiring first
Into the various sources whence
  This Myth of Christ is derivable;
Demanding from the evidence,   860
  (Since plainly no such life was liveable)
How these phenomena should class?
Whether 't were best opine Christ was,
Or never was at all, or whether
He was and was not, both together—   865
It matters little for the name,
So the idea be left the same.
Only, for practical purpose' sake,
'T was obviously as well to take
The popular story,—understanding   870
  How the ineptitude of the time,
And the penman's prejudice, expanding
  Fact into fable fit for the clime,
Had, by slow and sure degrees, translated it
  Into this myth, this Individuum,—   875
Which, when reason had strained and abated it
  Of foreign matter, left, for residuum,
A Man!—a right true man, however,
Whose work was worthy a man's endeavour:
Work, that gave warrant almost sufficient   880

To his disciples, for rather believing
He was just omnipotent and omniscient,
    As it gives to us, for as frankly receiving
His word, their tradition,—which, though it meant
Something entirely different   885
From all that those who only heard it,
In their simplicity thought and averred it,
Had yet a meaning quite as respectable:
For, among other doctrines delectable,
Was he not surely the first to insist on   890
    The natural sovereignty of our race?—
    Here the lecturer came to a pausing-place.
And while his cough, like a drouthy piston,
Tried to dislodge the husk that grew to him,
I seized the occasion of bidding adieu to him,   895
The vesture still within my hand.

XVI

I could interpret its command.
This time he would not bid me enter
The exhausted air-bell of the Critic.
Truth's atmosphere may grow mephitic   900
When Papist struggles with Dissenter,
Impregnating its pristine clarity,
—One, by his daily fare's vulgarity,
    Its gust of broken meat and garlic;
—One, by his soul's too-much presuming   905
To turn the frankincense's fuming
    And vapours of the candle starlike
Into the cloud her wings she buoys on.
    Each, that thus sets the pure air seething,
    May poison it for healthy breathing—   910
But the Critic leaves no air to poison;
Pumps out with ruthless ingenuity
Atom by atom, and leaves you—vacuity.
Thus much of Christ does he reject?
And what retain? His intellect?   915
What is it I must reverence duly?
Poor intellect for worship, truly,
Which tells me simply what was told

(If mere morality, bereft
Of the God in Christ, be all that's left)   920
Elsewhere by voices manifold;
With this advantage, that the stater
  Made nowise the important stumble
  Of adding, he, the sage and humble,
Was also one with the Creator.   925
You urge Christ's followers' simplicity:
  But how does shifting blame, evade it?
Have wisdom's words no more felicity?
  The stumbling-block, his speech—who laid it?
How comes it that for one found able   930
To sift the truth of it from fable,
Millions believe it to the letter?
Christ's goodness, then—does that fare better?
Strange goodness, which upon the score
  Of being goodness, the mere due   935
Of man to fellow-man, much more
  To God,—should take another view
Of its possessor's privilege,
And bid him rule his race! You pledge
Your fealty to such rule? What, all—   940
From heavenly John and Attic Paul,
And that brave weather-battered Peter,
Whose stout faith only stood completer
For buffets, sinning to be pardoned,
As, more his hands hauled nets, they hardened,—   945
All, down to you, the man of men,
Professing here at Göttingen,
Compose Christ's flock! They, you and I,
Are sheep of a good man! And why?
The goodness,—how did he acquire it?   950
Was it self-gained, did God inspire it?
Choose which; then tell me, on what ground
Should its possessor dare propound
His claim to rise o'er us an inch?
  Were goodness all some man's invention,   955
  Who arbitrarily made mention
What we should follow, and whence flinch,—
What qualities might take the style

s

Of right and wrong,—and had such guessing
Met with as general acquiescing   960
As graced the alphabet erewhile,
When A got leave an Ox to be,
No Camel (quoth the Jews) like G,—
For thus inventing thing and title
Worship were that man's fit requital.   965
But if the common conscience must
Be ultimately judge, adjust
Its apt name to each quality
Already known,—I would decree
Worship for such mere demonstration   970
  And simple work of nomenclature,
Only the day I praised, not nature,
  But Harvey, for the circulation.
I would praise such a Christ, with pride
And joy, that he, as none beside,   975
Had taught us how to keep the mind
God gave him, as God gave his kind,
Freer than they from fleshly taint:
I would call such a Christ our Saint,
As I declare our Poet, him   980
Whose insight makes all others dim:
A thousand poets pried at life,
And only one amid the strife
Rose to be Shakespeare: each shall take
His crown, I'd say, for the world's sake—   985
Though some objected—'Had we seen
'The heart and head of each, what screen
'Was broken there to give them light,
'While in ourselves it shuts the sight,
'We should no more admire, perchance,   990
'That these found truth out at a glance,
'Than marvel how the bat discerns
'Some pitch-dark cavern's fifty turns,
'Led by a finer tact, a gift
'He boasts, which other birds must shift   995
'Without, and grope as best they can.'
No, freely I would praise the man,—
Nor one whit more, if he contended

That gift of his, from God descended.
Ah friend, what gift of man's does not?   1000
No nearer something, by a jot,
Rise an infinity of nothings
   Than one: take Euclid for your teacher:
Distinguish kinds: do crownings, clothings,
   Make that creator which was creature?   1005
Multiply gifts upon man's head,
And what, when all's done, shall be said
But—the more gifted he, I ween!
   That one's made Christ, this other, Pilate,
And this might be all that has been,—   1010
   So what is there to frown or smile at?
What is left for us, save, in growth
Of soul, to rise up, far past both,
From the gift looking to the giver,
And from the cistern to the river,   1015
And from the finite to infinity,
And from man's dust to God's divinity?

                     XVII

Take all in a word: the truth in God's breast
Lies trace for trace upon ours impressed:
Though he is so bright and we so dim,   1020
We are made in his image to witness him:
And were no eye in us to tell,
   Instructed by no inner sense,
The light of heaven from the dark of hell,
   That light would want its evidence,—   1025
Though justice, good and truth were still
Divine, if, by some demon's will,
Hatred and wrong had been proclaimed
Law through the worlds, and right misnamed.
No mere exposition of morality   1030
Made or in part or in totality,
Should win you to give it worship, therefore:
And, if no better proof you will care for,
—Whom do you count the worst man upon earth?
   Be sure, he knows, in his conscience, more   1035
Of what right is, than arrives at birth

In the best man's acts that we bow before:
This last knows better—true, but my fact is,
'T is one thing to know, and another to practise.
And thence I conclude that the real God-function   1040
Is to furnish a motive and injunction
For practising what we know already.
And such an injunction and such a motive
As the God in Christ, do you waive, and 'heady,
'High-minded,' hang your tablet-votive   1045
Outside the fane on a finger-post?
Morality to the uttermost,
Supreme in Christ as we all confess,
Why need we prove would avail no jot
To make him God, if God he were not?   1050
What is the point where himself lays stress?
Does the precept run 'Believe in good,
'In justice, truth, now understood
'For the first time?'—or, 'Believe in me,
'Who lived and died, yet essentially   1055
'Am Lord of Life?' Whoever can take
The same to his heart and for mere love's sake
Conceive of the love,—that man obtains
A new truth; no conviction gains
Of an old one only, made intense   1060
By a fresh appeal to his faded sense.

XVIII

Can it be that he stays inside?
    Is the vesture left me to commune with?
    Could my soul find aught to sing in tune with
Even at this lecture, if she tried?   1065
Oh, let me at lowest sympathize
With the lurking drop of blood that lies
In the desiccated brain's white roots
Without throb for Christ's attributes,
As the lecturer makes his special boast!   1070
If love's dead there, it has left a ghost.
Admire we, how from heart to brain
    (Though to say so strike the doctors dumb)
One instinct rises and falls again,

Restoring the equilibrium.   1075
And how when the Critic had done his best,
And the pearl of price, at reason's test,
Lay dust and ashes levigable
On the Professor's lecture-table,—
When we looked for the inference and monition   1080
That our faith, reduced to such condition,
Be swept forthwith to its natural dust-hole,—
    He bids us, when we least expect it,
Take back our faith,—if it be not just whole,
    Yet a pearl indeed, as his tests affect it,   1085
Which fact pays damage done rewardingly,
So, prize we our dust and ashes accordingly!
'Go home and venerate the myth
'I thus have experimented with—
'This man, continue to adore him   1090
'Rather than all who went before him,
'And all who ever followed after!'—
    Surely for this I may praise you, my brother!
Will you take the praise in tears or laughter?
    That's one point gained: can I compass
            another?   1095
Unlearned love was safe from spurning—
Can't we respect your loveless learning?
Let us at least give learning honour!
What laurels had we showered upon her,
Girding her loins up to perturb   1100
Our theory of the Middle Verb;
Or Turk-like brandishing a scimitar
O'er anapæsts in comic-trimeter;
Or curing the halt and maimed 'Iketides,'
While we lounged on at our indebted ease: 1105
Instead of which, a tricksy demon
Sets her at Titus or Philemon!
When ignorance wags his ears of leather
And hates God's word, 't is altogether;
Nor leaves he his congenial thistles   1110
To go and browse on Paul's Epistles.
—And you, the audience, who might ravage
The world wide, enviably savage,

Nor heed the cry of the retriever,
More than Herr Heine (before his fever),—   1115
I do not tell a lie so arrant
    As say my passion's wings are furled up,
And, without plainest heavenly warrant,
    I were ready and glad to give the world up—
But still, when you rub brow meticulous,   1120
    And ponder the profit of turning holy
    If not for God's, for your own sake solely,
—God forbid I should find you ridiculous!
Deduce from this lecture all that eases you,
Nay, call yourselves, if the calling pleases you,   1125
'Christians,'—abhor the deist's pravity,—
Go on, you shall no more move my gravity
Than, when I see boys ride a-cockhorse,
I find it in my heart to embarrass them
By hinting that their stick's a mock horse,   1130
And they really carry what they say carries them.

XIX

So sat I talking with my mind.
    I did not long to leave the door
    And find a new church, as before,
But rather was quiet and inclined   1135
To prolong and enjoy the gentle resting
From further tracking and trying and testing.
'This tolerance is a genial mood!'
(Said I, and a little pause ensued).
'One trims the bark 'twixt shoal and shelf,   1140
    'And sees, each side, the good effects of it,
'A value for religion's self,
    'A carelessness about the sects of it.
'Let me enjoy my own conviction,
    'Not watch my neighbour's faith with fretfulness,   1145
'Still spying there some dereliction
    'Of truth, perversity, forgetfulness!
'Better a mild indifferentism,
    'Teaching that both our faiths (though duller
'His shine through a dull spirit's prism)   1150
    'Originally had one colour!

'Better pursue a pilgrimage
  'Through ancient and through modern times
  'To many peoples, various climes.
'Where I may see saint, savage, sage   1155
'Fuse their respective creeds in one
'Before the general Father's throne!'

XX

—'T was the horrible storm began afresh!
The black night caught me in his mesh,
Whirled me up, and flung me prone.   1160
I was left on the college-step alone.
I looked, and far there, ever fleeting
Far, far away, the receding gesture,
And looming of the lessening vesture!—
Swept forward from my stupid hand,   1165
While I watched my foolish heart expand
In the lazy glow of benevolence,
  O'er the various modes of man's belief.
I sprang up with fear's vehemence.
    Needs must there be one way, our chief   1170
Best way of worship: let me strive
To find it, and when found, contrive
My fellows also take their share!
This constitutes my earthly care:
God's is above it and distinct.   1175
For I, a man, with men am linked
And not a brute with brutes; no gain
That I experience, must remain
Unshared: but should my best endeavour
To share it, fail—subsisteth ever   1180
God's care above, and I exult
That God, by God's own ways occult,
May—doth, I will believe—bring back
All wanderers to a single track.
Meantime, I can but testify   1185
God's care for me—no more, can I—
It is but for myself I know;
  The world rolls witnessing around me
  Only to leave me as it found me;

Men cry there, but my ear is slow: 1190
Their races flourish or decay
—What boots it, while yon lucid way
Loaded with stars divides the vault?
But soon my soul repairs its fault
When, sharpening sense's hebetude,   1195
She turns on my own life! So viewed,
No mere mote's-breadth but teems immense
With witnessings of providence:
And woe to me if when I look
Upon that record, the sole book   1200
Unsealed to me, I take no heed
Of any warning that I read!
Have I been sure, this Christmas-Eve,
God's own hand did the rainbow weave,
Whereby the truth from heaven slid   1205
Into my soul?—I cannot bid
The world admit he stooped to heal
My soul, as if in a thunder-peal
Where one heard noise, and one saw flame,
I only knew he named my name: 1210
But what is the world to me, for sorrow
Or joy in its censure, when to-morrow
It drops the remark, with just-turned head
Then, on again, 'That man is dead'?
Yes, but for me—my name called,—drawn   1215
As a conscript's lot from the lap's black yawn,
He has dipt into on a battle-dawn:
Bid out of life by a nod, a glance,—
Stumbling, mute-mazed, at nature's chance,—
With a rapid finger circled round,   1220
Fixed to the first poor inch of ground
To fight from, where his foot was found;
Whose ear but a minute since lay free
To the wide camp's buzz and gossipry—
Summoned, a solitary man   1225
To end his life where his life began,
From the safe glad rear, to the dreadful van!
Soul of mine, hadst thou caught and held
By the hem of the vesture!—

XXI

And I caught
At the flying robe, and unrepelled   1230
Was lapped again in its folds full-fraught
With warmth and wonder and delight,
God's mercy being infinite.
For scarce had the words escaped my tongue,
When, at a passionate bound, I sprung,   1235
Out of the wandering world of rain,
Into the little chapel again.

XXII

How else was I found there, bolt upright
On my bench, as if I had never left it?
—Never flung out on the common at night,   1240
Nor met the storm and wedge-like cleft it,
Seen the raree-show of Peter's successor,
Or the laboratory of the Professor!
For the Vision, that was true, I wist,
True as that heaven and earth exist.   1245
There sat my friend, the yellow and tall,
With his neck and its wen in the selfsame place;
Yet my nearest neighbour's cheek showed gall.
She had slid away a contemptuous space:
And the old fat woman, late so placable,   1250
Eyed me with symptoms, hardly mistakable,
Of her milk of kindness turning rancid.
In short, a spectator might have fancied
That I had nodded, betrayed by slumber,
Yet kept my seat, a warning ghastly,   1255
Through the heads of the sermon, nine in number,
And woke up now at the tenth and lastly.
But again, could such disgrace have happened?
Each friend at my elbow had surely nudged it;
And, as for the sermon, where did my nap end?   1260
Unless I heard it, could I have judged it?
Could I report as I do at the close,
First, the preacher speaks through his nose:
Second, his gesture is too emphatic:
Thirdly, to waive what's pedagogic,   1265

The subject-matter itself lacks logic:
Fourthly, the English is ungrammatic.
Great news! the preacher is found no Pascal,
Whom, if I pleased, I might to the task call
Of making square to a finite eye   1270
The circle of infinity,
And find so all-but-just-succeeding!
Great news! the sermon proves no reading
Where bee-like in the flowers I bury me,
Like Taylor's the immortal Jeremy!   1275
And now that I know the very worst of him,
What was it I thought to obtain at first of him?
Ha! Is God mocked, as he asks?
Shall I take on me to change his tasks,
And dare, despatched to a river-head   1280
   For a simple draught of the element,
Neglect the thing for which he sent,
   And return with another thing instead?—
Saying, 'Because the water found
'Welling up from underground,   1285
'Is mingled with the taints of earth,
'While thou, I know, dost laugh at dearth,
'And couldst, at wink or word, convulse
'The world with the leap of a river-pulse,—
'Therefore I turned from the oozings muddy,   1290
   'And bring thee a chalice I found, instead:
'See the brave veins in the breccia ruddy!
   'One would suppose that the marble bled.
'What matters the water? A hope I have nursed:
'The waterless cup will quench my thirst.'   1295
—Better have knelt at the poorest stream
   That trickles in pain from the straitest rift!
For the less or the more is all God's gift,
Who blocks up or breaks wide the granite-seam.
And here, is there water or not, to drink?   1300
   I then, in ignorance and weakness,
Taking God's help, have attained to think
   My heart does best to receive in meekness
That mode of worship, as most to his mind,
Where earthly aids being cast behind,   1305

His All in All appears serene
With the thinnest human veil between,
Letting the mystic lamps, the seven,
   The many motions of his spirit,
Pass, as they list, to earth from heaven.   1310
   For the preacher's merit or demerit,
It were to be wished the flaws were fewer
   In the earthen vessel, holding treasure
Which lies as safe in a golden ewer;
   But the main thing is, does it hold good measure?   1315
Heaven soon sets right all other matters!—
   Ask, else, these ruins of humanity,
This flesh worn out to rags and tatters,
   This soul at struggle with insanity,
Who thence take comfort—can I doubt?—   1320
Which an empire gained, were a loss without.
May it be mine! And let us hope
That no worse blessing befall the Pope,
Turned sick at last of to-day's buffoonery,
   Of posturings and petticoatings,   1325
   Beside his Bourbon bully's gloatings
In the bloody orgies of drunk poltroonery!
Nor may the Professor forego its peace
   At Göttingen presently, when, in the dusk
Of his life, if his cough, as I fear, should increase,   1330
   Prophesied of by that horrible husk—
When thicker and thicker the darkness fills
The world through his misty spectacles,
And he gropes for something more substantial
   Than a fable, myth or personification,—   1335
May Christ do for him what no mere man shall,
   And stand confessed as the God of salvation!
Meantime, in the still recurring fear
   Lest myself, at unawares, be found,
    While attacking the choice of my neighbours
     round,   1340
With none of my own made—I choose here!
The giving out of the hymn reclaims me;
I have done: and if any blames me,
Thinking that merely to touch in brevity

The topics I dwell on, were unlawful,—   1345
Or worse, that I trench, with undue levity,
  On the bounds of the holy and the awful,—
I praise the heart, and pity the head of him,
And refer myself to THEE, instead of him,
Who head and heart alike discernest,   1350
  Looking below light speech we utter,
  When frothy spume and frequent sputter
Prove that the soul's depths boil in earnest!
May truth shine out, stand ever before us!
I put up pencil and join chorus   1355
To Hepzibah Tune, without further apology,
  The last five verses of the third section
  Of the seventeenth hymn of Whitfield's Collection,
To conclude with the doxology.

EASTER-DAY

I

How very hard it is to be
A Christian! Hard for you and me,
—Not the mere task of making real
That duty up to its ideal,
Effecting thus, complete and whole,   5
A purpose of the human soul—
For that is always hard to do;
But hard, I mean, for me and you
To realize it, more or less,
With even the moderate success   10
Which commonly repays our strife
To carry out the aims of life.
'This aim is greater,' you will say,
'And so more arduous every way.'
—But the importance of their fruits   15
Still proves to man, in all pursuits,
Proportional encouragement.
'Then, what if it be God's intent
'That labour to this one result

'Should seem unduly difficult?'   20
Ah, that's a question in the dark—
And the sole thing that I remark
Upon the difficulty, this;
We do not see it where it is,
At the beginning of the race: 25
As we proceed, it shifts its place,
And where we looked for crowns to fall,
We find the tug's to come,—that's all.

II

At first you say, 'The whole, or chief
'Of difficulties, is belief.   30
'Could I believe once thoroughly,
'The rest were simple. What? Am I
'An idiot, do you think,—a beast?
'Prove to me, only that the least
'Command of God is God's indeed,   35
'And what injunction shall I need
'To pay obedience? Death so nigh,
'When time must end, eternity
'Begin,—and cannot I compute,
'Weigh loss and gain together, suit   40
'My actions to the balance drawn,
'And give my body to be sawn
'Asunder, hacked in pieces, tied
'To horses, stoned, burned, crucified,
'Like any martyr of the list?   45
'How gladly!—if I make acquist,
'Through the brief minute's fierce annoy,
'Of God's eternity of joy.'

III

—And certainly you name the point
Whereon all turns: for could you joint   50
This flexile finite life once tight
Into the fixed and infinite,
You, safe inside, would spurn what's out,
With carelessness enough, no doubt—
Would spurn mere life: but when time brings   55

To their next stage your reasonings,
Your eyes, late wide, begin to wink
Nor see the path so well, I think.

IV

You say, 'Faith may be, one agrees,
'A touchstone for God's purposes,   60
'Even as ourselves conceive of them.
'Could he acquit us or condemn
'For holding what no hand can loose,
'Rejecting when we can't but choose?
'As well award the victor's wreath   65
'To whosoever should take breath
'Duly each minute while he lived—
'Grant heaven, because a man contrived
'To see its sunlight every day
'He walked forth on the public way.   70
'You must mix some uncertainty
'With faith, if you would have faith be.
'Why, what but faith, do we abhor
'And idolize each other for—
'Faith in our evil or our good,   75
'Which is or is not understood
'Aright by those we love or those
'We hate, thence called our friends or foes?
'Your mistress saw your spirit's grace,
'When, turning from the ugly face,   80
'I found belief in it too hard;
'And she and I have our reward.
'—Yet here a doubt peeps: well for us
'Weak beings, to go using thus
'A touchstone for our little ends,   85
'Trying with faith the foes and friends;
'—But God, bethink you! I would fain
'Conceive of the Creator's reign
'As based upon exacter laws
'Than creatures build by with applause.   90
'In all God's acts—(as Plato cries
'He doth)—he should geometrize.
'Whence, I desiderate . . .'

V

                    I see!
You would grow as a natural tree,
Stand as a rock, soar up like fire.   95
The world's so perfect and entire,
Quite above faith, so right and fit!
Go there, walk up and down in it!
No. The creation travails, groans—
Contrive your music from its moans,   100
Without or let or hindrance, friend!
That's an old story, and its end
As old—you come back (be sincere)
With every question you put here
(Here where there once was, and is still,   105
We think, a living oracle,
Whose answers you stand carping at)
This time flung back unanswered flat,—
Beside, perhaps, as many more
As those that drove you out before,   110
Now added, where was little need.
Questions impossible, indeed,
To us who sat still, all and each
Persuaded that our earth had speech,
Of God's, writ down, no matter if   115
In cursive type or hieroglyph,—
Which one fact freed us from the yoke
Of guessing why He never spoke.
You come back in no better plight
Than when you left us,—am I right?   120

VI

So, the old process, I conclude,
Goes on, the reasoning's pursued
Further. You own, ' 'T is well averred,
'A scientific faith's absurd,
'—Frustrates the very end 't was meant   125
'To serve. So, I would rest content
'With a mere probability,
'But, probable; the chance must lie

'Clear on one side,—lie all in rough,
'So long as there be just enough   130
'To pin my faith to, though it hap
'Only at points: from gap to gap
'One hangs up a huge curtain so,
'Grandly, nor seeks to have it go
'Foldless and flat along the wall.   135
'What care I if some interval
'Of life less plainly may depend
'On God? I'd hang there to the end;
'And thus I should not find it hard
'To be a Christian and debarred   140
'From trailing on the earth, till furled
'Away by death.—Renounce the world!
'Were that a mighty hardship? Plan
'A pleasant life, and straight some man
'Beside you, with, if he thought fit,   145
'Abundant means to compass it,
'Shall turn deliberate aside
'To try and live as, if you tried
'You clearly might, yet most despise.
'One friend of mine wears out his eyes,   150
'Slighting the stupid joys of sense,
'In patient hope that, ten years hence,
' "Somewhat completer," he may say,
' "My list of *coleoptera!*"
'While just the other who most laughs   155
'At him, above all epitaphs
'Aspires to have his tomb describe
'Himself as sole among the tribe
'Of snuffbox-fanciers, who possessed
'A Grignon with the Regent's crest.   160
'So that, subduing, as you want,
'Whatever stands predominant
'Among my earthly appetites
'For tastes and smells and sounds and sights,
'I shall be doing that alone,   165
'To gain a palm-branch and a throne,
'Which fifty people undertake
'To do, and gladly, for the sake

'Of giving a Semitic guess,
'Or playing pawns at blindfold chess.'   170

VII

Good: and the next thing is,—look round
For evidence enough! 'T is found,
No doubt: as is your sort of mind,
So is your sort of search: you'll find
What you desire, and that's to be   175
A Christian. What says history?
How comforting a point it were
To find some mummy-scrap declare
There lived a Moses! Better still,
Prove Jonah's whale translatable   180
Into some quicksand of the seas,
Isle, cavern, rock, or what you please,
That faith might flap her wings and crow
From such an eminence! Or, no—
The human heart's best; you prefer   185
Making that prove the minister
To truth; you probe its wants and needs,
And hopes and fears, then try what creeds
Meet these most aptly,—resolute
That faith plucks such substantial fruit   190
Wherever these two correspond,
She little needs to look beyond,
And puzzle out who Orpheus was,
Or Dionysius Zagrias.
You'll find sufficient, as I say,   195
To satisfy you either way;
You wanted to believe; your pains
Are crowned—you do: and what remains?
'Renounce the world!'—Ah, were it done
By merely cutting one by one   200
Your limbs off, with your wise head last,
How easy were it!—how soon past,
If once in the believing mood!
'Such is man's usual gratitude,
'Such thanks to God do we return,   205
'For not exacting that we spurn

'A single gift of life, forego
'One real gain,—only taste them so
'With gravity and temperance,
'That those mild virtues may enhance   210
'Such pleasures, rather than abstract—
'Last spice of which, will be the fact
'Of love discerned in every gift;
'While, when the scene of life shall shift,
'And the gay heart be taught to ache,   215
'As sorrows and privations take
'The place of joy,—the thing that seems
'Mere misery, under human schemes,
'Becomes, regarded by the light
'Of love, as very near, or quite   220
'As good a gift as joy before.
'So plain is it that, all the more
'A dispensation's merciful,
'More pettishly we try and cull
'Briers, thistles, from our private plot,   225
'To mar God's ground where thorns are not!'

VIII

Do you say this, or I?—Oh, you!
Then, what, my friend?—(thus I pursue
Our parley)—you indeed opine
That the Eternal and Divine   230
Did, eighteen centuries ago,
In very truth . . . Enough! you know
The all-stupendous tale,—that Birth,
That Life, that Death! And all, the earth
Shuddered at,—all, the heavens grew black   235
Rather than see; all, nature's rack
And throe at dissolution's brink
Attested,—all took place, you think,
Only to give our joys a zest,
And prove our sorrows for the best?   240
We differ, then! Were I, still pale
And heartstruck at the dreadful tale,
Waiting to hear God's voice declare
What horror followed for my share,

As implicated in the deed, 245
Apart from other sins,—concede
That if He blacked out in a blot
My brief life's pleasantness, 't were not
So very disproportionate!
Or there might be another fate— 250
I certainly could understand
(If fancies were the thing in hand)
How God might save, at that day's price,
The impure in their impurities,
Give licence formal and complete 255
To choose the fair and pick the sweet.
But there be certain words, broad, plain,
Uttered again and yet again,
Hard to mistake or overgloss—
Announcing this world's gain for loss, 260
And bidding us reject the same:
The whole world lieth (they proclaim)
In wickedness,—come out of it!
Turn a deaf ear, if you think fit,
But I who thrill through every nerve 265
At thought of what deaf ears deserve—
How do you counsel in the case?

IX

'I'd take, by all means, in your place,
'The safe side, since it so appears:
'Deny myself, a few brief years, 270
'The natural pleasure, leave the fruit
'Or cut the plant up by the root.
'Remember what a martyr said
'On the rude tablet overhead!
' "I was born sickly, poor and mean, 275
' "A slave: no misery could screen
' "The holders of the pearl of price
' "From Cæsar's envy; therefore twice
' "I fought with beasts, and three times saw
' "My children suffer by his law; 280
' "At last my own release was earned:
' "I was some time in being burned,

' "But at the close a Hand came through
' "The fire above my head, and drew
' "My soul to Christ, whom now I see.   285
' "Sergius, a brother, writes for me
' "This testimony on the wall—
' "For me, I have forgot it all."
'You say right; this were not so hard!
'And since one nowise is debarred   290
'From this, why not escape some sins
'By such a method?'

X

               Then begins
To the old point revulsion new—
(For 't is just this I bring you to)
If after all we should mistake,   295
And so renounce life for the sake
Of death and nothing else? You hear
Each friend we jeered at, send the jeer
Back to ourselves with good effect—
'There were my beetles to collect!   300
'My box—a trifle, I confess,
'But here I hold it, ne'ertheless!'
Poor idiots, (let us pluck up heart
And answer) we, the better part
Have chosen, though 't were only hope,—   305
Nor envy moles like you that grope
Amid your veritable muck,
More than the grasshoppers would truck,
For yours, their passionate life away,
That spends itself in leaps all day   310
To reach the sun, you want the eyes
To see, as they the wings to rise
And match the noble hearts of them!
Thus the contemner we contemn,—
And, when doubt strikes us, thus we ward   315
Its stroke off, caught upon our guard,
—Not struck enough to overturn
Our faith, but shake it—make us learn
What I began with, and, I wis,

End, having proved,—how hard it is   320
To be a Christian!

XI

'Proved, or not,
'Howe'er you wis, small thanks, I wot,
'You get of mine, for taking pains
'To make it hard to me. Who gains
'By that, I wonder? Here I live   325
'In trusting ease; and here you drive
'At causing me to lose what most
'Yourself would mourn for had you lost!'

XII

But, do you see, my friend, that thus
You leave Saint Paul for Æschylus?   330
—Who made his Titan's arch-device
The giving men *blind hopes* to spice
The meal of life with, else devoured
In bitter haste, while lo, death loured
Before them at the platter's edge!   335
If faith should be, as I allege,
Quite other than a condiment
To heighten flavours with, or meant
(Like that brave curry of his Grace)
To take at need the victuals' place?   340
If, having dined, you would digest
Besides, and turning to your rest
Should find instead . . .

XIII

Now, you shall see
And judge if a mere foppery
Pricks on my speaking! I resolve   345
To utter—yes, it shall devolve
On you to hear as solemn, strange
And dread a thing as in the range
Of facts,—or fancies, if God will—
E'er happened to our kind! I still   350
Stand in the cloud and, while it wraps
My face, ought not to speak perhaps;

Seeing that if I carry through
My purpose, if my words in you
Find a live actual listener,   355
My story, reason must aver
False after all—the happy chance!
While, if each human countenance
I meet in London day by day,
Be what I fear,—my warnings fray   360
No one, and no one they convert,
And no one helps me to assert
How hard it is to really be
A Christian, and in vacancy
I pour this story!

XIV

　 I commence   365
By trying to inform you, whence
It comes that every Easter-night
As now, I sit up, watch, till light,
Upon those chimney-stacks and roofs,
Give, through my window-pane, grey proofs   370
That Easter-day is breaking slow.
On such a night three years ago,
It chanced that I had cause to cross
The common, where the chapel was,
Our friend spoke of, the other day—   375
You've not forgotten, I dare say.
I fell to musing of the time
So close, the blessed matin-prime
All hearts leap up at, in some guise—
One could not well do otherwise.   380
Insensibly my thoughts were bent
Toward the main point; I overwent
Much the same ground of reasoning
As you and I just now. One thing
Remained, however—one that tasked   385
My soul to answer; and I asked,
Fairly and frankly, what might be
That History, that Faith, to me
—Me there—not me in some domain

Built up and peopled by my brain,   390
Weighing its merits as one weighs
Mere theories for blame or praise,
—The kingcraft of the Lucumons,
Or Fourier's scheme, its pros and cons,—
But my faith there, or none at all.   395
'How were my case, now, did I fall
'Dead here, this minute—should I lie
'Faithful or faithless?' Note that I
Inclined thus ever!—little prone
For instance, when I lay alone   400
In childhood, to go calm to sleep
And leave a closet where might keep
His watch perdue some murderer
Waiting till twelve o'clock to stir,
As good authentic legends tell: 405
'He might: but how improbable!
'How little likely to deserve
'The pains and trial to the nerve
'Of thrusting head into the dark!'—
Urged my old nurse, and bade me mark   410
Beside, that, should the dreadful scout
Really lie hid there, and leap out
At first turn of the rusty key,
Mine were small gain that she could see,
Killed not in bed but on the floor,   415
And losing one night's sleep the more.
I tell you, I would always burst
The door ope, know my fate at first.
This time, indeed, the closet penned
No such assassin: but a friend   420
Rather, peeped out to guard me, fit
For counsel, Common Sense, to wit,
Who said a good deal that might pass,—
Heartening, impartial too, it was,
Judge else: 'For, soberly now,—who   425
'Should be a Christian if not you?'
(Hear how he smoothed me down.) 'One takes
'A whole life, sees what course it makes
'Mainly, and not by fits and starts—

'In spite of stoppage which imparts 430
'Fresh value to the general speed.
'A life, with none, would fly indeed:
'Your progressing is slower—right!
'We deal with progress and not flight.
'Through baffling senses passionate, 435
'Fancies as restless,—with a freight
'Of knowledge cumbersome enough
'To sink your ship when waves grow rough,
'Though meant for ballast in the hold,—
'I find, 'mid dangers manifold, 440
'The good bark answers to the helm
'Where faith sits, easier to o'erwhelm
'Than some stout peasant's heavenly guide,
'Whose hard head could not, if it tried,
'Conceive a doubt, nor understand 445
'How senses hornier than his hand
'Should 'tice the Christian off his guard.
'More happy! But shall we award
'Less honour to the hull which, dogged
'By storms, a mere wreck, waterlogged, 450
'Masts by the board, her bulwarks gone
'And stanchions going, yet bears on,—
'Than to mere life-boats, built to save,
'And triumph o'er the breaking wave?
'Make perfect your good ship as these, 455
'And what were her performances!'
I added—'Would the ship reach home!
'I wish indeed "God's kingdom come—"
'The day when I shall see appear
'His bidding, as my duty, clear 460
'From doubt! And it shall dawn, that day,
'Some future season; Easter may
'Prove, not impossibly, the time—
'Yes, that were striking—fates would chime
'So aptly! Easter-morn, to bring 465
'The Judgment!—deeper in the spring
'Than now, however, when there's snow
'Capping the hills; for earth must show
'All signs of meaning to pursue

'Her tasks as she was wont to do 470
'—The skylark, taken by surprise
'As we ourselves, shall recognize
'Sudden the end. For suddenly
'It comes; the dreadfulness must be
'In that; all warrants the belief— 475
' "At night it cometh like a thief."
'I fancy why the trumpet blows;
'—Plainly, to wake one. From repose
'We shall start up, at last awake
'From life, that insane dream we take 480
'For waking now, because it seems.
'And as, when now we wake from dreams,
'We laugh, while we recall them, "Fool,
' "To let the chance slip, linger cool
' "When such adventure offered! Just 485
' "A bridge to cross, a dwarf to thrust
' "Aside, a wicked mage to stab—
' "And, lo ye, I had kissed Queen Mab!"
'So shall we marvel why we grudged
'Our labour here, and idly judged 490
'Of heaven, we might have gained, but lose!
'Lose? Talk of loss, and I refuse
'To plead at all! You speak no worse
'Nor better than my ancient nurse
'When she would tell me in my youth 495
'I well deserved that shapes uncouth
'Frighted and teased me in my sleep:
'Why could I not in memory keep
'Her precept for the evil's cure?
' "Pinch your own arm, boy, and be sure 500
' "You'll wake forthwith!" '

XV

And as I said
This nonsense, throwing back my head
With light complacent laugh, I found
Suddenly all the midnight round
One fire. The dome of heaven had stood 505
As made up of a multitude

Of handbreadth cloudlets, one vast rack
Of ripples infinite and black,
From sky to sky. Sudden there went,
Like horror and astonishment, 510
A fierce vindictive scribble of red
Quick flame across, as if one said
(The angry scribe of Judgment) 'There—
'Burn it!' And straight I was aware
That the whole ribwork round, minute 515
Cloud touching cloud beyond compute,
Was tinted, each with its own spot
Of burning at the core, till clot
Jammed against clot, and spilt its fire
Over all heaven, which 'gan suspire 520
As fanned to measure equable,—
Just so great conflagrations kill
Night overhead, and rise and sink,
Reflected. Now the fire would shrink
And wither off the blasted face 525
Of heaven, and I distinct might trace
The sharp black ridgy outlines left
Unburned like network—then, each cleft
The fire had been sucked back into,
Regorged, and out it surging flew 530
Furiously, and night writhed inflamed,
Till, tolerating to be tamed
No longer, certain rays world-wide
Shot downwardly. On every side
Caught past escape, the earth was lit; 535
As if a dragon's nostril split
And all his famished ire o'erflowed;
Then, as he winced at his lord's goad,
Back he inhaled: whereat I found
The clouds into vast pillars bound, 540
Based on the corners of the earth,
Propping the skies at top: a dearth
Of fire i' the violet intervals,
Leaving exposed the utmost walls
Of time, about to tumble in 545
And end the world.

XVI

I felt begin
The Judgment-Day: to retrocede
Was too late now. 'In very deed,'
(I uttered to myself) 'that Day!'
The intuition burned away   550
All darkness from my spirit too:
There, stood I, found and fixed, I knew,
Choosing the world. The choice was made;
And naked and disguiseless stayed,
And unevadable, the fact.   555
My brain held all the same compact
Its senses, nor my heart declined
Its office; rather, both combined
To help me in this juncture. I
Lost not a second,—agony   560
Gave boldness: since my life had end
And my choice with it—best defend,
Applaud both! I resolved to say,
'So was I framed by thee, such way
'I put to use thy senses here!   565
'It was so beautiful, so near,
'Thy world,—what could I then but choose
'My part there? Nor did I refuse
'To look above the transient boon
'Of time; but it was hard so soon   570
'As in a short life, to give up
'Such beauty: I could put the cup
'Undrained of half its fulness, by;
'But, to renounce it utterly,
'—That was too hard! Nor did the cry   575
'Which bade renounce it, touch my brain
'Authentically deep and plain
'Enough to make my lips let go.
'But Thou, who knowest all, dost know
'Whether I was not, life's brief while,   580
'Endeavouring to reconcile
'Those lips (too tardily, alas!)
'To letting the dear remnant pass,
'One day,—some drops of earthly good

'Untasted! Is it for this mood,   585
'That Thou, whose earth delights so well,
'Hast made its complement a hell?'

XVII

A final belch of fire like blood,
Overbroke all heaven in one flood
Of doom. Then fire was sky, and sky   590
Fire, and both, one brief ecstasy,
Then ashes. But I heard no noise
(Whatever was) because a voice
Beside me spoke thus, 'Life is done,
'Time ends, Eternity's begun,   595
'And thou art judged for evermore.'

XVIII

I looked up; all seemed as before;
Of that cloud-Tophet overhead
No trace was left: I saw instead
The common round me, and the sky   600
Above, stretched drear and emptily
Of life. 'T was the last watch of night,
Except what brings the morning quite;
When the armed angel, conscience-clear,
His task nigh done, leans o'er his spear   605
And gazes on the earth he guards,
Safe one night more through all its wards,
Till God relieve him at his post.
'A dream—a waking dream at most!'
(I spoke out quick, that I might shake   610
The horrid nightmare off, and wake.)
'The world gone, yet the world is here?
'Are not all things as they appear?
'Is Judgment past for me alone?
'—And where had place the great white throne? 615
'The rising of the quick and dead?
'Where stood they, small and great? Who read
'The sentence from the opened book?'
So, by degrees, the blood forsook
My heart, and let it beat afresh;   620

I knew I should break through the mesh
Of horror, and breathe presently:
When, lo, again, the voice by me!

XIX

I saw . . . Oh brother, 'mid far sands
The palm-tree-cinctured city stands,   625
Bright-white beneath, as heaven, bright-blue,
Leans o'er it, while the years pursue
Their course, unable to abate
Its paradisal laugh at fate!
One morn,—the Arab staggers blind   630
O'er a new tract of death, calcined
To ashes, silence, nothingness,—
And strives, with dizzy wits, to guess
Whence fell the blow. What if, 'twixt skies
And prostrate earth, he should surprise   635
The imaged vapour, head to foot,
Surveying, motionless and mute,
Its work, ere, in a whirlwind rapt
It vanish up again?—So hapt
My chance. HE stood there. Like the smoke   640
Pillared o'er Sodom, when day broke,—
I saw Him. One magnific pall
Mantled in massive fold and fall
His head, and coiled in snaky swathes
About His feet: night's black, that bathes   645
All else, broke, grizzled with despair,
Against the soul of blackness there.
A gesture told the mood within—
That wrapped right hand which based the chin,
That intense meditation fixed   650
On His procedure,—pity mixed
With the fulfilment of decree.
Motionless, thus, He spoke to me,
Who fell before His feet, a mass,
No man now.

XX

       'All is come to pass.   655
'Such shows are over for each soul

'They had respect to. In the roll
'Of Judgment which convinced mankind
'Of sin, stood many, bold and blind,
'Terror must burn the truth into: 660
'Their fate for them!—thou hadst to do
'With absolute omnipotence,
'Able its judgments to dispense
'To the whole race, as every one
'Were its sole object. Judgment done,   665
'God is, thou art,—the rest is hurled
'To nothingness for thee. This world,
'This finite life, thou hast preferred,
'In disbelief of God's plain word,
'To heaven and to infinity.   670
'Here the probation was for thee,
'To show thy soul the earthly mixed
'With heavenly, it must choose betwixt.
'The earthly joys lay palpable,—
'A taint, in each, distinct as well;   675
'The heavenly flitted, faint and rare,
'Above them, but as truly were
'Taintless, so, in their nature, best.
'Thy choice was earth: thou didst attest
' 'T was fitter spirit should subserve   680
'The flesh, than flesh refine to nerve
'Beneath the spirit's play. Advance
'No claim to their inheritance
'Who chose the spirit's fugitive
'Brief gleams, and yearned, "This were to live   685
' "Indeed, if rays, completely pure
' "From flesh that dulls them, could endure,—
' "Not shoot in meteor-light athwart
' "Our earth, to show how cold and swart
' "It lies beneath their fire, but stand   690
' "As stars do, destined to expand,
' "Prove veritable worlds, our home!"
'Thou saidst,—"Let spirit star the dome
' "Of sky, that flesh may miss no peak,
' "No nook of earth,—I shall not seek   695
' "Its service further!" Thou art shut

'Out of the heaven of spirit; glut
'Thy sense upon the world: 't is thine
'For ever—take it!'

XXI

       'How? Is mine,
'The world?' (I cried, while my soul broke   700
Out in a transport.) 'Hast Thou spoke
'Plainly in that? Earth's exquisite
'Treasures of wonder and delight,
'For me?'

XXII

    The austere voice returned,—
'So soon made happy? Hadst thou learned   705
'What God accounteth happiness,
'Thou wouldst not find it hard to guess
'What hell may be his punishment
'For those who doubt if God invent
'Better than they. Let such men rest   710
'Content with what they judged the best.
'Let the unjust usurp at will:
'The filthy shall be filthy still:
'Miser, there waits the gold for thee!
'Hater, indulge thine enmity!   715
'And thou, whose heaven self-ordained
'Was, to enjoy earth unrestrained,
'Do it! Take all the ancient show!
'The woods shall wave, the rivers flow,
'And men apparently pursue   720
'Their works, as they were wont to do,
'While living in probation yet.
'I promise not thou shalt forget
'The past, now gone to its account;
'But leave thee with the old amount   725
'Of faculties, nor less nor more,
'Unvisited, as heretofore,
'By God's free spirit, that makes an end.
'So, once more, take thy world! Expend
'Eternity upon its shows,   730
'Flung thee as freely as one rose

'Out of a summer's opulence,
'Over the Eden-barrier whence
'Thou art excluded. Knock in vain!'

XXIII

I sat up. All was still again.   735
I breathed free: to my heart, back fled
The warmth. 'But, all the world!'—I said.
I stooped and picked a leaf of fern,
And recollected I might learn
From books, how many myriad sorts   740
Of fern exist, to trust reports,
Each as distinct and beautiful
As this, the very first I cull.
Think, from the first leaf to the last!
Conceive, then, earth's resources! Vast   745
Exhaustless beauty, endless change
Of wonder! And this foot shall range
Alps, Andes,—and this eye devour
The bee-bird and the aloe-flower?

XXIV

Then the voice, 'Welcome so to rate   750
'The arras-folds that variegate
'The earth, God's antechamber, well!
'The wise, who waited there, could tell
'By these, what royalties in store
'Lay one step past the entrance-door.   755
'For whom, was reckoned, not too much,
'This life's munificence? For such
'As thou,—a race, whereof scarce one
'Was able, in a million,
'To feel that any marvel lay   760
'In objects round his feet all day;
'Scarce one, in many millions more,
'Willing, if able, to explore
'The secreter, minuter charm!
'—Brave souls, a fern-leaf could disarm   765
'Of power to cope with God's intent,—
'Or scared if the south firmament

'With north-fire did its wings refledge!
'All partial beauty was a pledge
'Of beauty in its plenitude: 770
'But since the pledge sufficed thy mood,
'Retain it! plenitude be theirs
'Who looked above!'

XXV

                    Though sharp despairs
Shot through me, I held up, bore on.
'What matter though my trust were gone   775
'From natural things? Henceforth my part
'Be less with nature than with art!
'For art supplants, gives mainly worth
'To nature; 't is man stamps the earth—
'And I will seek his impress. seek   780
'The statuary of the Greek,
'Italy's painting—there my choice
'Shall fix!'

XXVI

                'Obtain it!' said the voice.
'—The one form with its single act,
'Which sculptors laboured to abstract,   785
'The one face, painters tried to draw,
'With its one look, from throngs they saw.
'And that perfection in their soul,
'These only hinted at? The whole,
'They were but parts of? What each laid   790
'His claim to glory on?—afraid
'His fellow-men should give him rank
'By mere tentatives which he shrank
'Smitten at heart from, all the more,
'That gazers pressed in to adore!   795
' "Shall I be judged by only these?"
'If such his soul's capacities,
'Even while he trod the earth,—think, now,
'What pomp in Buonarroti's brow,
'With its new palace-brain where dwells   800
'Superb the soul, unvexed by cells
'That crumbled with the transient clay!

T

'What visions will his right hand's sway
'Still turn to forms, as still they burst
'Upon him? How will he quench thirst,   805
'Titanically infantine,
'Laid at the breast of the Divine?
'Does it confound thee,—this first page
'Emblazoning man's heritage?—
'Can this alone absorb thy sight,   810
'As pages were not infinite,—
'Like the omnipotence which tasks
'Itself to furnish all that asks
'The soul it means to satiate?
'What was the world, the starry state   815
'Of the broad skies,—what, all displays
'Of power and beauty intermixed,
'Which now thy soul is chained betwixt,—
'What else than needful furniture
'For life's first stage? God's work, be sure,   820
'No more spreads wasted, than falls scant!
'He filled, did not exceed, man's want
'Of beauty in this life. But through
'Life pierce,—and what has earth to do,
'Its utmost beauty's appanage,   825
'With the requirement of next stage?
'Did God pronounce earth "very good"?
'Needs must it be, while understood
'For man's preparatory state;
'Nought here to heighten nor abate;   830
'Transfer the same completeness here,
'To serve a new state's use,—and drear
'Deficiency gapes every side!
'The good, tried once, were bad, retried.
'See the enwrapping rocky niche,   835
'Sufficient for the sleep in which
'The lizard breathes for ages safe:
'Split the mould—and as light would chafe
'The creature's new world-widened sense,
'Dazzled to death at evidence   840
'Of all the sounds and sights that broke
'Innumerous at the chisel's stroke,—

'So, in God's eye, the earth's first stuff
'Was, neither more nor less, enough
'To house man's soul, man's need fulfil.   845
'Man reckoned it immeasurable?
'So thinks the lizard of his vault!
'Could God be taken in default,
'Short of contrivances, by you,—
'Or reached, ere ready to pursue   850
'His progress through eternity?
'That chambered rock, the lizard's world,
'Your easy mallet's blow has hurled
'To nothingness for ever; so,
'Has God abolished at a blow   855
'This world, wherein his saints were pent,—
'Who, though found grateful and content,
'With the provision there, as thou,
'Yet knew he would not disallow
'Their spirit's hunger, felt as well,—   860
'Unsated,—not unsatable,
'As paradise gives proof. Deride
'Their choice now, thou who sit'st outside!'

XXVII

I cried in anguish, 'Mind, the mind,
'So miserably cast behind,   865
'To gain what had been wisely lost!
'Oh, let me strive to make the most
'Of the poor stinted soul, I nipped
'Of budding wings, else now equipped
'For voyage from summer isle to isle!   870
'And though she needs must reconcile
'Ambition to the life on ground,
'Still, I can profit by late found
'But precious knowledge. Mind is best—
'I will seize mind, forego the rest,   875
'And try how far my tethered strength
'May crawl in this poor breadth and length.
'Let me, since I can fly no more,
'At least spin dervish-like about
'(Till giddy rapture almost doubt   880

'I fly) through circling sciences,
'Philosophies and histories!
'Should the whirl slacken there, then verse,
'Fining to music, shall asperse
'Fresh and fresh fire-dew, till I strain   885
'Intoxicate, half-break my chain!
'Not joyless, though more favoured feet
'Stand calm, where I want wings to beat
'The floor. At least earth's bond is broke!

XXVIII

Then, (sickening even while I spoke)   890
'Let me alone! No answer, pray,
'To this! I know what Thou wilt say!
'All still is earth's,—to know, as much
'As feel its truths, which if we touch
'With sense, or apprehend in soul,   895
'What matter? I have reached the goal—
' "Whereto does knowledge serve!" will burn
'My eyes, too sure, at every turn!
'I cannot look back now, nor stake
'Bliss on the race, for running's sake.   900
'The goal's a ruin like the rest!—
'And so much worse thy latter quest,'
(Added the voice) 'that even on earth—
'Whenever, in man's soul, had birth
'Those intuitions, grasps of guess,   905
'Which pull the more into the less,
'Making the finite comprehend
'Infinity,—the bard would spend
'Such praise alone, upon his craft,
'As, when wind-lyres obey the waft,   910
'Goes to the craftsman who arranged
'The seven strings, changed them and rechanged—
'Knowing it was the South that harped.
'He felt his song, in singing, warped;
'Distinguished his and God's part: whence   915
'A world of spirit as of sense
'Was plain to him, yet not too plain,
'Which he could traverse, not remain

'A guest in:—else were permanent
'Heaven on the earth its gleams were meant   920
'To sting with hunger for full light,—
'Made visible in verse, despite
'The veiling weakness,—truth by means
'Of fable, showing while it screens,—
'Since highest truth, man e'er supplied,   925
'Was ever fable on outside.
'Such gleams made bright the earth an age;
'Now the whole sun's his heritage!
'Take up thy world, it is allowed,
'Thou who hast entered in the cloud!'   930

XXIX

Then I—'Behold, my spirit bleeds,
'Catches no more at broken reeds,—
'But lilies flower those reeds above:
'I let the world go, and take love!
'Love survives in me, albeit those   935
'I love be henceforth masks and shows,
'Not living men and women: still
'I mind how love repaired all ill,
'Cured wrong, soothed grief, made earth amends
'With parents, brothers, children, friends!   940
'Some semblance of a woman yet
'With eyes to help me to forget,
'Shall look on me; and I will match
'Departed love with love, attach
'Old memories to new dreams, nor scorn   945
'The poorest of the grains of corn
'I save from shipwreck on this isle,
'Trusting its barrenness may smile
'With happy foodful green one day,
'More precious for the pains. I pray,—   950
'Leave to love, only!'

XXX

At the word,
The form, I looked to have been stirred
With pity and approval, rose
O'er me, as when the headsman throws

Axe over shoulder to make end—   955
I fell prone, letting Him expend
His wrath, while thus the inflicting voice
Smote me. 'Is this thy final choice?
'Love is the best? 'T is somewhat late!
'And all thou dost enumerate   960
'Of power and beauty in the world,
'The mightiness of love was curled
'Inextricably round about.
'Love lay within it and without,
'To clasp thee,—but in vain! Thy soul   965
'Still shrunk from Him who made the whole,
'Still set deliberate aside
'His love!—Now take love! Well betide
'Thy tardy conscience! Haste to take
'The show of love for the name's sake,   970
'Remembering every moment Who,
'Beside creating thee unto
'These ends, and these for thee, was said
'To undergo death in thy stead
'In flesh like thine: so ran the tale.   975
'What doubt in thee could countervail
'Belief in it? Upon the ground
' "That in the story had been found
' "Too much love! How could God love so?"
'He who in all his works below   980
'Adapted to the needs of man,
'Made love the basis of the plan,—
'Did love, as was demonstrated:
'While man, who was so fit instead
'To hate, as every day gave proof,—   985
'Man thought man, for his kind's behoof,
'Both could and did invent that scheme
'Of perfect love: 't would well beseem
'Cain's nature thou wast wont to praise,
'Not tally with God's usual ways!'   990

XXXI

And I cowered deprecatingly—
'Thou Love of God! Or let me die,

'Or grant what shall seem heaven almost!
'Let me not know that all is lost,
'Though lost it be—leave me not tied   995
'To this despair, this corpse-like bride!
'Let that old life seem mine—no more—
'With limitation as before,
'With darkness, hunger, toil, distress:
'Be all the earth a wilderness!   1000
'Only let me go on, go on,
'Still hoping ever and anon
'To reach one eve the Better Land!'

XXXII

Then did the form expand, expand—
I knew Him through the dread disguise   1005
As the whole God within His eyes
Embraced me.

XXXIII

       When I lived again,
The day was breaking,—the grey plain
I rose from, silvered thick with dew.
Was this a vision? False or true?   1010
Since then, three varied years are spent,
And commonly my mind is bent
To think it was a dream—be sure
A mere dream and distemperature—
The last day's watching: then the night,—   1015
The shock of that strange Northern Light
Set my head swimming, bred in me
A dream. And so I live, you see,
Go through the world, try, prove, reject,
Prefer, still struggling to effect   1020
My warfare; happy that I can
Be crossed and thwarted as a man,
Not left in God's contempt apart,
With ghastly smooth life, dead at heart,
Tame in earth's paddock as her prize.   1025
Thank God, she still each method tries
To catch me, who may yet escape,
She knows,—the fiend in angel's shape!

Thank God, no paradise stands barred
To entry, and I find it hard   1030
To be a Christian, as I said!
Still every now and then my head
Raised glad, sinks mournful—all grows drear
Spite of the sunshine, while I fear
And think, 'How dreadful to be grudged   1035
'No ease henceforth, as one that's judged.
'Condemned to earth for ever, shut
'From heaven!'
                    But Easter-Day breaks! But
Christ rises! Mercy every way
Is infinite,—and who can say?   1040

MEN AND WOMEN

MEN AND WOMEN
1855

[*First published in two volumes in 1855. Although the text given here is that of 1888–9, the arrangement follows the original edition. For Browning's later rearrangement and classification of the poems in the collection see Appendix D below.*]

LOVE AMONG THE RUINS

I

WHERE the quiet-coloured end of evening smiles,
    Miles and miles
On the solitary pastures where our sheep
    Half-asleep
Tinkle homeward thro' the twilight, stray or stop   5
    As they crop—
Was the site once of a city great and gay,
    (So they say)
Of our country's very capital, its prince
    Ages since   10
Held his court in, gathered councils, wielding far
    Peace or war.

II

Now,—the country does not even boast a tree,
    As you see,
To distinguish slopes of verdure, certain rills   15
    From the hills
Intersect and give a name to, (else they run
    Into one)
Where the domed and daring palace shot its spires
    Up like fires   20
O'er the hundred-gated circuit of a wall
    Bounding all,
Made of marble, men might march on nor be pressed,
    Twelve abreast.

III

And such plenty and perfection, see, of grass   25
    Never was!
Such a carpet as, this summer time, o'erspreads
    And embeds
Every vestige of the city, guessed alone,
    Stock or stone—   30
Where a multitude of men breathed joy and woe
    Long ago;
Lust of glory pricked their hearts up, dread of shame
    Struck them tame;
And that glory and that shame alike, the gold   35
    Bought and sold.

IV

Now,—the single little turret that remains
    On the plains,
By the caper overrooted, by the gourd
    Overscored,   40
While the patching houseleek's head of blossom winks
    Through the chinks—
Marks the basement whence a tower in ancient time
    Sprang sublime,
And a burning ring, all round, the chariots traced   45
    As they raced,
And the monarch and his minions and his dames
    Viewed the games.

V

And I know, while thus the quiet-coloured eve
    Smiles to leave   50
To their folding, all our many-tinkling fleece
    In such peace,
And the slopes and rills in undistinguished grey
    Melt away—
That a girl with eager eyes and yellow hair   55
    Waits me there
In the turret whence the charioteers caught soul
    For the goal,

When the king looked, where she looks now, breath-
                                            less, dumb
    Till I come. 60

VI

But he looked upon the city, every side,
    Far and wide,
All the mountains topped with temples, all the glades'
    Colonnades,
All the causeys, bridges, aqueducts,—and then, 65
    All the men!
When I do come, she will speak not, she will stand,
    Either hand
On my shoulder, give her eyes the first embrace
    Of my face, 70
Ere we rush, ere we extinguish sight and speech
    Each on each.

VII

In one year they sent a million fighters forth
    South and North,
And they built their gods a brazen pillar high 75
    As the sky,
Yet reserved a thousand chariots in full force—
    Gold, of course.
Oh heart! oh blood that freezes, blood that burns!
    Earth's returns 80
For whole centuries of folly, noise and sin!
    Shut them in,
With their triumphs and their glories and the rest!
    Love is best!

A LOVERS' QUARREL

I

Oh, what a dawn of day!
How the March sun feels like May!
    All is blue again
    After last night's rain,
And the South dries the hawthorn-spray. 5
    Only, my Love's away!
I'd as lief that the blue were grey.

II

Runnels, which rillets swell,
Must be dancing down the dell,
　　With a foaming head　　　　　　　　　　10
　　On the beryl bed
Paven smooth as a hermit's cell;
　　Each with a tale to tell,
Could my Love but attend as well.

III

Dearest, three months ago!　　　　　　　　15
When we lived blocked-up with snow,—
　　When the wind would edge
　　In and in his wedge,
In, as far as the point could go—
　　Not to our ingle, though,　　　　　　　　20
Where we loved each the other so!

IV

Laughs with so little cause!
We devised games out of straws.
　　We would try and trace
　　One another's face　　　　　　　　　　25
In the ash, as an artist draws;
　　Free on each other's flaws,
How we chattered like two church daws!

V

What's in the 'Times?'—a scold
At the emperor deep and cold;　　　　　　30
　　He has taken a bride
　　To his gruesome side,
That's as fair as himself is bold:
　　There they sit ermine-stoled,
And she powders her hair with gold.　　　35

VI

Fancy the Pampas' sheen!
Miles and miles of gold and green
　　Where the sunflowers blow
　　In a solid glow,

And—to break now and then the screen—   40
    Black neck and eyeballs keen,
Up a wild horse leaps between!

VII

 Try, will our table turn?
Lay your hands there light, and yearn
    Till the yearning slips   45
    Thro' the finger-tips
In a fire which a few discern,
    And a very few feel burn,
And the rest, they may live and learn!

VIII

Then we would up and pace,   50
For a change, about the place,
    Each with arm o'er neck:
    'Tis our quarter-deck,
We are seamen in woeful case.
    Help in the ocean-space!   55
Or, if no help, we'll embrace.

IX

See, how she looks now, dressed
In a sledging-cap and vest!
    'T is a huge fur cloak—
    Like a reindeer's yoke   60
Falls the lappet along the breast:
    Sleeves for her arms to rest,
Or to hang, as my Love likes best.

X

Teach me to flirt a fan
As the Spanish ladies can,   65
    Or I tint your lip
    With a burnt stick's tip
And you turn into such a man!'
    Just the two spots that span
Half the bill of the young male swan.   70

XI

Dearest, three months ago
When the mesmerizer Snow
    With his hand's first sweep
    Put the earth to sleep:
'T was a time when the heart could show   75
    All—how was earth to know,
'Neath the mute hand's to-and-fro?

XII

Dearest, three months ago
When we loved each other so,
    Lived and loved the same   80
    Till an evening came
When a shaft from the devil's bow
    Pierced to our ingle-glow,
And the friends were friend and foe!

XIII

Not from the heart beneath—   85
'T was a bubble born of breath,
    Neither sneer nor vaunt,
    Nor reproach nor taunt.
See a word, how it severeth!
    Oh, power of life and death   90
In the tongue, as the Preacher saith!

XIV

Woman, and will you cast
For a word, quite off at last
    Me, your own, your You,—
    Since, as truth is true,   95
I was You all the happy past—
    Me do you leave aghast
With the memories We amassed?

XV

Love, if you knew the light
That your soul casts in my sight,   100
    How I look to you
    For the pure and true,

And the beauteous and the right,—
   Bear with a moment's spite
When a mere mote threats the white!   105

XVI

What of a hasty word?
Is the fleshly heart not stirred
   By a worm's pin-prick
   Where its roots are quick?
See the eye, by a fly's foot blurred—   110
   Ear, when a straw is heard
Scratch the brain's coat of curd!

XVII

Foul be the world or fair
More or less, how can I care?
   'T is the world the same   115
   For my praise or blame,
And endurance is easy there.
   Wrong in the one thing rare—
Oh, it is hard to bear!

XVIII

Here's the spring back or close,   120
When the almond-blossom blows:
   We shall have the word
   In a minor third
There is none but the cuckoo knows:
   Heaps of the guelder-rose!   125
I must bear with it, I suppose.

XIX

Could but November come,
Were the noisy birds struck dumb
   At the warning slash
   Of his driver's-lash—   130
I would laugh like the valiant Thumb
   Facing the castle glum
And the giant's fee-faw-fum!

XX

Then, were the world well stripped
Of the gear wherein equipped   135
    We can stand apart,
    Heart dispense with heart
In the sun, with the flowers unnipped,—
    Oh, the world's hangings ripped,
We were both in a bare-walled crypt!   140

XXI

Each in the crypt would cry
'But one freezes here! and why?
    'When a heart, as chill
    'At my own would thrill
'Back to life, and its fires out-fly?   145
    'Heart, shall we live or die?
'The rest, . . . settle by-and-by!'

XXII

So, she'd efface the score,
And forgive me as before.
    It is twelve o' clock: 150
    I shall hear her knock
In the worst of a storm's uproar,
    I shall pull her through the door,
I shall have her for evermore!

EVELYN HOPE

I

BEAUTIFUL Evelyn Hope is dead!
    Sit and watch by her side an hour.
That is her book-shelf, this her bed;
    She plucked that piece of geranium-flower,
Beginning to die too, in the glass;   5
    Little has yet been changed, I think:
The shutters are shut, no light may pass
    Save two long rays thro' the hinge's chink.

II

Sixteen years old when she died!
  Perhaps she had scarcely heard my name;   10
It was not her time to love; beside,
  Her life had many a hope and aim,
Duties enough and little cares,
  And now was quiet, now astir,
Till God's hand beckoned unawares,—   15
  And the sweet white brow is all of her.

III

Is it too late then, Evelyn Hope?
  What, your soul was pure and true,
The good stars met in your horoscope,
  Made you of spirit, fire and dew—   20
And, just because I was thrice as old
  And our paths in the world diverged so wide,
Each was nought to each, must I be told?
  We were fellow mortals, nought beside?

IV

No, indeed! for God above   25
  Is great to grant, as mighty to make,
And creates the love to reward the love:
  I claim you still, for my own love's sake!
Delayed it may be for more lives yet,
  Through worlds I shall traverse, not a few: 30
Much is to learn, much to forget
  Ere the time be come for taking you.

V

But the time will come,—at last it will,
  When, Evelyn Hope, what meant (I shall say)
In the lower earth, in the years long still,   35
  That body and soul so pure and gay?
Why your hair was amber, I shall divine,
  And your mouth of your own geranium's red—
And what you would do with me, in fine,
  In the new life come in the old one's stead.   40

VI

I have lived (I shall say) so much since then,
    Given up myself so many times,
Gained me the gains of various men,
    Ransacked the ages, spoiled the climes;
Yet one thing, one, in my soul's full scope,   45
    Either I missed or itself missed me:
And I want and find you, Evelyn Hope!
    What is the issue? let us see!

VII

I loved you, Evelyn, all the while.
    My heart seemed full as it could hold?   50
There was place and to spare for the frank young smile,
    And the red young mouth, and the hair's young gold.
So, hush,—I will give you this leaf to keep:
    See, I shut it inside the sweet cold hand!
There, that is our secret: go to sleep!   55
    You will wake, and remember, and understand.

UP AT A VILLA—DOWN IN THE CITY

(AS DISTINGUISHED BY AN ITALIAN PERSON OF QUALITY)

I

HAD I but plenty of money, money enough and to spare,
The house for me, no doubt, were a house in the city-square;
Ah, such a life, such a life, as one leads at the window there!

II

Something to see, by Bacchus, something to hear, at least!
There, the whole day long, one's life is a perfect feast;   5
While up at a villa one lives, I maintain it, no more than a beast.

III

Well now, look at our villa! stuck like the horn of a bull
Just on a mountain-edge as bare as the creature's skull,
Save a mere shag of a bush with hardly a leaf to pull!
—I scratch my own, sometimes, to see if the hair's turned wool. 10

IV

But the city, oh the city—the square with the houses! Why?
They are stone-faced, white as a curd, there's something to take the
  eye!
Houses in four straight lines, not a single front awry;
You watch who crosses and gossips, who saunters, who hurries by;
Green blinds, as a matter of course, to draw when the sun gets high;
And the shops with fanciful signs which are painted properly.   16

V

What of a villa? Though winter be over in March by rights,
'T is May perhaps ere the snow shall have withered well off the
  heights:
You've the brown ploughed land before, where the oxen steam and
  wheeze,
And the hills over-smoked behind by the faint grey olive-trees.   20

VI

Is it better in May, I ask you? You've summer all at once;
In a day he leaps complete with a few strong April suns.
'Mid the sharp short emerald wheat, scarce risen three fingers well,
The wild tulip, at end of its tube, blows out its great red bell
Like a thin clear bubble of blood, for the children to pick and
  sell.   25

VII

Is it ever hot in the square? There's a fountain to spout and splash!
In the shade it sings and springs; in the shine such foam-bows
  flash
On the horses with curling fish-tails, that prance and paddle and
  pash
Round the lady atop in her conch—fifty gazers do not abash,
Though all that she wears is some weeds round her waist in a sort of
  sash.   30

VIII

All the year long at the villa, nothing to see though you linger,
Except yon cypress that points like death's lean lifted forefinger.
Some think fireflies pretty, when they mix i' the corn and mingle,
Or thrid the stinking hemp till the stalks of it seem a-tingle.

Late August or early September, the stunning cicala is shrill,   35
And the bees keep their tiresome whine round the resinous firs on
    the hill.
Enough of the seasons,—I spare you the months of the fever and chill.

IX

Ere you open your eyes in the city, the blessed church-bells begin:
No sooner the bells leave off than the diligence rattles in:
You get the pick of the news, and it costs you never a pin.   40
By-and-by there's the travelling doctor gives pills, lets blood, draws
    teeth;
Or the Pulcinello-trumpet breaks up the market beneath.
At the post-office such a scene-picture—the new play, piping hot!
And a notice how, only this morning, three liberal thieves were shot.
Above it, behold the Archbishop's most fatherly of rebukes,   45
And beneath, with his crown and his lion, some little new law of the
    Duke's!
Or a sonnet with flowery marge, to the Reverend Don So-and-so
Who is Dante, Boccaccio, Petrarca, Saint Jerome and Cicero,
'And moreover,' (the sonnet goes rhyming,) 'the skirts of Saint Paul
    has reached,
'Having preached us those six Lent-lectures more unctuous than ever
    he preached.'   50
Noon strikes,—here sweeps the procession! our Lady borne smiling
    and smart
With a pink gauze gown all spangles, and seven swords stuck in her
    heart!
Bang-whang-whang goes the drum, *tootle-te-tootle* the fife;
No keeping one's haunches still: it's the greatest pleasure in life.

X

But bless you, it's dear—it's dear! fowls, wine, at double the rate.   55
They have clapped a new tax upon salt, and what oil pays passing
    the gate
It's a horror to think of. And so, the villa for me, not the city!
Beggars can scarcely be choosers: but still—ah, the pity, the pity!
Look, two and two go the priests, then the monks with cowls and
    sandals,
And the penitents dressed in white shirts, a-holding the yellow
    candles;   60

One, he carries a flag up straight, and another a cross with handles,
And the Duke's guard brings up the rear, for the better prevention
    of scandals:
Bang-whang-whang goes the drum, *tootle-te-tootle* the fife.
Oh, a day in the city-square, there is no such pleasure in life!

A WOMAN'S LAST WORD

I

LET'S contend no more, Love,
    Strive nor weep:
All be as before, Love,
    —Only sleep!

II

What so wild as words are?   5
    I and thou
In debate, as birds are,
    Hawk on bough!

III

See the creature stalking
    While we speak!   10
Hush and hide the talking,
    Cheek on cheek!

IV

What so false as truth is,
    False to thee?
Where the serpent's tooth is   15
    Shun the tree—

V

Where the apple reddens
    Never pry—
Lest we lose our Edens,
    Eve and I.   20

VI

Be a god and hold me
  With a charm!
Be a man and fold me
  With thine arm!

VII

Teach me, only teach, Love!   25
  As I ought
I will speak thy speech, Love,
  Think thy thought—

VIII

Meet, if thou require it,
  Both demands,   30
Laying flesh and spirit
  In thy hands.

IX

That shall be to-morrow
  Not to-night:
I must bury sorrow   35
  Out of sight:

X

—Must a little weep, Love,
  (Foolish me!)
And so fall asleep, Love,
  Loved by thee.   40

FRA LIPPO LIPPI

I AM poor brother Lippo, by your leave!
You need not clap your torches to my face.
Zooks, what's to blame? you think you see a monk!
What, 't is past midnight, and you go the rounds,
And here you catch me at an alley's end   5
Where sportive ladies leave their doors ajar?
The Carmine's my cloister: hunt it up,

Do,—harry out, if you must show your zeal,
Whatever rat, there, haps on his wrong hole,
And nip each softling of a wee white mouse,   10
Weke, weke, that's crept to keep him company!
Aha, you know your betters? Then, you'll take
Your hand away that's fiddling on my throat,
And please to know me likewise. Who am I?
Why, one, sir, who is lodging with a friend   15
Three streets off—he's a certain . . . how d'ye call?
Master—a . . . Cosimo of the Medici,
I' the house that caps the corner. Boh! you were best!
Remember and tell me, the day you're hanged,
How you affected such a gullet's-gripe!   20
But you, sir, it concerns you that your knaves
Pick up a manner nor discredit you:
Zooks, are we pilchards, that they sweep the streets
And count fair prize what comes into their net?
He's Judas to a tittle, that man is!   25
Just such a face! Why, sir, you make amends.
Lord, I'm not angry! Bid your hangdogs go
Drink out this quarter-florin to the health
Of the munificent House that harbours me
(And many more beside, lads! more beside!)   30
And all's come square again. I'd like his face—
His, elbowing on his comrade in the door
With the pike and lantern,—for the slave that holds
John Baptist's head a-dangle by the hair
With one hand ('Look you, now,' as who should say)   35
And his weapon in the other, yet unwiped!
It's not your chance to have a bit of chalk,
A wood-coal or the like? or you should see!
Yes, I'm the painter, since you style me so.
What, brother Lippo's doings, up and down,   40
You know them and they take you? like enough!
I saw the proper twinkle in your eye—
'Tell you, I liked your looks at very first.
Let's sit and set things straight now, hip to haunch.
Here's spring come, and the nights one makes up bands   45
To roam the town and sing out carnival,
And I've been three weeks shut within my mew,

A-painting for the great man, saints and saints
And saints again. I could not paint all night—
Ouf! I leaned out of window for fresh air.   50
There came a hurry of feet and little feet,
A sweep of lute-strings, laughs, and whifts of song,—
Flower o' the broom,
Take away love, and our earth is a tomb!
Flower o' the quince,   55
I let Lisa go, and what good in life since?
Flower o' the thyme—and so on. Round they went.
Scarce had they turned the corner when a titter
Like the skipping of rabbits by moonlight,—three slim shapes,
And a face that looked up . . . zooks, sir, flesh and blood,   60
That's all I'm made of! Into shreds it went,
Curtain and counterpane and coverlet,
All the bed furniture—a dozen knots,
There was a ladder! Down I let myself,
Hands and feet, scrambling somehow, and so dropped,   65
And after them. I came up with the fun
Hard by St. Laurence, hail fellow, well met.—
Flower o' the rose,
If I've been merry, what matter who knows?
And so as I was stealing back again   70
To get to bed and have a bit of sleep
Ere I rise up to-morrow and go work
On Jerome knocking at his poor old breast
With his great round stone to subdue the flesh,
You snap me of the sudden. Ah, I see!   75
Though your eye twinkles still, you shake your head—
Mine's shaved,—a monk, you say—the sting's in that!
If Master Cosimo announced himself,
Mum's the word naturally; but a monk!
Come, what am I a beast for? tell us, now!   80
I was a baby when my mother died
And father died and left me in the street.
I starved there, God knows how, a year or two
On fig-skins, melon-parings, rinds and shucks,
Refuse and rubbish. One fine frosty day,   85
My stomach being empty as your hat,
The wind doubled me up and down I went.

Old Aunt Lapaccia trussed me with one hand,
(Its fellow was a stinger as I knew)
And so along the wall, over the bridge,   90
By the straight cut to the convent. Six words there,
While I stood munching my first bread that month:
'So, boy, you're minded,' quoth the good fat father
Wiping his own mouth, 'twas refection-time,—
'To quit this very miserable world?   95
'Will you renounce' . . . 'the mouthful of bread?' thought I;
By no means! Brief, they made a monk of me;
I did renounce the world, its pride and greed,
Palace, farm, villa, shop and banking-house,
Trash, such as these poor devils of Medici   100
Have given their hearts to—all at eight years old.
Well, sir, I found in time, you may be sure,
'Twas not for nothing—the good bellyful,
The warm serge and the rope that goes all round,
And day-long blessed idleness beside!   105
'Let's see what the urchin's fit for'—that came next.
Not overmuch their way, I must confess.
Such a to-do! they tried me with their books:
Lord, they'd have taught me Latin in pure waste!
Flower o' the clove,   110
All the Latin I construe is, 'amo' I love!
But, mind you, when a boy starves in the streets
Eight years together, as my fortune was,
Watching folk's faces to know who will fling
The bit of half-stripped grape-bunch he desires,   115
And who will curse or kick him for his pains,—
Which gentleman processional and fine,
Holding a candle to the Sacrament,
Will wink and let him lift a plate and catch
The droppings of the wax to sell again,   120
Or holla for the Eight and have him whipped,—
How say I?—nay, which dog bites, which lets drop
His bone from the heap of offal in the street,—
Why, soul and sense of him grow sharp alike,
He learns the look of things, and none the less   125
For admonition from the hunger-pinch.
I had a store of such remarks, be sure,

Which, after I found leisure, turned to use.
I drew men's faces on my copy-books,
Scrawled them within the antiphonary's marge,   130
Joined legs and arms to the long music-notes,
Found eyes and nose and chin for A's and B's,
And made a string of pictures of the world
Betwixt the ins and outs of verb and noun,
On the wall, the bench, the door. The monks looked black. 135
'Nay,' quoth the Prior, 'turn him out, d' ye say?
'In no wise. Lose a crow and catch a lark.
'What if at last we get our man of parts,
'We Carmelites, like those Camaldolese
'And Preaching Friars, to do our church up fine   140
'And put the front on it that ought to be!'
And hereupon he bade me daub away.
Thank you! my head being crammed, the walls a blank,
Never was such prompt disemburdening.
First, every sort of monk, the black and white,   145
I drew them, fat and lean: then, folk at church,
From good old gossips waiting to confess
Their cribs of barrel-droppings, candle-ends,—
To the breathless fellow at the altar-foot,
Fresh from his murder, safe and sitting there   150
With the little children round him in a row
Of admiration, half for his beard and half
For that white anger of his victim's son
Shaking a fist at him with one fierce arm,
Signing himself with the other because of Christ   155
(Whose sad face on the cross sees only this
After the passion of a thousand years)
Till some poor girl, her apron o'er her head,
(Which the intense eyes looked through) came at eve
On tiptoe, said a word, dropped in a loaf,   160
Her pair of earrings and a bunch of flowers
(The brute took growling), prayed, and so was gone.
I painted all, then cried, "'T is ask and have;
'Choose, for more's ready!'—laid the ladder flat,
And showed my covered bit of cloister-wall.   165
The monks closed in a circle and praised loud
Till checked, taught what to see and not to see,

Being simple bodies,—'That's the very man!
'Look at the boy who stoops to pat the dog!
'That woman's like the Prior's niece who comes   170
'To care about his asthma: it's the life!'
But there my triumph's straw-fire flared and funked;
Their betters took their turn to see and say:
The Prior and the learned pulled a face
And stopped all that in no time. 'How? what's here?   175
'Quite from the mark of painting, bless us all!
'Faces, arms, legs and bodies like the true
'As much as pea and pea! it's devil's-game!
'Your business is not to catch men with show,
'With homage to the perishable clay,   180
'But lift them over it, ignore it all,
'Make them forget there's such a thing as flesh.
'Your business is to paint the souls of men—
'Man's soul, and it's a fire, smoke . . . no, it's not . . .
'It's vapour done up like a new-born babe—   185
'(In that shape when you die it leaves your mouth)
'It's . . . well, what matters talking, it's the soul!
'Give us no more of body than shows soul!
'Here's Giotto, with his Saint a-praising God,
'That sets us praising,—why not stop with him?   190
'Why put all thoughts of praise out of our head
'With wonder at lines, colours, and what not?
'Paint the soul, never mind the legs and arms!
'Rub all out, try at it a second time.
'Oh, that white smallish female with the breasts,   195
'She's just my niece . . . Herodias, I would say,—
'Who went and danced and got men's heads cut off!
'Have it all out!' Now, is this sense, I ask?
A fine way to paint soul, by painting body
So ill, the eye can't stop there, must go further   200
And can't fare worse! Thus, yellow does for white
When what you put for yellow's simply black,
And any sort of meaning looks intense
When all beside itself means and looks nought.
Why can't a painter lift each foot in turn,   205
Left foot and right foot, go a double step,
Make his flesh liker and his soul more like,

Both in their order? Take the prettiest face,
The Prior's niece . . . patron-saint—is it so pretty
You can't discover if it means hope, fear,   210
Sorrow or joy? won't beauty go with these?
Suppose I've made her eyes all right and blue,
Can't I take breath and try to add life's flash,
And then add soul and heighten them threefold?
Or say there's beauty with no soul at all—   215
(I never saw it—put the case the same—)
If you get simple beauty and nought else,
You get about the best thing God invents:
That's somewhat: and you'll find the soul you have missed,
Within yourself, when you return him thanks.   220
'Rub all out!' Well, well, there's my life, in short,
And so the thing has gone on ever since.
I'm grown a man no doubt, I've broken bounds:
You should not take a fellow eight years old
And make him swear to never kiss the girls.   225
I'm my own master, paint now as I please—
Having a friend, you see, in the Corner-house!
Lord, it's fast holding by the rings in front—
Those great rings serve more purposes than just
To plant a flag in, or tie up a horse!   230
And yet the old schooling sticks, the old grave eyes
Are peeping o'er my shoulder as I work,
The heads shake still—'It's art's decline, my son!
'You're not of the true painters, great and old;
'Brother Angelico's the man, you'll find;   235
'Brother Lorenzo stands his single peer:
'Fag on at flesh, you'll never make the third!'
Flower o' the pine,
You keep your mistr . . . manners, and I'll stick to mine!
I'm not the third, then: bless us, they must know!   240
Don't you think they're the likeliest to know,
They with their Latin? So, I swallow my rage,
Clench my teeth, suck my lips in tight, and paint
To please them—sometimes do and sometimes don't;
For, doing most, there's pretty sure to come   245
A turn, some warm eve finds me at my saints—
A laugh, a cry, the business of the world—

(*Flower o' the peach,*
Death for us all, and his own life for each!)
And my whole soul revolves, the cup runs over,   250
The world and life's too big to pass for a dream,
And I do these wild things in sheer despite,
And play the fooleries you catch me at,
In pure rage! The old mill-horse, out at grass
After hard years, throws up his stiff heels so,   255
Although the miller does not preach to him
The only good of grass is to make chaff.
What would men have? Do they like grass or no—
May they or mayn't they? all I want's the thing
Settled for ever one way. As it is,   260
You tell too many lies and hurt yourself:
You don't like what you only like too much,
You do like what, if given you at your word,
You find abundantly detestable.
For me, I think I speak as I was taught;   265
I always see the garden and God there
A-making man's wife: and, my lesson learned,
The value and significance of flesh,
I can't unlearn ten minutes afterwards.

You understand me: I'm a beast, I know.   270
But see, now—why, I see as certainly
As that the morning-star's about to shine,
What will hap some day. We've a youngster here
Comes to our convent, studies what I do,
Slouches and stares and lets no atom drop: 275
His name is Guidi—he'll not mind the monks—
They call him Hulking Tom, he lets them talk—
He picks my practice up—he'll paint apace,
I hope so—though I never live so long,
I know what's sure to follow. You be judge!   280
You speak no Latin more than I, belike,
However, you're my man, you've seen the world
—The beauty and the wonder and the power,
The shapes of things, their colours, lights and shades,
Changes, surprises,—and God made it all!   285
—For what? Do you feel thankful, ay or no,

For this fair town's face, yonder river's line,
The mountain round it and the sky above,
Much more the figures of man, woman, child,
These are the frame to? What's it all about?   290
To be passed over, despised? or dwelt upon,
Wondered at? oh, this last of course!—you say.
But why not do as well as say,—paint these
Just as they are, careless what comes of it?
God's works—paint anyone, and count it crime   295
To let a truth slip. Don't object, 'His works
'Are here already; nature is complete:
'Suppose you reproduce her—(which you can't)
There's no advantage! you must beat her, then.'
For, don't you mark? we're made so that we love   300
First when we see them painted, things we have passed
Perhaps a hundred times nor cared to see;
And so they are better, painted—better to us,
Which is the same thing. Art was given for that;
God uses us to help each other so,   305
Lending our minds out. Have you noticed, now,
Your cullion's hanging face? A bit of chalk,
And trust me but you should, though! How much more,
If I drew higher things with the same truth!
That were to take the Prior's pulpit-place,   310
Interpret God to all of you! Oh, oh,
It makes me mad to see what men shall do
And we in our graves! This world's no blot for us,
Nor blank; it means intensely, and means good:
To find its meaning is my meat and drink.   315
'Ay, but you don't so instigate to prayer!'
Strikes in the Prior: 'when your meaning's plain
'It does not say to folk—remember matins,
'Or, mind you fast next Friday!' Why, for this
What need of art at all? A skull and bones,   320
Two bits of stick nailed crosswise, or, what's best,
A bell to chime the hour with, does as well.
I painted a Saint Laurence six months since
At Prato, splashed the fresco in fine style:
'How looks my painting, now the scaffold's down?'   325
I ask a brother: 'Hugely,' he returns—

'Already not one phiz of your three slaves
'Who turn the Deacon off his toasted side,
'But's scratched and prodded to our heart's content,
'The pious people have so eased their own   330
'With coming to say prayers there in a rage:
'We get on fast to see the bricks beneath.
'Expect another job this time next year,
'For pity and religion grow i' the crowd—
'Your painting serves its purpose!' Hang the fools!   335
   —That is—you'll not mistake an idle word
Spoke in a huff by a poor monk, God wot,
Tasting the air this spicy night which turns
The unaccustomed head like Chianti wine!
Oh, the church knows! don't misreport me, now!   340
It's natural a poor monk out of bounds
Should have his apt word to excuse himself:
And hearken how I plot to make amends.
I have bethought me: I shall paint a piece
. . . There's for you! Give me six months, then go, see   345
Something in Sant' Ambrogio's! Bless the nuns!
They want a cast o' my office. I shall paint
God in the midst, Madonna and her babe,
Ringed by a bowery flowery angel-brood,
Lilies and vestments and white faces, sweet   350
As puff on puff of grated orris-root
When ladies crowd to Church at midsummer.
And then i' the front, of course a saint or two—
Saint John, because he saves the Florentines,
Saint Ambrose, who puts down in black and white   355
The convent's friends and gives them a long day,
And Job, I must have him there past mistake,
The man of Uz (and Us without the z,
Painters who need his patience.) Well, all these
Secured at their devotion, up shall come   360
Out of a corner when you least expect,
As one by a dark stair into a great light,
Music and talking, who but Lippo! I!—
Mazed, motionless and moonstruck—I'm the man!
Back I shrink—what is this I see and hear?   365
I, caught up with my monk's things by mistake,

U

My old serge gown and rope that goes all round,
I, in this presence, this pure company!
Where's a hole, where's a corner for escape?
Then steps a sweet angelic slip of a thing   370
Forward, puts out a soft palm—'Not so fast!'
—Addresses the celestial presence, 'nay—
'He made you and devised you, after all,
'Though he's none of you! Could Saint John there draw—
'His camel-hair make up a painting-brush?   375
'We come to brother Lippo for all that,
'*Iste perfecit opus!*' So, all smile—
I shuffle sideways with my blushing face
Under the cover of a hundred wings
Thrown like a spread of kirtles when you're gay   380
And play hot cockles, all the doors being shut,
Till, wholly unexpected, in there pops
The hothead husband! Thus I scuttle off
To some safe bench behind, not letting go
The palm of her, the little lily thing   385
That spoke the good word for me in the nick,
Like the Prior's niece . . . Saint Lucy, I would say.
And so all's saved for me, and for the church
A pretty picture gained. Go, six months hence!
Your hand, sir, and good-bye: no lights, no lights!   390
The street's hushed, and I know my own way back,
Don't fear me! There's the grey beginning. Zooks!

A TOCCATA OF GALUPPI'S

I

OH Galuppi, Baldassaro, this is very sad to find!
I can hardly misconceive you; it would prove me deaf and blind;
But although I take your meaning, 'tis with such a heavy mind!

II

Here you come with your old music, and here's all the good it brings.
What, they lived once thus at Venice where the merchants were the
    kings,   5
Where Saint Mark's is, where the Doges used to wed the sea with
    rings?

III

Ay, because the sea's the street there; and 't is arched by . . . what
    you call
. . . Shylock's bridge with houses on it, where they kept the carnival:
I was never out of England—it's as if I saw it all.

IV

Did young people take their pleasure when the sea was warm in
    May?   10
Balls and masks begun at midnight, burning ever to mid-day,
When they made up fresh adventures for the morrow, do you say?

V

Was a lady such a lady, cheeks so round and lips so red,—
On her neck the small face buoyant, like a bell-flower on its bed,
O'er the breast's superb abundance where a man might base his
    head?   15

VI

Well, and it was graceful of them—they'd break talk off and afford
—She, to bite her mask's black velvet—he, to finger on his sword,
While you sat and played Toccatas, stately at the clavichord?

VII

What? Those lesser thirds so plaintive, sixths diminished, sigh on
    sigh,
Told them something? Those suspensions, those solutions—'Must
    we die?'   20
Those commiserating sevenths—'Life might last! we can but try!'

VIII

'Were you happy?'—'Yes.'—'And are you still as happy?'—'Yes.
    And you?'
—'Then, more kisses!'—'Did *I* stop them, when a million seemed
    so few?'
Hark, the dominant's persistence till it must be answered to!

IX

So, an octave struck the answer. Oh, they praised you, I dare say! 25
'Brave Galuppi! that was music! good alike at grave and gay!
'I can always leave off talking when I hear a master play!'

X

Then they left you for their pleasure: till in due time, one by one,
Some with lives that came to nothing, some with deeds as well
 undone,
Death stepped tacitly and took them where they never see the sun.

XI

But when I sit down to reason, think to take my stand nor swerve,
While I triumph o'er a secret wrung from nature's close reserve,
In you come with your cold music till I creep thro' every nerve.

XII

Yes, you, like a ghostly cricket, creaking where a house was burned:
'Dust and ashes, dead and done with, Venice spent what Venice
 earned.   35
'The soul, doubtless, is immortal—where a soul can be discerned.

XIII

'Yours for instance: you know physics, something of geology,
'Mathematics are your pastime; souls shall rise in their degree;
'Butterflies may dread extinction,—you'll not die, it cannot be!

XIV

'As for Venice and her people, merely born to bloom and drop, 40
'Here on earth they bore their fruitage, mirth and folly were the crop:
'What of soul was left, I wonder, when the kissing had to stop?

XV

'Dust and ashes!' So you creak it, and I want the heart to scold.
Dear dead women, with such hair, too—what's become of all the gold
Used to hang and brush their bosoms? I feel chilly and grown old. 45

BY THE FIRE-SIDE

I

How well I know what I mean to do
 When the long dark autumn-evenings come
And where, my soul, is thy pleasant hue?
 With the music of all thy voices, dumb
In life's November too!   5

II

I shall be found by the fire, suppose,
  O'er a great wise book as beseemeth age,
While the shutters flap as the cross-wind blows
  And I turn the page, and I turn the page,
Not verse now, only prose!   10

III

Till the young ones whisper, finger on lip,
  'There he is at it, deep in Greek:
'Now then, or never, out we slip
  'To cut from the hazels by the creek
'A mainmast for our ship!'   15

IV

I shall be at it indeed, my friends:
  Greek puts already on either side
Such a branch-work forth as soon extends
  To a vista opening far and wide,
And I pass out where it ends.   20

V

The outside-frame like your hazel-trees:
  But the inside-archway widens fast,
And a rarer sort succeeds to these,
  And we slope to Italy at last
And youth, by green degrees.   25

VI

I follow wherever I am led,
  Knowing so well the leader's hand:
Oh woman-country, wooed not wed,
  Loved all the more by earth's male-lands,
Laid to their hearts instead!   30

VII

Look at the ruined chapel again
  Half-way up in the Alpine gorge!
Is that a tower, I point you plain,
  Or is it a mill, or an iron-forge
Breaks solitude in vain?   35

VIII

A turn, and we stand in the heart of things;
   The woods are round us, heaped and dim;
From slab to slab how it slips and springs,
   The thread of water single and slim,
Through the ravage some torrent brings!   40

IX

Does it feed the little lake below?
   That speck of white just on its marge
Is Pella; see, in the evening glow,
   How sharp the silver spear-heads charge
When Alp meets heaven in snow!   45

X

On our other side is the straight-up rock;
   And a path is kept 'twixt the gorge and it
By boulder-stones where lichens mock
   The marks on a moth, and small ferns fit
Their teeth to the polished block.   50

XI

Oh the sense of the yellow mountain flowers,
   And thorny balls, each three in one,
The chestnuts throw on our path in showers!
   For the drop of the woodland fruit's begun,
These early November hours,   55

XII

That crimson the creeper's leaf across
   Like a splash of blood, intense, abrupt,
O'er a shield else gold from rim to boss,
   And lay it for show on the fairy-cupped
Elf-needled mat of moss,   60

XIII

By the rose-flesh mushrooms, undivulged
   Last evening—nay, in to-day's first dew
Yon sudden coral nipple bulged,
   Where a freaked fawn-coloured flaky crew
Of toadstools peep indulged.   65

XIV

And yonder, at foot of the fronting ridge
   That takes the turn to a range beyond,
Is the chapel reached by the one-arched bridge
   Where the water is stopped in a stagnant pond
Danced over by the midge.   70

XV

The chapel and bridge are of stone alike,
   Blackish-grey and mostly wet;
Cut hemp-stalks steep in the narrow dyke.
   See here again, how the lichens fret
And the roots of the ivy strike!   75

XVI

Poor little place, where its one priest comes
   On a festa-day, if he comes at all,
To the dozen folk from their scattered homes,
   Gathered within that precinct small
By the dozen ways one roams—   80

XVII

To drop from the charcoal-burners' huts,
   Or climb from the hemp-dressers' low shed,
Leave the grange where the woodman stores his nuts,
   Or the wattled cote where the fowlers spread
Their gear on the rock's bare juts.   85

XVIII

It has some pretension too, this front,
   With its bit of fresco half-moon-wise
Set over the porch, Art's early wont:
   'T is John in the Desert, I surmise,
But has borne the weather's brunt—   90

XIX

Not from the fault of the builder, though,
   For a pent-house properly projects
Where three carved beams make a certain show,
   Dating—good thought of our architect's—
'Five, six, nine, he lets you know.   95

XX

And all day long a bird sings there,
　　And a stray sheep drinks at the pond at times;
The place is silent and aware;
　　It has had its scenes, its joys and crimes,
But that is its own affair.　　　　　　　　　　100

XXI

My perfect wife, my Leonor,
　　Oh heart, my own, oh eyes, mine too,
Whom else could I dare look backward for,
　　With whom beside should I dare pursue
The path grey heads abhor?　　　　　　　　　　105

XXII

For it leads to a crag's sheer edge with them;
　　Youth, flowery all the way, there stops—
Not they; age threatens and they contemn,
　　Till they reach the gulf wherein youth drops,
One inch from life's safe hem!　　　　　　　　　110

XXIII

With me, youth led . . . I will speak now,
　　No longer watch you as you sit
Reading by fire-light, that great brow
　　And the spirit-small hand propping it,
Mutely, my heart knows how—　　　　　　　　　115

XXIV

When, if I think but deep enough,
　　You are wont to answer, prompt as rhyme;
And you, too, find without rebuff
　　Response your soul seeks many a time
Piercing its fine flesh-stuff.　　　　　　　　　120

XXV

My own, confirm me! If I tread
　　This path back, is it not in pride
To think how little I dreamed it led
　　To an age so blest that, by its side,
Youth seems the waste instead?　　　　　　　　125

XXVI

My own, see where the years conduct!
  At first, 't was something our two souls
Should mix as mists do; each is sucked
  Into each now: on, the new stream rolls,
Whatever rocks obstruct.   130

XXVII

Think, when our one soul understands
  The great Word which makes all things new,
When earth breaks up and heaven expands,
  How will the change strike me and you
In the house not made with hands?   135

XXVIII

Oh I must feel your brain prompt mine,
  Your heart anticipate my heart,
You must be just before, in fine,
  See and make me see, for your part,
New depths of the divine!   140

XXIX

But who could have expected this
  When we two drew together first
Just for the obvious human bliss,
  To satisfy life's daily thirst
With a thing men seldom miss?   145

XXX

Come back with me to the first of all,
  Let us lean and love it over again,
Let us now forget and now recall,
  Break the rosary in a pearly rain,
And gather what we let fall!   150

XXXI

What did I say?—that a small bird sings
  All day long, save when a brown pair
Of hawks from the wood float with wide wings
  Strained to a bell: 'gainst noon-day glare
You count the streaks and rings.   155

XXXII

But at afternoon or almost eve
　'T is better; then the silence grows
To that degree, you half believe
　It must get rid of what it knows,
Its bosom does so heave.　　　　　　　　　　160

XXXIII

Hither we walked then, side by side,
　Arm in arm and cheek to cheek,
And still I questioned or replied,
　While my heart, convulsed to really speak,
Lay choking in its pride.　　　　　　　　　　165

XXXIV

Silent the crumbling bridge we cross,
　And pity and praise the chapel sweet,
And care about the fresco's loss,
　And wish for our souls a like retreat,
And wonder at the moss.　　　　　　　　　　170

XXXV

Stoop and kneel on the settle under,
　Look through the window's grated square:
Nothing to see! For fear of plunder,
　The cross is down and the altar bare,
As if thieves don't fear thunder.　　　　　　　175

XXXVI

We stoop and look in through the grate,
　See the little porch and rustic door,
Read duly the dead builder's date;
　Then cross the bridge that we crossed before,
Take the path again—but wait!　　　　　　　180

XXXVII

Oh moment, one and infinite!
　The water slips o'er stock and stone;
The West is tender, hardly bright:
　How grey at once is the evening grown—
One star, its chrysolite!　　　　　　　　　　185

XXXVIII

We two stood there with never a third,
  But each by each, as each knew well:
The sights we saw and the sounds we heard,
  The lights and the shades·made up a spell
Till the trouble grew and stirred.   190

XXXIX

Oh, the little more, and how much it is!
And the little less, and what worlds away!
How a sound shall quicken content to bliss,
  Or a breath suspend the blood's best play,
And life be a proof of this!   195

XL

Had she willed it, still had stood the screen
  So slight, so sure, 'twixt my love and her:
I could fix her face with a guard between,
  And find her soul as when friends confer,
Friends—lovers that might have been.   200

XLI

For my heart had a touch of the woodland-time,
  Wanting to sleep now over its best.
Shake the whole tree in the summer-prime,
  But bring to the last leaf no such test!
'Hold the last fast!' runs the rhyme.   205

XLII

For a chance to make your little much,
  To gain a lover and lose a friend,
Venture the tree and a myriad such,
  When nothing you mar but the year can mend:
But a last leaf—fear to touch!   210

XLIII

Yet should it unfasten itself and fall
  Eddying down till it find your face
At some slight wind—best chance of all!
  Be your heart henceforth its dwelling-place
You trembled to forestall!   215

XLIV

Worth how well, those dark grey eyes,
  That hair so dark and dear, how worth
That a man should strive and agonize,
  And taste a veriest hell on earth
For the hope of such a prize!   220

XLV

You might have turned and tried a man,
  Set him a space to weary and wear,
And prove which suited more your plan,
  His best of hope or his worst despair,
Yet end as he began.   225

XLVI

But you spared me this, like the heart you are,
  And filled my empty heart at a word.
If two lives join, there is oft a scar,
  They are one and one, with a shadowy third;
One near one is too far.   230

XLVII

A moment after, and hands unseen
  Were hanging the night around us fast;
But we knew that a bar was broken between
  Life and life: we were mixed at last
In spite of the mortal screen.   235

XLVIII

The forests had done it; there they stood;
  We caught for a moment the powers at play:
They had mingled us so, for once and good,
  Their work was done—we might go or stay,
They relapsed to their ancient mood.   240

XLIX

How the world is made for each of us!
  How all we perceive and know in it
Tends to some moment's product thus,
  When a soul declares itself—to wit,
By its fruit, the thing it does!   245

L

Be hate that fruit or love that fruit,
　　It forwards the general deed of man,
And each of the Many helps to recruit
　　The life of the race by a general plan;
Each living his own, to boot.　　　　　　　250

LI

I am named and known by that moment's feat;
　　There took my station and degree;
So grew my own small life complete,
　　As nature obtained her best of me—
One born to love you, sweet!　　　　　　　255

LII

And to watch you sink by the fire-side now
　　Back again, as you mutely sit
Musing by fire-light, that great brow
　　And the spirit-small hand propping it,
Yonder, my heart knows how!　　　　　　　260

LIII

So, earth has gained by one man the more,
　　And the gain of earth must be heaven's gain too;
And the whole is well worth thinking o'er
　　When autumn comes: which I mean to do
One day, as I said before.　　　　　　　265

ANY WIFE TO ANY HUSBAND

I

My love, this is the bitterest, that thou—
Who art all truth, and who dost love me now
　　As thine eyes say, as thy voice breaks to say—
Shouldst love so truly, and couldst love me still
A whole long life through, had but love its will,　　　5
　　Would death that leads me from thee brook delay.

II

I have but to be by thee, and thy hand
Would never let mine go, nor heart withstand
 The beating of my heart to reach its place.
When shall I look for thee and feel thee gone?   10
When cry for the old comfort and find none?
 Never, I know! Thy soul is in thy face.

III

Oh, I should fade—'t is willed so! Might I save,
Gladly I would, whatever beauty gave
 Joy to thy sense, for that was precious too.   15
It is not to be granted. But the soul
Whence the love comes, all ravage leaves that whole;
 Vainly the flesh fades; soul makes all things new.

IV

It would not be because my eye grew dim
Thou couldst not find the love there, thanks to Him   20
 Who never is dishonoured in the spark
He gave us from his fire of fires, and bade
Remember whence it sprang, nor be afraid
 While that burns on, though all the rest grow dark.

V

So, how thou wouldst be perfect, white and clean   25
Outside as inside, soul and soul's demesne
 Alike, this body given to show it by!
Oh, three-parts through the worst of life's abyss,
What plaudits from the next world after this,
 Couldst thou repeat a stroke and gain the sky!   30

VI

And is it not the bitterer to think
That, disengage our hands and thou wilt sink
 Although thy love was love in very deed?
I know that nature! Pass a festive day,
Thou dost not throw its relic-flower away   35
 Nor bid its music's loitering echo speed.

VII

Thou let'st the stranger's glove lie where it fell;
If old things remain old things all is well,
   For thou art grateful as becomes man best:
And hadst thou only heard me play one tune,   40
Or viewed me from a window, not so soon
   With thee would such things fade as with the rest.

VIII

I seem to see! We meet and part; 't is brief;
The book I opened keeps a folded leaf,
   The very chair I sat on, breaks the rank;   45
That is a portrait of me on the wall—
Three lines, my face comes at so slight a call:
   And for all this, one little hour to thank!

IX

But now, because the hour through years was fixed,
Because our inmost beings met and mixed,   50
   Because thou once hast loved me—wilt thou dare
Say to thy soul and Who may list beside,
   'Therefore she is immortally my bride;
   'Chance cannot change my love, nor time impair.

X

'So, what if in the dusk of life that's left,   55
'I, a tired traveller of my sun bereft,
   'Look from my path when, mimicking the same,
'The fire-fly glimpses past me, come and gone?
'—Where was it till the sunset? where anon
   'It will be at the sunrise! What's to blame?'   60

XI

Is it so helpful to thee? Canst thou take
The mimic up, nor, for the true thing's sake,
   Put gently by such efforts at a beam?
Is the remainder of the way so long,
Thou need'st the little solace, thou the strong?   65
   Watch out thy watch, let weak ones doze and dream!

XII

—Ah, but the fresher faces! 'Is it true,'
Thou'lt ask, 'some eyes are beautiful and new?
  'Some hair,—how can one choose but grasp such wealth?
'And if a man would press his lips to lips   70
'Fresh as the wilding hedge-rose-cup there slips
  'The dew-drop out of, must it be by stealth?

XIII

'It cannot change the love kept still for Her,
'More than if such a picture I prefer
  'Passing a day with, to a room's bare side: 75
'The painted form takes nothing she possessed,
'Yet, while the Titian's Venus lies at rest,
  'A man looks. Once more, what is there to chide?'

XIV

So must I see, from where I sit and watch,
My own self sell myself, my hand attach   80
  Its warrant to the very thefts from me—
Thy singleness of soul that made me proud,
Thy purity of heart I loved aloud,
  Thy man's-truth I was bold to bid God see!

XV

Love so, then, if thou wilt! Give all thou canst   85
Away to the new faces—disentranced,
  (Say it and think it) obdurate no more:
Re-issue looks and words from the old mint,
Pass them afresh, no matter whose the print
  Image and superscription once they bore!   90

XVI

Re-coin thyself and give it them to spend,—
It all comes to the same thing at the end,
  Since mine thou wast, mine art and mine shalt be,
Faithful or faithless, sealing up the sum
Or lavish of my treasure, thou must come   95
  Back to the heart's place here I keep for thee!

XVII

Only, why should it be with stain at all?
Why must I, 'twixt the leaves of coronal,
   Put any kiss of pardon on thy brow?
Why need the other women know so much,   100
And talk together, 'Such the look and such
   'The smile he used to love with, then as now!'

XVIII

Might I die last and show thee! Should I find
Such hardship in the few years left behind,
   If free to take and light my lamp, and go   105
Into thy tomb, and shut the door and sit,
Seeing thy face on those four sides of it
   The better that they are so blank, I know!

XIX

Why, time was what I wanted, to turn o'er
Within my mind each look, get more and more   110
   By heart each word, too much to learn at first;
And join thee all the fitter for the pause
'Neath the low doorway's lintel. That were cause
   For lingering, though thou calledst, if I durst!

XX

And yet thou art the nobler of us two: 115
What dare I dream of, that thou canst not do,
   Outstripping my ten small steps with one stride?
I'll say then, here's a trial and a task—
Is it to bear?—if easy, I'll not ask:
   Though love fail, I can trust on in thy pride.   120

XXI

Pride?—when those eyes forestall the life behind
The death I have to go through!—when I find,
   Now that I want thy help most, all of thee!
What did I fear? Thy love shall hold me fast
Until the little minute's sleep is past   125
   And I wake saved.—And yet it will not be!

AN EPISTLE

CONTAINING THE
STRANGE MEDICAL EXPERIENCE OF KARSHISH,
THE ARAB PHYSICIAN

KARSHISH, the picker-up of learning's crumbs,
The not-incurious in God's handiwork
(This man's-flesh he hath admirably made,
Blown like a bubble, kneaded like a paste,
To coop up and keep down on earth a space   5
That puff of vapour from his mouth, man's soul)
—To Abib, all-sagacious in our art,
Breeder in me of what poor skill I boast,
Like me inquisitive how pricks and cracks
Befall the flesh through too much stress and strain,   10
Whereby the wily vapour fain would slip
Back and rejoin its source before the term,—
And aptest in contrivance (under God)
To baffle it by deftly stopping such:—
The vagrant Scholar to his Sage at home   15
Sends greeting (health and knowledge, fame with peace)
Three samples of true snakestone—rarer still,
One of the other sort, the melon-shaped,
(But fitter, pounded fine, for charms than drugs)
And writeth now the twenty-second time.   20

My journeyings were brought to Jericho:
Thus I resume. Who studious in our art
Shall count a little labour unrepaid?
I have shed sweat enough, left flesh and bone
On many a flinty furlong of this land.   25
Also, the country-side is all on fire
With rumours of a marching hitherward:
Some say Vespasian cometh, some, his son.
A black lynx snarled and pricked a tufted ear;
Lust of my blood inflamed his yellow balls: 30
I cried and threw my staff and he was gone.
Twice have the robbers stripped and beaten me,
And once a town declared me for a spy;

But at the end, I reach Jerusalem,
Since this poor covert where I pass the night, 35
This Bethany, lies scarce the distance thence
A man with plague-sores at the third degree
Runs till he drops down dead. Thou laughest here!
'Sooth, it elates me, thus reposed and safe,
To void the stuffing of my travel-scrip 40
And share with thee whatever Jewry yields.
A viscid choler is observable
In tertians, I was nearly bold to say;
And falling-sickness hath a happier cure
Than our school wots of: there's a spider here 45
Weaves no web, watches on the ledge of tombs,
Sprinkled with mottles on an ash-grey back;
Take five and drop them . . . but who knows his mind,
The Syrian runagate I trust this to?
His service payeth me a sublimate 50
Blown up his nose to help the ailing eye.
Best wait: I reach Jerusalem at morn,
There set in order my experiences,
Gather what most deserves, and give thee all—
Or I might add, Judæa's gum-tragacanth 55
Scales off in purer flakes, shines clearer-grained,
Cracks 'twixt the pestle and the porphyry,
In fine exceeds our produce. Scalp-disease
Confounds me, crossing so with leprosy—
Thou hadst admired one sort I gained at Zoar— 60
But zeal outruns discretion. Here I end.

Yet stay: my Syrian blinketh gratefully,
Protesteth his devotion is my price—
Suppose I write what harms not, though he steal?
I half resolve to tell thee, yet I blush, 65
What set me off a-writing first of all.
An itch I had, a sting to write, a tang!
For, be it this town's barrenness—or else
The Man had something in the look of him—
His case has struck me far more than 't is worth. 70
So, pardon if—(lest presently I lose
In the great press of novelty at hand

The care and pains this somehow stole from me)
I bid thee take the thing while fresh in mind,
Almost in sight—for, wilt thou have the truth?   75
The very man is gone from me but now,
Whose ailment is the subject of discourse.
Thus then, and let thy better wit help all!

'T is but a case of mania—subinduced
By epilepsy, at the turning-point   80
Of trance prolonged unduly some three days:
When, by the exhibition of some drug
Or spell, exorcization, stroke of art
Unknown to me and which 't were well to know,
The evil thing out-breaking all at once   85
Left the man whole and sound of body indeed,—
But, flinging (so to speak) life's gates too wide,
Making a clear house of it too suddenly,
The first conceit that entered might inscribe
Whatever it was minded on the wall   90
So plainly at that vantage, as it were,
(First come, first served) that nothing subsequent
Attaineth to erase those fancy-scrawls
The just-returned and new-established soul
Hath gotten now so thoroughly by heart   95
That henceforth she will read or these or none.
And first—the man's own firm conviction rests
That he was dead (in fact they buried him)
—That he was dead and then restored to life
By a Nazarene physician of his tribe: 100
—'Sayeth, the same bade 'Rise,' and he did rise.
'Such cases are diurnal,' thou wilt cry.
Not so this figment!—not, that such a fume,
Instead of giving way to time and health,
Should eat itself into the life of life,   105
As saffron tingeth flesh, blood, bones and all!
For see, how he takes up the after-life.
The man—it is one Lazarus a Jew,
Sanguine, proportioned, fifty years of age,
The body's habit wholly laudable,   110
As much, indeed, beyond the common health

As he were made and put aside to show.
Think, could we penetrate by any drug
And bathe the wearied soul and worried flesh,
And bring it clear and fair, by three days' sleep!   115
Whence has the man the balm that brightens all?
This grown man eyes the world now like a child.
Some elders of his tribe, I should premise,
Led in their friend, obedient as a sheep,
To bear my inquisition. While they spoke,   120
Now sharply, now with sorrow,—told the case,—
He listened not except I spoke to him,
But folded his two hands and let them talk,
Watching the flies that buzzed: and yet no fool.
And that's a sample how his years must go.   125
Look, if a beggar, in fixed middle-life,
Should find a treasure,—can he use the same
With straitened habits and with tastes starved small,
And take at once to his impoverished brain
The sudden element that changes things,   130
That sets the undreamed-of rapture at his hand
And puts the cheap old joy in the scorned dust?
Is he not such an one as moves to mirth—
Warily parsimonious, when no need,
Wasteful as drunkenness at undue times?   135
All prudent counsel as to what befits
The golden mean, is lost on such an one:
The man's fantastic will is the man's law.
So here—we call the treasure knowledge, say,
Increased beyond the fleshly faculty—   140
Heaven opened to a soul while yet on earth,
Earth forced on a soul's use while seeing heaven:
The man is witless of the size, the sum,
The value in proportion of all things,
Or whether it be little or be much.   145
Discourse to him of prodigious armaments
Assembled to besiege his city now,
And of the passing of a mule with gourds—
'T is one! Then take it on the other side,
Speak of some trifling fact,—he will gaze rapt   150
With stupor at its very littleness,

(Far as I see) as if in that indeed
He caught prodigious import, whole results;
And so will turn to us the bystanders
In ever the same stupor (note this point)   155
That we too see not with his opened eyes.
Wonder and doubt come wrongly into play,
Preposterously, at cross purposes.
Should his child sicken unto death,—why, look
For scarce abatement of his cheerfulness,   160
Or pretermission of the daily craft!
While a word, gesture, glance, from that same child
At play or in the school or laid asleep,
Will startle him to an agony of fear,
Exasperation, just as like. Demand   165
The reason why—' 't is but a word,' object—
'A gesture'—he regards thee as our lord
Who lived there in the pyramid alone,
Looked at us (dost thou mind?) when, being young,
We both would unadvisedly recite   170
Some charm's beginning, from that book of his,
Able to bid the sun throb wide and burst
All into stars, as suns grown old are wont.
Thou and the child have each a veil alike
Thrown o'er your heads, from under which ye both   175
Stretch your blind hands and trifle with a match
Over a mine of Greek fire, did ye know!
He holds on firmly to some thread of life—
(It is the life to lead perforcedly)
Which runs across some vast distracting orb   180
Of glory on either side that meagre thread,
Which, conscious of, he must not enter yet—
The spiritual life around the earthly life:
The law of that is known to him as this,
His heart and brain move there, his feet stay here.   185
So is the man perplext with impulses
Sudden to start off crosswise, not straight on,
Proclaiming what is right and wrong across,
And not along, this black thread through the blaze--
'It should be' baulked by 'here it cannot be.'   190
And oft the man's soul springs into his face

As if he saw again and heard again
His sage that bade him 'Rise' and he did rise.
Something, a word, a tick o' the blood within
Admonishes: then back he sinks at once   195
To ashes, who was very fire before,
In sedulous recurrence to his trade
Whereby he earneth him the daily bread;
And studiously the humbler for that pride,
Professedly the faultier that he knows   200
God's secret, while he holds the thread of life.
Indeed the especial marking of the man
Is prone submission to the heavenly will—
Seeing it, what it is, and why it is.
'Sayeth, he will wait patient to the last   205
For that same death which must restore his being
To equilibrium, body loosening soul
Divorced even now by premature full growth:
He will live, nay, it pleaseth him to live
So long as God please, and just how God please.   210
He even seeketh not to please God more
(Which meaneth, otherwise) than as God please.
Hence, I perceive not he affects to preach
The doctrine of his sect whate'er it be,
Make proselytes as madmen thirst to do: 215
How can he give his neighbour the real ground,
His own conviction? Ardent as he is—
Call his great truth a lie, why, still the old
'Be it as God please' reassureth him.
I probed the sore as thy disciple should:
'How, beast,' said I, 'this stolid carelessness   220
'Sufficeth thee, when Rome is on her march
'To stamp out like a little spark thy town,
'Thy tribe, thy crazy tale and thee at once?'
He merely looked with his large eyes on me.   225
The man is apathetic, you deduce?
Contrariwise, he loves both old and young,
Able and weak, affects the very brutes
And birds—how say I? flowers of the field—
As a wise workman recognizes tools   230
In a master's workshop, loving what they make.

Thus is the man as harmless as a lamb:
Only impatient, let him do his best,
At ignorance and carelessness and sin—
An indignation which is promptly curbed: 235
As when in certain travel I have feigned
To be an ignoramus in our art
According to some preconceived design,
And happed to hear the land's practitioners
Steeped in conceit sublimed by ignorance,   240
Prattle fantastically on disease,
Its cause and cure—and I must hold my peace!

     Thou wilt object—Why have I not ere this
Sought out the sage himself, the Nazarene
Who wrought this cure, enquiring at the source,   245
Conferring with the frankness that befits?
Alas! it grieveth me, the learned leech
Perished in a tumult many years ago,
Accused,—our learning's fate,—of wizardry,
Rebellion, to the setting up a rule   250
And creed prodigious as described to me.
His death, which happened when the earthquake fell
(Prefiguring, as soon appeared, the loss
To occult learning in our lord the sage
Who lived there in the pyramid alone)   255
Was wrought by the mad people—that's their wont!
On vain recourse, as I conjecture it,
To his tried virtue, for miraculous help—
How could he stop the earthquake? That's their way!
The other imputations must be lies: 260
But take one, though I loathe to give it thee,
In mere respect for any good man's fame.
(And after all, our patient Lazarus
Is stark mad; should we count on what he says?
Perhaps not: though in writing to a leech   265
'T is well to keep back nothing of a case.)
This man so cured regards the curer, then,
As—God forgive me! who but God himself,
Creator and sustainer of the world,
That came and dwelt in flesh on it awhile!   270

—'Sayeth that such an one was born and lived,
Taught, healed the sick, broke bread at his own house,
Then died, with Lazarus by, for aught I know,
And yet was . . . what I said nor choose repeat,
And must have so avouched himself, in fact,   275
In hearing of this very Lazarus
Who saith—but why all this of what he saith?
Why write of trivial matters, things of price
Calling at every moment for remark?
I noticed on the margin of a pool   280
Blue-flowering borage, the Aleppo sort,
Aboundeth, very nitrous. It is strange!

Thy pardon for this long and tedious case,
Which, now that I review it, needs must seem
Unduly dwelt on, prolixly set forth!   285
Nor I myself discern in what is writ
Good cause for the peculiar interest
And awe indeed this man has touched me with.
Perhaps the journey's end, the weariness
Had wrought upon me first. I met him thus: 290
I crossed a ridge of short sharp broken hills
Like an old lion's cheek teeth. Out there came
A moon made like a face with certain spots
Multiform, manifold and menacing:
Then a wind rose behind me. So we met   295
In this old sleepy town at unaware,
The man and I. I send thee what is writ.
Regard it as a chance, a matter risked
To this ambiguous Syrian—he may lose,
Or steal, or give it thee with equal good.   300
Jerusalem's repose shall make amends
For time this letter wastes, thy time and mine;
Till when, once more thy pardon and farewell!

The very God! think, Abib; dost thou think?
So, the All-Great, were the All-Loving too—   305
So, through the thunder comes a human voice
Saying, 'O heart I made, a heart beats here!
'Face, my hands fashioned, see it in myself!

'Thou hast no power nor mayst conceive of mine,
'But love I gave thee, with myself to love,   310
'And thou must love me who have died for thee!'
The madman saith He said so: it is strange.

MESMERISM

I

ALL I believed is true!
  I am able yet
  All I want, to get
By a method as strange as new:
Dare I trust the same to you?   5

II

If at night, when doors are shut,
  And the wood-worm picks,
  And the death-watch ticks,
And the bar has a flag of smut,
And a cat's in the water-butt—   10

III

And the socket floats and flares,
  And the house-beams groan,
  And a foot unknown
Is surmised on the garret-stairs,
And the locks slip unawares—   15

IV

And the spider, to serve his ends,
  By a sudden thread,
  Arms and legs outspread,
On the table's midst descends,
Comes to find, God knows what friends!—   20

V

If since eve drew in, I say,
  I have sat and brought
  (So to speak) my thought
To bear on the woman away,
Till I felt my hair turn grey—   25

VI

Till I seemed to have and hold,
  In the vacancy
    'Twixt the wall and me,
From the hair-plait's chestnut-gold
To the foot in its muslin fold—   30

VII

Have and hold, then and there,
  Her, from head to foot,
    Breathing and mute,
Passive and yet aware,
In the grasp of my steady stare—   35

VIII

Hold and have, there and then,
  All her body and soul
    That completes my whole,
All that women add to men,
In the clutch of my steady ken—   40

IX

Having and holding, till
  I imprint her fast
    On the void at last
As the sun does whom he will
By the calotypist's skill—   45

X

Then,—if my heart's strength serve,
  And through all and each
    Of the veils I reach
To her soul and never swerve,
Knitting an iron nerve—   50

XI

Command her soul to advance
  And inform the shape
    Which has made escape
And before my countenance
Answers me glance for glance—   55

XII

I, still with a gesture fit
   Of my hands that best
   Do my soul's behest,
Pointing the power from it,
While myself do steadfast sit—   60

XIII

Steadfast and still the same
   On my object bent,
   While the hands give vent
To my ardour and my aim
And break into very flame—   65

XIV

Then I reach, I must believe,
   Not her soul in vain,
   For to me again
It reaches, and past retrieve
Is wound in the toils I weave;   70

XV

And must follow as I require,
   As befits a thrall,
   Bringing flesh and all,
Essence and earth-attire,
To the source of the tractile fire: 75

XVI

Till the house called hers, not mine,
   With a growing weight
   Seems to suffocate
If she break not its leaden line
And escape from its close confine.   80

XVII

Out of doors into the night!
   On to the maze
   Of the wild wood-ways,
Not turning to left nor right
From the pathway, blind with sight—   85

XVIII

Making thro' rain and wind
    O'er the broken shrubs,
    'Twixt the stems and stubs,
With a still, composed, strong mind,
Nor a care for the world behind—   90

XIX

Swifter and still more swift,
    As the crowding peace
    Doth to joy increase
In the wide blind eyes uplift
Thro' the darkness and the drift!   95

XX

While I—to the shape, I too
    Feel my soul dilate
    Nor a whit abate,
And relax not a gesture due,
As I see my belief come true.   100

XXI

For, there! have I drawn or no
    Life to that lip?
    Do my fingers dip
In a flame which again they throw
On the cheek that breaks a-glow?   105

XXII

Ha! was the hair so first?
    What, unfilleted,
    Made alive, and spread
Through the void with a rich outburst,
Chestnut gold-interspersed?   110

XXIII

Like the doors of a casket-shrine,
    See, on either side,
    Her two arms divide
Till the heart betwixt makes sign,
Take me, for I am thine!   115

XXIV

'Now—now'—the door is heard!
  Hark, the stairs! and near—
  Nearer—and here—
'Now!' and at call the third
She enters without a word.   120

XXV

On doth she march and on
  To the fancied shape;
  It is, past escape,
Herself, now: the dream is done
And the shadow and she are one.   125

XXVI

First I will pray. Do Thou
  That ownest the soul,
  Yet wilt grant control
To another, nor disallow
For a time, restrain me now!   130

XXVII

I admonish me while I may,
  Not to squander guilt,
  Since require Thou wilt
At my hand its price one day!
What the price is, who can say?   135

A SERENADE AT THE VILLA

I

That was I, you heard last night,
  When there rose no moon at all,
Nor, to pierce the strained and tight
  Tent of heaven, a planet small:
Life was dead and so was light.   5

II

Not a twinkle from the fly,
  Not a glimmer from the worm;

When the crickets stopped their cry,
  When the owls forbore a term,
You heard music; that was I.   10

III

Earth turned in her sleep with pain,
  Sultrily suspired for proof:
In at heaven and out again,
  Lightning!—where it broke the roof,
Bloodlike, some few drops of rain.   15

IV

What they could my words expressed,
  O my love, my all, my one!
Singing helped the verses best,
  And when singing's best was done,
To my lute I left the rest.   20

V

So wore night; the East was gray,
  White the broad-faced hemlock flowers:
There would be another day;
  Ere its first of heavy hours
Found me, I had passed away.   25

VI

What became of all the hopes,
  Words and song and lute as well?
Say, this struck you—'When life gropes
  'Feebly for the path where fell
'Light last on the evening slopes,   30

VII

'One friend in that path shall be,
  'To secure my step from wrong;
'One to count night day for me,
  'Patient through the watches long,
'Serving most with none to see.'   35

VIII

Never say—as something bodes—
  'So, the worst has yet a worse!

'When life halts 'neath double loads,
  'Better the taskmaster's curse
'Than such music on the roads!   40

IX

'When no moon succeeds the sun,
  'Nor can pierce the midnight's tent,
'Any star, the smallest one,
  'While some drops, where lightning rent,
'Show the final storm begun—   45

X

'When the fire-fly hides its spot,
  'When the garden-voices fail
'In the darkness thick and hot,—
  'Shall another voice avail,
'That shape be where these are not?   50

XI

'Has some plague a longer lease,
  'Proffering its help uncouth?
'Can't one even die in peace?
  'As one shuts one's eyes on youth,
'Is that face the last one sees?'   55

XII

Oh how dark your villa was,
  Windows fast and obdurate!
How the garden grudged me grass
  Where I stood—the iron gate
Ground its teeth to let me pass!   60

MY STAR

ALL that I know
  Of a certain star
Is, it can throw
  (Like the angled spar)
Now a dart of red,   5
  Now a dart of blue;

Till my friends have said
They would fain see, too,
My star that dartles the red and the blue!
Then it stops like a bird; like a flower, hangs furled: 10
They must solace themselves with the Saturn above it.
What matter to me if their star is a world?
Mine has opened its soul to me; therefore I love it.

INSTANS TYRANNUS

I

OF the million or two, more or less,
I rule and possess,
One man, for some cause undefined,
Was least to my mind.

II

I struck him, he grovelled of course—   5
For, what was his force?
I pinned him to earth with my weight
And persistence of hate:
And he lay, would not moan, would not curse,
As his lot might be worse.   10

III

'Were the object less mean, would he stand
'At the swing of my hand!
'For obscurity helps him and blots
'The hole where he squats.'
So, I set my five wits on the stretch   15
To inveigle the wretch.
All in vain! gold and jewels I threw,
Still he couched there perdue;
I tempted his blood and his flesh,
Hid in roses my mesh,   20
Choicest cates and the flagon's best spilth:
Still he kept to his filth.

X

IV

Had he kith now or kin, were access
To his heart, did I press:
Just a son or a mother to seize!   25
No such booty as these.
Were it simply a friend to pursue
'Mid my million or two,
Who could pay me in person or pelf
What he owes me himself!   30
No: I could not but smile through my chafe:
For the fellow lay safe
As his mates do, the midge and the nit,
—Through minuteness, to wit.

V

Then a humour more great took its place   35
At the thought of his face,
The droop, the low cares of the mouth,
The trouble uncouth
'Twixt the brows, all that air one is fain
To put out of its pain.   40
And, 'no!' I admonished myself,
'Is one mocked by an elf,
'Is one baffled by toad or by rat?
'The gravamen's in that!
'How the lion, who crouches to suit   45
'His back to my foot,
'Would admire that I stand in debate!
'But the small turns the great
'If it vexes you,—that is the thing!
'Toad or rat vex the king?   50
'Though I waste half my realm to unearth
'Toad or rat, 't is well worth!'

VI

So, I soberly laid my last plan
To extinguish the man.
Round his creep-hole, with never a break   55
Ran my fires for his sake;
Over-head, did my thunder combine

With my underground mine:
Till I looked from my labour content
To enjoy the event.   60

VII

When sudden . . . how think ye, the end?
Did I say 'without friend?'
Say rather, from marge to blue marge
The whole sky grew his targe
With the sun's self for visible boss,   65
While an Arm ran across
Which the earth heaved beneath like a breast
Where the wretch was safe prest!
Do you see? Just my vengeance complete,
The man sprang to his feet,   70
Stood erect, caught at God's skirts, and prayed!
—So, *I* was afraid!

A PRETTY WOMAN

I

THAT fawn-skin-dappled hair of hers,
    And the blue eye
    Dear and dewy,
And that infantine fresh air of hers!

II

To think men cannot take you, Sweet,   5
    And enfold you,
    Ay, and hold you,
And so keep you what they make you, Sweet!

III

You like us for a glance, you know—
    For a word's sake   10
    Or a sword's sake,
All's the same, whate'er the chance, you know.

IV

And in turn we make you ours, we say—
    You and youth too,
    Eyes and mouth too,   15
All the face composed of flowers, we say.

V

All's our own, to make the most of, Sweet—
    Sing and say for,
    Watch and pray for,
Keep a secret or go boast of, Sweet!   20

VI

But for loving, why, you would not, Sweet,
    Though we prayed you,
    Paid you, brayed you
In a mortar—for you could not, Sweet!

VII

So, we leave the sweet face fondly there: 25
    Be its beauty
    Its sole duty!
Let all hope of grace beyond, lie there!

VIII

And while the face lies quiet there,
    Who shall wonder   30
    That I ponder
A conclusion? I will try it there.

IX

As,—why must one, for the love foregone,
    Scout mere liking?
    Thunder-striking   35
Earth,—the heaven, we looked above for, gone!

X

Why, with beauty, needs there money be,
    Love with liking?
    Crush the fly-king
In his gauze, because no honey-bee?   40

XI

May not liking be so simple-sweet,
　　If love grew there
　　'T would undo there
All that breaks the cheek to dimples sweet?

XII

Is the creature too imperfect, say?　　　　　45
　　Would you mend it
　　And so end it?
Since not all addition perfects aye!

XIII

Or is it of its kind, perhaps,
　　Just perfection—　　　　　　　　　50
　　Whence, rejection
Of a grace not to its mind, perhaps?

XIV

Shall we burn up, tread that face at once
　　Into tinder,
　　And so hinder　　　　　　　　　55
Sparks from kindling all the place at once?

XV

Or else kiss away one's soul on her?
　　Your love-fancies!
　　—A sick man sees
Truer, when his hot eyes roll on her!　　　　60

XVI

Thus the craftsman thinks to grace the rose,—
　　Plucks a mould-flower
　　For his gold flower,
Uses fine things that efface the rose:

XVII

Rosy rubies make its cup more rose,　　　　65
　　Precious metals
　　Ape the petals,—
Last, some old king locks it up, morose!

XVIII

Then how grace a rose? I know a way!
  Leave it, rather.   70
  Must you gather?
Smell, kiss, wear it—at last, throw away!

'CHILDE ROLAND TO THE DARK TOWER CAME'

(See Edgar's Song in 'LEAR')

I

My first thought was, he lied in every word,
  That hoary cripple, with malicious eye
  Askance to watch the working of his lie
On mine, and mouth scarce able to afford
Suppression of the glee, that pursed and scored   5
  Its edge, at one more victim gained thereby.

II

What else should he be set for, with his staff?
  What, save to waylay with his lies, ensnare
  All travellers who might find him posted there,
And ask the road? I guessed what skull-like laugh   10
Would break, what crutch 'gin write my epitaph
  For pastime in the dusty thoroughfare,

III

If at his counsel I should turn aside
  Into that ominous tract which, all agree,
  Hides the Dark Tower. Yet acquiescingly   15
I did turn as he pointed: neither pride
Nor hope rekindling at the end descried,
  So much as gladness that some end might be.

IV

For, what with my whole world-wide wandering,
  What with my search drawn out thro' years, my hope   20
  Dwindled into a ghost not fit to cope
With that obstreperous joy success would bring,—

I hardly tried now to rebuke the spring
My heart made, finding failure in its scope.

V

As when a sick man very near to death   25
  Seems dead indeed, and feels begin and end
  The tears and takes the farewell of each friend,
And hears one bid the other go, draw breath
Freelier outside, ('since all is o'er,' he saith,
  'And the blow fallen no grieving can amend;')   30

VI

While some discuss if near the other graves
  Be room enough for this, and when a day
  Suits best for carrying the corpse away,
With care about the banners, scarves and staves:
And still the man hears all, and only craves   35
  He may not shame such tender love and stay.

VII

Thus, I had so long suffered in this quest,
  Heard failure prophesied so oft, been writ
  So many times among 'The Band'—to wit,
The knights who to the Dark Tower's search addressed   40
Their steps—that just to fail as they, seemed best,
  And all the doubt was now—should I be fit?

VIII

So, quiet as despair, I turned from him,
  That hateful cripple, out of his highway
  Into the path he pointed. All the day   45
Had been a dreary one at best, and dim
Was settling to its close, yet shot one grim
  Red leer to see the plain catch its estray.

IX

For mark! no sooner was I fairly found
  Pledged to the plain, after a pace or two,   50
  Than, pausing to throw backward a last view
O'er the safe road, 't was gone; grey plain all round:

Nothing but plain to the horizon's bound.
I might go on; nought else remained to do.

X

So, on I went. I think I never saw   55
  Such starved ignoble nature; nothing throve:
  For flowers—as well expect a cedar grove!
But cockle, spurge, according to their law
Might propagate their kind, with none to awe,
  You'd think; a burr had been a treasure-trove.   60

XI

No! penury, inertness and grimace,
  In some strange sort, were the land's portion. 'See
  Or shut your eyes,' said Nature peevishly,
'It nothing skills: I cannot help my case:
' 'T is the Last Judgment's fire must cure this place,   65
  'Calcine its clods and set my prisoners free.'

XII

If there pushed any ragged thistle-stalk
  Above its mates, the head was chopped; the bents
  Were jealous else. What made those holes and rents
In the dock's harsh swarth leaves, bruised as to baulk   70
All hope of greenness? 't is a brute must walk
  Pashing their life out, with a brute's intents.

XIII

As for the grass, it grew as scant as hair
  In leprosy; thin dry blades pricked the mud
  Which underneath looked kneaded up with blood.   75
One stiff blind horse, his every bone a-stare,
Stood stupefied, however he came there:
  Thrust out past service from the devil's stud!

XIV

Alive? he might be dead for aught I know,
  With that red gaunt and colloped neck a-strain,   80
  And shut eyes underneath the rusty mane;
Seldom went such grotesqueness with such woe;

I never saw a brute I hated so;
    He must be wicked to deserve such pain.

XV

I shut my eyes and turned them on my heart.   85
    As a man calls for wine before he fights,
    I asked one draught of earlier, happier sights,
Ere fitly I could hope to play my part.
Think first, fight afterwards—the soldier's art:
    One taste of the old time sets all to rights.   90

XVI

Not it! I fancied Cuthbert's reddening face
    Beneath its garniture of curly gold,
    Dear fellow, till I almost felt him fold
An arm in mine to fix me to the place,
That way he used. Alas, one night's disgrace!   95
    Out went my heart's new fire and left it cold.

XVII

Giles then, the soul of honour—there he stands
    Frank as ten years ago when knighted first.
    What honest men should dare (he said) he durst.   99
Good—but the scene shifts—faugh! what hangman-hands
Pin to his breast a parchment? his own bands
    Read it. Poor traitor, spit upon and curst!

XVIII

Better this present than a past like that;
    Back therefore to my darkening path again!
    No sound, no sight as far as eye could strain.   105
Will the night send a howlet or a bat?
I asked: when something on the dismal flat
    Came to arrest my thoughts and change their train.

XIX

A sudden little river crossed my path
    As unexpected as a serpent comes.   110
    No sluggish tide congenial to the glooms;

This, as it frothed by, might have been a bath
  For the fiend's glowing hoof—to see the wrath
  Of its black eddy bespate with flakes and spumes.

XX

So petty yet so spiteful! All along,   115
  Low scrubby alders kneeled down over it;
  Drenched willows flung them headlong in a fit
Of mute despair, a suicidal throng:
The river which had done them all the wrong,
  Whate'er that was, rolled by, deterred no whit.   120

XXI

Which, while I forded,—good saints, how I feared
  To set my foot upon a dead man's cheek,
  Each step, or feel the spear I thrust to seek
For hollows, tangled in his hair or beard!
—It may have been a water-rat I speared,   125
  But, ugh! it sounded like a baby's shriek.

XXII

Glad was I when I reached the other bank.
  Now for a better country. Vain presage!
  Who were the strugglers, what war did they wage,
Whose savage trample thus could pad the dank   130
Soil to a plash? Toads in a poisoned tank,
  Or wild cats in a red-hot iron cage—

XXIII

The fight must so have seemed in that fell cirque.
  What penned them there, with all the plain to choose?
  No foot-print leading to that horrid mews,   135
None out of it. Mad brewage set to work
Their brains, no doubt, like galley-slaves the Turk
  Pits for his pastime, Christians against Jews.

XXIV

And more than that—a furlong on—why, there!
  What bad use was that engine for, that wheel,   140
  Or brake, not wheel—that harrow fit to reel

Men's bodies out like silk? with all the air
Of Tophet's tool, on earth left unaware,
  Or brought to sharpen its rusty teeth of steel.

XXV

Then came a bit of stubbed ground, once a wood,   145
  Next a marsh, it would seem, and now mere earth
  Desperate and done with; (so a fool finds mirth,
Makes a thing and then mars it, till his mood
Changes and off he goes!) within a rood—
  Bog, clay and rubble, sand and stark black dearth.   150

XXVI

Now blotches rankling, coloured gay and grim,
  Now patches where some leanness of the soil's
  Broke into moss or substances like boils;
Then came some palsied oak, a cleft in him
Like a distorted mouth that splits its rim   155
  Gaping at death, and dies while it recoils.

XXVII

And just as far as ever from the end!
  Nought in the distance but the evening, nought
  To point my footstep further! At the thought,
A great black bird, Apollyon's bosom-friend,   160
Sailed past, nor beat his wide wing dragon-penned
  That brushed my cap—perchance the guide I sought.

XXVIII

For, looking up, aware I somehow grew,
  'Spite of the dusk, the plain had given place
  All round to mountains—with such name to grace   165
Mere ugly heights and heaps now stolen in view.
How thus they had surprised me,—solve it, you!
  How to get from them was no clearer case.

XXIX

Yet half I seemed to recognize some trick
  Of mischief happened to me, God knows when—   170
  In a bad dream perhaps. Here ended, then,

Progress this way. When, in the very nick
Of giving up, one time more, came a click
　　As when a trap shuts—you're inside the den!

XXX

Burningly it came on me all at once,　　175
　　This was the place! those two hills on the right,
　　Crouched like two bulls locked horn in horn in fight;
While to the left, a tall scalped mountain . . . Dunce,
Dotard, a-dozing at the very nonce,
　　After a life spent training for the sight!　　180

XXXI

What in the midst lay but the Tower itself?
　　The round squat turret, blind as the fool's heart,
　　Built of brown stone, without a counterpart
In the whole world. The tempest's mocking elf
Points to the shipman thus the unseen shelf　　185
　　He strikes on, only when the timbers start.

XXXII

Not see? because of night perhaps?—why, day
　　Came back again for that! before it left,
　　The dying sunset kindled through a cleft:
The hills, like giants at a hunting, lay,　　190
Chin upon hand, to see the game at bay,—
　　'Now stab and end the creature—to the heft!'

XXXIII

Not hear? when noise was everywhere! it tolled
　　Increasing like a bell. Names in my ears
　　Of all the lost adventurers my peers,—　　195
How such a one was strong, and such was bold,
And such was fortunate, yet each of old
　　Lost, lost! one moment knelled the woe of years.

XXXIV

There they stood, ranged along the hill-sides, met
　　To view the last of me, a living frame　　200
　　For one more picture! in a sheet of flame

I saw them and I knew them all. And yet
Dauntless the slug-horn to my lips I set,
    And blew. '*Childe Roland to the Dark Tower came.*'

RESPECTABILITY

I

DEAR, had the world in its caprice
    Deigned to proclaim 'I know you both,
    'Have recognized your plighted troth,
'Am sponsor for you: live in peace!'—
How many precious months and years   5
    Of youth had passed, that speed so fast,
    Before we found it out at last,
The world, and what it fears?

II

How much of priceless life were spent
    With men that every virtue decks,   10
    And women models of their sex,
Society's true ornament,—
Ere we dared wander, nights like this,
    Thro' wind and rain, and watch the Seine,
    And feel the Boulevart break again   15
To warmth and light and bliss?

III

I know! the world proscribes not love;
    Allows my finger to caress
    Your lips' contour and downiness,
Provided it supply a glove.   20
The world's good word!—the Institute!
    Guizot receives Montalembert!
    Eh? down the court three lampions flare:
Put forward your best foot!

A LIGHT WOMAN

I

So far as our story approaches the end,
   Which do you pity the most of us three?—
My friend, or the mistress of my friend
   With her wanton eyes, or me?

II

My friend was already too good to lose,   5
   And seemed in the way of improvement yet,
When she crossed his path with her hunting-noose
   And over him drew her net.

III

When I saw him tangled in her toils,
   A shame, said I, if she adds just him   10
To her nine-and-ninety other spoils,
   The hundredth for a whim!

IV

And before my friend be wholly hers,
   How easy to prove to him, I said,
An eagle's the game her pride prefers,   15
   Though she snaps at a wren instead!

V

So, I gave her eyes my own eyes to take,
   My hand sought hers as in earnest need,
And round she turned for my noble sake,
   And gave me herself indeed.   20

VI

The eagle am I, with my fame in the world,
   The wren is he, with his maiden face.
—You look away and your lip is curled?
   Patience, a moment's space!

VII

For see, my friend goes shaking and white;   25
   He eyes me as the basilisk:
I have turned, it appears, his day to night,
   Eclipsing his sun's disk.

VIII

And I did it, he thinks, as a very thief:
  'Though I love her—that, he comprehends—   30
'One should master one's passions, (love, in chief)
  'And be loyal to one's friends!'

IX

And she,—she lies in my hand as tame
  As a pear late basking over a wall;
Just a touch to try and off it came;   35
  'T is mine,—can I let it fall?

X

With no mind to eat it, that's the worst!
  Were it thrown in the road, would the case assist?
'T was quenching a dozen blue-flies' thirst
  When I gave its stalk a twist.   40

XI

And I,—what I seem to my friend, you see:
  What I soon shall seem to his love, you guess:
What I seem to myself, do you ask of me?
  No hero, I confess.

XII

'T is an awkward thing to play with souls,   45
  And matter enough to save one's own:
Yet think of my friend, and the burning coals
  He played with for bits of stone!

XIII

One likes to show the truth for the truth;
  That the woman was light is very true: 50
But suppose she says,—Never mind that youth!
  What wrong have I done to you?

XIV

Well, any how, here the story stays,
  So far at least as I understand;
And, Robert Browning, you writer of plays,   55
  Here's a subject made to your hand!

THE STATUE AND THE BUST

THERE's a palace in Florence, the world knows well,
And a statue watches it from the square,
And this story of both do our townsmen tell.

Ages ago, a lady there,
At the farthest window facing the East   5
Asked, 'Who rides by with the royal air?'

The bridesmaids' prattle around her ceased;
She leaned forth, one on either hand;
They saw how the blush of the bride increased—

They felt by its beats her heart expand—   10
As one at each ear and both in a breath
Whispered, 'The Great-Duke Ferdinand.'

That self-same instant, underneath,
The Duke rode past in his idle way,
Empty and fine like a swordless sheath.   15

Gay he rode, with a friend as gay,
Till he threw his head back—'Who is she?'
—'A Bride the Riccardi brings home to-day.'

Hair in heaps lay heavily
Over a pale brow spirit-pure—   20
Carved like the heart of the coal-black tree,

Crisped like a war-steed's encolure—
And vainly sought to dissemble her eyes
Of the blackest black our eyes endure.

And lo, a blade for a knight's emprise   25
Filled the fine empty sheath of a man,—
The Duke grew straightway brave and wise.

He looked at her, as a lover can;
She looked at him, as one who awakes:
The past was a sleep, and her life began.   30

Now, love so ordered for both their sakes,
A feast was held that selfsame night
In the pile which the mighty shadow makes.

(For Via Larga is three-parts light,
But the palace overshadows one,   35
Because of a crime which may God requite!

To Florence and God the wrong was done,
Through the first republic's murder there
By Cosimo and his cursed son.)

The Duke (with the statue's face in the square)   40
Turned in the midst of his multitude
At the bright approach of the bridal pair.

Face to face the lovers stood
A single minute and no more,
While the bridegroom bent as a man subdued—   45

Bowed till his bonnet brushed the floor—
For the Duke on the lady a kiss conferred,
As the courtly custom was of yore.

In a minute can lovers exchange a word?
If a word did pass, which I do not think,   50
Only one out of the thousand heard.

That was the bridegroom. At day's brink
He and his bride were alone at last
In a bedchamber by a taper's blink.

Calmly he said that her lot was cast,   55
That the door she had passed was shut on her
Till the final catafalk repassed.

The world meanwhile, its noise and stir,
Through a certain window facing the East,
She could watch like a convent's chronicler.   60

Since passing the door might lead to a feast,
And a feast might lead to so much beside,
He, of many evils, chose the least.

'Freely I choose too,' said the bride—
'Your window and its world suffice,'   65
Replied the tongue, while the heart replied—

'If I spend the night with that devil twice,
'May his window serve as my loop of hell
'Whence a damned soul looks on paradise!

'I fly to the Duke who loves me well,   70
'Sit by his side and laugh at sorrow
'Ere I count another ave-bell.

' 'T is only the coat of a page to borrow,
And tie my hair in a horse-boy's trim,
And I save my soul—but not to-morrow'—   75

(She checked herself and her eye grew dim)
'My father tarries to bless my state:
'I must keep it one day more for him.

'Is one day more so long to wait?
'Moreover the Duke rides past, I know;   80
'We shall see each other, sure as fate.'

She turned on her side and slept. Just so!
So we resolve on a thing and sleep:
So did the lady, ages ago.

That night the Duke said, 'Dear or cheap   85
'As the cost of this cup of bliss may prove
'To body or soul, I will drain it deep.'

And on the morrow, bold with love,
He beckoned the bridegroom (close on call,
As his duty bade, by the Duke's alcove)   90

And smiled ' 'T was a very funeral,
'Your lady will think, this feast of ours,—
'A shame to efface, whate'er befall!

'What if we break from the Arno bowers,
'And try if Petraja, cool and green,   95
'Cure last night's fault with this morning's flowers?'

The bridegroom, not a thought to be seen
On his steady brow and quiet mouth,
Said, 'Too much favour for me so mean!

'But, alas! my lady leaves the South;   100
'Each wind that comes from the Apennine
'Is a menace to her tender youth:

'Nor a way exists, the wise opine,
'If she quits her palace twice this year,
'To avert the flower of life's decline.'   105

Quoth the Duke, 'A sage and a kindly fear.
'Moreover Petraja is cold this spring:
'Be our feast to-night as usual here!'

And then to himself—'Which night shall bring
'Thy bride to her lover's embraces, fool—   110
'Or I am the fool, and thou art the king!

'Yet my passion must wait a night, nor cool—
'For to-night the Envoy arrives from France
'Whose heart I unlock with thyself, my tool.

'I need thee still and might miss perchance.   115
'To-day is not wholly lost, beside,
'With its hope of my lady's countenance:

'For I ride—what should I do but ride?
'And passing her palace, if I list,
'May glance at its window—well betide!'   120

So said, so done: nor the lady missed
One ray that broke from the ardent brow,
Nor a curl of the lips where the spirit kissed.

Be sure that each renewed the vow,
No morrow's sun should arise and set   125
And leave them then as it left them now.

But next day passed, and next day yet,
With still fresh cause to wait one day more
Ere each leaped over the parapet.

And still, as love's brief morning wore,   130
With a gentle start, half smile, half sigh,
They found love not as it seemed before.

They thought it would work infallibly,
But not in despite of heaven and earth:
The rose would blow when the storm passed by.   135

Meantime they could profit in winter's dearth
By store of fruits that supplant the rose:
The world and its ways have a certain worth:

And to press a point while these oppose
Were simple policy; better wait: 140
We lose no friends and we gain no foes.

Meantime, worse fates than a lover's fate,
Who daily may ride and pass and look
Where his lady watches behind the grate!

And she—she watched the square like a book   145
Holding one picture and only one,
Which daily to find she undertook:

When the picture was reached the book was done,
And she turned from the picture at night to scheme
Of tearing it out for herself next sun.   150

So weeks grew months, years; gleam by gleam
The glory dropped from their youth and love,
And both perceived they had dreamed a dream;

Which hovered as dreams do, still above:
But who can take a dream for a truth?   155
Oh, hide our eyes from the next remove!

One day as the lady saw her youth
Depart, and the silver thread that streaked
Her hair, and, worn by the serpent's tooth,

The brow so puckered, the chin so peaked,—   160
And wondered who the woman was,
Hollow-eyed and haggard-cheeked,

Fronting her silent in the glass—
'Summon here,' she suddenly said,
'Before the rest of my old self pass,   165

'Him, the Carver, a hand to aid,
'Who fashions the clay no love will change,
'And fixes a beauty never to fade.

'Let Robbia's craft so apt and strange
'Arrest the remains of young and fair,   170
'And rivet them while the seasons range.

'Make me a face on the window there,
'Waiting as ever, mute the while,
'My love to pass below in the square!

'And let me think that it may beguile   175
'Dreary days which the dead must spend
'Down in their darkness under the aisle,

'To say, "What matters it at the end?
' "I did no more while my heart was warm
' "Than does that image, my pale-faced friend."   180

'Where is the use of the lip's red charm,
'The heaven of hair, the pride of the brow,
'And the blood that blues the inside arm—

'Unless we turn, as the soul knows how,
'The earthly gift to an end divine?   185
'A lady of clay is as good, I trow.'

But long ere Robbia's cornice, fine
With flowers and fruits which leaves enlace,
Was set where now is the empty shrine—

(And, leaning out of a bright blue space,   190
As a ghost might lean from a chink of sky,
The passionate pale lady's face—

Eyeing ever, with earnest eye
And quick-turned neck at its breathless stretch,
Some one who ever is passing by—)   195

The Duke had sighed like the simplest wretch
In Florence, 'Youth—my dream escapes!
'Will its record stay?' And he bade them fetch

Some subtle moulder of brazen shapes—
'Can the soul, the will, die out of a man   200
'Ere his body find the grave that gapes?

'John of Douay shall effect my plan,
'Set me on horseback here aloft,
'Alive, as the crafty sculptor can,

'In the very square I have crossed so oft: 205
'That men may admire, when future suns
'Shall touch the eyes to a purpose soft,

'While the mouth and the brow stay brave in bronze—
'Admire and say, "When he was alive
' "How he would take his pleasure once!"   210

'And it shall go hard but I contrive
'To listen the while, and laugh in my tomb
'At idleness which aspires to strive.'

———————

So! While these wait the trump of doom,
How do their spirits pass, I wonder,   215
Nights and days in the narrow room?

Still, I suppose, they sit and ponder
What a gift life was, ages ago,
Six steps out of the chapel yonder.

Only they see not God, I know,   220
Nor all that chivalry of his,
The soldier-saints who, row on row,

Burn upward each to his point of bliss—
Since, the end of life being manifest,
He had burned his way thro' the world to this.   225

I hear you reproach, 'But delay was best,
'For their end was a crime.'—Oh, a crime will do
As well, I reply, to serve for a test,

As a virtue golden through and through,
Sufficient to vindicate itself   230
And prove its worth at a moment's view!

Must a game be played for the sake of pelf?
Where a button goes, 't were an epigram
To offer the stamp of the very Guelph.

The true has no value beyond the sham: 235
As well the counter as coin, I submit,
When your table's a hat, and your prize a dram.

Stake your counter as boldly every whit,
Venture as warily, use the same skill,
Do your best, whether winning or losing it,   240

If you choose to play!—is my principle.
Let a man contend to the uttermost
For his life's set prize, be it what it will!

The counter our lovers staked was lost
As surely as if it were lawful coin: 245
And the sin I impute to each frustrate ghost

Is—the unlit lamp and the ungirt loin,
Though the end in sight was a vice, I say.
You of the virtue (we issue join)
How strive you? *De te, fabula.*   250

LOVE IN A LIFE

I

ROOM after room,
I hunt the house through
We inhabit together.
Heart, fear nothing, for, heart, thou shalt find her—
Next time, herself!—not the trouble behind her   5
Left in the curtain, the couch's perfume!
As she brushed it, the cornice-wreath blossomed anew:
Yon looking-glass gleamed at the wave of her feather.

II

Yet the day wears,
And door succeeds door;   10
I try the fresh fortune—
Range the wide house from the wing to the centre.
Still the same chance! she goes out as I enter.
Spend my whole day in the quest,—who cares?
But 't is twilight, you see,—with such suites to explore,   15
Such closets to search, such alcoves to importune!

LIFE IN A LOVE

ESCAPE me?
Never—
Beloved!
While I am I, and you are you,

So long as the world contains us both,   5
  Me the loving and you the loth,
While the one eludes, must the other pursue.
My life is a fault at last, I fear:
  It seems too much like a fate, indeed!
Though I do my best I shall scarce succeed.   10
But what if I fail of my purpose here?
It is but to keep the nerves at strain,
  To dry one's eyes and laugh at a fall,
And, baffled, get up and begin again,—
  So the chace takes up one's life, that's all.   15
While, look but once from your farthest bound
  At me so deep in the dust and dark,
No sooner the old hope goes to ground
  Than a new one, straight to the self-same mark,
I shape me—   20
Ever
Removed!

HOW IT STRIKES A CONTEMPORARY

I ONLY knew one poet in my life:
And this, or something like it, was his way.

  You saw go up and down Valladolid,
A man of mark, to know next time you saw.
His very serviceable suit of black   5
Was courtly once and conscientious still,
And many might have worn it, though none did:
The cloak, that somewhat shone and showed the threads,
Had purpose, and the ruff, significance.
He walked and tapped the pavement with his cane,   10
Scenting the world, looking it full in face,
An old dog, bald and blindish, at his heels.
They turned up, now, the alley by the church,
That leads nowhither; now, they breathed themselves
On the main promenade just at the wrong time: 15
You'd come upon his scrutinizing hat,
Making a peaked shade blacker than itself
Against the single window spared some house

Intact yet with its mouldered Moorish work,—
Or else surprise the ferrel of his stick   20
Trying the mortar's temper 'tween the chinks
Of some new shop a-building, French and fine.
He stood and watched the cobbler at his trade,
The man who slices lemons into drink,
The coffee-roaster's brazier, and the boys   25
That volunteer to help him turn its winch.
He glanced o'er books on stalls with half an eye,
And fly-leaf ballads on the vendor's string,
And broad-edge bold-print posters by the wall.
He took such cognizance of men and things,   30
If any beat a horse, you felt he saw;
If any cursed a woman, he took note;
Yet stared at nobody,—you stared at him,
And found, less to your pleasure than surprise,
He seemed to know you and expect as much.   35
So, next time that a neighbour's tongue was loosed,
It marked the shameful and notorious fact,
We had among us, not so much a spy,
As a recording chief-inquisitor,
The town's true master if the town but knew!   40
We merely kept a governor for form,
While this man walked about and took account
Of all thought, said and acted, then went home,
And wrote it fully to our Lord the King
Who has an itch to know things, he knows why,   45
And reads them in his bedroom of a night.
Oh, you might smile! there wanted not a touch,
A tang of . . . well, it was not wholly ease
As back into your mind the man's look came.
Stricken in years a little,—such a brow   50
His eyes had to live under!—clear as flint
On either side the formidable nose
Curved, cut and coloured like an eagle's claw.
Had he to do with A.'s surprising fate?
When altogether old B. disappeared   55
And young C. got his mistress,—was 't our friend,
His letter to the King, that did it all?
What paid the bloodless man for so much pains?

Our Lord the King has favourites manifold,
And shifts his ministry some once a month;   60
Our city gets new governors at whiles,—
But never word or sign, that I could hear,
Notified to this man about the streets
The King's approval of those letters conned
The last thing duly at the dead of night.   65
Did the man love his office? Frowned our Lord,
Exhorting when none heard—'Beseech me not!
'Too far above my people,—beneath me!
'I set the watch,—how should the people know?
'Forget them, keep me all the more in mind!'   70
Was some such understanding 'twixt the two?

    I found no truth in one report at least—
That if you tracked him to his home, down lanes
Beyond the Jewry, and as clean to pace,
You found he ate his supper in a room   75
Blazing with lights, four Titians on the wall,
And twenty naked girls to change his plate!
Poor man, he lived another kind of life
In that new stuccoed third house by the bridge,
Fresh-painted, rather smart than otherwise!   80
The whole street might o'erlook him as he sat,
Leg crossing leg, one foot on the dog's back,
Playing a decent cribbage with his maid
(Jacynth, you 're sure her name was) o'er the cheese
And fruit, three red halves of starved winter-pears,   85
Or treat of radishes in April. Nine,
Ten, struck the church clock, straight to bed went he.

    My father, like the man of sense he was,
Would point him out to me a dozen times;
' 'St—'St,' he'd whisper, 'the Corregidor!'   90
I had been used to think that personage
Was one with lacquered breeches, lustrous belt,
And feathers like a forest in his hat,
Who blew a trumpet and proclaimed the news,
Announced the bull-fights, gave each church its turn,   95
And memorized the miracle in vogue!

He had a great observance from us boys;
We were in error; that was not the man.

I'd like now, yet had haply been afraid,
To have just looked, when this man came to die,   100
And seen who lined the clean gay garret-sides
And stood about the neat low truckle-bed,
With the heavenly manner of relieving guard.
Here had been, mark, the general-in-chief,
Thro' a whole campaign of the world's life and death,   105
Doing the King's work all the dim day long,
In his old coat and up to knees in mud,
Smoked like a herring, dining on a crust,—
And, now the day was won, relieved at once!
No further show or need for that old coat,   110
You are sure, for one thing! Bless us, all the while
How sprucely we are dressed out, you and I!
A second, and the angels alter that.
Well, I could never write a verse,—could you?
Let's to the Prado and make the most of time.   115

THE LAST RIDE TOGETHER

I

I said—Then, dearest, since 't is so,
Since now at length my fate I know,
Since nothing all my love avails,
Since all, my life seemed meant for, fails,
  Since this was written and needs must be—   5
My whole heart rises up to bless
Your name in pride and thankfulness!
Take back the hope you gave,—I claim
Only a memory of the same,
—And this beside, if you will not blame,   10
  Your leave for one more last ride with me.

II

My mistress bent that brow of hers;
Those deep dark eyes where pride demurs
When pity would be softening through,

Fixed me a breathing-while or two   15
  With life or death in the balance: right!
The blood replenished me again;
My last thought was at least not vain:
I and my mistress, side by side
Shall be together, breathe and ride,   20
So, one day more am I deified.
  Who knows but the world may end to-night?

III

Hush! if you saw some western cloud
All billowy-bosomed, over-bowed
By many benedictions—sun's   25
And moon's and evening-star's at once—
  And so, you, looking and loving best,
Conscious grew, your passion drew
Cloud, sunset, moonrise, star-shine too,
Down on you, near and yet more near,   30
Till flesh must fade for heaven was here!—
Thus leant she and lingered—joy and fear!
  Thus lay she a moment on my breast.

IV

Then we began to ride. My soul
Smoothed itself out, a long-cramped scroll   35
Freshening and fluttering in the wind.
Past hopes already lay behind.
  What need to strive with a life awry?
Had I said that, had I done this,
So might I gain, so might I miss.   40
Might she have loved me? just as well
She might have hated, who can tell!
Where had I been now if the worst befell?
  And here we are riding, she and I.

V

Fail I alone, in words and deeds?   45
Why, all men strive and who succeeds?
We rode; it seemed my spirit flew,
Saw other regions, cities new,
  As the world rushed by on either side.

I thought,—All labour, yet no less 50
Bear up beneath their unsuccess.
Look at the end of work, contrast
The petty done, the undone vast,
This present of theirs with the hopeful past!
 I hoped she would love me; here we ride. 55

VI

What hand and brain went ever paired?
What heart alike conceived and dared?
What act proved all its thought had been?
What will but felt the fleshly screen?
 We ride and I see her bosom heave. 60
There's many a crown for who can reach.
Ten lines, a statesman's life in each!
The flag stuck on a heap of bones,
A soldier's doing! what atones?
They scratch his name on the Abbey-stones. 65
 My riding is better, by their leave.

VII

What does it all mean, poet? Well,
Your brains beat into rhythm, you tell
What we felt only; you expressed
You hold things beautiful the best, 70
 And pace them in rhyme so, side by side.
'T is something, nay 't is much: but then,
Have you yourself what's best for men?
Are you—poor, sick, old ere your time—
Nearer one whit your own sublime 75
Than we who never have turned a rhyme?
 Sing, riding's a joy! For me, I ride.

VIII

And you, great sculptor—so, you gave
A score of years to Art, her slave,
And that's your Venus, whence we turn 80
To yonder girl that fords the burn!
 You acquiesce, and shall I repine?
What, man of music, you grown grey
With notes and nothing else to say,

Is this your sole praise from a friend,   85
'Greatly his opera's strains intend,
'But in music we know how fashions end!'
    I gave my youth; but we ride, in fine.

IX

Who knows what's fit for us? Had fate
Proposed bliss here should sublimate   90
My being—had I signed the bond—
Still one must lead some life beyond,
    Have a bliss to die with, dim-descried.
This foot once planted on the goal,
This glory-garland round my soul,   95
Could I descry such? Try and test!
I sink back shuddering from the quest.
Earth being so good, would heaven seem best?
    Now, heaven and she are beyond this ride.

X

And yet—she has not spoke so long!   100
What if heaven be that, fair and strong
At life's best, with our eyes upturned
Whither life's flower is first discerned,
    We, fixed so, ever should so abide?
What if we still ride on, we two,   105
With life for ever old yet new,
Changed not in kind but in degree,
The instant made eternity,—
And heaven just prove that I and she
    Ride, ride together, for ever ride?   110

THE PATRIOT

AN OLD STORY

I

IT was roses, roses, all the way,
    With myrtle mixed in my path like mad:
The house-roofs seemed to heave and sway,
    The church-spires flamed, such flags they had,
A year ago on this very day.   5

II

The air broke into a mist with bells,
  The old walls rocked with the crowd and cries.
Had I said, 'Good folk, mere noise repels—
  'But give me your sun from yonder skies!'
They had answered, 'And afterward, what else?'   10

III

Alack, it was I who leaped at the sun
  To give it my loving friends to keep!
Nought man could do, have I left undone:
  And you see my harvest, what I reap
This very day, now a year is run.   15

IV

There's nobody on the house-tops now—
  Just a palsied few at the windows set;
For the best of the sight is, all allow,
  At the Shambles' Gate—or, better yet,
By the very scaffold's foot, I trow.   20

V

I go in the rain, and, more than needs,
  A rope cuts both my wrists behind;
And I think, by the feel, my forehead bleeds,
  For they fling, whoever has a mind,
Stones at me for my year's misdeeds.   25

VI

Thus I entered, and thus I go!
  In triumphs, people have dropped down dead.
'Paid by the world, what dost thou owe
  'Me?'—God might question; now instead,
'T is God shall repay: I am safer so.   30

MASTER HUGUES OF SAXE-GOTHA

I

Hist, but a word, fair and soft!
  Forth and be judged, Master Hugues!

Answer the question I've put you so oft:—
　What do you mean by your mountainous fugues?
See, we're alone in the loft,—　　　　　　　　5

II

I, the poor organist here,
　Hugues, the composer of note,
Dead though, and done with, this many a year:
　Let's have a colloquy, something to quote,
Make the world prick up its ear!　　　　　10

III

See, the church empties apace:
　Fast they extinguish the lights.
Hallo there, sacristan! Five minutes' grace!
　Here's a crank pedal wants setting to rights,
Baulks one of holding the base.　　　　　15

IV

See, our huge house of the sounds,
　Hushing its hundreds at once,
Bids the last loiterer back to his bounds!
　—O you may challenge them, not a response
Get the church-saints on their rounds!　　20

V

(Saints go their rounds, who shall doubt?
　—March, with the moon to admire,
Up nave, down chancel, turn transept about,
　Supervise all betwixt pavement and spire,
Put rats and mice to the rout—　　　　　25

VI

Aloys and Jurien and Just—
　Order things back to their place,
Have a sharp eye lest the candlesticks rust,
　Rub the church-plate, darn the sacrament-lace,
Clear the desk-velvet of dust.)　　　　　30

VII

Here's your book, younger folks shelve!
　Played I not off-hand and runningly,

Y

Just now, your masterpiece, hard number twelve?
  Here's what should strike, could one handle it cunningly:
Help the axe, give it a helve!   35

VIII

Page after page as I played,
  Every bar's rest, where one wipes
Sweat from one's brow, I looked up and surveyed,
  O'er my three claviers, yon forest of pipes
Whence you still peeped in the shade.   40

IX

Sure you were wishful to speak?
  You, with brow ruled like a score,
Yes, and eyes buried in pits on each cheek,
  Like two great breves, as they wrote them of yore,
Each side that bar, your straight beak!   45

X

Sure you said—'Good, the mere notes!
  'Still, couldst thou take my intent,
'Know what procured me our Company's votes—
  'A master were lauded and sciolists shent,
'Parted the sheep from the goats!'   50

XI

Well then, speak up, never flinch!
  Quick, ere my candle's a snuff
—Burnt, do you see? to its uttermost inch—
  I believe in you, but that's not enough:
Give my conviction a clinch!   55

XII

First you deliver your phrase
  —Nothing propound, that I see,
Fit in itself for much blame or much praise—
  Answered no less, where no answer needs be:
Off start the Two on their ways.   60

XIII

Straight must a Third interpose,
  Volunteer needlessly help;

In strikes a Fourth, a Fifth thrusts in his nose,
  So the cry's open, the kennel's a-yelp,
Argument's hot to the close.   65

XIV

One dissertates, he is candid;
  Two must discept,—has distinguished;
Three helps the couple, if ever yet man did;
  Four protests; Five makes a dart at the thing wished:
Back to One, goes the case bandied.   70

XV

One says his say with a difference;
  More of expounding, explaining!
All now is wrangle, abuse, and vociferance;
  Now there's a truce, all's subdued, self-restraining;
Five, though, stands out all the stiffer hence.   75

XVI

One is incisive, corrosive;
  Two retorts, nettled, curt, crepitant;
Three makes rejoinder, expansive, explosive;
  Four overbears them all, strident and strepitant:
Five . . . O Danaides, O Sieve!   80

XVII

Now, they ply axes and crowbars;
  Now, they prick pins at a tissue
Fine as a skein of the casuist Escobar's
  Worked on the bone of a lie. To what issue?
Where is our gain at the Two-bars?   85

XVIII

Est fuga, volvitur rota.
  On we drift: where looms the dim port?
One, Two, Three, Four, Five, contribute their quota;
  Something is gained, if one caught but the import—
Show it us, Hugues of Saxe-Gotha!   90

XIX

What with affirming, denying,
  Holding, risposting, subjoining,

All's like . . . it's like . . . for an instance I'm trying . . .
　　There! See our roof, its gilt moulding and groining
Under those spider-webs lying!　　　　　　　　　　　　95

XX

So your fugue broadens and thickens,
　　Greatens and deepens and lengthens,
Till we exclaim—'But where's music, the dickens?
　　'Blot ye the gold, while your spider-web strengthens
'—Blacked to the stoutest of tickens?'　　　　　　　100

XXI

I for man's effort am zealous:
　　Prove me such censure unfounded!
Seems it surprising a lover grows jealous—
　　Hopes 't was for something, his organ-pipes sounded,
Tiring three boys at the bellows?　　　　　　　　　105

XXII

Is it your moral of Life?
　　Such a web, simple and subtle,
Weave we on earth here in impotent strife,
　　Backward and forward each throwing his shuttle,
Death ending all with a knife?　　　　　　　　　110

XXIII

Over our heads truth and nature—
　　Still our life's zigzags and dodges,
Ins and outs, weaving a new legislature—
　　God's gold just shining its last where that lodges,
Palled beneath man's usurpature.　　　　　　　　115

XXIV

So we o'ershroud stars and roses,
　　Cherub and trophy and garland;
Nothings grow something which quietly closes
　　Heaven's earnest eye: not a glimpse of the far land
Gets through our comments and glozes.　　　　　　120

XXV

Ah but traditions, inventions,
　　(Say we and make up a visage)

So many men with such various intentions,
   Down the past ages, must know more than this age!
Leave we the web its dimensions! 125

XXVI

Who thinks Hugues wrote for the deaf,
   Proved a mere mountain in labour?
Better submit; try again; what's the clef?
   'Faith, 't is no trifle for pipe and for tabor—
Four flats, the minor in F. 130

XXVII

Friend, your fugue taxes the finger:
   Learning it once, who would lose it?
Yet all the while a misgiving will linger,
   Truth's golden o'er us although we refuse it—
Nature, thro' cobwebs we string her. 135

XXVIII

Hugues! I advise *meâ pœnâ*
   (Counterpoint glares like a Gorgon)
Bid One, Two, Three, Four, Five, clear the arena!
   Say the word, straight I unstop the full-organ,
Blare out the *mode Palestrina.* 140

XXIX

While in the roof, if I'm right there,
   . . . Lo you, the wick in the socket!
Hallo, you sacristan, show us a light there!
   Down it dips, gone like a rocket.
What, you want, do you, to come unawares, 145
Sweeping the church up for first morning-prayers,
And find a poor devil has ended his cares
At the foot of your rotten-runged rat-riddled stairs?
   Do I carry the moon in my pocket?

BISHOP BLOUGRAM'S APOLOGY

No more wine? then we'll push back chairs and talk.
A final glass for me, though: cool, i' faith!
We ought to have our Abbey back, you see.

It's different, preaching in basilicas,
And doing duty in some masterpiece   5
Like this of brother Pugin's, bless his heart!
I doubt if they're half baked, those chalk rosettes,
Ciphers and stucco-twiddlings everywhere;
It 's just like breathing in a lime-kiln: eh?
These hot long ceremonies of our church   10
Cost us a little—oh, they pay the price,
You take me—amply pay it! Now, we'll talk.

So, you despise me, Mr. Gigadibs.
No deprecation,—nay, I beg you, sir!
Beside 't is our engagement: don't you know,   15
I promised, if you'd watch a dinner out,
We'd see truth dawn together?—truth that peeps
Over the glasses' edge when dinner's done,
And body gets its sop and holds its noise
And leaves soul free a little. Now's the time: 20
Truth's break of day! You do despise me then.
And if I say, 'despise me,'—never fear!
I know you do not in a certain sense—
Not in my arm-chair, for example: here,
I well imagine you respect my place   25
(*Status, entourage*, worldly circumstance)
Quite to its value—very much indeed:
—Are up to the protesting eyes of you
In pride at being seated here for once—
You'll turn it to such capital account!   30
When somebody, through years and years to come,
Hints of the bishop,—names me—that's enough:
'Blougram? I knew him'—(into it you slide)
'Dined with him once, a Corpus Christi Day,
'All alone, we two; he's a clever man: 35
'And after dinner,—why, the wine you know,—
'Oh, there was wine, and good!—what with the wine . . .
' 'Faith, we began upon all sorts of talk!
'He's no bad fellow, Blougram; he had seen
'Something of mine he relished, some review: 40
'He's quite above their humbug in his heart,
'Half-said as much, indeed—the thing's his trade.

'I warrant, Blougram 's sceptical at times:
'How otherwise? I liked him, I confess!'
Che che, my dear sir, as we say at Rome,   45
Don't you protest now! It's fair give and take;
You have had your turn and spoken your home-truths:
The hand's mine now, and here you follow suit.

   Thus much conceded, still the first fact stays—
You do despise me; your ideal of life   50
Is not the bishop's: you would not be I.
You would like better to be Goethe, now,
Or Buonaparte, or, bless me, lower still,
Count D'Orsay,—so you did what you preferred,
Spoke as you thought, and, as you cannot help,   55
Believed or disbelieved, no matter what,
So long as on that point, whate'er it was,
You loosed your mind, were whole and sole yourself.
—That, my ideal never can include,
Upon that element of truth and worth   60
Never be based! for say they make me Pope—
(They can't—suppose it for our argument!)
Why, there I'm at my tether's end, I've reached
My height, and not a height which pleases you:
An unbelieving Pope won't do, you say.   65
It's like those eerie stories nurses tell,
Of how some actor on a stage played Death,
With pasteboard crown, sham orb and tinselled dart,
And called himself the monarch of the world;
Then, going in the tire-room afterward,   70
Because the play was done, to shift himself,
Got touched upon the sleeve familiarly,
The moment he had shut the closet door,
By Death himself. Thus God might touch a Pope
At unawares, ask what his baubles mean,   75
And whose part he presumed to play just now.
Best be yourself, imperial, plain and true!

So, drawing comfortable breath again,
You weigh and find, whatever more or less
I boast of my ideal realized   80

Is nothing in the balance when opposed
To your ideal, your grand simple life,
Of which you will not realize one jot.
I am much, you are nothing; you would be all,
I would be merely much: you beat me there.   85

No, friend, you do not beat me: hearken why!
The common problem, yours, mine, every one's,
Is—not to fancy what were fair in life
Provided it could be,—but, finding first
What may be, then find how to make it fair   90
Up to our means: a very different thing!
No abstract intellectual plan of life
Quite irrespective of life's plainest laws,
But one, a man, who is man and nothing more,
May lead within a world which (by your leave)   95
Is Rome or London, not Fool's-paradise.
Embellish Rome, idealize away,
Make paradise of London if you can,
You're welcome, nay, you're wise.

                              A simile!
We mortals cross the ocean of this world   100
Each in his average cabin of a life;
The best's not big, the worst yields elbow-room.
Now for our six months' voyage—how prepare?
You come on shipboard with a landsman's list
Of things he calls convenient: so they are!   105
An India screen is pretty furniture,
A piano-forte is a fine resource,
All Balzac's novels occupy one shelf,
The new edition fifty volumes long;
And little Greek books, with the funny type   110
They get up well at Leipsic, fill the next:
Go on! slabbed marble, what a bath it makes!
And Parma's pride, the Jerome, let us add!
'T were pleasant could Correggio's fleeting glow
Hang full in face of one where'er one roams,   115
Since he more than the others brings with him
Italy's self,—the marvellous Modenese!—

Yet was not on your list before, perhaps.
—Alas, friend, here's the agent . . . is 't the name?
The captain, or whoever's master here—   120
You see him screw his face up; what's his cry
Ere you set foot on shipboard? 'Six feet square!'
If you won't understand what six feet mean,
Compute and purchase stores accordingly—
And if, in pique because he overhauls   125
Your Jerome, piano, bath, you come on board
Bare—why, you cut a figure at the first
While sympathetic landsmen see you off;
Not afterward, when long ere half seas over,
You peep up from your utterly naked boards   130
Into some snug and well-appointed berth,
Like mine for instance (try the cooler jug—
Put back the other, but don't jog the ice!)
And mortified you mutter 'Well and good;
'He sits enjoying his sea-furniture;   135
' 'T is stout and proper, and there's store of it:
'Though I've the better notion, all agree,
'Of fitting rooms up. Hang the carpenter,
'Neat ship-shape fixings and contrivances—
'I would have brought my Jerome, frame and all!'   140
And meantime you bring nothing: never mind—
You've proved your artist-nature: what you don't
You might bring, so despise me, as I say.

Now come, let's backward to the starting-place.
See my way: we're two college friends, suppose.   145
Prepare together for our voyage, then;
Each note and check the other in his work,—
Here's mine, a bishop's outfit; criticize!
What's wrong? why won't you be a bishop too?

Why first, you don't believe, you don't and can't,   150
(Not statedly, that is, and fixedly
And absolutely and exclusively)
In any revelation called divine.
No dogmas nail your faith; and what remains
But say so, like the honest man you are?   155

First, therefore, overhaul theology!
Nay, I too, not a fool, you please to think,
Must find believing every whit as hard:
And if I do not frankly say as much,
The ugly consequence is clear enough.   160

　　Now wait, my friend: well, I do not believe—
If you'll accept no faith that is not fixed,
Absolute and exclusive, as you say.
You're wrong—I mean to prove it in due time.
Meanwhile, I know where difficulties lie   165
I could not, cannot solve, nor ever shall,
So give up hope accordingly to solve—
(To you, and over the wine). Our dogmas then
With both of us, though in unlike degree,
Missing full credence—overboard with them!   170
I mean to meet you on your own premise:
Good, there go mine in company with yours!

　　And now what are we? unbelievers both,
Calm and complete, determinately fixed
To-day, to-morrow and for ever, pray?   175
You'll guarantee me that? Not so, I think!
In no wise! all we've gained is, that belief,
As unbelief before, shakes us by fits,
Confounds us like its predecessor. Where's
The gain? how can we guard our unbelief,   180
Make it bear fruit to us?—the problem here.
Just when we are safest, there's a sunset-touch,
A fancy from a flower-bell, some one's death,
A chorus-ending from Euripides,—
And that's enough for fifty hopes and fears   185
As old and new at once as nature's self,
To rap and knock and enter in our soul,
Take hands and dance there, a fantastic ring,
Round the ancient idol, on his base again,—
The grand Perhaps! We look on helplessly.   190
There the old misgivings, crooked questions are—
This good God,—what he could do, if he would,
Would, if he could—then must have done long since:

If so, when, where and how? some way must be,—
Once feel about, and soon or late you hit   195
Some sense, in which it might be, after all.
Why not, 'The Way, the Truth, the Life?'

                                        —That way
Over the mountain, which who stands upon
Is apt to doubt if it be meant for a road;
While, if he views it from the waste itself,   200
Up goes the line there, plain from base to brow,
Not vague, mistakeable! what's a break or two
Seen from the unbroken desert either side?
And then (to bring in fresh philosophy)
What if the breaks themselves should prove at last   205
The most consummate of contrivances
To train a man's eye, teach him what is faith?
And so we stumble at truth's very test!
All we have gained then by our unbelief
Is a life of doubt diversified by faith,   210
For one of faith diversified by doubt:
We called the chess-board white,—we call it black.

'Well,' you rejoin, 'the end's no worse, at least;
'We've reason for both colours on the board:
'Why not confess then, where I drop the faith   215
'And you the doubt, that I'm as right as you?'

Because, friend, in the next place, this being so,
And both things even,—faith and unbelief
Left to a man's choice,—we'll proceed a step,
Returning to our image, which I like.   220

A man's choice, yes—but a cabin-passenger's—
The man made for the special life o' the world—
Do you forget him? I remember though!
Consult our ship's conditions and you find
One and but one choice suitable to all;   225
The choice, that you unluckily prefer,
Turning things topsy-turvy—they or it
Going to the ground. Belief or unbelief
Bears upon life, determines its whole course,
Begins at its beginning. See the world   230

Such as it is,—you made it not, nor I;
I mean to take it as it is,—and you,
Not so you'll take it,—though you get nought else.
I know the special kind of life I like,
What suits the most my idiosyncrasy,　　　　　235
Brings out the best of me and bears me fruit
In power, peace, pleasantness and length of days.
I find that positive belief does this
For me, and unbelief, no whit of this.
—For you, it does, however?—that, we'll try!　　　240
'T is clear, I cannot lead my life, at least,
Induce the world to let me peaceably,
Without declaring at the outset, 'Friends,
'I absolutely and peremptorily
'Believe!'—I say, faith is my waking life:　　　245
One sleeps, indeed, and dreams at intervals,
We know, but waking's the main point with us
And my provision's for life's waking part.
Accordingly, I use heart, head and hand
All day, I build, scheme, study, and make friends;　　　250
And when night overtakes me, down I lie,
Sleep, dream a little, and get done with it,
The sooner the better, to begin afresh.
What's midnight doubt before the dayspring's faith?
You, the philosopher, that disbelieve,　　　255
That recognize the night, give dreams their weight—
To be consistent you should keep your bed,
Abstain from healthy acts that prove you man,
For fear you drowse perhaps at unawares!
And certainly at night you'll sleep and dream,　　　260
Live through the day and bustle as you please.
And so you live to sleep as I to wake,
To unbelieve as I still believe?
Well, and the common sense o' the world calls you
Bed-ridden,—and its good things come to me.　　　265
Its estimation, which is half the fight,
That's the first-cabin comfort I secure:
The next . . . but you perceive with half an eye!
Come, come, it's best believing, if we may;
You can't but own that!

                              Next, concede again,   270
If once we choose belief, on all accounts
We can't be too decisive in our faith,
Conclusive and exclusive in its terms,
To suit the world which gives us the good things.
In every man's career are certain points   275
Whereon he dares not be indifferent;
The world detects him clearly, if he dare,
As baffled at the game, and losing life.
He may care little or he may care much
For riches, honour, pleasure, work, repose,   280
Since various theories of life and life's
Success are extant which might easily
Comport with either estimate of these;
And whoso chooses wealth or poverty,
Labour or quiet, is not judged a fool   285
Because his fellow would choose otherwise:
We let him choose upon his own account
So long as he's consistent with his choice.
But certain points, left wholly to himself,
When once a man has arbitrated on,   290
We say he must succeed there or go hang.
Thus, he should wed the woman he loves most
Or needs most, whatsoe'er the love or need—
For he can't wed twice. Then, he must avouch,
Or follow, at the least, sufficiently,   295
The form of faith his conscience holds the best,
Whate'er the process of conviction was:
For nothing can compensate his mistake
On such a point, the man himself being judge:
He cannot wed twice, nor twice lose his soul.   300

    Well now, there's one great form of Christian faith
I happened to be born in—which to teach
Was given me as I grew up, on all hands,
As best and readiest means of living by;
The same on examination being proved   305
The most pronounced moreover, fixed, precise
And absolute form of faith in the whole world—
Accordingly, most potent of all forms

For working on the world. Observe, my friend!
Such as you know me, I am free to say,   310
In these hard latter days which hamper one,
Myself—by no immoderate exercise
Of intellect and learning, but the tact
To let external forces work for me,
—Bid the street's stones be bread and they are bread;   315
Bid Peter's creed, or rather, Hildebrand's,
Exalt me o'er my fellows in the world
And make my life an ease and joy and pride;
It does so,—which for me's a great point gained,
Who have a soul and body that exact   320
A comfortable care in many ways.
There's power in me and will to dominate
Which I must exercise, they hurt me else:
In many ways I need mankind's respect,
Obedience, and the love that's born of fear: 325
While at the same time, there's a taste I have,
A toy of soul, a titillating thing,
Refuses to digest these dainties crude.
The naked life is gross till clothed upon:
I must take what men offer, with a grace   330
As though I would not, could I help it, take!
An uniform I wear though over-rich—
Something imposed on me, no choice of mine;
No fancy-dress worn for pure fancy's sake
And despicable therefore! now folk kneel   335
And kiss my hand—of course the Church's hand.
Thus I am made, thus life is best for me,
And thus that it should be I have procured;
And thus it could not be another way,
I venture to imagine.
                              You'll reply,   340
So far my choice, no doubt, is a success;
But were I made of better elements,
With nobler instincts, purer tastes, like you,
I hardly would account the thing success
Though it did all for me I say.
                                        But, friend,   345
We speak of what is; not of what might be,

And how 't were better if 't were otherwise.
I am the man you see here plain enough:
Grant I'm a beast, why, beasts must lead beasts'
    lives!
Suppose I own: at once to tail and claws;   350
The tailless man exceeds me: but being tailed
I'll lash out lion fashion, and leave apes
To dock their stump and dress their haunches up.
My business is not to remake myself,
But make the absolute best of what God made.   355
Or—our first simile—though you prove me doomed
To a viler berth still, to the steerage-hole,
The sheep-pen or the pig-stye, I should strive
To make what use of each were possible;
And as this cabin gets upholstery,   360
That hutch should rustle with sufficient straw.

    But, friend, I don't acknowledge quite so fast
I fail of all your manhood's lofty tastes
Enumerated so complacently,
On the mere ground that you forsooth can find   365
In this particular life I choose to lead
No fit provision for them. Can you not?
Say you, my fault is I address myself
To grosser estimators than should judge?
And that's no way of holding up the soul,   370
Which, nobler, needs men's praise perhaps, yet knows
One wise man's verdict outweighs all the fools'—
Would like the two, but, forced to choose, takes that.
I pine among my million imbeciles
(You think) aware some dozen men of sense   375
Eye me and know me, whether I believe
In the last winking Virgin, as I vow,
And am a fool, or disbelieve in her
And am a knave,—approve in neither case,
Withhold their voices though I look their way: 380
Like Verdi when, at his worst opera's end
(The thing they gave at Florence,—what's its name?)
While the mad houseful's plaudits near out-bang
His orchestra of salt-box, tongs and bones,

He looks through all the roaring and the wreaths   385
Where sits Rossini patient in his stall.

Nay, friend, I meet you with an answer here—
That even your prime men who appraise their kind
Are men still, catch a wheel within a wheel,
See more in a truth than the truth's simple self,   390
Confuse themselves. You see lads walk the street
Sixty the minute; what's to note in that?
You see one lad o'erstride a chimney-stack;
Him you must watch—he's sure to fall, yet stands!
Our interest's on the dangerous edge of things.   395
The honest thief, the tender murderer,
The superstitious atheist, demirep
That loves and saves her soul in new French books—
We watch while these in equilibrium keep
The giddy line midway: one step aside,   400
They're classed and done with. I, then, keep the line
Before your sages,—just the men to shrink
From the gross weights, coarse scales and labels broad
You offer their refinement. Fool or knave?
Why needs a bishop be a fool or knave   405
When there's a thousand diamond weights between?
So, I enlist them. Your picked twelve, you'll find,
Profess themselves indignant, scandalized
At thus being held unable to explain
How a superior man who disbelieves   410
May not believe as well: that's Schelling's way!
It's through my coming in the tail of time,
Nicking the minute with a happy tact.
Had I been born three hundred years ago
They'd say, 'What's strange? Blougram of course
        believes;'   415
And, seventy years since, 'disbelieves of course.'
But now, 'He may believe; and yet, and yet
'How can he?' All eyes turn with interest.
Whereas, step off the line on either side—
You, for example, clever to a fault,   420
The rough and ready man who write apace,
Read somewhat seldomer, think perhaps even less—

You disbelieve! Who wonders and who cares?
Lord So-and-so—his coat bedropped with wax,
All Peter's chains about his waist, his back   425
Brave with the needlework of Noodledom—
Believes! Again, who wonders and who cares?
But I, the man of sense and learning too,
The able to think yet act, the this, the that,
I, to believe at this late time of day!   430
Enough; you see, I need not fear contempt.

—Except it's yours! Admire me as these may,
You don't. But whom at least do you admire?
Present your own perfection, your ideal,
Your pattern man for a minute—oh, make haste,   435
Is it Napoleon you would have us grow?
Concede the means; allow his head and hand,
(A large concession, clever as you are)
Good! In our common primal element
Of unbelief (we can't believe, you know—   440
We're still at that admission, recollect!)
Where do you find—apart from, towering o'er
The secondary temporary aims
Which satisfy the gross taste you despise—
Where do you find his star?—his crazy trust   445
God knows through what or in what? it's alive
And shines and leads him, and that's all we want.
Have we aught in our sober night shall point
Such ends as his were, and direct the means
Of working out our purpose straight as his,   450
Nor bring a moment's trouble on success
With after-care to justify the same?
—Be a Napoleon, and yet disbelieve—
Why, the man's mad, friend, take his light away!
What's the vague good o' the world, for which you dare   455
With comfort to yourself blow millions up?
We neither of us see it! we do see
The blown-up millions—spatter of their brains
And writhing of their bowels and so forth,
In that bewildering entanglement   460
Of horrible eventualities

Past calculation to the end of time!
Can I mistake for some clear word of God
(Which were my ample warrant for it all)
His puff of hazy instinct, idle talk,   465
'The State, that's I,' quack-nonsense about crowns,
And (when one beats the man to his last hold)
A vague idea of setting things to rights,
Policing people efficaciously,
More to their profit, most of all to his own;   470
The whole to end that dismallest of ends
By an Austrian marriage, cant to us the Church,
And resurrection of the old *régime?*
Would I, who hope to live a dozen years,
Fight Austerlitz for reasons such and such?   475
No: for, concede me but the merest chance
Doubt may be wrong—there's judgment, life to come!
With just that chance, I dare not. Doubt proves right?
This present life is all?—you offer me
Its dozen noisy years, without a chance   480
That wedding an archduchess, wearing lace,
And getting called by divers new-coined names,
Will drive off ugly thoughts and let me dine,
Sleep, read and chat in quiet as I like!
Therefore I will not.

                    Take another case;   485
Fit up the cabin yet another way.
What say you to the poets? shall we write
Hamlet, Othello—make the world our own,
Without a risk to run of either sort?
I can't!—to put the strongest reason first.   490
'But try,' you urge, 'the trying shall suffice;
'The aim, if reached or not, makes great the life:
'Try to be Shakespeare, leave the rest to fate!'
Spare my self-knowledge—there's no fooling me!
If I prefer remaining my poor self,   495
I say so not in self-dispraise but praise.
If I'm a Shakespeare, let the well alone;
Why should I try to be what now I am?
If I'm no Shakespeare, as too probable,—

His power and consciousness and self-delight   500
And all we want in common, shall I find—
Trying for ever? while on points of taste
Wherewith, to speak it humbly, he and I
Are dowered alike—I'll ask you, I or he,
Which in our two lives realizes most?   505
Much, he imagined—somewhat, I possess.
He had the imagination; stick to that!
Let him say, 'In the face of my soul's works
'Your world is worthless and I touch it not
'Lest I should wrong them'—I'll withdraw my plea.   510
But does he say so? look upon his life!
Himself, who only can, gives judgment there.
He leaves his towers and gorgeous palaces
To build the trimmest house in Stratford town;
Saves money, spends it, owns the worth of things,   515
Giulio Romano's pictures, Dowland's lute;
Enjoys a show, respects the puppets, too,
And none more, had he seen its entry once,
Than 'Pandulph, of fair Milan cardinal.'
Why then should I who play that personage,   520
The very Pandulph Shakespeare's fancy made,
Be told that had the poet chanced to start
From where I stand now (some degree like mine
Being just the goal he ran his race to reach)
He would have run the whole race back, forsooth,   525
And left being Pandulph, to begin write plays?
Ah, the earth's best can be but the earth's best!
Did Shakespeare live, he could but sit at home
And get himself in dreams the Vatican,
Greek busts, Venetian paintings, Roman walls,   530
And English books, none equal to his own,
Which I read, bound in gold (he never did).
—Terni's fall, Naples' bay and Gothard's top—
Eh, friend? I could not fancy one of these;
But, as I pour this claret, there they are: 535
I've gained them—crossed St. Gothard last July
With ten mules to the carriage and a bed
Slung inside; is my hap the worse for that?
We want the same things, Shakespeare and myself,

And what I want, I have: he, gifted more,   540
Could fancy he too had them when he liked,
But not so thoroughly that, if fate allowed,
He would not have them also in my sense.
We play one game; I send the ball aloft
No less adroitly that of fifty strokes   545
Scarce five go o'er the wall so wide and high
Which sends them back to me: I wish and get.
He struck balls higher and with better skill,
But at a poor fence level with his head,
And hit—his Stratford house, a coat of arms,   550
Successful dealings in his grain and wool,—
While I receive heaven's incense in my nose
And style myself the cousin of Queen Bess.
Ask him, if this life's all, who wins the game?

Believe—and our whole argument breaks up.   555
Enthusiasm's the best thing, I repeat;
Only, we can't command it; fire and life
Are all, dead matter's nothing, we agree:
And be it a mad dream or God's very breath,
The fact's the same,—belief's fire, once in us,   560
Makes of all else mere stuff to show itself:
We penetrate our life with such a glow
As fire lends wood and iron—this turns steel,
That burns to ash—all's one, fire proves its power
For good or ill, since men call flare success.   565
But paint a fire, it will not therefore burn.
Light one in me, I'll find it food enough!
Why, to be Luther—that's a life to lead,
Incomparably better than my own.
He comes, reclaims God's earth for God, he says,   570
Sets up God's rule again by simple means,
Re-opens a shut book, and all is done.
He flared out in the flaring of mankind;
Such Luther's luck was: how shall such be mine?
If he succeeded, nothing's left to do: 575
And if he did not altogether—well,
Strauss is the next advance. All Strauss should be
I might be also. But to what result?

He looks upon no future: Luther did.
What can I gain on the denying side?   580
Ice makes no conflagration. State the facts,
Read the text right, emancipate the world—
The emancipated world enjoys itself
With scarce a thank-you: Blougram told it first
It could not owe a farthing,—not to him   585
More than Saint Paul! 't would press its pay, you think?
Then add there's still that plaguy hundredth chance
Strauss may be wrong. And so a risk is run—
For what gain? not for Luther's, who secured
A real heaven in his heart throughout his life,   590
Supposing death a little altered things.

   'Ay, but since really you lack faith,' you cry,
'You run the same risk really on all sides,
'In cool indifference as bold unbelief.
'As well be Strauss as swing 'twixt Paul and him.   595
'It's not worth having, such imperfect faith,
'No more available to do faith's work
'Than unbelief like mine. Whole faith, or none!'

   Softly, my friend! I must dispute that point.
Once own the use of faith, I'll find you faith.   600
We're back on Christian ground. You call for faith:
I show you doubt, to prove that faith exists.
The more of doubt, the stronger faith, I say,
If faith o'ercomes doubt. How I know it does?
By life and man's free will, God gave for that!   605
To mould life as we choose it, shows our choice:
That's our one act, the previous work's his own.
You criticize the soil? it reared this tree—
This broad life and whatever fruit it bears!
What matter though I doubt at every pore,   610
Head-doubts, heart-doubts, doubts at my fingers' ends,
Doubts in the trivial work of every day,
Doubts at the very bases of my soul
In the grand moments when she probes herself—
If finally I have a life to show,   615
The thing I did, brought out in evidence
Against the thing done to me underground

By hell and all its brood, for aught I know?
I say, whence sprang this? shows it faith or doubt?
All's doubt in me; where's break of faith in this?   620
It is the idea, the feeling and the love,
God means mankind should strive for and show forth
Whatever be the process to that end,—
And not historic knowledge, logic sound,
And metaphysical acumen, sure!   625
'What think ye of Christ,' friend? when all's done and said,
Like you this Christianity or not?
It may be false, but will you wish it true?
Has it your vote to be so if it can?
Trust you an instinct silenced long ago   630
That will break silence and enjoin you love
What mortified philosophy is hoarse,
And all in vain, with bidding you despise?
If you desire faith—then you've faith enough:
What else seeks God—nay, what else seek ourselves?   635
You form a notion of me, we'll suppose,
On hearsay; it's a favourable one:
'But still' (you add), 'there was no such good man,
'Because of contradiction in the facts.
'One proves, for instance, he was born in Rome,   640
'This Blougram; yet throughout the tales of him
'I see he figures as an Englishman.'
Well, the two things are reconcileable.
But would I rather you discovered that,
Subjoining—'Still, what matter though they be?   645
'Blougram concerns me nought, born here or there.'

      Pure faith indeed—you know not what you ask!
Naked belief in God the Omnipotent,
Omniscient, Omnipresent, sears too much
The sense of conscious creatures to be borne.   650
It were the seeing him, no flesh shall dare.
Some think, Creation's meant to show him forth:
I say it's meant to hide him all it can,
And that's what all the blessed evil's for.   655
Its use in Time is to environ us,
Our breath, our drop of dew, with shield enough

Against that sight till we can bear its stress.
Under a vertical sun, the exposed brain
And lidless eye and disemprisoned heart
Less certainly would wither up at once 660
Than mind, confronted with the truth of him.
But time and earth case-harden us to live;
The feeblest sense is trusted most; the child
Feels God a moment, ichors o'er the place,
Plays on and grows to be a man like us. 665
With me, faith means perpetual unbelief
Kept quiet like the snake 'neath Michael's foot
Who stands calm just because he feels it writhe.
Or, if that's too ambitious,—here's my box—
I need the excitation of a pinch 670
Threatening the torpor of the inside-nose
Nigh on the imminent sneeze that never comes.
'Leave it in peace' advise the simple folk:
Make it aware of peace by itching-fits,
Say I—let doubt occasion still more faith! 675

You'll say, once all believed, man, woman, child,
In that dear middle-age these noodles praise.
How you'd exult if I could put you back
Six hundred years, blot out cosmogony,
Geology, ethnology, what not, 680
(Greek endings, each the little passing-bell
That signifies some faith's about to die),
And set you square with Genesis again,—
When such a traveller told you his last news,
He saw the ark a-top of Ararat 685
But did not climb there since 't was getting dusk
And robber-bands infest the mountain's foot!
How should you feel, I ask, in such an age,
How act? As other people felt and did;
With soul more blank than this decanter's knob, 690
Believe—and yet lie, kill, rob, fornicate
Full in belief's face, like the beast you'd be!

No, when the fight begins within himself,
A man's worth something. God stoops o'er his head,

Satan looks up between his feet—both tug—   695
He's left, himself, i' the middle: the soul wakes
And grows. Prolong that battle through his life!
Never leave growing till the life to come!
Here, we've got callous to the Virgin's winks
That used to puzzle people wholesomely: 700
Men have outgrown the shame of being fools.
What are the laws of nature, not to bend
If the Church bid them?—brother Newman asks.
Up with the Immaculate Conception, then—
On to the rack with faith!—is my advice.   705
Will not that hurry us upon our knees,
Knocking our breasts, 'It can't be—yet it shall!
'Who am I, the worm, to argue with my Pope?
'Low things confound the high things!' and so forth.
That's better than acquitting God with grace   710
As some folk do. He's tried—no case is proved,
Philosophy is lenient—he may go!

      You'll say, the old system's not so obsolete
But men believe still: ay, but who and where?
King Bomba's lazzaroni foster yet   715
The sacred flame, so Antonelli writes;
But even of these, what ragamuffin-saint
Believes God watches him continually,
As he believes in fire that it will burn,
Or rain that it will drench him? Break fire's law,   720
Sin against rain, although the penalty
Be just a singe or soaking? 'No,' he smiles;
'Those laws are laws that can enforce themselves.'

      The sum of all is—yes, my doubt is great,
My faith's still greater, then my faith's enough.   725
I have read much, thought much, experienced much,
Yet would die rather than avow my fear
The Naples' liquefaction may be false,
When set to happen by the palace-clock
According to the clouds or dinner-time.   730
I hear you recommend, I might at least
Eliminate, decrassify my faith

Since I adopt it; keeping what I must
And leaving what I can— such points as this.
I won't—that is, I can't throw one away.   735
Supposing there's no truth in what I hold
About the need of trial to man's faith,
Still, when you bid me purify the same,
To such a process I discern no end.
Clearing off one excrescence to see two,   740
There's ever a next in size, now grown as big,
That meets the knife: I cut and cut again!
First cut the Liquefaction, what comes last
But Fichte's clever cut at God himself?
Experimentalize on sacred things!   745
I trust nor hand nor eye nor heart nor brain
To stop betimes: they all get drunk alike.
The first step, I am master not to take.

   You'd find the cutting-process to your taste
As much as leaving growths of lies unpruned,   750
Nor see more danger in it,—you retort.
Your taste's worth mine; but my taste proves more wise
When we consider that the steadfast hold
On the extreme end of the chain of faith
Gives all the advantage, makes the difference   755
With the rough purblind mass we seek to rule:
We are their lords, or they are free of us,
Just as we tighten or relax our hold.
So, other matters equal, we'll revert
To the first problem—which, if solved my way   760
And thrown into the balance, turns the scale—
How we may lead a comfortable life,
How suit our luggage to the cabin's size.

   Of course you are remarking all this time
How narrowly and grossly I view life,   765
Respect the creature-comforts, care to rule
The masses, and regard complacently
'The cabin,' in our old phrase. Well, I do.
I act for, talk for, live for this world now,
As this world prizes action, life and talk: 770
No prejudice to what next world may prove,

Whose new laws and requirements, my best pledge
To observe then, is that I observe these now,
Shall do hereafter what I do meanwhile.
Let us concede (gratuitously though)   775
Next life relieves the soul of body, yields
Pure spiritual enjoyment: well, my friend,
Why lose this life i' the meantime, since its use
May be to make the next life more intense?

Do you know, I have often had a dream   780
(Work it up in your next month's article)
Of man's poor spirit in its progress, still
Losing true life for ever and a day
Through ever trying to be and ever being—
In the evolution of successive spheres—   785
Before its actual sphere and place of life,
Halfway into the next, which having reached,
It shoots with corresponding foolery
Halfway into the next still, on and off!
As when a traveller, bound from North to South,   790
Scouts fur in Russia: what's its use in France?
In France spurns flannel: where's its need in Spain?
In Spain drops cloth, too cumbrous for Algiers!
Linen goes next, and last the skin itself,
A superfluity at Timbuctoo.   795
When, through his journey, was the fool at ease?
I'm at ease now, friend; worldly in this world,
I take and like its way of life; I think
My brothers, who administer the means,
Live better for my comfort—that's good too;   800
And God, if he pronounce upon such life,
Approves my service, which is better still.
If he keep silence,—why, for you or me
Or that brute beast pulled-up in to-day's 'Times,'
What odds is 't, save to ourselves, what life we lead?   805

You meet me at this issue: you declare,—
All special-pleading done with—truth is truth,
And justifies itself by undreamed ways.
You don't fear but it's better, if we doubt,

To say so, act up to our truth perceived 810
However feebly. Do then,—act away!
'T is there I'm on the watch for you. How one acts
Is, both of us agree, our chief concern:
And how you'll act is what I fain would see
If, like the candid person you appear, 815
You dare to make the most of your life's scheme
As I of mine, live up to its full law
Since there's no higher law that counterchecks.
Put natural religion to the test
You've just demolished the revealed with—quick, 820
Down to the root of all that checks your will,
All prohibition to lie, kill and thieve,
Or even to be an atheistic priest!
Suppose a pricking to incontinence—
Philosophers deduce you chastity 825
Or shame, from just the fact that at the first
Whoso embraced a woman in the field,
Threw club down and forewent his brains beside,
So, stood a ready victim in the reach
Of any brother savage, club in hand; 830
Hence saw the use of going out of sight
In wood or cave to prosecute his loves:
I read this in a French book t' other day.
Does law so analysed coerce you much?
Oh, men spin clouds of fuzz where matters end, 835
But you who reach where the first thread begins,
You'll soon cut that!—which means you can, but won't,
Through certain instincts, blind, unreasoned-out,
You dare not set aside, you can't tell why,
But there they are, and so you let them rule. 840
Then, friend, you seem as much a slave as I,
A liar, conscious coward and hypocrite,
Without the good the slave expects to get,
In case he has a master after all!
You own your instincts? why, what else do I, 845
Who want, am made for, and must have a God
Ere I can be aught, do aught?—no mere name
Want, but the true thing with what proves its truth,
To wit, a relation from that thing to me,

Touching from head to foot—which touch I feel,   850
And with it take the rest, this life of ours!
I live my life here; yours you dare not live.

—Not as I state it, who (you please subjoin)
Disfigure such a life and call it names,
While, to your mind, remains another way   855
For simple men: knowledge and power have rights,
But ignorance and weakness have rights too.
There needs no crucial effort to find truth
If here or there or anywhere about:
We ought to turn each side, try hard and see,   860
And if we can't, be glad we've earned at least
The right, by one laborious proof the more,
To graze in peace earth's pleasant pasturage.
Men are not angels, neither are they brutes:
Something we may see, all we cannot see.   865
What need of lying? I say, I see all,
And swear to each detail the most minute
In what I think a Pan's face—you, mere cloud:
I swear I hear him speak and see him wink,
For fear, if once I drop the emphasis,   870
Mankind may doubt there's any cloud at all.
You take the simple life—ready to see,
Willing to see (for no cloud's worth a face)—
And leaving quiet what no strength can move,
And which, who bids you move? who has the right?   875
I bid you; but you are God's sheep, not mine:
'Pastor est tui Dominus.' You find
In this the pleasant pasture of our life
Much you may eat without the least offence,
Much you don't eat because your maw objects,   880
Much you would eat but that your fellow-flock
Open great eyes at you and even butt,
And thereupon you like your mates so well
You cannot please yourself, offending them;
Though when they seem exorbitantly sheep,   885
You weigh your pleasure with their butts and bleats
And strike the balance. Sometimes certain fears
Restrain you, real checks since you find them so;

Sometimes you please yourself and nothing checks:
And thus you graze through life with not one lie,   890
And like it best.

                         But do you, in truth's name?
If so, you beat—which means you are not I—
Who needs must make earth mine and feed my fill
Not simply unbutted at, unbickered with,
But motioned to the velvet of the sward   895
By those obsequious wethers' very selves.
Look at me, sir; my age is double yours:
At yours, I knew beforehand, so enjoyed,
What now I should be—as, permit the word,
I pretty well imagine your whole range   900
And stretch of tether twenty years to come.
We both have minds and bodies much alike:
In truth's name, don't you want my bishopric,
My daily bread, my influence and my state?
You're young. I'm old; you must be old one day;   905
Will you find then, as I do hour by hour,
Women their lovers kneel to, who cut curls
From your fat lap-dog's ear to grace a brooch—
Dukes, who petition just to kiss your ring—
With much beside you know or may conceive?   910
Suppose we die to-night: well, here am I,
Such were my gains, life bore this fruit to me,
While writing all the same my articles
On music, poetry, the fictile vase
Found at Albano, chess, Anacreon's Greek.   915
But you—the highest honour in your life,
The thing you'll crown yourself with, all your days,
Is—dining here and drinking this last glass
I pour you out in sign of amity
Before we part for ever. Of your power   920
And social influence, worldly worth in short,
Judge what's my estimation by the fact,
I do not condescend to enjoin, beseech,
Hint secrecy on one of all these words!
You're shrewd and know that should you publish one   925
The world would brand the lie—my enemies first,

Who'd sneer—'the bishop's an arch-hypocrite
'And knave perhaps, but not so frank a fool.'
Whereas I should not dare for both my ears
Breathe one such syllable, smile one such smile,　　930
Before the chaplain who reflects myself—
My shade's so much more potent than your flesh.
What's your reward, self-abnegating friend?
Stood you confessed of those exceptional
And privileged great natures that dwarf mine—　　935
A zealot with a mad ideal in reach,
A poet just about to print his ode,
A statesman with a scheme to stop this war,
An artist whose religion is his art—
I should have nothing to object: such men　　940
Carry the fire, all things grow warm to them,
Their drugget's worth my purple, they beat me.
But you,—you're just as little those as I—
You, Gigadibs, who, thirty years of age,
Write stately for Blackwood's Magazine,　　945
Believe you see two points in Hamlet's soul
Unseized by the Germans yet—which view you'll print—
Meantime the best you have to show being still
That lively lightsome article we took
Almost for the true Dickens,—what's its name?　　950
'The Slum and Cellar, or Whitechapel life
'Limned after dark!' it made me laugh, I know,
And pleased a month, and brought you in ten pounds.
—Success I recognize and compliment,
And therefore give you, if you choose, three words　　955
(The card and pencil-scratch is quite enough)
Which whether here, in Dublin or New York,
Will get you, prompt as at my eyebrow's wink,
Such terms as never you aspired to get
In all our own reviews and some not ours.　　960
Go write your lively sketches! be the first
'Blougram, or The Eccentric Confidence'—
Or better simply say, 'The Outward-bound.'
Why, men as soon would throw it in my teeth
As copy and quote the infamy chalked broad　　965
About me on the church-door opposite.

You will not wait for that experience though,
I fancy, howsoever you decide,
To discontinue—not detesting, not
Defaming, but at least—despising me!   970

   Over his wine so smiled and talked his hour
Sylvester Blougram, styled *in partibus*
Episcopus, nec non—(the deuce knows what
It's changed to by our novel hierarchy)
With Gigadibs the literary man,   975
Who played with spoons, explored his plate's design,
And ranged the olive-stones about its edge,
While the great bishop rolled him out a mind
Long crumpled, till creased consciousness lay smooth.

   For Blougram, he believed, say, half he spoke.   980
The other portion, as he shaped it thus
For argumentatory purposes,
He felt his foe was foolish to dispute.
Some arbitrary accidental thoughts
That crossed his mind, amusing because new,   985
He chose to represent as fixtures there,
Invariable convictions (such they seemed
Beside his interlocutor's loose cards
Flung daily down, and not the same way twice)
While certain hell-deep instincts, man's weak tongue   990
Is never bold to utter in their truth
Because styled hell-deep ('t is an old mistake
To place hell at the bottom of the earth)
He ignored these,—not having in readiness
Their nomenclature and philosophy: 995
He said true things, but called them by wrong names.
'On the whole,' he thought, 'I justify myself
'On every point where cavillers like this
'Oppugn my life: he tries one kind of fence,
'I close, he's worsted, that's enough for him.   1000
'He's on the ground: if ground should break away
'I take my stand on, there's a firmer yet
'Beneath it, both of us may sink and reach.

'His ground was over mine and broke the first:
'So, let him sit with me this many a year!'   1005

He did not sit five minutes. Just a week
Sufficed his sudden healthy vehemence.
Something had struck him in the 'Outward-bound'
Another way than Blougram's purpose was:
And having bought, not cabin-furniture   1010
But settler's-implements (enough for three)
And started for Australia—there, I hope,
By this time he has tested his first plough,
And studied his last chapter of St. John.

MEMORABILIA

I

AH, did you once see Shelley plain,
    And did he stop and speak to you,
And did you speak to him again?
    How strange it seems and new!

II

But you were living before that,   5
    And also you are living after;
And the memory I started at—
    My starting moves your laughter.

III

I crossed a moor, with a name of its own
    And a certain use in the world no doubt,   10
Yet a hand's-breadth of it shines alone
    'Mid the blank miles round about:

IV

For there I picked up on the heather
    And there I put inside my breast
A moulted feather, an eagle-feather!   15
    Well, I forget the rest.

ANDREA DEL SARTO

(CALLED 'THE FAULTLESS PAINTER')[1]

BUT do not let us quarrel any more,
No, my Lucrezia; bear with me for once:
Sit down and all shall happen as you wish.
You turn your face, but does it bring your heart?
I'll work then for your friend's friend, never fear,   5
Treat his own subject after his own way,
Fix his own time, accept too his own price,
And shut the money into this small hand
When next it takes mine. Will it? tenderly?
Oh, I'll content him,—but to-morrow, Love!   10
I often am much wearier than you think,
This evening more than usual, and it seems
As if—forgive now—should you let me sit
Here by the window with your hand in mine
And look a half-hour forth on Fiesole,   15
Both of one mind, as married people use,
Quietly, quietly the evening through,
I might get up to-morrow to my work
Cheerful and fresh as ever. Let us try.
To-morrow, how you shall be glad for this!   20
Your soft hand is a woman of itself,
And mine the man's bared breast she curls inside.
Don't count the time lost, neither; you must serve
For each of the five pictures we require:
It saves a model. So! keep looking so—   25
My serpentining beauty, rounds on rounds!
—How could you ever prick those perfect ears,
Even to put the pearl there! oh, so sweet—
My face, my moon, my everybody's moon,
Which everybody looks on and calls his,   30
And, I suppose, is looked on by in turn,
While she looks—no one's: very dear, no less.
You smile? why, there's my picture ready made,
There's what we painters call our harmony!
A common greyness silvers everything,—   35

[1] In *Men and Women* (1855) this poem is the first in the second volume.

z

All in a twilight, you and I alike
—You, at the point of your first pride in me
(That's gone you know),—but I, at every point;
My youth, my hope, my art, being all toned down
To yonder sober pleasant Fiesole.   40
There's the bell clinking from the chapel-top;
That length of convent-wall across the way
Holds the trees safer, huddled more inside;
The last monk leaves the garden; days decrease,
And autumn grows, autumn in everything.   45
Eh? the whole seems to fall into a shape
As if I saw alike my work and self
And all that I was born to be and do,
A twilight-piece. Love, we are in God's hand.
How strange now, looks the life he makes us lead;   50
So free we seem, so fettered fast we are!
I feel he laid the fetter: let it lie!
This chamber for example—turn your head—
All that's behind us! You don't understand
Nor care to understand about my art,   55
But you can hear at least when people speak:
And that cartoon, the second from the door
—It is the thing, Love! so such things should be—
Behold Madonna!—I am bold to say.
I can do with my pencil what I know,   60
What I see, what at bottom of my heart
I wish for, if I ever wish so deep—
Do easily, too—when I say, perfectly,
I do not boast, perhaps: yourself are judge,
Who listened to the Legate's talk last week,   65
And just as much they used to say in France.
At any rate 't is easy, all of it!
No sketches first, no studies, that's long past:
I do what many dream of, all their lives,
—Dream? strive to do, and agonize to do,   70
And fail in doing. I could count twenty such
On twice your fingers, and not leave this town,
Who strive—you don't know how the others strive
To paint a little thing like that you smeared
Carelessly passing with your robes afloat,—   75

Yet do much less, so much less, Someone says,
(I know his name, no matter)—so much less!
Well, less is more, Lucrezia: I am judged.
There burns a truer light of God in them,
In their vexed beating stuffed and stopped-up brain, 80
Heart, or whate'er else, than goes on to prompt
This low-pulsed forthright craftsman's hand of mine.
Their works drop groundward, but themselves, I know,
Reach many a time a heaven that's shut to me,
Enter and take their place there sure enough, 85
Though they come back and cannot tell the world.
My works are nearer heaven, but I sit here.
The sudden blood of these men! at a word—
Praise them, it boils, or blame them, it boils too.
I, painting from myself and to myself, 90
Know what I do, am unmoved by men's blame
Or their praise either. Somebody remarks
Morello's outline there is wrongly traced,
His hue mistaken; what of that? or else,
Rightly traced and well ordered; what of that? 95
Speak as they please, what does the mountain care?
Ah, but a man's reach should exceed his grasp,
Or what's a heaven for? All is silver-grey
Placid and perfect with my art: the worse!
I know both what I want and what might gain, 100
And yet how profitless to know, to sigh
'Had I been two, another and myself,
'Our head would have o'erlooked the world!' No doubt.
Yonder's a work now, of that famous youth
The Urbinate who died five years ago. 105
('T is copied, George Vasari sent it me.)
Well, I can fancy how he did it all,
Pouring his soul, with kings and popes to see,
Reaching, that heaven might so replenish him,
Above and through his art—for it gives way; 110
That arm is wrongly put—and there again—
A fault to pardon in the drawing's lines,
Its body, so to speak: its soul is right,
He means right—that, a child may understand.
Still, what an arm! and I could alter it: 115

But all the play, the insight and the stretch—
Out of me, out of me! And wherefore out?
Had you enjoined them on me, given me soul,
We might have risen to Rafael, I and you!
Nay, Love, you did give all I asked, I think—   120
More than I merit, yes, by many times.
But had you—oh, with the same perfect brow,
And perfect eyes, and more than perfect mouth,
And the low voice my soul hears, as a bird
The fowler's pipe, and follows to the snare—   125
Had you, with these the same, but brought a mind!
Some women do so. Had the mouth there urged
'God and the glory! never care for gain.
'The present by the future, what is that?
'Live for fame, side by side with Agnolo!   130
'Rafael is waiting: up to God, all three!'
I might have done it for you. So it seems:
Perhaps not. All is as God over-rules.
Beside, incentives come from the soul's self;
The rest avail not. Why do I need you?   135
What wife had Rafael, or has Agnolo?
In this world, who can do a thing, will not;
And who would do it, cannot, I perceive:
Yet the will's somewhat—somewhat, too, the power—
And thus we half-men struggle. At the end,   140
God, I conclude, compensates, punishes.
'T is safer for me, if the award be strict,
That I am something underrated here,
Poor this long while, despised, to speak the truth.
I dared not, do you know, leave home all day,   145
For fear of chancing on the Paris lords.
The best is when they pass and look aside;
But they speak sometimes; I must bear it all.
Well may they speak! That Francis, that first time,
And that long festal year at Fontainebleau!   150
I surely then could sometimes leave the ground,
Put on the glory, Rafael's daily wear,
In that humane great monarch's golden look,—
One finger in his beard or twisted curl
Over his mouth's good mark that made the smile,   155

One arm about my shoulder, round my neck,
The jingle of his gold chain in my ear,
I painting proudly with his breath on me,
All his court round him, seeing with his eyes,
Such frank French eyes, and such a fire of souls 160
Profuse, my hand kept plying by those hearts,—
And, best of all, this, this, this face beyond,
This in the background, waiting on my work,
To crown the issue with a last reward!
A good time, was it not, my kingly days? 165
And had you not grown restless . . . but I know—
'T is done and past; 't was right, my instinct said;
Too live the life grew, golden and not grey,
And I'm the weak-eyed bat no sun should tempt
Out of the grange whose four walls make his world. 170
How could it end in any other way?
You called me, and I came home to your heart.
The triumph was—to reach and stay there; since
I reached it ere the triumph, what is lost?
Let my hands frame your face in your hair's gold, 175
You beautiful Lucrezia that are mine!
'Rafael did this, Andrea painted that;
'The Roman's is the better when you pray,
'But still the other's Virgin was his wife—'
Men will excuse me. I am glad to judge 180
Both pictures in your presence; clearer grows
My better fortune, I resolve to think.
For, do you know, Lucrezia, as God lives,
Said one day Agnolo, his very self,
To Rafael . . . I have known it all these years . . . 185
(When the young man was flaming out his thoughts
Upon a palace-wall for Rome to see,
Too lifted up in heart because of it)
'Friend, there's a certain sorry little scrub
'Goes up and down our Florence, none cares how, 190
'Who, were he set to plan and execute
'As you are, pricked on by your popes and kings,
'Would bring the sweat into that brow of yours!'
To Rafael's!—And indeed the arm is wrong.
I hardly dare . . . yet, only you to see, 195

Give the chalk here—quick, thus the line should go!
Ay, but the soul! he's Rafael! rub it out!
Still, all I care for, if he spoke the truth,
(What he? why, who but Michel Agnolo?
Do you forget already words like those?)　　　　　200
If really there was such a chance, so lost,—
Is, whether you're—not grateful—but more pleased.
Well, let me think so. And you smile indeed!
This hour has been an hour! Another smile?
If you would sit thus by me every night　　　　　205
I should work better, do you comprehend?
I mean that I should earn more, give you more.
See, it is settled dusk now; there's a star;
Morello's gone, the watch-lights show the wall,
The cue-owls speak the name we call them by.　　　　210
Come from the window, love,—come in, at last,
Inside the melancholy little house
We built to be so gay with. God is just.
King Francis may forgive me: oft at nights
When I look up from painting, eyes tired out,　　　　215
The walls become illumined, brick from brick
Distinct, instead of mortar, fierce bright gold,
That gold of his I did cement them with!
Let us but love each other. Must you go?
That Cousin here again? he waits outside?　　　　220
Must see you—you, and not with me? Those loans?
More gaming debts to pay? you smiled for that?
Well, let smiles buy me! have you more to spend?
While hand and eye and something of a heart
Are left me, work's my ware, and what's it worth?　　　　225
I'll pay my fancy. Only let me sit
The grey remainder of the evening out,
Idle, you call it, and muse perfectly
How I could paint, were I but back in France,
One picture, just one more—the Virgin's face,　　　　230
Not yours this time! I want you at my side
To hear them—that is, Michel Agnolo—
Judge all I do and tell you of its worth.
Will you? To-morrow, satisfy your friend.
I take the subjects for his corridor,　　　　235

Finish the portrait out of hand—there, there,
And throw him in another thing or two
If he demurs; the whole should prove enough
To pay for this same Cousin's freak. Beside,
What's better and what's all I care about,   240
Get you the thirteen scudi for the ruff!
Love, does that please you? Ah, but what does he,
The Cousin! what does he to please you more?

   I am grown peaceful as old age to-night.
I regret little, I would change still less.   245
Since there my past life lies, why alter it?
The very wrong to Francis!—it is true
I took his coin, was tempted and complied,
And built this house and sinned, and all is said.
My father and my mother died of want.   250
Well, had I riches of my own? you see
How one gets rich! Let each one bear his lot.
They were born poor, lived poor, and poor they died:
And I have laboured somewhat in my time
And not been paid profusely. Some good son   255
Paint my two hundred pictures—let him try!
No doubt, there's something strikes a balance. Yes,
You loved me quite enough, it seems to-night.
This must suffice me here. What would one have?
In heaven, perhaps, new chances, one more chance—   260
Four great walls in the New Jerusalem,
Meted on each side by the angel's reed,
For Leonard, Rafael, Agnolo and me
To cover—the three first without a wife,
While I have mine! So—still they overcome   265
Because there's still Lucrezia,—as I choose.

Again the Cousin's whistle! Go, my Love.

BEFORE

I

Let them fight it out, friend! things have gone too far.
God must judge the couple: leave them as they are
—Whichever one's the guiltless, to his glory,
And whichever one the guilt's with, to my story!

II

Why, you would not bid men, sunk in such a slough,   5
Strike no arm out further, stick and stink as now,
Leaving right and wrong to settle the embroilment,
Heaven with snaky hell, in torture and entoilment?

III

Who's the culprit of them? How must he conceive
God—the queen he caps to, laughing in his sleeve,   10
' 'T is but decent to profess oneself beneath her:
'Still, one must not be too much in earnest either!'

IV

Better sin the whole sin, sure that God observes;
Then go live his life out! Life will try his nerves,
When the sky, which noticed all, makes no disclosure,   15
And the earth keeps up her terrible composure.

V

Let him pace at pleasure, past the walls of rose,
Pluck their fruits when grape-trees graze him as he goes!
For he 'gins to guess the purpose of the garden,
With the sly mute thing, beside there, for a warden.   20

VI

What's the leopard-dog-thing, constant at his side,
A leer and lie in every eye of its obsequious hide?
When will come an end to all the mock obeisance,
And the price appear that pays for the misfeasance?

VII

So much for the culprit. Who's the martyred man?   25
Let him bear one stroke more, for be sure he can!
He that strove thus evil's lump with good to leaven,
Let him give his blood at last and get his heaven!

VIII

All or nothing, stake it! Trusts he God or no?
Thus far and no farther? farther? be it so!   30
Now, enough of your chicane of prudent pauses,
Sage provisos, sub-intents and saving-clauses!

IX

Ah, 'forgive' you bid him? While God's champion lives,
Wrong shall be resisted: dead, why, he forgives.
But you must not end my friend ere you begin him; 35
Evil stands not crowned on earth, while breath is in him.

X

Once more—Will the wronger, at this last of all,
Dare to say, 'I did wrong,' rising in his fall?
No?—Let go, then! Both the fighters to their places!
While I count three, step you back as many paces! 40

AFTER

TAKE the cloak from his face, and at first
    Let the corpse do its worst!

How he lies in his rights of a man!
    Death has done all death can.
And, absorbed in the new life he leads, 5
    He recks not, he heeds
Nor his wrong nor my vengeance; both strike
    On his senses alike,
And are lost in the solemn and strange
    Surprise of the change. 10

Ha, what avails death to erase
    His offence, my disgrace?
I would we were boys as of old
    In the field, by the fold:
His outrage, God's patience, man's scorn 15
    Were so easily borne!

I stand here now, he lies in his place:
    Cover the face!

IN THREE DAYS

I

So, I shall see her in three days
And just one night, but nights are short,
Then two long hours, and that is morn.

See how I come, unchanged, unworn!
Feel, where my life broke off from thine,   5
How fresh the splinters keep and fine,—
Only a touch and we combine!

II

Too long, this time of year, the days!
But nights, at least the nights are short.
As night shows where her one moon is,   10
A hand's-breadth of pure light and bliss,
So life's night gives my lady birth
And my eyes hold her! What is worth
The rest of heaven, the rest of earth?

III

O loaded curls, release your store   15
Of warmth and scent, as once before
The tingling hair did, lights and darks
Outbreaking into fairy sparks,
When under curl and curl I pried
After the warmth and scent inside,   20
Thro' lights and darks how manifold—
The dark inspired, the light controlled!
As early Art embrowns the gold.

IV

What great fear, should one say, 'Three days
'That change the world might change as well   25
'Your fortune; and if joy delays,
'Be happy that no worse befell!'
What small fear, if another says,
'Three days and one short night beside
'May throw no shadow on your ways;   30
'But years must teem with change untried,
'With chance not easily defied,
'With an end somewhere undescried.'
No fear!—or if a fear be born
This minute, it dies out in scorn.   35
Fear? I shall see her in three days
And one night, now the nights are short,
Then just two hours, and that is morn.

IN A YEAR

I

NEVER any more,
 While I live,
Need I hope to see his face
 As before.
Once his love grown chill, 5
 Mine may strive:
Bitterly we re-embrace,
 Single still.

II

Was it something said,
 Something done, 10
Vexed him? was it touch of hand,
 Turn of head?
Strange! that very way
 Love begun:
I as little understand 15
 Love's decay.

III

When I sewed or drew,
 I recall
How he looked as if I sung,
 —Sweetly too. 20
If I spoke a word,
 First of all
Up his cheek the colour sprung,
 Then he heard.

IV

Sitting by my side, 25
 At my feet,
So he breathed but air I breathed,
 Satisfied!
I, too, at love's brim
 Touched the sweet: 30
I would die if death bequeathed
 Sweet to him.

V

'Speak, I love thee best!'
 He exclaimed:
'Let thy love my own foretell!'   35
 I confessed:
'Clasp my heart on thine
 'Now unblamed,
'Since upon thy soul as well
 'Hangeth mine!'   40

VI

Was it wrong to own,
 Being truth?
Why should all the giving prove
 His alone?
I had wealth and ease,   45
 Beauty, youth:
Since my lover gave me love,
 I gave these.

VII

That was all I meant,
 —To be just,   50
And the passion I had raised,
 To content.
Since he chose to change
 Gold for dust,
If I gave him what he praised   55
 Was it strange?

VIII

Would he loved me yet,
 On and on,
While I found some way undreamed
 —Paid my debt!   60
Gave more life and more,
 Till, all gone,
He should smile 'She never seemed
 'Mine before.

IX

'What, she felt the while,   65
   'Must I think?
'Love's so different with us men!'
   He should smile:
'Dying for my sake—
   'White and pink!   70
'Can't we touch these bubbles then
   'But they break?'

X

Dear, the pang is brief,
   Do thy part,
Have thy pleasure! How perplexed   75
   Grows belief!
Well, this cold clay clod
   Was man's heart:
Crumble it, and what comes next?
   Is it God?   80

OLD PICTURES IN FLORENCE

I

THE morn when first it thunders in March,
   The eel in the pond gives a leap, they say:
As I leaned and looked over the aloed arch
   Of the villa-gate this warm March day,
No flash snapped, no dumb thunder rolled   5
   In the valley beneath where, white and wide
And washed by the morning water-gold,
   Florence lay out on the mountain-side.

II

River and bridge and street and square
   Lay mine, as much at my beck and call,   10
Through the live translucent bath of air,
   As the sights in a magic crystal ball.
And of all I saw and of all I praised,
   The most to praise and the best to see
Was the startling bell-tower Giotto raised: 15
   But why did it more than startle me?

III

Giotto, how, with that soul of yours,
  Could you play me false who loved you so?
Some slights if a certain heart endures
  Yet it feels, I would have your fellows know!   20
I' faith, I perceive not why I should care
  To break a silence that suits them best,
But the thing grows somewhat hard to bear
  When I find a Giotto join the rest.

IV

On the arch where olives overhead   25
  Print the blue sky with twig and leaf,
(That sharp-curled leaf which they never shed)
  'Twixt the aloes, I used to lean in chief,
And mark through the winter afternoons,
  By a gift God grants me now and then,   30
In the mild decline of those suns like moons,
  Who walked in Florence, besides her men.

V

They might chirp and chaffer, come and go
  For pleasure or profit, her men alive—
My business was hardly with them, I trow,   35
  But with empty cells of the human hive;
—With the chapter-room, the cloister-porch,
  The church's apsis, aisle or nave,
Its crypt, one fingers along with a torch,
  Its face set full for the sun to shave.   40

VI

Wherever a fresco peels and drops,
  Wherever an outline weakens and wanes
Till the latest life in the painting stops,
  Stands One whom each fainter pulse-tick pains:
One, wishful each scrap should clutch the brick,   45
  Each tinge not wholly escape the plaster,
—A lion who dies of an ass's kick,
  The wronged great soul of an ancient Master.

VII

For oh, this world and the wrong it does!
   They are safe in heaven with their backs to it,   50
The Michaels and Rafaels, you hum and buzz
   Round the works of, you of the little wit!
Do their eyes contract to the earth's old scope,
   Now that they see God face to face,
And have all attained to be poets, I hope?   55
   'T is their holiday now, in any case.

VIII

Much they reck of your praise and you!
   But the wronged great souls—can they be quit
Of a world where their work is all to do,
   Where you style them, you of the little wit,   60
Old Master This and Early the Other,
   Not dreaming that Old and New are fellows:
A younger succeeds to an elder brother,
   Da Vincis derive in good time from Dellos.

IX

And here where your praise might yield returns,   65
   And a handsome word or two give help,
Here, after your kind, the mastiff girns
   And the puppy pack of poodles yelp.
What, not a word for Stefano there,
   Of brow once prominent and starry,   70
Called Nature's Ape and the world's despair
   For his peerless painting? (See Vasari.)

X

There stands the Master. Study, my friends,
   What a man's work comes to! So he plans it,
Performs it, perfects it, makes amends   75
   For the toiling and moiling, and then, *sic transit!*
Happier the thrifty blind-folk labour,
   With upturned eye while the hand is busy,
Not sidling a glance at the coin of their neighbour!
   'T is looking downward that makes one dizzy.   80

XI

'If you knew their work you would deal your dole.'
    May I take upon me to instruct you?
When Greek Art ran and reached the goal,
    Thus much had the world to boast *in fructu*—
The Truth of Man, as by God first spoken,   85
    Which the actual generations garble,
Was re-uttered, and Soul (which Limbs betoken)
    And Limbs (Soul informs) made new in marble.

XII

So, you saw yourself as you wished you were,
    As you might have been, as you cannot be;   90
Earth here, rebuked by Olympus there:
    And grew content in your poor degree
With your little power, by those statues' godhead,
    And your little scope, by their eyes' full sway,
And your little grace, by their grace embodied,   95
    And your little date, by their forms that stay.

XIII

You would fain be kinglier, say, than I am?
    Even so, you will not sit like Theseus.
You would prove a model? The Son of Priam
    Has yet the advantage in arms' and knees' use.   100
You're wroth—can you slay your snake like Apollo?
    You're grieved—still Niobe's the grander!
You live—there's the Racers' frieze to follow:
    You die—there's the dying Alexander.

XIV

So, testing your weakness by their strength,   105
    Your meagre charms by their rounded beauty,
Measured by Art in your breadth and length,
    You learned—to submit is a mortal's duty.
—When I say 'you' 't is the common soul,
    The collective, I mean: the race of Man   110
That receives life in parts to live in a whole,
    And grow here according to God's clear plan.

XV

Growth came when, looking your last on them all,
    You turned your eyes inwardly one fine day
And cried with a start—What if we so small   115
    Be greater and grander the while than they?
Are they perfect of lineament, perfect of stature?
    In both, of such lower types are we
Precisely because of our wider nature;
    For time, theirs—ours, for eternity.   120

XVI

To-day's brief passion limits their range;
    It seethes with the morrow for us and more.
They are perfect—how else? they shall never change:
    We are faulty—why not? we have time in store.
The Artificer's hand is not arrested   125
    With us; we are rough-hewn, nowise polished:
They stand for our copy, and, once invested
    With all they can teach, we shall see them abolished.

XVII

'T is a life-long toil till our lump be leaven—
    The better! What's come to perfection perishes.   130
Things learned on earth, we shall practise in heaven:
    Works done least rapidly, Art most cherishes.
Thyself shalt afford the example, Giotto!
    Thy one work, not to decrease or diminish,
Done at a stroke, was just (was it not?) 'O!'   135
    Thy great Campanile is still to finish.

XVIII

Is it true that we are now, and shall be hereafter,
    But what and where depend on life's minute?
Hails heavenly cheer or infernal laughter
    Our first step out of the gulf or in it?   140
Shall Man, such step within his endeavour,
    Man's face, have no more play and action
Than joy which is crystallized for ever,
    Or grief, an eternal petrifaction?

XIX

On which I conclude, that the early painters,   145
    To cries of 'Greek Art and what more wish you?'—
Replied, 'To become now self-acquainters,
    'And paint man man, whatever the issue!
'Make new hopes shine through the flesh they fray,
    'New fears aggrandize the rags and tatters: 150
'To bring the invisible full into play!
    'Let the visible go to the dogs—what matters?'

XX

Give these, I exhort you, their guerdon and glory
    For daring so much, before they well did it.
The first of the new, in our race's story,   155
    Beats the last of the old; 't is no idle quiddit.
The worthies began a revolution,
    Which if on earth you intend to acknowledge,
Why, honour them now! (ends my allocution)
    Nor confer your degree when the folk leave college.   160

XXI

There's a fancy some lean to and others hate—
    That, when this life is ended, begins
New work for the soul in another state,
    Where it strives and gets weary, loses and wins:
Where the strong and the weak, this world's congeries,   165
    Repeat in large what they practised in small,
Through life after life in unlimited series;
    Only the scale's to be changed, that's all.

XXII

Yet I hardly know. When a soul has seen
    By the means of Evil that Good is best,   170
And, through earth and its noise, what is heaven's
        serene,—
    When our faith in the same has stood the test—
Why, the child grown man, you burn the rod,
    The uses of labour are surely done;
There remaineth a rest for the people of God: 175
    And I have had troubles enough, for one.

XXIII

But at any rate I have loved the season
  Of Art's spring-birth so dim and dewy;
My sculptor is Nicolo the Pisan,
  My painter—who but Cimabue?   180
Nor ever was man of them all indeed,
  From these to Ghiberti and Ghirlandajo,
Could say that he missed my critic-meed.
  So, now to my special grievance—heigh ho!

XXIV

Their ghosts still stand, as I said before,   185
  Watching each fresco flaked and rasped,
Blocked up, knocked out, or whitewashed o'er:
  —No getting again what the church has grasped!
The works on the wall must take their chance;
  'Works never conceded to England's thick clime!'   190
(I hope they prefer their inheritance
  Of a bucketful of Italian quick-lime.)

XXV

When they go at length, with such a shaking
  Of heads o'er the old delusion, sadly
Each master his way through the black streets taking,   195
  Where many a lost work breathes though badly—
Why don't they bethink them of who has merited?
  Why not reveal, while their pictures dree
Such doom, how a captive might be out-ferreted?
  Why is it they never remember me?   200

XXVI

Not that I expect the great Bigordi,
  Nor Sandro to hear me, chivalric, bellicose;
Nor the wronged Lippino; and not a word I
  Say of a scrap of Frà Angelico's:
But are you too fine, Taddeo Gaddi,   205
  To grant me a taste of your intonaco,
Some Jerome that seeks the heaven with a sad eye?
  Not a churlish saint, Lorenzo Monaco?

XXVII

Could not the ghost with the close red cap,
  My Pollajolo, the twice a craftsman,   210
Save me a sample, give me the hap
  Of a muscular Christ that shows the draughtsman?
No Virgin by him the somewhat petty,
  Of finical touch and tempera crumbly—
Could not Alesso Baldovinetti   215
  Contribute so much, I ask him humbly?

XXVIII

Margheritone of Arezzo,
  With the grave-clothes garb and swaddling barret
(Why purse up mouth and beak in a pet so,
  You bald old saturnine poll-clawed parrot?)   220
Not a poor glimmering Crucifixion,
  Where in the foreground kneels the donor?
If such remain, as is my conviction,
  The hoarding it does you but little honour.

XXIX

They pass; for them the panels may thrill,   225
  The tempera grow alive and tinglish;
Their pictures are left to the mercies still
  Of dealers and stealers, Jews and the English,
Who, seeing mere money's worth in their prize,
  Will sell it to somebody calm as Zeno   230
At naked High Art, and in ecstasies
  Before some clay-cold vile Carlino!

XXX

No matter for these! But Giotto, you,
  Have you allowed, as the town-tongues babble it,—
Oh, never! it shall not be counted true—   235
  That a certain precious little tablet
Which Buonarroti eyed like a lover,—
  Was buried so long in oblivion's womb
And, left for another than I to discover,
  Turns up at last! and to whom?—to whom?   240

XXXI

I, that have haunted the dim San Spirito,
  (Or was it rather the Ognissanti?)
Patient on altar-step planting a weary toe!
  Nay, I shall have it yet! *Detur amanti!*
My Koh-i-noor—or (if that's a platitude)   245
  Jewel of Giamschid, the Persian Sofi's eye;
So, in anticipative gratitude,
  What if I take up my hope and prophesy?

XXXII

When the hour grows ripe, and a certain dotard
  Is pitched, no parcel that needs invoicing,   250
To the worse side of the Mont Saint Gothard,
  We shall begin by way of rejoicing;
None of that shooting the sky (blank cartridge),
  Nor a civic guard, all plumes and lacquer,
Hunting Radetzky's soul like a partridge   255
  Over Morello with squib and cracker.

XXXIII

This time we'll shoot better game and bag 'em hot—
  No mere display at the stone of Dante,
But a kind of sober Witanagemot
  (Ex: 'Casa Guidi,' *quod videas ante*)   260
Shall ponder, once Freedom restored to Florence,
  How Art may return that departed with her.
Go, hated house, go each trace of the Loraine's,
  And bring us the days of Orgagna hither!

XXXIV

How we shall prologize, how we shall perorate,   265
  Utter fit things upon art and history,
Feel truth at blood-heat and falsehood at zero rate,
  Make of the want of the age no mystery;
Contrast the fructuous and sterile eras,
  Show—monarchy ever its uncouth cub licks   270
Out of the bear's shape into Chimæra's,
  While Pure Art's birth is still the republic's.

XXXV

Then one shall propose in a speech (curt Tuscan,
    Expurgate and sober, with scarcely an *'issimo,'*)
To end now our half-told tale of Cambuscan,   275
    And turn the bell-tower's *alt* to *altissimo*:
And fine as the beak of a young beccaccia
    The Campanile, the Duomo's fit ally,
Shall soar up in gold full fifty braccia,
    Completing Florence, as Florence Italy.   280

XXXVI

Shall I be alive that morning the scaffold
    Is broken away, and the long-pent fire,
Like the golden hope of the world, unbaffled
    Springs from its sleep, and up goes the spire
While 'God and the People' plain for its motto,   285
    Thence the new tricolour flaps at the sky?
At least to foresee that glory of Giotto
    And Florence together, the first am I!

IN A BALCONY

1853

PERSONS

NORBERT.

CONSTANCE.

THE QUEEN.

CONSTANCE *and* NORBERT.

NORBERT. Now!
CONSTANCE.   Not now!
NORBERT.   Give me them again, those hands:
    Put them upon my forehead, how it throbs!
    Press them before my eyes, the fire comes through!
    You cruellest, you dearest in the world,
    Let me! The Queen must grant whate'er I ask—   5
    How can I gain you and not ask the Queen?

There she stays waiting for me, here stand you;
Some time or other this was to be asked;
Now is the one time—what I ask, I gain:
Let me ask now, Love!

CONSTANCE.   Do, and ruin us.   10

NORBERT. Let it be now, Love! All my soul breaks forth.
How I do love you! Give my love its way!
A man can have but one life and one death,
One heaven, one hell. Let me fulfil my fate—
Grant me my heaven now! Let me know you mine,   15
Prove you mine, write my name upon your brow,
Hold you and have you, and then die away,
If God please, with completion in my soul!

CONSTANCE. I am not yours then? How content this man!
I am not his—who change into himself,   20
Have passed into his heart and beat its beats,
Who give my hands to him, my eyes, my hair,
Give all that was of me away to him—
So well, that now, my spirit turned his own,
Takes part with him against the woman here,   25
Bids him not stumble at so mere a straw
As caring that the world be cognizant
How he loves her and how she worships him.
You have this woman, not as yet that world.
Go on, I bid, nor stop to care for me   30
By saving what I cease to care about,
The courtly name and pride of circumstance—
The name you'll pick up and be cumbered with
Just for the poor parade's sake, nothing more;
Just that the world may slip from under you—   35
Just that the world may cry 'So much for him—
'The man predestined to the heap of crowns:
'There goes his chance of winning one, at least!'

NORBERT. The world!

CONSTANCE.   You love it. Love me quite as well,
And see if I shall pray for this in vain!   40
Why must you ponder what it knows or thinks?

NORBERT. You pray for—what, in vain?

CONSTANCE.   Oh my heart's heart,
How I do love you, Norbert! That is right:

But listen, or I take my hands away!
You say, 'let it be now': you would go now   45
And tell the Queen, perhaps six steps from us,
You love me—so you do, thank God!
NORBERT.   Thank God!
CONSTANCE. Yes, Norbert,—but you fain would tell your love,
  And, what succeeds the telling, ask of her
  My hand. Now take this rose and look at it,   50
  Listening to me. You are the minister,
  The Queen's first favourite, nor without a cause.
  To-night completes your wonderful year's-work
  (This palace-feast is held to celebrate)
  Made memorable by her life's success,   55
  The junction of two crowns, on her sole head,
  Her house had only dreamed of anciently:
  That this mere dream is grown a stable truth,
  To-night's feast makes authentic. Whose the praise?
  Whose genius, patience, energy, achieved   60
  What turned the many heads and broke the hearts?
  You are the fate, your minute's in the heaven.
  Next comes the Queen's turn. 'Name your own reward!'
  With leave to clench the past, chain the to-come,
  Put out an arm and touch and take the sun   65
  And fix it ever full-faced on your earth,
  Possess yourself supremely of her life,—
  You choose the single thing she will not grant;
  Nay, very declaration of which choice
  Will turn the scale and neutralize your work: 70
  At best she will forgive you, if she can.
  You think I'll let you choose—her cousin's hand?
NORBERT. Wait. First, do you retain your old belief
  The Queen is generous,—nay, is just?
CONSTANCE.   There, there!
  So men make women love them, while they know   75
  No more of women's hearts than . . . look you here,
  You that are just and generous beside,
  Make it your own case! For example now,
  I'll say—I let you kiss me, hold my hands—
  Why? do you know why? I'll instruct you, then—   80
  The kiss, because you have a name at court;

This hand and this, that you may shut in each
A jewel, if you please to pick up such.
That's horrible? Apply it to the Queen—
Suppose I am the Queen to whom you speak: 85
'I was a nameless man; you needed me:
'Why did I proffer you my aid? there stood
'A certain pretty cousin at your side.
'Why did I make such common cause with you?
'Access to her had not been easy else. 90
'You give my labour here abundant praise?
' 'Faith, labour, which she overlooked, grew play.
'How shall your gratitude discharge itself?
'Give me her hand!'
NORBERT And still I urge the same.
Is the Queen just? just—generous or no! 95
CONSTANCE. Yes, just. You love a rose; no harm in that:
But was it for the rose's sake or mine
You put it in your bosom? mine, you said—
Then, mine you still must say or else be false.
You told the Queen you served her for herself; 100
If so, to serve her was to serve yourself,
She thinks, for all your unbelieving face!
I know her. In the hall, six steps from us,
One sees the twenty pictures; there's a life
Better than life, and yet no life at all. 105
Conceive her born in such a magic dome,
Pictures all round her! why, she sees the world,
Can recognize its given things and facts,
The fight of giants or the feast of gods,
Sages in senate, beauties at the bath, 110
Chases and battles, the whole earth's display,
Landscape and sea-piece, down to flowers and fruit—
And who shall question that she knows them all,
In better semblance than the things outside?
Yet bring into the silent gallery 115
Some live thing to contrast in breath and blood,
Some lion, with the painted lion there—
You think she'll understand composedly?
—Say, 'that's his fellow in the hunting-piece
'Yonder, I've turned to praise a hundred times?' 120

Not so. Her knowledge of our actual earth,
Its hopes and fears, concerns and sympathies,
Must be too far, too mediate, too unreal.
The real exists for us outside, not her:
How should it, with that life in these four walls—   125
That father and that mother, first to last
No father and no mother—friends, a heap,
Lovers, no lack—a husband in due time,
And every one of them alike a lie!
Things painted by a Rubens out of nought   130
Into what kindness, friendship, love should be;
All better, all more grandiose than the life,
Only no life; mere cloth and surface-paint,
You feel, while you admire. How should she feel?
Yet now that she has stood thus fifty years   135
The sole spectator in that gallery,
You think to bring this warm real struggling love
In to her of a sudden, and suppose
She'll keep her state untroubled? Here's the truth—
She'll apprehend truth's value at a glance,   140
Prefer it to the pictured loyalty?
You only have to say, 'so men are made,
'For this they act; the thing has many names,
'But this the right one: and now, Queen, be just!'
Your life slips back; you lose her at the word: 145
You do not even for amends gain me.
He will not understand; oh, Norbert, Norbert,
Do you not understand?
NORBERT   The Queen's the Queen:
I am myself—no picture, but alive
In every nerve and every muscle, here   150
At the palace-window o'er the people's street,
As she in the gallery where the pictures glow:
The good of life is precious to us both.
She cannot love; what do I want with rule?
When first I saw your face a year ago   155
I knew my life's good, my soul heard one voice—
'The woman yonder, there's no use of life
'But just to obtain her! heap earth's woes in one
'And bear them—make a pile of all earth's joys

'And spurn them, as they help or help not this;   160
'Only, obtain her!' How was it to be?
I found you were the cousin of the Queen;
I must then serve the Queen to get to you.
No other way. Suppose there had been one,
And I, by saying prayers to some white star   165
With promise of my body and my soul,
Might gain you,—should I pray the star or no?
Instead, there was the Queen to serve! I served,
Helped, did what other servants failed to do.
Neither she sought nor I declared my end.   170
Her good is hers, my recompense be mine,—
I therefore name you as that recompense.
She dreamed that such a thing could never be?
Let her wake now. She thinks there was more cause
In love of power, high fame, pure loyalty?   175
Perhaps she fancies men wear out their lives
Chasing such shades. Then, I've a fancy too;
I worked because I want you with my soul:
I therefore ask your hand. Let it be now!
CONSTANCE. Had I not loved you from the very first,   180
Were I not yours, could we not steal out thus
So wickedly, so wildly, and so well,
You might become impatient. What's conceived
Of us without here, by the folk within?
Where are you now? immersed in cares of state—   185
Where am I now? intent on festal robes—
We two, embracing under death's spread hand!
What was this thought for, what that scruple of yours
Which broke the council up?—to bring about
One minute's meeting in the corridor!   190
And then the sudden sleights, strange secrecies,
Complots inscrutable, deep telegraphs,
Long-planned chance-meetings, hazards of a look,
'Does she know! does she not know? saved or lost?'
A year of this compression's ecstasy   195
All goes for nothing! you would give this up
For the old way, the open way, the world's,
His way who beats, and his who sells his wife!
What tempts you?—their notorious happiness

Makes you ashamed of ours? The best you'll gain   200
Will be—the Queen grants all that you require,
Concedes the cousin, rids herself of you
And me at once, and gives us ample leave
To live like our five hundred happy friends.
The world will show us with officious hand   205
Our chamber-entry, and stand sentinel
Where we so oft have stolen across its traps!
Get the world's warrant, ring the falcon's feet,
And make it duty to be bold and swift,
Which long ago was nature. Have it so!   210
We never hawked by rights till flung from fist?
Oh, the man's thought! no woman's such a fool.
NORBERT. Yes, the man's thought and my thought, which is
    more—
One made to love you, let the world take note!
Have I done worthy work? be love's the praise,   215
Though hampered by restrictions, barred against
By set forms, blinded by forced secrecies!
Set free my love, and see what love can do
Shown in my life—what work will spring from that!
The world is used to have its business done   220
On other grounds, find great effects produced
For power's sake, fame's sake, motives in men's mouth.
So, good: but let my low ground shame their high!
Truth is the strong thing. Let man's life be true!
And love's the truth of mine. Time prove the rest!   225
I choose to wear you stamped all over me,
Your name upon my forehead and my breast,
You, from the sword's blade to the ribbon's edge,
That men may see, all over, you in me—
That pale loves may die out of their pretence   230
In face of mine, shames thrown on love fall off.
Permit this, Constance! Love has been so long
Subdued in me, eating me through and through,
That now 't is all of me and must have way.
Think of my work, that chaos of intrigues,   235
Those hopes and fears, surprises and delays,
That long endeavour, earnest, patient, slow,
Trembling at last to its assured result:

Then think of this revulsion! I resume
Life after death, (it is no less than life,   240
After such long unlovely labouring days)
And liberate to beauty life's great need
O' the beautiful, which, while it prompted work,
Suppressed itself erewhile. This eve's the time,
This eve intense with yon first trembling star   245
We seem to pant and reach; scarce aught between
The earth that rises and the heaven that bends;
All nature self-abandoned, every tree
Flung as it will, pursuing its own thoughts
And fixed so, every flower and every weed,   250
No pride, no shame, no victory, no defeat;
All under God, each measured by itself.
These statues round us stand abrupt, distinct,
The strong in strength, the weak in weakness fixed,
The Muse for ever wedded to her lyre,   255
Nymph to her fawn, and Silence to her rose:
See God's approval on his universe!
Let us do so—aspire to live as these
In harmony with truth, ourselves being true!
Take the first way, and let the second come!   260
My first is to possess myself of you;
The music sets the march-step—forward, then!
And there's the Queen, I go to claim you of,
The world to witness, wonder and applaud.
Our flower of life breaks open. No delay!   265
CONSTANCE. And so shall we be ruined, both of us.
Norbert, I know her to the skin and bone:
You do not know her, were not born to it,
To feel what she can see or cannot see.
Love, she is generous,—ay, despite your smile,   270
Generous as you are: for, in that thin frame
Pain-twisted, punctured through and through with cares,
There lived a lavish soul until it starved,
Debarred of healthy food. Look to the soul—
Pity that, stoop to that, ere you begin   275
(The true man's-way) on justice and your rights,
Exactions and acquittance of the past!
Begin so—see what justice she will deal!

We women hate a debt as men a gift.
Suppose her some poor keeper of a school   280
Whose business is to sit thro' summer months
And dole out children leave to go and play,
Herself superior to such lightness—she
In the arm-chair's state and pædagogic pomp—
To the life, the laughter, sun and youth outside: 285
We wonder such a face looks black on us?
I do not bid you wake her tenderness,
(That were vain truly—none is left to wake)
But let her think her justice is engaged
To take the shape of tenderness, and mark   290
If she'll not coldly pay its warmest debt!
Does she love me, I ask you? not a whit:
Yet, thinking that her justice was engaged
To help a kinswoman, she took me up—
Did more on that bare ground than other loves   295
Would do on greater argument. For me,
I have no equivalent of such cold kind
To pay her with, but love alone to give
If I give anything. I give her love:
I feel I ought to help her, and I will.   300
So, for her sake, as yours, I tell you twice
That women hate a debt as men a gift.
If I were you, I could obtain this grace—
Could lay the whole I did to love's account,
Nor yet be very false as courtiers go—   305
Declaring my success was recompense;
It would be so, in fact: what were it else?
And then, once loose her generosity,—
Oh, how I see it!—then, were I but you,
To turn it, let it seem to move itself,   310
And make it offer what I really take,
Accepting just, in the poor cousin's hand,
Her value as the next thing to the Queen's—
Since none love Queens directly, none dare that,
And a thing's shadow or a name's mere echo   315
Suffices those who miss the name and thing!
You pick up just a ribbon she has worn,
To keep in proof how near her breath you came.

Say, I'm so near I seem a piece of her—
Ask for me that way—(oh, you understand)   320
You'd find the same gift yielded with a grace,
Which, if you make the least show to extort . . .
—You'll see! and when you have ruined both of us,
Dissertate on the Queen's ingratitude!
NORBERT. Then, if I turn it that way, you consent?   325
'T is not my way; I have more hope in truth:
Still, if you won't have truth—why, this indeed,
Were scarcely false, as I'd express the sense.
Will you remain here?
CONSTANCE.   O best heart of mine,
How I have loved you! then, you take my way?   330
Are mine as you have been her minister,
Work out my thought, give it effect for me,
Paint plain my poor conceit and make it serve?
I owe that withered woman everything—
Life, fortune, you, remember! Take my part—   335
Help me to pay her! Stand upon your rights?
You, with my rose, my hands, my heart on you?
Your rights are mine—you have no rights but mine.
NORBERT. Remain here. How you know me!
CONSTANCE.   Ah, but still——
                    [*He breaks from her: she remains. Dance-music
                    from within.*

                    Enter the QUEEN.

QUEEN. Constance? She is here as he said. Speak quick! 340
Is it so? Is it true or false? One word!
CONSTANCE. True.
QUEEN.   Mercifullest Mother, thanks to thee!
CONSTANCE. Madam?
QUEEN.   I love you, Constance, from my soul.
Now say once more, with any words you will,
'T is true, all true, as true as that I speak.   345
CONSTANCE. Why should you doubt it?
QUEEN.   Ah, why doubt? why doubt?
Dear, make me see it! Do you see it so?
None see themselves; another sees them best.
You say 'why doubt it?'—you see him and me.

It is because the Mother has such grace   350
That if we had but faith—wherein we fail—
Whate'er we yearn for would be granted us;
Yet still we let our whims prescribe despair,
Our fancies thwart and cramp our will and power,
And while, accepting life, abjure its use.   355
Constance, I had abjured the hope of love
And being loved, as truly as yon palm
The hope of seeing Egypt from that plot.
CONSTANCE. Heaven!
QUEEN.   But it was so, Constance, it was so!
Men say—or do men say it? fancies say—   360
'Stop here, your life is set, you are grown old.
'Too late—no love for you, too late for love—
'Leave love to girls. Be queen: let Constance love.'
One takes the hint—half meets it like a child,
Ashamed at any feelings that oppose.   365
'Oh love, true, never think of love again!
'I am a queen: I rule, not love forsooth.'
So it goes on; so a face grows like this,
Hair like this hair, poor arms as lean as these,
Till,—nay, it does not end so, I thank God!   370
CONSTANCE. I cannot understand—
QUEEN.   The happier you!
Constance, I know not how it is with men:
For women (I am a woman now like you)
There is no good of life but love—but love!
What else looks good, is some shade flung from love;   375
Love gilds it, gives it worth. Be warned by me,
Never you cheat yourself one instant! Love,
Give love, ask only love, and leave the rest!
O Constance, how I love you!
CONSTANCE.   I love you.
QUEEN. I do believe that all is come through you.   380
I took you to my heart to keep it warm
When the last chance of love seemed dead in me;
I thought your fresh youth warmed my withered heart.
Oh, I am very old now, am I not?
Not so! it is true and it shall be true!   385
CONSTANCE. Tell it me: let me judge if true or false.

QUEEN. Ah, but I fear you! you will look at me
    And say, 'she's old, she's grown unlovely quite
    'Who ne'er was beauteous: men want beauty still.'
    Well, so I feared—the curse! so I felt sure!   390
CONSTANCE. Be calm. And now you feel not sure, you say?
QUEEN. Constance, he came,—the coming was not strange—
    Do not I stand and see men come and go?
    I turned a half-look from my pedestal
    Where I grow marble—'one young man the more!   395
    'He will love some one; that is nought to me:
    'What would he with my marble stateliness?'
    Yet this seemed somewhat worse than heretofore;
    The man more gracious, youthful, like a god,
    And I still older, with less flesh to change—   400
    We two those dear extremes that long to touch.
    It seemed still harder when he first began
    To labour at those state-affairs, absorbed
    The old way for the old end—interest.
    Oh, to live with a thousand beating hearts   405
    Around you, swift eyes, serviceable hands,
    Professing they've no care but for your cause,
    Thought but to help you, love but for yourself,—
    And you the marble statue all the time
    They praise and point at as preferred to life,   410
    Yet leave for the first breathing woman's smile,
    First dancer's, gipsy's or street baladine's!
    Why, how I have ground my teeth to hear men's speech
    Stifled for fear it should alarm my ear,
    Their gait subdued lest step should startle me,   415
    Their eyes declined, such queendom to respect,
    Their hands alert, such treasure to preserve,
    While not a man of them broke rank and spoke,
    Wrote me a vulgar letter all of love,
    Or caught my hand and pressed it like a hand!   420
    There have been moments, if the sentinel
    Lowering his halbert to salute the queen,
    Had flung it brutally and clasped my knees,
    I would have stooped and kissed him with my soul.
CONSTANCE. Who could have comprehended?
QUEEN.   Ay, who—who?   425

A a

Why, no one, Constance, but this one who did.
Not they, not you, not I. Even now perhaps
It comes too late—would you but tell the truth.
CONSTANCE. I wait to tell it.
QUEEN.   Well, you see, he came,
Outfaced the others, did a work this year   430
Exceeds in value all was ever done,
You know—it is not I who say it—all
Say it. And so (a second pang and worse)
I grew aware not only of what he did,
But why so wondrously. Oh, never work   435
Like his was done for work's ignoble sake—
Souls need a finer aim to light and lure!
I felt, I saw, he loved—loved somebody.
And Constance, my dear Constance, do you know,
I did believe this while 't was you he loved.   440
CONSTANCE. Me, madam?
QUEEN.   It did seem to me, your face
Met him where'er he looked: and whom but you
Was such a man to love? It seemed to me,
You saw he loved you, and approved his love,
And both of you were in intelligence.   445
You could not loiter in that garden, step
Into this balcony, but I straight was stung
And forced to understand. It seemed so true,
So right, so beautiful, so like you both,
That all this work should have been done by him   450
Not for the vulgar hope of recompense,
But that at last—suppose, some night like this—
Borne on to claim his due reward of me,
He might say 'Give her hand and pay me so.'
And I (O Constance, you shall love me now!)   455
I thought, surmounting all the bitterness,
—'And he shall have it. I will make her blest,
'My flower of youth, my woman's self that was,
'My happiest woman's self that might have been!
'These two shall have their joy and leave me here.'   460
Yes—yes!
CONSTANCE. Thanks!
QUEEN.   And the word was on my lips

When he burst in upon me. I looked to hear
A mere calm statement of his just desire
For payment of his labour. When—O heaven,
How can I tell you? lightning on my eyes   465
And thunder in my ears proved that first word
Which told 't was love of me, of me, did all—
He loved me—from the first step to the last,
Loved me!

CONSTANCE. You hardly saw, scarce heard him speak
Of love: what if you should mistake?

QUEEN.   No, no—   470
No mistake! Ha, there shall be no mistake!
He had not dared to hint the love he felt—
You were my reflex—(how I understood!)
He said you were the ribbon I had worn,
He kissed my hand, he looked into my eyes,   475
And love, love came at end of every phrase.
Love is begun; this much is come to pass:
The rest is easy. Constance, I am yours!
I will learn, I will place my life on you,
Teach me but how to keep what I have won!   480
Am I so old? This hair was early grey;
But joy ere now has brought hair brown again,
And joy will bring the cheek's red back, I feel.
I could sing once too; that was in my youth.
Still, when men paint me, they declare me . . . yes,   485
Beautiful—for the last French painter did!
I know they flatter somewhat; you are frank—
I trust you. How I loved you from the first!
Some queens would hardly seek a cousin out
And set her by their side to take the eye: 490
I must have felt that good would come from you.
I am not generous—like him—like you!
But he is not your lover after all:
It was not you he looked at. Saw you him?
You have not been mistaking words or looks?   495
He said you were the reflex of myself.
And yet he is not such a paragon
To you, to younger women who may choose
Among a thousand Norberts. Speak the truth!

You know you never named his name to me: 500
You know, I cannot give him up—ah God,
Not up now, even to you!
CONSTANCE.   Then calm yourself.
QUEEN. See, I am old—look here, you happy girl!
I will not play the fool, deceive—ah, whom?
'T is all gone: put your cheek beside my cheek   505
And what a contrast does the moon behold!
But then I set my life upon one chance,
The last chance and the best—am *I* not left,
My soul, myself? All women love great men
If young or old; it is in all the tales: 510
Young beauties love old poets who can love—
Why should not he, the poems in my soul,
The passionate faith, the pride of sacrifice,
Life-long, death-long? I throw them at his feet.
Who cares to see the fountain's very shape,   515
Whether it be a Triton's or a Nymph's
That pours the foam, makes rainbows all around?
You could not praise indeed the empty conch;
But I'll pour floods of love and hide myself.
How I will love him! Cannot men love love?   520
Who was a queen and loved a poet once
Humpbacked, a dwarf? ah, women can do that!
Well, but men too; at least, they tell you so.
They love so many women in their youth,
And even in age they all love whom they please;   525
And yet the best of them confide to friends
That 't is not beauty makes the lasting love—
They spend a day with such and tire the next:
They like soul,—well then, they like phantasy,
Novelty even. Let us confess the truth,   530
Horrible though it be, that prejudice,
Prescription . . . curses! they will love a queen.
They will, they do: and will not, does not—he?
CONSTANCE. How can he? You are wedded: 't is a name
We know, but still a bond. Your rank remains,   535
His rank remains. How can he, nobly souled
As you believe and I incline to think,
Aspire to be your favourite, shame and all?

QUEEN. Hear her! There, there now—could she love like me?
    What did I say of smooth-cheeked youth and grace?   540
    See all it does or could do! so youth loves!
    Oh, tell him, Constance, you could never do
    What I will,—you, it was not born in! I
    Will drive these difficulties far and fast
    As yonder mists curdling before the moon.   545
    I'll use my light too, gloriously retrieve
    My youth from its enforced calamity,
    Dissolve that hateful marriage, and be his,
    His own in the eyes alike of God and man.
CONSTANCE. You will do—dare do . . . pause on what you say! 550
QUEEN. Hear her! I thank you, sweet, for that surprise.
    You have the fair face: for the soul, see mine!
    I have the strong soul: let me teach you, here.
    I think I have borne enough and long enough,
    And patiently enough, the world remarks,   555
    To have my own way now, unblamed by all.
    It does so happen (I rejoice for it)
    This most unhoped-for issue cuts the knot.
    There's not a better way of settling claims
    Than this; God sends the accident express: 560
    And were it for my subjects' good, no more,
    'T were best thus ordered. I am thankful now,
    Mute, passive, acquiescent. I receive,
    And bless God simply, or should almost fear
    To walk so smoothly to my ends at last.   565
    Why, how I baffle obstacles, spurn fate!
    How strong I am! Could Norbert see me now!
CONSTANCE. Let me consider. It is all too strange.
QUEEN. You, Constance, learn of me; do you, like me!
    You are young, beautiful: my own, best girl,   570
    You will have many lovers, and love one—
    Light hair, not hair like Norbert's, to suit yours:
    Taller than he is, since yourself are tall.
    Love him, like me! Give all away to him;
    Think never of yourself; throw by your pride,   575
    Hope, fear,—your own good as you saw it once,
    And love him simply for his very self.
    Remember, I (and what am I to you?)

Would give up all for one, leave throne, lose life,
Do all but just unlove him! He loves me.   580
CONSTANCE. He shall.
QUEEN.   You, step inside my inmost heart!
Give me your own heart: let us have one heart!
I'll come to you for counsel; 'this he says,
'This he does; what should this amount to, pray?
'Beseech you, change it into current coin!   585
'Is that worth kisses? Shall I please him there?'
And then we'll speak in turn of you—what else?
Your love, according to your beauty's worth,
For you shall have some noble love, all gold:
Whom choose you? we will get him at your choice.   590
—Constance, I leave you. Just a minute since,
I felt as I must die or be alone
Breathing my soul into an ear like yours:
Now, I would face the world with my new life,
Wear my new crown. I'll walk around the rooms,   595
And then come back and tell you how it feels.
How soon a smile of God can change the world!
How we are made for happiness—how work
Grows play, adversity a winning fight!
True, I have lost so many years: what then?   600
Many remain: God has been very good.
You, stay here! 'T is as different from dreams,
From the mind's cold calm estimate of bliss,
As these stone statues from the flesh and blood.
The comfort thou hast caused mankind, God's moon!   605
    [*She goes out, leaving* CONSTANCE. *Dance-music from within.*
                    NORBERT *enters.*

NORBERT. Well? we have but one minute and one word!
CONSTANCE. I am yours, Norbert!
NORBERT.   Yes, mine.
CONSTANCE.   Not till now!
You were mine. Now I give myself to you.
NORBERT. Constance?
CONSTANCE.   Your own! I know the thriftier way
Of giving—haply, 't is the wiser way.   610
Meaning to give a treasure, I might dole
Coin after coin out (each, as that were all,

With a new largess still at each despair)
And force you keep in sight the deed, preserve
Exhaustless till the end my part and yours,   615
My giving and your taking; both our joys
Dying together. Is it the wiser way?
I choose the simpler; I give all at once.
Know what you have to trust to, trade upon!
Use it, abuse it,—anything but think   620
Hereafter, 'Had I known she loved me so,
'And what my means, I might have thriven with it.'
This is your means. I give you all myself.
NORBERT. I take you and thank God.
CONSTANCE.   Look on through years!
We cannot kiss, a second day like this;   625
Else were this earth no earth.
NORBERT.   With this day's heat
We shall go on through years of cold.
CONSTANCE.   So, best!
   —I try to see those years—I think I see.
You walk quick and new warmth comes; you look back
And lay all to the first glow—not sit down   630
For ever brooding on a day like this
While seeing embers whiten and love die.
Yes, love lives best in its effect; and mine,
Full in its own life, yearns to live in yours.
NORBERT. Just so. I take and know you all at once.   635
Your soul is disengaged so easily,
Your face is there, I know you; give me time,
Let me be proud and think you shall know me.
My soul is slower: in a life I roll
The minute out whereto you condense yours—   640
The whole slow circle round you I must move,
To be just you. I look to a long life
To decompose this minute, prove its worth.
'T is the sparks' long succession one by one
Shall show you, in the end, what fire was crammed   645
In that mere stone you struck: how could you know,
If it lay ever unproved in your sight,
As now my heart lies? your own warmth would hide
Its coldness, were it cold.

CONSTANCE.   But how prove, how?
NORBERT. Prove in my life, you ask?
CONSTANCE.   Quick, Norbert—how? 650
NORBERT. That's easy told. I count life just a stuff
    To try the soul's strength on, educe the man.
    Who keeps one end in view makes all things serve.
    As with the body—he who hurls a lance
    Or heaps up stone on stone, shows strength alike: 655
    So must I seize and task all means to prove
    And show this soul of mine, you crown as yours,
    And justify us both.
CONSTANCE.   Could you write books,
    Paint pictures! One sits down in poverty
    And writes or paints, with pity for the rich.   660
NORBERT. And loves one's painting and one's writing, then,
    And not one's mistress! All is best, believe,
    And we best as no other than we are.
    We live, and they experiment on life—
    Those poets, painters, all who stand aloof   665
    To overlook the farther. Let us be
    The thing they look at! I might take your face
    And write of it and paint it—to what end?
    For whom? what pale dictatress in the air
    Feeds, smiling sadly, her fine ghost-like form   670
    With earth's real blood and breath, the beauteous life
    She makes despised for ever? You are mine,
    Made for me, not for others in the world,
    Nor yet for that which I should call my art,
    The cold calm power to see how fair you look.   675
    I come to you; I leave you not, to write
    Or paint. You are, I am: let Rubens there
    Paint us!
CONSTANCE. So, best!
NORBERT.   I understand your soul.
    You live, and rightly sympathize with life,
    With action, power, success. This way is straight;   680
    And time were short beside, to let me change
    The craft my childhood learnt: my craft shall serve.
    Men set me here to subjugate, enclose,
    Manure their barren lives, and force thence fruit

First for themselves, and afterward for me   685
In the due tithe; the task of some one soul,
Through ways of work appointed by the world.
I am not bid create—men see no star
Transfiguring my brow to warrant that—
But find and bind and bring to bear their wills.   690
So I began: to-night sees how I end.
What if it see, too, power's first outbreak here
Amid the warmth, surprise and sympathy,
And instincts of the heart that teach the head?
What if the people have discerned at length   695
The dawn of the next nature, novel brain
Whose will they venture in the place of theirs,
Whose work, they trust, shall find them as novel ways
To untried heights which yet he only sees?
I felt it when you kissed me. See this Queen,   700
This people—in our phrase, this mass of men—
See how the mass lies passive to my hand
Now that my hand is plastic, with you by
To make the muscles iron! Oh, an end
Shall crown this issue as this crowns the first!   705
My will be on this people! then, the strain,
The grappling of the potter with his clay,
The long uncertain struggle,—the success
And consummation of the spirit-work,
Some vase shaped to the curl of the god's lip,   710
While rounded fair for human sense to see
The Graces in a dance men recognize
With turbulent applause and laughs of heart!
So triumph ever shall renew itself;
Ever shall end in efforts higher yet,   715
Ever begin . . .
CONSTANCE.   I ever helping?
NORBERT.   Thus!
              [*As he embraces her, the* QUEEN *enters.*
CONSTANCE. Hist, madam! So have I performed my part.
    You see your gratitude's true decency,
    Norbert? A little slow in seeing it!
    Begin, to end the sooner! What's a kiss?   720
NORBERT. Constance?

CONSTANCE.   Why, must I teach it you again?
  You want a witness to your dulness, sir?
  What was I saying these ten minutes long?
  Then I repeat—when some young handsome man
  Like you has acted out a part like yours,   725
  Is pleased to fall in love with one beyond,
  So very far beyond him, as he says—
  So hopelessly in love that but to speak
  Would prove him mad,—he thinks judiciously,
  And makes some insignificant good soul,   730
  Like me, his friend, adviser, confidant,
  And very stalking-horse to cover him
  In following after what he dares not face.
  When his end's gained—(sir, do you understand?)
  When she, he dares not face, has loved him first,   735
  —May I not say so, madam?—tops his hope,
  And overpasses so his wildest dream,
  With glad consent of all, and most of her
  The confidant who brought the same about—
  Why, in the moment when such joy explodes,   740
  I do hold that the merest gentleman
  Will not start rudely from the stalking-horse,
  Dismiss it with a 'There, enough of you!'
  Forget it, show his back unmannerly:
  But like a liberal heart will rather turn   745
  And say, 'A tingling time of hope was ours;
  'Betwixt the fears and falterings, we two lived
  'A chanceful time in waiting for the prize:
  'The confidant, the Constance, served not ill.
  'And though I shall forget her in due time,   750
  'Her use being answered now, as reason bids,
  'Nay as herself bids from her heart of hearts,—
  'Still, she has rights, the first thanks go to her,
  'The first good praise goes to the prosperous tool,
  'And the first—which is the last—rewarding kiss.'   755
NORBERT. Constance, it is a dream—ah, see, you smile!
CONSTANCE. So, now his part being properly performed,
  Madam, I turn to you and finish mine
  As duly; I do justice in my turn.
  Yes, madam, he has loved you—long and well;   760

He could not hope to tell you so—'t was I
Who served to prove your soul accessible,
I led his thoughts on, drew them to their place
When they had wandered else into despair,
And kept love constant toward its natural aim.　　765
Enough, my part is played; you stoop half-way
And meet us royally and spare our fears:
'T is like yourself. He thanks you, so do I.
Take him—with my full heart! my work is praised
By what comes of it. Be you happy, both!　　770
Yourself—the only one on earth who can—
Do all for him, much more than a mere heart
Which though warm is not useful in its warmth
As the silk vesture of a queen! fold that
Around him gently, tenderly. For him—　　775
For him,—he knows his own part!
NORBERT.　　　　　　　　　　Have you done?
I take the jest at last. Should I speak now?
Was yours the wager, Constance, foolish child,
Or did you but accept it? Well—at least
You lose by it.
CONSTANCE.　　Nay, madam, 't is your turn!　　780
Restrain him still from speech a little more,
And make him happier as more confident!
Pity him, madam, he is timid yet!
Mark, Norbert! Do not shrink now! Here I yield
My whole right in you to the Queen, observe!　　785
With her go put in practice the great schemes
You teem with, follow the career else closed—
Be all you cannot be except by her!
Behold her!—Madam, say for pity's sake
Anything—frankly say you love him! Else　　790
He'll not believe it: there's more earnest in
His fear than you conceive: I know the man!
NORBERT. I know the woman somewhat, and confess
I thought she had jested better: she begins
To overcharge her part. I gravely wait　　795
Your pleasure, madam: where is my reward?
QUEEN. Norbert, this wild girl (whom I recognize
Scarce more than you do, in her fancy-fit,

Eccentric speech and variable mirth,
Not very wise perhaps and somewhat bold, 800
Yet suitable, the whole night's work being strange)
—May still be right: I may do well to speak
And make authentic what appears a dream
To even myself. For, what she says, is true:
Yes, Norbert—what you spoke just now of love, 805
Devotion, stirred no novel sense in me,
But justified a warmth felt long before.
Yes, from the first—I loved you, I shall say:
Strange! but I do grow stronger, now 't is said.
Your courage helps mine: you did well to speak 810
To-night, the night that crowns your twelvemonths' toil:
But still I had not waited to discern
Your heart so long, believe me! From the first
The source of so much zeal was almost plain,
In absence even of your own words just now 815
Which hazarded the truth. 'T is very strange,
But takes a happy ending—in your love
Which mine meets: be it so! as you chose me,
So I choose you.
NORBERT.   And worthily you choose.
I will not be unworthy your esteem, 820
No, madam. I do love you; I will meet
Your nature, now I know it. This was well.
I see,—you dare and you are justified:
But none had ventured such experiment,
Less versed than you in nobleness of heart, 825
Less confident of finding such in me.
I joy that thus you test me ere you grant
The dearest richest beauteousest and best
Of women to my arms: 't is like yourself.
So—back again into my part's set words— 830
Devotion to the uttermost is yours,
But no, you cannot, madam, even you,
Create in me the love our Constance does.
Or—something truer to the tragic phrase—
Not yon magnolia-bell superb with scent 835
Invites a certain insect—that's myself—
But the small eye-flower nearer to the ground.

I take this lady.

CONSTANCE.   Stay—not hers, the trap—
Stay, Norbert—that mistake were worst of all!
He is too cunning, madam! It was I,   840
I, Norbert, who . . .

NORBERT.   You, was it, Constance? Then,
But for the grace of this divinest hour
Which gives me you, I might not pardon here!
I am the Queen's; she only knows my brain:
She may experiment upon my heart   845
And I instruct her too by the result.
But you, sweet, you who know me, who so long
Have told my heart-beats over, held my life
In those white hands of yours,—it is not well!

CONSTANCE. Tush! I have said it, did I not say it all?   850
The life, for her—the heart-beats, for her sake!

NORBERT. Enough! my cheek grows red, I think. Your test?
There's not the meanest woman in the world,
Not she I least could love in all the world,
Whom, did she love me, had love proved itself,   855
I dare insult as you insult me now.
Constance, I could say, if it must be said,
'Take back the soul you offer, I keep mine!'
But—'Take the soul still quivering on your hand,
'The soul so offered, which I cannot use,   860
'And, please you, give it to some playful friend,
'For—what's the trifle he requites me with?'
I, tempt a woman, to amuse a man,
That two may mock her heart if it succumb?
No: fearing God and standing 'neath his heaven,   865
I would not dare insult a woman so,
Were she the meanest woman in the world,
And he, I cared to please, ten emperors!

CONSTANCE. Norbert!

NORBERT.   I love once as I live but once.
What case is this to think or talk about?   870
I love you. Would it mend the case at all
If such a step as this killed love in me?
Your part were done: account to God for it!
But mine—could murdered love get up again,

And kneel to whom you please to designate,   875
And make you mirth? It is too horrible.
You did not know this, Constance? now you know
That body and soul have each one life, but one:
And here's my love, here, living, at your feet.
CONSTANCE. See the Queen! Norbert—this one more last word— 880
If thus you have taken jest for earnest—thus
Loved me in earnest . . .
NORBERT.   Ah, no jest holds here!
Where is the laughter in which jests break up,
And what this horror that grows palpable?
Madam—why grasp you thus the balcony?   885
Have I done ill? Have I not spoken truth?
How could I other? Was it not your test,
To try me, what my love for Constance meant?
Madam, your royal soul itself approves,
The first, that I should choose thus! so one takes   890
A beggar,—asks him, what would buy his child?
And then approves the expected laugh of scorn
Returned as something noble from the rags.
Speak, Constance, I'm the beggar! Ha, what's this?
You two glare each at each like panthers now.   895
Constance, the world fades; only you stand there!
You did not, in to-night's wild whirl of things,
Sell me—your soul of souls, for any price?
No—no—'t is easy to believe in you!
Was it your love's mad trial to o'ertop   900
Mine by this vain self-sacrifice? well, still—
Though I might curse, I love you. I am love
And cannot change: love's self is at your feet!
                              [*The* QUEEN *goes out.*
CONSTANCE. Feel my heart; let it die against your own!
NORBERT. Against my own. Explain not; let this be!   905
This is life's height.
CONSTANCE.   Yours, yours, yours!
NORBERT.   You and I—
Why care by what meanders we are here
I' the centre of the labyrinth? Men have died
Trying to find this place, which we have found.
CONSTANCE. Found, found!

NORBERT.   Sweet, never fear what she can do! 910
  We are past harm now.
CONSTANCE.   On the breast of God.
  I thought of men—as if you were a man.
  Tempting him with a crown!
NORBERT.   This must end here:
  It is too perfect.
CONSTANCE.   There's the music stopped.
  What measured heavy tread? It is one blaze   915
  About me and within me.
NORBERT.   Oh, some death
  Will run its sudden finger round this spark
  And sever us from the rest!
CONSTANCE.   And so do well.
  Now the doors open.
NORBERT.   'T is the guard comes.
CONSTANCE.   Kiss!

SAUL[1]

I

Said Abner, 'At last thou art come! Ere I tell, ere thou speak,
'Kiss my cheek, wish me well!' Then I wished it, and did kiss his
    cheek.
And he, 'Since the King, O my friend, for thy countenance sent,
'Neither drunken nor eaten have we; nor until from his tent
'Thou return with the joyful assurance the King liveth yet,   5
'Shall our lip with the honey be bright, with the water be wet.
'For out of the black mid-tent's silence, a space of three days,
'Not a sound hath escaped to thy servants, of prayer nor of praise,
'To betoken that Saul and the Spirit have ended their strife,
'And that, faint in his triumph, the monarch sinks back upon life. 10

II

'Yet now my heart leaps, O beloved! God's child with his dew
'On thy gracious gold hair, and those lilies still living and blue
'Just broken to twine round thy harp-strings, as if no wild heat
'Were now raging to torture the desert!'

III

                              Then I, as was meet,
Knelt down to the God of my fathers, and rose on my feet,   15

[1] For the earlier version of this poem, see p. 474, above.

And ran o'er the sand burnt to powder. The tent was unlooped;
I pulled up the spear that obstructed, and under I stooped;
Hands and knees on the slippery grass-patch, all withered and gone,
That extends to the second enclosure, I groped my way on
Till I felt where the foldskirts fly open. Then once more I prayed, 20
And opened the foldskirts and entered, and was not afraid
But spoke, 'Here is David, thy servant!' And no voice replied.
At the first I saw nought but the blackness; but soon I descried
A something more black than the blackness—the vast, the upright
Main prop which sustains the pavilion: and slow into sight   25
Grew a figure against it, gigantic and blackest of all.
Then a sunbeam, that burst thro' the tent-roof, showed Saul.

IV

He stood as erect as that tent-prop, both arms stretched out wide
On the great cross-support in the centre, that goes to each side;
He relaxed not a muscle, but hung there as, caught in his pangs   30
And waiting his change, the king-serpent all heavily hangs,
Far away from his kind, in the pine, till deliverance come
With the spring-time,—so agonized Saul, drear and stark, blind and
    dumb.

V

Then I tuned my harp,—took off the lilies we twine round its
    chords
Lest they snap 'neath the stress of the noontide—those sunbeams
    like swords!   35
And I first played the tune all our sheep know, as, one after one,
So docile they come to the pen-door till folding be done.
They are white and untorn by the bushes, for lo, they have fed
Where the long grasses stifle the water within the stream's bed;
And now one after one seeks its lodging, as star follows star   40
Into eve and the blue far above us,—so blue and so far!

VI

—Then the tune, for which quails on the cornland will each leave
    his mate
To fly after the player; then, what makes the crickets elate
Till for boldness they fight one another: and then, what has weight
To set the quick jerboa a-musing outside his sand house—   45
There are none such as he for a wonder, half bird and half mouse!

God made all the creatures and gave them our love and our fear,
To give sign, we and they are his children, one family here.

VII

Then I played the help-tune of our reapers, their wine-song, when
    hand
Grasps at hand, eye lights eye in good friendship, and great hearts
    expand   50
And grow one in the sense of this world's life.—And then, the last
    song
When the dead man is praised on his journey—'Bear, bear him
    along
'With his few faults shut up like dead flowerets! Are balm-seeds not
    here
'To console us? The land has none left such as he on the bier.
'Oh, would we might keep thee, my brother!'—And then, the glad
    chaunt   55
Of the marriage,—first go the young maidens, next, she whom we
    vaunt
As the beauty, the pride of our dwelling.—And then, the great
    march
Wherein man runs to man to assist him and buttress an arch
Nought can break; who shall harm them, our friends?—Then, the
    chorus intoned
As the Levites go up to the altar in glory enthroned.   60
But I stopped here: for here in the darkness Saul groaned.

VIII

And I paused, held my breath in such silence, and listened apart;
And the tent shook, for mighty Saul shuddered: and sparkles 'gan
    dart
From the jewels that woke in his turban, at once with a start,
All its lordly male-sapphires, and rubies courageous at heart.   65
So the head: but the body still moved not, still hung there erect.
And I bent once again to my playing, pursued it unchecked,
As I sang,—

IX

    'Oh, our manhood's prime vigour! No spirit feels waste,
'Not a muscle is stopped in its playing nor sinew unbraced.
'Oh, the wild joys of living! the leaping from rock up to rock,   70

'The strong rending of boughs from the fir-tree, the cool silver
    shock
'Of the plunge in a pool's living water, the hunt of the bear,
'And the sultriness showing the lion is couched in his lair.
'And the meal, the rich dates yellowed over with gold dust divine,
'And the locust-flesh steeped in the pitcher, the full draught of
    wine,   75
'And the sleep in the dried river-channel where bulrushes tell
'That the water was wont to go warbling so softly and well.
'How good is man's life, the mere living! how fit to employ
'All the heart and the soul and the senses for ever in joy!
'Hast thou loved the white locks of thy father, whose sword thou
    didst guard   80
'When he trusted thee forth with the armies, for glorious reward?
'Didst thou see the thin hands of thy mother, held up as men sung
'The low song of the nearly-departed, and hear her faint tongue
'Joining in while it could to the witness, "Let one more attest,
' "I have lived, seen God's hand thro' a lifetime, and all was for
    best"?   85
'Then they sung thro' their tears in strong triumph, not much, but
    the rest.
'And thy brothers, the help and the contest, the working whence
    grew
'Such result as, from seething grape-bundles, the spirit strained
    true:
'And the friends of thy boyhood—that boyhood of wonder and hope,
'Present promise and wealth of the future beyond the eye's
    scope,—   90
'Till lo, thou art grown to a monarch; a people is thine;
'And all gifts, which the world offers singly, on one head combine!
'On one head, all the beauty and strength, love and rage (like the
    throe
'That, a-work in the rock, helps its labour and lets the gold go)
'High ambition and deeds which surpass it, fame crowning them,—
    all   95
'Brought to blaze on the head of one creature—King Saul!'

X

And lo, with that leap of my spirit,—heart, hand, harp and voice,
Each lifting Saul's name out of sorrow, each bidding rejoice

Saul's fame in the light it was made for—as when, dare I say,
The Lord's army, in rapture of service, strains through its
    array,   100
And upsoareth the cherubim-chariot—'Saul!' cried I, and stopped,
And waited the thing that should follow. Then Saul, who hung
    propped
By the tent's cross-support in the centre, was struck by his name.
Have ye seen when Spring's arrowy summons goes right to the
    aim,
And some mountain, the last to withstand her, that held (he
    alone,   105
While the vale laughed in freedom and flowers) on a broad bust of
    stone
A year's snow bound about for a breastplate,—leaves grasp of the
    sheet?
Fold on fold all at once it crowds thunderously down to his feet,
And there fronts you, stark, black, but alive yet, your mountain of
    old,
With his rents, the successive bequeathings of ages untold—   110
Yea, each harm got in fighting your battles, each furrow and scar
Of his head thrust 'twixt you and the tempest—all hail, there they
    are!
—Now again to be softened with verdure, again hold the nest
Of the dove, tempt the goat and its young to the green on his crest
For their food in the ardours of summer. One long shudder
    thrilled   115
All the tent till the very air tingled, then sank and was stilled
At the King's self left standing before me, released and aware.
What was gone, what remained? All to traverse, 'twixt hope and
    despair;
Death was past, life not come: so he waited. Awhile his right hand
Held the brow, helped the eyes left too vacant forthwith to
    remand   120
To their place what new objects should enter: 't was Saul as before.
I looked up and dared gaze at those eyes, nor was hurt any more
Than by slow pallid sunsets in autumn, ye watch from the shore,
At their sad level gaze o'er the ocean—a sun's slow decline
Over hills which, resolved in stern silence, o'erlap and entwine   125
Base with base to knit strength more intensely: so, arm folded arm
O'er the chest whose slow heavings subsided.

XI

What spell or what charm,
(For, awhile there was trouble within me) what next should I urge
To sustain him where song had restored him?—Song filled to the
    verge
His cup with the wine of this life, pressing all that it yields   130
Of mere fruitage, the strength and the beauty: beyond, on what
    fields,
Glean a vintage more potent and perfect to brighten the eye
And bring blood to the lip, and commend them the cup they put by?
He saith, 'It is good;' still he drinks not: he lets me praise life,
Gives assent, yet would die for his own part.

XII

Then fancies grew rife   135
Which had come long ago on the pasture, when round me the sheep
Fed in silence—above, the one eagle wheeled slow as in sleep;
And I lay in my hollow and mused on the world that might lie
'Neath his ken, though I saw but the strip 'twixt the hill and the sky:
And I laughed—'Since my days are ordained to be passed with my
    flocks,   140
'Let me people at least, with my fancies, the plains and the rocks,
'Dream the life I am never to mix with, and image the show
'Of mankind as they live in those fashions I hardly shall know!
'Schemes of life, its best rules and right uses, the courage that gains,
'And the prudence that keeps what men strive for.' And now these
    old trains   145
Of vague thought came again; I grew surer; so, once more the string
Of my harp made response to my spirit, as thus—

XIII

'Yea, my King,'
I began—'thou dost well in rejecting mere comforts that spring
'From the mere mortal life held in common by man and by brute:
'In our flesh grows the branch of this life, in our soul it bears
    fruit.   150
'Thou hast marked the slow rise of the tree,—how its stem trembled
    first
'Till it passed the kid's lip, the stag's antler; then safely outburst
'The fan-branches all round; and thou mindest when these too, in
    turn

'Broke a-bloom and the palm-tree seemed perfect: yet more was to
    learn,
'E'en the good that comes in with the palm-fruit. Our dates shall we
    slight,   155
'When their juice brings a cure for all sorrow? or care for the plight
'Of the palm's self whose slow growth produced them? Not so!
    stem and branch
'Shall decay, nor be known in their place, while the palm-wine shall
    staunch
'Every wound of man's spirit in winter. I pour thee such wine.
'Leave the flesh to the fate it was fit for! the spirit be thine!   160
'By the spirit, when age shall o'ercome thee, thou still shalt enjoy
'More indeed, than at first when inconscious, the life of a boy.
'Crush that life, and behold its wine running! Each deed thou hast
    done
'Dies, revives, goes to work in the world; until e'en as the sun
'Looking down on the earth, though clouds spoil him, though
    tempests efface,   165
'Can find nothing his own deed produced not, must everywhere
    trace
'The results of his past summer-prime,—so, each ray of thy will,
'Every flash of thy passion and prowess, long over, shall thrill
'Thy whole people, the countless, with ardour, till they too give
    forth
'A like cheer to their sons, who in turn, fill the South and the
    North   170
'With the radiance thy deed was the germ of. Carouse in the past!
'But the license of age has its limit; thou diest at last:
'As the lion when age dims his eyeball, the rose at her height,
'So with man—so his power and his beauty for ever take flight.
'No! Again a long draught of my soul-wine! Look forth o'er the
    years!   175
'Thou hast done now with eyes for the actual; begin with the seer's!
'Is Saul dead? In the depth of the vale make his tomb—bid arise
'A grey mountain of marble heaped four-square, till, built to the
    skies,
'Let it mark where the great First King slumbers: whose fame
    would ye know?
'Up above see the rock's naked face, where the record shall go   180
'In great characters cut by the scribe,—Such was Saul, so he did;

'With the sages directing the work, by the populace chid,—
'For not half, they'll affirm, is comprised there! Which fault to
    amend,
'In the grove with his kind grows the cedar, whereon they shall
    spend
'(See, in tablets 't is level before them) their praise, and record 185
'With the gold of the graver, Saul's story,—the statesman's great
    word
'Side by side with the poet's sweet comment. The river's a-wave
'With smooth paper-reeds grazing each other when prophet-winds
    rave:
'So the pen gives unborn generations their due and their part
'In thy being! Then, first of the mighty, thank God that thou
    art!'   190

XIV

And behold while I sang . . . but O Thou who didst grant me that
    day,
And before it not seldom hast granted thy help to essay,
Carry on and complete an adventure,—my shield and my sword
In that act where my soul was thy servant, thy word was my word,—
Still be with me, who then at the summit of human endeavour 195
And scaling the highest, man's thought could, gazed hopeless as
    ever
On the new stretch of heaven above me—till, mighty to save,
Just one lift of thy hand cleared that distance—God's throne from
    man's grave!
Let me tell out my tale to its ending—my voice to my heart
Which can scarce dare believe in what marvels last night I took
    part,   200
As this morning I gather the fragments, alone with my sheep,
And still fear lest the terrible glory evanish like sleep!
For I wake in the grey dewy covert, while Hebron up-heaves
The dawn struggling with night on his shoulder, and Kidron
    retrieves
Slow the damage of yesterday's sunshine.

XV

                                       I say then,—my song 205
While I sang thus, assuring the monarch, and ever more strong
Made a proffer of good to console him—he slowly resumed

His old motions and habitudes kingly. The right-hand replumed
His black locks to their wonted composure, adjusted the swathes
Of his turban, and see—the huge sweat that his countenance
    bathes,   210
He wipes off with the robe; and he girds now his loins as of yore,
And feels slow for the armlets of price, with the clasp set before.
He is Saul, ye remember in glory,—ere error had bent
The broad brow from the daily communion; and still, though much
    spent
Be the life and the bearing that front you, the same, God did
    choose,   215
To receive what a man may waste, desecrate, never quite lose.
So sank he along by the tent-prop till, stayed by the pile
Of his armour and war-cloak and garments, he leaned there awhile,
And sat out my singing,—one arm round the tent-prop, to raise
His bent head, and the other hung slack—till I touched on the
    praise   220
I foresaw from all men in all time, to the man patient there;
And thus ended, the harp falling forward. Then first I was 'ware
That he sat, as I say, with my head just above his vast knees
Which were thrust out on each side around me, like oak-roots which
    please
To encircle a lamb when it slumbers. I looked up to know   225
If the best I could do had brought solace: he spoke not, but slow
Lifted up the hand slack at his side, till he laid it with care
Soft and grave, but in mild settled will, on my brow: thro' my hair
The large fingers were pushed, and he bent back my head, with
    kind power—
All my face back, intent to peruse it, as men do a flower.   230
Thus held he me there with his great eyes that scrutinized mine—
And oh, all my heart how it loved him! but where was the sign?
I yearned—'Could I help thee, my father, inventing a bliss,
'I would add, to that life of the past, both the future and this;
'I would give thee new life altogether, as good, ages hence,   235
'As this moment,—had love but the warrant, love's heart to dis-
    pense!'

XVI

Then the truth came upon me. No harp more—no song more!
    outbroke—

XVII

'I have gone the whole round of creation: I saw and I spoke:
'I, a work of God's hand for that purpose, received in my brain
'And pronounced on the rest of his handwork—returned him
     again   240
'His creation's approval or censure: I spoke as I saw:
'I report, as a man may of God's work—all's love, yet all's law.
'Now I lay down the judgeship he lent me. Each faculty tasked
'To perceive him, has gained an abyss, where a dew-drop was asked.
'Have I knowledge? confounded it shrivels at Wisdom laid bare. 245
'Have I forethought? how purblind, how blank, to the Infinite Care!
'Do I task any faculty highest, to image success?
'I but open my eyes,—and perfection, no more and no less,
'In the kind I imagined, full-fronts me, and God is seen God
'In the star, in the stone, in the flesh, in the soul and the clod. 250
'And thus looking within and around me, I ever renew
'(With that stoop of the soul which in bending upraises it too)
'The submission of man's nothing-perfect to God's all-complete,
'As by each new obeisance in spirit, I climb to his feet.
'Yet with all this abounding experience, this deity known,   255
'I shall dare to discover some province, some gift of my own.
'There's a faculty pleasant to exercise, hard to hoodwink,
'I am fain to keep still in abeyance, (I laugh as I think)
'Lest, insisting to claim and parade in it, wot ye, I worst
'E'en the Giver in one gift.—Behold, I could love if I durst!   260
'But I sink the pretension as fearing a man may o'ertake
'God's own speed in the one way of love: I abstain for love's sake.
'—What, my soul? see thus far and no farther? when doors great
     and small,
'Nine-and-ninety flew ope at our touch, should the hundredth
     appal?
'In the least things have faith, yet distrust in the greatest of all? 265
'Do I find love so full in my nature, God's ultimate gift,
'That I doubt his own love can compete with it? Here, the parts
     shift?
'Here, the creature surpass the Creator,—the end, what Began?
'Would I fain in my impotent yearning do all for this man,
'And dare doubt he alone shall not help him, who yet alone can? 270
'Would it ever have entered my mind, the bare will, much less
     power,

'To bestow on this Saul what I sang of, the marvellous dower
'Of the life he was gifted and filled with? to make such a soul,
'Such a body, and then such an earth for insphering the whole?
'And doth it not enter my mind (as my warm tears attest)   275
'These good things being given, to go on, and give one more, the
      best?
'Ay, to save and redeem and restore him, maintain at the height
'This perfection,—succeed with life's dayspring, death's minute of
      night?
'Interpose at the difficult minute, snatch Saul the mistake,
'Saul the failure, the ruin he seems now,—and bid him awake   280
'From the dream, the probation, the prelude, to find himself set
'Clear and safe in new light and new life,—a new harmony yet
'To be run, and continued, and ended—who knows?—or endure!
'The man taught enough, by life's dream, of the rest to make
      sure;
'By the pain-throb, triumphantly winning intensified bliss,   285
'And the next world's reward and repose, by the struggles in this.

XVIII

'I believe it! 'T is thou, God, that givest, 't is I who receive:
'In the first is the last, in thy will is my power to believe.
'All's one gift: thou canst grant it moreover, as prompt to my
      prayer
'As I breathe out this breath, as I open these arms to the air.   290
'From thy will, stream the worlds, life and nature, thy dread
      Sabaoth:
'*I* will?—the mere atoms despise me! Why am I not loth
'To look that, even that in the face too? Why is it I dare
'Think but lightly of such impuissance? What stops my despair?
'This;—'t is not what man Does which exalts him, but what man
      Would do!   295
'See the King—I would help him but cannot, the wishes fall
      through.
'Could I wrestle to raise him from sorrow, grow poor to enrich,
'To fill up his life, starve my own out, I would—knowing which,
'I know that my service is perfect. Oh, speak through me now!
'Would I suffer for him that I love? So wouldst thou—so wilt
      thou!   300
'So shall crown thee the topmost, ineffablest, uttermost crown—

'And thy love fill infinitude wholly, nor leave up nor down
'One spot for the creature to stand in! It is by no breath,
'Turn of eye, wave of hand, that salvation joins issue with death!
'As thy Love is discovered almighty, almighty be proved   305
'Thy power, that exists with and for it, of being Beloved!
'He who did most, shall bear most; the strongest shall stand the
          most weak.
' 'T is the weakness in strength, that I cry for! my flesh, that I seek
'In the Godhead! I seek and I find it. O Saul, it shall be
'A Face like my face that receives thee; a Man like to me,   310
'Thou shalt love and be loved by, for ever: a Hand like this hand
'Shall throw open the gates of new life to thee! See the Christ stand!'

XIX

I know not too well how I found my way home in the night.
There were witnesses, cohorts about me, to left and to right,
Angels, powers, the unuttered, unseen, the alive, the aware: 315
I repressed, I got through them as hardly, as strugglingly there,
As a runner beset by the populace famished for news—
Life or death. The whole earth was awakened, hell loosed with her
          crews;
And the stars of night beat with emotion, and tingled and shot
Out in fire the strong pain of pent knowledge: but I fainted not, 320
For the Hand still impelled me at once and supported, suppressed
All the tumult, and quenched it with quiet, and holy behest,
Till the rapture was shut in itself, and the earth sank to rest.
Anon at the dawn, all that trouble had withered from earth—
Not so much, but I saw it die out in the day's tender birth;   325
In the gathered intensity brought to the grey of the hills;
In the shuddering forests' held breath; in the sudden wind-thrills;
In the startled wild beasts that bore off, each with eye sidling still
Though averted with wonder and dread; in the birds stiff and
          chill
That rose heavily, as I approached them, made stupid with awe: 330
E'en the serpent that slid away silent,—he felt the new law.
The same stared in the white humid faces upturned by the flowers;
The same worked in the heart of the cedar and moved the vine-
          bowers:
And the little brooks witnessing murmured, persistent and low,
With their obstinate, all but hushed voices—'E'en so, it is so!' 335

'DE GUSTIBUS—'

I

YOUR ghost will walk, you lover of trees,
    (If our loves remain)
    In an English lane,
By a cornfield-side a-flutter with poppies.
Hark, those two in the hazel coppice—   5
A boy and a girl, if the good fates please,
    Making love, say,—
    The happier they!
Draw yourself up from the light of the moon,
And let them pass, as they will too soon,   10
    With the beanflowers' boon,
    And the blackbird's tune,
    And May, and June!

II

What I love best in all the world
Is a castle, precipice-encurled,   15
In a gash of the wind-grieved Apennine.
Or look for me, old fellow of mine,
(If I get my head from out the mouth
O' the grave, and loose my spirit's bands,
And come again to the land of lands)—   20
In a sea-side house to the farther South,
Where the baked cicala die of drouth,
And one sharp tree—'tis a cypress—stands,
By the many hundred years red-rusted,
Rough iron-spiked, ripe fruit-o'ercrusted,   25
My sentinel to guard the sands
To the water's edge. For, what expands
Before the house, but the great opaque
Blue breadth of sea without a break?
While, in the house, for ever crumbles   30
Some fragment of the frescoed walls,
From blisters where a scorpion sprawls.
A girl bare-footed brings, and tumbles
Down on the pavement, green-flesh melons,

And says there's news to-day—the king   35
Was shot at, touched in the liver-wing,
Goes with his Bourbon arm in a sling:
—She hopes they have not caught the felons.
Italy, my Italy!
Queen Mary's saying serves for me—   40
    (When fortune's malice
    Lost her—Calais)—
Open my heart and you will see
Graved inside of it, 'Italy.'
Such lovers old are I and she: 45
So it always was, so shall ever be!

WOMEN AND ROSES

I

I DREAM of a red-rose tree.
And which of its roses three
Is the dearest rose to me?

II

Round and round, like a dance of snow
In a dazzling drift, as its guardians, go   5
Floating the women faded for ages,
Sculptured in stone, on the poet's pages.
Then follow women fresh and gay,
Living and loving and loved to-day.
Last, in the rear, flee the multitude of maidens,   10
Beauties yet unborn. And all, to one cadence,
They circle their rose on my rose tree.

III

Dear rose, thy term is reached,
Thy leaf hangs loose and bleached:
Bees pass it unimpeached.   15

IV

Stay then, stoop, since I cannot climb,
You, great shapes of the antique time!
How shall I fix you, fire you, freeze you,
Break my heart at your feet to please you?

Oh, to possess and be possessed!   20
Hearts that beat 'neath each pallid breast!
Once but of love, the poesy, the passion,
Drink but once and die!—In vain, the same fashion,
They circle their rose on my rose tree.

V

Dear rose, thy joy's undimmed,   25
Thy cup is ruby-rimmed,
Thy cup's heart nectar-brimmed.

VI

Deep, as drops from a statue's plinth
The bee sucked in by the hyacinth,
So will I bury me while burning,   30
Quench like him at a plunge my yearning,
Eyes in your eyes, lips on your lips!
Fold me fast where the cincture slips,
Prison all my soul in eternities of pleasure,
Girdle me for once! But no—the old measure,   35
They circle their rose on my rose tree.

VII

Dear rose without a thorn,
Thy bud's the babe unborn:
First streak of a new morn.

VIII

Wings, lend wings for the cold, the clear!   40
What is far conquers what is near.
Roses will bloom nor want beholders,
Sprung from the dust where our flesh moulders.
What shall arrive with the cycle's change?
A novel grace and a beauty strange.   45
I will make an Eve, be the artist that began her,
Shaped her to his mind!—Alas! in like manner
They circle their rose on my rose tree.

PROTUS

AMONG these latter busts we count by scores,
Half-emperors and quarter-emperors,

Each with his bay-leaf fillet, loose-thonged vest,
Loric and low-browed Gorgon on the breast,—
One loves a baby face, with violets there,　　　　5
Violets instead of laurel in the hair,
As those were all the little locks could bear.

Now read here. 'Protus ends a period
'Of empery beginning with a god;
'Born in the porphyry chamber at Byzant,　　　10
'Queens by his cradle, proud and ministrant:
'And if he quickened breath there, 't would like fire
'Pantingly through the dim vast realm transpire.
'A fame that he was missing spread afar:
'The world from its four corners, rose in war,　　　15
'Till he was borne out on a balcony
'To pacify the world when it should see.
'The captains ranged before him, one, his hand
'Made baby points at, gained the chief command.
'And day by day more beautiful he grew　　　20
'In shape, all said, in feature and in hue,
'While young Greek sculptors, gazing on the child,
'Became with old Greek sculpture reconciled.
'Already sages laboured to condense
'In easy tomes a life's experience:　　　25
'And artists took grave counsel to impart
'In one breath and one hand-sweep, all their art—
'To make his graces prompt as blossoming
'Of plentifully-watered palms in spring:
'Since well beseems it, whoso mounts the throne,　　　30
'For beauty, knowledge, strength, should stand alone,
'And mortals love the letters of his name.'

—Stop! Have you turned two pages? Still the same.
New reign, same date. The scribe goes on to say
How that same year, on such a month and day,　　　35
'John the Pannonian, groundedly believed
'A blacksmith's bastard, whose hard hand reprieved
'The Empire from its fate the year before,—
'Came, had a mind to take the crown, and wore
'The same for six years (during which the Huns　　　40

'Kept off their fingers from us), till his sons
'Put something in his liquor'—and so forth.
Then a new reign. Stay—'Take at its just worth'
(Subjoins an annotator) 'what I give
'As hearsay. Some think, John let Protus live   45
'And slip away. 'T is said, he reached man's age
'At some blind northern court; made, first a page,
'Then tutor to the children; last, of use
'About the hunting-stables. I deduce
'He wrote the little tract "On worming dogs,"   50
'Whereof the name in sundry catalogues
'Is extant yet. A Protus of the race
'Is rumoured to have died a monk in Thrace,—
'And if the same, he reached senility.'

Here's John the Smith's rough-hammered head. Great
    eye,   55
Gross jaw and griped lips do what granite can
To give you the crown-grasper. What a man!

HOLY-CROSS DAY

ON WHICH THE JEWS WERE FORCED TO ATTEND AN ANNUAL
CHRISTIAN SERMON IN ROME

['Now was come about Holy-Cross Day, and now must my lord preach his first
sermon to the Jews: as it was of old cared for in the merciful bowels of the
Church, that, so to speak, a crumb at least from her conspicuous table here in
Rome should be, though but once yearly, cast to the famishing dogs, under-
trampled and bespitten-upon beneath the feet of the guests. And a moving
sight in truth, this, of so many of the besotted blind restif and ready-to-perish
Hebrews! now maternally brought—nay (for He saith, 'Compel them to come
in') haled, as it were, by the head and hair, and against their obstinate hearts,
to partake of the heavenly grace. What awakening, what striving with tears,
what working of a yeasty conscience! Nor was my lord wanting to himself on
so apt an occasion; witness the abundance of conversions which did incontinently
reward him: though not to my lord be altogether the glory.'—

                Diary by the Bishop's Secretary, 1600.]

What the Jews really said, on thus being driven to church, was rather to this
                    effect:—

I

FEE, faw, fum! bubble and squeak!
Blessedest Thursday's the fat of the week.

Rumble and tumble, sleek and rough,
Stinking and savoury, smug and gruff,
Take the church-road, for the bell's due chime   5
Gives us the summons—'t is sermon-time!

II

Boh, here's Barnabas! Job, that's you?
Up stumps Solomon—bustling too?
Shame, man! greedy beyond your years
To handsel the bishop's shaving-shears?   10
Fair play's a jewel! Leave friends in the lurch?
Stand on a line ere you start for the church!

III

Higgledy piggledy, packed we lie,
Rats in a hamper, swine in a stye,
Wasps in a bottle, frogs in a sieve,   15
Worms in a carcase, fleas in a sleeve.
Hist! square shoulders, settle your thumbs
And buzz for the bishop—here he comes.

IV

Bow, wow, wow—a bone for the dog!
I liken his Grace to an acorned hog.   20
What, a boy at his side, with the bloom of a lass,
To help and handle my lord's hour-glass!
Didst ever behold so lithe a chine?
His cheek hath laps like a fresh-singed swine.

V

Aaron's asleep—shove hip to haunch,   25
Or somebody deal him a dig in the paunch!
Look at the purse with the tassel and knob,
And the gown with the angel and thingumbob!
What's he at, quotha? reading his text!
Now you've his curtsey—and what comes next.   30

VI

See to our converts—you doomed black dozen—
No stealing away—nor cog nor cozen!
You five, that were thieves, deserve it fairly;

You seven, that were beggars, will live less sparely;
You took your turn and dipped in the hat, 35
Got fortune—and fortune gets you; mind that!

VII

Give your first groan—compunction's at work;
And soft! from a Jew you mount to a Turk.
Lo, Micah,—the selfsame beard on chin
He was four times already converted in! 40
Here's a knife, clip quick—it's a sign of grace—
Or he ruins us all with his hanging-face.

VIII

Whom now is the bishop a-leering at?
I know a point where his text falls pat.
I'll tell him to-morrow, a word just now 45
Went to my heart and made me vow
I meddle no more with the worst of trades—
Let somebody else pay his serenades.

IX

Groan all together now, whee—hee—hee!
It's a-work, it's a-work, ah, woe is me! 50
It began, when a herd of us, picked and placed,
Were spurred through the Corso, stripped to the waist;
Jew-brutes, with sweat and blood well spent
To usher in worthily Christian Lent.

X

It grew, when the hangman entered our bounds, 55
Yelled, pricked us out to this church like hounds:
It got to a pitch, when the hand indeed
Which gutted my purse would throttle my creed:
And it overflows when, to even the odd,
Men I helped to their sins help me to their God. 60

XI

But now, while the scapegoats leave our flock,
And the rest sit silent and count the clock,
Since forced to muse the appointed time
On these precious facts and truths sublime,—

Let us fitly employ it, under our breath,   65
In saying Ben Ezra's Song of Death.

XII

For Rabbi Ben Ezra, the night he died,
Called sons and sons' sons to his side,
And spoke, 'This world has been harsh and strange;
'Something is wrong: there needeth a change.   70
'But what, or where? at the last or first?
'In one point only we sinned, at worst.

XIII

'The Lord will have mercy on Jacob yet,
'And again in his border see Israel set.
'When Judah beholds Jerusalem,   75
'The stranger-seed shall be joined to them:
'To Jacob's House shall the Gentiles cleave.
'So the Prophet saith and his sons believe.

XIV

'Ay, the children of the chosen race
'Shall carry and bring them to their place: 80
'In the land of the Lord shall lead the same,
'Bondsmen and handmaids. Who shall blame,
'When the slaves enslave, the oppressed ones o'er
'The oppressor triumph for evermore?

XV

'God spoke, and gave us the word to keep,   85
'Bade never fold the hands nor sleep
' 'Mid a faithless world,—at watch and ward,
'Till Christ at the end relieve our guard.
'By His servant Moses the watch was set:
'Though near upon cock-crow, we keep it yet.   90

XVI

'Thou! if thou wast He, who at mid-watch came,
'By the starlight, naming a dubious name!
'And if, too heavy with sleep—too rash
'With fear—O Thou, if that martyr-gash
'Fell on Thee coming to take thine own,   95
'And we gave the Cross, when we owed the Throne—

XVII

'Thou art the Judge. We are bruised thus.
'But, the Judgment over, join sides with us!
'Thine too is the cause! and not more thine
'Than ours, is the work of these dogs and swine,   100
'Whose life laughs through and spits at their creed!
'Who maintain Thee in word, and defy Thee in deed!

XVIII

'We withstood Christ then? Be mindful how
'At least we withstand Barabbas now!
'Was our outrage sore? but the worst we spared,   105
'To have called these—Christians, had we dared!
'Let defiance to them pay mistrust of Thee,
'And Rome make amends for Calvary!

XIX

'By the torture, prolonged from age to age,
'By the infamy, Israel's heritage,   110
'By the Ghetto's plague, by the garb's disgrace,
'By the badge of shame, by the felon's place,
'By the branding-tool, the bloody whip,
'And the summons to Christian fellowship,—

XX

'We boast our proof that at least the Jew   115
'Would wrest Christ's name from the Devil's crew.
'Thy face took never so deep a shade
'But we fought them in it, God our aid!
'A trophy to bear, as we march, thy band,
'South, East, and on to the Pleasant Land!'   120

[*Pope Gregory XVI. abolished this bad business of the Sermon.*—R. B.]

THE GUARDIAN-ANGEL

A PICTURE AT FANO

I

DEAR and great Angel, wouldst thou only leave
    That child, when thou hast done with him, for me!

Let me sit all the day here, that when eve
  Shall find performed thy special ministry,
And time come for departure, thou, suspending   5
Thy flight, mayst see another child for tending,
  Another still, to quiet and retrieve.

II

Then I shall feel thee step one step, no more,
  From where thou standest now, to where I gaze,
—And suddenly my head is covered o'er   10
  With those wings, white above the child who prays
Now on that tomb—and I shall feel thee guarding
Me, out of all the world; for me, discarding
  Yon heaven thy home, that waits and opes its door.

III

I would not look up thither past thy head   15
  Because the door opes, like that child, I know,
For I should have thy gracious face instead,
  Thou bird of God! And wilt thou bend me low
Like him, and lay, like his, my hands together,
And lift them up to pray, and gently tether   20
  Me, as thy lamb there, with thy garment's spread?

IV

If this was ever granted, I would rest
  My head beneath thine, while thy healing hands
Close-covered both my eyes beside thy breast,
  Pressing the brain, which too much thought expands,   25
Back to its proper size again, and smoothing
Distortion down till every nerve had soothing,
  And all lay quiet, happy and suppressed.

V

How soon all worldly wrong would be repaired!
  I think how I should view the earth and skies   30
And sea, when once again my brow was bared
  After thy healing, with such different eyes.
O world, as God has made it! All is beauty:
And knowing this, is love, and love is duty.
  What further may be sought for or declared?   35

VI

Guercino drew this angel I saw teach
   (Alfred, dear friend!)—that little child to pray,
Holding the little hands up, each to each
   Pressed gently,—with his own head turned away
Over the earth where so much lay before him   40
Of work to do, though heaven was opening o'er him,
   And he was left at Fano by the beach.

VII

We were at Fano, and three times we went
   To sit and see him in his chapel there,
And drink his beauty to our soul's content
   —My angel with me too: and since I care   45
For dear Guercino's fame (to which in power
And glory comes this picture for a dower,
   Fraught with a pathos so magnificent)—

VIII

And since he did not work thus earnestly   50
   At all times, and has else endured some wrong—
I took one thought his picture struck from me,
   And spread it out, translating it to song.
My love is here. Where are you, dear old friend?
How rolls the Wairoa at your world's far end?   55
   This is Ancona, yonder is the sea.

CLEON
'As certain also of your own poets have said'—

CLEON the poet (from the sprinkled isles,
   Lily on lily, that o'erlace the sea,
   And laugh their pride when the light wave lisps
      'Greece')—
To Protus in his Tyranny: much health!

   They give thy letter to me, even now: 5
I read and seem as if I heard thee speak.
The master of thy galley still unlades
Gift after gift; they block my court at last
And pile themselves along its portico

Royal with sunset, like a thought of thee: 10
And one white she-slave from the group dispersed
Of black and white slaves (like the chequer-work
Pavement, at once my nation's work and gift,
Now covered with this settle-down of doves),
One lyric woman, in her crocus vest 15
Woven of sea-wools, with her two white hands
Commends to me the strainer and the cup
Thy lip hath bettered ere it blesses mine.

Well-counselled, king, in thy munificence!
For so shall men remark, in such an act 20
Of love for him whose song gives life its joy,
Thy recognition of the use of life;
Nor call thy spirit barely adequate
To help on life in straight ways, broad enough
For vulgar souls, by ruling and the rest. 25
Thou, in the daily building of thy tower,—
Whether in fierce and sudden spasms of toil,
Or through dim lulls of unapparent growth,
Or when the general work 'mid good acclaim
Climbed with the eye to cheer the architect,— 30
Didst ne'er engage in work for mere work's sake—
Hadst ever in thy heart the luring hope
Of some eventual rest a-top of it,
Whence, all the tumult of the building hushed,
Thou first of men mightst look out to the East: 35
The vulgar saw thy tower, thou sawest the sun.
For this, I promise on thy festival
To pour libation, looking o'er the sea,
Making this slave narrate thy fortunes, speak
Thy great words, and describe thy royal face—
Wishing thee wholly where Zeus lives the most, 40
Within the eventual element of calm.

Thy letter's first requirement meets me here.
It is as thou hast heard: in one short life
I, Cleon, have effected all those things 45
Thou wonderingly dost enumerate.
That epos on thy hundred plates of gold

Is mine,—and also mine the little chant,
So sure to rise from every fishing-bark
When, lights at prow, the seamen haul their net.   50
The image of the sun-god on the phare,
Men turn from the sun's self to see, is mine;
The Pœcile, o'er-storied its whole length,
As thou didst hear, with painting, is mine too.
I know the true proportions of a man   55
And woman also, not observed before;
And I have written three books on the soul,
Proving absurd all written hitherto,
And putting us to ignorance again.
For music,—why, I have combined the moods,   60
Inventing one. In brief, all arts are mine;
Thus much the people know and recognize,
Throughout our seventeen islands. Marvel not.
We of these latter days, with greater mind
Than our forerunners, since more composite,   65
Look not so great, beside their simple way,
To a judge who only sees one way at once,
One mind-point and no other at a time,—
Compares the small part of a man of us
With some whole man of the heroic age,   70
Great in his way—not ours, nor meant for ours.
And ours is greater, had we skill to know:
For, what we call this life of men on earth,
This sequence of the soul's achievements here
Being, as I find much reason to conceive,   75
Intended to be viewed eventually
As a great whole, not analyzed to parts,
But each part having reference to all,—
How shall a certain part, pronounced complete,
Endure effacement by another part?   80
Was the thing done?—then, what's to do again?
See, in the chequered pavement opposite,
Suppose the artist made a perfect rhomb,
And next a lozenge, then a trapezoid—
He did not overlay them, superimpose   85
The new upon the old and blot it out,
But laid them on a level in his work,

Making at last a picture; there it lies.
So, first the perfect separate forms were made,
The portions of mankind; and after, so,   90
Occurred the combination of the same.
For where had been a progress, otherwise?
Mankind, made up of all the single men,—
In such a synthesis the labour ends.
Now mark me! those divine men of old time   95
Have reached, thou sayest well, each at one point
The outside verge that rounds our faculty;
And where they reached, who can do more than reach?
It takes but little water just to touch
At some one point the inside of a sphere,   100
And, as we turn the sphere, touch all the rest
In due succession: but the finer air
Which not so palpably nor obviously,
Though no less universally, can touch
The whole circumference of that emptied sphere,   105
Fills it more fully than the water did;
Holds thrice the weight of water in itself
Resolved into a subtler element.
And yet the vulgar call the sphere first full
Up to the visible height—and after, void;   110
Not knowing air's more hidden properties.
And thus our soul, misknown, cries out to Zeus
To vindicate his purpose in our life:
Why stay we on the earth unless to grow?
Long since, I imaged, wrote the fiction out,   115
That he or other god descended here
And, once for all, showed simultaneously
What, in its nature, never can be shown,
Piecemeal or in succession;—showed, I say,
The worth both absolute and relative   120
Of all his children from the birth of time,
His instruments for all appointed work.
I now go on to image,—might we hear
The judgment which should give the due to each,
Show where the labour lay and where the ease,   125
And prove Zeus' self, the latent everywhere!
This is a dream:—but no dream, let us hope,

That years and days, the summers and the springs,
Follow each other with unwaning powers.
The grapes which dye thy wine are richer far,   130
Through culture, than the wild wealth of the rock;
The suave plum than the savage-tasted drupe;
The pastured honey-bee drops choicer sweet;
The flowers turn double, and the leaves turn flowers;
That young and tender crescent-moon, thy slave,   135
Sleeping above her robe as buoyed by clouds,
Refines upon the women of my youth.
What, and the soul alone deteriorates?
I have not chanted verse like Homer, no—
Nor swept string like Terpander, no—nor carved   140
And painted men like Phidias and his friend:
I am not great as they are, point by point.
But I have entered into sympathy
With these four, running these into one soul,
Who, separate, ignored each other's art.   145
Say, is it nothing that I know them all?
The wild flower was the larger; I have dashed
Rose-blood upon its petals, pricked its cup's
Honey with wine, and driven its seed to fruit,
And show a better flower if not so large: 150
I stand myself. Refer this to the gods
Whose gift alone it is! which, shall I dare
(All pride apart) upon the absurd pretext
That such a gift by chance lay in my hand,
Discourse of lightly or depreciate?   155
It might have fallen to another's hand: what then?
I pass too surely: let at least truth stay!

And next, of what thou followest on to ask.
This being with me as I declare, O king,
My works, in all these varicoloured kinds,   160
So done by me, accepted so by men—
Thou askest, if (my soul thus in men's hearts)
I must not be accounted to attain
The very crown and proper end of life?
Inquiring thence how, now life closeth up,   165
I face death with success in my right hand:

Whether I fear death less than dost thyself
The fortunate of men? 'For' (writest thou)
'Thou leavest much behind, while I leave nought.
'Thy life stays in the poems men shall sing,　　　　170
'The pictures men shall study; while my life,
'Complete and whole now in its power and joy,
'Dies altogether with my brain and arm,
'Is lost indeed; since, what survives myself?
'The brazen statue to o'erlook my grave,　　　　175
'Set on the promontory which I named.
'And that—some supple courtier of my heir
'Shall use its robed and sceptred arm, perhaps,
'To fix the rope to, which best drags it down.
'I go then: triumph thou, who dost not go!'　　　　180

　　Nay, thou art worthy of hearing my whole mind.
Is this apparent, when thou turn'st to muse
Upon the scheme of earth and man in chief,
That admiration grows as knowledge grows?
That imperfection means perfection hid,　　　　185
Reserved in part, to grace the after-time?
If, in the morning of philosophy,
Ere aught had been recorded, nay perceived,
Thou, with the light now in thee, couldst have looked
On all earth's tenantry, from worm to bird,　　　　190
Ere man, her last, appeared upon the stage—
Thou wouldst have seen them perfect, and deduced
The perfectness of others yet unseen.
Conceding which,—had Zeus then questioned thee
'Shall I go on a step, improve on this,　　　　195
'Do more for visible creatures than is done?'
Thou wouldst have answered, 'Ay, by making each
'Grow conscious in himself—by that alone.
'All's perfect else: the shell sucks fast the rock,
'The fish strikes through the sea, the snake both swims　200
'And slides, forth range the beasts, the birds take flight,
'Till life's mechanics can no further go—
'And all this joy in natural life is put
'Like fire from off thy finger into each,
'So exquisitely perfect is the same.　　　　205

'But 't is pure fire, and they mere matter are;
'It has them, not they it: and so I choose
'For man, thy last premeditated work
'(If I might add a glory to the scheme)
'That a third thing should stand apart from both,   210
'A quality arise within his soul,
'Which, intro-active, made to supervise
'And feel the force it has, may view itself,
'And so be happy.' Man might live at first
The animal life: but is there nothing more?   215
In due time, let him critically learn
How he lives; and, the more he gets to know
Of his own life's adaptabilities,
The more joy-giving will his life become.
Thus man, who hath this quality, is best.   220

But thou, king, hadst more reasonably said:
'Let progress end at once,—man make no step
'Beyond the natural man, the better beast,
'Using his senses, not the sense of sense.'
In man there's failure, only since he left   225
The lower and inconscious forms of life.
We called it an advance, the rendering plain
Man's spirit might grow conscious of man's life,
And, by new lore so added to the old,
Take each step higher over the brute's head.   230
This grew the only life, the pleasure-house,
Watch-tower and treasure-fortress of the soul,
Which whole surrounding flats of natural life
Seemed only fit to yield subsistence to;
A tower that crowns a country. But alas,   235
The soul now climbs it just to perish there!
For thence we have discovered ('t is no dream—
We know this, which we had not else perceived)
That there's a world of capability
For joy, spread round about us, meant for us,   240
Inviting us; and still the soul craves all,
And still the flesh replies, 'Take no jot more
'Than ere thou clombst the tower to look abroad!
'Nay, so much less as that fatigue has brought

'Deduction to it.' We struggle, fain to enlarge   245
Our bounded physical recipiency,
Increase our power, supply fresh oil to life,
Repair the waste of age and sickness: no,
It skills not! life's inadequate to joy,
As the soul sees joy, tempting life to take.   250
They praise a fountain in my garden here
Wherein a Naiad sends the water-bow
Thin from her tube; she smiles to see it rise.
What if I told her, it is just a thread
From that great river which the hills shut up,   255
And mock her with my leave to take the same?
The artificer has given her one small tube
Past power to widen or exchange—what boots
To know she might spout oceans if she could?
She cannot lift beyond her first thin thread: 260
And so a man can use but a man's joy
While he sees God's. Is it for Zeus to boast,
'See, man, how happy I live, and despair—
'That I may be still happier—for thy use!'
If this were so, we could not thank our lord,   265
As hearts beat on to doing: 't is not so—
Malice it is not. Is it carelessness?
Still, no. If care—where is the sign? I ask,
And get no answer, and agree in sum,
O king, with thy profound discouragement,   270
Who seest the wider but to sigh the more.
Most progress is most failure: thou sayest well.

    The last point now:—thou dost except a case—
Holding joy not impossible to one
With artist-gifts—to such a man as I   275
Who leave behind me living works indeed;
For, such a poem, such a painting lives.
What? dost thou verily trip upon a word,
Confound the accurate view of what joy is
(Caught somewhat clearer by my eyes than thine)   280
With feeling joy? confound the knowing how
And showing how to live (my faculty)
With actually living?—Otherwise

Where is the artist's vantage o'er the king?
Because in my great epos I display   285
How divers men young, strong, fair, wise, can act—
Is this as though I acted? if I paint,
Carve the young Phœbus, am I therefore young?
Methinks I'm older that I bowed myself
The many years of pain that taught me art!   290
Indeed, to know is something, and to prove
How all this beauty might be enjoyed, is more:
But, knowing nought, to enjoy is something too.
Yon rower, with the moulded muscles there,
Lowering the sail, is nearer it than I.   295
I can write love-odes: thy fair slave's an ode.
I get to sing of love, when grown too grey
For being beloved: she turns to that young man
The muscles all a-ripple on his back.
I know the joy of kingship: well, thou art king!   300

    'But,' sayest thou—(and I marvel, I repeat,
To find thee trip on such a mere word) 'what
'Thou writest, paintest, stays; that does not die:
'Sappho survives, because we sing her songs,
'And Æschylus, because we read his plays!'   305
Why, if they live still, let them come and take
Thy slave in my despite, drink from thy cup,
Speak in my place. Thou diest while I survive?
Say rather that my fate is deadlier still,
In this, that every day my sense of joy   310
Grows more acute, my soul (intensified
In power and insight) more enlarged, more keen;
While every day my hairs fall more and more,
My hand shakes, and the heavy years increase—
The horror quickening still from year to year,   315
The consummation coming past escape
When I shall know most, and yet least enjoy—
When all my works wherein I prove my worth,
Being present still to mock me in men's mouths,
Alive still, in the praise of such as thou,   320
I, I the feeling, thinking, acting man,
The man who loved his life so over-much,

Sleep in my urn. It is so horrible,
I dare at times imagine to my need
Some future state revealed to us by Zeus, 325
Unlimited in capability
For joy, as this is in desire for joy,
—To seek which, the joy-hunger forces us:
That, stung by straitness of our life, made strait
On purpose to make prized the life at large— 330
Freed by the throbbing impulse we call death,
We burst there as the worm into the fly,
Who, while a worm still, wants his wings. But no!
Zeus has not yet revealed it; and alas,
He must have done so, were it possible! 335

Live long and happy, and in that thought die:
Glad for what was! Farewell. And for the rest,
I cannot tell thy messenger aright
Where to deliver what he bears of thine
To one called Paulus; we have heard his fame 340
Indeed, if Christus be not one with him—
I know not, nor am troubled much to know.
Thou canst not think a mere barbarian Jew
As Paulus proves to be, one circumcized,
Hath access to a secret shut from us? 345
Thou wrongest our philosophy, O king,
In stooping to inquire of such an one,
As if his answer could impose at all!
He writeth, doth he? well, and he may write.
Oh, the Jew findeth scholars! certain slaves 350
Who touched on this same isle, preached him and Christ;
And (as I gathered from a bystander)
Their doctrine could be held by no sane man.

THE TWINS[1]
'Give' and 'It-shall-be-given-unto-you'.

I

GRAND rough old Martin Luther
Bloomed fables—flowers on furze,

[1] First published in a pamphlet entitled *Two Poems, by Elizabeth Barrett and Robert Browning*, and sold at a bazaar in aid of a 'Refuge for young destitute girls' (1854).

The better the uncouther:
  Do roses stick like burrs?

II

A beggar asked an alms   5
  One day at an abbey-door,
Said Luther; but, seized with qualms,
  The Abbot replied, 'We're poor!

III

'Poor, who had plenty once,
  'When gifts fell thick as rain: 10
'But they give us nought, for the nonce,
  'And how should we give again?'

IV

Then the beggar, 'See your sins!
  'Of old, unless I err,
'Ye had brothers for inmates, twins,   15
  'Date and Dabitur.

V

'While Date was in good case
  'Dabitur flourished too:
'For Dabitur's lenten face
  'No wonder if Date rue.   20

VI

'Would ye retrieve the one?
  'Try and make plump the other!
'When Date's penance is done,
  'Dabitur helps his brother.

VII

'Only, beware relapse!'   25
  The Abbot hung his head.
This beggar might be perhaps
  An angel, Luther said.

POPULARITY

I

STAND still, true poet that you are!
 I know you; let me try and draw you.
Some night you'll fail us: when afar
 You rise, remember one man saw you,
Knew you, and named a star!   5

II

My star, God's glow-worm! Why extend
 That loving hand of his which leads you,
Yet locks you safe from end to end
 Of this dark world, unless he needs you,
Just saves your light to spend?   10

III

His clenched hand shall unclose at last,
 I know, and let out all the beauty:
My poet holds the future fast,
 Accepts the coming ages' duty,
Their present for this past.   15

IV

That day, the earth's feast-master's brow
 Shall clear, to God the chalice raising;
'Others give best at first, but thou
 'Forever set'st our table praising,
'Keep'st the good wine till now!'   20

V

Meantime, I'll draw you as you stand,
 With few or none to watch and wonder:
I'll say—a fisher, on the sand
 By Tyre the old, his ocean-plunder,
A netful, brought to land.   25

VI

Who has not heard how Tyrian shells
 Enclosed the blue, that dye of dyes

Whereof one drop worked miracles,
  And coloured like Astarte's eyes
Raw silk the merchant sells?   30

VII

And each bystander of them all
  Could criticize, and quote tradition
How depths of blue sublimed some pall
  —To get which, pricked a king's ambition;
Worth sceptre, crown and ball.   35

VIII

Yet there's the dye, in that rough mesh,
  The sea has only just o'erwhispered!
Live whelks, each lip's beard dripping fresh,
  As if they still the water's lisp heard
Through foam the rock-weeds thresh.   40

IX

Enough to furnish Solomon
  Such hangings for his cedar-house,
That, when gold-robed he took the throne
  In that abyss of blue, the Spouse
Might swear his presence shone   45

X

Most like the centre-spike of gold
  Which burns deep in the blue-bell's womb,
What time, with ardours manifold,
  The bee goes singing to her groom,
Drunken and overbold.   50

XI

Mere conchs! not fit for warp or woof!
  Till cunning come to pound and squeeze
And clarify,—refine to proof
  The liquor filtered by degrees,
While the world stands aloof.   55

XII

And there's the extract, flasked and fine,
  And priced and saleable at last!

And Hobbs, Nobbs, Stokes and Nokes combine
  To paint the future from the past,
Put blue into their line.   60

XIII

Hobbs hints blue,—straight he turtle eats:
  Nobbs prints blue,—claret crowns his cup:
Nokes outdares Stokes in azure feats,—
  Both gorge. Who fished the murex up?
What porridge had John Keats?   65

THE HERETIC'S TRAGEDY

A MIDDLE-AGE INTERLUDE

ROSA MUNDI; SEU, FULCITE ME FLORIBUS. A CONCEIT OF MASTER GYS-
BRECHT, CANON-REGULAR OF SAINT JODOCUS-BY-THE-BAR, YPRES CITY.
CANTUQUE, *Virgilius*. AND HATH OFTEN BEEN SUNG AT HOCK-TIDE AND
FESTIVALS. GAVISUS ERAM, *Jessides*.

(It would seem to be a glimpse from the burning of Jacques du Bourg-Molay, at
Paris, A.D. 1314; as distorted by the refraction from Flemish brain to brain,
during the course of a couple of centuries.)

I

PREADMONISHETH THE ABBOT DEODAET.

THE Lord, we look to once for all,
  Is the Lord we should look at, all at once:
He knows not to vary, saith Saint Paul,
  Nor the shadow of turning, for the nonce.
See him no other than as he is!   5
  Give both the infinitudes their due—
Infinite mercy, but, I wis,
  As infinite a justice too.

                               [Organ: plagal-cadence.

  As infinite a justice too.

II

ONE SINGETH.

John, Master of the Temple of God,   10
  Falling to sin the Unknown Sin,
What he bought of Emperor Aldabrod,
  He sold it to Sultan Saladin:

Till, caught by Pope Clement, a-buzzing there,
 Hornet-prince of the mad wasps' hive,   15
And clipt of his wings in Paris square,
 They bring him now to be burned alive.

 [*And wanteth there grace of lute or clavicithern,*
  ye shall say to confirm him who singeth—

We bring John now to be burned alive.

III

In the midst is a goodly gallows built;
 'Twixt fork and fork, a stake is stuck;   20
But first they set divers tumbrils a-tilt,
 Make a trench all round with the city muck;
Inside they pile log upon log, good store;
 Faggots no few, blocks great and small,
Reach a man's mid-thigh, no less, no more,—   25
 For they mean he should roast in the sight of all.

CHORUS.
We mean he should roast in the sight of all.

IV

Good sappy bavins that kindle forthwith;
 Billets that blaze substantial and slow;
Pine-stump split deftly, dry as pith;   30
 Larch-heart that chars to a chalk-white glow:
Then up they hoist me John in a chafe,
 Sling him fast like a hog to scorch,
Spit in his face, then leap back safe,
 Sing 'Laudes' and bid clap-to the torch.   35

CHORUS.
Laus Deo—who bids clap-to the torch.

V

John of the Temple, whose fame so bragged,
 Is burning alive in Paris square!
How can he curse, if his mouth is gagged?
 Or wriggle his neck, with a collar there?   40
Or heave his chest, which a band goes round?
 Or threat with his fist, since his arms are spliced?

Or kick with his feet, now his legs are bound?
　—Thinks John, I will call upon Jesus Christ.

[Here one crosseth himself.

VI

Jesus Christ—John had bought and sold,　　　　　45
　Jesus Christ—John had eaten and drunk;
To him, the Flesh meant silver and gold.
　(*Salvâ reverentiâ.*)
Now it was, 'Saviour, bountiful lamb,
　'I have roasted thee Turks, though men roast me!　50
'See thy servant, the plight wherein I am!
　'Art thou a saviour? Save thou me!'

CHORUS.

'T is John the mocker cries, 'Save thou me!'

VII

Who maketh God's menace an idle word?
　—Saith, it no more means what it proclaims,　　55
Than a damsel's threat to her wanton bird?—
　For she too prattles of ugly names.
—Saith, he knoweth but one thing,—what he knows?
　That God is good and the rest is breath;
Why else is the same styled Sharon's rose?　　　60
　Once a rose, ever a rose, he saith.

CHORUS.

O, John shall yet find a rose, he saith!

VIII

Alack, there be roses and roses, John!
　Some, honied of taste like your leman's tongue:
Some, bitter; for why? (roast gaily on!)　　　　65
　Their tree struck root in devil's dung.
When Paul once reasoned of righteousness
　And of temperance and of judgment to come,
Good Felix trembled, he could no less:
　John, snickering, crook'd his wicked thumb.　　70

CHORUS.

What cometh to John of the wicked thumb?

IX

Ha ha, John pluckem now at his rose
  To rid himself of a sorrow at heart!
Lo,—petal on petal, fierce rays unclose;
  Anther on anther, sharp spikes outstart;   75
And with blood for dew, the bosom boils;
  And a gust of sulphur is all its smell;
And lo, he is horribly in the toils
  Of a coal-black giant flower of hell!

CHORUS.

What maketh heaven, That maketh hell.   80

X

So, as John called now, through the fire amain,
  On the Name, he had cursed with, all his life—
To the Person, he bought and sold again—
  For the Face, with his daily buffets rife—
Feature by feature It took its place: 85
  And his voice, like a mad dog's choking bark,
At the steady whole of the Judge's face—
  Died. Forth John's soul flared into the dark.

SUBJOINETH THE ABBOT DEODAET.

God help all poor souls lost in the dark!

TWO IN THE CAMPAGNA

I

I WONDER do you feel to-day
  As I have felt since, hand in hand,
We sat down on the grass, to stray
  In spirit better through the land,
This morn of Rome and May?   5

II

For me, I touched a thought, I know,
  Has tantalized me many times,
(Like turns of thread the spiders throw
  Mocking across our path) for rhymes
To catch at and let go.   10

III

Help me to hold it! First it left
   The yellowing fennel, run to seed
There, branching from the brickwork's cleft,
   Some old tomb's ruin: yonder weed
Took up the floating weft,   15

IV

Where one small orange cup amassed
   Five beetles,—blind and green they grope
Among the honey-meal: and last,
   Everywhere on the grassy slope
I traced it. Hold it fast!   20

V

The champaign with its endless fleece
   Of feathery grasses everywhere!
Silence and passion, joy and peace,
   An everlasting wash of air—
Rome's ghost since her decease.   25

VI

Such life here, through such lengths of hours,
   Such miracles performed in play,
Such primal naked forms of flowers,
   Such letting nature have her way
While heaven looks from its towers!   30

VII

How say you? Let us, O my dove,
   Let us be unashamed of soul,
As earth lies bare to heaven above!
   How is it under our control
To love or not to love?   35

VIII

I would that you were all to me,
   You that are just so much, no more.
Nor yours nor mine, nor slave nor free!
   Where does the fault lie? What the core
O' the wound, since wound must be?   40

IX

I would I could adopt your will,
  See with your eyes, and set my heart
Beating by yours, and drink my fill
  At your soul's springs,—your part my part
In life, for good and ill.　　　　　　　　　45

X

No. I yearn upward, touch you close,
  Then stand away. I kiss your cheek,
Catch your soul's warmth,—I pluck the rose
  And love it more than tongue can speak—
Then the good minute goes.　　　　　　　50

XI

Already how am I so far
  Out of that minute? Must I go
Still like the thistle-ball, no bar,
  Onward, whenever light winds blow, ·
Fixed by no friendly star?　　　　　　　55

XII

Just when I seemed about to learn!
  Where is the thread now? Off again!
The old trick! Only I discern—
  Infinite passion, and the pain
Of finite hearts that yearn.　　　　　　　60

A GRAMMARIAN'S FUNERAL,

SHORTLY AFTER THE REVIVAL OF LEARNING IN EUROPE

Let us begin and carry up this corpse,
    Singing together.
Leave we the common crofts, the vulgar thorpes
    Each in its tether
Sleeping safe on the bosom of the plain,　　5
    Cared-for till cock-crow:
Look out if yonder be not day again
    Rimming the rock-row!

That's the appropriate country; there, man's thought,
    Rarer, intenser,   10
Self-gathered for an outbreak, as it ought,
    Chafes in the censer.
Leave we the unlettered plain its herd and crop;
    Seek we sepulture
On a tall mountain, citied to the top,   15
    Crowded with culture!
All the peaks soar, but one the rest excels;
    Clouds overcome it;
No! yonder sparkle is the citadel's
    Circling its summit.   20
Thither our path lies; wind we up the heights:
    Wait ye the warning?
Our low life was the level's and the night's;
    He's for the morning.
Step to a tune, square chests, erect the head,   25
    'Ware the beholders!
This is our master, famous calm and dead,
    Borne on our shoulders.

Sleep, crop and herd! sleep, darkling thorpe and croft,
    Safe from the weather!   30
He, whom we convoy to his grave aloft,
    Singing together,
He was a man born with thy face and throat,
    Lyric Apollo!
Long he lived nameless: how should spring take note   35
    Winter would follow?
Till lo, the little touch, and youth was gone!
    Cramped and diminished,
Moaned he, 'New measures, other feet anon!
    My dance is finished?'   40
No, that's the world's way: (keep the mountain-side,
    Make for the city!)
He knew the signal, and stepped on with pride
    Over men's pity;
Left play for work, and grappled with the world   45
    Bent on escaping:

'What's in the scroll,' quoth he, 'thou keepest furled?
　　'Show me their shaping,
'Theirs who most studied man, the bard and sage,—
　　'Give!'—So, he gowned him,　　　　　　　　50
Straight got by heart that book to its last page:
　　Learned, we found him.
Yea, but we found him bald too, eyes like lead,
　　Accents uncertain:
'Time to taste life,' another would have said,　　55
　　'Up with the curtain!'
This man said rather, 'Actual life comes next?
　　'Patience a moment!
'Grant I have mastered learning's crabbed text,
　　'Still there's the comment.　　　　　　　　60
'Let me know all! Prate not of most or least,
　　'Painful or easy!
'Even to the crumbs I'd fain eat up the feast,
　　Ay, nor feel queasy.'
Oh, such a life as he resolved to live,　　　　65
　　When he had learned it,
When he had gathered all books had to give!
　　Sooner, he spurned it.
Image the whole, then execute the parts—
　　Fancy the fabric　　　　　　　　　　　70
Quite, ere you build, ere steel strike fire from quartz,
　　Ere mortar dab brick!

(Here's the town-gate reached: there's the market-place
　　Gaping before us.)
Yea, this in him was the peculiar grace　　　75
　　(Hearten our chorus!)
Still before living he'd learn how to live—
　　No end to learning:
Earn the means first—God surely will contrive
　　Use for our earning.　　　　　　　　　80
Others mistrust and say, 'But time escapes:
　　'Live now or never!'
He said, 'What's time? Leave Now for dogs and apes!
　　'Man has Forever.'

Back to his book then: deeper drooped his head: 85
    Calculus racked him:
Leaden before, his eyes grew dross of lead:
    Tussis attacked him.
'Now, master, take a little rest!'—not he!
    (Caution redoubled,   90
Step two abreast, the way winds narrowly!)
    Not a whit troubled
Back to his studies, fresher than at first,
    Fierce as a dragon
He (soul-hydroptic with a sacred thirst)   95
    Sucked at the flagon.
Oh, if we draw a circle premature,
    Heedless of far gain,
Greedy for quick returns of profit, sure
    Bad is our bargain!   100
Was it not great? did not he throw on God,
    (He loves the burthen)—
God's task to make the heavenly period
    Perfect the earthen?
Did not he magnify the mind, show clear   105
    Just what it all meant?
He would not discount life, as fools do here,
    Paid by instalment.
He ventured neck or nothing—heaven's success
    Found, or earth's failure: 110
'Wilt thou trust death or not?' He answered 'Yes:
    'Hence with life's pale lure!'
That low man seeks a little thing to do,
    Sees it and does it:
This high man, with a great thing to pursue,   115
    Dies ere he knows it.
That low man goes on adding one to one,
    His hundred's soon hit:
This high man, aiming at a million,
    Misses an unit.   120
That, has the world here—should he need the next,
    Let the world mind him!
This, throws himself on God, and unperplexed
    Seeking shall find him.

So, with the throttling hands of death at strife,   125
  Ground he at grammar;
Still, thro' the rattle, parts of speech were rife:
  While he could stammer
He settled *Hoti's* business—let it be!—
  Properly based *Oun*—   130
Gave us the doctrine of the enclitic *De*,
  Dead from the waist down.
Well, here's the platform, here's the proper place:
  Hail to your purlieus,
All ye highfliers of the feathered race,   135
  Swallows and curlews!
Here's the top-peak; the multitude below
  Live, for they can, there:
This man decided not to Live but Know—
  Bury this man there?   140
Here—here's his place, where meteors shoot, clouds form,
  Lightnings are loosened,
Stars come and go! Let joy break with the storm,
  Peace let the dew send!
Lofty designs must close in like effects: 145
  Loftily lying,
Leave him—still loftier than the world suspects,
  Living and dying.

ONE WAY OF LOVE

I

ALL June I bound the rose in sheaves.
Now, rose by rose, I strip the leaves
And strew them where Pauline may pass.
She will not turn aside? Alas!
Let them lie. Suppose they die?   5
The chance was they might take her eye.

II

How many a month I strove to suit
These stubborn fingers to the lute!
To-day I venture all I know.

She will not hear my music? So!   10
Break the string; fold music's wing:
Suppose Pauline had bade me sing!

III

My whole life long I learned to love.
This hour my utmost art I prove
And speak my passion—heaven or hell?   15
She will not give me heaven? 'T is well!
Lose who may—I still can say,
Those who win heaven, blest are they!

ANOTHER WAY OF LOVE

I

JUNE was not over
   Though past the full,
And the best of her roses
   Had yet to blow,
     When a man I know   5
(But shall not discover,
   Since ears are dull,
  And time discloses)
Turned him and said with a man's true air,
Half sighing a smile in a yawn, as 't were,—   10
'If I tire of your June, will she greatly care?'

II

Well, dear, in-doors with you!
   True! serene deadness
Tries a man's temper.
   What's in the blossom   15
  June wears on her bosom?
Can it clear scores with you?
    Sweetness and redness.
    Eadem semper!
Go, let me care for it greatly or slightly!   20
If June mend her bower now, your hand left unsightly
By plucking the roses,—my June will do rightly.

III

And after, for pastime,
   If June be refulgent
With flowers in completeness,   25
   All petals, no prickles,
   Delicious as trickles
Of wine poured at mass-time,—
   And choose One indulgent
   To redness and sweetness: 30
Or if, with experience of man and of spider,
June use my June-lightning, the strong insect-ridder,
And stop the fresh film-work,—why, June will consider.

'TRANSCENDENTALISM: A POEM IN
TWELVE BOOKS'

STOP playing, poet! May a brother speak?
'T is you speak, that's your error. Song's our art:
Whereas you please to speak these naked thoughts
Instead of draping them in sights and sounds.
—True thoughts, good thoughts, thoughts fit to treasure
   up!   5
But why such long prolusion and display,
Such turning and adjustment of the harp,
And taking it upon your breast, at length,
Only to speak dry words across its strings?
Stark-naked thought is in request enough: 10
Speak prose and hollo it till Europe hears!
The six-foot Swiss tube, braced about with bark,
Which helps the hunter's voice from Alp to Alp—
Exchange our harp for that,—who hinders you?

But here's your fault; grown men want thought, you
   think;   15
Thought's what they mean by verse, and seek in verse.
Boys seek for images and melody,
Men must have reason—so, you aim at men.
Quite otherwise! Objects throng our youth, 't is true;

We see and hear and do not wonder much:　　　　20
If you could tell us what they mean, indeed!
As German Boehme never cared for plants
Until it happed, a-walking in the fields,
He noticed all at once that plants could speak,
Nay, turned with loosened tongue to talk with him.　　　25
That day the daisy had an eye indeed—
Colloquized with the cowslip on such themes!
We find them extant yet in Jacob's prose.
But by the time youth slips a stage or two
While reading prose in that tough book he wrote　　　30
(Collating and emendating the same
And settling on the sense most to our mind),
We shut the clasps and find life's summer past.
Then, who helps more, pray, to repair our loss—
Another Boehme with a tougher book　　　35
And subtler meanings of what roses say,—
Or some stout Mage like him of Halberstadt,
John, who made things Boehme wrote thoughts about?
He with a 'look you!' vents a brace of rhymes,
And in there breaks the sudden rose herself,　　　40
Over us, under, round us every side,
Nay, in and out the tables and the chairs
And musty volumes, Boehme's book and all,—
Buries us with a glory, young once more,
Pouring heaven into this shut house of life.　　　45

So come, the harp back to your heart again!
You are a poem, though your poem's naught.
The best of all you showed before, believe,
Was your own boy-face o'er the finer chords
Bent, following the cherub at the top　　　50
That points to God with his paired half-moon wings.

MISCONCEPTIONS

I

THIS is a spray the Bird clung to,
　　Making it blossom with pleasure,

Ere the high tree-top she sprung to,
    Fit for her nest and her treasure.
    Oh, what a hope beyond measure   5
Was the poor spray's, which the flying feet hung to,—
So to be singled out, built in, and sung to!

                  II

This is a heart the Queen leant on,
    Thrilled in a minute erratic,
Ere the true bosom she bent on,   10
    Meet for love's regal dalmatic.
    Oh, what a fancy ecstatic
Was the poor heart's, ere the wanderer went on—
Love to be saved for it, proffered to, spent on!

ONE WORD MORE

TO E. B. B.

1855

                  I

THERE they are, my fifty men and women
Naming me the fifty poems finished!
Take them, Love, the book and me together:
Where the heart lies, let the brain lie also.

                  II

Rafael made a century of sonnets,   5
Made and wrote them in a certain volume
Dinted with the silver-pointed pencil
Else he only used to draw Madonnas:
These, the world might view—but one, the volume.
Who that one, you ask? Your heart instructs you.   10
Did she live and love it all her life-time?
Did she drop, his lady of the sonnets,
Die, and let it drop beside her pillow
Where it lay in place of Rafael's glory,
Rafael's cheek so duteous and so loving—   15

Cheek, the world was wont to hail a painter's,
Rafael's cheek, her love had turned a poet's?

III

You and I would rather read that volume,
(Taken to his beating bosom by it)
Lean and list the bosom-beats of Rafael,   20
Would we not? than wonder at Madonnas—
Her, San Sisto names, and Her, Foligno,
Her, that visits Florence in a vision,
Her, that's left with lilies in the Louvre—
Seen by us and all the world in circle.   25

IV

You and I will never read that volume.
Guido Reni, like his own eye's apple
Guarded long the treasure-book and loved it.
Guido Reni dying, all Bologna
Cried, and the world cried too, 'Ours, the treasure!'   30
Suddenly, as rare things will, it vanished.

V

Dante once prepared to paint an angel:
Whom to please? You whisper 'Beatrice.'
While he mused and traced it and retraced it,
(Peradventure with a pen corroded   35
Still by drops of that hot ink he dipped for,
When, his left-hand i' the hair o' the wicked,
Back he held the brow and pricked its stigma,
Bit into the live man's flesh for parchment,
Loosed him, laughed to see the writing rankle,   40
Let the wretch go festering through Florence)—
Dante, who loved well because he hated,
Hated wickedness that hinders loving,
Dante standing, studying his angel,—
In there broke the folk of his Inferno.   45
Says he—'Certain people of importance'
(Such he gave his daily dreadful line to)
'Entered and would seize, forsooth, the poet.'
Says the poet—'Then I stopped my painting.'

VI

You and I would rather see that angel,   50
Painted by the tenderness of Dante,
Would we not?—than read a fresh Inferno.

VII

You and I will never see that picture.
While he mused on love and Beatrice,
While he softened o'er his outlined angel,   55
In they broke, those 'people of importance:'
We and Bice bear the loss for ever.

VIII

What of Rafael's sonnets, Dante's picture?
This: no artist lives and loves, that longs not
Once, and only once, and for one only,   60
(Ah, the prize!) to find his love a language
Fit and fair and simple and sufficient—
Using nature that's an art to others,
Not, this one time, art that's turned his nature.
Ay, of all the artists living, loving,   65
None but would forego his proper dowry,—
Does he paint? he fain would write a poem,—
Does he write? he fain would paint a picture,
Put to proof art alien to the artist's,
Once, and only once, and for one only,   70
So to be the man and leave the artist,
Save the man's joy, miss the artist's sorrow.

IX

Wherefore? Heaven's gift takes earth's abatement!
He who smites the rock and spreads the water,
Bidding drink and live a crowd beneath him,   75
Even he, the minute makes immortal,
Proves, perchance, but mortal in the minute,
Desecrates, belike, the deed in doing.
While he smites, how can he but remember,
So he smote before, in such a peril,   80
When they stood and mocked—'Shall smiting help us?'
When they drank and sneered—'A stroke is easy!'

When they wiped their mouths and went their journey,
Throwing him for thanks—'But drought was pleasant.'
Thus old memories mar the actual triumph;   85
Thus the doing savours of disrelish;
Thus achievement lacks a gracious somewhat;
O'er-importuned brows becloud the mandate,
Carelessness or consciousness—the gesture.
For he bears an ancient wrong about him,   90
Sees and knows again those phalanxed faces,
Hears, yet one time more, the 'customed prelude—
'How shouldst thou, of all men, smite, and save us?'
Guesses what is like to prove the sequel—
'Egypt's flesh-pots—nay, the drought was better.'   95

X

Oh, the crowd must have emphatic warrant!
Theirs, the Sinai-forehead's cloven brilliance,
Right-arm's rod-sweep, tongue's imperial fiat.
Never dares the man put off the prophet.

XI

Did he love one face from out the thousands,   100
(Were she Jethro's daughter, white and wifely,
Were she but the Æthiopian bondslave,)
He would envy yon dumb patient camel,
Keeping a reserve of scanty water
Meant to save his own life in the desert;   105
Ready in the desert to deliver
(Kneeling down to let his breast be opened)
Hoard and life together for his mistress.

XII

I shall never, in the years remaining,
Paint you pictures, no, nor carve you statues,   110
Make you music that should all-express me;
So it seems: I stand on my attainment.
This of verse alone, one life allows me;
Verse and nothing else have I to give you.
Other heights in other lives, God willing: 115
All the gifts from all the heights, your own, Love!

XIII

Yet a semblance of resource avails us—
Shade so finely touched, love's sense must seize it.
Take these lines, look lovingly and nearly,
Lines I write the first time and the last time.   120
He who works in fresco, steals a hair-brush,
Curbs the liberal hand, subservient proudly,
Cramps his spirit, crowds its all in little,
Makes a strange art of an art familiar,
Fills his lady's missal-marge with flowerets.   125
He who blows thro' bronze, may breathe thro' silver,
Fitly serenade a slumbrous princess.
He who writes, may write for once as I do.

XIV

Love, you saw me gather men and women,
Live or dead or fashioned by my fancy,   130
Enter each and all, and use their service,
Speak from every mouth,—the speech, a poem.
Hardly shall I tell my joys and sorrows,
Hopes and fears, belief and disbelieving:
I am mine and yours—the rest be all men's,   135
Karshish, Cleon, Norbert and the fifty.
Let me speak this once in my true person,
Not as Lippo, Roland or Andrea,
Though the fruit of speech be just this sentence:
Pray you, look on these my men and women,   140
Take and keep my fifty poems finished;
Where my heart lies, let my brain lie also!
Poor the speech; be how I speak, for all things.

XV

Not but that you know me! Lo, the moon's self!
Here in London, yonder late in Florence,   145
Still we find her face, the thrice-transfigured.
Curving on a sky imbrued with colour,
Drifted over Fiesole by twilight,
Came she, our new crescent of a hair's-breadth.
Full she flared it, lamping Samminiato,   150

Rounder 'twixt the cypresses and rounder,
Perfect till the nightingales applauded.
Now, a piece of her old self, impoverished,
Hard to greet, she traverses the houseroofs,
Hurries with unhandsome thrift of silver,   155
Goes dispiritedly, glad to finish.

XVI

What, there's nothing in the moon noteworthy?
Nay: for if that moon could love a mortal,
Use, to charm him (so to fit a fancy),
All her magic ('t is the old sweet mythos)   160
She would turn a new side to her mortal,
Side unseen of herdsman, huntsman, steersman—
Blank to Zoroaster on his terrace,
Blind to Galileo on his turret,
Dumb to Homer, dumb to Keats—him, even!   165
Think, the wonder of the moonstruck mortal—
When she turns round, comes again in heaven,
Opens out anew for worse or better!
Proves she like some portent of an iceberg
Swimming full upon the ship it founders,   170
Hungry with huge teeth of splintered crystals?
Proves she as the paved work of a sapphire
Seen by Moses when he climbed the mountain?
Moses, Aaron, Nadab and Abihu
Climbed and saw the very God, the Highest,   175
Stand upon the paved work of a sapphire.
Like the bodied heaven in his clearness
Shone the stone, the sapphire of that paved work,
When they ate and drank and saw God also!

XVII

What were seen? None knows, none ever shall know.   180
Only this is sure—the sight were other,
Not the moon's same side, born late in Florence,
Dying now impoverished here in London.
God be thanked, the meanest of his creatures
Boasts two soul-sides, one to face the world with,   185
One to show a woman when he loves her!

XVIII

This I say of me, but think of you, Love!
This to you—yourself my moon of poets!
Ah, but that's the world's side, there's the wonder,
Thus they see you, praise you, think they know you!   190
There, in turn I stand with them and praise you—
Out of my own self, I dare to phrase it.
But the best is when I glide from out them,
Cross a step or two of dubious twilight,
Come out on the other side, the novel   195
Silent silver lights and darks undreamed of,
Where I hush and bless myself with silence.

XIX

Oh, their Rafael of the dear Madonnas,
Oh, their Dante of the dread Inferno,
Wrote one song—and in my brain I sing it,   200
Drew one angel—borne, see, on my bosom!

R. B.

DRAMATIS PERSONÆ

DRAMATIS PERSONÆ

1864

[In the second edition, which appeared later in 1864, there were considerable revisions in a number of the poems (notably 'James Lee'). Further revisions were made in The Poetical Works *of 1868 (where the title of that poem was changed to 'James Lee's Wife'), and in 1888-9.]*

JAMES LEE'S WIFE[1]

I—JAMES LEE'S WIFE SPEAKS AT THE WINDOW

I

Ah, Love, but a day
   And the world has changed!
The sun's away,
   And the bird estranged;
The wind has dropped,   5
   And the sky's deranged:
Summer has stopped.

II

Look in my eyes!
   Wilt thou change too?
Should I fear surprise?   10
   Shall I find aught new
In the old and dear,
   In the good and true,
With the changing year?

III

Thou art a man,   15
   But I am thy love.
For the lake, its swan;
   For the dell, its dove;

---

[1] The first six stanzas of section VI were first printed in the *Monthly Repository* for May 1836.

And for thee—(oh, haste!)
    Me, to bend above,   20
    Me, to hold embraced.

II—BY THE FIRESIDE

I

Is all our fire of shipwreck wood,
    Oak and pine?
Oh, for the ills half-understood,
    The dim dead woe   25
      Long ago
Befallen this bitter coast of France!
Well, poor sailors took their chance;
    I take mine.

II

A ruddy shaft our fire must shoot   30
    O'er the sea:
Do sailors eye the casement—mute,
    Drenched and stark,
      From their bark—
And envy, gnash their teeth for hate   35
O' the warm safe house and happy freight
    —Thee and me?

III

God help you, sailors, at your need!
    Spare the curse!
For some ships, safe in port indeed,   40
    Rot and rust,
      Run to dust,
All through worms i' the wood, which crept,
Gnawed our hearts out while we slept:
    That is worse.   45

IV

Who lived here before us two?
    Old-world pairs.

Did a woman ever—would I knew!—
    Watch the man
    With whom began   50
Love's voyage full-sail,—(now, gnash your
      teeth!)
When planks start, open hell beneath
    Unawares?

III—IN THE DOORWAY

I

THE swallow has set her six young on the rail,
    And looks sea-ward: 55
The water's in stripes like a snake, olive-pale
    To the leeward,—
On the weather-side, black, spotted white with the wind.
  'Good fortune departs, and disaster's behind,'—
Hark, the wind with its wants and its infinite wail!   60

II

Our fig-tree, that leaned for the saltness, has furled
    Her five fingers,
Each leaf like a hand opened wide to the world
    Where there lingers
No glint of the gold, Summer sent for her sake: 65
How the vines writhe in rows, each impaled on its stake!
My heart shrivels up and my spirit shrinks curled.

III

Yet here are we two; we have love, house enough,
    With the field there,
This house of four rooms, that field red and rough,   70
    Though it yield there,
For the rabbit that robs, scarce a blade or a bent;
If a magpie alight now, it seems an event;
And they both will be gone at November's rebuff.

IV

But why must cold spread? but wherefore bring change 75
    To the spirit,

God meant should mate his with an infinite range,
    And inherit
His power to put life in the darkness and cold?
Oh, live and love worthily, bear and be bold!   80
Whom Summer made friends of, let Winter estrange!

IV—ALONG THE BEACH

I

I WILL be quiet and talk with you,
    And reason why you are wrong.
You wanted my love—is that much true?
And so I did love, so I do: 85
    What has come of it all along?

II

I took you—how could I otherwise?
    For a world to me, and more;
For all, love greatens and glorifies
Till God's a-glow, to the loving eyes,   90
    In what was mere earth before.

III

Yes, earth—yes, mere ignoble earth!
    Now do I mis-state, mistake?
Do I wrong your weakness and call it worth?
Expect all harvest, dread no dearth,   95
    Seal my sense up for your sake?

IV

Oh, Love, Love, no, Love! not so, indeed!
    You were just weak earth, I knew:
With much in you waste, with many a weed,
And plenty of passions run to seed,   100
    But a little good grain too.

V

And such as you were, I took you for mine:
    Did not you find me yours,
To watch the olive and wait the vine,

And wonder when rivers of oil and wine 105
  Would flow, as the Book assures?

VI

Well, and if none of these good things came,
  What did the failure prove?
The man was my whole world, all the same,
With his flowers to praise or his weeds to blame, 110
  And, either or both, to love.

VII

Yet this turns now to a fault—there! there!
  That I do love, watch too long,
And wait too well, and weary and wear;
And 't is all an old story, and my despair 115
  Fit subject for some new song:

VIII

'How the light, light love, he has wings to fly
  'At suspicion of a bond:
'My wisdom has bidden your pleasure good-bye,
'Which will turn up next in a laughing eye, 120
  'And why should you look beyond?'

V—ON THE CLIFF

I

I LEANED on the turf,
I looked at a rock
Left dry by the surf;
For the turf, to call it grass were to mock: 125
Dead to the roots, so deep was done
The work of the summer sun.

II

And the rock lay flat
As an anvil's face:
No iron like that! 130
Baked dry; of a weed, of a shell, no trace:
Sunshine outside, but ice at the core,
Death's altar by the lone shore.

III

On the turf, sprang gay
With his films of blue,   135
No cricket, I'll say,
But a warhorse, barded and chanfroned too,
The gift of a quixote-mage to his knight,
Real fairy, with wings all right.

IV

On the rock, they scorch   140
Like a drop of fire
From a brandished torch,
Fall two red fans of a butterfly:
No turf, no rock: in their ugly stead,
See, wonderful blue and red!   145

V

Is it not so
With the minds of men?
The level and low,
The burnt and bare, in themselves; but then
With such a blue and red grace, not theirs,—   150
Love settling unawares!

VI—READING A BOOK, UNDER THE CLIFF

I

'Still ailing, Wind? Wilt be appeased or no?
  'Which needs the other's office, thou or I?
'Dost want to be disburthened of a woe,
  'And can, in truth, my voice untie   155
'Its links, and let it go?

II

'Art thou a dumb wronged thing that would be
    righted,
  'Entrusting thus thy cause to me? Forbear!
'No tongue can mend such pleadings; faith, requited
  'With falsehood,—love, at last aware   160
'Of scorn,—hopes, early blighted,—

III

'We have them; but I know not any tone
  'So fit as thine to falter forth a sorrow:
'Dost think men would go mad without a moan,
  'If they knew any way to borrow   165
'A pathos like thy own?

IV

'Which sigh wouldst mock, of all the sighs? The one
  'So long escaping from lips starved and blue,
'That lasts while on her pallet-bed the nun
  'Stretches her length; her foot comes through   170
'The straw she shivers on;

V

'You had not thought she was so tall: and spent,
  'Her shrunk lids open, her lean fingers shut
'Close, close, their sharp and livid nails indent
  'The clammy palm; then all is mute: 175
'That way, the spirit went.

VI

'Or wouldst thou rather that I understand
  'Thy will to help me?—like the dog I found
'Once, pacing sad this solitary strand,
  'Who would not take my food, poor hound,   180
'But whined and licked my hand.'

VII

All this, and more, comes from some young man's pride
  Of power to see,—in failure and mistake,
Relinquishment, disgrace, on every side,—
  Merely examples for his sake,   185
Helps to his path untried:

VIII

Instances he must—simply recognize?
  Oh, more than so!—must, with a learner's zeal,

Make doubly prominent, twice emphasize,
   By added touches that reveal   190
The god in babe's disguise.

IX

Oh, he knows what defeat means, and the rest!
   Himself the undefeated that shall be:
Failure, disgrace, he flings them you to test,—
   His triumph, in eternity   195
Too plainly manifest!

X

Whence, judge if he learn forthwith what the wind
   Means in its moaning—by the happy prompt
Instinctive way of youth, I mean; for kind
   Calm years, exacting their accompt   200
Of pain, mature the mind:

XI

And some midsummer morning, at the lull
   Just about daybreak, as he looks across
A sparkling foreign country, wonderful
   To the sea's edge for gloom and gloss,   205
Next minute must annul,—

XII

Then, when the wind begins among the vines,
   So low, so low, what shall it say but this?
'Here is the change beginning, here the lines
   'Circumscribe beauty, set to bliss   210
'The limit time assigns.'

XIII

Nothing can be as it has been before;
   Better, so call it, only not the same.
To draw one beauty into our hearts' core,
   And keep it changeless! such our claim;   215
So answered,—Never more!

XIV

Simple? Why this is the old woe o' the world;
   Tune, to whose rise and fall we live and die.

Rise with it, then! Rejoice that man is hurled
   From change to change unceasingly,   220
His soul's wings never furled!

XV

That's a new question; still replies the fact,
   Nothing endures: the wind moans, saying so;
We moan in acquiescence: there's life's pact,
   Perhaps probation—do *I* know?   225
God does: endure his act!

XVI

Only, for man, how bitter not to grave
   On his soul's hands' palms one fair good wise thing
Just as he grasped it! For himself, death's wave;
   While time first washes—ah, the sting!—   230
O'er all he'd sink to save.

VII—AMONG THE ROCKS

I

OH, good gigantic smile o' the brown old earth,
   This autumn morning! How he sets his bones
To bask i' the sun, and thrusts out knees and feet
For the ripple to run over in its mirth;   235
   Listening the while, where on the heap of stones
The white breast of the sea-lark twitters sweet.

II

That is the doctrine, simple, ancient, true;
   Such is life's trial, as old earth smiles and knows.
If you loved only what were worth your love,   240
Love were clear gain, and wholly well for you:
   Make the low nature better by your throes!
Give earth yourself, go up for gain above!

VIII—BESIDE THE DRAWING BOARD

I

'As like as a Hand to another Hand!'
   Whoever said that foolish thing,   245

Could not have studied to understand
  The counsels of God in fashioning,
Out of the infinite love of his heart,
This Hand, whose beauty I praise, apart
From the world of wonder left to praise,   250
If I tried to learn the other ways
Of love in its skill, or love in its power.
  'As like as a Hand to another Hand':
    Who said that, never took his stand,
Found and followed, like me, an hour,   255
The beauty in this,—how free, how fine
To fear, almost,—of the limit-line!
As I looked at this, and learned and drew,
  Drew and learned, and looked again,
While fast the happy minutes flew,   260
    Its beauty mounted into my brain,
    And a fancy seized me; I was fain
To efface my work, begin anew,
Kiss what before I only drew;
Ay, laying the red chalk 'twixt my lips,   265
    With soul to help if the mere lips failed,
    I kissed all right where the drawing ailed,
Kissed fast the grace that somehow slips
Still from one's soulless finger-tips.

II

'T is a clay cast, the perfect thing,   270
  From Hand live once, dead long ago:
Princess-like it wears the ring
  To fancy's eye, by which we know
That here at length a master found
  His match, a proud lone soul its mate,   275
As soaring genius sank to ground,
  And pencil could not emulate
The beauty in this,—how free, how fine
To fear almost!—of the limit-line.
Long ago the god, like me   280
The worm, learned, each in our degree:
Looked and loved, learned and drew,
  Drew and learned and loved again,

While fast the happy minutes flew,
   Till beauty mounted into his brain   285
And on the finger which outvied
   His·art he placed the ring that's there,
Still by fancy's eye descried,
   In token of a marriage rare:
   For him on earth, his art's despair,   290
For him in heaven, his soul's fit bride.

III

Little girl with the poor coarse hand
   I turned from to a cold clay cast—
I have my lesson, understand
   The worth of flesh and blood at last.   295
Nothing but beauty in a Hand?
   Because he could not change the hue,
   Mend the lines and make them true
To this which met his soul's demand,—
   Would Da Vinci turn from you?   300
I hear him laugh my woes to scorn—
'The fool forsooth is all forlorn
'Because the beauty, she thinks best,
'Lived long ago or was never born,—
'Because no beauty bears the test   305
'In this rough peasant Hand! Confessed!
' "Art is null and study void!"
   'So sayest thou? So said not I,
   'Who threw the faulty pencil by,
'And years instead of hours employed,   310
'Learning the veritable use
   'Of flesh and bone and nerve beneath
   'Lines and hue of the outer sheath,
'If haply I might reproduce
'One motive of the powers profuse,   315
'Flesh and bone and nerve that make
   'The poorest coarsest human hand
   'An object worthy to be scanned
'A whole life long for their sole sake.
'Shall earth and the cramped moment-space   320
'Yield the heavenly crowning grace?

'Now the parts and then the whole!
'Who art thou, with stinted soul
   'And stunted body, thus to cry
' "I love,—shall that be life's strait dole?   325
   ' "I must live beloved or die!"
'This peasant hand that spins the wool
   'And bakes the bread, why lives it on,
   'Poor and coarse with beauty gone,—
'What use survives the beauty?' Fool!   330

Go, little girl with the poor coarse hand!
I have my lesson, shall understand.

IX—ON DECK

I

THERE is nothing to remember in me,
   Nothing I ever said with a grace,
Nothing I did that you care to see,   335
   Nothing I was that deserves a place
In your mind, now I leave you, set you free.

II

Conceded! In turn, concede to me,
   Such things have been as a mutual flame.
Your soul's locked fast; but, love for a key,   340
   You might let it loose, till I grew the same
In your eyes, as in mine you stand: strange plea!

III

For then, then, what would it matter to me
   That I was the harsh ill-favoured one?
We both should be like as pea and pea;   345
   It was ever so since the world begun:
So, let me proceed with my reverie.

IV

How strange it were if you had all me,
   As I have all you in my heart and brain,
You, whose least word brought gloom or glee,   350
   Who never lifted the hand in vain—
Will hold mine yet, from over the sea!

V

Strange, if a face, when you thought of me,
   Rose like your own face present now,
With eyes as dear in their due degree,   355
   Much such a mouth, and as bright a brow,
Till you saw yourself, while you cried ' 'T is She!'

VI

Well, you may, you must, set down to me
   Love that was life, life that was love;
A tenure of breath at your lips' decree,   360
   A passion to stand as your thoughts approve,
A rapture to fall where your foot might be.

VII

But did one touch of such love for me
   Come in a word or a look of yours,
Whose words and looks will, circling, flee   365
   Round me and round while life endures,—
Could I fancy 'As I feel, thus feels he';

VIII

Why, fade you might to a thing like me,
   And your hair grow these coarse hanks of hair,
Your skin, this bark of a gnarled tree,—   370
   You might turn myself!—should I know or care
When I should be dead of joy, James Lee?

GOLD HAIR:

A STORY OF PORNIC[1]

I

OH, the beautiful girl, too white,
   Who lived at Pornic, down by the sea,
Just where the sea and the Loire unite!
   And a boasted name in Brittany
She bore, which I will not write.   5

[1] 'Gold Hair' was first published in the American *Atlantic Monthly* for May 1864.

II

Too white, for the flower of life is red;
   Her flesh was the soft seraphic screen
Of a soul that is meant (her parents said)
   To just see earth, and hardly be seen,
And blossom in heaven instead.   10

III

Yet earth saw one thing, one how fair!
   One grace that grew to its full on earth:
Smiles might be sparse on her cheek so spare,
   And her waist want half a girdle's girth,
But she had her great gold hair.   15

IV

Hair, such a wonder of flix and floss,
   Freshness and fragrance—floods of it, too!
Gold, did I say? Nay, gold's mere dross:
   Here, Life smiled, 'Think what I meant to do!'
And Love sighed, 'Fancy my loss!'   20

V

So, when she died, it was scarce more strange
   Than that, when delicate evening dies,
And you follow its spent sun's pallid range,
   There's a shoot of colour startles the skies
With sudden, violent change,—   25

VI

That, while the breath was nearly to seek,
   As they put the little cross to her lips,
She changed; a spot came out on her cheek,
   A spark from her eye in mid-eclipse,
And she broke forth, 'I must speak!'   30

VII

'Not my hair!' made the girl her moan—
   'All the rest is gone or to go;
'But the last, last grace, my all, my own,
   'Let it stay in the grave, that the ghosts may know!
'Leave my poor gold hair alone!'   35

VIII

The passion thus vented, dead lay she;
  Her parents sobbed their worst on that;
All friends joined in, nor observed degree:
  For indeed the hair was to wonder at,
As it spread—not flowing free,   40

IX

But curled around her brow, like a crown,
  And coiled beside her cheeks, like a cap,
And calmed about her neck—ay, down
  To her breast, pressed flat, without a gap
I' the gold, it reached her gown.   45

X

All kissed that face, like a silver wedge
  Mid the yellow wealth, nor disturbed its hair:
E'en the priest allowed death's privilege,
  As he planted the crucifix with care
On her breast, 'twixt edge and edge.   50

XI

And thus was she buried, inviolate
  Of body and soul, in the very space
By the altar; keeping saintly state
  In Pornic church, for her pride of race,
Pure life and piteous fate.   55

XII

And in after-time would your fresh tear fall,
  Though your mouth might twitch with a dubious smile,
As they told you of gold, both robe and pall,
  How she prayed them leave it alone awhile,
So it never was touched at all.   60

XIII

Years flew; this legend grew at last
  The life of the lady; all she had done,
All been, in the memories fading fast
  Of lover and friend, was summed in one
Sentence survivors passed: 65

XIV

To wit, she was meant for heaven, not earth;
   Had turned an angel before the time:
Yet, since she was mortal, in such dearth
   Of frailty, all you could count a crime
Was—she knew her gold hair's worth.   70

XV

At little pleasant Pornic church,
   It chanced, the pavement wanted repair,
Was taken to pieces: left in the lurch,
   A certain sacred space lay bare,
And the boys began research.   75

XVI

'T was the space where our sires would lay a saint,
   A benefactor,—a bishop, suppose,
A baron with armour-adornments quaint,
   Dame with chased ring and jewelled rose,
Things sanctity saves from taint;   80

XVII

So we come to find them in after-days
   When the corpse is presumed to have done with
      gauds
Of use to the living, in many ways:
   For the boys get pelf, and the town applauds,
And the church deserves the praise.   85

XVIII

They grubbed with a will: and at length—*O cor*
   Humanum, pectora cœca, and the rest!—
They found—no gaud they were prying for,
   No ring, no rose, but—who would have guessed?—
A double Louis-d'or!   90

XIX

Here was a case for the priest: he heard,
   Marked, inwardly digested, laid

Finger on nose, smiled, 'There's a bird
  'Chirps in my ear': then, 'Bring a spade,
Dig deeper!'—he gave the word.   95

XX

And lo, when they came to the coffin-lid,
  Or rotten planks which composed it once,
Why, there lay the girl's skull wedged amid
  A mint of money, it served for the nonce
To hold in its hair-heaps hid!   100

XXI[1]

Hid there? Why? Could the girl be wont
  (She the stainless soul) to treasure up
Money, earth's trash and heaven's affront?
  Had a spider found out the communion-cup,
Was a toad in the christening-font?   105

XXII

Truth is truth: too true it was.
  Gold! She hoarded and hugged it first,
Longed for it, leaned o'er it, loved it—alas—
  Till the humour grew to a head and burst,
And she cried, at the final pass,—   110

XXIII

'Talk not of God, my heart is stone!
  'Nor lover nor friend—be gold for both!
'Gold I lack; and, my all, my own,
  'It shall hide in my hair. I scarce die loth
'If they let my hair alone!'   115

XXIV

Louis-d'or, some six times five,
  And duly double, every piece.
Now do you see? With the priest to shrive,
  With parents preventing her soul's release
By kisses that kept alive,—   120

[1] Stanzas XXI–XXIII were added in the second edition of *Dramatis Personæ*, at the suggestion of George Eliot.

XXV

With heaven's gold gates about to ope,
  With friends' praise, gold-like, lingering still,
An instinct had bidden the girl's hand grope
  For gold, the true sort—'Gold in heaven, if you will;
'But I keep earth's too, I hope.'   125

XXVI

Enough! The priest took the grave's grim yield:
  The parents, they eyed that price of sin
As if *thirty pieces* lay revealed
  On the place *to bury strangers in,*
The hideous Potter's Field.   130

XXVII

But the priest bethought him: ' "Milk that's spilt"
  '—You know the adage! Watch and pray!
'Saints tumble to earth with so slight a tilt!
  'It would build a new altar; that, we may!'
And the altar therewith was built.   135

XXVIII

Why I deliver this horrible verse?
  As the text of a sermon, which now I preach:
Evil or good may be better or worse
  In the human heart, but the mixture of each
Is a marvel and a curse.   140

XXIX

The candid incline to surmise of late
  That the Christian faith proves false, I find:
For our Essays-and-Reviews' debate
  Begins to tell on the public mind,
And Colenso's words have weight: 145

XXX

I still, to suppose it true, for my part,
  See reasons and reasons; this, to begin:
'T is the faith that launched point-blank her dart
  At the head of a lie—taught Original Sin,
The Corruption of Man's Heart.   150

THE WORST OF IT

I

WOULD it were I had been false, not you!
    I that am nothing, not you that are all:
I, never the worse for a touch or two
    On my speckled hide; not you, the pride
Of the day, my swan, that a first fleck's fall   5
    On her wonder of white must unswan, undo!

II

I had dipped in life's struggle and out again,
    Bore specks of it here, there, easy to see,
When I found my swan and the cure was plain;
    The dull turned bright as I caught your white   10
On my bosom: you saved me—saved in vain
    If you ruined yourself, and all through me!

III

Yes, all through the speckled beast that I am,
    Who taught you to stoop; you gave me yourself,
And bound your soul by the vows that damn: 15
    Since on better thought you break, as you ought,
Vows—words, no angel set down, some elf
    Mistook,—for an oath, an epigram!

IV

Yes, might I judge you, here were my heart,
    And a hundred its like, to treat as you pleased!   20
I choose to be yours, for my proper part,
    Yours, leave or take, or mar me or make;
If I acquiesce, why should you be teased
    With the conscience-prick and the memory-smart?

V

But what will God say? Oh, my sweet,   25
    Think, and be sorry you did this thing
Though earth were unworthy to feel your feet,
    There's a heaven above may deserve your love:
Should you forfeit heaven for a snapt gold ring
    And a promise broke, were it just or meet?   30

VI

And I to have tempted you! I, who tried
  Your soul, no doubt, till it sank! Unwise,
I loved and was lowly, loved and aspired,
  Loved, grieving or glad, till I made you mad,
And you meant to have hated and despised—   35
  Whereas, you deceived me nor inquired!

VII

She, ruined? How? No heaven for her?
  Crowns to give, and none for the brow
That looked like marble and smelt like myrrh?
  Shall the robe be worn, and the palm-branch borne,   40
And she go graceless, she graced now
  Beyond all saints, as themselves aver?

VIII

Hardly! That must be understood!
  The earth is your place of penance, then;
And what will it prove? I desire your good,   45
  But, plot as I may, I can find no way
How a blow should fall, such as falls on men,
  Nor prove too much for your womanhood.

IX

It will come, I suspect, at the end of life,
  When you walk alone, and review the past;   50
And I, who so long shall have done with strife,
  And journeyed my stage and earned my wage
And retired as was right,—I am called at last
  When the devil stabs you, to lend the knife.

X

He stabs for the minute of trivial wrong,   55
  Nor the other hours are able to save,
The happy, that lasted my whole life long:
  For a promise broke, not for first words spoke,
The true, the only, that turn my grave
  To a blaze of joy and a crash of song.   60

XI

Witness beforehand! Off I trip
  On a safe path gay through the flowers you flung:
My very name made great by your lip,
  And my heart a-glow with the good I know
Of a perfect year when we both were young,   65
  And I tasted the angels' fellowship.

XII

And witness, moreover . . . Ah, but wait!
  I spy the loop whence an arrow shoots!
It may be for yourself, when you meditate,
  That you grieve—for slain ruth, murdered truth.   70
'Though falsehood escape in the end, what boots?
  'How truth would have triumphed!'—you sigh too
    late.

XIII

Ay, who would have triumphed like you, I say!
  Well, it is lost now; well, you must bear,
Abide and grow fit for a better day: 75
  You should hardly grudge, could I be your judge!
But hush! For you, can be no despair:
  There's amends: 't is a secret: hope and pray!

XIV

For I was true at least—oh, true enough!
  And, Dear, truth is not as good as it seems!   80
Commend me to conscience! Idle stuff!
  Much help is in mine, as I mope and pine,
And skulk through day, and scowl in my dreams
  At my swan's obtaining the crow's rebuff.

XV

Men tell me of truth now—'False!' I cry: 85
  Of beauty—'A mask, friend! Look beneath!'
We take our own method, the devil and I,
  With pleasant and fair and wise and rare:
And the best we wish to what lives, is—death;
  Which even in wishing, perhaps we lie!   90

XVI

Far better commit a fault and have done—
    As you, Dear!—for ever; and choose the pure,
And look where the healing waters run,
    And strive and strain to be good again,
And a place in the other world ensure,   95
    All glass and gold, with God for its sun.

XVII

Misery! What shall I say or do?
    I cannot advise, or, at least, persuade:
Most like, you are glad you deceived me—rue
    No whit of the wrong: you endured too long,   100
Have done no evil and want no aid,
    Will live the old life out and chance the new.

XVIII

And your sentence is written all the same,
    And I can do nothing,—pray, perhaps:
But somehow the world pursues its game,—   105
    If I pray, if I curse,—for better or worse:
And my faith is torn to a thousand scraps,
    And my heart feels ice while my words breathe flame.

XIX

Dear, I look from my hiding-place.
    Are you still so fair? Have you still the eyes?   110
Be happy! Add but the other grace,
    Be good! Why want what the angels vaunt?
I knew you once: but in Paradise,
    If we meet, I will pass nor turn my face.

DÎS ALITER VISUM; OR, LE BYRON
DE NOS JOURS

I

STOP, let me have the truth of that!
    Is that all true? I say, the day
Ten years ago when both of us
    Met on a morning, friends—as thus
We meet this evening, friends or what?—   5

II

Did you—because I took your arm
  And sillily smiled, 'A mass of brass
'That sea looks, blazing underneath!'
  While up the cliff-road edged with heath,
We took the turns nor came to harm—   10

III

Did you consider 'Now makes twice
  'That I have seen her, walked and talked
'With this poor pretty thoughtful thing,
  'Whose worth I weigh: she tries to sing;
'Draws, hopes in time the eye grows nice;   15

IV

'Reads verse and thinks she understands;
  'Loves all, at any rate, that's great,
'Good, beautiful; but much as we
  'Down at the bath-house love the sea,
'Who breathe its salt and bruise its sands: 20

V

'While . . . do but follow the fishing-gull
  'That flaps and floats from wave to cave!
'There's the sea-lover, fair my friend!
  'What then? Be patient, mark and mend!
'Had you the making of your scull?'   25

VI

And did you, when we faced the church
  With spire and sad slate roof, aloof
From human fellowship so far,
  Where a few graveyard crosses are,
And garlands for the swallows' perch,—   30

VII

Did you determine, as we stepped
  O'er the lone stone fence, 'Let me get

'Her for myself, and what's the earth
  'With all its art, verse, music, worth—
'Compared with love, found, gained, and kept?   35

VIII

'Schumann's our music-maker now;
  'Has his march-movement youth and mouth?
'Ingres 's the modern man that paints;
  'Which will lean on me, of his saints?
'Heine for songs; for kisses, how?'   40

IX

And did you, when we entered, reached
  The votive frigate, soft aloft
Riding on air this hundred years,
  Safe-smiling at old hopes and fears,—
Did you draw profit while she preached?   45

X

Resolving, 'Fools we wise men grow!
  'Yes, I could easily blurt out curt
'Some question that might find reply
  'As prompt in her stopped lips, dropped eye,
'And rush of red to cheek and brow: 50

XI

'Thus were a match made, sure and fast,
  ' 'Mid the blue weed-flowers round the mound
'Where, issuing, we shall stand and stay
  'For one more look at baths and bay,
'Sands, sea-gulls, and the old church last—   55

XII

'A match 'twixt me, bent, wigged and lamed,
  'Famous, however, for verse and worse,
'Sure of the Fortieth spare Arm-chair
  'When gout and glory seat me there,
'So, one whose love-freaks pass unblamed,—   60

XIII

'And this young beauty, round and sound
  'As a mountain-apple, youth and truth

'With loves and doves, at all events
  'With money in the Three per Cents;
'Whose choice of me would seem profound:—   65

XIV

'She might take me as I take her.
  'Perfect the hour would pass, alas!
'Climb high, love high, what matter? Still,
  'Feet, feelings, must descend the hill:
'An hour's perfection can't recur.   70

XV

'Then follows Paris and full time
  'For both to reason: "Thus with us!"
'She'll sigh, "Thus girls give body and soul
  ' "At first word, think they gain the goal,
' "When 't is the starting-place they climb!   75

XVI

' "My friend makes verse and gets renown;
  ' "Have they all fifty years, his peers?
' "He knows the world, firm, quiet and gay;
  ' "Boys will become as much one day:
' "They're fools; he cheats, with beard less brown.   80

XVII

' "For boys say, *Love me or I die!*
  ' "He did not say, *The truth is, youth*
' "*I want, who am old and know too much;*
  ' "*I'd catch youth: lend me sight and touch!*
' "*Drop heart's blood where life's wheels grate dry!*"   85

XVIII

'While I should make rejoinder'—(then
  It was, no doubt, you ceased that least
Light pressure of my arm in yours)
  ' "I can conceive of cheaper cures
' "For a yawning-fit o'er books and men.   90

XIX

' "What? All I am, was, and might be,
  ' "All, books taught, art brought, life's whole strife,

D d

' "Painful results since precious, just
  ' "Were fitly exchanged, in wise disgust,
' "For two cheeks freshened by youth and sea?   95

XX

' "All for a nosegay!—what came first;
  ' "With fields on flower, untried each side;
' "I rally, need my books and men,
  ' "And find a nosegay": drop it, then,
'No match yet made for best or worst!'   100

XXI

That ended me. You judged the porch
  We left by, Norman; took our look
At sea and sky; wondered so few
  Find out the place for air and view;
Remarked the sun began to scorch;   105

XXII

Descended, soon regained the baths,
  And then, good-bye! Years ten since then:
Ten years! We meet: you tell me, now,
  By a window-seat for that cliff-brow,
On carpet-stripes for those sand-paths.   110

XXIII

Now I may speak: you fool, for all
  Your lore! WHO made things plain in vain?
What was the sea for? What, the grey
  Sad church, that solitary day,
Crosses and graves and swallows' call?   115

XXIV

Was there nought better than to enjoy?
  No feat which, done, would make time break,
And let us pent-up creatures through
  Into eternity, our due?
No forcing earth teach heaven's employ?   120

XXV

No wise beginning, here and now,
  What cannot grow complete (earth's feat)

And heaven must finish, there and then?
  No tasting earth's true food for men,
Its sweet in sad, its sad in sweet?   125

XXVI

No grasping at love, gaining a share
  O' the sole spark from God's life at strife
With death, so, sure of range above
  The limits here? For us and love,
Failure; but, when God fails, despair.   130

XXVII

This you call wisdom? Thus you add
  Good unto good again, in vain?
You loved, with body worn and weak;
  I loved, with faculties to seek:
Were both loves worthless since ill-clad?   135

XXVIII

Let the mere star-fish in his vault
  Crawl in a wash of weed, indeed,
Rose-jacynth to the finger-tips:
  He, whole in body and soul, outstrips
Man, found with either in default.   140

XXIX

But what's whole, can increase no more,
  Is dwarfed and dies, since here's its sphere.
The devil laughed at you in his sleeve!
  You knew not? That I well believe;
Or you had saved two souls: nay, four.   145

XXX

For Stephanie sprained last night her wrist,
  Ankle or something. 'Pooh,' cry you?
At any rate she danced, all say,
  Vilely; her vogue has had its day.
Here comes my husband from his whist.   150

TOO LATE

I

HERE was I with my arm and heart
   And brain, all yours for a word, a want
Put into a look—just a look, your part,—
   While mine, to repay it . . . vainest vaunt,
Were the woman, that's dead, alive to hear,   5
   Had her lover, that's lost, love's proof to show!
But I cannot show it; you cannot speak
   From the churchyard neither, miles removed,
Though I feel by a pulse within my cheek,
   Which stabs and stops, that the woman I loved   10
Needs help in her grave and finds none near,
   Wants warmth from the heart which sends it—so!

II

Did I speak once angrily, all the drear days
   You lived, you woman I loved so well,
Who married the other? Blame or praise,   15
   Where was the use then? Time would tell,
And the end declare what man for you,
   What woman for me, was the choice of God.
But, Edith dead! no doubting more!
   I used to sit and look at my life   20
As it rippled and ran till, right before,
   A great stone stopped it: oh, the strife
Of waves at the stone some devil threw
   In my life's midcurrent, thwarting God!

III

But either I thought, 'They may churn and chide   25
   'Awhile, my waves which came for their joy
'And found this horrible stone full-tide:
   'Yet I see just a thread escape, deploy
'Through the evening-country, silent and safe,
   'And it suffers no more till it finds the sea.'   30
Or else I would think, 'Perhaps some night
   'When new things happen, a meteor-ball

'May slip through the sky in a line of light,
  'And earth breathe hard, and landmarks fall,
'And my waves no longer champ nor chafe,   35
  'Since a stone will have rolled from its place: let be!'

IV

But, dead! All's done with: wait who may,
  Watch and wear and wonder who will.
Oh, my whole life that ends to-day!
  Oh, my soul's sentence, sounding still,   40
'The woman is dead that was none of his;
  'And the man that was none of hers may go!'
There's only the past left: worry that!
  Wreak, like a bull, on the empty coat,
Rage, its late wearer is laughing at!   45
  Tear the collar to rags, having missed his throat;
Strike stupidly on—'This, this and this,
  'Where I would that a bosom received the blow!'

V

I ought to have done more: once my speech,
  And once your answer, and there, the end,   50
And Edith was henceforth out of reach!
  Why, men do more to deserve a friend,
Be rid of a foe, get rich, grow wise,
  Nor, folding their arms, stare fate in the face.
Why, better even have burst like a thief   55
  And borne you away to a rock for us two,
In a moment's horror, bright, bloody and brief:
  Then changed to myself again—'I slew
'Myself in that moment; a ruffian lies
  'Somewhere: your slave, see, born in his place!'   60

VI

What did the other do? You be judge!
  Look at us, Edith! Here are we both!
Give him his six whole years: I grudge
  None of the life with you, nay, loathe
Myself that I grudged his start in advance   65
  Of me who could overtake and pass.

But, as if he loved you! No, not he,
    Nor anyone else in the world, 't is plain:
Who ever heard that another, free
    As I, young, prosperous, sound and sane,   70
Poured life out, proffered it—'Half a glance
    'Of those eyes of yours and I drop the glass!'

VII

Handsome, were you? 'T is more than they held,
    More than they said; I was 'ware and watched:
I was the 'scapegrace, this rat belled   75
    The cat, this fool got his whiskers scratched:
The others? No head that was turned, no heart
    Broken, my lady, assure yourself!
Each soon made his mind up; so and so
    Married a dancer, such and such   80
Stole his friend's wife, stagnated slow,
    Or maundered, unable to do as much,
And muttered of peace where he had no part:
    While, hid in the closet, laid on the shelf,—

VIII

On the whole, you were let alone, I think!   85
    So, you looked to the other, who acquiesced;
My rival, the proud man,—prize your pink
    Of poets! A poet he was! I've guessed:
He rhymed you his rubbish nobody read,
    Loved you and doved you—did not I laugh!   90
There was a prize! But we both were tried.
    Oh, heart of mine, marked broad with her mark,
Tekel, found wanting, set aside,
    Scorned! See, I bleed these tears in the dark
Till comfort come and the last be bled: 95
    He? He is tagging your epitaph.

IX

If it would only come over again!
    —Time to be patient with me, and probe
This heart till you punctured the proper vein,
    Just to learn what blood is: twitch the robe   100

From that blank lay-figure your fancy draped,
   Prick the leathern heart till the—verses spirt!
And late it was easy; late, you walked
   Where a friend might meet you; Edith's name
Arose to one's lip if one laughed or talked;   105
   If I heard good news, you heard the same;
When I woke, I knew that your breath escaped;
   I could bide my time, keep alive, alert.

X

And alive I shall keep and long, you will see!
   I knew a man, was kicked like a dog   110
From gutter to cesspool; what cared he
   So long as he picked from the filth his prog?
He saw youth, beauty and genius die,
   And jollily lived to his hundredth year.
But I will live otherwise: none of such life!   115
   At once I begin as I mean to end.
Go on with the world, get gold in its strife,
   Give your spouse the slip and betray your friend!
There are two who decline, a woman and I,
   And enjoy our death in the darkness here.   120

XI

I liked that way you had with your curls
   Wound to a ball in a net behind:
Your cheek was chaste as a quaker-girl's,
   And your mouth—there was never, to my mind,
Such a funny mouth, for it would not shut;   125
   And the dented chin too—what a chin!
There were certain ways when you spoke, some words
   That you know you never could pronounce:
You were thin, however; like a bird's
   Your hand seemed—some would say, the pounce   130
Of a scaly-footed hawk—all but!
   The world was right when it called you thin.

XII

But I turn my back on the world: I take
   Your hand, and kneel, and lay to my lips.

Bid me live, Edith! Let me slake   135
   Thirst at your presence! Fear no slips:
'T is your slave shall pay, while his soul endures,
   Full due, love's whole debt, *summum jus.*
My queen shall have high observance, planned
   Courtship made perfect, no least line   140
Crossed without warrant. There you stand,
   Warm too, and white too: would this wine
Had washed all over that body of yours,
   Ere I drank it, and you down with it, thus!

ABT VOGLER

(AFTER HE HAS BEEN EXTEMPORIZING UPON THE MUSICAL INSTRUMENT OF HIS INVENTION)

I

WOULD that the structure brave, the manifold music I build,
   Bidding my organ obey, calling its keys to their work,
Claiming each slave of the sound, at a touch, as when Solomon willed
   Armies of angels that soar, legions of demons that lurk,
Man, brute, reptile, fly,—alien of end and of aim,   5
   Adverse, each from the other heaven-high, hell-deep removed,—
Should rush into sight at once as he named the ineffable Name,
   And pile him a palace straight, to pleasure the princess he loved!

II

Would it might tarry like his, the beautiful building of mine,
   This which my keys in a crowd pressed and importuned to raise!   10
Ah, one and all, how they helped, would dispart now and now combine,
   Zealous to hasten the work, heighten their master his praise!
And one would bury his brow with a blind plunge down to hell,
   Burrow awhile and build, broad on the roots of things,
Then up again swim into sight, having based me my palace well,   15
   Founded it, fearless of flame, flat on the nether springs.

III

And another would mount and march, like the excellent minion he
    was,
    Ay, another and yet another, one crowd but with many a crest,
Raising my rampired walls of gold as transparent as glass,
    Eager to do and die, yield each his place to the rest: 20
For higher still and higher (as a runner tips with fire,
    When a great illumination surprises a festal night—
Outlining round and round Rome's dome from space to spire)
    Up, the pinnacled glory reached, and the pride of my soul was in
    sight.

IV

In sight? Not half! for it seemed, it was certain, to match man's
    birth,   25
    Nature in turn conceived, obeying an impulse as I;
And the emulous heaven yearned down, made effort to reach the
    earth,
    As the earth had done her best, in my passion, to scale the sky:
Novel splendours burst forth, grew familiar and dwelt with mine,
    Not a point nor peak but found and fixed its wandering star;   30
Meteor-moons, balls of blaze: and they did not pale nor pine,
    For earth had attained to heaven, there was no more near nor far.

V

Nay more; for there wanted not who walked in the glare and glow,
    Presences plain in the place; or, fresh from the Protoplast,
Furnished for ages to come, when a kindlier wind should blow,   35
    Lured now to begin and live, in a house to their liking at last;
Or else the wonderful Dead who have passed through the body and
    gone,
    But were back once more to breathe in an old world worth their
    new:
What never had been, was now; what was, as it shall be anon;
    And what is,—shall I say, matched both? for I was made perfect
    too.   40

VI

All through my keys that gave their sounds to a wish of my soul,
    All through my soul that praised as its wish flowed visibly forth,
All through music and me! For think, had I painted the whole,

Why, there it had stood, to see, nor the process so wonder-worth:
Had I written the same, made verse—still, effect proceeds from
    cause,   45
Ye know why the forms are fair, ye hear how the tale is told;
It is all triumphant art, but art in obedience to laws,
    Painter and poet are proud in the artist-list enrolled:—

VII

But here is the finger of God, a flash of the will that can,
    Existent behind all laws, that made them and, lo, they are!   50
And I know not if, save in this, such gift be allowed to man,
    That out of three sounds he frame, not a fourth sound, but a star.
Consider it well: each tone of our scale in itself is nought;
    It is everywhere in the world—loud, soft, and all is said:
Give it to me to use! I mix it with two in my thought: 55
    And, there! Ye have heard and seen: consider and bow the head!

VIII

Well, it is gone at last, the palace of music I reared;
    Gone! and the good tears start, the praises that come too slow;
For one is assured at first, one scarce can say that he feared,
    That he even gave it a thought, the gone thing was to go.   60
Never to be again! But many more of the kind
    As good, nay, better perchance: is this your comfort to me?
To me, who must be saved because I cling with my mind
    To the same, same self, same love, same God: ay, what was, shall
    be.

IX

Therefore to whom turn I but to thee, the ineffable Name?   65
    Builder and maker, thou, of houses not made with hands!
What, have fear of change from thee who art ever the same?
    Doubt that thy power can fill the heart that thy power expands?
There shall never be one lost good! What was, shall live as before;
    The evil is null, is nought, is silence implying sound;   70
What was good shall be good, with, for evil, so much good more;
    On the earth the broken arcs; in the heaven, a perfect round.

X

All we have willed or hoped or dreamed of good shall exist;
    Not its semblance, but itself; no beauty, nor good, nor power

Whose voice has gone forth, but each survives for the melodist 75
  When eternity affirms the conception of an hour.
The high that proved too high, the heroic for earth too hard,
  The passion that left the ground to lose itself in the sky,
Are music sent up to God by the lover and the bard;
  Enough that he heard it once: we shall hear it by-and-by. 80

XI

And what is our failure here but a triumph's evidence
  For the fulness of the days? Have we withered or agonized?
Why else was the pause prolonged but that singing might issue
    thence?
  Why rushed the discords in but that harmony should be prized?
Sorrow is hard to bear, and doubt is slow to clear, 85
  Each sufferer says his say, his scheme of the weal and woe:
But God has a few of us whom he whispers in the ear;
  The rest may reason and welcome: 't is we musicians know.

XII

Well, it is earth with me; silence resumes her reign:
  I will be patient and proud, and soberly acquiesce. 90
Give me the keys. I feel for the common chord again,
  Sliding by semitones, till I sink to the minor,—yes,
And I blunt it into a ninth, and I stand on alien ground,
  Surveying awhile the heights I rolled from into the deep;
Which, hark, I have dared and done, for my resting-place is
    found, 95
  The C Major of this life: so, now I will try to sleep.

RABBI BEN EZRA

I

    GROW old along with me!
      The best is yet to be,
The last of life, for which the first was made:
      Our times are in His hand
      Who saith 'A whole I planned, 5
'Youth shows but half; trust God: see all nor be afraid!'

II

Not that, amassing flowers,
Youth sighed 'Which rose make ours,
'Which lily leave and then as best recall?'
Not that, admiring stars,   10
It yearned 'Nor Jove, nor Mars;
'Mine be some figured flame which blends, transcends
    them all!'

III

Not for such hopes and fears
Annulling youth's brief years,
Do I remonstrate: folly wide the mark!   15
Rather I prize the doubt
Low kinds exist without,
Finished and finite clods, untroubled by a spark.

IV

Poor vaunt of life indeed,
Were man but formed to feed   20
On joy, to solely seek and find and feast:
Such feasting ended, then
As sure an end to men;
Irks care the crop-full bird? Frets doubt the maw-
    crammed beast?

V

Rejoice we are allied   25
To That which doth provide
And not partake, effect and not receive!
A spark disturbs our clod;
Nearer we hold of God
Who gives, than of His tribes that take, I must believe.   30

VI

Then, welcome each rebuff
That turns earth's smoothness rough,
Each sting that bids nor sit nor stand but go!
Be our joys three-parts pain!
Strive, and hold cheap the strain;   35
Learn, nor account the pang; dare, never grudge the throe!

VII

For thence,—a paradox
Which comforts while it mocks,—
Shall life succeed in that it seems to fail:
    What I aspired to be,   40
    And was not, comforts me:
A brute I might have been, but would not sink i' the scale.

VIII

    What is he but a brute
    Whose flesh has soul to suit,
Whose spirit works lest arms and legs want play?   45
    To man, propose this test—
    Thy body at its best,
How far can that project thy soul on its lone way?

IX

    Yet gifts should prove their use:
    I own the Past profuse   50
Of power each side, perfection every turn:
    Eyes, ears took in their dole,
    Brain treasured up the whole;
Should not the heart beat once 'How good to live and
    learn?'

X

    Not once beat 'Praise be Thine!   55
    'I see the whole design,
'I, who saw power, see now love perfect too:
    'Perfect I call Thy plan:
    'Thanks that I was a man!
'Maker, remake, complete,—I trust what Thou shalt
    do!'   60

XI

    For pleasant is this flesh;
    Our soul, in its rose-mesh
Pulled ever to the earth, still yearns for rest;
    Would we some prize might hold
    To match those manifold   65
Possessions of the brute,—gain most, as we did best!

XII

Let us not always say
'Spite of this flesh to-day
'I strove, made head, gained ground upon the whole!'
As the bird wings and sings,   70
Let us cry 'All good things
'Are ours, nor soul helps flesh more, now, than flesh
    helps soul!'

XIII

Therefore I summon age
To grant youth's heritage,
Life's struggle having so far reached its term: 75
Thence shall I pass, approved
A man, for aye removed
From the developed brute; a god though in the germ.

XIV

And I shall thereupon
Take rest, ere I be gone   80
Once more on my adventure brave and new:
Fearless and unperplexed,
When I wage battle next,
What weapons to select, what armour to indue.

XV

Youth ended, I shall try   85
My gain or loss thereby;
Leave the fire ashes, what survives is gold:
And I shall weigh the same,
Give life its praise or blame:
Young, all lay in dispute; I shall know, being old.   90

XVI

For note, when evening shuts,
A certain moment cuts
The deed off, calls the glory from the grey:
A whisper from the west
Shoots—'Add this to the rest,   95
'Take it and try its worth: here dies another day.'

XVII

So, still within this life,
Though lifted o'er its strife,
Let me discern, compare, pronounce at last,
  'This rage was right i' the main,   100
  'That acquiescence vain:
'The Future I may face now I have proved the Past.'

XVIII

For more is not reserved
To man, with soul just nerved
To act to-morrow what he learns to-day: 105
  Here, work enough to watch
  The Master work, and catch
Hints of the proper craft, tricks of the tool's true play.

XIX

As it was better, youth
Should strive, through acts uncouth,   110
Toward making, than repose on aught found made:
  So, better, age, exempt
  From strife, should know, than tempt
Further. Thou waitedest age: wait death nor be afraid!

XX

Enough now, if the Right   115
And Good and Infinite
Be named here, as thou callest thy hand thine own,
  With knowledge absolute,
  Subject to no dispute
From fools that crowded youth, nor let thee feel alone. 120

XXI

Be there, for once and all,
Severed great minds from small,
Announced to each his station in the Past!
  Was I, the world arraigned,
  Were they, my soul disdained,   125
Right? Let age speak the truth and give us peace at
    last!

XXII

Now, who shall arbitrate?
Ten men love what I hate,
Shun what I follow, slight what I receive;
    Ten, who in ears and eyes   130
    Match me: we all surmise,
They this thing, and I that: whom shall my soul
    believe?

XXIII

Not on the vulgar mass
Called 'work,' must sentence pass,
Things done, that took the eye and had the price;   135
    O'er which, from level stand,
    The low world laid its hand,
Found straightway to its mind, could value in a trice:

XXIV

But all, the world's coarse thumb
And finger failed to plumb,   140
So passed in making up the main account;
    All instincts immature,
    All purposes unsure,
That weighed not as his work, yet swelled the man's
    amount:

XXV

Thoughts hardly to be packed   145
Into a narrow act,
Fancies that broke through language and escaped;
    All I could never be,
    All, men ignored in me,
This, I was worth to God, whose wheel the pitcher
    shaped.   150

XXVI

Ay, note that Potter's wheel,
That metaphor! and feel
Why time spins fast, why passive lies our clay,—
    Thou, to whom fools propound,
    When the wine makes its round,   155
'Since life fleets, all is change; the Past gone, seize to-day!'

XXVII

Fool! All that is, at all,
Lasts ever, past recall;
Earth changes, but thy soul and God stand sure:
What entered into thee,   160
That was, is, and shall be:
Time's wheel runs back or stops: Potter and clay endure.

XXVIII

He fixed thee mid this dance
Of plastic circumstance,
This Present, thou, forsooth, wouldst fain arrest: 165
Machinery just meant
To give thy soul its bent,
Try thee and turn thee forth, sufficiently impressed.

XXIX

What though the earlier grooves
Which ran the laughing loves   170
Around thy base, no longer pause and press?
What though, about thy rim,
Scull-things in order grim
Grow out, in graver mood, obey the sterner stress?

XXX

Look not thou down but up!   175
To uses of a cup,
The festal board, lamp's flash and trumpet's peal,
The new wine's foaming flow,
The Master's lips a-glow!
Thou, heaven's consummate cup, what need'st thou with
    earth's wheel?   180

XXXI

But I need, now as then,
Thee, God, who mouldest men;
And since, not even while the whirl was worst,
Did I,—to the wheel of life
With shapes and colours rife,   185
Bound dizzily,—mistake my end, to slake Thy thirst:

XXXII

So, take and use Thy work:
Amend what flaws may lurk,
What strain o' the stuff, what warpings past the aim!
My times be in Thy hand!   190
Perfect the cup as planned!
Let age approve of youth, and death complete the
        same!

A DEATH IN THE DESERT

[SUPPOSED of Pamphylax the Antiochene:
It is a parchment, of my rolls the fifth,
Hath three skins glued together, is all Greek
And goeth from *Epsilon* down to *Mu*:
Lies second in the surnamed Chosen Chest,   5
Stained and conserved with juice of terebinth,
Covered with cloth of hair, and lettered *Xi*,
From Xanthus, my wife's uncle, now at peace:
Mu and *Epsilon* stand for my own name.
I may not write it, but I make a cross   10
To show I wait His coming, with the rest,
And leave off here: beginneth Pamphylax.]

I said, 'If one should wet his lips with wine,
'And slip the broadest plantain-leaf we find,
'Or else the lappet of a linen robe,   15
'Into the water-vessel, lay it right,
'And cool his forehead just above the eyes,
'The while a brother, kneeling either side,
'Should chafe each hand and try to make it warm,—
'He is not so far gone but he might speak.'   20

This did not happen in the outer cave,
Nor in the secret chamber of the rock
Where, sixty days since the decree was out,
We had him, bedded on a camel-skin,
And waited for his dying all the while;   25
But in the midmost grotto: since noon's light
Reached there a little, and we would not lose
The last of what might happen on his face.

I at the head, and Xanthus at the feet,
With Valens and the Boy, had lifted him, 30
And brought him from the chamber in the depths,
And laid him in the light where we might see:
For certain smiles began about his mouth,
And his lids moved, presageful of the end.

Beyond, and half way up the mouth o' the cave, 35
The Bactrian convert, having his desire,
Kept watch, and made pretence to graze a goat
That gave us milk, on rags of various herb,
Plantain and quitch, the rocks' shade keeps alive:
So that if any thief or soldier passed, 40
(Because the persecution was aware)
Yielding the goat up promptly with his life,
Such man might pass on, joyful at a prize,
Nor care to pry into the cool o' the cave.
Outside was all noon and the burning blue. 45

'Here is wine,' answered Xanthus,—dropped a drop;
I stooped and placed the lap of cloth aright,
Then chafed his right hand, and the Boy his left:
But Valens had bethought him, and produced
And broke a ball of nard, and made perfume. 50
Only, he did—not so much wake, as—turn
And smile a little, as a sleeper does
If any dear one call him, touch his face—
And smiles and loves, but will not be disturbed.

Then Xanthus said a prayer, but still he slept: 55
It is the Xanthus that escaped to Rome,
Was burned, and could not write the chronicle.

Then the Boy sprang up from his knees, and ran,
Stung by the splendour of a sudden thought,
And fetched the seventh plate of graven lead 60
Out of the secret chamber, found a place,
Pressing with finger on the deeper dints,
And spoke, as 't were his mouth proclaiming first,
'I am the Resurrection and the Life.'

Whereat he opened his eyes wide at once,   65
And sat up of himself, and looked at us;
And thenceforth nobody pronounced a word:
Only, outside, the Bactrian cried his cry
Like the lone desert-bird that wears the ruff,
As signal we were safe, from time to time.   70

First he said, 'If a friend declared to me,
'This my son Valens, this my other son,
'Were James and Peter,—nay, declared as well
'This lad was very John,—I could believe!
'—Could, for a moment, doubtlessly believe: 75
'So is myself withdrawn into my depths,
'The soul retreated from the perished brain
'Whence it was wont to feel and use the world
'Through these dull members, done with long ago.
'Yet I myself remain; I feel myself: 80
'And there is nothing lost. Let be, awhile!'

[This is the doctrine he was wont to teach,
How divers persons witness in each man,
Three souls which make up one soul: first, to wit,
A soul of each and all the bodily parts,   85
Seated therein, which works, and is what Does,
And has the use of earth, and ends the man
Downward: but, tending upward for advice,
Grows into, and again is grown into
By the next soul, which, seated in the brain,   90
Useth the first with its collected use,
And feeleth, thinketh, willeth,—is what Knows:
Which, duly tending upward in its turn,
Grows into, and again is grown into
By the last soul, that uses both the first,   95
Subsisting whether they assist or no,
And, constituting man's self, is what Is—
And leans upon the former, makes it play,
As that played off the first: and, tending up,
Holds, is upheld by, God, and ends the man   100
Upward in that dread point of intercourse,
Nor needs a place, for it returns to Him.

What Does, what Knows, what Is; three souls, one man.
I give the glossa of Theotypas.]

And then, 'A stick, once fire from end to end;   105
'Now, ashes save the tip that holds a spark!
'Yet, blow the spark, it runs back, spreads itself
'A little where the fire was: this I urge
'The soul that served me, till it task once more
'What ashes of my brain have kept their shape,   110
'And these make effort on the last o' the flesh,
'Trying to taste again the truth of things—'
(He smiled)—'their very superficial truth;
'As that ye are my sons, that it is long
'Since James and Peter had release by death,   115
'And I am only he, your brother John,
'Who saw and heard, and could remember all.
'Remember all! It is not much to say.
'What if the truth broke on me from above
'As once and oft-times? Such might hap again: 120
'Doubtlessly He might stand in presence here,
'With head wool-white, eyes flame, and feet like brass,
'The sword and the seven stars, as I have seen—
'I who now shudder only and surmise
' "How did your brother bear that sight and live?"   125

'If I live yet, it is for good, more love
'Through me to men: be nought but ashes here
'That keep awhile my semblance, who was John,—
'Still, when they scatter, there is left on earth
'No one alive who knew (consider this!)   130
'—Saw with his eyes and handled with his hands
'That which was from the first, the Word of Life.
'How will it be when none more saith "I saw"?

'Such ever was love's way: to rise, it stoops.
'Since I, whom Christ's mouth taught, was bidden
      teach,   135
'I went, for many years, about the world,
'Saying "It was so; so I heard and saw,"
'Speaking as the case asked: and men believed.

'Afterward came the message to myself
'In Patmos isle; I was not bidden teach,   140
'But simply listen, take a book and write,
'Nor set down other than the given word,
'With nothing left to my arbitrament
'To choose or change: I wrote, and men believed.
'Then, for my time grew brief, no message more,   145
'No call to write again, I found a way,
'And, reasoning from my knowledge, merely taught
'Men should, for love's sake, in love's strength
        believe;
'Or I would pen a letter to a friend
'And urge the same as friend, nor less nor more: 150
'Friends said I reasoned rightly, and believed.
'But at the last, why, I seemed left alive
'Like a sea-jelly weak on Patmos strand,
'To tell dry sea-beach gazers how I fared
'When there was mid-sea, and the mighty things;   155
'Left to repeat, "I saw, I heard, I knew,"
'And go all over the old ground again,
'With Antichrist already in the world,
'And many Antichrists, who answered prompt
' "Am I not Jasper as thyself art John?   160
' "Nay, young, whereas through age thou mayest forget:
' "Wherefore, explain, or how shall we believe?"
'I never thought to call down fire on such,
'Or, as in wonderful and early days,
'Pick up the scorpion, tread the serpent dumb;   165
'But patient stated much of the Lord's life
'Forgotten or misdelivered, and let it work:
'Since much that at the first, in deed and word,
'Lay simply and sufficiently exposed,
'Had grown (or else my soul was grown to match,   170
'Fed through such years, familiar with such light,
'Guarded and guided still to see and speak)
'Of new significance and fresh result;
'What first were guessed as points, I now knew stars,
'And named them in the Gospel I have writ.   175
'For men said, "It is getting long ago:"
' "Where is the promise of His coming?"—asked

'These young ones in their strength, as loth to wait,
'Of me who, when their sires were born, was old.
'I, for I loved them, answered, joyfully,   180
'Since I was there, and helpful in my age;
'And, in the main, I think such men believed.
'Finally, thus endeavouring, I fell sick,
'Ye brought me here, and I supposed the end,
'And went to sleep with one thought that, at least,   185
'Though the whole earth should lie in wickedness,
'We had the truth, might leave the rest to God.
'Yet now I wake in such decrepitude
'As I had slidden down and fallen afar,
'Past even the presence of my former self,   190
'Grasping the while for stay at facts which snap,
'Till I am found away from my own world,
'Feeling for foot-hold through a blank profound,
'Along with unborn people in strange lands,
'Who say—I hear said or conceive they say—   195
' "Was John at all, and did he say he saw?
' "Assure us, ere we ask what he might see!"

'And how shall I assure them? Can they share
'—They, who have flesh, a veil of youth and strength
'About each spirit, that needs must bide its time,   200
'Living and learning still as years assist
'Which wear the thickness thin, and let man see—
'With me who hardly am withheld at all,
'But shudderingly, scarce a shred between,
'Lie bare to the universal prick of light?   205
'Is it for nothing we grow old and weak,
'We whom God loves? When pain ends, gain ends too.
'To me, that story—ay, that Life and Death
'Of which I wrote "it was"—to me, it is;
'—Is, here and now: I apprehend nought else.   210
'Is not God now i' the world His power first made?
'Is not His love at issue still with sin
'Visibly when a wrong is done on earth?
'Love, wrong, and pain, what see I else around?
'Yea, and the Resurrection and Uprise   215
'To the right hand of the throne—what is it beside,

'When such truth, breaking bounds, o'erfloods my soul,
'And, as I saw the sin and death, even so
'See I the need yet transiency of both,
'The good and glory consummated thence? 220
'I saw the power; I see the Love, once weak,
'Resume the Power: and in this word "I see,"
'Lo, there is recognized the Spirit of both
'That moving o'er the spirit of man, unblinds
'His eye and bids him look. These are, I see; 225
'But ye, the children, His beloved ones too,
'Ye need,—as I should use an optic glass
'I wondered at erewhile, somewhere i' the world,
'It had been given a crafty smith to make;
'A tube, he turned on objects brought too close, 230
'Lying confusedly insubordinate
'For the unassisted eye to master once:
'Look through his tube, at distance now they lay,
'Become succinct, distinct, so small, so clear!
'Just thus, ye needs must apprehend what truth 235
'I see, reduced to plain historic fact,
'Diminished into clearness, proved a point
'And far away: ye would withdraw your sense
'From out eternity, strain it upon time,
'Then stand before that fact, that Life and Death, 240
'Stay there at gaze, till it dispart, dispread,
'As though a star should open out, all sides,
'Grow the world on you, as it is my world.

'For life, with all it yields of joy and woe,
'And hope and fear,—believe the aged friend,— 245
'Is just our chance o' the prize of learning love,
'How love might be, hath been indeed, and is;
'And that we hold thenceforth to the uttermost
'Such prize despite the envy of the world,
'And, having gained truth, keep truth: that is all. 250
'But see the double way wherein we are led,
'How the soul learns diversely from the flesh!
'With flesh, that hath so little time to stay,
'And yields mere basement for the soul's emprise,
'Expect prompt teaching. Helpful was the light, 255

'And warmth was cherishing and food was choice
'To every man's flesh, thousand years ago,
'As now to yours and mine; the body sprang
'At once to the height, and stayed: but the soul,—no!
'Since sages who, this noontide, meditate   260
'In Rome or Athens, may descry some point
'Of the eternal power, hid yestereve;
'And, as thereby the power's whole mass extends,
'So much extends the æther floating o'er,
'The love that tops the might, the Christ in God.   265
'Then, as new lessons shall be learned in these
'Till earth's work stop and useless time run out,
'So duly, daily, needs provision be
'For keeping the soul's prowess possible,
'Building new barriers as the old decay,   270
'Saving us from evasion of life's proof,
'Putting the question ever, "Does God love,
' "And will ye hold that truth against the world?"
'Ye know there needs no second proof with good
'Gained for our flesh from any earthly source: 275
'We might go freezing, ages,—give us fire,
'Thereafter we judge fire at its full worth,
'And guard it safe through every chance, ye know!
'That fable of Prometheus and his theft,
'How mortals gained Jove's fiery flower, grows old   280
'(I have been used to hear the pagans own)
'And out of mind; but fire, howe'er its birth,
'Here is it, precious to the sophist now
'Who laughs the myth of Æschylus to scorn,
'As precious to those satyrs of his play,   285
'Who touched it in gay wonder at the thing.
'While were it so with the soul,—this gift of truth
'Once grasped, were this our soul's gain safe, and sure
'To prosper as the body's gain is wont,—
'Why, man's probation would conclude, his earth   290
'Crumble; for he both reasons and decides,
'Weighs first, then chooses: will he give up fire
'For gold or purple once he knows its worth?
'Could he give Christ up were His worth as plain?
'Therefore, I say, to test man, the proofs shift,   295

'Nor may he grasp that fact like other fact,
'And straightway in his life acknowledge it,
'As, say, the indubitable bliss of fire.
'Sigh ye, "It had been easier once than now"?
'To give you answer I am left alive;   300
'Look at me who was present from the first!
'Ye know what things I saw; then came a test,
'My first, befitting me who so had seen:
' "Forsake the Christ thou sawest transfigured, Him
' "Who trod the sea and brought the dead to life?   305
' "What should wring this from thee!"—ye laugh and
      ask.
'What wrung it? Even a torchlight and a noise,
'The sudden Roman faces, violent hands,
'And fear of what the Jews might do! Just that,
'And it is written, "I forsook and fled:"   310
'There was my trial, and it ended thus.
'Ay, but my soul had gained its truth, could grow:
'Another year or two,—what little child,
'What tender woman that had seen no least
'Of all my sights, but barely heard them told,   315
'Who did not clasp the cross with a light laugh,
'Or wrap the burning robe round, thanking God?
'Well, was truth safe for ever, then? Not so.
'Already had begun the silent work
'Whereby truth, deadened of its absolute blaze,   320
'Might need love's eye to pierce the o'erstretched doubt.
'Teachers were busy, whispering "All is true
' "As the aged ones report; but youth can reach
' "Where age gropes dimly, weak with stir and strain,
' "And the full doctrine slumbers till to-day."   325
'Thus, what the Roman's lowered spear was found,
'A bar to me who touched and handled truth,
'Now proved the glozing of some new shrewd tongue,
'This Ebion, this Cerinthus or their mates,
'Till imminent was the outcry "Save our Christ!"   330
'Whereon I stated much of the Lord's life
'Forgotten or misdelivered, and let it work.
'Such work done, as it will be, what comes next?
'What do I hear say, or conceive men say,

' "Was John at all, and did he say he saw?   335
' "Assure us, ere we ask what he might see!"

'Is this indeed a burthen for late days,
'And may I help to bear it with you all,
'Using my weakness which becomes your strength?
'For if a babe were born inside this grot,   340
'Grew to a boy here, heard us praise the sun,
'Yet had but yon sole glimmer in light's place,—
'One loving him and wishful he should learn,
'Would much rejoice himself was blinded first
'Month by month here, so made to understand   345
'How eyes, born darkling, apprehend amiss:
'I think I could explain to such a child
'There was more glow outside than gleams he caught,
'Ay, nor need urge "I saw it, so believe!"
'It is a heavy burthen you shall bear   350
'In latter days, new lands, or old grown strange,
'Left without me, which must be very soon.
'What is the doubt, my brothers? Quick with it!
'I see you stand conversing, each new face,
'Either in fields, of yellow summer eves,   355
'On islets yet unnamed amid the sea;
'Or pace for shelter 'neath a portico
'Out of the crowd in some enormous town
'Where now the larks sing in a solitude;
'Or muse upon blank heaps of stone and sand   360
'Idly conjectured to be Ephesus:
'And no one asks his fellow any more
' "Where is the promise of His coming?" but
' "Was he revealed in any of His lives,
' "As Power, as Love, as Influencing Soul?"   365

'Quick, for time presses, tell the whole mind out,
'And let us ask and answer and be saved!
'My book speaks on, because it cannot pass;
'One listens quietly, nor scoffs but pleads
' "Here is a tale of things done ages since;   370
' "What truth was ever told the second day?
' "Wonders, that would prove doctrine, go for nought.

' "Remains the doctrine, love; well, we must love,
' "And what we love most, power and love in one,
' "Let us acknowledge on the record here,   375
' "Accepting these in Christ: must Christ then be?
' "Has He been? Did not we ourselves make Him?
' "Our mind receives but what it holds, no more.
' "First of the love, then; we acknowledge Christ—
' "A proof we comprehend His love, a proof   380
' "We had such love already in ourselves,
' "Knew first what else we should not recognize.
' " 'T is mere projection from man's inmost mind,
' "And, what he loves, thus falls reflected back,
' "Becomes accounted somewhat out of him;   385
' "He throws it up in air, it drops down earth's,
' "With shape, name, story added, man's old way.
' "How prove you Christ came otherwise at least?
' "Next try the power: He made and rules the world:
' "Certes there is a world once made, now ruled,   390
' "Unless things have been ever as we see.
' "Our sires declared a charioteer's yoked steeds
' "Brought the sun up the east and down the west,
' "Which only of itself now rises, sets,
' "As if a hand impelled it and a will,—   395
' "Thus they long thought, they who had will and hands:
' "But the new question's whisper is distinct,
' "Wherefore must all force needs be like ourselves?
' "We have the hands, the will; what made and drives
' "The sun is force, is law, is named, not known,   400
' "While will and love we do know; marks of these,
' "Eye-witnesses attest, so books declare—
' "As that, to punish or reward our race,
' "The sun at undue times arose or set
' "Or else stood still: what do not men affirm?   405
' "But earth requires as urgently reward
' "Or punishment to-day as years ago,
' "And none expects the sun will interpose:
' "Therefore it was mere passion and mistake,
' "Or erring zeal for right, which changed the truth.   410
' "Go back, far, farther, to the birth of things;
' "Ever the will, the intelligence, the love,

' "Man's!—which he gives, supposing he but finds,
' "As late he gave head, body, hands and feet,
' "To help these in what forms he called his gods.   415
' "First, Jove's brow, Juno's eyes were swept away,
' "But Jove's wrath, Juno's pride continued long;
' "As last, will, power, and love discarded these,
' "So law in turn discards power, love, and will.
' "What proveth God is otherwise at least?   420
' "All else, projection from the mind of man!"

'Nay, do not give me wine, for I am strong,
'But place my gospel where I put my hands.

'I say that man was made to grow, not stop;
'That help, he needed once, and needs no more,   425
'Having grown but an inch by, is withdrawn:
'For he hath new needs, and new helps to these.
'This imports solely, man should mount on each
'New height in view; the help whereby he mounts,
'The ladder-rung his foot has left, may fall,   430
'Since all things suffer change save God the Truth.
'Man apprehends Him newly at each stage
'Whereat earth's ladder drops, its service done;
'And nothing shall prove twice what once was proved.
'You stick a garden-plot with ordered twigs   435
'To show inside lie germs of herbs unborn,
'And check the careless step would spoil their birth;
'But when herbs wave, the guardian twigs may go,
'Since should ye doubt of virtues, question kinds,
'It is no longer for old twigs ye look,   440
'Which proved once underneath lay store of seed,
'But to the herb's self, by what light ye boast,
'For what fruit's signs are. This book's fruit is plain,
'Nor miracles need prove it any more.
'Doth the fruit show? Then miracles bade 'ware   445
'At first of root and stem, saved both till now
'From trampling ox, rough boar and wanton goat.
'What? Was man made a wheelwork to wind up,
'And be discharged, and straight wound up anew?

'No!—grown, his growth lasts; taught, he ne'er for-
    gets: 450
'May learn a thousand things, not twice the same.

'This might be pagan teaching: now hear mine.

'I say, that as the babe, you feed awhile,
'Becomes a boy and fit to feed himself,
'So, minds at first must be spoon-fed with truth: 455
'When they can eat, babe's-nurture is withdrawn.
'I fed the babe whether it would or no:
'I bid the boy or feed himself or starve.
'I cried once, "That ye may believe in Christ,
' "Behold this blind man shall receive his sight!"   460
'I cry now, "Urgest thou, *for I am shrewd*
' "*And smile at stories how John's word could cure*—
' "*Repeat that miracle and take my faith?*"
'I say, that miracle was duly wrought
'When, save for it, no faith was possible.   465
'Whether a change were wrought i' the shows o' the
    world,
'Whether the change came from our minds which see
'Of shows o' the world so much as and no more
'Than God wills for his purpose,—(what do I
'See now, suppose you, there where you see rock   470
'Round us?)—I know not; such was the effect,
'So faith grew, making void more miracles
'Because too much: they would compel, not help.
'I say, the acknowledgment of God in Christ
'Accepted by thy reason, solves for thee   475
'All questions in the earth and out of it,
'And has so far advanced thee to be wise.
'Wouldst thou unprove this to re-prove the proved?
'In life's mere minute, with power to use that proof,
'Leave knowledge and revert to how it sprung?   480
'Thou hast it; use it and forthwith, or die!

'For I say, this is death and the sole death,
'When a man's loss comes to him from his gain,
'Darkness from light, from knowledge ignorance,

'And lack of love from love made manifest;   485
'A lamp's death when, replete with oil, it chokes;
'A stomach's when, surcharged with food, it starves.
'With ignorance was surety of a cure.
'When man, appalled at nature, questioned first
' "What if there lurk a might behind this might?"   490
'He needed satisfaction God could give,
'And did give, as ye have the written word:
'But when he finds might still redouble might,
'Yet asks, "Since all is might, what use of will?"
'—Will, the one source of might,—he being man   495
'With a man's will and a man's might, to teach
'In little how the two combine in large,—
'That man has turned round on himself and stands,
'Which in the course of nature is, to die.

'And when man questioned, "What if there be love   500
' "Behind the will and might, as real as they?"—
'He needed satisfaction God could give,
'And did give, as ye have the written word:
'But when, beholding that love everywhere,
'He reasons, "Since such love is everywhere,   505
' "And since ourselves can love and would be loved,
' "We ourselves make the love, and Christ was not,"—
'How shall ye help this man who knows himself,
'That he must love and would be loved again,
'Yet, owning his own love that proveth Christ,   510
'Rejecteth Christ through very need of Him?
'The lamp o'erswims with oil, the stomach flags
'Loaded with nurture, and that man's soul dies.

'If he rejoin, "But this was all the while
' "A trick; the fault was, first of all, in thee,   515
' "Thy story of the places, names and dates,
' "Where, when and how the ultimate truth had rise,
' "—Thy prior truth, at last discovered none,
' "Whence now the second suffers detriment.
' "What good of giving knowledge if, because   520
' "O' the manner of the gift, its profit fail?
' "And why refuse what modicum of help

' "Had stopped the after-doubt, impossible
' "'I' the face of truth—truth absolute, uniform?
' "Why must I hit of this and miss of that,   525
' "Distinguish just as I be weak or strong,
' "And not ask of thee and have answer prompt,
' "Was this once, was it not once?—then and now
' "And evermore, plain truth from man to man.
' "Is John's procedure just the heathen bard's?   530
' "Put question of his famous play again
' "How for the ephemerals' sake Jove's fire was filched,
' "And carried in a cane and brought to earth:
' "*The fact is in the fable*, cry the wise,
' "*Mortals obtained the boon, so much is fact*,   535
' "*Though fire be spirit and produced on earth.*
' "As with the Titan's, so now with thy tale:
' "Why breed in us perplexity, mistake,
' "Nor tell the whole truth in the proper words?"

'I answer, Have ye yet to argue out   540
'The very primal thesis, plainest law,
'—Man is not God but hath God's end to serve,
'A master to obey, a course to take,
'Somewhat to cast off, somewhat to become?
'Grant this, then man must pass from old to new,   545
'From vain to real, from mistake to fact,
'From what once seemed good, to what now proves best.
'How could man have progression otherwise?
'Before the point was mooted "What is God?"
'No savage man inquired "What am myself?"   550
'Much less replied, "First, last, and best of things."
'Man takes that title now if he believes
'Might can exist with neither will nor love,
'In God's case—what he names now Nature's Law—
'While in himself he recognizes love   555
'No less than might and will: and rightly takes.
'Since if man prove the sole existent thing
'Where these combine, whatever their degree,
'However weak the might or will or love,
'So they be found there, put in evidence,—   560
'He is as surely higher in the scale

'Than any might with neither love nor will,
'As life, apparent in the poorest midge,
'(When the faint dust-speck flits, ye guess its wing)
'Is marvellous beyond dead Atlas' self—   565
'Given to the nobler midge for resting-place!
'Thus, man proves best and highest—God, in fine,
'And thus the victory leads but to defeat,
'The gain to loss, best rise to the worst fall,
'His life becomes impossible, which is death.   570

'But if, appealing thence, he cower, avouch
'He is mere man, and in humility
'Neither may know God nor mistake himself;
'I point to the immediate consequence
'And say, by such confession straight he falls   575
'Into man's place, a thing nor God nor beast,
'Made to know that he can know and not more:
'Lower than God who knows all and can all,
'Higher than beasts which know and can so far
'As each beast's limit, perfect to an end,   580
'Nor conscious that they know, nor craving more;
'While man knows partly but conceives beside,
'Creeps ever on from fancies to the fact,
'And in this striving, this converting air
'Into a solid he may grasp and use,   585
'Finds progress, man's distinctive mark alone,
'Not God's, and not the beasts': God is, they are,
'Man partly is and wholly hopes to be.
'Such progress could no more attend his soul
'Were all it struggles after found at first   590
'And guesses changed to knowledge absolute,
'Than motion wait his body, were all else
'Than it the solid earth on every side,
'Where now through space he moves from rest to rest.
'Man, therefore, thus conditioned, must expect   595
'He could not, what he knows now, know at first;
'What he considers that he knows to-day,
'Come but to-morrow, he will find misknown;
'Getting increase of knowledge, since he learns
'Because he lives, which is to be a man,   600

E e

'Set to instruct himself by his past self:
'First, like the brute, obliged by facts to learn,
'Next, as man may, obliged by his own mind,
'Bent, habit, nature, knowledge turned to law.
'God's gift was that man should conceive of truth   605
'And yearn to gain it, catching at mistake,
'As midway help till he reach fact indeed.
'The statuary ere he mould a shape
'Boasts a like gift, the shape's idea, and next
'The aspiration to produce the same;   610
'So, taking clay, he calls his shape thereout,
'Cries ever "Now I have the thing I see":
'Yet all the while goes changing what was wrought,
'From falsehood like the truth, to truth itself.
'How were it had he cried "I see no face,   615
' "No breast, no feet i' the ineffectual clay"?
'Rather commend him that he clapped his hands,
'And laughed "It is my shape and lives again!"
'Enjoyed the falsehood, touched it on to truth,
'Until yourselves applaud the flesh indeed   620
'In what is still flesh-imitating clay.
'Right in you, right in him, such way be man's!
'God only makes the live shape at a jet.
'Will ye renounce this pact of creatureship?
'The pattern on the Mount subsists no more,   625
'Seemed awhile, then returned to nothingness;
'But copies, Moses strove to make thereby,
'Serve still and are replaced as time requires:
'By these, make newest vessels, reach the type!
'If ye demur, this judgment on your head,   630
'Never to reach the ultimate, angels' law,
'Indulging every instinct of the soul
'There where law, life, joy, impulse are one thing!

'Such is the burthen of the latest time.
'I have survived to hear it with my ears,   635
'Answer it with my lips: does this suffice?
'For if there be a further woe than such,
'Wherein my brothers struggling need a hand,
'So long as any pulse is left in mine,

'May I be absent even longer yet,   640
'Plucking the blind ones back from the abyss,
'Though I should tarry a new hundred years!'

But he was dead; 't was about noon, the day
Somewhat declining: we five buried him
That eve, and then, dividing, went five ways,   645
And I, disguised, returned to Ephesus.

By this, the cave's mouth must be filled with sand.
Valens is lost, I know not of his trace;
The Bactrian was but a wild childish man,
And could not write nor speak, but only loved: 650
So, lest the memory of this go quite,
Seeing that I to-morrow fight the beasts,
I tell the same to Phœbas, whom believe!
For many look again to find that face,
Beloved John's to whom I ministered,   655
Somewhere in life about the world; they err:
Either mistaking what was darkly spoke
At ending of his book, as he relates,
Or misconceiving somewhat of this speech
Scattered from mouth to mouth, as I suppose.   660
Believe ye will not see him any more
About the world with his divine regard!
For all was as I say, and now the man
Lies as he lay once, breast to breast with God.

———

[Cerinthus read and mused; one added this: 665

'If Christ, as thou affirmest, be of men
'Mere man, the first and best but nothing more,—
'Account Him, for reward of what He was,
'Now and for ever, wretchedest of all.
'For see; Himself conceived of life as love,   670
'Conceived of love as what must enter in,
'Fill up, make one with His each soul He loved:
'Thus much for man's joy, all men's joy for Him.
'Well, He is gone, thou sayest, to fit reward.

'But by this time are many souls set free,   675
'And very many still retained alive:
'Nay, should His coming be delayed awhile,
'Say, ten years longer (twelve years, some compute)
'See if, for every finger of thy hands,
'There be not found, that day the world shall end,   680
'Hundreds of souls, each holding by Christ's word
'That He will grow incorporate with all,
'With me as Pamphylax, with him as John,
'Groom for each bride! Can a mere man do this?
'Yet Christ saith, this He lived and died to do.   685
'Call Christ, then, the illimitable God,
'Or lost!'

But 't was Cerinthus that is lost.]

CALIBAN UPON SETEBOS; OR, NATURAL
THEOLOGY IN THE ISLAND

'Thou thoughtest that I was altogether such a one as thyself.'

['WILL sprawl, now that the heat of day is best,
Flat on his belly in the pit's much mire,
With elbows wide, fists clenched to prop his chin.
And, while he kicks both feet in the cool slush,
And feels about his spine small eft-things course,   5
Run in and out each arm, and make him laugh:
And while above his head a pompion-plant,
Coating the cave-top as a brow its eye,
Creeps down to touch and tickle hair and beard,
And now a flower drops with a bee inside,   10
And now a fruit to snap at, catch and crunch,—
He looks out o'er yon sea which sunbeams cross
And recross till they weave a spider-web
(Meshes of fire, some great fish breaks at times)
And talks to his own self, howe'er he please,   15
Touching that other, whom his dam called God.
Because to talk about Him, vexes—ha,
Could He but know! and time to vex is now,
When talk is safer than in winter-time.

Moreover Prosper and Miranda sleep   20
In confidence he drudges at their task,
And it is good to cheat the pair, and gibe,
Letting the rank tongue blossom into speech.]

Setebos, Setebos, and Setebos!
'Thinketh, He dwelleth i' the cold o' the moon.   25

'Thinketh He made it, with the sun to match,
But not the stars; the stars came otherwise;
Only made clouds, winds, meteors, such as that:
Also this isle, what lives and grows thereon,
And snaky sea which rounds and ends the same.   30

'Thinketh, it came of being ill at ease:
He hated that He cannot change His cold,
Nor cure its ache. 'Hath spied an icy fish
That longed to 'scape the rock-stream where she lived,
And thaw herself within the lukewarm brine   35
O' the lazy sea her stream thrusts far amid,
A crystal spike 'twixt two warm walls of wave;
Only, she ever sickened, found repulse
At the other kind of water, not her life,
(Green-dense and dim-delicious, bred o' the sun)   40
Flounced back from bliss she was not born to breathe,
And in her old bounds buried her despair,
Hating and loving warmth alike: so He.

'Thinketh, He made thereat the sun, this isle,
Trees and the fowls here, beast and creeping thing.   45
Yon otter, sleek-wet, black, lithe as a leech;
Yon auk, one fire-eye in a ball of foam,
That floats and feeds; a certain badger brown
He hath watched hunt with that slant white-wedge eye
By moonlight; and the pie with the long tongue   50
That pricks deep into oakwarts for a worm,
And says a plain word when she finds her prize,
But will not eat the ants; the ants themselves
That build a wall of seeds and settled stalks
About their hole—He made all these and more,   55
Made all we see, and us, in spite: how else?
He could not, Himself, make a second self

To be His mate; as well have made Himself:
He would not make what he mislikes or slights,
An eyesore to Him, or not worth His pains: 60
But did, in envy, listlessness or sport,
Make what Himself would fain, in a manner, be—
Weaker in most points, stronger in a few,
Worthy, and yet mere playthings all the while,
Things He admires and mocks too,—that is it.   65
Because, so brave, so better though they be,
It nothing skills if He begin to plague.
Look now, I melt a gourd-fruit into mash,
Add honeycomb and pods, I have perceived,
Which bite like finches when they bill and kiss,—   70
Then, when froth rises bladdery, drink up all,
Quick, quick, till maggots scamper through my brain;
Last, throw me on my back i' the seeded thyme,
And wanton, wishing I were born a bird.
Put case, unable to be what I wish,   75
I yet could make a live bird out of clay:
Would not I take clay, pinch my Caliban
Able to fly?—for, there, see, he hath wings,
And great comb like the hoopoe's to admire,
And there, a sting to do his foes offence,   80
There, and I will that he begin to live,
Fly to yon rock-top, nip me off the horns
Of grigs high up that make the merry din,
Saucy through their veined wings, and mind me not.
In which feat, if his leg snapped, brittle clay,   85
And he lay stupid-like,—why, I should laugh;
And if he, spying me, should fall to weep,
Beseech me to be good, repair his wrong,
Bid his poor leg smart less or grow again,—
Well, as the chance were, this might take or else   90
Not take my fancy: I might hear his cry,
And give the mankin three sound legs for one,
Or pluck the other off, leave him like an egg,
And lessoned he was mine and merely clay.
Were this no pleasure, lying in the thyme,   95
Drinking the mash, with brain become alive,
Making and marring clay at will? So He.

'Thinketh, such shows nor right nor wrong in Him,
Nor kind, nor cruel: He is strong and Lord.
'Am strong myself compared to yonder crabs 100
That march now from the mountain to the sea,
'Let twenty pass, and stone the twenty-first,
Loving not, hating not, just choosing so.
'Say, the first straggler that boasts purple spots
Shall join the file, one pincer twisted off; 105
'Say, this bruised fellow shall receive a worm,
And two worms he whose nippers end in red;
As it likes me each time, I do: so He.

Well then, 'supposeth He is good i' the main,
Placable if His mind and ways were guessed, 110
But rougher than His handiwork, be sure!
Oh, He hath made things worthier than Himself,
And envieth that, so helped, such things do more
Than He who made them! What consoles but this?
That they, unless through Him, do nought at all, 115
And must submit: what other use in things?
'Hath cut a pipe of pithless elder-joint
That, blown through, gives exact the scream o' the jay
When from her wing you twitch the feathers blue:
Sound this, and little birds that hate the jay 120
Flock within stone's throw, glad their foe is hurt:
Put case such pipe could prattle and boast forsooth
'I catch the birds, I am the crafty thing,
'I make the cry my maker cannot make
'With his great round mouth; he must blow through
    mine!' 125
Would not I smash it with my foot? So He.

But wherefore rough, why cold and ill at ease?
Aha, that is a question! Ask, for that,
What knows,—the something over Setebos
That made Him, or He, may be, found and fought, 130
Worsted, drove off and did to nothing, perchance.
There may be something quiet o'er His head,
Out of His reach, that feels nor joy nor grief,
Since both derive from weakness in some way.

I joy because the quails come; would not joy 135
Could I bring quails here when I have a mind:
This Quiet, all it hath a mind to, doth.
'Esteemeth stars the outposts of its couch,
But never spends much thought nor care that way.
It may look up, work up,—the worse for those 140
It works on! 'Careth but for Setebos
The many-handed as a cuttle-fish,
Who, making Himself feared through what He does,
Looks up, first, and perceives He cannot soar
To what is quiet and hath happy life; 145
Next looks down here, and out of very spite
Makes this a bauble-world to ape yon real,
These good things to match those as hips do grapes.
'T is solace making baubles, ay, and sport.
Himself peeped late, eyed Prosper at his books 150
Careless and lofty, lord now of the isle:
Vexed, 'stitched a book of broad leaves, arrow-shaped,
Wrote thereon, he knows what, prodigious words;
Has peeled a wand and called it by a name;
Weareth at whiles for an enchanter's robe 155
The eyed skin of a supple ocelot;
And hath an ounce sleeker than youngling mole,
A four-legged serpent he makes cower and couch,
Now snarl, now hold its breath and mind his eye,
And saith she is Miranda and my wife: 160
'Keeps for his Ariel a tall pouch-bill crane
He bids go wade for fish and straight disgorge;
Also a sea-beast, lumpish, which he snared,
Blinded the eyes of, and brought somewhat tame,
And split its toe-webs, and now pens the drudge 165
In a hole o' the rock and calls him Caliban;
A bitter heart that bides its time and bites.
'Plays thus at being Prosper in a way,
Taketh his mirth with make-believes: so He.

His dam held that the Quiet made all things 170
Which Setebos vexed only: 'holds not so.
Who made them weak, meant weakness He might vex.
Had He meant other, while His hand was in,

Why not make horny eyes no thorn could prick,
Or plate my scalp with bone against the snow,   175
Or overscale my flesh 'neath joint and joint,
Like an orc's armour? Ay,—so spoil His sport!
He is the One now: only He doth all.

'Saith, He may like, perchance, what profits Him.
Ay, himself loves what does him good; but why?   180
'Gets good no otherwise. This blinded beast
Loves whoso places flesh-meat on his nose,
But, had he eyes, would want no help, but hate
Or love, just as it liked him: He hath eyes.
Also it pleaseth Setebos to work,   185
Use all His hands, and exercise much craft,
By no means for the love of what is worked.
'Tasteth, himself, no finer good i' the world
When all goes right, in this safe summer-time,
And he wants little, hungers, aches not much,   190
Than trying what to do with wit and strength.
'Falls to make something: 'piled yon pile of turfs,
And squared and stuck there squares of soft white chalk,
And, with a fish-tooth, scratched a moon on each,
And set up endwise certain spikes of tree,   195
And crowned the whole with a sloth's skull a-top,
Found dead i' the woods, too hard for one to kill.
No use at all i' the work, for work's sole sake;
'Shall some day knock it down again: so He.

'Saith He is terrible: watch His feats in proof!   200
One hurricane will spoil six good months' hope.
He hath a spite against me, that I know,
Just as He favours Prosper, who knows why?
So it is, all the same, as well I find.
'Wove wattles half the winter, fenced them firm   205
With stone and stake to stop she-tortoises
Crawling to lay their eggs here: well, one wave,
Feeling the foot of Him upon its neck,
Gaped as a snake does, lolled out its large tongue,
And licked the whole labour flat: so much for spite.   210
'Saw a ball flame down late (yonder it lies)

Where, half an hour before, I slept i' the shade:
Often they scatter sparkles: there is force!
'Dug up a newt He may have envied once
And turned to stone, shut up inside a stone.   215
Please Him and hinder this?—What Prosper does?
Aha, if He would tell me how! Not He!
There is the sport: discover how or die!
All need not die, for of the things o' the isle
Some flee afar, some dive, some run up trees;   220
Those at His mercy,—why, they please Him most
When . . when . . well, never try the same way twice!
Repeat what act has pleased, He may grow wroth.
You must not know His ways, and play Him off,
Sure of the issue. 'Doth the like himself: 225
'Spareth a squirrel that it nothing fears
But steals the nut from underneath my thumb,
And when I threat, bites stoutly in defence:
'Spareth an urchin that contrariwise,
Curls up into a ball, pretending death   230
For fright at my approach: the two ways please.
But what would move my choler more than this,
That either creature counted on its life
To-morrow and next day and all days to come,
Saying, forsooth, in the inmost of its heart,   235
'Because he did so yesterday with me,
'And otherwise with such another brute,
'So must he do henceforth and always.'—Ay?
Would teach the reasoning couple what 'must' means!
'Doth as he likes, or wherefore Lord? So He.   240

'Conceiveth all things will continue thus,
And we shall have to live in fear of Him
So long as He lives, keeps His strength: no change,
If He have done His best, make no new world
To please Him more, so leave off watching this,—   245
If He surprise not even the Quiet's self
Some strange day,—or, suppose, grow into it
As grubs grow butterflies: else, here are we,
And there is He, and nowhere help at all.

'Believeth with the life, the pain shall stop. 250
His dam held different, that after death
He both plagued enemies and feasted friends:
Idly! He doth His worst in this our life,
Giving just respite lest we die through pain,
Saving last pain for worst,—with which, an end. 255
Meanwhile, the best way to escape His ire
Is, not to seem too happy. 'Sees, himself,
Yonder two flies, with purple films and pink,
Bask on the pompion-bell above: kills both.
'Sees two black painful beetles roll their ball 260
On head and tail as if to save their lives:
Moves them the stick away they strive to clear.

Even so, 'would have Him misconceive, suppose
This Caliban strives hard and ails no less,
And always, above all else, envies Him; 265
Wherefore he mainly dances on dark nights,
Moans in the sun, gets under holes to laugh,
And never speaks his mind save housed as now:
Outside, 'groans, curses. If He caught me here,
O'erheard this speech, and asked 'What chucklest at?' 270
'Would, to appease Him, cut a finger off,
Or of my three kid yearlings burn the best,
Or let the toothsome apples rot on tree,
Or push my tame beast for the orc to taste:
While myself lit a fire, and made a song 275
And sung it, '*What I hate, be consecrate*
'*To celebrate Thee and Thy state, no mate*
'*For Thee; what see for envy in poor me?*'
Hoping the while, since evils sometimes mend,
Warts rub away and sores are cured with slime, 280
That some strange day, will either the Quiet catch
And conquer Setebos, or likelier He
Decrepit may doze, doze, as good as die.

[What, what? A curtain o'er the world at once!
Crickets stop hissing; not a bird—or, yes, 285
There scuds His raven that has told Him all!
It was fool's play, this prattling! Ha! The wind
Shoulders the pillared dust, death's house o' the move,

And fast invading fires begin! White blaze—
A tree's head snaps—and there, there, there, there,
    there,   290
His thunder follows! Fool to gibe at Him!
Lo! 'Lieth flat and loveth Setebos!
'Maketh his teeth meet through his upper lip,
Will let those quails fly, will not eat this month
One little mess of whelks, so he may 'scape!]   295

CONFESSIONS

I

WHAT is he buzzing in my ears?
    'Now that I come to die,
'Do I view the world as a vale of tears?'
    Ah, reverend sir, not I!

II

What I viewed there once, what I view again   5
    Where the physic bottles stand
On the table's edge,—is a suburb lane,
    With a wall to my bedside hand.

III

That lane sloped, much as the bottles do,
    From a house you could descry   10
O'er the garden-wall: is the curtain blue
    Or green to a healthy eye?

IV

To mine, it serves for the old June weather
    Blue above lane and wall;
And that farthest bottle labelled 'Ether'   15
    Is the house o'ertopping all.

V

At a terrace, somewhere near the stopper,
    There watched for me, one June,
A girl: I know, sir, it's improper,
    My poor mind's out of tune.   20

VI

Only, there was a way . . . you crept
  Close by the side, to dodge
Eyes in the house, two eyes except:
  They styled their house 'The Lodge.'

VII

What right had a lounger up their lane?   25
  But, by creeping very close,
With the good wall's help,—their eyes might strain
  And stretch themselves to Oes,

VIII

Yet never catch her and me together,
  As she left the attic, there,   30
By the rim of the bottle labelled 'Ether,'
  And stole from stair to stair,

IX

And stood by the rose-wreathed gate. Alas,
  We loved, sir—used to meet:
How sad and bad and mad it was—   35
  But then, how it was sweet!

MAY AND DEATH [1]

I

I wish that when you died last May,
  Charles, there had died along with you
Three parts of spring's delightful things;
  Ay, and, for me, the fourth part too.

II

A foolish thought, and worse, perhaps!   5
  There must be many a pair of friends
Who, arm in arm, deserve the warm
  Moon-births and the long evening-ends.

[1] 'May and Death' was first published in *The Keepsake* for 1857.

III

So, for their sake, be May still May!
   Let their new time, as mine of old,   10
Do all it did for me: I bid
   Sweet sights and sounds throng manifold.

IV

Only, one little sight, one plant,
   Woods have in May, that starts up green
Save a sole streak which, so to speak,   15
   Is spring's blood, spilt its leaves between,—

V

That, they might spare; a certain wood
   Might miss the plant; their loss were small:
But I,—whene'er the leaf grows there,
   Its drop comes from my heart, that's all.   20

PROSPICE [1]

FEAR death?—to feel the fog in my throat,
   The mist in my face,
When the snows begin, and the blasts denote
   I am nearing the place,
The power of the night, the press of the storm,   5
   The post of the foe;
Where he stands, the Arch Fear in a visible form,
   Yet the strong man must go:
For the journey is done and the summit attained,
   And the barriers fall,   10
Though a battle's to fight ere the guerdon be gained,
   The reward of it all.
I was ever a fighter, so—one fight more,
   The best and the last!
I would hate that death bandaged my eyes, and forbore, 15
   And bade me creep past.

---

[1] 'Prospice' was first published in the American *Atlantic Monthly* in May 1864, in the June number.

No! let me taste the whole of it, fare like my peers
    The heroes of old,
Bear the brunt, in a minute pay glad life's arrears
    Of pain, darkness and cold.   20
For sudden the worst turns the best to the brave,
    The black minute's at end,
And the elements' rage, the fiend-voices that rave,
    Shall dwindle, shall blend,
Shall change, shall become first a peace out of pain,   25
    Then a light, then thy breast,
O thou soul of my soul! I shall clasp thee again,
    And with God be the rest!

YOUTH AND ART

I

It once might have been, once only:
    We lodged in a street together,
You, a sparrow on the housetop lonely,
    I, a lone she-bird of his feather.

II

Your trade was with sticks and clay,   5
    You thumbed, thrust, patted and polished,
Then laughed 'They will see some day
    'Smith made, and Gibson demolished.'

III

My business was song, song, song;
    I chirped, cheeped, trilled and twittered,   10
'Kate Brown's on the boards ere long,
    'And Grisi's existence embittered!'

IV

I earned no more by a warble
    Than you by a sketch in plaster;
You wanted a piece of marble,   15
    I needed a music-master.

V

We studied hard in our styles,
   Chipped each at a crust like Hindoos,
For air looked out on the tiles,
   For fun watched each other's windows.   20

VI

You lounged, like a boy of the South,
   Cap and blouse—nay, a bit of beard too;
Or you got it, rubbing your mouth
   With fingers the clay adhered to.

VII

And I—soon managed to find   25
   Weak points in the flower-fence facing,
Was forced to put up a blind
   And be safe in my corset-lacing.

VIII

No harm! It was not my fault
   If you never turned your eye's tail up   30
As I shook upon E *in alt*,
   Or ran the chromatic scale up:

IX

For spring bade the sparrows pair,
   And the boys and girls gave guesses,
And stalls in our street looked rare   35
   With bulrush and watercresses.

X

Why did not you pinch a flower
   In a pellet of clay and fling it?
Why did not I put a power
   Of thanks in a look, or sing it?   40

XI

I did look, sharp as a lynx,
   (And yet the memory rankles)
When models arrived, some minx
   Tripped up-stairs, she and her ankles.

XII

But I think I gave you as good!
　'That foreign fellow,—who can know   45
'How she pays, in a playful mood,
　'For his tuning her that piano?'

XIII

Could you say so, and never say
　'Suppose we join hands and fortunes,   50
'And I fetch her from over the way,
　'Her, piano, and long tunes and short tunes?'

XIV

No, no: you would not be rash,
　Nor I rasher and something over:
You've to settle yet Gibson's hash,   55
　And Grisi yet lives in clover.

XV

But you meet the Prince at the Board,
　I'm queen myself at *bals-paré*,
I've married a rich old lord,
　And you 're dubbed knight and an R.A.   60

XVI

Each life unfulfilled, you see;
　It hangs still, patchy and scrappy:
We have not sighed deep, laughed free,
　Starved, feasted, despaired,—been happy.

XVII

And nobody calls you a dunce,   65
　And people suppose me clever:
This could but have happened once,
　And we missed it, lost it for ever.

A FACE

If one could have that little head of hers
  Painted upon a background of pale gold,
Such as the Tuscan's early art prefers!
  No shade encroaching on the matchless mould
Of those two lips, which should be opening soft   5
  In the pure profile; not as when she laughs,
For that spoils all: but rather as if aloft
  Yon hyacinth, she loves so, leaned its staff's
Burthen of honey-coloured buds to kiss
And capture 'twixt the lips apart for this.   10
Then her lithe neck, three fingers might surround,
How it should waver on the pale gold ground
Up to the fruit-shaped, perfect chin it lifts!
I know, Correggio loves to mass, in rifts
Of heaven, his angel faces, orb on orb   15
Breaking its outline, burning shades absorb:
But these are only massed there, I should think,
  Waiting to see some wonder momently
  Grow out, stand full, fade slow against the sky
  (That's the pale ground you'd see this sweet face by), 20
  All heaven, meanwhile, condensed into one eye
Which fears to lose the wonder, should it wink.

A LIKENESS

Some people hang portraits up
In a room where they dine or sup:
  And the wife clinks tea-things under,
And her cousin, he stirs his cup,
  Asks, 'Who was the lady, I wonder?'   5
' 'T is a daub John bought at a sale,'
  Quoth the wife,—looks black as thunder:
'What a shade beneath her nose!
'Snuff-taking, I suppose,—'
Adds the cousin, while John's corns ail.   10

Or else, there's no wife in the case,
But the portrait's queen of the place,
Alone mid the other spoils
Of youth,—masks, gloves and foils,

And pipe-sticks, rose, cherry-tree, jasmine,   15
   And the long whip, the tandem-lasher,
And the cast from a fist ('not, alas! mine,
   'But my master's, the Tipton Slasher'),
And the cards where pistol-balls mark ace,
And a satin shoe used for cigar-case,   20
And the chamois-horns ('shot in the Chablais')
   And prints—Rarey drumming on Cruiser,
   And Sayers, our champion, the bruiser,
And the little edition of Rabelais:
Where a friend, with both hands in his pockets,   25
   May saunter up close to examine it,
   And remark a good deal of Jane Lamb in it,
'But the eyes are half out of their sockets;
'That hair's not so bad, where the gloss is,
'But they've made the girl's nose a proboscis: 30
'Jane Lamb, that we danced with at Vichy!
'What, is not she Jane? Then, who is she?'

All that I own is a print,
An etching, a mezzotint;
'T is a study, a fancy, a fiction,   35
Yet a fact (take my conviction)
Because it has more than a hint
   Of a certain face, I never
Saw elsewhere touch or trace of
In women I've seen the face of: 40
   Just an etching, and, so far, clever.

I keep my prints, an imbroglio,
Fifty in one portfolio.
When somebody tries my claret,
We turn round chairs to the fire,   45
Chirp over days in a garret,
   Chuckle o'er increase of salary,
Taste the good fruits of our leisure,
Talk about pencil and lyre,
   And the National Portrait Gallery: 50
Then I exhibit my treasure.
After we 've turned over twenty,

And the debt of wonder my crony owes
Is paid to my Marc Antonios,
He stops me—'*Festina lentè!*   55
'What's that sweet thing there, the etching?'
How my waistcoat-strings want stretching,
　　How my cheeks grow red as tomatos,
How my heart leaps! But hearts, after leaps,
　　ache.

'By the by, you must take, for a keepsake,   60
　　'That other, you praised, of Volpato's.'
The fool! would he try a flight further and say—
He never saw, never before to-day,
What was able to take his breath away,
A face to lose youth for, to occupy age   65
With the dream of, meet death with,—why, I 'll
　　not engage
But that, half in a rapture and half in a rage,
I should toss him the thing's self—' 'T is only a
　　duplicate,
'A thing of no value! Take it, I supplicate!'

MR. SLUDGE, 'THE MEDIUM'

Now, don't, sir! Don't expose me! Just this once!
This was the first and only time, I 'll swear,—
Look at me,—see, I kneel,—the only time,
I swear, I ever cheated,—yes, by the soul
Of Her who hears—(your sainted mother, sir!)   5
All, except this last accident, was truth—
This little kind of slip!—and even this,
It was your own wine, sir, the good champagne,
(I took it for Catawba, you 're so kind)
Which put the folly in my head!

　　　　　　　　　　　'Get up?'   10
You still inflict on me that terrible face?
You show no mercy?—Not for Her dear sake,
The sainted spirit's, whose soft breath even now
Blows on my cheek—(don't you feel something, sir?)
You 'll tell?

Go tell, then! Who the devil cares   15
What such a rowdy chooses to . . .
                        Aie—aie—aie!
Please, sir! your thumbs are through my windpipe, sir!
Ch—ch!

            Well, sir, I hope you 've done it now!
Oh Lord! I little thought, sir, yesterday,
When your departed mother spoke those words   20
Of peace through me, and moved you, sir, so much,
You gave me—(very kind it was of you)
These shirt-studs—(better take them back again,
Please, sir)—yes, little did I think so soon
A trifle of trick, all through a glass too much   25
Of his own champagne, would change my best of friends
Into an angry gentleman!

                   Though, 't was wrong.
I don't contest the point; your anger 's just:
Whatever put such folly in my head,
I know 't was wicked of me. There 's a thick   30
Dusk undeveloped spirit (I 've observed)
Owes me a grudge—a negro's, I should say,
Or else an Irish emigrant's; yourself
Explained the case so well last Sunday, sir,
When we had summoned Franklin to clear up   35
A point about those shares i' the telegraph:
Ay, and he swore . . . or might it be Tom Paine? . . .
Thumping the table close by where I crouched,
He 'd do me soon a mischief: that 's come true!
Why, now your face clears! I was sure it would!   40
Then, this one time . . . don't take your hand away,
Through yours I surely kiss your mother's hand . . .
You 'll promise to forgive me?—or, at least,
Tell nobody of this? Consider, sir!
What harm can mercy do? Would but the shade   45
Of the venerable dead-one just vouchsafe
A rap or tip! What bit of paper 's here?
Suppose we take a pencil, let her write,
Make the least sign, she urges on her child

Forgiveness? There now! Eh? Oh! 'T was your foot,   50
And not a natural creak, sir?

                           Answer, then!
Once, twice, thrice . . . see, I'm waiting to say 'thrice!'
All to no use? No sort of hope for me?
It 's all to post to Greeley's newspaper?

What? If I told you all about the tricks?   55
Upon my soul!—the whole truth, and nought else,
And how there 's been some falsehood—for your part,
Will you engage to pay my passage out,
And hold your tongue until I'm safe on board?
England 's the place, not Boston—no offence!   60
I see what makes you hesitate: don't fear!
I mean to change my trade and cheat no more,
Yes, this time really it 's upon my soul!
Be my salvation!—under Heaven, of course.
I 'll tell some queer things. Sixty Vs must do.   65
A trifle, though, to start with! We 'll refer
The question to this table?

                        How you 're changed!
Then split the difference; thirty more, we 'll say.
Ay, but you leave my presents! Else I 'll swear
'T was all through those: you wanted yours again,   70
So, picked a quarrel with me, to get them back!
Tread on a worm, it turns, sir! If I turn,
Your fault! 'T is you 'll have forced me! Who 's obliged
To give up life yet try no self-defence?
At all events, I 'll run the risk. Eh?

                        Done!   75
May I sit, sir? This dear old table, now!
Please, sir, a parting egg-nogg and cigar!
I 've been so happy with you! Nice stuffed chairs,
And sympathetic sideboards; what an end
To all the instructive evenings! (It 's alight.)   80
Well, nothing lasts, as Bacon came and said.
Here goes,—but keep your temper, or I 'll scream!

Fol-lol-the-rido-liddle-iddle-ol!
You see, sir, it's your own fault more than mine;
It's all your fault, you curious gentlefolk!   85
You're prigs,—excuse me,—like to look so spry,
So clever, while you cling by half a claw
To the perch whereon you puff yourselves at roost,
Such piece of self-conceit as serves for perch
Because you chose it, so it must be safe.   90
Oh, otherwise you're sharp enough! You spy
Who slips, who slides, who holds by help of wing,
Wanting real foothold,—who can't keep upright
On the other perch, your neighbour chose, not you:
There's no outwitting you respecting him!   95
For instance, men love money—that, you know
And what men do to gain it: well, suppose
A poor lad, say a help's son in your house,
Listening at keyholes, hears the company
Talk grand of dollars, V-notes, and so forth,   100
How hard they are to get, how good to hold,
How much they buy,—if, suddenly, in pops he—
'*I*'ve got a V-note!'—what do you say to him?
What's your first word which follows your last kick?
'Where did you steal it, rascal?' That's because   105
He finds you, fain would fool you, off your perch,
Not on the special piece of nonsense, sir,
Elected your parade-ground: let him try
Lies to the end of the list,—'He picked it up,
'His cousin died and left it him by will,   110
'The President flung it to him, riding by,
'An actress trucked it for a curl of his hair,
'He dreamed of luck and found his shoe enriched,
'He dug up clay, and out of clay made gold'—
How would you treat such possibilities?   115
Would not you, prompt, investigate the case
With cow-hide? 'Lies, lies, lies,' you'd shout: and why?
Which of the stories might not prove mere truth?
This last, perhaps, that clay was turned to coin!
Let's see, now, give him me to speak for him!   120
How many of your rare philosophers,
In plaguy books I've had to dip into,

Believed gold could be made thus, saw it made
And made it? Oh, with such philosophers
You 're on your best behaviour! While the lad—   125
With him, in a trice, you settle likelihoods,
Nor doubt a moment how he got his prize:
In his case, you hear, judge and execute,
All in a breath: so would most men of sense.

But let the same lad hear you talk as grand   130
At the same keyhole, you and company,
Of signs and wonders, the invisible world;
How wisdom scouts our vulgar unbelief
More than our vulgarest credulity;
How good men have desired to see a ghost,   135
What Johnson used to say, what Wesley did,
Mother Goose thought, and fiddle-diddle-dee:—
If he breaks in with, 'Sir, *I* saw a ghost!'
Ah, the ways change! He finds you perched and prim;
It 's a conceit of yours that ghosts may be: 140
There 's no talk now of cow-hide. 'Tell it out!
'Don't fear us! Take your time and recollect!
'Sit down first: try a glass of wine, my boy!
'And, David, (is not that your Christian name?)
'Of all things, should this happen twice—it may—   145
'Be sure, while fresh in mind, you let us know!'
Does the boy blunder, blurt out this, blab that,
Break down in the other, as beginners will?
All 's candour, all 's considerateness—'No haste!
'Pause and collect yourself! We understand!   150
'That 's the bad memory, or the natural shock,
'Or the unexplained *phenomena*!'

                                    Egad,
The boy takes heart of grace; finds, never fear,
The readiest way to ope your own heart wide,
Show—what I call your peacock-perch, pet post   155
To strut, and spread the tail, and squawk upon!
'Just as you thought, much as you might expect!
'There be more things in heaven and earth, Horatio,' . .
And so on. Shall not David take the hint,

Grow bolder, stroke you down at quickened rate?   160
If he ruffle a feather, it 's 'Gently, patiently!
'Manifestations are so weak at first!
'Doubting, moreover, kills them, cuts all short,
'Cures with a vengeance!'

          There, sir, that 's your style!
You and your boy—such pains bestowed on him,   165
Or any headpiece of the average worth,
To teach, say, Greek, would perfect him apace,
Make him a Person ('Porson?' thank you, sir!)
Much more, proficient in the art of lies.
You never leave the lesson! Fire alight,   170
Catch you permitting it to die! You 've friends;
There 's no withholding knowledge,—least from those
Apt to look elsewhere for their souls' supply:
Why should not you parade your lawful prize?
Who finds a picture, digs a medal up,   175
Hits on a first edition,—he henceforth
Gives it his name, grows notable: how much more,
Who ferrets out a 'medium'? 'David 's yours,
'You highly-favoured man? Then, pity souls
'Less privileged! Allow us share your luck!'   180
So, David holds the circle, rules the roast,
Narrates the vision, peeps in the glass ball,
Sets-to the spirit-writing, hears the raps,
As the case may be.

          Now mark! To be precise—
Though I say, 'lies' all these, at this first stage,   185
'T is just for science' sake: I call such grubs
By the name of what they 'll turn to, dragonflies.
Strictly, it 's what good people style untruth;
But yet, so far, not quite the full-grown thing:
It 's fancying, fable-making, nonsense-work—   190
What never meant to be so very bad—
The knack of story-telling, brightening up
Each dull old bit of fact that drops its shine.
One does see somewhat when one shuts one's eyes,
If only spots and streaks; tables do tip   195

In the oddest way of themselves: and pens, good Lord,
Who knows if you drive them or they drive you?
'T is but a foot in the water and out again;
Not that duck-under which decides your dive.
Note this, for it 's important: listen why. 200
I 'll prove, you push on David till he dives
And ends the shivering. Here 's your circle, now:
Two-thirds of them, with heads like you their host,
Turn up their eyes, and cry, as you expect,
'Lord, who 'd have thought it!' But there 's always one 205
Looks wise, compassionately smiles, submits
'Of your veracity no kind of doubt,
'But—do you feel so certain of that boy's?
'Really, I wonder! I confess myself
'More chary of my faith!' That 's galling, sir! 210
What, he the investigator, he the sage,
When all 's done? Then, you just have shut your eyes,
Opened your mouth, and gulped down David whole,
You! Terrible were such catastrophe!
So, evidence is redoubled, doubled again, 215
And doubled besides; once more, 'He heard, we heard,
'You and they heard, your mother and your wife,
'Your children and the stranger in your gates:
'Did they or did they not?' So much for him,
The black sheep, guest without the wedding-garb, 220
The doubting Thomas! Now 's your turn to crow:
'He 's kind to think you such a fool: Sludge cheats?
Leave you alone to take precautions!'
                                 Straight
The rest join chorus. Thomas stands abashed,
Sips silent some such beverage as this, 225
Considers if it be harder, shutting eyes
And gulping David in good fellowship,
Than going elsewhere, getting, in exchange,
With no egg-nogg to lubricate the food,
Some just as tough a morsel. Over the way, 230
Holds Captain Sparks his court: is it better there?
Have not you hunting-stories, scalping-scenes,
And Mexican War exploits to swallow plump
If you 'd be free o' the stove-side, rocking-chair,

And trio of affable daughters?

                        Doubt succumbs!   235
Victory! All your circle 's yours again!
Out of the clubbing of submissive wits,
David's performance rounds, each chink gets patched,
Every protrusion of a point 's filed fine,
All 's fit to set a-rolling round the world,   240
And then return to David finally,
Lies seven-feet thick about his first half-inch.
Here 's a choice birth o' the supernatural,
Poor David 's pledged to! You 've employed no tool
That laws exclaim at, save the devil's own,   245
Yet screwed him into henceforth gulling you
To the top o' your bent,—all out of one half-lie!

You hold, if there 's one half or a hundredth part
Of a lie, that 's his fault,—his be the penalty!
I dare say! You 'd prove firmer in his place?   250
You 'd find the courage,—that first flurry over,
That mild bit of romancing-work at end,—
To interpose with 'It gets serious, this;
'Must stop here. Sir, I saw no ghost at all.
'Inform your friends I made . . . well, fools of them,   255
'And found you ready-made. I 've lived in clover
'These three weeks: take it out in kicks of me!'
I doubt it. Ask your conscience! Let me know,
Twelve months hence, with how few embellishments
You 've told almighty Boston of this passage   260
Of arms between us, your first taste o' the foil
From Sludge who could not fence, sir! Sludge, your boy!
I lied, sir,—there! I got up from my gorge
On offal in the gutter, and preferred
Your canvas-backs: I took their carver's size,   265
Measured his modicum of intelligence,
Tickled him on the cockles of his heart
With a raven feather, and next week found myself
Sweet and clean, dining daintily, dizened smart,
Set on a stool buttressed by ladies' knees,   270
Every soft smiler calling me her pet,
Encouraging my story to uncoil

And creep out from its hole, inch after inch,
'How last night, I no sooner snug in bed,
'Tucked up, just as they left me,—than came raps!   275
'While a light whisked' . . . 'Shaped somewhat like a star?'
'Well, like some sort of stars, ma'am.'—'So we thought!
'And any voice? Not yet? Try hard, next time,
'If you can't hear a voice; we think you may:
'At least, the Pennsylvanian "mediums" did.'   280
Oh, next time comes the voice! 'Just as we hoped!'
Are not the hopers proud now, pleased, profuse
O' the natural acknowledgment?

                                        Of course!
So, off we push, illy-oh-yo, trim the boat,
On we sweep with a cataract ahead,   285
We 're midway to the Horseshoe: stop, who can,
The dance of bubbles gay about our prow!
Experiences become worth waiting for,
Spirits now speak up, tell their inmost mind,
And compliment the 'medium' properly,   290
Concern themselves about his Sunday coat,
See rings on his hand with pleasure. Ask yourself
How you'd receive a course of treats like these!
Why, take the quietest hack and stall him up,
Cram him with corn a month, then out with him   295
Among his mates on a bright April morn,
With the turf to tread; see if you find or no
A caper in him, if he bucks or bolts!
Much more a youth whose fancies sprout as rank
As toadstool-clump from melon-bed. 'T is soon,   300
'Sirrah, you spirit, come, go, fetch and carry,
'Read, write, rap, rub-a-dub, and hang yourself!'
I 'm spared all further trouble; all 's arranged;
Your circle does my business; I may rave
Like an epileptic dervish in the books,   305
Foam, fling myself flat, rend my clothes to shreds;
No matter: lovers, friends and countrymen
Will lay down spiritual laws, read wrong things right
By the rule o' reverse. If Francis Verulam
Styles himself Bacon, spells the name beside   310

With a *y* and a *k*, says he drew breath in York,
Gave up the ghost in Wales when Cromwell reigned,
(As, sir, we somewhat fear he was apt to say,
Before I found the useful book that knows)
Why, what harm 's done? The circle smiles apace,   315
'It was not Bacon, after all, you see!
'We understand; the trick 's but natural:
'Such spirits' individuality
'Is hard to put in evidence: they incline
'To gibe and jeer, these undeveloped sorts.   320
'You see, their world 's much like a jail broke loose,
'While this of ours remains shut, bolted, barred,
'With a single window to it. Sludge, our friend,
'Serves as this window, whether thin or thick,
'Or stained or stainless; he 's the medium-pane   325
'Through which, to see us and be seen, they peep:
'They crowd each other, hustle for a chance,
'Tread on their neighbour's kibes, play tricks enough!
'Does Bacon, tired of waiting, swerve aside?
'Up in his place jumps Barnum—"I 'm your man,   330
' "I 'll answer you for Bacon!" Try once more!'

Or else it 's—'What 's a "medium"? He 's a means,
'Good, bad, indifferent, still the only means
'Spirits can speak by; he may misconceive,
'Stutter and stammer,—he 's their Sludge and drudge,   335
'Take him or leave him; they must hold their peace,
'Or else, put up with having knowledge strained
'To half-expression through his ignorance.
'Suppose, the spirit Beethoven wants to shed
'New music he 's brimful of; why, he turns   340
'The handle of this organ, grinds with Sludge,
'And what he poured in at the mouth o' the mill
'As a Thirty-third Sonata, (fancy now!)
'Comes from the hopper as bran-new Sludge, nought else,
'The Shakers' Hymn in G, with a natural F,   345
'Or the "Stars and Stripes" set to consecutive fourths.'

Sir, where 's the scrape you did not help me through,
You that are wise? And for the fools, the folk
Who came to see,—the guests, (observe that word!)

Pray do you find guests criticize your wine,   350
Your furniture, your grammar, or your nose?
Then, why your 'medium'? What 's the difference?
Prove your madeira red-ink and gamboge,—
Your Sludge, a cheat—then, somebody 's a goose
For vaunting both as genuine. 'Guests!' Don't fear!   355
They 'll make a wry face, nor too much of that,
And leave you in your glory.

                              'No, sometimes
'They doubt and say as much!' Ay, doubt they do!
And what 's the consequence? 'Of course they doubt'—
(You triumph) 'that explains the hitch at once!   360
'Doubt posed our "medium," puddled his pure mind;
'He gave them back their rubbish: pitch chaff in,
'Could flour come out o' the honest mill?' So, prompt
Applaud the faithful: cases flock in point,
'How, when a mocker willed a "medium" once   365
'Should name a spirit James whose name was George,
' "James" cried the "medium",—'t was the test of truth!'
In short, a hit proves much, a miss proves more.
Does this convince? The better: does it fail?
Time for the double-shotted broadside, then—   370
The grand means, last resource. Look black and big!
'You style us idiots, therefore—why stop short?
'Accomplices in rascality: this we hear
'In our own house, from our invited guest
'Found brave enough to outrage a poor boy   375
'Exposed by our good faith! Have you been heard?
'Now, then, hear us; one man 's not quite worth twelve.
'You see a cheat? Here 's some twelve see an ass:
'Excuse me if I calculate: good day!'
Out slinks the sceptic, all the laughs explode.   380
Sludge waves his hat in triumph!

                              Or—he don't.
There 's something in real truth (explain who can!)
One casts a wistful eye at, like the horse
Who mopes beneath stuffed hay-racks and won't munch
Because he spies a corn-bag: hang that truth,   385

It spoils all dainties proffered in its place!
I 've felt at times when, cockered, cosseted
And coddled by the aforesaid company,
Bidden enjoy their bullying,—never fear,
But o'er their shoulders spit at the flying man,—   390
I 've felt a child; only, a fractious child
That, dandled soft by nurse, aunt, grandmother,
Who keep him from the kennel, sun and wind,
Good fun and wholesome mud,—enjoined be sweet,
And comely and superior,—eyes askance   395
The ragged sons o' the gutter at their game,
Fain would be down with them i' the thick o' the filth,
Making dirt-pies, laughing free, speaking plain,
And calling granny the grey old cat she is.
I 've felt a spite, I say, at you, at them,   400
Huggings and humbug—gnashed my teeth to mark
A decent dog pass! It 's too bad, I say,
Ruining a soul so!

       But what 's 'so,' what 's fixed,
Where may one stop? Nowhere! The cheating 's nursed
Out of the lying, softly and surely spun   405
To just your length, sir! I 'd stop soon enough:
But you 're for progress. 'All old, nothing new?
'Only the usual talking through the mouth,
'Or writing by the hand? I own, I thought
'This would develop, grow demonstrable,   410
'Make doubt absurd, give figures we might see,
'Flowers we might touch. There 's no one doubts you,
    Sludge!
'You dream the dreams, you see the spiritual sights,
'The speeches come in your head, beyond dispute.
'Still, for the sceptics' sake, to stop all mouths,   415
'We want some outward manifestation!—well,
'The Pennsylvanians gained such; why not Sludge?
'He may improve with time!'

           Ay, that he may!
He sees his lot: there 's no avoiding fate.
'T is a trifle at first. 'Eh, David? Did you hear?   420

'You jogged the table, your foot caused the squeak,
'This time you're . . . joking, are you not, my boy?'
'N-n-no!'—and I 'm done for, bought and sold henceforth.
The old good easy jog-trot way, the . . . eh?
The . . . not so very false, as falsehood goes,   425
The spinning out and drawing fine, you know,—
Really mere novel-writing of a sort,
Acting, or improvising, make-believe,
Surely not downright cheatery,—any how,
'T is done with and my lot cast; Cheat 's my name: 430
The fatal dash of brandy in your tea
Has settled what you 'll have the souchong's smack:
The caddy gives way to the dram-bottle.

Then, it 's so cruel easy! Oh, those tricks
That can't be tricks, those feats by sleight of hand,   435
Clearly no common conjuror's!—no indeed!
A conjuror? Choose me any craft i' the world
A man puts hand to; and with six months' pains
I 'll play you twenty tricks miraculous
To people untaught the trade: have you seen glass
       blown,   440
Pipes pierced? Why, just this biscuit that I chip,
Did you ever watch a baker toss one flat
To the oven? Try and do it! Take my word,
Practise but half as much, while limbs are lithe,
To turn, shove, tilt a table, crack your joints,   445
Manage your feet, dispose your hands aright,
Work wires that twitch the curtains, play the glove
At end o' your slipper,—then put out the lights
And . . . there, there, all you want you 'll get, I hope!
I found it slip, easy as an old shoe.   450

Now, lights on table again! I 've done my part,
You take my place while I give thanks and rest.
'Well, Judge Humgruffin, what 's your verdict, sir?
'You, hardest head in the United States,—
'Did you detect a cheat here? Wait! Let 's see!   455
'Just an experiment first, for candour's sake!
'I 'll try and cheat you, Judge! The table tilts:

'Is it I that move it? Write! I'll press your hand:
'Cry when I push, or guide your pencil, Judge!'
Sludge still triumphant! 'That a rap, indeed?   460
'That, the real writing? Very like a whale!
'Then, if, sir, you—a most distinguished man,
'And, were the Judge not here, I'd say, . . . no matter!
'Well, sir, if you fail, you can't take us in,—
'There's little fear that Sludge will!'

                            Won't he, ma'am?   465
But what if our distinguished host, like Sludge,
Bade God bear witness that he played no trick,
While you believed that what produced the raps
Was just a certain child who died, you know,
And whose last breath you thought your lips had felt?   470
Eh? That's a capital point, ma'am: Sludge begins
At your entreaty with your dearest dead,
The little voice set lisping once again,
The tiny hand made feel for yours once more,
The poor lost image brought back, plain as dreams,   475
Which image, if a word had chanced recall,
The customary cloud would cross your eyes,
Your heart return the old tick, pay its pang!
A right mood for investigation, this!
One's at one's ease with Saul and Jonathan,   480
Pompey and Cæsar: but one's own lost child . . .
I wonder, when you heard the first clod drop
From the spadeful at the grave-side, felt you free
To investigate who twitched your funeral scarf
Or brushed your flounces? Then, it came of course   485
You should be stunned and stupid; then, (how else?)
Your breath stopped with your blood, your brain struck
    work.
But now, such causes fail of such effects,
All's changed,—the little voice begins afresh,
Yet you, calm, consequent, can test and try   490
And touch the truth. 'Tests? Didn't the creature tell
'Its nurse's name, and say it lived six years,
'And rode a rocking-horse? Enough of tests!
'Sludge never could learn that!'
                    F f

                                        He could not, eh?
You compliment him. 'Could not?' Speak for yourself!   495
I'd like to know the man I ever saw
Once,—never mind where, how, why, when,—once saw,
Of whom I do not keep some matter in mind
He'd swear I 'could not' know, sagacious soul!
What? Do you live in this world's blow of blacks,   500
Palaver, gossipry, a single hour
Nor find one smut has settled on your nose,
Of a smut's worth, no more, no less?—one fact
Out of the drift of facts, whereby you learn
What someone was, somewhere, somewhen, somewhy?   505
You don't tell folk—'See what has stuck to me!
'Judge Humgruffin, our most distinguished man,
'Your uncle was a tailor, and your wife
'Thought to have married Miggs, missed him, hit you!'—
Do you, sir, though you see him twice a-week?   510
'No,' you reply, 'what use retailing it?
'Why should I?' But, you see, one day you *should*,
Because one day there's much use,—when this fact
Brings you the Judge upon both gouty knees
Before the supernatural; proves that Sludge   515
Knows, as you say, a thing he 'could not' know:
Will not Sludge thenceforth keep an outstretched face
The way the wind drives?

                                        'Could not!' Look you now,
I'll tell you a story! There's a whiskered chap,
A foreigner, that teaches music here   520
And gets his bread,—knowing no better way:
He says, the fellow who informed of him
And made him fly his country and fall West
Was a hunchback cobbler, sat, stitched soles and sang,
In some outlandish place, the city Rome,   525
In a cellar by their Broadway, all day long;
Never asked questions, stopped to listen or look,
Nor lifted nose from lapstone; let the world
Roll round his three-legged stool, and news run in
The ears he hardly seemed to keep pricked up.   530
Well, that man went on Sundays, touched his pay,

And took his praise from government, you see;
For something like two dollars every week,
He'd engage tell you some one little thing
Of some one man, which led to many more,   535
(Because one truth leads right to the world's end)
And make you that man's master—when he dined
And on what dish, where walked to keep his health
And to what street. His trade was, throwing thus
His sense out, like an ant-eater's long tongue,   540
Soft, innocent, warm, moist, impassible,
And when 't was crusted o'er with creatures—slick,
Their juice enriched his palate. 'Could not Sludge!'

I'll go yet a step further, and maintain,
Once the imposture plunged its proper depth   545
I' the rotten of your natures, all of you,—
(If one's not mad nor drunk, and hardly then)
It's impossible to cheat—that's, be found out!
Go tell your brotherhood this first slip of mine,
All to-day's tale, how you detected Sludge,   550
Behaved unpleasantly, till he was fain confess,
And so has come to grief! You'll find, I think,
Why Sludge still snaps his fingers in your face.
There now, you've told them! What's their prompt reply?
'Sir, did that youth confess he had cheated me,   555
'I'd disbelieve him. He may cheat at times;
'That's in the "medium"-nature, thus they're made,
'Vain and vindictive, cowards, prone to scratch.
'And so all cats are; still, a cat's the beast
'You coax the strange electric sparks from out,   560
'By rubbing back its fur; not so a dog,
'Nor lion, nor lamb: 't is the cat's nature, sir!
'Why not the dog's? Ask God, who made them beasts!
'D'ye think the sound, the nicely-balanced man
'Like me'—(aside)—'like you yourself,'—(aloud)   565
'—He's stuff to make a "medium"? Bless your soul,
' 'T is these hysteric, hybrid half-and-halfs,
'Equivocal, worthless vermin yield the fire!
'We take such as we find them, 'ware their tricks,
'Wanting their service. Sir, Sludge took in you—   570

'How, I can't say, not being there to watch:
'He was tried, was tempted by your easiness,—
'He did not take in me!'

                   Thank you for Sludge!
I'm to be grateful to such patrons, eh,
When what you hear's my best word? 'T is a challenge   575
'Snap at all strangers, half-tamed prairie-dog,
'So you cower duly at your keeper's beck!
'Cat, show what claws were made for, muffling them
'Only to me! Cheat others if you can,
'Me, if you dare!' And, my wise sir, I dared—   580
Did cheat you first, made you cheat others next,
And had the help o' your vaunted manliness
To bully the incredulous. You used me?
Have not I used you, taken full revenge,
Persuaded folk they knew not their own name,   585
And straight they'd own the error! Who was the fool
When, to an awe-struck wide-eyed open-mouthed
Circle of sages, Sludge would introduce
Milton composing baby-rhymes, and Locke
Reasoning in gibberish, Homer writing Greek   590
In noughts and crosses, Asaph setting psalms
To crotchet and quaver? I've made a spirit squeak
In sham voice for a minute, then outbroke
Bold in my own, defying the imbeciles—
Have copied some ghost's pothooks, half a page,   595
Then ended with my own scrawl undisguised.
'All right! The ghost was merely using Sludge,
'Suiting itself from his imperfect stock!'
Don't talk of gratitude to me! For what?
For being treated as a showman's ape,   600
Encouraged to be wicked and make sport,
Fret or sulk, grin or whimper, any mood
So long as the ape be in it and no man—
Because a nut pays every mood alike.
Curse your superior, superintending sort,   605
Who, since you hate smoke, send up boys that climb
To cure your chimney, bid a 'medium' lie
To sweep you truth down! Curse your women too,

Your insolent wives and daughters, that fire up
Or faint away if a male hand squeeze theirs,   610
Yet, to encourage Sludge, may play with Sludge
As only a 'medium,' only the kind of thing
They must humour, fondle . . . oh, to misconceive
Were too preposterous! But I've paid them out!
They've had their wish—called for the naked truth,   615
And in she tripped, sat down and bade them stare:
They had to blush a little and forgive!
'The fact is, children talk so; in next world
'All our conventions are reversed,—perhaps
'Made light of: something like old prints, my dear!   620
'The Judge has one, he brought from Italy,
'A metropolis in the background,—o'er a bridge,
'A team of trotting roadsters,—cheerful groups
'Of wayside travellers, peasants at their work,
'And, full in front, quite unconcerned, why not?   625
'Three nymphs conversing with a cavalier,
'And never a rag among them: "fine," folk cry—
'And heavenly manners seem not much unlike!
'Let Sludge go on; we'll fancy it's in print!'
If such as came for wool, sir, went home shorn,   630
Where is the wrong I did them? 'T was their choice;
They tried the adventure, ran the risk, tossed up
And lost, as some one's sure to do in games;
They fancied I was made to lose,—smoked glass
Useful to spy the sun through, spare their eyes: 635
And had I proved a red-hot iron plate
They thought to pierce, and, for their pains, grew blind,
Whose were the fault but theirs? While, as things go,
Their loss amounts to gain, the more's the shame!
They've had their peep into the spirit-world,   640
And all this world may know it! They've fed fat
Their self-conceit which else had starved: what chance
Save this, of cackling o'er a golden egg
And compassing distinction from the flock,
Friends of a feather? Well, they paid for it,   645
And not prodigiously; the price o' the play,
Not counting certain pleasant interludes,
Was scarce a vulgar play's worth. When you buy

The actor's talent, do you dare propose
For his soul beside? Whereas my soul you buy!   650
Sludge acts Macbeth, obliged to be Macbeth,
Or you'll not hear his first word! Just go through
That slight formality, swear himself's the Thane,
And thenceforth he may strut and fret his hour,
Spout, spawl, or spin his target, no one cares!   655
Why hadn't I leave to play tricks, Sludge as Sludge?
Enough of it all! I've wiped out scores with you—
Vented your fustian, let myself be streaked
Like tom-fool with your ochre and carmine,
Worn patchwork your respectable fingers sewed   660
To metamorphose somebody,—yes, I've earned
My wages, swallowed down my bread of shame,
And shake the crumbs off—where but in your face?

As for religion—why, I served it, sir!
I'll stick to that! With my *phenomena*   665
I laid the atheist sprawling on his back,
Propped up Saint Paul, or, at least, Swedenborg!
In fact, it's just the proper way to baulk
These troublesome fellows—liars, one and all,
Are not these sceptics? Well, to baffle them,   670
No use in being squeamish: lie yourself!
Erect your buttress just as wide o' the line,
Your side, as they build up the wall on theirs;
Where both meet, midway in a point, is truth
High overhead: so, take your room, pile bricks,   675
Lie! Oh, there's titillation in all shame!
What snow may lose in white, snow gains in rose!
Miss Stokes turns—Rahab,—nor a bad exchange!
Glory be on her, for the good she wrought,
Breeding belief anew 'neath ribs of death,   680
Browbeating now the unabashed before,
Ridding us of their whole life's gathered straws
By a live coal from the altar! Why, of old,
Great men spent years and years in writing books
To prove we've souls, and hardly proved it then: 685
Miss Stokes with her live coal, for you and me!
Surely, to this good issue, all was fair—

Not only fondling Sludge, but, even suppose
He let escape some spice of knavery,—well,
In wisely being blind to it! Don't you praise   690
Nelson for setting spy-glass to blind eye
And saying . . . what was it—that he could not see
The signal he was bothered with? Ay, indeed!

I'll go beyond: there's a real love of a lie,
Liars find ready-made for lies they make,   695
As hand for glove, or tongue for sugar-plum.
At best, 't is never pure and full belief;
Those furthest in the quagmire,—don't suppose
They strayed there with no warning, got no chance
Of a filth-speck in their face, which they clenched teeth,   700
Bent brow against! Be sure they had their doubts,
And fears, and fairest challenges to try
The floor o' the seeming solid sand! But no!
Their faith was pledged, acquaintance too apprised,
All but the last step ventured, kerchiefs waved,   705
And Sludge called 'pet': 't was easier marching on
To the promised land, join those who, Thursday next,
Meant to meet Shakespeare; better follow Sludge—
Prudent, oh sure!—on the alert, how else?—
But making for the mid-bog, all the same!   710
To hear your outcries, one would think I caught
Miss Stokes by the scruff o' the neck, and pitched her flat,
Foolish-face-foremost! Hear these simpletons,
That's all I beg, before my work's begun,
Before I've touched them with my finger-tip!   715
Thus they await me (do but listen, now!
It's reasoning, this is,—I can't imitate
The baby voice, though) 'In so many tales
'Must be some truth, truth though a pin-point big,
'Yet, some: a single man's deceived, perhaps—   720
'Hardly, a thousand: to suppose one cheat
'Can gull all these, were more miraculous far
'Than aught we should confess a miracle'—
And so on. Then the Judge sums up—(it's rare)
Bids you respect the authorities that leap   725
To the judgment-seat at once,—why don't you note

The limpid nature, the unblemished life,
The spotless honour, indisputable sense
Of the first upstart with his story? What—
Outrage a boy on whom you ne'er till now   730
Set eyes, because he finds raps trouble him?
Fools, these are: ay, and how of their opposites
Who never did, at bottom of their hearts,
Believe for a moment?—Men emasculate,
Blank of belief, who played, as eunuchs use,   735
With superstition safely,—cold of blood,
Who saw what made for them i' the mystery,
Took their occasion, and supported Sludge
—As proselytes? No, thank you, far too shrewd!
—But promisers of fair play, encouragers   740
O' the claimant; who in candour needs must hoist
Sludge up on Mars' Hill, get speech out of Sludge
To carry off, criticize, and cant about!
Didn't Athens treat Saint Paul so?—at any rate,
It's 'a new thing' philosophy fumbles at.   745
Then there's the other picker-out of pearl
From dung-heaps,—ay, your literary man,
Who draws on his kid gloves to deal with Sludge
Daintily and discreetly,—shakes a dust
O' the doctrine, flavours thence, he well knows how,   750
The narrative or the novel,—half-believes,
All for the book's sake, and the public's stare,
And the cash that's God's sole solid in this world!
Look at him! Try to be too bold, too gross
For the master! Not you! He's the man for muck;   755
Shovel it forth, full-splash, he'll smooth your brown
Into artistic richness, never fear!
Find him the crude stuff; when you recognize
Your lie again, you'll doff your hat to it,
Dressed out for company! 'For company,'   760
I say, since there's the relish of success:
Let all pay due respect, call the lie truth,
Save the soft silent smirking gentleman
Who ushered in the stranger: you must sigh
'How melancholy, he, the only one   765
'Fails to perceive the bearing of the truth

'Himself gave birth to!'—There's the triumph's smack!
That man would choose to see the whole world roll
I' the slime o' the slough, so he might touch the tip
Of his brush with what I call the best of browns—   770
Tint ghost-tales, spirit-stories, past the power
Of the outworn umber and bistre!

                                    Yet I think
There's a more hateful form of foolery—
The social sage's, Solomon of saloons
And philosophic diner-out, the fribble   775
Who wants a doctrine for a chopping-block
To try the edge of his faculty upon,
Prove how much common sense he'll hack and hew
I' the critical minute 'twixt the soup and fish!
These were my patrons: these, and the like of them   780
Who, rising in my soul now, sicken it,—
These I have injured! Gratitude to these?
The gratitude, forsooth, of a prostitute
To the greenhorn and the bully—friends of hers,
From the wag that wants the queer jokes for his club,   785
To the snuff-box-decorator, honest man,
Who just was at his wits' end where to find
So genial a Pasiphae! All and each
Pay, compliment, protect from the police:
And how she hates them for their pains, like me!   790
So much for my remorse at thanklessness
Toward a deserving public!

                                    But, for God?
Ay, that's a question! Well, sir, since you press—
(How you do tease the whole thing out of me!
I don't mean you, you know, when I say 'them':   795
Hate you, indeed! But that Miss Stokes, that Judge!
Enough, enough—with sugar: thank you, sir!)
Now for it, then! Will you believe me, though?
You've heard what I confess; I don't unsay
A single word: I cheated when I could,   800
Rapped with my toe-joints, set sham hands at work,
Wrote down names weak in sympathetic ink,

Rubbed odic lights with ends of phosphor-match,
And all the rest; believe that: believe this,
By the same token, though it seem to set   805
The crooked straight again, unsay the said,
Stick up what I've knocked down; I can't help that
It's truth! I somehow vomit truth to-day.
This trade of mine—I don't know, can't be sure
But there was something in it, tricks and all!   810
Really, I want to light up my own mind.
They were tricks,—true, but what I mean to add
Is also true. First,—don't it strike you, sir?
Go back to the beginning,—the first fact
We're taught is, there's a world beside this world,   815
With spirits, not mankind, for tenantry;
That much within that world once sojourned here,
That all upon this world will visit there,
And therefore that we, bodily here below,
Must have exactly such an interest   820
In learning what may be the ways o' the world
Above us, as the disembodied folk
Have (by all analogic likelihood)
In watching how things go in the old home
With us, their sons, successors, and what not.   825
Oh yes, with added powers probably,
Fit for the novel state,—old loves grown pure,
Old interests understood aright,—they watch!
Eyes to see, ears to hear, and hands to help,
Proportionate to advancement: they're ahead,   830
That's all—do what we do, but nobler done—
Use plate, whereas we eat our meals off delf,
(To use a figure).

     Concede that, and I ask
Next what may be the mode of intercourse
Between us men here, and those once-men there?   835
First comes the Bible's speech; then, history
With the supernatural element,—you know—
All that we sucked in with our mothers' milk,
Grew up with, got inside of us at last,
Till it's found bone of bone and flesh of flesh.   840

See now, we start with the miraculous,
And know it used to be, at all events:
What's the first step we take, and can't but take,
In arguing from the known to the obscure?
Why this: 'What was before, may be to-day.   845
'Since Samuel's ghost appeared to Saul, of course
'My brother's spirit may appear to me.'
Go tell your teacher that! What's his reply?
What brings a shade of doubt for the first time
O'er his brow late so luminous with faith?   850
'Such things have been,' says he, 'and there's no doubt
'Such things may be: but I advise mistrust
'Of eyes, ears, stomach, and, more than all, your brain,
'Unless it be of your great-grandmother,
'Whenever they propose a ghost to you!'   855
The end is, there's a composition struck;
'T is settled, we've some way of intercourse
Just as in Saul's time; only, different:
How, when and where, precisely,—find it out!
I want to know, then, what's so natural   860
As that a person born into this world
And seized on by such teaching, should begin
With firm expectancy and a frank look-out
For his own allotment, his especial share
I' the secret,—his particular ghost, in fine?   865
I mean, a person born to look that way,
Since natures differ: take the painter-sort,
One man lives fifty years in ignorance
Whether grass be green or red,—'No kind of eye
'For colour,' say you; while another picks   870
And puts away even pebbles, when a child,
Because of bluish spots and pinky veins—
'Give him forthwith a paint-box!' Just the same
Was I born . . . 'medium,' you won't let me say,—
Well, seer of the supernatural   875
Everywhen, everyhow and everywhere,—
Will that do?

            I and all such boys of course
Started with the same stock of Bible-truth;

Only,—what in the rest you style their sense,
Instinct, blind reasoning but imperative,   880
This, betimes, taught them the old world had one law
And ours another: 'New world, new laws,' cried they:
'None but old laws, seen everywhere at work,'
Cried I, and by their help explained my life
The Jews' way, still a working way to me.   885
Ghosts made the noises, fairies waved the lights,
Or Santa Claus slid down on New Year's Eve
And stuffed with cakes the stocking at my bed,
Changed the worn shoes, rubbed clean the fingered slate
O' the sum that came to grief the day before.   890

This could not last long: soon enough I found
Who had worked wonders thus, and to what end:
But did I find all easy, like my mates?
Henceforth no supernatural any more?
Not a whit: what projects the billiard-balls?   895
'A cue,' you answer: 'Yes, a cue,' said I;
'But what hand, off the cushion, moved the cue?
'What unseen agency, outside the world,
'Prompted its puppets to do this and that,
'Put cakes and shoes and slates into their mind,   900
'These mothers and aunts, nay even schoolmasters?'
Thus high I sprang, and there have settled since.
Just so I reason, in sober earnest still,
About the greater godsends, what you call
The serious gains and losses of my life.   905
What do I know or care about your world
Which either is or seems to be? This snap
O' my fingers, sir! My care is for myself;
Myself am whole and sole reality
Inside a raree-show and a market-mob   910
Gathered about it: that's the use of things.
'T is easy saying they serve vast purposes,
Advantage their grand selves: be it true or false,
Each thing may have two uses. What's a star?
A world, or a world's sun: doesn't it serve   915
As taper also, time-piece, weather-glass,
And almanac? Are stars not set for signs

When we should shear our sheep, sow corn, prune trees?
The Bible says so.

                Well, I add one use
To all the acknowledged uses, and declare   920
If I spy Charles's Wain at twelve to-night,
It warns me, 'Go, nor lose another day,
'And have your hair cut, Sludge!' You laugh: and why?
Were such a sign too hard for God to give?
No: but Sludge seems too little for such grace: 925
Thank you, sir! So you think, so does not Sludge!
When you and good men gape at Providence,
Go into history and bid us mark
Not merely powder-plots prevented, crowns
Kept on kings' heads by miracle enough,   930
But private mercies—oh, you've told me, sir,
Of such interpositions! How yourself
Once, missing on a memorable day
Your handkerchief—just setting out, you know,—
You must return to fetch it, lost the train,   935
And saved your precious self from what befell
The thirty-three whom Providence forgot.
You tell, and ask me what I think of this?
Well, sir, I think then, since you needs must know,
What matter had you and Boston city to boot   940
Sailed skyward, like burnt onion-peelings? Much
To you, no doubt: for me—undoubtedly
The cutting of my hair concerns me more,
Because, however sad the truth may seem,
Sludge is of all-importance to himself.   945
You set apart that day in every year
For special thanksgiving, were a heathen else:
Well, I who cannot boast the like escape,
Suppose I said 'I don't thank Providence
'For my part, owing it no gratitude'?   950
'Nay, but you owe as much'—you'd tutor me,
'You, every man alive, for blessings gained
'In every hour o' the day, could you but know!
'I saw my crowning mercy: all have such,
'Could they but see!' Well, sir, why don't they see?   955

'Because they won't look,—or perhaps, they can't.'
Then, sir, suppose I can, and will, and do
Look, microscopically as is right,
Into each hour with its infinitude
Of influences at work to profit Sludge?   960
For that's the case: I've sharpened up my sight
To spy a providence in the fire's going out,
The kettle's boiling, the dime's sticking fast
Despite the hole i' the pocket. Call such facts
Fancies, too petty a work for Providence,   965
And those same thanks which you exact from me
Prove too prodigious payment: thanks for what,
If nothing guards and guides us little men?
No, no, sir! You must put away your pride,
Resolve to let Sludge into partnership!   970
I live by signs and omens: looked at the roof
Where the pigeons settle—'If the further bird,
'The white, takes wing first, I'll confess when thrashed;
'Not, if the blue does'—so I said to myself
Last week, lest you should take me by surprise: 975
Off flapped the white,—and I'm confessing, sir!
Perhaps 't is Providence's whim and way
With only me, i' the world: how can you tell?
'Because unlikely!' Was it likelier, now,
That this our one out of all worlds beside,   980
That what-d'you-call-'em millions, should be just
Precisely chosen to make Adam for,
And the rest o' the tale? Yet the tale's true, you know:
Such undeserving clod was graced so once;
Why not graced likewise undeserving Sludge?   985
Are we merit-mongers, flaunt we filthy rags?
All you can bring against my privilege
Is, that another way was taken with you,—
Which I don't question. It's pure grace, my luck:
I'm broken to the way of nods and winks,   990
And need no formal summoning. You've a help;
Holloa his name or whistle, clap your hands,
Stamp with your foot or pull the bell: all's one,
He understands you want him, here he comes.
Just so, I come at the knocking: you, sir, wait   995

The tongue o' the bell, nor stir before you catch
Reason's clear tingle, nature's clapper brisk,
Or that traditional peal was wont to cheer
Your mother's face turned heavenward: short of these
There's no authentic intimation, eh?   1000
Well, when you hear, you'll answer them, start up
And stride into the presence, top of toe,
And there find Sludge beforehand, Sludge that sprang
At noise o' the knuckle on the partition-wall!
I think myself the more religious man.   1005
Religion's all or nothing; it's no mere smile
O' contentment, sigh of aspiration, sir—
No quality o' the finelier-tempered clay
Like its whiteness or its lightness; rather, stuff
O' the very stuff, life of life, and self of self.   1010
I tell you, men won't notice; when they do,
They'll understand. I notice nothing else:
I'm eyes, ears, mouth of me, one gaze and gape,
Nothing eludes me, everything's a hint,
Handle and help. It's all absurd, and yet   1015
There's something in it all, I know: how much?
No answer! What does that prove? Man's still man,
Still meant for a poor blundering piece of work
When all's done; but, if somewhat's done, like this,
Or not done, is the case the same? Suppose   1020
I blunder in my guess at the true sense
O' the knuckle-summons, nine times out of ten,—
What if the tenth guess happen to be right?
If the tenth shovel-load of powdered quartz
Yield me the nugget? I gather, crush, sift all,   1025
Pass o'er the failure, pounce on the success.
To give you a notion, now—(let who wins, laugh!)
When first I see a man, what do I first?
Why, count the letters which make up his name,
And as their number chances, even or odd,   1030
Arrive at my conclusion, trim my course:
Hiram H. Horsefall is your honoured name,
And haven't I found a patron, sir, in you?
'Shall I cheat this stranger?' I take apple-pips,
Stick one in either canthus of my eye,   1035

And if the left drops first—(your left, sir, stuck)
I'm warned, I let the trick alone this time.
You, sir, who smile, superior to such trash,
You judge of character by other rules:
Don't your rules sometimes fail you? Pray, what rule   1040
Have you judged Sludge by hitherto?

                              Oh, be sure,
You, everybody blunders, just as I,
In simpler things than these by far! For see:
I knew two farmers,—one, a wiseacre
Who studied seasons, rummaged almanacs,   1045
Quoted the dew-point, registered the frost,
And then declared, for outcome of his pains,
Next summer must be dampish: 't was a drought.
His neighbour prophesied such drought would fall,
Saved hay and corn, made cent. per cent. thereby,   1050
And proved a sage indeed: how came his lore?
Because one brindled heifer, late in March,
Stiffened her tail of evenings, and somehow
He got into his head that drought was meant!
I don't expect all men can do as much: 1055
Such kissing goes by favour. You must take
A certain turn of mind for this,—a twist
I' the flesh, as well. Be lazily alive,
Open-mouthed, like my friend the ant-eater,
Letting all nature's loosely-guarded motes   1060
Settle and, slick, be swallowed! Think yourself
The one i' the world, the one for whom the world
Was made, expect it tickling at your mouth!
Then will the swarm of busy buzzing flies,
Clouds of coincidence, break egg-shell, thrive,   1065
Breed, multiply, and bring you food enough.

I can't pretend to mind your smiling, sir!
Oh, what you mean is this! Such intimate way,
Close converse, frank exchange of offices,
Strict sympathy of the immeasurably great   1070
With the infinitely small, betokened here
By a course of signs and omens, raps and sparks,—

How does it suit the dread traditional text
O' the 'Great and Terrible Name'? Shall the Heaven of
    Heavens
Stoop to such child's play?

                    Please, sir, go with me   1075
A moment, and I'll try to answer you.
The '*Magnum et terribile*' (is that right?)
Well, folk began with this in the early day;
And all the acts they recognized in proof
Were thunders, lightnings, earthquakes, whirlwinds,
    dealt   1080
Indisputably on men whose death they caused.
There, and there only, folk saw Providence
At work,—and seeing it, 't was right enough
All heads should tremble, hands wring hands amain,
And knees knock hard together at the breath   1085
O' the Name's first letter; why, the Jews, I'm told,
Won't write it down, no, to this very hour,
Nor speak aloud: you know best if 't be so.
Each ague-fit of fear at end, they crept
(Because somehow people once born must live)   1090
Out of the sound, sight, swing and sway o' the Name,
Into a corner, the dark rest of the world,
And safe space where as yet no fear had reached;
'T was there they looked about them, breathed again,
And felt indeed at home, as we might say.   1095
The current o' common things, the daily life,
This had their due contempt; no Name pursued
Man from the mountain-top where fires abide,
To his particular mouse-hole at its foot
Where he ate, drank, digested, lived in short: 1100
Such was man's vulgar business, far too small
To be worth thunder: 'small,' folk kept on, 'small,'
With much complacency in those great days!
A mote of sand, you know, a blade of grass—
What was so despicable as mere grass,   1105
Except perhaps the life o' the worm or fly
Which fed there? These were 'small' and men were great.
Well, sir, the old way's altered somewhat since,

And the world wears another aspect now:
Somebody turns our spyglass round, or else   1110
Puts a new lens in it: grass, worm, fly grow big:
We find great things are made of little things,
And little things go lessening till at last
Comes God behind them. Talk of mountains now?
We talk of mould that heaps the mountain, mites   1115
That throng the mould, and God that makes the mites.
The Name comes close behind a stomach-cyst,
The simplest of creations, just a sac
That's mouth, heart, legs and belly at once, yet lives
And feels, and could do neither, we conclude,   1120
If simplified still further one degree:
The small becomes the dreadful and immense!
Lightning, forsooth? No word more upon that!
A tin-foil bottle, a strip of greasy silk,
With a bit of wire and knob of brass, and there's   1125
Your dollar's-worth of lightning! But the cyst—
The life of the least of the little things?

                               No, no!
Preachers and teachers try another tack,
Come near the truth this time: they put aside
Thunder and lightning: 'That's mistake,' they cry,   1130
'Thunderbolts fall for neither fright nor sport,
'But do appreciable good, like tides,
'Changes o' the wind, and other natural facts—
' "Good" meaning good to man, his body or soul.
'Mediate, immediate, all things minister   1135
'To man,—that's settled: be our future text
' "We are His children!" ' So, they now harangue
About the intention, the contrivance, all
That keeps up an incessant play of love,—
See the Bridgewater book.

                            Amen to it!   1140
Well, sir, I put this question: I'm a child?
I lose no time, but take you at your word:
How shall I act a child's part properly?

Your sainted mother, sir,—used you to live
With such a thought as this a-worrying you?   1145
'She has it in her power to throttle me,
'Or stab or poison: she may turn me out,
'Or lock me in,—nor stop at this to-day,
'But cut me off to-morrow from the estate
'I look for'—(long may you enjoy it, sir!)   1150
'In brief, she may unchild the child I am.'
You never had such crotchets? Nor have I!
Who, frank confessing childship from the first,
Cannot both fear and take my ease at once,
So, don't fear,—know what might be, well enough,   1155
But know too, child-like, that it will not be,
At least in my case, mine, the son and heir
O' the kingdom, as yourself proclaim my style.
But do you fancy I stop short at this?
Wonder if suit and service, son and heir   1160
Needs must expect, I dare pretend to find?
If, looking for signs proper to such an one,
I straight perceive them irresistible?
Concede that homage is a son's plain right,
And, never mind the nods and raps and winks,   1165
'T is the pure obvious supernatural
Steps forward, does its duty: why, of course!
I have presentiments; my dreams come true:
I fancy a friend stands whistling all in white
Blithe as a boblink, and he's dead I learn.   1170
I take dislike to a dog my favourite long,
And sell him; he goes mad next week and snaps.
I guess that stranger will turn up to-day
I have not seen these three years; there's his knock
I wager 'sixty peaches on that tree!'—   1175
That I pick up a dollar in my walk,
That your wife's brother's cousin's name was George—
And win on all points. Oh, you wince at this?
You'd fain distinguish between gift and gift,
Washington's oracle and Sludge's itch   1180
O' the elbow when at whist he ought to trump?
With Sludge it's too absurd? *Fine, draw the line
Somewhere, but, sir, your somewhere is not mine!*

Bless us, I'm turning poet! It's time to end.
How you have drawn me out, sir! All I ask   1185
Is—am I heir or not heir? If I'm he,
Then, sir, remember, that same personage
(To judge by what we read i' the newspaper)
Requires, beside one nobleman in gold
To carry up and down his coronet,   1190
Another servant, probably a duke,
To hold egg-nogg in readiness: why want
Attendance, sir, when helps in his father's house
Abound, I'd like to know?

       Enough of talk!
My fault is that I tell too plain a truth.   1195
Why, which of those who say they disbelieve,
Your clever people, but has dreamed his dream,
Caught his coincidence, stumbled on his fact
He can't explain, (he'll tell you smilingly)
Which he's too much of a philosopher   1200
To count as supernatural, indeed,
So calls a puzzle and problem, proud of it,
Bidding you still be on your guard, you know,
Because one fact don't make a system stand,
Nor prove this an occasional escape   1205
Of spirit beneath the matter: that's the way!
Just so wild Indians picked up, piece by piece,
The fact in California, the fine gold
That underlay the gravel—hoarded these,
But never made a system stand, nor dug!   1210
So wise men hold out in each hollowed palm
A handful of experience, sparkling fact
They can't explain; and since their rest of life
Is all explainable, what proof in this?
Whereas I take the fact, the grain of gold,   1215
And fling away the dirty rest of life,
And add this grain to the grain each fool has found
O' the million other such philosophers,—
Till I see gold, all gold and only gold,
Truth questionless though unexplainable,   1220
And the miraculous proved the commonplace!

The other fools believed in mud, no doubt—
Failed to know gold they saw: was that so strange?
Are all men born to play Bach's fiddle-fugues,
'Time' with the foil in carte, jump their own height,   1225
Cut the mutton with the broadsword, skate a five,
Make the red hazard with the cue, clip nails
While swimming, in five minutes row a mile,
Pull themselves three feet up with the left arm,
Do sums of fifty figures in their head,   1230
And so on, by the scores of instances?
The Sludge with luck, who sees the spiritual facts
His fellows strive and fail to see, may rank
With these, and share the advantage.

                                 Ay, but share
The drawback! Think it over by yourself;   1235
I have not heart, sir, and the fire's gone grey.
Defect somewhere compensates for success,
Everyone knows that. Oh, we're equals, sir!
The big-legged fellow has a little arm
And a less brain, though big legs win the race: 1240
Do you suppose I 'scape the common lot?
Say, I was born with flesh so sensitive,
Soul so alert, that, practice helping both,
I guess what's going on outside the veil,
Just as a prisoned crane feels pairing-time   1245
In the islands where his kind are, so must fall
To capering by himself some shiny night,
As if your back-yard were a plot of spice—
Thus am I 'ware o'. the spirit-world: while you,
Blind as a beetle that way,—for amends,   1250
Why, you can double fist and floor me, sir!
Ride that hot hardmouthed horrid horse of yours,
Laugh while it lightens, play with the great dog,
Speak your mind though it vex some friend to hear,
Never brag, never bluster, never blush,—   1255
In short, you've pluck, when I'm a coward—there!
I know it, I can't help it,—folly or no,
I'm paralyzed, my hand's no more a hand,
Nor my head a head, in danger: you can smile

And change the pipe in your cheek. Your gift's not
    mine.   1260
Would you swap for mine? No! but you'd add my gift
To yours: I dare say! I too sigh at times,
Wish I were stouter, could tell truth nor flinch,
Kept cool when threatened, did not mind so much
Being dressed gaily, making strangers stare,   1265
Eating nice things; when I'd amuse myself,
I shut my eyes and fancy in my brain
I'm—now the President, now Jenny Lind,
Now Emerson, now the Benicia Boy—
With all the civilized world a-wondering   1270
And worshipping. I know it's folly and worse;
I feel such tricks sap, honeycomb the soul,
But I can't cure myself: despond, despair,
And then, hey, presto, there's a turn o' the wheel,
Under comes uppermost, fate makes full amends;   1275
Sludge knows and sees and hears a hundred things
You all are blind to,—I've my taste of truth,
Likewise my touch of falsehood,—vice no doubt,
But you've your vices also: I'm content.

What, sir? You won't shake hands? 'Because I cheat!'   1280
'You've found me out in cheating!' That's enough
To make an apostle swear! Why, when I cheat,
Mean to cheat, do cheat, and am caught in the act,
Are you, or, rather, am I sure o' the fact?
(There's verse again, but I'm inspired somehow.)   1285
Well then I'm not sure! I may be, perhaps,
Free as a babe from cheating: how it began,
My gift,—no matter; what 't is got to be
In the end now, that's the question; answer that!
Had I seen, perhaps, what hand was holding mine,   1290
Leading me whither, I had died of fright:
So, I was made believe I led myself.
If I should lay a six-inch plank from roof
To roof, you would not cross the street, one step,
Even at your mother's summons: but, being shrewd,   1295
If I paste paper on each side the plank
And swear 't is solid pavement, why, you'll cross

Humming a tune the while, in ignorance
Beacon Street stretches a hundred feet below:
I walked thus, took the paper-cheat for stone.   1300
Some impulse made me set a thing o' the move
Which, started once, ran really by itself;
Beer flows thus, suck the siphon; toss the kite,
It takes the wind and floats of its own force.
Don't let truth's lump rot stagnant for the lack   1305
Of a timely helpful lie to leaven it!
Put a chalk-egg beneath the clucking hen,
She'll lay a real one, laudably deceived,
Daily for weeks to come. I've told my lie,
And seen truth follow, marvels none of mine;   1310
All was not cheating, sir, I'm positive!
I don't know if I move your hand sometimes
When the spontaneous writing spreads so far,
If my knee lifts the table all that height,
Why the inkstand don't fall off the desk a-tilt,   1315
Why the accordion plays a prettier waltz
Than I can pick out on the piano-forte,
Why I speak so much more than I intend,
Describe so many things I never saw.
I tell you, sir, in one sense, I believe   1320
Nothing at all,—that everybody can,
Will, and does cheat: but in another sense
I'm ready to believe my very self—
That every cheat's inspired, and every lie
Quick with a germ of truth.

      You ask perhaps   1325
Why I should condescend to trick at all
If I know a way without it? This is why!
There's a strange secret sweet self-sacrifice
In any desecration of one's soul
To a worthy end,—isn't it Herodotus   1330
(I wish I could read Latin!) who describes
The single gift o' the land's virginity,
Demanded in those old Egyptian rites,
(I've but a hazy notion—help me, sir!)
For one purpose in the world, one day in a life,   1335

One hour in a day—thereafter, purity,
And a veil thrown o'er the past for evermore!
Well, now, they understood a many things
Down by Nile city, or wherever it was!
I've always vowed, after the minute's lie,   1340
And the end's gain,—truth should be mine henceforth.
This goes to the root o' the matter, sir,—this plain
Plump fact: accept it and unlock with it
The wards of many a puzzle!

                  Or, finally,
Why should I set so fine a gloss on things?   1345
What need I care? I cheat in self-defence,
And there's my answer to a world of cheats!
Cheat? To be sure, sir! What's the world worth else?
Who takes it as he finds, and thanks his stars?
Don't it want trimming, turning, furbishing up   1350
And polishing over? Your so-styled great men,
Do they accept one truth as truth is found,
Or try their skill at tinkering? What's your world?
Here are you born, who are, I'll say at once,
Of the luckiest kind, whether in head and heart,   1355
Body and soul, or all that helps them both.
Well, now, look back: what faculty of yours
Came to its full, had ample justice done
By growing when rain fell, biding its time,
Solidifying growth when earth was dead,   1360
Spiring up, broadening wide, in seasons due?
Never! You shot up and frost nipped you off,
Settled to sleep when sunshine bade you sprout;
One faculty thwarted its fellow: at the end,
All you boast is 'I had proved a topping tree   1365
'In other climes'—yet this was the right clime
Had you foreknown the seasons. Young, you've force
Wasted like well-streams: old,—oh, then indeed,
Behold a labyrinth of hydraulic pipes
Through which you'd play off wondrous waterwork;   1370
Only, no water's left to feed their play.
Young,—you've a hope, an aim, a love: it's tossed
And crossed and lost: you struggle on, some spark

Shut in your heart against the puffs around,
Through cold and pain; these in due time subside,   1375
Now then for age's triumph, the hoarded light
You mean to loose on the altered face of things,—
Up with it on the tripod! It's extinct.
Spend your life's remnant asking, which was best,
Light smothered up that never peeped forth once,   1380
Or the cold cresset with full leave to shine?
Well, accept this too,—seek the fruit of it
Not in enjoyment, proved a dream on earth,
But knowledge, useful for a second chance,
Another life,—you've lost this world—you've gained   1385
Its knowledge for the next. What knowledge, sir,
Except that you know nothing? Nay, you doubt
Whether 't were better have made you man or brute,
If aught be true, if good and evil clash.
No foul, no fair, no inside, no outside,   1390
There's your world!

                    Give it me! I slap it brisk
With harlequin's pasteboard sceptre: what's it now?
Changed like a rock-flat, rough with rusty weed,
At first wash-over o' the returning wave!
All the dry dead impracticable stuff   1395
Starts into life and light again; this world
Pervaded by the influx from the next.
I cheat, and what's the happy consequence?
You find full justice straightway dealt you out,
Each want supplied, each ignorance set at ease,   1400
Each folly fooled. No life-long labour now
As the price of worse than nothing! No mere film
Holding you chained in iron, as it seems,
Against the outstretch of your very arms
And legs i' the sunshine moralists forbid!   1405
What would you have? Just speak and, there, you see!
You're supplemented, made a whole at last,
Bacon advises, Shakespeare writes you songs,
And Mary Queen of Scots embraces you.
Thus it goes on, not quite like life perhaps,   1410
But so near, that the very difference piques,

Shows that e'en better than this best will be—
This passing entertainment in a hut
Whose bare walls take your taste since, one stage more,
And you arrive at the palace: all half real,   1415
And you, to suit it, less than real beside,
In a dream, lethargic kind of death in life,
That helps the interchange of natures, flesh
Transfused by souls, and such souls! Oh, 't is choice!
And if at whiles the bubble, blown too thin,   1420
Seem nigh on bursting,—if you nearly see
The real world through the false,—what *do* you see?
Is the old so ruined? You find you're in a flock
O' the youthful, earnest, passionate—genius, beauty,
Rank and wealth also, if you care for these: 1425
And all depose their natural rights, hail you,
(That's me, sir) as their mate and yoke-fellow,
Participate in Sludgehood—nay, grow mine,
I veritably possess them—banish doubt,
And reticence and modesty alike!   1430
Why, here's the Golden Age, old Paradise
Or new Eutopia! Here's true life indeed,
And the world well won now, mine for the first time!

And all this might be, may be, and with good help
Of a little lying shall be: so, Sludge lies!   1435
Why, he's at worst your poet who sings how Greeks
That never were, in Troy which never was,
Did this or the other impossible great thing!
He's Lowell—it's a world (you smile applause),
Of his own invention—wondrous Longfellow,   1440
Surprising Hawthorne! Sludge does more than they,
And acts the books they write: the more his praise!

But why do I mount to poets? Take plain prose—
Dealers in common sense, set these at work,
What can they do without their helpful lies?   1445
Each states the law and fact and face o' the thing
Just as he'd have them, finds what he thinks fit,
Is blind to what missuits him, just records
What makes his case out, quite ignores the rest.

It's a History of the World, the Lizard Age,   1450
The Early Indians, the Old Country War,
Jerome Napoleon, whatsoever you please,
All as the author wants it. Such a scribe
You pay and praise for putting life in stones,
Fire into fog, making the past your world.   1455
There's plenty of 'How did you contrive to grasp
'The thread which led you through this labyrinth?
'How build such solid fabric out of air?
'How on so slight foundation found this tale,
'Biography, narrative?' or, in other words,   1460
'How many lies did it require to make
'The portly truth you here present us with?'
'Oh,' quoth the penman, purring at your praise,
' 'T is fancy all; no particle of fact:
'I was poor and threadbare when I wrote that book   1465
' "Bliss in the Golden City." I, at Thebes?
'We writers paint out of our heads, you see!'
'—Ah, the more wonderful the gift in you,
'The more creativeness and godlike craft!'
But I, do I present you with my piece,   1470
It's 'What, Sludge? When my sainted mother spoke
'The verses Lady Jane Grey last composed
'About the rosy bower in the seventh heaven
'Where she and Queen Elizabeth keep house,—
'You made the raps? 'T was your invention that?   1475
'Cur, slave and devil!'—eight fingers and two thumbs
Stuck in my throat!

                    Well, if the marks seem gone
'T is because stiffish cock-tail, taken in time,
Is better for a bruise than arnica.
There, sir! I bear no malice: 't isn't in me.   1480
I know I acted wrongly: still, I've tried
What I could say in my excuse,—to show
The devil's not all devil . . . I don't pretend,
He's angel, much less such a gentleman
As you, sir! And I've lost you, lost myself,   1485
Lost all-l-l-l- . . .

    No—are you in earnest, sir?
O yours, sir, is an angel's part! I know
What prejudice prompts, and what's the common course
Men take to soothe their ruffled self-conceit:
Only you rise superior to it all!   1490
No, sir, it don't hurt much; it's speaking long
That makes me choke a little: the marks will go!
What? Twenty V-notes more, and outfit too,
And not a word to Greeley? One—one kiss
O' the hand that saves me! You'll not let me speak, 1495
I well know, and I've lost the right, too true!
But I must say, sir, if She hears (she does)
Your sainted . . . Well, sir,—be it so! That's, I think,
My bed-room candle. Good-night! Bl-l-less you, sir!

R-r-r, you brute-beast and blackguard! Cowardly
  scamp!   1500
I only wish I dared burn down the house
And spoil your sniggering! Oh what, you're the man?
You're satisfied at last? You've found out Sludge?
We'll see that presently: my turn, sir, next!
I too can tell my story: brute,—do you hear?— 1505
You throttled your sainted mother, that old hag,
In just such a fit of passion: no, it was . . .
To get this house of hers, and many a note
Like these . . . I'll pocket them, however . . . five,
Ten, fifteen . . . ay, you gave her throat the twist, 1510
Or else you poisoned her! Confound the cuss!
Where was my head? I ought to have prophesied
He'll die in a year and join her: that's the way.
I don't know where my head is: what had I done?
How did it all go? I said he poisoned her, 1515
And hoped he'd have grace given him to repent,
Whereon he picked this quarrel, bullied me
And called me cheat: I thrashed him,—who could help?
He howled for mercy, prayed me on his knees
To cut and run and save him from disgrace: 1520
I do so, and once off, he slanders me.
An end of him! Begin elsewhere anew!

Boston's a hole, the herring-pond is wide,
V-notes are something, liberty still more.
Beside, is he the only fool in the world?   1525

APPARENT FAILURE

'We shall soon lose a celebrated building.'
Paris Newspaper.

I

No, for I'll save it! Seven years since,
    I passed through Paris, stopped a day
To see the baptism of your Prince;
    Saw, made my bow, and went my way:
Walking the heat and headache off,   5
    I took the Seine-side, you surmise,
Thought of the Congress, Gortschakoff,
    Cavour's appeal and Buol's replies,
So sauntered till—what met my eyes?

II

Only the Doric little Morgue!   10
    The dead-house where you show your drowned:
Petrarch's Vaucluse makes proud the Sorgue,
    Your Morgue has made the Seine renowned.
One pays one's debt in such a case;
    I plucked up heart and entered,—stalked,   15
Keeping a tolerable face
    Compared with some whose cheeks were chalked:
Let them! No Briton's to be baulked!

III

First came the silent gazers; next,
    A screen of glass, we're thankful for;   20
Last, the sight's self, the sermon's text,
    The three men who did most abhor
Their life in Paris yesterday,
    So killed themselves: and now, enthroned
Each on his copper couch, they lay   25
    Fronting me, waiting to be owned.
I thought, and think, their sin's atoned.

IV

Poor men, God made, and all for that!
　The reverence struck me; o'er each head
Religiously was hung its hat,   30
　Each coat dripped by the owner's bed,
Sacred from touch: each had his berth,
　His bounds, his proper place of rest,
Who last night tenanted on earth
　Some arch, where twelve such slept abreast,—   35
Unless the plain asphalte seemed best.

V

How did it happen, my poor boy?
　You wanted to be Buonaparte
And have the Tuileries for toy,
　And could not, so it broke your heart?   40
You, old one by his side, I judge,
　Were, red as blood, a socialist,
A leveller! Does the Empire grudge
　You've gained what no Republic missed?
Be quiet, and unclench your fist!   45

VI

And this—why, he was red in vain,
　Or black,—poor fellow that is blue!
What fancy was it turned your brain?
　Oh, women were the prize for you!
Money gets women, cards and dice   50
　Get money, and ill-luck gets just
The copper couch and one clear nice
　Cool squirt of water o'er your bust,
The right thing to extinguish lust!

VII

It's wiser being good than bad;   55
　It's safer being meek than fierce:
It's fitter being sane than mad.
　My own hope is, a sun will pierce
The thickest cloud earth ever stretched;
　That, after Last, returns the First,   60

Though a wide compass round be fetched;
   That what began best, can't end worst,
Nor what God blessed once, prove accurst.

EPILOGUE

I

ON the first of the Feast of Feasts,
   The Dedication Day,
When the Levites joined the Priests
   At the Altar in robed array,
Gave signal to sound and say,—   5

II

When the thousands, rear and van,
   Swarming with one accord
Became as a single man
   (Look, gesture, thought and word)
In praising and thanking the Lord,—   10

III

When the singers lift up their voice,
   And the trumpets made endeavour,
Sounding, 'In God rejoice!'
   Saying, 'In Him rejoice
'Whose mercy endureth for ever!'—   15

IV

Then the Temple filled with a cloud,
   Even the House of the Lord;
Porch bent and pillar bowed:
   For the presence of the Lord,
In the glory of His cloud,   20
   Had filled the House of the Lord.

SECOND SPEAKER, *as Renan.*

Gone now! All gone across the dark so far,
   Sharpening fast, shuddering ever, shutting still,

Dwindling into the distance, dies that star
    Which came, stood, opened once! We gazed our fill   25
With upturned faces on as real a Face
    That, stooping from grave music and mild fire,
Took in our homage, made a visible place
    Through many a depth of glory, gyre on gyre,
For the dim human tribute. Was this true?   30
    Could man indeed avail, mere praise of his,
To help by rapture God's own rapture too,
    Thrill with a heart's red tinge that pure pale bliss?
Why did it end? Who failed to beat the breast,
    And shriek, and throw the arms protesting wide,   35
When a first shadow showed the star addressed
    Itself to motion, and on either side
The rims contracted as the rays retired;
    The music, like a fountain's sickening pulse,
Subsided on itself; awhile transpired   40
    Some vestige of a Face no pangs convulse,
No prayers retard; then even this was gone,
    Lost in the night at last. We, lone and left
Silent through centuries, ever and anon
    Venture to probe again the vault bereft   45
Of all now save the lesser lights, a mist
    Of multitudinous points, yet suns, men say—
And this leaps ruby, this lurks amethyst,
    But where may hide what came and loved our clay?
How shall the sage detect in yon expanse   50
    The star which chose to stoop and stay for us?
Unroll the records! Hailed ye such advance
    Indeed, and did your hope evanish thus?
Watchers of twilight, is the worst averred?
    We shall not look up, know ourselves are seen,   55
Speak, and be sure that we again are heard,
    Acting or suffering, have the disk's serene
Reflect our life, absorb an earthly flame,
    Nor doubt that, were mankind inert and numb,
Its core had never crimsoned all the same,   60
    Nor, missing ours, its music fallen dumb?
Oh, dread succession to a dizzy post,
    Sad sway of sceptre whose mere touch appals,

Ghastly dethronement, cursed by those the most
  On whose repugnant brow the crown next falls!   65

THIRD SPEAKER.

I

Witless alike of will and way divine,
How heaven's high with earth's low should intertwine!
Friends, I have seen through your eyes: now use mine!

II

Take the least man of all mankind, as I;
Look at his head and heart, find how and why   70
He differs from his fellows utterly:

III

Then, like me, watch when nature by degrees
Grows alive round him, as in Arctic seas
(They said of old) the instinctive water flees

IV

Toward some elected point of central rock,   75
As though, for its sake only, roamed the flock
Of waves about the waste: awhile they mock

V

With radiance caught for the occasion,—hues
Of blackest hell now, now such reds and blues
As only heaven could fitly interfuse,—   80

VI

The mimic monarch of the whirlpool, king
O' the current for a minute: then they wring
Up by the roots and oversweep the thing,

VII

And hasten off, to play again elsewhere
The same part, choose another peak as bare,   85
They find and flatter, feast and finish there.

VIII

When you see what I tell you,—nature dance
About each man of us, retire, advance,
As though the pageant's end were to enhance

IX

His worth, and—once the life, his product, gained—   90
Roll away elsewhere, keep the strife sustained,
And show thus real, a thing the North but feigned—

X

When you acknowledge that one world could do
All the diverse work, old yet ever new,
Divide us, each from other, me from you,—   95

XI

Why, where's the need of Temple, when the walls
O' the world are that? What use of swells and falls
From Levites' choir, Priests' cries, and trumpet-calls?

XII

That one Face, far from vanish, rather grows,
Or decomposes but to recompose,   100
Become my universe that feels and knows.

APPENDIX A

PAULINE AS FIRST PUBLISHED

PAULINE;

A

FRAGMENT OF A CONFESSION.

Plus ne suis ce que j'ai été,
Et ne le sçaurois jamais être.
MAROT.

LONDON:
SAUNDERS AND OTLEY, CONDUIT STREET.
1833.

NON dubito, quin titulus libri nostri raritate suâ quamplurimos alliciat ad legendum: inter quos nonnulli obliquæ opinionis, mente languidi, multi etiam maligni, et in ingenium nostrum ingrati accedent, qui temerariâ suâ ignorantiâ, vix conspecto titulo clamabunt: Nos vetita docere, hæresium semina jacere: piis auribus offendiculo, præclaris ingeniis scandalo esse: .... adeò conscientiæ suæ consulentes, ut nec Apollo, nec Musæ omnes, neque Angelus de cœlo me ab illorum execratione vindicare queant: quibus et ego nunc consulo, ne scripta nostra legant, nec intelligant, nec meminerint: nam noxia sunt, venenosa sunt: Acherontis ostium est in hoc libro, lapides loquitur, caveant, ne cerebrum illis excutiat. Vos autem, qui æquâ mente ad legendum venitis, si tantam prudentiæ discretionem adhibueritis, quantam in melle legendo apes, jam securi legite. Puto namque vos et utilitatis haud parùm et voluptatis plurimùm accepturos. Quod si qua repereritis, quæ vobis non placeant, mittite illa, nec utimini. NAM ET EGO VOBIS ILLA NON PROBO, SED NARRO. Cætera tamen propterea non respuite. ......Ideo, si quid liberius dictum sit, ignoscite adolescentiæ nostræ, qui minor quam adolescens hoc opus composui.—*H. Cor. Agrippa, De Occult. Phil.*

London, January, 1833.
V. A. XX.

PAULINE

PAULINE, mine own, bend o'er me—thy soft breast
Shall pant to mine—bend o'er me—thy sweet eyes,
And loosened hair, and breathing lips, and arms
Drawing me to thee—these build up a screen
To shut me in with thee, and from all fear,   5
So that I might unlock the sleepless brood
Of fancies from my soul, their lurking place,
Nor doubt that each would pass, ne'er to return
To one so watched, so loved, and so secured.
But what can guard thee but thy naked love?   10
Ah, dearest! whoso sucks a poisoned wound
Envenoms his own veins,—thou art so good,
So calm—if thou should'st wear a brow less light
For some wild thought which, but for me, were kept
From out thy soul, as from a sacred star.   15
Yet till I have unlocked them it were vain
To hope to sing; some woe would light on me;
Nature would point at one, whose quivering lip
Was bathed in her enchantments—whose brow burned
Beneath the crown, to which her secrets knelt;   20
Who learned the spell which can call up the dead,
And then departed, smiling like a fiend
Who has deceived God. If such one should seek
Again her altars, and stand robed and crowned
Amid the faithful: sad confession first.   25
Remorse and pardon, and old claims renewed,
Ere I can be—as I shall be no more.

I had been spared this shame, if I had sate
By thee for ever, from the first, in place
Of my wild dreams of beauty and of good,   30
Or with them, as an earnest of their truth.
No thought nor hope, having been shut from thee,
No vague wish unexplained—no wandering aim
Sent back to bind on Fancy's wings, and seek
Some strange fair world, where it might be a law;   35
But doubting nothing, had been led by thee,
Thro' youth, and saved, as one at length awaked.
Who has slept thro' a peril. Ah! vain, vain!

Thou lovest me—the past is in its grave,
Tho' its ghost haunts us—still this much is ours,   40
To cast away restraint, lest a worse thing
Wait for us in the darkness. Thou lovest me,
And thou art to receive not love, but faith,
For which thou wilt be mine, and smile, and take
All shapes, and shames, and veil without a fear   45
That form which music follows like a slave;
And I look to thee, and I trust in thee,
As in a Northern night one looks alway
Unto the East for morn, and spring and joy.
Thou seest then my aimless, hopeless state,   50
And resting on some few old feelings, won
Back by thy beauty, would'st that I essay
The task, which was to me what now thou art:
And why should I conceal one weakness more?

Thou wilt remember one warm morn, when Winter   55
Crept aged from the earth, and Spring's first breath
Blew soft from the moist hills—the black-thorn
        boughs,
So dark in the bare wood, when glistening
In the sunshine were white with coming buds,
Like the bright side of a sorrow—and the banks   60
Had violets opening from sleep like eyes—
I walked with thee, who knew not a deep shame
Lurked beneath smiles and careless words, which
        sought
To hide it—till they wandered and were mute;
As we stood listening on a sunny mound   65
To the wind murmuring in the damp copse,
Like heavy breathings of some hidden thing
Betrayed by sleep—until the feeling rushed
That I was low indeed, yet not so low
As to endure the calmness of thine eyes;   70
And so I told thee all, while the cool breast
I leaned on altered not its quiet beating;
And long ere words, like a hurt bird's complaint,
Bade me look up and be what I had been,
I felt despair could never live by thee.   75
Thou wilt remember:—thou art not more dear
Than song was once to me; and I ne'er sung
But as one entering bright halls, where all

Will rise and shout for him. Sure I must own
That I am fallen—having chosen gifts   80
Distinct from theirs—that I am sad—and fain
Would give up all to be but where I was;
Not high as I had been, if faithful found—
But low and weak, yet full of hope, and sure
Of goodness as of life—that I would lose   85
All this gay mastery of mind, to sit
Once more with them, trusting in truth and love,
And with an aim—not being what I am.
Oh, Pauline! I am ruined! who believed
That tho' my soul had floated from its sphere   90
Of wide dominion into the dim orb
Of self—that it was strong and free as ever:—
It has conformed itself to that dim orb,
Reflecting all its shades and shapes, and now
Must stay where it alone can be adored.   95
I have felt this in dreams—in dreams in which
I seemed the fate from which I fled; I felt
A strange delight in causing my decay;
I was a fiend, in darkness chained for ever
Within some ocean-cave; and ages rolled,   100
Till thro' the cleft rock, like a moonbeam, came
A white swan to remain with me; and ages
Rolled, yet I tired not of my first joy
In gazing on the peace of its pure wings.
And then I said, 'It is most fair to me,   105
'Yet its soft wings must sure have suffered change
'From the thick darkness—sure its eyes are dim—
'Its silver pinions must be cramped and numbed
'With sleeping ages here; it cannot leave me,
'For it would seem, in light, beside its kind,   110
'Withered—tho' here to me most beautiful.'
And then I was a young witch, whose blue eyes,
As she stood naked by the river springs,
Drew down a god—I watched his radiant form
Growing less radiant—and it gladdened me;   115
Till one morn, as he sat in the sunshine
Upon my knees, singing to me of heaven,
He turned to look at me, ere I could lose
The grin with which I viewed his perishing.
And he shrieked and departed, and sat long   120
By his deserted throne—but sunk at last,

Murmuring, as I kissed his lips and curled
Around him, 'I am still a god—to thee.'
Still I can lay my soul bare in its fall,
For all the wandering and all the weakness   125
Will be a saddest comment on the song.
And if, that done, I can be young again,
I will give up all gained as willingly
As one gives up a charm which shuts him out
From hope, or part, or care, in human kind.   130
As life wanes, all its cares, and strife, and toil,
Seem strangely valueless, while the old trees
Which grew by our youth's home—the waving mass
Of climbing plants, heavy with bloom and dew—
The morning swallows with their songs like words,—   135
All these seem clear and only worth our thoughts.
So aught connected with my early life———
My rude songs or my wild imaginings,
How I look on them—most distinct amid
The fever and the stir of after years!   140

I ne'er had ventured e'en to hope for this,
Had not the glow I felt at His award,
Assured me all was not extinct within.
Him whom all honor—whose renown springs up
Like sunlight which will visit all the world;   145
So that e'en they who sneered at him at first,
Come out to it, as some dark spider crawls
From his foul nets, which some lit torch invades,
Yet spinning still new films for his retreat.—
Thou didst smile, poet,—but, can *we* forgive?   150

Sun-treader—life and light be thine for ever;
Thou art gone from us—years go by—and spring
Gladdens, and the young earth is beautiful,
Yet thy songs come not—other bards arise,
But none like thee—they stand—thy majesties,   155
Like mighty works which tell some Spirit there
Hath sat regardless of neglect and scorn,
Till, its long task completed, it hath risen
And left us, never to return: and all
Rush in to peer and praise when all in vain.   160
The air seems bright with thy past presence yet,
But thou art still for me, as thou hast been

When I have stood with thee, as on a throne
With all thy dim creations gathered round
Like mountains,—and I felt of mould like them,   165
And creatures of my own were mixed with them,
Like things half-lived, catching and giving life.
But thou art still for me, who have adored,
Tho' single, panting but to hear thy name,
Which I believed a spell to me alone,   170
Scarce deeming thou wert as a star to men—
As one should worship long a sacred spring
Scarce worth a moth's flitting, which long grasses cross,
And one small tree embowers droopingly,
Joying to see some wandering insect won,   175
To live in its few rushes—or some locust
To pasture on its boughs—or some wild bird
Stoop for its freshness from the trackless air,
And then should find it but the fountain-head,
Long lost, of some great river—washing towns   180
And towers, and seeing old woods which will live
But by its banks, untrod of human foot,
Which, when the great sun sinks, lie quivering
In light as some thing lieth half of life
Before God's foot—waiting a wondrous change   185
—Then girt with rocks which seek to turn or stay
Its course in vain, for it does ever spread
Like a sea's arm as it goes rolling on,
Being the pulse of some great country—so
Wert thou to me—and art thou to the world.   190
And I, perchance, half feel a strange regret,
That I am not what I have been to thee:
Like a girl one has loved long silently,
In her first loveliness, in some retreat,
When first emerged, all gaze and glow to view   195
Her fresh eyes, and soft hair, and lips which bleed
Like a mountain berry. Doubtless it is sweet
To see her thus adored—but there have been
Moments, when all the world was in his praise,
Sweeter than all the pride of after hours.   200
Yet, Sun-treader, all hail!—from my heart's heart
I bid thee hail!—e'en in my wildest dreams,
I am proud to feel I would have thrown up all
The wreathes of fame which seemed o'erhanging me,
To have seen thee, for a moment, as thou art.   205

And if thou livest—if thou lovest, spirit!
Remember me, who set this final seal
To wandering thought—that one so pure as thou
Could never die. Remember me, who flung
All honor from my soul—yet paused and said,   210
'There is one spark of love remaining yet,
'For I have nought in common with him—shapes
'Which followed him avoid me, and foul forms
'Seek me, which ne'er could fasten on his mind;
'And tho' I feel how low I am to him,   215
'Yet I aim not even to catch a tone
'Of all the harmonies which he called up,
'So one gleam still remains, altho' the last.'
Remember me—who praise thee e'en with tears,
For never more shall I walk calm with thee;   220
Thy sweet imaginings are as an air,
A melody, some wond'rous singer sings,
Which, though it haunt men oft in the still eve,
They dream not to essay; yet it no less,
But more is honored. I was thine in shame,   225
And now when all thy proud renown is out,
I am a watcher, whose eyes have grown dim
With looking for some star—which breaks on him,
Altered, and worn, and weak, and full of tears.

Autumn has come—like Spring returned to us,   230
Won from her girlishness—like one returned
A friend that was a lover—nor forgets
The first warm love, but full of sober thoughts
Of fading years; whose soft mouth quivers yet
With the old smile—but yet so changed and still!   235
And here am I the scoffer, who have probed
Life's vanity, won by a word again
Into my old life—for one little word
Of this sweet friend, who lives in loving me,
Lives strangely on my thoughts, and looks, and words, 240
As fathoms down some nameless ocean thing
Its silent course of quietness and joy.
O dearest, if, indeed, I tell the past,
May'st thou forget it as a sad sick dream;
Or if it linger—my lost soul too soon   245
Sinks to itself, and whispers, we shall be
But closer linked—two creatures whom the earth

Bears singly—with strange feelings, unrevealed
But to each other; or two lonely things
Created by some Power, whose reign is done,   250
Having no part in God, or his bright world,
I am to sing; whilst ebbing day dies soft,
As a lean scholar dies, worn o'er his book,
And in the heaven stars steal out one by one,
As hunted men steal to their mountain watch.   255
I must not think—lest this new impulse die
In which I trust. I have no confidence,
So I will sing on—fast as fancies come
Rudely—the verse being as the mood it paints.

I strip my mind bare—whose first elements   260
I shall unveil—not as they struggled forth
In infancy, nor as they now exist,
That I am grown above them, and can rule them,
But in that middle stage, when they were full,
Yet ere I had disposed them to my will;   265
And then I shall show how these elements
Produced my present state, and what it is.
I am made up of an intensest life,
Of a most clear idea of consciousness
Of self—distinct from all its qualities,   270
From all affections, passions, feelings, powers;
And thus far it exists, if tracked in all,
But linked in me, to self-supremacy,
Existing as a centre to all things,
Most potent to create, and rule, and call   275
Upon all things to minister to it;
And to a principle of restlessness
Which would be all, have, see, know, taste, feel, all—
This is myself; and I should thus have been,
Though gifted lower than the meanest soul.   280

And of my powers, one springs up to save
From utter death a soul with such desires
Confined to clay—which is the only one
Which marks me—an imagination which
Has been an angel to me—coming not   285
In fitful visions, but beside me ever,
And never failing me; so tho' my mind
Forgets not—not a shred of life forgets—

Yet I can take a secret pride in calling
The dark past up—to quell it regally.   290

A mind like this must dissipate itself,
But I have always had one lode-star; now,
As I look back, I see that I have wasted,
Or progressed as I looked toward that star—
A need, a trust, a yearning after God,   295
A feeling I have analysed but late,
But it existed, and was reconciled
With a neglect of all I deemed his laws,
Which yet, when seen in others, I abhorred.
I felt as one beloved, and so shut in   300
From fear—and thence I date my trust in signs
And omens—for I saw God every where;
And I can only lay it to the fruit
Of a sad after-time that I could doubt
Even his being—having always felt   305
His presence—never acting from myself,
Still trusting in a hand that leads me through
All danger; and this feeling still has fought
Against my weakest reason and resolves.

And I can love nothing—and this dull truth   310
Has come the last—but sense supplies a love
Encircling me and mingling with my life.

These make myself—for I have sought in vain
To trace how they were formed by circumstance,
For I still find them—turning my wild youth   315
Where they alone displayed themselves, converting
All objects to their use—now see their course!

They came to me in my first dawn of life,
Which passed alone with wisest ancient books,
All halo-girt with fancies of my own,   320
And I myself went with the tale—a god,
Wandering after beauty—or a giant,
Standing vast in the sunset—an old hunter,
Talking with gods—or a high-crested chief,
Sailing with troops of friends to Tenedos;—   325
I tell you, nought has ever been so clear
As the place, the time, the fashion of those lives.

I had not seen a work of lofty art,
Nor woman's beauty, nor sweet nature's face,
Yet, I say, never morn broke clear as those   330
On the dim clustered isles in the blue sea:
The deep groves, and white temples, and wet caves—
And nothing ever will surprise me now—
Who stood beside the naked Swift-footed,
Who bound my forehead with Proserpine's hair.   335

An' strange it is, that I who could so dream,
Should e'er have stooped to aim at aught beneath—
Aught low, or painful, but I never doubted;
So as I grew, I rudely shaped my life
To my immediate wants, yet strong beneath   340
Was a vague sense of powers folded up—
A sense that tho' those shadowy times were past,
Their spirit dwelt in me, and I should rule.

Then came a pause, and long restraint chained down
My soul, till it was changed. I lost myself,   345
And were it not that I so loathe that time,
I could recall how first I learned to turn
My mind against itself; and the effects,
In deeds for which remorse were vain, as for
The wanderings of delirious dream; yet thence   350
Came cunning, envy, falsehood, which so long
Have spotted me—at length I was restored,
Yet long the influence remained; and nought
But the still life I led, apart from all,
Which left my soul to seek its old delights,   355
Could e'er have brought me thus far back to peace.
As peace returned, I sought out some pursuit:
And song rose—no new impulse—but the one
With which all others best could be combined.
My life has not been that of those whose heaven   360
Was lampless, save where poesy shone out;
But as a clime, where glittering mountain-tops,
And glancing sea, and forests steeped in light,
Give back reflected the far-flashing sun;
For music, (which is earnest of a heaven,   365
Seeing we know emotions strange by it,
Not else to be revealed,) is as a voice,
A low voice calling Fancy, as a friend,

To the green woods in the gay summer time.
And she fills all the way with dancing shapes,   370
Which have made painters pale; and they go on
While stars look at them, and winds call to them,
As they leave life's path for the twilight world,
Where the dead gather. This was not at first,
For I scarce knew what I would do. I had   375
No wish to paint, no yearning—but I sang.

   And first I sang, as I in dream have seen,
Music wait on a lyrist for some thought,
Yet singing to herself until it came.
I turned to those old times and scenes, where all   380
That's beautiful had birth for me, and made
Rude verses on them all; and then I paused—
I had done nothing, so I sought to know
What mind had yet achieved. No fear was mine
As I gazed on the works of mighty bards,   385
In the first joy at finding my own thoughts
Recorded, and my powers exemplified,
And feeling their aspirings were my own.
And then I first explored passion and mind;
And I began afresh; I rather sought   390
To rival what I wondered at, than form
Creations of my own; so much was light
Lent back by others, yet much was my own.

   I paused again—a change was coming on,
I was no more a boy—the past was breaking   395
Before the coming, and like fever worked.
I first thought on myself—and here my powers
Burst out. I dreamed not of restraint, but gazed
On all things: schemes and systems went and came,
And I was proud (being vainest of the weak),   400
In wandering o'er them, to seek out some one
To be my own; as one should wander o'er
The white way for a star.

     *   *   *   *

On one, whom praise of mine would not offend,
Who was as calm as beauty—being such   405
Unto mankind as thou to me, Pauline,
Believing in them, and devoting all
His soul's strength to their winning back to peace;

Who sent forth hopes and longings for their sake,
Clothed in all passion's melodies, which first   410
Caught me, and set me, as to a sweet task,
To gather every breathing of his songs.
And woven with them there were words, which seemed
A key to a new world; the muttering
Of angels, of some thing unguessed by man.   415
How my heart beat, as I went on, and found
Much there! I felt my own mind had conceived,
But there living and burning; soon the whole
Of his conceptions dawned on me; their praise
Is in the tongues of men; men's brows are high   420
When his name means a triumph and a pride;
So my weak hands may well forbear to dim
What then seemed my bright fate: I threw myself
To meet it. I was vowed to liberty,
Men were to be as gods, and earth as heaven.   425
And I—ah! what a life was mine to be,
My whole soul rose to meet it. Now, Pauline,
I shall go mad, if I recall that time.

                    *   *   *   *

    O let me look back, e'er I leave for ever
The time, which was an hour, that one waits   430
For a fair girl, that comes a withered hag.
And I was lonely,—far from woods and fields,
And amid dullest sights, who should be loose
As a stag—yet I was full of joy—who lived
With Plato—and who had the key to life.   435
And I had dimly shaped my first attempt,
And many a thought did I build up on thought,
As the wild bee hangs cell to cell—in vain;
For I must still go on: my mind rests not.

'Twas in my plan to look on real life,   440
Which was all new to me; my theories
Were firm, so I left them, to look upon
Men, and their cares, and hopes, and fears, and joys;
And, as I pondered on them all, I sought
How best life's end might be attained—an end   445
Comprising every joy. I deeply mused.

And suddenly, without heart-wreck, I awoke
As from a dream—I said, 'twas beautiful,

Yet but a dream; and so adieu to it.
As some world-wanderer sees in a far meadow   450
Strange towers, and walled gardens, thick with trees,
Where singing goes on, and delicious mirth,
And laughing fairy creatures peeping over,
And on the morrow, when he comes to live
For ever by those springs, and trees, fruit-flushed   455
And fairy bowers—all his search is vain.
Well I remember * * * *
First went my hopes of perfecting mankind,
And faith in them—then freedom in itself,
And virtue in itself—and then my motives' ends,   460
And powers and loves; and human love went last.
I felt this no decay, because new powers
Rose as old feelings left—wit, mockery,
And happiness; for I had oft been sad,
Mistrusting my resolves: but now I cast   465
Hope joyously away—I laughed and said,
'No more of this'—I must not think; at length
I look'd again to see how all went on.

My powers were greater—as some temple seemed
My soul, where nought is changed, and incense rolls   470
Around the altar—only God is gone,
And some dark spirit sitteth in his seat!
So I passed through the temple; and to me
Knelt troops of shadows; and they cried, 'Hail, king!
'We serve thee now, and thou shalt serve no more!   475
'Call on us, prove us, let us worship thee!'
And I said, 'Are ye strong—let fancy bear me
'Far from the past.'—And I was borne away
As Arab birds float sleeping in the wind,
O'er deserts, towers, and forests, I being calm;   480
And I said, 'I have nursed up energies,
'They will prey on me.' And a band knelt low,
And cried, 'Lord, we are here, and we will make
'A way for thee—in thine appointed life
'O look on us!' And I said, 'Ye will worship   485
'Me; but my heart must worship too.' They shouted,
'Thyself—thou art our king!' So I stood there
Smiling * * * * * *
And buoyant and rejoicing was the spirit
With which I looked out how to end my days;   490

I felt once more myself—my powers were mine;
I found that youth or health so lifted me,
That, spite of all life's vanity, no grief
Came nigh me—I must ever be light-hearted;
And that this feeling was the only veil   495
Betwixt me and despair: so if age came,
I should be as a wreck linked to a soul
Yet fluttering, or mind-broken, and aware
Of my decay. So a long summer morn
Found me; and e'er noon came, I had resolved   500
No age should come on me, ere youth's hopes went,
For I would wear myself out—like that morn
Which wasted not a sunbeam—every joy
I would make mine, and die; and thus I sought
To chain my spirit down, which I had fed   505
With thoughts of fame. I said, the troubled life
Of genius seen so bright when working forth
Some trusted end, seems sad, when all in vain—
Most sad, when men have parted with all joy
For their wild fancy's sake, which waited first,   510
As an obedient spirit, when delight
Came not with her alone, but alters soon,
Coming darkened, seldom, hasting to depart,
Leaving a heavy darkness and warm tears.

But I shall never lose her; she will live   515
Brighter for such seclusion—I but catch
A hue, a glance of what I sing, so pain
Is linked with pleasure, for I ne'er may tell
The radiant sights which dazzle me; but now
They shall be all my own, and let them fade   520
Untold—others shall rise as fair, as fast.
And when all's done, the few dim gleams transferred,—
(For a new thought sprung up—that it were well
To leave all shadowy hopes, and weave such lays
As would encircle me with praise and love;   525
So I should not die utterly—I should bring
One branch from the gold forest, like the knight
Of old tales, witnessing I had been there,)—
And when all's done, how vain seems e'en success,
And all the influence poets have o'er men!   530
'Tis a fine thing that one, weak as myself,
Should sit in his lone room, knowing the words

He utters in his solitude shall move
Men like a swift wind—that tho' he be forgotten,
Fair eyes shall glisten when his beauteous dreams   535
Of love come true in happier frames than his.
Ay, the still night brought thoughts like these, but
        morn
Came, and the mockery again laughed out
At hollow praises, and smiles, almost sneers;
And my soul's idol seemed to whisper me   540
To dwell with him and his unhonoured name—
And I well knew my spirit, that would be
First in the struggle, and again would make
All bow to it; and I would sink again.

            *   *   *   *   *

And then know that this curse will come on us,   545
To see our idols perish—we may wither,
Nor marvel—we are clay; but our low fate
Should not extend them, whom trustingly
We sent before into Time's yawning gulf,
To face what e'er may lurk in darkness there—   550
To see the painters' glory pass, and feel
Sweet music move us not as once, or worst,
To see decaying wits ere the frail body
Decays. Nought makes me trust in love so really,
As the delight of the contented lowness   555
With which I gaze on souls I'd keep for ever
In beauty—I'd be sad to equal them;
I'd feed their fame e'en from my heart's best blood,
Withering unseen, that they might flourish still.

            *   *   *   *

Pauline, my sweet friend, thou dost not forget   560
How this mood swayed me, when thou first wert
        mine,
When I had set myself to live this life,
Defying all opinion. Ere thou camest
I was most happy, sweet, for old delights
Had come like birds again; music, my life,   565
I nourished more than ever, and old lore
Loved for itself, and all it shows—the king
Treading the purple calmly to his death,
—While round him, like the clouds of eve, all dusk,

The giant shades of fate, silently flitting,   570
Pile the dim outline of the coming doom,
—And him sitting alone in blood, while friends
Are hunting far in the sunshine; and the boy,
With his white breast and brow and clustering curls
Streaked with his mother's blood, and striving hard   575
To tell his story ere his reason goes.
And when I loved thee, as I've loved so oft,
Thou lovedst me, and I wondered, and looked in
My heart to find some feeling like such love,
Believing I was still what I had been;   580
And soon I found all faith had gone from me,
And the late glow of life—changing like clouds,
'Twas not the morn-blush widening into day,
But evening, coloured by the dying sun
While darkness is quick hastening:—I will tell   585
My state as though 'twere none of mine—despair
Cannot come near me—thus it is with me.
Souls alter not, and mine must progress still;
And this I knew not when I flung away
My youth's chief aims. I ne'er supposed the loss   590
Of what few I retained; for no resource
Awaits me—now behold the change of all.
I cannot chain my soul, it will not rest
In its clay prison; this most narrow sphere—
It has strange powers, and feelings, and desires,   595
Which I cannot account for, nor explain,
But which I stifle not, being bound to trust
All feelings equally—to hear all sides:
Yet I cannot indulge them, and they live,
Referring to some state or life unknown. . . .   600

My selfishness is satiated not,
It wears me like a flame; my hunger for
All pleasure, howsoe'er minute, is pain;
I envy—how I envy him whose mind
Turns with its energies to some one end!   605
To elevate a sect, or a pursuit,
However mean—so my still baffled hopes
Seek out abstractions; I would have but one
Delight on earth, so it were wholly mine;
One rapture all my soul could fill—and this   610
Wild feeling places me in dream afar,

In some wide country, where the eye can see
No end to the far hills and dales bestrewn
With shining towers and dwellings. I grow mad
Well-nigh, to know not one abode but holds   615
Some pleasure—for my soul could grasp them all,
But must remain with this vile form. I look
With hope to age at last, which quenching much,
May let me concentrate the sparks it spares.

This restlessness of passion meets in me   620
A craving after knowledge: the sole proof
Of a commanding will is in that power
Repressed; for I beheld it in its dawn,
That sleepless harpy, with its budding wings,
And I considered whether I should yield   625
All hopes and fears, to live alone with it,
Finding a recompence in its wild eyes;
And when I found that I should perish so,
I bade its wild eyes close from me for ever;—
And I am left alone with my delights,—   630
So it lies in me a chained thing—still ready
To serve me, if I loose its slightest bond—
I cannot but be proud of my bright slave.

And thus I know this earth is not my sphere,
For I cannot so narrow me, but that   635
I still exceed it; in their elements
My love would pass my reason—but since here
Love must receive its objects from this earth,
While reason will be chainless, the few truths
Caught from its wanderings have sufficed to quell   640
All love below;—then what must be that love
Which, with the object it demands, would quell
Reason, tho' it soared with the seraphim?
No—what I feel may pass all human love,
Yet fall far short of what my love should be;   645
And yet I seem more warped in this than aught,
For here myself stands out more hideously.
I can forget myself in friendship, fame,
Or liberty, or love of mighty souls.

                    *   *   *   *

But I begin to know what thing hate is—   650
To sicken, and to quiver, and grow white,

And I myself have furnished its first prey.
All my sad weaknesses, this wavering will,
This selfishness, this still decaying frame . . .
But I must never grieve while I can pass   655
Far from such thoughts—as now—Andromeda!
And she is with me—years roll, I shall change,
But change can touch her not—so beautiful
With her dark eyes, earnest and still, and hair
Lifted and spread by the salt-sweeping breeze;   660
And one red-beam, all the storm leaves in heaven,
Resting upon her eyes and face and hair,
As she awaits the snake on the wet beach,
By the dark rock, and the white wave just breaking
At her feet; quite naked and alone,—a thing   665
You doubt not, nor fear for, secure that God
Will come in thunder from the stars to save her.
Let it pass—I will call another change.
I will be gifted with a wond'rous soul,
Yet sunk by error to men's sympathy,   670
And in the wane of life; yet only so
As to call up their fears, and there shall come
A time requiring youth's best energies;
And strait I fling age, sorrow, sickness off,
And I rise triumphing over my decay.   675

*   *   *   *

And thus it is that I supply the chasm
'Twixt what I am and all that I would be.
But then to know nothing—to hope for nothing—
To seize on life's dull joys from a strange fear,
Lest, losing them, all's lost, and nought remains.   680

*   *   *   *

There's some vile juggle with my reason here—
I feel I but explain to my own loss
These impulses—they live no less the same.
Liberty! what though I despair—my blood
Rose not at a slave's name proudlier than now,   685
And sympathy obscured by sophistries.
Why have not I sought refuge in myself,
But for the woes I saw and could not stay—
And love!—do I not love thee, my Pauline?

*   *   *   *

I cherish prejudice, lest I be left   690
Utterly loveless—witness this belief
In poets, tho' sad change has come there too;
No more I leave myself to follow them:
Unconsciously I measure me by them.
Let me forget it; and I cherish most   695
My love of England—how her name—a word
Of her's in a strange tongue makes my heart beat! . .

                      *   *   *   *

Pauline, I could do any thing—not now—
All's fever—but when calm shall come again—
I am prepared—I have made life my own—   700
I would not be content with all the change
One frame should feel—but I have gone in thought
Thro' all conjuncture—I have lived all life
When it is most alive—where strangest fate
New shapes it past surmise—the tales of men   705
Bit by some curse—or in the grasps of doom
Half-visible and still increasing round,
Or crowning their wide being's general aim. . . .

                      *   *   *   *

These are wild fancies, but I feel, sweet friend,
As one breathing his weakness to the ear   710
Of pitying angel—dear as a winter flower;
A slight flower growing alone, and offering
Its frail cup of three leaves to the cold sun,
Yet joyous and confiding, like the triumph
Of a child—and why am I not worthy thee?   715

                      *   *   *   *

I can live all the life of plants, and gaze
Drowsily on the bees that flit and play,
Or bare my breast for sunbeams which will kill,
Or open in the night of sounds, to look
For the dim stars; I can mount with the bird,   720
Leaping airily his pyramid of leaves
And twisted boughs of some tall mountain tree,
Or rise cheerfully springing to the heavens—
Or like a fish breathe in the morning air
In the misty sun-warm water—or with flowers   725
And trees can smile in light at the sinking sun,

Just as the storm comes—as a girl would look
On a departing lover—most serene.

Pauline, come with me—see how I could build
A home for us, out of the world; in thought—   730
I am inspired—come with me, Pauline!

Night, and one single ridge of narrow path
Between the sullen river and the woods
Waving and muttering—for the moonless night
Has shaped them into images of life,   735
Like the upraising of the giant-ghosts,
Looking on earth to know how their sons fare.
Thou art so close by me, the roughest swell
Of wind in the tree-tops hides not the panting
Of thy soft breasts; no—we will pass to morning—   740
Morning—the rocks, and vallies, and old woods.
How the sun brightens in the mist, and here,—
Half in the air, like creatures of the place,
Trusting the element—living on high boughs
That swing in the wind—look at the golden spray,   745
Flung from the foam-sheet of the cataract,
Amid the broken rocks—shall we stay here
With the wild hawks?—no, ere the hot noon come
Dive we down—safe;—see this our new retreat
Walled in with a sloped mound of matted shrubs,   750
Dark, tangled, old and green—still sloping down
To a small pool whose waters lie asleep
Amid the trailing boughs turned water-plants
And tall trees over-arch to keep us in,
Breaking the sunbeams into emerald shafts,   755
And in the dreamy water one small group
Of two or three strange trees are got together,
Wondering at all around—as strange beasts herd
Together far from their own land—all wildness—
No turf nor moss, for boughs and plants pave all,   760
And tongues of bank go shelving in the waters,
Where the pale-throated snake reclines his head,
And old grey stones lie making eddies there;
The wild mice cross them dry-shod—deeper in—
Shut thy soft eyes—now look—still deeper in: 765
This is the very heart of the woods—all round,
Mountain-like, heaped above us; yet even here

One pond of water gleams—far off the river
Sweeps like a sea, barred out from land; but one—
One thin clear sheet has over-leaped and wound   770
Into this silent depth, which gained, it lies
Still, as but let by sufferance; the trees bend
O'er it as wild men watch a sleeping girl,
And thro' their roots long creeping plants stretch out
Their twined hair, steeped and sparkling; farther on,   775
Tall rushes and thick flag-knots have combined
To narrow it; so, at length, a silver thread
It winds, all noiselessly, thro' the deep wood,
Till thro' a cleft way, thro' the moss and stone,
It joins its parent-river with a shout.   780
Up for the glowing day—leave the old woods:
See, they part, like a ruined arch, the sky!
Nothing but sky appears, so close the root
And grass of the hill-top level with the air—
Blue sunny air, where a great cloud floats, laden   785
With light, like a dead whale that white birds pick,
Floating away in the sun in some north sea.
Air, air—fresh life-blood—thin and searching air—
The clear, dear breath of God, that loveth us:
Where small birds reel and winds take their delight.   790
Water is beautiful, but not like air.
See, where the solid azure waters lie,
Made as of thickened air, and down below,
The fern-ranks, like a forest spread themselves,
As tho' each pore could feel the element;   795
Where the quick glancing serpent winds his way—
Float with me there, Pauline, but not like air.
Down the hill—stop—a clump of trees, see, set
On a heap of rocks, which look o'er the far plains,
And envious climbing shrubs would mount to rest,   800
And peer from their spread boughs. There they wave,
        looking
At the muleteers, who whistle as they go
To the merry chime of their morning bells, and all
The little smoking cots, and fields, and banks,
And copses, bright in the sun; my spirit wanders.   805
Hedge-rows for me—still, living, hedge-rows, where
The bushes close, and clasp above, and keep
Thought in—I am concentrated—I feel;—
But my soul saddens when it looks beyond;

I cannot be immortal, nor taste all.   810
O God! where does this tend—these struggling aims!*
What would I have? what is this 'sleep,' which seems
To bound all? can there be a 'waking' point
Of crowning life? The soul would never rule—
It would be first in all things—it would have   815
Its utmost pleasure filled,—but that complete
Commanding for commanding sickens it.
The last point that I can trace is, rest beneath
Some better essence than itself—in weakness;
This is 'myself'—not what I think should be,   820
And what is that I hunger for but God?
My God, my God! let me for once look on thee
As tho' nought else existed: we alone.
And as creation crumbles, my soul's spark
Expands till I can say, 'Even from myself   825
'I need thee, and I feel thee, and I love thee;
'I do not plead my rapture in thy works
'For love of thee—or that I feel as one
'Who cannot die—but there is that in me
'Which turns to thee, which loves, or which should
    love.'   830

* Je crains bien que mon pauvre ami ne soit pas toujours parfaitement compris dans
ce qui reste à lire de cet étrange fragment — mais il est moins propre que tout autre à
éclaircir ce qui de sa nature ne peut jamais être que songe et confusion. D'ailleurs je ne
sais trop si en cherchant à mieux co-ordonner certaines parties l'on ne courrait pas le
risque de nuire au seul mérite auquel une production si singuliere peut prétendre —
celui de donner une idée assez précise du genre qu'elle n'a fait qu'ébaucher. — Ce
début sans prétention, ce remuement des passions qui va d'abord en accroissant et puis
s'appaise par degrés, ces élans de l'ame, ce retour soudain sur soi-même. — Et par
dessus tout, la tournure d'esprit toute particulière de mon ami rendent les changemens
presque impossibles. Les raisons qu'il fait valoir ailleurs, et d'autres encore plus
puissantes, ont fait trouver grâce à mes yeux pour cet écrit qu' autrement je lui eusse
conseillé de jeter au feu — Je n'en crois pas moins au grand principe de toute composi-
tion — à ce principe de Shakspeare, de Raffaelle, de Beethoven, d'où il suit que la
concentration des idées est dûe bien plus à leur conception, qu'à leur mise en exécution
. . . j'ai tout lieu de craindre que la première de ces qualités ne soit encore étrangère à
mon ami — et je doute fort qu'un redoublement de travail lui fasse acquérir la seconde.
Le mieux serait de bruler ceci; mais que faire?
    Je crois que dans ce qui suit il fait allusion à un certain examen qu'il fit autrefois de
l'âme ou plutot de son âme, pour découvrir la suite des objets auxquels il lui serait
possible d'atteindre, et dont chacun une fois obtenu devait former une espèce de plateau
d'où l'on pouvait apercevoir d'autres buts, d'autres projets, d'autres jouissances, qui,
à leur tour, devaient être surmontés. Il en résultait que l'oubli et le sommeil devaient
tout terminer. Cette idée que je ne saisis pas parfaitement lui est peutêtre aussi intelligible
qu'à moi.

                                                                   PAULINE.

Why have I girt myself with this hell-dress?
Why have I laboured to put out my life?
Is it not in my nature to adore,
And e'en for all my reason do I not
Feel him, and thank him, and pray to him?—*Now.*   835
Can I forego the trust that he loves me?
Do I not feel a love which only O N E . . . . .
O thou pale form, so dimly seen, deep-eyed,
I have denied thee calmly—do I not
Pant when I read of thy consummate deeds,   840
And burn to see thy calm, pure truths out-flash
The brightest gleams of earth's philosophy?
Do I not shake to hear aught question thee? . . . .

If I am erring save me, madden me,
Take from me powers, and pleasures—let me die   845
Ages, so I see thee: I am knit round
As with a charm, by sin and lust and pride,
Yet tho' my wandering dreams have seen all shapes
Of strange delight, oft have I stood by thee—
Have I been keeping lonely watch with thee,   850
In the damp night by weeping Olivet,
Or leaning on thy bosom, proudly less—
Or dying with thee on the lonely cross—
Or witnessing thy bursting from the tomb!

A mortal, sin's familiar friend doth here   855
Avow that he will give all earth's reward,
But to believe and humbly teach the faith,
In suffering, and poverty, and shame,
Only believing he is not unloved . . . .

And now, my Pauline, I am thine for ever!   860
I feel the spirit which has buoyed me up
Deserting me: and old shades gathering on;
Yet while its last light waits, I would say much,
And chiefly, I am glad that I have said
That love which I have ever felt for thee,   865
But seldom told; our hearts so beat together,
That speech is mockery, but when dark hours come;
And I feel sad; and thou, sweet, deem'st it strange;
A sorrow moves me, thou canst not remove.
Look on this lay I dedicate to thee,   870

Which thro' thee I began, and which I end,
Collecting the last gleams to strive to tell
That I am thine, and more than ever now—
That I am sinking fast—yet tho' I sink,
No less I feel that thou hast brought me bliss,   875
And that I still may hope to win it back.
Thou know'st, dear friend, I could not think all calm,
For wild dreams followed me, and bore me off,
And all was indistinct. Ere one was caught
Another glanced: so dazzled by my wealth,   880
Knowing not which to leave nor which to choose,
For all my thoughts so floated, nought was fixed—
And then thou said'st a perfect bard was one
Who shadowed out the stages of all life,
And so thou badest me tell this my first stage;—   885
'Tis done: and even now I feel all dim the shift
Of thought. These are my last thoughts; I discern
Faintly immortal life, and truth, and good.
And why thou must be mine is, that e'en now,
In the dim hush of night—that I have done—   890
With fears and sad forebodings: I look thro'
And say, 'E'en at the last I have her still,
'With her delicious eyes as clear as heaven,
'When rain in a quick shower has beat down mist,
'And clouds float white in the sun like broods of
          swans.'   895
How the blood lies upon her cheek, all spread
As thinned by kisses; only in her lips
It wells and pulses like a living thing,
And her neck looks, like marble misted o'er
With love-breath, a dear thing to kiss and love,   900
Standing beneath me—looking out to me,
As I might kill her and be loved for it.

Love me—love me, Pauline, love nought but me;
Leave me not. All these words are wild and weak,
Believe them not, Pauline. I stooped so low   905
But to behold thee purer by my side,
To show thou art my breath—my life—a last
Resource—an extreme want: never believe
Aught better could so look to thee, nor seek
Again the world of good thoughts left for me.   910
There were bright troops of undiscovered suns,

Each equal in their radiant course. There were
Clusters of far fair isles, which ocean kept
For his own joy, and his waves broke on them
Without a choice. And there was a dim crowd   915
Of visions, each a part of the dim whole.
And a star left his peers and came with peace
Upon a storm, and all eyes pined for him.
And one isle harboured a sea-beaten ship,
And the crew wandered in its bowers, and plucked   920
Its fruits, and gave up all their hopes for home.
And one dream came to a pale poet's sleep,
And he said, 'I am singled out by God,
'No sin must touch me.' I am very weak,
But what I would express is,—Leave me not,   925
Still sit by me—with beating breast, and hair
Loosened—watching earnest by my side,
Turning my books, or kissing me when I
Look up—like summer wind. Be still to me
A key to music's mystery, when mind fails,   930
A reason, a solution and a clue.
You see I have thrown off my prescribed rules:
I hope in myself—and hope, and pant, and love—
You'll find me better—know me more than when
You loved me as I was. Smile not; I have   935
Much yet to gladden you—to dawn on you.

No more of the past—I'll look within no more—
I have too trusted to my own wild wants—
Too trusted to myself—to intuition.
Draining the wine alone in the still night,   940
And seeing how—as gathering films arose,
As by an inspiration life seemed bare
And grinning in its vanity, and ends
Hard to be dreamed of, stared at me as fixed,
And others suddenly became all foul,   945
As a fair witch turned an old hag at night.
No more of this—we will go hand in hand,
I will go with thee, even as a child,
Looking no further than thy sweet commands.
And thou hast chosen where this life shall be—   950
The land which gave me thee shall be our home,
Where nature lies all wild amid her lakes
And snow-swathed mountains, and vast pines all girt

With ropes of snow—where nature lies all bare,
Suffering none to view her but a race 955
Most stinted and deformed—like the mute dwarfs
Which wait upon a naked Indian queen.
And there (the time being when the heavens are thick
With storms) I'll sit with thee while thou dost sing
Thy native songs, gay as a desert bird 960
Who crieth as he flies for perfect joy,
Or telling me old stories of dead knights.
Or I will read old lays to thee—how she,
The fair pale sister, went to her chill grave
With power to love, and to be loved, and live. 965
Or we will go together, like twin gods
Of the infernal world, with scented lamp
Over the dead—to call and to awake—
Over the unshaped images which lie
Within my mind's cave—only leaving all 970
That tells of the past doubts. So when spring comes,
And sunshine comes again like an old smile,
And the fresh waters, and awakened birds,
And budding woods await us—I shall be
Prepared, and we will go and think again, 975
And all old loves shall come to us—but changed
As some sweet thought which harsh words veiled before;
Feeling God loves us, and that all that errs,
Is a strange dream which death will dissipate;
And then when I am firm we'll seek again 980
My own land, and again I will approach
My old designs, and calmly look on all
The works of my past weakness, as one views
Some scene where danger met him long before.
Ah! that such pleasant life should be but dreamed! 985

But whate'er come of it—and tho' it fade,
And tho' ere the cold morning all be gone
As it will be;—tho' music wait for me,
And fair eyes and bright wine, laughing like sin,
Which steals back softly on a soul half saved; 990
And I be first to deny all, and despise
This verse, and these intents which seem so fair;
Still this is all my own, this moment's pride,
No less I make an end in perfect joy.
E'en in my brightest time, a lurking fear 995

Possessed me. I well knew my weak resolves,
I felt the witchery that makes mind sleep
Over its treasures—as one half afraid
To make his riches definite—but now
These feelings shall not utterly be lost,   1000
I shall not know again that nameless care,
Lest leaving all undone in youth, some new
And undreamed end reveal itself too late:
For this song shall remain to tell for ever,
That when I lost all hope of such a change,   1005
Suddenly Beauty rose on me again.
No less I make an end in perfect joy,
For I, having thus again been visited,
Shall doubt not many another bliss awaits,
And tho' this weak soul sink, and darkness come,   1010
Some little word shall light it up again,
And I shall see all clearer and love better;
I shall again go o'er the tracts of thought,
As one who has a right; and I shall live
With poets—calmer—purer still each time,   1015
And beauteous shapes will come to me again,
And unknown secrets will be trusted me,
Which were not mine when wavering—but now
I shall be priest and lover, as of old.

Sun-treader, I believe in God, and truth,   1020
And love; and as one just escaped from death
Would bind himself in bands of friends to feel
He lives indeed—so, I would lean on thee;
Thou must be ever with me—most in gloom
When such shall come—but chiefly when I die,   1025
For I seem dying, as one going in the dark
To fight a giant—and live thou for ever,
And be to all what thou hast been to me—
All in whom this wakes pleasant thoughts of me,
Know my last state is happy—free from doubt,   1030
Or touch of fear. Love me and wish me well!

RICHMOND,
October 22, 1832.

APPENDIX B

JUVENILIA AND FUGITIVE POEMS
WRITTEN BEFORE 1864

THE FIRST-BORN OF EGYPT[1]

THAT night came on in Egypt with a step
So calmly stealing in the gorgeous train
Of sunset glories flooding the pale clouds
With liquid gold, until at length the glow
Sank to its shadowy impulse and soft sleep   5
Bent o'er the world to curtain it from life—
Vitality was hushed beneath her wing—
Pomp sought his couch of purple—care-worn grief
Flung slumber's mantle o'er him. At that hour
He in whose brain the burning fever fiend   10
Held revelry—his hot cheek turn'd awhile
Upon the cooler pillow. In his cell
The captive wrapped him in his squalid rags,
And sank amid his straw. Circean sleep!
Bathed in thine opiate dew false hope vacates   15
Her seat in the sick soul, leaving awhile
Her dreamy fond imaginings—pale fear
His wild misgivings, and the warm life-springs
Flow in their wonted channels—and the train—
The harpy train of care forsakes the heart.   20

Was it the passing sigh of the night wind
Or some lorn spirit's wail—that moaning cry
That struck the ear? 'tis hushed—no! it swells on
On—as the thunder peal when it essays
To wreck the summer sky—that fearful shriek   25
Still it increases—'tis the dolorous plaint,
The death cry of a nation—

It was a fearful thing—that hour of night.
I have seen many climes, but that dread hour

[1] This and the following poem are the only examples of Browning's very early work which he failed to destroy. They were written in his fourteenth year.

Hath left its burning impress on my soul   30
Never to be erased. Not the loud crash
When the shuddering forest swings to the red bolt
Or march of the fell earthquake when it whelms
A city in its yawning gulf, could quell
That deep voice of despair. Pharaoh arose   35
Startled from slumber, and in anger sought
The reason of the mighty rushing throng
At that dark hour around the palace gates,
—And then he dashed his golden crown away
And tore his hair in frenzy when he knew   40
That Egypt's heir was dead—From every home,
The marbled mansion of regality
To the damp dungeon's walls—gay pleasure's seat
And poverty's lone hut, that cry was heard
As guided by the Seraph's vengeful arm   45
The hand of death held on its withering course,
Blighting the hopes of thousands.—

I sought the street to gaze upon the grief
Of congregated Egypt—there the slave
Stood by him late his master, for that hour   50
Made vain the world's distinctions—for could wealth
Or power arrest the woe?—Some were there
As sculptured marble from the quarry late
Of whom the foot first in the floating dance,
The glowing cheek hued with the deep'ning flush   55
In the night revel—told the young and gay.
No kindly moisture dewed their stony eye,
Or damp'd their ghastly glare—for they felt not.
The chain of torpor bound around the heart
Had stifled it for ever. Tears stole down   60
The furrow'd channels of those withered cheeks
Whose fount had long been chill'd, but that night's term
Had loosed the springs—for 'twas a fearful thing
To see a nation's hope so blasted. One
Press'd his dead child unto his heart—no spot   65
Of livid plague was nigh—no purple cloud
Of scathing fever—and he struck his brow
To rouse himself from that wild phantasy
Deeming it but a vision of the night.
I marked one old man with his only son   70
Lifeless within his arms—his withered hand

Wandering o'er the features of his child
Bidding him [wake] from that long dreary sleep,
And lead his old blind father from the crowd
To the green meadows[1]—but he answer'd not;   75
And then the terrible truth flash'd on his brain,
And when the throng roll'd on some bade him rise
And cling not so unto the dead one there,
Nor voice nor look made answer—he was gone.
But one thought chain'd the powers of each mind   80
Amid that night's felt horror—each one owned
In silence the dread majesty—the might
Of Israel's God, whose red hand had avenged
His servants' cause so fearfully.

THE DANCE OF DEATH

And as they footed it around,
They sang their triumphs o'er mankind!
                              de Stael.

FEVER

Bow to me, bow to me;
Follow me in my burning breath,
Which brings as the simoom destruction and death.
My spirit lives in the hectic glow
When I bid the life streams tainted flow   5
In the fervid sun's deep brooding beam
When seething vapours in volumes steam,
And they fall—the young, the gay—as the flower
'Neath the fiery wind's destructive power.
This day I have gotten a noble prize—   10
There was one who saw the morning rise,
And watch'd fair Cynthia's golden streak
Kiss the misty mountain peak,
But I was there, and my pois'nous flood
Envenom'd the gush of the youth's warm blood.   15
They hastily bore him to his bed,
But o'er him death his swart pennons spread:
The skilléd leech's art was vain,
Delirium revelled in each vein.

---

[1] These lines were probably underlined by Sarah Flower because she considered them particularly good.

I mark'd each deathly change in him;   20
I watch'd his lustrous eye grow dim,
The purple cloud on his deep swol'n brow,
The gathering death sweat's chilly flow,
The dull dense film obscure the eye,
Heard the last quick gasp and saw him die.   25

PESTILENCE

My spirit has past on the lightning's wing
O'er city and land with its withering;
In the crowded street, in the flashing hall
My tramp has been heard: they are lonely all.
A nation has swept at my summons away   30
As mists before the glare of day.
See how proudly reigns my hand
In the black'ning heaps on the surf-beat strand
[Where][1] the rank grass grows in deserted streets
[Where] the terrified stranger no passer meets   35
[And all] around the putrid air
[Gleams] lurid and red in Erinnys stare
Where silence reigns, where late swell'd the lute,
Thrilling lyre, mellifluous flute.
There if my prowess ye would know   40
Seek ye—and bow to your rival low.

AGUE

Bow to me, bow to me;
My influence is in the freezing deeps
Where the icy power of torpor sleeps,
Where the frigid waters flow   45
My marble chair is more cold below;
When the Grecian brav'd the Hellespont's flood
How did I curdle his fever'd blood,
And sent his love in tumescent wave
To meet with her lover an early grave.   50
When Hellas' victor sought the rush
Of the river to lave in its cooling gush,
Did he not feel my iron clutch
When he fainted and sank at my algid touch?
These are the least of the trophies I claim—   55
Bow to me then, and own my fame.

[1] Paper removed where sealed.

MADNESS

Hear ye not the gloomy yelling
Or the tide of anguish swelling,
Hear ye the clank of fetter and chain,
Hear ye the wild cry of grief and pain,   60
Followed by the shuddering laugh
As when fiends the life blood quaff?
See! see that band,
See how their bursting eyeballs gleam,
As the tiger's when crouched in the jungle's lair,   65
In India's sultry land.
Now they are seized in the rabies fell,
Hark! 'tis a shriek as from fiends of hell;
Now there is a plaining moan,
As the flow of the sullen river—   70
List! there is a hollow groan.
Doth it not make e'en *you* to shiver—
These are they struck of the barbs of my quiver.
Slaves before my haughty throne,
Bow then, bow to me alone.   75

CONSUMPTION

'Tis for me, 'tis for me;
Mine the prize of Death must be;
My spirit is o'er the young and gay
As on snowy wreaths in the bright noonday
They wear a melting and vermeille flush   80
E'en while I bid their pulses hush,
Hueing o'er their dying brow
With the spring [?] of health's best roseate glow
When the lover watches the full dark eye
Robed in tints of ianthine dye,   85
Beaming eloquent as to declare
The passions that deepen the glories there.
The frost in its tide of dazzling whiteness,
As Juno's brow of chrystal brightness,
Such as the Grecian's hand could give   90
When he bade the sculptured marble 'live,'
The ruby suffusing the Hebe cheek,
The pulses that love and pleasure speak
Can his fond heart claim but another day,
And the loathsome worm on her form shall prey.   95

She is scathed as the tender flower,
When mildews o'er its chalice lour.
Tell me not of her balmy breath,
Its tide shall be shut in the fold of death;
Tell me not of her honied lip,   100
The reptile's fangs shall its fragrance sip.
Then will I say triumphantly
Bow to the deadliest—bow to me!

VERSES IN MEMORY OF JAMES DOW[1]

Words we might else have been compelled to say
In silence to our hearts, great love, great praise,
Of thee, our father, have been freely said
By those whom none shall blame; and while thy life
Endures, a beauteous thing in their record,   5
We may desist; but thou art not alone:
A part of those thou lovedst here so well
Repose beside thee, and the eyes that saw
Thy daily course of good could never see
The light their presence cast upon thy path: 10
Soft Sanctuary-tapers of thy house
Close-curtained when the Priest came forth; on these
Let peace be, Peace on thee our Mother too!
Serenest Spirit; do we vainly dream
Some portion of the constant joy you spread   15
Around you living, comforts even yet
The Child that never knew you, and the Girl
In whom your gentle soul seemed born again
To bless us longer? Peace like yours be ours
Till the same quiet home receive us all!   20

SONNET[2]

EYES calm beside thee (Lady, could'st thou know!)
May turn away thick with fast-gathering tears:
I glance not where all gaze: thrilling and low
Their passionate praises reach thee—my cheek wears

[1] A shorter version of this poem is given in *New Poems by Robert Browning and Elizabeth Barrett Browning* (1914), with the title 'Lines to the Memory of his Parents (1866)'. As E. G. Bayford pointed out in *Notes and Queries* for 12 June 1948, however, the lines printed above are engraved on a tombstone in the additional burying ground belonging to St. Mary's Church, Barnsley, Yorkshire. According to Bayford, James Dow's son William Alexander Dow and Browning 'were great friends and . . . the latter wrote the lines at the request of his friend'. James Dow died on 9 October 1832.

[2] Published in *The Monthly Repository*, October 1834, under the initial 'Z'.

Alone no wonder when thou passest by;   5
Thy tremulous lids bent and suffused reply
To the irrepressible homage which doth glow
On every lip but mine: if in thine ears
Their accents linger—and thou dost recall
Me as I stood, still, guarded, very pale,   10
Beside each votarist whose lighted brow
Wore worship like an aureole, 'O'er them all
My beauty,' thou wilt murmur, 'did prevail
Save that one only':—Lady, could'st thou know!

Aug. 17, 1834.

A FOREST THOUGHT[1]

Written and inscribed to W. A. and A. D. by their Sincere Friend, Robert
Browning, 13 Nelson Sq., November 4, 1837.

IN far Esthonian solitudes
The parent-firs of future woods
Gracefully, airily spire at first
Up to the sky, by the soft sand nurst;
Self-sufficient are they, and strong   5
With outspread arms, broad level and long;
But soon in the sunshine and the storm
They darken, changing fast their form—
Low boughs fall off, and in the bole
Each tree spends all its strenuous soul—   10
Till the builder gazes wistfully
Such noble ship-mast wood to see,
And cares not for its soberer hue,
Its rougher bark and leaves more few.

But just when beauty passes away   15
And you half regret it could not stay,
For all their sap and vigorous life,—
Under the shade, secured from strife
A seedling springs—the forest-tree
In miniature, and again we see   20
The delicate leaves that will fade one day,
The fan-like shoots that will drop away,

[1] Written in an album when Browning stood godfather to the eldest son of his friend
William Alexander Dow.

The taper stem a breath could strain—
Which shall foil one day the hurricane:
We turn from this infant of the copse   25
To the parent-firs,—in their waving tops
To find some trace of the light green tuft
A breath could stir,—in the bole aloft
Column-like set against the sky,
The spire that flourished airily   30
And the marten bent as she rustled by.
So shall it be, dear Friends, when days
Pass, and in this fair child we trace
Goodness, full-formed in you, tho' dim
Faint-budding, just astir in him: 35
When rudiments of generous worth
And frankest love in him have birth,
We'll turn to love and worth full-grown,
And learn their fortune from your own.
Nor shall we vainly search to see   40
His gentleness—simplicity—
Not lost in your maturer grace—
Perfected, but not changing place.

May this grove be a charmed retreat . . .
May northern winds and savage sleet   45
Leave the good trees untouched, unshorn
A crowning pride of woods unborn:
And gracefully beneath their shield
May the seedling grow! All pleasures yield
Peace below and peace above,   50
The glancing squirrels' summer love,
And the brood-song of the cushat-dove!

THE 'MOSES' OF MICHAEL ANGELO[1]

AND who is He that, sculptured in huge stone,
    Sitteth a giant, where no works arrive
Of straining Art, and hath so prompt and live
The lips, I listen to their very tone?
Moses is He—Ay, that, makes clearly known   5
    The chin's thick boast, and brow's prerogative

---

[1] This translation of a sonnet by G. B. F. Zappi was marked by Browning 'From Zappi, R.B. (Given to Ba "for love's sake," Siena. Sept. 27, '50.)'

Of double ray: so did the mountain give
Back to the world that visage, God was grown
Great part of! Such was he when he suspended
    Round him the sounding and vast waters; such   10
When he shut sea on sea o'er Mizraïm.
And ye, his hordes, a vile calf raised, and bended
    The knee? This Image had ye raised, not **much**
Had been your error in adoring Him.

BEN KARSHOOK'S WISDOM[1]

I

'WOULD a man 'scape the rod?'
    Rabbi Ben Karshook saith,
'See that he turn to God
    'The day before his death.'

'Ay, could a man inquire   5
    'When it shall come!' I say.
The Rabbi's eye shoots fire—
    'Then let him turn to-day!'

II

Quoth a young Sadducee:
    'Reader of many rolls,   10
'Is it so certain we
    'Have, as they tell us, souls?'

'Son, there is no reply!'
    The Rabbi bit his beard;
'Certain, a soul have *I*—   15
    '*We* may have none,' he sneer'd.

    .   .   .   .   .

Thus Karshook, the Hiram's-Hammer,
    The Right-hand Temple-column,
Taught babes in grace their grammar,
    And struck the simple, solemn.   20

Rome, *April* 27, 1854.

[1] First printed in *The Keepsake*, 1856. Not reprinted by Browning.

DEAF AND DUMB

A GROUP BY WOOLNER[1]

ONLY the prism's obstruction shows aright
The secret of a sunbeam, breaks its light
Into the jewelled bow from blankest white;
 So may a glory from defect arise:
Only by Deafness may the vexed Love wreak
Its insuppressive sense on brow and cheek,
Only by Dumbness adequately speak
 As favoured mouth could never, through the eyes.

EURYDICE TO ORPHEUS

A PICTURE BY LEIGHTON[2]

BUT give them me, the mouth, the eyes, the brow!
Let them once more absorb me! One look now
 Will lap me round for ever, not to pass
Out of its light, though darkness lie beyond:
Hold me but safe again within the bond
 Of one immortal look! All woe that was,
Forgotten, and all terror that may be,
Defied,—no past is mine, no future: look at me!

[1] Written in 1862 to accompany Thomas Woolner's group of the deaf and dumb children of Sir Thomas Fairbairn. First printed in *The Poetical Works*, 1868, among the *Dramatis Personæ* poems.

[2] First published in the catalogue of the Royal Academy Exhibition for 1864, where it was printed as prose and entitled 'A Fragment'. Included in *A Selection from the Works of Robert Browning* in 1865, and among the *Dramatis Personæ* poems in *The Poetical Works* of 1868.

APPENDIX C

THE CONTENTS OF THE EARLY
COLLECTED EDITIONS

POEMS BY ROBERT BROWNING. In Two Volumes. Vol. I. (II.) A New Edition. 1849.

'Many of these pieces were out of print, the rest had been withdrawn from circulation, when the corrected edition, now submitted to the reader, was prepared. The various Poems and Dramas have received the author's most careful revision. December, 1848.'

Vol. I: Paracelsus; Pippa Passes. A Drama; King Victor and King Charles. A Tragedy; Colombe's Birthday. A Play.

Vol. II: A Blot in the 'Scutcheon. A Tragedy; The Return of the Druses. A Tragedy; Luria. A Tragedy; A Soul's Tragedy; Dramatic Romances and Lyrics (see p. 941 below).

THE POETICAL WORKS OF ROBERT BROWNING. Vol. I. (II. III.) Third Edition. 1863. (Dedication to John Forster, dated 21 April 1863. For the note facing the first page of the text, and that at the foot of the first page, see p. 941 below and p. 365 n. above.)

Vol. I: Lyrics, Romances, Men, and Women.

Vol. II: Tragedies and other Plays (Pippa Passes—A Drama; King Victor and King Charles—A Tragedy; The Return of the Druses—A Tragedy; A Blot in the 'Scutcheon—A Tragedy; Colombe's Birthday—A Play; Luria—A Tragedy; A Soul's Tragedy; In A Balcony—A Scene; Strafford—A Tragedy.

Vol. III: Paracelsus; Christmas-Eve and Easter-Day; Sordello.

THE POETICAL WORKS OF ROBERT BROWNING, M.A., Honorary Fellow of Balliol College, Oxford. 1868. (Dedication to John Forster, as in 1863. Prefatory note, as reprinted on p. 1 above.)

Vol. I: Pauline; Paracelsus; Strafford.

Vol. II: Sordello; Pippa Passes.

Vol. III: King Victor and King Charles; Dramatic Lyrics; The Return of the Druses.

Vol. IV: A Blot in the 'Scutcheon; Colombe's Birthday; Dramatic Romances.

Vol. V: A Soul's Tragedy; Luria; Christmas-Eve and Easter-Day; Men and Women.

Vol. VI: In A Balcony; Dramatis Personæ. (General Index.)

THE POETICAL WORKS OF ROBERT BROWNING. 1889 (1888–9).
(Prefatory matter as in the present edition.)

Vol. I: Pauline; Sordello.

Vol. II: Paracelsus; Strafford.

Vol. III: Pippa Passes; King Victor and King Charles; The Return of the Druses; A Soul's Tragedy.

Vol. IV: A Blot in the 'Scutcheon; Colombe's Birthday; Men and Women.

Vol. V: Dramatic Romances; Christmas-Eve and Easter-Day.

Vol. VI: Dramatic Lyrics; Luria.

Vol. VII: In A Balcony; Dramatis Personæ.

Vols. VIII–X: The Ring and the Book.

Vol. XI: Balaustion's Adventure; Prince Hohenstiel-Schwangau; Fifine at the Fair.

Vol. XII: Red Cotton Night-Cap Country; The Inn Album.

Vol. XIII: Aristophanes' Apology: The Agamemnon of Æschylus.

Vol. XIV: Pacchiarotto and How He Worked in Distemper with other poems.

Vol. XV: Dramatic Idyls [First and Second Series]; Jocoseria.

Vol. XVI: Ferishtah's Fancies; Parleyings with Certain People.

Note: Vol. XVII appeared in 1894. It contains *Asolando*, Biographical and Historical Notes to the Poems, a General Index, and an Index to First Lines of Shorter Poems. A further uniform volume, NEW POEMS BY ROBERT BROWNING AND ELIZABETH BARRETT BROWNING, edited by Sir Frederic G. Kenyon, K.C.B., D.Litt. With Two Portraits, was published in 1914.

APPENDIX D

TABLE OF POEMS CLASSIFIED
BY BROWNING AS 'DRAMATIC LYRICS', 'DRAMATIC ROMANCES', AND 'MEN AND WOMEN'

In Vol. II of the *Poems* of 1849 Browning printed the contents of *Bells and Pomegranates No. III* (*Dramatic Lyrics*) and *No. VII* (*Dramatic Romances and Lyrics*) under the general heading 'Dramatic Romances and Lyrics', retaining the original order of the poems and making no distinction between Romances and Lyrics. Two poems were dropped, 'Claret and Tokay' and 'Home-Thoughts, from Abroad II'.

Vol. I of *The Poetical Works*, 1863, bears the sub-title: *Lyrics, Romances, Men, and Women*. The following note appears opposite the first page of the text: 'In this Volume are collected and redistributed the pieces first published in 1842, 1845, and 1855, respectively, under the titles of "Dramatic Lyrics," "Dramatic Romances," and "Men and Women."/Part of these were inscribed to my dear friend John Kenyon: I hope the whole may obtain the honour of an association with his memory./R. B.' For the footnote on the first page of the text, see p. 365 above. The contents are as follows:

Lyrics
Cavalier Tunes
    I. Marching along
    II. Give a rouse
    III. Boot and saddle

The Lost Leader

'How they brought the good news from Ghent to Aix'

Through the Metidja to Abd-el-Kadr

Nationality in drinks [see note on p. 473 above]

Garden Fancies
    I. The Flower's name
    II. Sibrandus Schafnaburgensis
    III. Soliloquy of the Spanish cloister

The Laboratory

The Confessional

Cristina

The Lost Mistress

Earth's Immortalities [Fame, Love]

Meeting at Night

Parting at Morning
Song ['Nay but you, who do not love her']
A Woman's Last Word
Evelyn Hope
Love among the Ruins
A Lovers' Quarrel
Up at a Villa—down in the City
A Toccata of Galuppi's
Old Pictures in Florence
'De gustibus—'
Home-Thoughts, from Abroad
Home-Thoughts, from the Sea
Saul
My Star
By the Fire-Side
Any Wife to any Husband
Two in the Campagna
Misconceptions
A Serenade at the Villa
One Way of Love
Another Way of Love
A Pretty Woman
Respectability
Love in a Life
Life in a Love
In three Days
In a Year
Women and Roses
Before
After
The Guardian-Angel—A Picture at Fano
Memorabilia
Popularity
Master Hugues of Saxe-Gotha

Romances
Incident of the French Camp
The Patriot. An Old Story
My last Duchess.—Ferrara
Count Gismond.—Aix in Provence

The Boy and the Angel
Instans Tyrannus
Mesmerism
The Glove
Time's Revenges
The Italian in England. Piano di Sorrento
The Englishman in Italy
In a Gondola
Waring
The Twins
A light Woman
The last Ride together
The Pied Piper of Hamelin; A Child's Story
The Flight of the Duchess
A Grammarian's Funeral
Johannes Agricola in Meditation
The Heretic's Tragedy. A Middle Age Interlude
Holy-Cross Day
Protus
The Statue and the Bust
Porphyria's Lover
'Childe Roland to the Dark Tower Came'

Men, and Women
'Transcendentalism:' A Poem in Twelve Books
How it strikes a Contemporary
Artemis Prologizes
An Epistle containing the strange medical Experience of Karshish, the Arab
  Physician
Pictor Ignotus
Fra Lippo Lippi
Andrea del Sarto
The Bishop orders his Tomb at Saint Praxed's Church
Bishop Blougram's Apology
Cleon
Rudel to the Lady of Tripoli
One Word More.

Note: In 1868 and subsequently 'Johannes Agricola in Meditation' was
removed from the *Romances* and printed among the *Men, and Women*, before
'Pictor Ignotus'.

APPENDIX E

TRANSLATIONS OF LATIN AND FRENCH NOTES

Page 6: I have no doubt that the title of our book may by its unusual character entice very many to read it, and that among them some of biassed opinions, with weak minds—many even hostile and churlish—will attack our genius, who in the rashness of their ignorance will cry out, almost before they have read the title, that we are teaching forbidden things, are scattering the seeds of heresies, that we are an annoyance to righteous ears, to enlightened minds an object of offence; so taking care for their consciences that neither Apollo, nor all the Muses, nor an angel from heaven could save me from their execration. To these I now give counsel not to read our book, neither to understand it nor remember it; for it is harmful, poisonous; the gate of Hell is in this book; it speaks of stones—let them beware lest by them it beat out their brains. But if you who come to its perusal with unprejudiced minds will exercise as much discernment and prudence as bees in gathering honey, then read with safety. For I think you will receive not a little of instruction and a great deal of enjoyment. On the other hand, if you find things which do not please you, pass over them and make no use of them. For I do not recommend these things to you: i merely Tell you of them. Yet do not on that account reject the rest. Therefore if anything has been said rather freely, forgive my youth; I wrote this work when I was less than a youth.

(Translation by Frederick A. Pottle, in *Shelley and Browning: A Myth and Some Facts*, Chicago, 1923.)

Page 28 *n.*: I am very much afraid that my poor friend will not always be perfectly understood in what remains to be read of this strange fragment, but he is less fitted than anyone else to make clear what from its very nature must always remain a confused dream. Besides, I am not at all sure that in attempting better to co-ordinate certain parts one would not run the risk of damaging the only merit to which so singular a production can lay claim, that of giving a pretty exact idea of the type which has merely been sketched. This unpretentious opening, this stirring of the passions which increases at first and then is gradually allayed—these impulses of the soul, this sudden return upon himself, and above all the altogether exceptional cast of mind of my friend make alterations almost impossible. The reasons that he puts forward elsewhere, and others still more powerful, have led me to look with favour on this piece of writing, which I would otherwise have advised him to throw into the fire. This does not mean that I do not believe in the great principle of all composition—that principle of Shakespeare, of Raphael, of Beethoven, from which it follows that the concentration of ideas is due much more to their conception than to their execution. I have good reason for fearing that the first of these qualities is still unfamiliar to my friend, and I very much doubt whether a doubling of his effort would lead him to acquire the second. The best thing would be to burn this; but what can one do?

I believe that in what follows he alludes to a certain examination of the soul, or rather of his own soul, which he carried out formerly, in order to discover the sequence of objectives which it would be possible for him to attain, and of which each one (once attained) should form a sort of plateau from which one could discern other aims, other projects, other pleasures which (in their turn) should be surmounted. The conclusion was that oblivion and sleep should bring an end to everything. This idea, which I do not altogether understand, is perhaps equally incomprehensible to him.

Page 149 *n.*: He (Erastus) states that at the age of three Paracelsus was castrated by a certain soldier, others state that it was by a boar: at all events he was beardless, and a hater of women.   I scarcely believe that he was a Swiss, for that region would scarcely have produced such a monster.

Page 150 *n.*: For I know that I am sufficiently and more than sufficiently fortified against you and all your great men, Avicenna, Galen, Aristotle and the rest. And my bald and hairless head contains more extensive and lofty knowledge than either your Avicenna or all the academies together. Come forth and give an indication of what men you are, what strength you possess. In fact what are you? Doctors and master physicians, combing lice and rubbing the anus.

Page 151 (2): When I recently conversed with you at some length, R. P., in your cloister at Herbipolis (Würzburg), and we had had much discussion together about chemistry, magic, occultism and those other sciences and arts which still lie hidden in darkness, etc.

Page 151 (3): That insatiable appetite for investigating the secrets of nature and enriching the mind with a store of strange information did not allow him to remain for any length of time in one and the same place, but kept goading him to travel through all lands and peoples and cities, like Mercury, so that he might confer by word of mouth with the investigators of nature, especially the chemists, and learn from them in a conversation or two what they had discovered through their strenuous efforts by day and by night. With the assistance of his father at first, and subsequently by his own efforts, he obtained as his teachers the most learned men of

Germany, Italy, France, Spain and the rest of Europe. As a result of their generous teaching, but especially through his own inquiries, as one would expect of a man possessing such a very keen and almost superhuman intellect, he made such strides in knowledge that many have testified that no mortal man in the whole realm of philosophy ever brought to light such difficult, such secret and hidden matters.   Paracelsus who entered so deeply into the innermost recesses of nature, who explored and examined the powers and virtues of minerals and plants with such an unbelievable keenness of intellect, to the point of curing completely all kinds of diseases, even those given up as hopeless and generally considered by mankind as incurable; so that the art of medicine seems not only to have been born with Theophrastus, but also to have been perfected.   Behold a young man in love does not shrink from the most difficult journey in order to behold a girl or a woman if she is truly beautiful. How much less will one shrink from labour or from any amount of tedious work when seized by a passion for the noblest arts?

Page 152, *line* 21: He is the founder not only of a new art of medicine, but even of a new theology.   partly atheists, partly heretics . . . It must be admitted, nevertheless, that many theological statements in the writings of that man openly reek of atheism and ring rather harshly in the ears of one who is truly Christian.   Oporinus says that he (Paracelsus) would sometimes boast that one day he would deflate the reputation of Luther and the Pope, no less than that of Galen and Hippocrates: claiming that none of those who had hitherto written upon sacred scripture, whether in the past or more recently, had extracted the kernel of the truth—they had merely penetrated as far as the outer shell and skin. He bade a long farewell to him (Paracelsus), since he feared that because of the terrifying blasphemies of his master, who was in other respects most dear to him, he too might incur the punishments of Almighty God.

Page 152 (5): This is a weakness of the race, not of the individual, a weakness that has come down without interruption from the age of Tacitus to our own time: perhaps as old a trait of the Germans as their honesty, a hereditary characteristic.   At home, as his secretary Oporinus often reported, he never set out to expound his ideas unless he was drunk: then, leaning against a column in the centre of the room, 'possessed' as it were, he grasped in his hands the hilt of his sword, the hollowed-out interior of which gave lodging (so they say) to a friendly spirit, and in this condition he revealed his inspirations or ideas. Others think that what he had in the handle (he called it Azoth) was a most extraordinary medicine, or the Philosopher's stone.

Page 153, *line* 15: Theophrastus was living at Nuremberg when he was summoned by the doctors of that city and proclaimed a boaster and a charlatan. In order to prop up his tottering reputation he approached certain men of the highest authority in that state and promised that without asking any payment or fee he would give a demonstration of his art for the purpose of refuting the slander and proving his skill. They granted him a favourable hearing; and at their bidding a number of lepers, who had been banished from society and confined in an infirmary, were selected by impartial judges. By the unique potency of his medicine Theophrastus cured these men from the foul Greek scurvy and restored them to their former state of health. The city preserves in its archives a record which testifies to these cures.   But at length he came to his senses again and honoured and venerated the man, now dead, whom he had attacked with abuse during his lifetime. The infamous backbiting at the fame of his master was converted by repentance into remorse of conscience—alas too late—which closed the wounds of the dead man which had been inflicted while he was alive.   This noble branch of medical science, buried long since in the time of our forefathers, was recalled from the underworld, as it were, by Theophrastus Paracelsus.

Page 153 *n.*: There are some too who dismiss for physical reasons the objection that Paracelsus did not live long. They say that a man's life can be cut short in such cases, as a result of the tincture's being taken too often or in excessive doses, so that the natural heat of the body is stifled by its extremely active and penetrating power.

Page 154, *line* 13: As regards the number of Paracelsus's books, I hear that almost three hundred are counted by the Germans.   What a fertile intellect!   excluding the works whose only claim to distinction is that they have been associated with his name, of which a huge number are in circulation   a most esteemed and precious memorial of their author, but one stolen from him rather than bestowed.   These writings of his seem very seldom to have reached the light of day as a result of his own wishes and instructions, since they were surreptitiously pilfered and taken away in his absence with the aid of a servant who showed the place in the wall where they had been hidden.

Page 154 (6): Who, I ask, would now honour a profession which is infested and controlled by such good-for-nothing scoundrels?   He left his possessions to be distributed among the poor and applied for their benefit.

INDEX OF TITLES

INDEX OF FIRST LINES